Social Networking
Law, Rights and Policy

Contributors

Gary Kovacs (CEO Mozilla Corporation); **Andrew Harbison** (Digital & Cybercrime Investigator, Grant Thornton); **Aisling McMahon** (University Edinburgh. Editor SCRIPT-ed); **Peggy Valcke** (Professor ICRI-iMinds-KU Leuven); **Aleksandra Kuczerawy** (Assistant Editor International Encyclopedia of Law); **Claire Wallace** (Maples & Calder); **Damien McCallig** (PhD candidate, *The law of digital remains: reconciling the dignity and interests of the deceased with those of the living*); **Cáit Brennan** (BSc, Dip IT, MTOPRA); **Max Schrems** (Founder *Europe versus Facebook.* Winner EPIC 2013 International Privacy Champion Award); **José Maria Baño Fos** (Adjunct Professor Instituto de Empresa Law School Madrid. Practised in Brussels (now Madrid), including on the Spanish Google case); **Donnacha O'Sullivan** (BL, LLM); **Gary Madden** (studied law, economics, technology and governance); **Sara Fernández Castedo (Lugo)** (studied at Santiago de Compostela University (business law) and University of Padova. Attorney); **Paul Lambert** (BA, LLB, LLM, CTMA, lawyer, adjunct lecturer, author of data protection and courtroom broadcasting books).

social
employee
data
privacy
issues
user
networking
personal
employees
internet
policy
online
stalking
protection
bandwidth
abuse
potential
educational
education
harassment
marketing
relationships
liability
advertising
safety
settings
children
security
telecommuting
resources
breaches
blogs
new
P2P
Privacy
Security
business for Statements

SOCIAL NETWORKING
LAW, RIGHTS AND POLICY

Edited by

PAUL LAMBERT
BA, LL.B, LL.M, CTMA, Solicitor

CLARUS
PRESS

Published by
Clarus Press Ltd,
Griffith Campus,
South Circular Road,
Dublin 8.
www.claruspress.ie

Typeset by
Gough Typesetting Services,
Dublin

Printed by
CPI Antony Rowe,
Chippenham,
Wiltshire

Production Credits
Publisher David McCartney
Front Cover designed by Fabrice Robin
Word Cloud designed by Steve O'Neill

ISBN
978-1-905536-55-9

A catalogue record for this book is available from the British Library

Dedication
To Maureen, Robert and Oisín

PREFACE

Social networking is the new modern zeitgeist. It is the unpredicted "killer-app" of the internet. There are billions of regular users. In fact the social networking user population of some websites is even greater than the populations of nation States.

The popularity is without doubt. There are tremendous and wonderful uses and benefits to online social networking. However, in a small number of instances there are less than welcome activities going on, most notably certain instances of online abuse. The small but 'dark side' is gaining prominence and undermining the many positives to social networking.

We should also note that social networks are not alone. There are many related websites which are not strictly speaking social networks but which very much related, interacting and sharing some of the same space.

As the size, popularity and indeed complexity of social networks evolved further, the number of legal, technical, policy and other issues involved will also increase. Indeed, on occasion these become headline news, and sometimes for the wrong reasons.

While sometimes there may be continuity with certain legal precedent, increasingly, with increasing frequency, courts, policymakers, employers, schools, and other are faced with entirely new legal issues stemming from social networking.

Frequently, the scale, complexity and expedition of the issues are at a level unprecedented in collective memory.

The number of sections, chapters and topics herein are just one indication of the breath of issues developing in relation to and arising from social networking.

Paul Lambert
March 2014

ACKNOWLEDGEMENTS

It is not possible to mention everyone whom made this possible but special appreciation and acknowledgement must go to all of the expert contributors to this book, and also to those luminaries who took the time to read the book in its draft stage and kindly furnish their review comments, to Rónán Kennedy, TJ McIntyre, the data protection masters students, the wonder and creativity of new technological developments and to learned judges whom sometimes have to grapple with new social hostilities.

TABLE OF CONTENTS

PART IV: SOCIAL NETWORKING AND EVIDENTIAL ISSUES

PART V: EMPLOYEES AND EDUCATION

PART XI: SOCIAL NETWORKING AND COURTS

PART XII: DATA PROTECTION: THE FUTURE

SOCIAL NETWORKING WEBSITES SAMPLE

Some example of various social networking and related websites are referred to below. This is illustrative only. It is not a definitive list nor is it listed in any order of priority. Neither should this be interpreted as any specific endorsement. (Note: dating websites not included).

Social Networking and Related Websites (Social)

MySpace (launched July 2003); Facebook (launched February 2004); Orkut; Zorpia; Netlog; Hi5; Perfspot; Sina Weibo; Renren; Tencent; Douban; Odnoklassniki; VKontakte; Twitter; YouTube; Bebo; Google+; Ping; Dailymotion; gURL; Friendster; LiveJournal; Xanga; Bolt; Grouper; Google video; Scribd; Blogger; Flickr; Amazon (eg book reviews); FourSquare; Yelp; Second Life; MyLife; Ning; Pinterest; Tagged; Reddit; Ask.com; Badoo; Imgur; Spotify, VK.com, Snapchat

Social Networking Websites (Business)

LinkedIn; Plaxo; Ecademy; Partner Up; StartUpNation; Xing; Twitter; Ecademy; Viadeo; Ryze; Efactor

Social Networking Websites (Online Instant Updates and Messaging)

Twitter; WhatsApp, WebChat, KakoaTalk, SnapChat, WeChat,, LINE, Kik, Yammer; Presnent.ly; LiveJournal; WordPress; Pinger

Social Networking Websites (News)

Journal.ie; Huffington Post; Mashable; Reddit; Breakingnews.ie; Guardian

Social Networking Websites (Document Resources: Pictures)

Flickr; PhotoBucket; Picture Social; Multiply; Fotolog; Zooomr

Social Networking Websites (Document Resources: Documents)

Google Docs; Docstoc; Dropbox; Windows Live Folders; Box.net; Mozy; Onmidrive; Xdrive; AmazonS3; Anobii.com; Scribd; Issuu; Slideshare; Docstoc; Pdfcast; Keepandshare; Slideboom; Slideserve

Statistics of Social Networking

In order to appreciate the importance of social networking it is necessary to appreciate its size, scale and speed of development. It is useful, therefore, to consider the following:

- Number of YouTube videos uploaded daily: 144,000(minutes)
- Number of hours uploaded to YouTube per minute: 50 million
- Number of YouTube users (pm): 1 billion
- YouTube Videos uploaded daily/minutes: 100 hours
- YouTube video hours of video uploaded per year: 52,560,000
- Number of Google users/monthly: 192 million
- Number of Facebook members 2004: 1 million
- Number of Facebook members 2008: 100 million
- Number of Facebook members: 1.11 billion
- Number of Twitter users: 200 million
- Number of Tweets per day: 400 million
- Number of annual online retail transactions (est): $318 billion
- Google purchase of YouTube in 2006: $1.6bn.[1]
- Number of social networking websites in 2007 (approx): 350[2]
- Value Google (est): $294.03 billion
- Value Facebook (est): $58.08 billion
- Value YouTube (est 2012): $8.7 billion
- Facebook revenue [Q1 2013]: $1,458 million
- YouTube revenue [Q1 2013 est]: $1.4 billion
- Google website revenue including YouTube [Q1 2013]: $8,640 million

However, given the speed of ongoing change and development, any reference to statistics is liable to be instantly out of date. Therefore, it may be more useful for readers to consider some information and statistical references which can be perused directly from sources such as, for example,

- GlobalWebIndex; Nielsen NetRatings; Techcrunch; Pew internet research; KantarcomTech; Amarach; Olytico (formerly O'Leary Analytics); Social Networking Watch; Web-strategist.com; Slide Share; Web.resourceshelf; Socialnomics; Tyntec; Gartner; social networking websites themselves; official sources.[3]

1 Flint, D, "Computers and Internet," *Business Law Review*, December 2006, 292 at 294.

2 Sharma, D, "Social Networking God: 350+ Social Networking Sites," *Mashable Social Networking News* (October 2007), available at http://mashable.com/2007/10/23/social-networking-god/, referred to in Mann, BL, "Social Networking Websites – A Concentration of Impersonation, Denigration, Sexual Aggressive Solicitation, Cyber-Bullying or Happy Slapping Videos," *International Journal of Law & Information Technology* (2009)(17) 252.

3 The above were compiled by Sara Fernández Castedo (Lugo).

ABBREVIATIONS AND MEANINGS

Abuse/Online Abuse:	Abuse and attacks carried out online including cyberbullying, defamation, attacks, threats, invasions and breaches of privacy and data protection, cyberstalking, grooming, etc;
Cyberbullying:	Abuse, defamation, threats, attacks, blackmailing, etc of children and teenagers online. Can be carried out by children, teenagers and adults
Cookies:	A cookie is a small piece of software generated by a website and saved by a user's computer web browser. The purpose is to remember information about the user, similar to a preference file created by a software application. It can help to speed up internet use and searches;
Data protection:	The law relating to the collection, processing and storing of personal data, in Ireland governed by the DPA 1988 and DPA 2003, and governed in the EU primarily by the Data Protection Directive 1995 and understood to be soon replaced by a draft Data Protection Regulation following an official modernisation review;
Data subject:	The individual to whom the personal data relates, sometimes referred to as the owner of the personal data;
Data controller:	Generally the entity which is collecting, processing and or storing the individual's personal data;
Data processor:	Generally an entity working for and on behalf of a Data Controller to undertake a specified data processing activity;
DP:	Data Protection;
DPA:	Data Protection Act 1988 as amended by Data Protection (Amendment) Act 2003;
Data Protection Act:	Data Protection Act 1988 as amended by Data Protection (Amendment) Act 2003;

Friend:	Means a linked fellow user on a social networking website; can be an actual friend, acquaintance or stranger;
Friend request:	Requesting a user on a social networking website to become your "friend"; to permit a link and access between respective social networking profile pages;
Like:	Frequently an icon whereby a user of a social networking website indicated that the like or appreciate a particular post, comment, picture or video on the website;
DPA 1988:	Data Protection Act 1988;
DPA 2003:	Data Protection (Amendment) Act 2003;
DPD/DPD 1995:	Data Protection Directive 1995 (Directive 95/46/EC);
Data Protection Directive 1995:	Data Protection Directive 1995 (Directive 95/46/EC);
DPC:	Data Protection Commissioner and or Data Protection Commissioner's Office;
Information Commissioner:	The UK equivalent of the Data Protection Commissioner;
ICO:	The UK Information Commissioner's Office;
Personal data:	Generally means any information relating to an identifiable natural person, the data subject. An identifiable person is one who can be identified, directly or indirectly, in particular by reference to an identification number or to one or more factors specific to his or her physical, physiological, mental, economic, cultural or social identity;
Post:	To upload a comment, photo or video onto a social networking website;
Social network(ing):	Means a website or application which is dedicated to enabling users to communicate with each other by posting information, comments, messages,

	images, etc onto a dedicated user section or page on the website;[1]
Tag/tagging:	A text label, description or comment attached to a photo on a social networking website;
Web 2.0:	Second generation internet and internet service applications. The range of activities and data processing possible with second generation internet (Web 2.0) is significantly greater than was possible with Web 1.0. Research is also being carried out in relation Web 3.0 and Web 4.0;
Article 29 Working Party:	An official EU data protection research and policy group, comprised of members from the Data Protection Commissioner's Offices (or equivalent, known as Data Protection Authorities) in each EU member state pursuant to the Data Protection Directive Article 29 Working Party;
WP29:	Article 29 Working Party;
2.0:	Similar to Web 2.0 above.

1 See variation of this definition in Oxford Dictionaries, at http://oxforddictionaries.com/definition/social+network.

PART I: INTRODUCTION

Chapter 1

INTRODUCTION

Introduction

Whether we are consumers, social networkers, parents, educators, policymakers, individuals or organisations, we are all interested in the control, safety and protection of personal information online.

No one is immune from the internet. Even if we do not use the internet, or do not know how to go online,[1] some of our personal information is most likely used by others who are online. Even if we have never accessed a website, our house is on Google Earth satellite images, on Google Maps and in real video images on Google Street View.

However, concern with the internet and social networking has taken on a new importance with the wider appreciation of the dark side of the internet. Online abuse and cyberbullying are particularly troubling. In the worst cases, victims of online abuse are being driven to suicide. The case involving the online video of Amanda Todd,[2] a victim of online abuse, is beneficial viewing for any parent, educator or policymaker who is considering social networking and the welfare and safety of young people.[3]

In the US, Canada,[4] UK[5] and Ireland[6] there have been a number suicides linked to online abuse and cyberbullying.

We increasingly access the internet, whether as individuals, students, employees or consumers. As part of this process we place our personal information online ((upload), eg uploading our photographs on social networks), have to disclose our personal information online to third-party websites (eg booking a flight online) or see the personal information of third parties (eg online dating websites).

There is frequently a perception and concern that personal information are less secure

---

1 We should not yet assume that everyone in every country and of every age has internet access. There is a distinct literature as regards the use by older people of the internet; internet access as between developed and non-developed countries; and even access to high-speed broadband within developed countries.

2 Amanda Todd is a (Canadian) victim of online abuse. She left flash-card messages on a YouTube video before she took her life after years of online abuse and related physical abuse.

3 Available at http://www.youtube.com/watch?v=KRxfTyNa24A.

4 For example, Rehtaeh Parsons, aged 17. She was the victim of online abuse after photos were distributed online of her alleged rape.

5 The most recent example relates to Hannah Smith, aged 14, and Ask.fm. Daniel Perry in Scotland, aged 17, is also reported to have committed suicide after being blackmailed online.

6 Ask.fm was also linked to the deaths of Erin Gallagher, aged 13, and Ciara Pugsley, aged 15.

online than in hardcopy or the non-internet connected world.[7] Certainly, the ways in which personal information are collected and used are amplified in the internet age.[8] The increasing scale of data loss and data security breaches legitimately concerns us. Indeed, examples of data loss, which were once a media backwater, are now front-page news. This should not be a surprise, given that some of the examples of individual data loss encompass the personal data of tens of millions of individuals, and involve personal medical, financial and social security information. Hacking, the existence of markets in databases of illegally obtained personal information and impersonation/identity theft are related issues and are the focus of mainstream media as well as legal and policy attention. The UK Leveson Inquiry, amongst others things, was concerned with the illicit and unlawful trade in personal data.[9]

Any consideration of these concerns must involve the area of law that is potentially most relevant, namely, the legal data protection regime. Understanding this important field also involves many definitions and terms of art, such as "personal identifiable information", "data protection" and "personal data" as outlined in legislation.

Concepts

The concerns relating to online personal information cannot be monopolised individually by media discussion, social discussion, policy discussion or legal discussion. While each will have their own perspective, there is an inevitable crossover.

Given that readers may look at individual sections and chapters in isolation, these are written to be as self-contained as possible and also to include "Headline Issues" at the beginning of each chapter.

While data protection and indeed privacy are sometimes viewed as relatively discrete areas in and of themselves, an analysis of the concerns in relation to personal data online reveals a number of separate stand-alone sub-areas and issues. While some of these are quite well defined, others are still evolving. Given that the law is being changed by and is reacting to technological developments and new business models, there is an inevitable theme of the law lagging behind technology. This pressure is evident in the commentary and observation of existing and developing internet activity.

Having said that, with online abuse having escalated to a stage where some users of social networks and related websites are taking their own lives, and others are suffering horrific online abuse and internet experiences, it behoves responsible websites as well as parents, educators, employers, organisations and policymakers to pay more attention to personal data and safer internet experiences. National

---

7 Than personal data which remains off-line or off-electronic copy.

8 Personal information and personal data are referred to in the plural in the data protection regime.

9 UK Leveson Inquiry. *An Inquiry into the Culture, Practices and Ethics of the Press: Report, The Right Honourable Lord Justice Leveson* (November 2012). Available at http://www.official-documents.gov.uk/document/hc1213/hc07/0780/0780.asp. Also see the main inquiry website at http://www.levesoninquiry.org.uk/.

data protection authorities as well as courts also have an important role to play, as appropriate.

Critics suggest that (some) social networking and related websites have not been doing everything that they can in terms of tackling these problems. Some are argued not to have (robust) online abuse policies, whereas others may have inadequate policies. Standards naturally vary across the range of such websites.

Finally, given the diverse nature of these issues, and the inevitable interface of technology, social issues, commerce and law, various expert contributors assist to elucidate this dynamic and evolving tapestry. We cannot hope to cover absolutely everything, but we do hope to provide a useful text in an area that is often neglected in the literature.

PART II: INTERNET AND SOCIAL NETWORKING

Chapter 2

INTERNET AND TECHNOLOGY

Headline of Issues

- Setting and context
- Concerns
- Social networking
- Definitions of social networking
- Examples and categories of social networking

Introduction

> "[N]ew conceptions must emerge to recognize the *electronic lives* that members of society lead today"[1]

> "[W]e are all just a few clicks away from internet infamy".[2]

> "Whether you are thinking in terms of your own … firm or your clients, you must now consider these new technologies".[3]

> "After I got home all i saw was on facebook – she deserved it did you wash the mud out of your hair? – I hope shes dead … Nobody cared … I moved away to another city to my moms … another school … people are posting pics of bleach, clorex, and ditches … tagging me … They said … She should try a different bleach, I hope she dies this time and isn't so stupid … They said I hope she sees this and kills herself … Why do I get this? I messed up but why follow me … I left your guys city … Im constantly crying now … Everyday I think why am I still here? … My anxiety is horrible now … never went out this summer … All from my past … lifes never getting better … cant go to school … meet or be with people … constantly cutting. I'm really depressed … Im on anti deppresants now and councelling and a month ago this summer … I overdosed … In hospital for 2 days … Im stuck … whats left of me now … nothing stops … I have nobody … I need someone :(… My name is Amanda Todd...."[4]

Social networking has arrived. It allows individuals to interact socially online through websites dedicated to facilitating such social contacts and relationships. It

---

1 D Findlay, "Tag! Now You're 'It.' What Photographs on Social Networking Sites Mean for the Fourth Amendment" (2008) (10) *North Carolina Journal of Law & Technology* 171 at 192. Emphasis in original.

2 J Sabin, "Every Click You Make: How The Proposed Disclosure of Law Students' Online Identities Violates Their First Amendment Right to Free Association" (2008–2009) (17) *Journal of Law and Policy* 699.

3 S Nelson, J Simek and J Foltin, "The Legal Implications of Social Networking" (2009–2010) (22) *Regent Law Review* 1 at 16.

4 Amanda Todd, a 15 year old Canadian teenager, is just another victim of online abuse. She left these flash-card messages on a YouTube video before she killed herself after years of social networking abuse and related physical abuse. If anyone is in any doubt as to the dark and feral side of social networking, this should be interesting viewing: http://youtu.be/vOHXGNx-E7E.

is important to note that "friends" on a social network may not actually be existing friends or acquaintances. The best-known (English-language) social network is Facebook. The significance of social networking cannot be understated. More people are registered social networkers than are involved in any other type of internet use. It now forms a growing part in social activity, relations, entertainment, electronic contracts,[5] business, commerce, electioneering and tourism,[6] to name but a few. To many, it is now part of growing up.

The value of many social networkings is now greater than the gross domestic product (GDP) of many nations. President Barack Obama visited the Facebook headquarters.[7] Few technology (or indeed other) companies can command a personal visit from the US President. Social network advertising is becoming more successful and more popular than traditional avenues for advertising.[8] The launch of Facebook (and now Twitter) on the stock exchange[9] has also enhanced the near hysteria surrounding social networking. It was valued at $104 billion.[10] It now has over 1 billion regular users.[11] Social networking is popular in almost every country[12] and language.

These are just some of the reasons why lawyers, business, the public, parents, educators and policymakers must take cognizance of the arrival of social networking and its implications. Social networking affects everyone (and every organisation) — whether directly or indirectly. Social networking has numerous advantages and benefits. However, while beneficial, sometimes bad things happen. It brings many legal and social concerns, many relating to online abuse, privacy and personal data. These concerns are not limited to one country.

> "Data borders continually merge and the privacy landscape mutates at an increasing pace ... Of course just because something can be done, does not mean that it is right or indeed legal to do it. This is a point all too often lost on those [websites] holding personal data".[13]

President Obama has also echoed similar concerns more recently, partly in light of the Snowden NSA revelations. Individuals disclose more and more information online and via social networking. Websites also collect more and more personal

---

5 D Looijen, "The Schema of Contract in the Digital Era" (2010) (8) *Journal on Telecommunications & High Technology* 547 at 562.

6 I Campbell, "Smartphone Guide to Put Dublin on the Map, 1,400 Points of Interest in 'Augmented Reality' Guide," *Irish Times*, 3 September 2010.

7 "Barack Obama and Mark Zuckerberg's Facebook 'Face Time'," BBC, available at www.bbc.co.uk/news/world-us-canada-13151889.

8 One example is referred to in S O'Connell, "We Get More Traffic on Facebook, Social Networks Could Take Over from the More Traditional Forms of E-selling," *Sunday Times*, 1 May 2011.

9 See, for example, "Goldman to Limit Facebook Deal," *Irish Times*, 18 January 2011, available at www.irishtimes.com/newspaper/breaking/2011/0118/breaking28.html.

10 K Rushton, "Facebook Valued at $104b on Record Breaking Stock Market Debut," *Daily Telegraph*, 17 May 2012, available at http://www.telegraph.co.uk/technology/facebook/9273583/Facebook-valued-at-104bn-on-record-breaking-stock-market-debut.html.

11 J Kiss, "Facebook Hits 1 Billion Users a Month," *Guardian*, 4 October 2012, available at http://www.guardian.co.uk/technology/2012/oct/04/facebook-hits-billion-users-a-month.

12 Irish people regularly use social networking and Ireland is well-served in terms of social networking. The European headquarters of Google and Facebook are in Dublin. The founder of Bebo chose Ireland to launch a new political social networking website (see A Maguire, "Bebo Founder Picks Ireland to Test Political Networking Site," *Irish Times*, 3 September 2010).

13 Irish Data Protection Commissioner, *Privacy Through the Years – 21 Years of Data Protection*, available at http://www.dataprivacy.ie/docs/27/01/2010_-_Privacy_through_the_Years_-_21_Y.

data, both explicitly and less explicitly. Regardless of where we are, people are legitimately concerned as to how secure their online personal data are, who can see it, who is collecting it, for what purposes, to whom they may be disclosing or *selling* it, and where these third-party recipients may be. Are they in jurisdictions that may have less secure data protection practices than apply in the EU,[14] or under specific national or state laws? These are all legitimate issues of concern, to individuals and the data protection regime.

A New Second Generation of Internet Activities

The commercial internet emerged during the 1960s and 1970s.[15] Now a second-generation internet is rising with the advent of social networking popularity and other developments such as cloud computing. Increasingly individuals, organisations and employees use electronic communications and social networking. There are ever increasing amounts personal data available online and or alternatively transmitted electronically. The continuing expansion of social networking and the new wave of cloud computing will expand the amounts of personal data held online and electronically in an exponential manner. Increasing amounts of social-networking documents and materials are discoverable in legal cases.[16] There are inevitably increasing privacy issues for individuals, both for private and public figures. David Cameron, the UK Prime Minister, felt the need to defend the right to a private life for public figures.[17] There is also the new category of person between the private individual and the public or celebrity figure, sometimes referred to as the "micro-celebrity".[18] It is now easier to become famous for a short period than at any time previous. Equally, is it reasonable to expect that individuals must abandon (permanently) their privacy and data protection rights as a result of temporary or limited publicity, which on occasion is not deliberate? Is it also reasonable to expect children to have to live the entirety of their lives with information, comments or photographs that they, or their friends, may have put online, but which they later regret?[19] Should the internet forget? Some suggest the debate is not should but rather when and in what circumstances it should delete and forget particular information.

We must not just consider the "normal" internet but also the second-generation

---

14 See, for example, the commentary of Andrew Harbison in relation to Cloud computing in Chapter 17.

15 AE Horton, "Beyond Control?: The Rise and Fall of Defamation Regulation on the Internet" (2009) (43) *Valparaiso University Law Review* 1265 at 1274. See also DC Davis, "MySpace Isn't Your Space: Expanding the Fair Credit Reporting Act to Ensure Accountability and Fairness in Employer Searches of Online Social Networking Services" (2006–2007) (XVI) *Kansas Journal of Law and Public Policy* 237 at 238–241.

16 See, for example, A Blank, "On the Precipe of E-Discovery: Can Litigants Obtain Employee Social Networking Web Site Information Through Employers?" (2010) (18) *CommLaw Conspectus* 487 at 488.

17 A Brown, "Facebook Data Concerns," *Society of Computers and Law*, 1 February 2008, available at http://www.scl.org/site.aspx?i=ed1035. This was even before the UK Leveson Inquiry into phone hacking, media ethics and media practices.

18 B Kane, "Balancing Anonymity, Popularity, & Micro-Celebrity: The Crosswords of Social Networking & Privacy" (2010) *Alb Law Journal of Science & Technology* 327.

19 Note the draft EU Data Protection Regulation, which includes, for example, an enhanced right to delete and be forgotten. Available at http://ec.europa.eu/justice/data-protection/document/review2012/com_2012_11_en.pdf.

internet (known as Web 2.0 internet). Web 2.0 encompasses social networking[20] website applications, user participation, encyclopaedias (eg Wikipedia), content-sharing websites (eg YouTube and Dailymotion),[21] new mainstream political campaigning via social networking (eg by Howard Dean and Barack Obama in the US, the UK and also in Irish political and presidential elections[22]), and increasing (mobile) internet-led democracy revolutions relying on social networking (sometimes labelled the Arab Spring), etc. The "emergence of social networking"[23] also means that we must consider how children and teenagers are using social networking,[24] in addition to our concerns regarding our own personal data. It is important to address the issue of online abuse, including cyberbullying, both for the instant harm it can inflict and for the ultimate harm it brings to our use of the internet. Corporates may arguably be concerned with the cost of diminished internet user experience which online abuse causes. This pertains in relation to victims, users, society generally and more recently advertisers. There have been calls for criminal sanctions against those who knowingly or recklessly engage in online abuse.

One of the reasons or enablers for Web 2.0 and its new myriad of websites and applications (ie uses), including social networking, is the reducing cost of rolling out new technologies and services.[25] "Decreased costs of production and distribution in the digital age enable widespread access to a greater variety of content"[26] and services. It is now less expensive to establish social networks and to transmit information electronically. It is also less expensive to store information electronically, including the storage of vast information online in new internet cloud services.[27]

What does social networking mean for privacy rights and data protection rights in the Web 2.0 era? Will Web 2.0 and social networking become the perfect manifestation of George Orwell's prophesy in *1984*[28]? Do NSA revelations mean that *1984* has been surpassed? Eric Schmidt, the chairman of Google, raises the possibility that some people may have to change their name in future as a result of particular online information relating to them.[29] Facebook suggests that the age of privacy is over[30]

---

20 In relation to the rise of Facebook and MySpace generally, see for example, I Byrnside, "Six Clicks of Separation: The Legal Ramifications of Employers Using Social Networking Sites to Research Applicants" (2008) (10) *Vanderbilt Journal of Entertainment and Technology Law* 445 at 454 *et seq*.

21 See Y Poullet, "Data Protection Legislation: What Is At Stake for Our Society and Democracy?" (2009) (25) *Computer Law & Security Review* 211 at 219.

22 See NJ Slabbert, "Orwell's Ghost: How Teletechnology is Reshaping Civil Society" (2008) (16) *CommLaw Conspectus* 349 at 355, 356–357.

23 L Thomas, "Social Networking in the Workplace: Are Private Employers Prepared to Comply with Discovery Requests for Posts and Tweets?" (2010) (63) *SMU Law Review* 1373 at 1379–1382.

24 Sometimes child and teenager internet users are referred to as "Generation Y".

25 Sometimes known as deployment.

26 See R Tushnet, "Power Without Responsibility: Intermediaries and the First Amendment" (2007–2008) (76) *George Washington Law Review* 986 at 990.

27 See Andrew Harbison at Chapter 17.

28 G Orwell, *1984* (London: Secker and Walburg, 1949).

29 "Young Will Have to Change Names to Escape 'Cyber Past' Warns Google's Eric Schmidt. The private lives of young people are now so well documented on the internet that many will have to change their names on reaching adulthood, Google's CEO has claimed," *Daily Telegraph*, 18 August 2010, available at http://www.telegraph.co.uk/technology/google/7951269/Young-will-have-to-change-names-to-escape-cyber-past-warns-Googles-Eric-Schmidt.html.

30 M Kirkpatrick, "Facebook's Zuckerberg Says the Age of Privacy is Over," Readwrite.com, 9

and that privacy is no longer a social norm.[31] Google has been criticised in relation to the apparent admission that users should not have any expectation of privacy in their Gmail accounts.[32] Yet, might a change of name be useful at all if someone can tag and link a new name to an old name, not to mention the issue of increasingly sophisticated search engine technology? As Mr Schmidt acknowledges, however, these are all evolving issues to be fully discussed, considered and debated.[33]

Describing Social Networking

Definitions

Social media have been described as the most powerful thing on the planet.[34] The scale of its popularity is quite staggering. It allows "users to publish their private lives on a world stage."[35] Social media have become the new "soda fountain"[36] or water-cooler social discussion point in offices, with a host of possibilities for interactive communication and sharing information and content (eg photographs, videos).[37] It can also be significantly more dangerous than a soda fountain. Life, quality of life and quality of internet experience are now sometimes at stake. Rightly or wrongly, there has been a fundamental shift in how social networks and related websites, and the (multinational) companies behind such websites, are perceived. We also need to be more considered and nuanced in our assessment of responses to these developments. Some argue that social networks and related websites are not doing, and have not done, everything that they can to deal with the dark side of the internet. Equally, some might argue that there is a business case, as well as a societal, ethical and legal case, for a safe internet experience. What is clear is that these issues continue to evolve.

However, what is social networking? Brown describes social networking as follows:

> "'Web 2.0' technologies allow users to share text, audio and video on blogs, photo and video sites such as Flicker and YouTube, and the now-ubiquitous social networks such as MySpace and Facebook. Combined with the still and video cameras present in most mobile phones, this has allowed individuals to share information about themselves and those around them to an unprecedented degree. Users can search for (possibly live) video feeds from specified locations or containing specific individuals. Supposedly 'anonymous' data

January 2010, available at http://readwrite.com/2010/01/09/facebooks_zuckerberg_says_the_age_of_privacy_is_ov.

31 B Johnson, "Privacy No Longer a Social Norm, Says Facebook Founder," *Guardian*, 11 January 2010, available at http://www.guardian.co.uk/technology/2010/jan/11/facebook-privacy.

32 D. Rusche, "Google: Don't Expect Privacy When Sending to Gmail, Critics Call Revelation 'A Stunning Admission' as Google Makes Claim in Court Filing in Attempt to Head Off Class Action Lawsuit", *Guardian*, 15 August 2013.

33 E. Schmidt, and J. Cohen, *The New Digital Age: Reshaping the Future of People, Nations and Business* (New York: Knopf Doubleday, 2013).

34 Louise McSharry, blogger, interviewed by Orla Barry on *The Green Room*, Newstalk, 21 March 2010; blog available at http://louisemcsharry.wordpress.com/2010/04/08/hello-and-welcome/; and http://twitter.com/#!/louisemcsharry.

35 LL Baughman, "Friend Request or Foe? Confirming the Misuse of Internet and Social Networking Sites By Domestic Violence Perpetrators" (2010) (19) *Widener Law Journal* 933.

36 *ibid.*

37 JS Groppe, "A Child's Playground or a Predator's Hunting Ground? – How to Protect Children on Internet Social Networking Sites" (2007) (16) *CommLaw Conspectus* 215 at 224.

can increasingly be linked back to individuals based on their profiles and set of 'friends' revealed by these services.

Social networks now have hundreds of millions of members around the world, while high-profile blogs [personal websites] like Boing Boing have readerships to rival national newspapers. Universities and companies have admitted checking the social network profiles of potential students and employees. Solicitors have warned that insurers are now monitoring social network [web]sites before paying claims.

In general, it seems that individuals (especially young people) are often privacy-unaware or prefer short-term gains from providing personal data over longer-term less tangible concerns over the resulting privacy impact. While many social networking [web]sites feature highly configurable privacy settings that allow information to be restricted to specific groups of friends, users rarely alter defaults allowing widespread sharing. It is likely to be many years before social norms fully adjust to these new possibilities for self-disclosure and the use of personal information by potential employers, educators and insurers".[38]

One definition refers to social networks as:

> "web-based services that allow individuals to,
> (1) construct a public or semi-public profile within a bounded system;
> (2) articulate a list of other users with whom they share a connection; and
> (3) view and traverse their list of connections and those made by others within the system".[39]

Gurney states:

> "Social networking [web]sites, or 'friend sites,' are vast gathering areas on the internet that allow users to create online profiles where they can list personal information and post photographs and other content. Profiles resemble the dating service advertisements that spawned them: They are created by filling out generic forms the [web]site makes available, and contain demographic details, likes and dislikes, and carefully selected personal photographs or video. A user can link her profile to those of her friends, compiling long lists of contacts, and post public messages on friends' profiles as well as send private messages to other users. The websites typically have search functions that allow members to look up other users on the [web]sites, or join groups of people with similar interests. Although other websites may also offer some of these features, social networking [web]sites are distinguished by the way they create an online society with clearly drawn connections where 'friends are publicly articulated, profiles are publicly viewed, and comments are publicly visible'".[40]

Zarsky describes social networks as websites "that allow individuals to exchange messages and information, and in some instances to work together as a group or team toward various objectives."[41] He further differentiates between different forms of social networks. There can be open and closed groups of communication and

38 I Brown, "Data Protection: The New Technical and Political Environment," *Society of Computers and Law*, available at http://www.scl.org/site.aspx?i=ed14331.

39 DM Boyd and NB Ellison, "Social Network Sites: Definition, History, and Scholarship" (2007) (13)(1) *Journal Computer-Mediated Comm.* 11, available at http://jcmc.indiana.edu/vol13/issue1/boyd.ellison.html. Referred to in J Grimmelmann, "Saving Facebook" (2009) (94) *Iowa Law Review* 1137 at 1142.

40 KM Gurney, "MySpace, Your Reputation: A Call to Change Libel Laws for Juveniles Using Social Networking Sites" (2009) (82) *Temple Law Review* 241 at 245–246.

41 TZ Zarsky, "Law and Online Social Networks: Mapping the Challenges and Promises of User-generated Information Flows" (2008)(18) *Fordham Intellectual Property Media & Entertainment Law Journal* 741 at 746. See also A Blank, "On the Precipe of E-Discovery: Can Litigants Obtain Employee Social Networking Web Site Information Through Employers?" (2010) (18) *CommLaw Conspectus* 487 at 489–490.

contact. These can also be in family (close ties), social, public and commercial settings. The connectivity or ties can vary between very strong to very weak social ties. Discourse can also be single comments or alternatively a stream of discussion.[42] There are significant issues and avenues for research.

In addition:

> "Social-networking [web]sites have been defined as 'web-based services that allow individuals to (1) construct a public or semi-public profile within a bounded system, (2) articulate a list of other users with whom they share a connection, and (3) view and traverse their list of connections and those made by others within the system.' This definition emphasizes three primary activities on such [web]sites: users create a unique online identity, establish relationships with other users, and join various communities of users who share connections".[43]

Some Categories of Social Networking

There are different categories of social networking. Below are just some examples:

Friend Websites
These are websites where individuals seek to become friends with others whether for personal or business reasons. Examples of friend social networks[44] include Facebook,[45] Friendster,[46] MySpace,[47] Plaxo[48] and LinkedIn.[49] It has been suggested that the most surprising uses of Facebook have been by the police, schools and employers, not individual users[50]

Blogs
Blogs are generally websites established with individuals posting personal information, comments and information about almost any topic, whether personal about themselves, status updates, or general commentary on a particular subject or theme.[51]

Blawging
The emergence of blogging by lawyers and legal academics has even coined its own phrase, blawging. Blawgs are blogs that relate specifically to law or particular legal subjects. There are now many well-known lawyers' and academics' blogs, such as those of Jeremy Philips, TJ McIntyre, Eoin O'Dell and Scotus (re US Supreme Court) as well as blawgs by well-established

---

42 See discussion in Zarsky, *op. cit.*, 747.
43 EE North, "Facebook Isn't Your Space Anymore: Discovery of Social Networking Websites" (2010) (58) *University of Kansas Law Review* 1281 at 1284.
44 See generally, *ibid*, 748–752.
45 U Munukutla-Parker, "Unsolicited Commercial Email, Privacy Concerns Relating to Social Network Services, Online Protection of Children, and Cyberbullying" (2006) (2) *I/S: A Journal of Law and Policy* 627 at 634.
46 *ibid*, 636.
47 *ibid*, 637.
48 *ibid*, 639.
49 *ibid*, 639–640.
50 *ibid*, 635.
51 DC Bechstrom, "Who's Looking at Your Facebook Profile? The Use of Student Conduct Codes to Censor College Students' Online Speech" (2008) (45) *Williamette Law Review* 261 at 269.

legal organisations, including the American Bar Association (ABA). Blawgs, as well as the interest and public service many of them provide, can also be used with marketing and advertising of a lawyer or firm in mind.[52] The same legal and ethical concerns can arise, including vicarious liability, ethical violations, anonymous blogging, advertising compliance, formalising client-lawyer relations (even inadvertently), legal advice issues, conflicts and confidentiality.[53] Confidentiality can be of particular concern.[54]

Tweets
Tweets are similar to blogs but are more instantaneous and are limited to 140 characters.

Message Boards
Message boards and bulletin boards[55] are another form of social networking. Here groups of people share information, comments and conversation on a specific topic. The comments are made within a "group" setting.

Gaming
There are numerous gaming websites where significant numbers of users interact and participate in online gaming and related discussion.

This is by no means a definitive categorisation and is meant merely as an illustrative sampling. Romantic and dating-type websites are not within the compass of the current discussion. Gambling-related websites are also popular but are also beyond the present discussion. These later categories are, however, significant on a variety of levels, not least on risk issues.

Depending on the category and type of website, there will be perceptibly more or less risk attaching. Even within categories, a lack of nuanced regulation and standards can mean that there are vast disparities in standards and a perceptible lack of any best practice within a given category. One website can be more or less responsible than another.

Conclusion

The examples above cannot be wholly definitive of all internet and social networking categories. This is in part because the area is always evolving. However, we need to distinguish different activities and different websites, as inevitably there will be certain privacy and data protection nuances to each. Some will inherently have greater risks, others less. We begin to look at some of these more specifically below.

---

52 See for instance JM Cornett, "The Ethics of Blawging: A Genre Analysis" (2009) (41) *Loyola University Chicago Law Journal* 221 at 244–249. Note also, KE Vinson, "The Blurred Boundaries of Social Networking in the Legal Field: Just 'Face' It" (2010–2011) *University of Memphis Law Review* 355.

53 See, for instance, Cornett, *op. cit.* at 235.

54 On confidentiality issues generally, see for example Cornett, *op.cit.* at 254–258.

55 Bechstrom, *op. cit.* at 269–270.

CHAPTER 3

CONCERNS

HEADLINE OF ISSUES

- The issue of more and more personal data being used online, in particular on social networkings
- Second-generation internet (Web 2.0)
- Data protection and EU data protection review
- Data loss
- Data theft and identity theft
- Misuse, direct marketing, etc
- Sensitive personal data
- Peer to peer, and the music file-sharing wars
- Children
- The Cloud
- Location data

SOCIAL NETWORKING: A NEW INTERNET AND NEW CONCERNS

The new second-generation internet (Web 2.0) and social networking use create a whole new tapestry of changes in society and in law. The growth of new media,[1] social networks[2] and new service applications (such as new business marketing tools[3]) raise new issues and concerns. There are obvious concerns regarding child safety. This is especially so when we consider that frequently all one needs to register an account is a valid email address, without any further verification[4] of name or age. There are, therefore, frequently no direct age checks. It is possible for almost any age of person to join, and worse still to pretend to be someone they are not.

While originally developed for music bands and students, social networks are now being fully embraced by all kinds of individuals, companies and organisations.[5] People judge others according to their online popularity, "social networking IQ,"[6]

---

1 See, for example H Jenkins, *Convergence Culture: Where Old and New Media Collide* (New York University Press, New York, 2006).

2 DC Bechstrom, "Who's Looking at Your Facebook Profile? The Use of Student Conduct Codes to Censor College Students' Online Speech" (2008) (45) *Williamette Law Review* 261 at 267–270.

3 R Barrett, "A Story of Social Capital Invested Wisely in Linked In" (Jan-Feb 2008) (34) *Law Practice* 43.

4 M Maher, "You've Got Messages: Modern Technology Recruiting Through Text-Messaging and the Intrusiveness of Facebook" (2007) (8) *Texas Review of Entertainment and Sports Law* 125 at 137.

5 C Barnes, "Social Networking: Not Just for Youngsters Anymore" (2008–2009) (33) *Bar Technology* 19.

6 MA Behnke, "What is Your Social Networking IQ" (2008–2009) (33) *Bar Leader* 2.

etc. One can even be accused of being antisocial if not widely connected on social networks.[7] Other commentators openly speak of social networking and networking tools for the 21st century.[8] There can be a perception that one is not "normal" without fully engaging in social networking, including on occasion the dark side of the internet.

Social networking has many advantages, such as communications, maintaining contact from a distance, entertainment, rich content, personal development and socialising skills.[9] A website was used by a school in Bolton, Lancashire during a period of heavy snow to assist schoolchildren with online lessons.[10] The students' grades were reported to have increased.[11] Using social networks can possibly educate younger people in the use of technology, increase confidence and enhance interpersonal skills.[12]

The use of social networks play an increasing part in peoples' daily lives.[13] Social networking makes changes to "evolving social norms".[14] Some of these can be obviously undesirable. An example referred to by some would be social networks collecting and storing categories of personal data that users were not made aware of and had not consented to. Concerns are most notable in the case of children and teenagers. The "new world" pitfalls[15] include online abuse, misuse of personal data and safety risks for children being perhaps those most emphasised.

The age profile for social networking is much lower than the average age for internet usage.[16] There are obvious concerns, therefore, in terms of children as well as teenagers using social networking. Amanda Todd is just one tragic example. The US, Canada, UK and Ireland all have tragic examples of online abuse.

MySpace began in 2003[17] and originally focused on providing personalised webpages for music bands and facilitating communications between bands.[18] Facebook was

---

7 LS Rosen, "Are You Antisocial?" (2008–2009) (31) *Family Advocate* 6.

8 L Glankler, "Networking Tools for the Twenty-First Century" (2009) (19) *Trends in Law Library Management and Technology* 29.

9 "Facebook Interactions Can Help Boost Personal Ones, Study Finds," *Irish Times*, 26 November 2010, available at http://www.irishtimes.com/newspaper/finance/2010/1126/1224284180450.html.

10 I Knight, "Illiteracy? Try Blogging," *Sunday Times*, 13 February 2011, News Review section, 4.

11 *ibid.*

12 "Benefits of Online Social Networking," ParentFurther, available at http://www.parentfurther.com/technology-media/social-networking/benefits.

13 S Nelson, J Simek and J Foltin, "The Legal Implications of Social Networking" (2009–2010) (22) *Regent Law Review* 1 at 2.

14 "Facebook, Facebook Principles," at www.facebook.com/principles.php, as referred to in A Blank, "On the Precipe of E-Discovery: Can Litigants Obtain Employee Social Networking Web Site Information Through Employers?" (2010) (18) *CommLaw Conspectus* 487 at 490.

15 *ibid.*

16 KM Gurney, "MySpace, Your Reputation: A Call to Change Libel Laws for Juveniles Using Social Networking Sites" (2009) (82) *Temple Law Review* 241 at 246.

17 For a brief history of MySpace see, for example, EP Stedman, "MySpace, But Whose Responsibility? Liability of Social-Networking Websites When Offline Sexual Assault of Minors Follows Online Interaction" (2007) (14) *Villanova Sports & Entertainment Law Journal* 363 at 363–364.

18 *ibid*, 367.

established on 4 February 2004 by a college student at Harvard University as a means of its students communicating with each other.[19] In 2006 Facebook had over 6.6 billion friend requests on its website.[20] It grew to 750 million active users,[21] and now has over 1 billion regular active users.[22] The scale of social networking popularity can mean that where things do go wrong, eg online abuse, that it can occur on a significant scale. Some might say that traditional bullying ends at the school yard. However, texting, calls, emails, online abuse and the internet do not.

There are increasing calls for empirical research of the effects of social networking and the relationship between law and social networking.[23] While many concerns are apparent, the full extent of the (problem) issues social networking raises — and how to deal with them — is only just beginning to be seen. One example of this occurred recently with the Irish Data Protection Commissioner's Office first data protection audit of Facebook on foot of several complaints in relation to its practices.[24] The Data Protection Commissioner's re-audit report[25] included two requirements: Facebook should be more transparent as to what it wished to do with users' personal data; and certain practices, such as automated facial recognition features for photographs, were not permissible under the EU data protection regime and should be discontinued. More recently, the UK Leveson Inquiry was critical of the trade in illegally obtained personal data.[26] Some argue that more transparency is needed of social networks and related websites as regards online abuse, abuse reports and abuse-reporting tools, procedures, protocols and resolutions, as well as preventative measures. Obviously, some are better than others.

One of the concerns relating to online abuse relates to its nature. Whereas traditional abuse and bullying, not condoning either, were limited to a location and a rather defined number of people, the advent of social networking brings a whole new escalation in damage, scale and permanence. It also brings a new set of problems for victims and parents seeking to deal with, prevent and take down online abuse.

Grimmelmann describes how social networking users,

---

19 RM Groves, "Facebook 2 Blackberry and Database Trading Systems: Morphing Social Networking to Business Growth in a Global Recession" (2009–2010) (112) *West Virginia Law Review* 153 at 160.

20 Referred to in JJ Ator, "Got Facebook?" *GPSOLO*, March 2009, 4.

21 Facebook statistics, available at www.facebook.com/press/info.php?statistics.

22 J Kiss, "Facebook Hits 1 Billion Users a Month," *Guardian*, 4 October 2012, available at http://www.guardian.co.uk/technology/2012/oct/04/facebook-hits-billion-users-a-month. There are some concerns that there are significant numbers of false and non-real accounts, thus distorting this figure.

23 Highlighted by Zarsky, *op. cit*, 782–783. The author also refers to the lack of empirical research in relation to television cameras and new social networking activities in court, such as Twitter. See P Lambert, *Courting Publicity, Twitter and Television Cameras in Court* (Bloomsbury, West Sussex, 2011).

24 See *Facebook Ireland Limited, Report of Audit*, Irish Data Protection Commissioner, 21 December 2011, available at www.dataprotection.ie.

25 See *Facebook Ireland Limited, Report of Re-Audit*, Irish Data Protection Commissioner, 21 September 2012, available at www.dataprotection.ie.

26 UK *Leveson Inquiry. An Inquiry into the Culture, Practices and Ethics of the Press: Report*, The Right Honourable Lord Justice Leveson, November 2012. Available at http://www.official-documents.gov.uk/document/hc1213/hc07/0780/0780.asp. Also see the main inquiry website at http://www.levesoninquiry.org.uk/.

> "socialize on the [web]site, why they misunderstand the risks involved, and how their privacy suffers as a result. Facebook offers a socially compelling platform that also facilitates peer-to-peer privacy violations: users harming each others' privacy interests. These two facts are inextricably linked; people use Facebook with the goal of sharing information about themselves. Policymakers cannot make Facebook completely safe, but they can help people use it safely".[27]

The argument for doing more has escalated with the tragic results of some of the online abuse occurring. The UK Prime Minister David Cameron, for instance, has called for a boycott of certain "vile" websites. He has also been putting pressure on websites to block and deal with child pornography.

Social networking "harms" can include cyberbullying, threats, abuse, grooming, defamation, privacy and data protection infringements, disclosure, surveillance, instability, disagreements, spillovers and denigration.[28] "While online social networking is nothing new, its legal ramifications are just beginning to come into focus."[29] Our critical analytical skills in assessing social networks and the nuances need to improve. That goes for parents, educators, policymakers, those representing victims, etc. Data protection authorities also need to be properly resourced. The Irish Data Protection Commissioner is on record a number of times highlighting his office's lack of resources. However, the problem is multifaceted, as will be the solutions. This will of course inevitably include legal recourse, as this will sometimes be the only avenue, or only timely avenue, available. However, other solutions can equally be looked at in particular circumstances.

We "cannot overstate the pervasive nature and rampant use of social-networking websites."[30] Social networking has literally changed how we socialise.[31] The opposite is also true. Many victims of online and social networking abuse become more isolated and cannot easily connect with real friends online or in person. They are prevented from availing of what should be a safe online experience. Today, "relationships now exist in an alternative online world and communal responsibilities thus have changed forever."[32] Teenagers and school children now routinely communicate in a way which up until now would have been reserved for evenings and weekends.[33] Social networks "represent the fastest growing segment of internet usage."[34] The amount of information gathered and made available is significant. However, the amount and level of detailed information is increasing rapidly. This

---

27 J Grimmelmann, "Saving Facebook" (2009) (94) *Iowa Law Review* 1137.

28 *ibid.*

29 EE North, "Facebook Isn't Your Space Anymore: Discovery of Social Networking Websites" (2010) (58) *University of Kansas Law Review* 1279 at 1286.

30 EP Stedman, "MySpace, But Whose Responsibility? Liability of Social-Networking Websites When Offline Sexual Assault of Minors Follows Online Interaction" (2007) (14) *Villanova Sports & Entertainment Law Journal* 363 at 366.

31 DC Davis, "MySpace Isn't Your Space: Expanding the Fair Credit Reporting Act to Ensure Accountability and Fairness in Employer Searches of Online Social Networking Services" (2006–2007) (XVI) *Kansas Journal of Law and Public Policy* 237.

32 Stedman, *op. cit*, 365.

33 KD Williams, "Public Schools Vs MySpace: The Newest Challenge to Student Rights" (2008) (76) *University of Cincinnati Law Review* 707 at 708.

34 *The Social Media Guide Website*, http://mashable.com/2009/04/20/the-fastest-growing-social-sites/, referred to in AJ Bojorquez and D Shores, "Open Government and the Net: Bringing Social Media into the Light" (2009–2010) (11) *Texas Tech Administrative Law Journal* 45 at 46.

is due to the popularity of social networking. It is also due to the increasing number and variety of "apps" or applications (services and features) on social networkings.[35]

There has been ongoing controversy in relation to the impact of social networking and mobile telephones on education and language.[36] Is it having a positive or detrimental effect? While pertinent, this is beyond the scope of the present discussion.[37]

One of the fastest growing social networking activities involves individuals connecting on video chat (discussion) with completely random strangers.[38] Does this create personal safety issues for adults, not just children?

Nelson *et al* state that:

> "Social networking and social media websites represent a shift in how people discover, read, and share news, information, and content; they are a fusion of sociology and technology, transforming monologues (one-to-many) into dialogues (many-to-many), and they are 'the democratization information, transforming people from content readers into content publishers.' The social nature of these websites helps to build online communities of people who share interests, activities, or both, or people interested in exploring the interests and activities of others".[39]

The pace of change can be frightening and our knowledge catch-up lags behind. There is a generational gap. In addition, policymakers and laws frequently tend to react to issues as they arise as opposed to being proactive. It also means that issues like online abuse are considered only when they make front-page headlines and there is a political or business imperative. Some social networks and related websites can sometimes be more proactive and more supportive in relation to victims and dealing with online abuse. Where websites do have measures in place, they need to be transparent and user friendly to achieve optimum benefit. Some websites need to improve more than others.

There are many privacy and data protection concerns, in particular those brought about by social networking and second-generation internet (Web 2.0). In some instances we are only beginning to see the problems which are arising. Only time will tell what solutions will follow and which ones will be successful. In other instances, there remains an education deficit in terms of compliance issues. For example, one political party in Ireland launched a new website in apparent breach of data protection compliance rules.[40]

---

35 Nelson *et al., op. cit*, 21.

36 As just one example, see N Bramhill, "Exams in Text: CU in 10 Years," *Sunday Times*, 20 February 2011. On a separate but not altogether unrelated note, given advertising, marketing and children on social networks, note G Farrell, "McDonald's Sued Over Toys With Meals," *Financial Times*, 16 December 2010, 27.

37 There is, however, a lot of literature available on this subject.

38 See ChatRoulette.com. There is also a ChatXRoulette.com.

39 AJ Bojorquez and D Shores, "Open Government and the Net: Bringing Social Media into the Light" (2009–2010) (11) *Texas Tech Administrative Law Journal* 45 at 47. References omitted.

40 Referring to Fine Gael. See E Edwards, "Fine Gael Website May Breach Privacy Laws, Warns Expert," *Irish Times*, 8 January 2011, 6. See separate incident referred to in "Two Held in Fine Gael Hacking Inquiry," RTE, 1 September 2011, available at http://www.rte.ie/news/2011/0901/hacking.html.

Data Protection Update

The arrival of Web 2.0 and websites such as social networks escalates the issues and concerns of traditional data protection law, such as online abuse, consent, transparency and fairness, and data security. However, the ease of transfer, loss and disclosure of personal data on social networking (and other new services) means that even greater strains are being put on the traditional data protection regime. Resources can also be an issue for official regulators. Public concerns and a slow but growing awareness of data-processing activities by websites, in conjunction with well-publicised examples of massive personal data loss (at a scale of millions of individuals' personal data), mean that there is a perceived need for updating the EU Data Protection Directive 1995.[41] The directive predates social networking and the second-generation internet. There are, therefore, new proposals to update the EU data protection regime.[42]

New laws, however, do not negate the need for individuals to engage positively in personal awareness and education as regards their own personal data online. Part of the solution involves individuals proactively seeking to protect their own personal data. That means that they must be educated as to the risks in the first instance, which in the case of children may not be immediately obvious. Parents, educators and policymakers also need to be educated. That includes the need to learn about social networks, the sometimes dark side of social networking, what social networks can and cannot do, etc. This can sometimes involve having to engage in an analysis of the nuances of exact terminology. What a particular person may say at first blush may not always convey the entirety of what is and is not happening. Sometimes it is critical to appreciate the business policy decisions and strategies behind what a given website may say as to what it can and cannot do. As always, these issues are evolving. Avenues for positive co-operation, partnering and research also arise.

Data Theft and Identity Theft

The theft of information, files, etc has always been an issue. However, the advent of digital data, second-generation internet and social networking emphasises problems of data theft, password theft, identity theft, hacking and malevolent software such as viruses. A breach in a website's security or a corporate computer system could result in the disclosure of the personal details of millions of individuals. Identity theft is identified as the fastest-growing offence in the US but equally as one of the most "daunting set of challenges" to address.[43] As indicated above, Lord Justice Leveson was concerned at the extent of the illicit trade in personal data in the UK.[44]

41 Directive 95/46/EC of the European Parliament and of the Council of 24 October 1995 on the protection of individuals with regard to the processing of personal data and on the free movement of such data.

42 A review culminated in a draft measure to update EU data protection regime to be implemented by way of an EU Regulation, as opposed to the current EU Directive format. See proposed Data Protection Regulation at http://ec.europa.eu/justice/data-protection/document/review2012/com_2012_11_en.pdf.

43 J Winn and K Govern, "Identity Theft: Risks and Challenges to Business of Data Compromise" (2009) *Temple Journal of Science, Technology & Environmental Law* 49.

44 UK Leveson Inquiry. *An Inquiry into the Culture, Practices and Ethics of the Press: Report, The Right Honourable Lord Justice Leveson*, November 2012. Available at http://www.official-

There is concern that many service apps or applications for social networks are easily vulnerable to hackers who use them to vacuum up the personal details of users and to impersonate (some of) those individuals.[45] Facebook has been criticised for not testing and verifying the security of its third-party apps suppliers.[46] The US Federal Trade Commission (FTC) described this as "deceptive".[47] The FTC also filed various other privacy complaints against Facebook.[48] In a settlement Facebook agreed to 20 years of FTC privacy audits.[49] Google was fined $22.5m in a settlement with the FTC in relation to its having bypassed privacy security settings.[50] The FTC states:

> "The settlement is part of the FTC's ongoing efforts make sure companies live up to the privacy promises they make to consumers, and is the largest penalty the agency has ever obtained for a violation of a Commission order. In addition to the civil penalty, the order also requires Google to disable all the tracking cookies it had said it would not place on consumers' computers".[51]

At the time this was the largest such penalty. Social networks as well as other websites have also been targeted directly by hackers searching for personal user details.[52]

Personal details such as name, address, date of birth and credit card are all targets for hackers. There is growing evidence of the vast market involved in the sale of whole databases containing personal details that have been illicitly obtained.

One of the reasons for websites, etc being targeted by hackers is that hackers can sell the personal data to third parties, seek to blackmail the website company or use the personal information directly to try to access bank accounts or charge purchases to the accounts of third-party individuals. In another example, as yet unreleased pop songs are hacked and then sold.[53] Attempts to access or charge an individual's bank account using their stolen personal data is known as identity theft. The UK Leveson

---

documents.gov.uk/document/hc1213/hc07/0780/0780.asp. Also see the main inquiry website at http://www.levesoninquiry.org.uk/.

45 C Soghoian, "Hackers Target Facebook Apps," *CNET News*, 27 March 2008, http://news.cnet.com/8301-13739_3-9904331-46.html, referred to in Nelson *et al., op. cit*, 32.

46 J Halliday, "Facebook Accused of Deceiving Developers Over Security. Social Networking Site Allegedly Did Nothing to Verify Security of Applications It Was Paid Tens of Thousands of Dollars to Review," *Guardian*, 30 November 2012, available at http://www.guardian.co.uk/technology/2012/aug/13/facebook-developers.

47 *ibid.*

48 FTC complaint available at http://www.ftc.gov/os/caselist/0923184/111129facebookcmpt.pdf.

49 F Lardinois, "Facebook and FTC Settle Privacy Charges – No Fine, But 20 Years of Privacy Audits," *Techcrunch*, 10 August 2012, available at http://techcrunch.com/2012/08/10/facebook-ftc-settlement-12/. The FTC settlement agreement is available at http://www.ftc.gov/os/caselist/0923184/111129facebookagree.pdf.

50 F Lardinois, "Google Settles With FTC, Agrees to Pay $22.5m Penalty for Bypassing Safari Privacy Settings," *Techcrunch*, 9 August 2012, available at http://techcrunch.com/2012/08/09/google-settles-with-ftc-agrees-to-pay-22-5m-penalty-for-bypassing-safari-privacy-settings/. The FTC settlement is available at http://ftc.gov/opa/2012/08/google.shtm.

51 At http://ftc.gov/opa/2012/08/google.shtm.

52 A Lyly, "Twitter Hacked, Personal Documents Leak," *Neowin.net*, 17 July 2009, http://neowin.net/news/main/09/07/17/twitter-hacked-personal-documents-leak; Siderr, "Facebook Applications Revealed" (Winter 2007–2008) (13) *2600: Hacker Quarterly* 32–33, each as referred to in Nelson *et al., op. cit*, 32.

53 J Clark, "Hackers Convicted of Stealing Lady GaGa Songs," *ZD Net UK*, 18 June 2011, available at http://www.zdnet.co.uk/blogs/mapping-babel-10017967/hackers-convicted-of-stealing-new-lady-gaga-songs-10022764/.

Inquiry, as well as referring to the illicit trade in personal data, also referred to the press blackmailing of a football manager with personal data that was obviously sensitive to him.[54]

There is now also an increasing practice of hacking the closed, or private, social networking accounts of well-known individuals such as actors and sports stars. The hackers will then contact and seek to blackmail the individual in order not to make the information, comments, photographs or videos public.

One of the more recent hacking examples involved Sony. Sony PlayStation is reported to have been breached, with over 70 million customers' personal details and accounts being illegally accessed.[55] There is also discussion in relation to whether various national data protection authorities will investigate and or impose sanctions, including monetary sanctions.[56] The UK Information Commissioner's Office (ICO) (the equivalent of the Irish Data Protection Commissioner) contacted Sony to investigate the issues further.[57] It eventually fined Sony £250,000. Certain US states' Attorneys General are also reported as investigating the breach.[58] The amount of data lost in this instance has been described as "extraordinary".[59] It was also reported as including credit card data.[60] The ICO has imposed a number of other significant fines in relation to data loss. These include fining a police force £150,000 (Greater Manchester Police), a charity £70,000 (Norwood Ravenswood), a health authority £70,000 (Aneurin Bevan Health Board), a council £140,000 (Midlothian Council), hospitals £375,000 (Brighton and Sussex University Hospitals NHS Trust) and a medical entity £225,000 (Belfast Health and Social Care Trust).[61] A spam text marketing firm was fined £440,000.[62] A local authority was fined £60,000 for sending a child-related report to the wrong person.[63] Separately, the ICO also imposed the

---

54 UK Leveson Inquiry. *An Inquiry into the Culture, Practices and Ethics of the Press: Report, The Right Honourable Lord Justice Leveson*, November 2012. Available at http://www.official-documents.gov.uk/document/hc1213/hc07/0780/0780.asp. Also see the main inquiry website at http://www.levesoninquiry.org.uk/. Note also the case of Daniel Perry in Scotland who is reported to have committed suicide after online blackmail.

55 See for, example, "Hacker Steals PlayStation Data," *Irish Times*, 27 April 2011, available at http://irishtimescom/newspaper/breaking/2011/0427/breaking2.html; "Sony PlayStation Suffers Breach," *Reuters*, available at http://reuters.com/article/2011/04/us-sony-stolendata-idUSTRE73P6WB20110.

56 See, for example, "Sony May Face Legal Action over Data Breach," *Irish Times*, http://www/irishtimes.com/newspaper/breaking/2011/0428/breaking7.html.

57 *ibid.*

58 *ibid.*

59 Rory Cellan-Jones and Rupert Goodwins , interviewed on *BBC News*, "'Long Term Damage' from Sony PlayStation Scandal," available at http://news.bbc.co.uk/today/hi/today/newsid_9468000/9468943.stm.

60 See, for example, "Sony: Credit Data Risked in PlayStation Outage," *Forbes*, available at http://www.forbes/ffeds/ap/2011/04/26/technology-specialized-consumer-services-u....

61 A Deighton, "ICO Fines Police and Charity for Data Breaches," *Lexology*, 29 October 2012, available at http://www.lexology.com/library/detail.aspx?g=7adda7a8-ba0c-4404-adba-1e6121b0824a; S Evans, "Huge Increase in ICO Fines for Data Breaches," *Computer Business Review*, 13 August 2012, available at http://www.cbronline.com/news/huge-increase-in-ico-fines-for-data-breaches-130812; "Data Breaches 10 Times Worse, Say ICO Figures," BBC, 30 August 2012, available at http://www.bbc.co.uk/news/technology-19424197.

62 "Spam Texters Fined Nearly Half a Million Pounds as ICO Cracks Down on Illegal Marketing Industry," ICO, 28 November 2012, available at http://www.ico.gov.uk/news/latest_news/2012/spam-texters-fined-nearly-half-a-million-pounds-28112012.aspx.

63 "Plymouth City Council Fined £60,000 for Sending Child Neglect Report to the Wrong Person,"

first fine for inaccurate and incorrect storage of personal data. Prudential was fined £50,000 for mixing up the account data of customers, which could have resulted in pension-related financial loss for one of the customers.[64]

More recently still, the Leveson Inquiry Report has recommended a more robust approach to implementing (and understanding) the data protection regime, including criticising the UK ICO for not being more proactive in policing the data protection regime.[65] The report also highlights the needs for a greater appreciation of the data protection regime at judicial level.[66]

Misuse, Marketing, Direct Marketing, Targeted Behavioural Marketing

Websites request ever more detailed information from individuals on registration. They can also gather personal data without users having to input details directly, which can occur on an ongoing basis and sometimes without the user's knowledge. This is sometimes prefaced with an official statement that furnishing the information will assist the website in profiling and in directing ever more useful targeted advertising and marketing to the individual.[67] It should be appreciated that using a website, for example, is one activity and can be distinguished from secondary activities such as the website targeting marketing at them based on a secondary profile or "shadow profile". The issue of such secondary, non-transparent data collections and profiling by organisations is an increasingly important issue. Much of the modern commercial internet, including social networking, depends on advertising. Many will readily accept and understand this. However, when the advertising and marketing received is based on a secondary hidden profile created by the website, or even based on our online activities, searches, emails, chat and preferences, greater concern may be raised. The profile may come from secondary unnecessary information that we are requested to provide; it may be gathered in a secondary profile request from the website; or it may be built up through observing individuals' activities, searches, communications and preferences. Tailoring or targeting marketing materials based on such profiles is referred to as targeted advertising.[68] The extent to which such issues are legal, fair and transparent requires detailed consideration in each instance.

One observer comments that:

ICO, 22 November 2012, available at http://www.ico.gov.uk/news/latest_news/2012/plymouth-city-council-fined-60000-for-sending-child-neglect-report-to-wrong-person-22112012.aspx.

64 "Prudential Fined £50,000 for Customer Account Confusion," ICO, 6 November 2012, available at http://www.ico.gov.uk/news/latest_news/2012/prudential-fined-50000-for-customer-account-confusion-06112012.aspx.

65 UK Leveson Inquiry. *An Inquiry into the Culture, Practices and Ethics of the Press: Report, The Right Honourable Lord Justice Leveson*, November 2012. Available at http://www.official-documents.gov.uk/document/hc1213/hc07/0780/0780.asp. Also see the main inquiry website at http://www.levesoninquiry.org.uk/.

66 *ibid.*

67 See A Brown and L Pownall, "Facebook Data Concerns," *Society of Computers and Law* 1 February 2008, available at www.scl.org/site.aspx?i=ed1035.

68 N Gleicher, "Neither a Customer Nor a Subscriber Be: Regulating the Release of User Information on the World Wide Web" (2008–2009) (118) *Yale Law Journal* 1945 at 1949.

> "marketers could send personalized promotional messages featuring an ordinary customer to that customer's friends. Because they reveal a customer's browsing and buying patterns, and because they feature implied endorsements, the messages raise significant concerns about disclosure of personal matters, information quality, and individuals' ability to control the commercial exploitation of their identity. Yet social marketing falls through the cracks between several different legal paradigms that might allow its regulation – spanning from privacy to trademark and unfair competition to consumer protection to the appropriation tort and rights of publicity … none of the existing legal paradigms, which all evolved in response to particular problems, addresses the unique new challenges posed by social marketing".[69]

As one commentator states:

> "It is obvious why social networking [web]sites seek to gather so much personal information about their users: they are driving the development of targeted advertising models. Whilst targeted advertising is crucial to push forward a more efficient advertising model, the line between personal and private is blurred".[70]

In one instance Sears was investigated in an enforcement action because it was obliging customers to download software onto their computers which enabled Sears TV to monitor and track all of the users' online activity, browsing, purchases and certain emails and instant messaging (IM) communications.[71] While Sears did seek consent in its terms and privacy statement, some authors would see the issue as purely a right to contract electronically and wonder why the FTC would have sought to investigate the wide tracking system in this instance.[72] They arguably ignore the concerns (and rights) of individual customers and users. The "Sears action serves as a reminder for advertisers about the necessity of providing effective disclosures to consumers."[73] "[C]urrent industry standard practices for obtaining consent may no longer be posted only in an online contract or privacy policy."[74] Sears "is prohibited from including material disclosures *only* in a privacy policy or user license agreement."[75]

Four telecommunications companies (telcos), UPC, Vodafone, O2 and Eircom, were fined in the Dublin District Court following breached of the Data Protection Acts. All four telcos pleaded guilty. The fines totalled €15,000. The largest fine was €7,100 for UPC, which continued to direct-market one person 225 times in less than three weeks, despite being requested to stop. The Assistant Irish Data Protection Commissioner indicated that this was "one of the most serious cases" of breach and persistence in unsolicited direct marketing.[76] This was before the Loyalty Build breach.

---

69 W McGeveran, "Disclosure, Endorsement, and Identity in Social Marketing" (2009) *University of Illinois Law Review* 1105.

70 A Brown, "Facebook Data Concerns," *Society of Computers and Law*, 1 February 2008, available at www.scl.org/site.aspx?i=ed1035.

71 Sears Holdings Management Corp, File No 082 3099 (Federal Trade Commission 4 June 2009), as referred to in SE Gindin, "Nobody Reads Your Privacy Policy or Online Contract? Lessons Learned and Questions Raised by the FTC's Action Against Sears" (2009) (8) *Northwestern Journal of Technology and Intellectual Property* 1.

72 Namely, Gindin, *op. cit*, 1–2.

73 Sears Holdings Management Corp, File No 082 3099 (Federal Trade Commission 4 June 2009), as referred to in Gindin, *op. cit*, 6.

74 Gindin, *op. cit*, 18.

75 Sears Holdings Management Corp, File No 082 3099 (Federal Trade Commission 4 June 2009), as referred to in Gindin, *op. cit*, 18.

76 See C O'Keefe, "Customer 'Harassed' by 225 Calls from UPC," *Irish Examiner*, 22 March

There have also been warnings in Ireland of a telephone scam where people receive calls from someone purporting to be from Microsoft and advising on IT security and upgrades, but really trying to obtain personal details.[77] The Irish police (Gardai) have also warned against phishing scams.[78]

There have been similar phishing scams using emails purporting to be from the Revenue Commissioners. An email headed "You are eligible to receive a tax refund" is sent to recipients and then asks them to access a scam website link and input personal details.[79] One asked users for their passport number and expiry date, name, address and date of birth.[80] Another phishing email is headed "Calculate Now Your … Taxes."[81]

The Irish Central Bank has also made proposals to regulate further direct marketing and calls to customers by financial institutions. It is proposing that they be restricted from such calls after 7pm and at weekends.[82] There are reports that the financial institutions, however, are resisting such proposals.[83]

Facebook has also agreed to make a settlement in the US in relation to its now discontinued Beacon advertising application of approximately $20m. In a Court of Appeals decision in California, Facebook was criticised in a dissenting judgment. The majority judgment upheld the amount. There was a possibility that the amount would not have been deemed sufficient to settle the case.[84] The minority dissenting judge states:

> "This settlement perverts the class action into a device for depriving victims of remedies for wrongs, while enriching … the wrongdoers ....
>
> The majority approves ratification of a class action settlement in which class members get no compensation at all. They do not get one cent. They do not get even an injunction against Facebook doing exactly the same thing to them again … Facebook gets a bar against any claims any of them might make for breach of their privacy rights. The most we could say for the cy pres award is that in exchange for giving up any claims they may have, the exposed Facebook users get the satisfaction of contributing to a charity to be funded by Facebook, partially controlled by Facebook, and advised by a legal team consisting of Facebook's counsel and their own purported counsel whom they did not hire and have never met.
>
> Facebook deprived its users of their privacy. And now they are deprived of a remedy"[85]

2011, available at www.irishexaminer.com/ireland/crime/customer-harassed-by-225-calls-from-upc-148895.html.

77 See "National Consumer Agency and Microsoft Warn of Cybercrime Scam," available at www.ncte.ie/NewsandEvents/Newsletter/title,19495,en.html.

78 Interview, *RTE News*, 16 August 2013.

79 See Revenue Commissioners, "Revenue Warning on New Phising Email Scam," 13 October 2009, available at www.revenue.ie/en/press/archive/2009/pr-131009-further-email-fraud.html.

80 "Warning Over Fake Revenue Email," *Irish Times*, 21 October 2011, available at www.irishtimes.com/newspaper/breaking/2010/1021/breaking40.html.

81 Revenue Commissioners, "Warning: Latest Email Scam," 12 April 2011, available at www.revenue.ie/en/spotlights/email-scam-warning.html.

82 A Sheehan, "Banks Dig Heels in on Proposals to Restrict Cold-Calling," *Irish Independent*, 23 March 2011.

83 *ibid.*

84 *McCall v Facebook*, United States Court of Appeals for the Ninth Circuit, 29 September 2012, available at http://www.ca9.uscourts.gov/datastore/opinions/2012/09/20/10-16380.pdf.

85 It may also be partly recognised in the USA. In the USA it appears that there is sometimes a recognition of higher obligations for sensitive personal data, eg FTC in the Sears investigation.

The issue of US class actions is increasingly contentious.

Sensitive Personal Data

Certain categories of personal data are deemed to be more important and personal to individuals. An example is personal heath data. This is recognised in the data protection legal regime.[86] Article 8 of the EU Data Protection Directive 1995 prohibits the processing of personal data revealing racial or ethnic origin, political opinions, religious or philosophical beliefs, trade-union membership, and the processing of data concerning health or sex life unless specified conditions are satisfied.[87] These conditions are the sensitive personal data legitimised processing conditions.[88] Organisations are obliged to comply with these rules.

Social networking can easily reveal sensitive personal data and, as such, issues of compliance with consent and the sensitive personal data legitimate processing conditions arise. Individuals, of course, need to be vigilant. However, social networks also need to work to protect the sensitive personal data of their users. Separately, websites need to consider whether they really need to request sensitive personal details from users, in particular for profiling and marketing purposes, whether directly or indirectly.

Peer to Peer (P2P)

There is also a new class of content creator lying between traditional content and media companies and individual users: namely "amateur content creators"[89] or "peer production".[90] Bloggers are an example. They can now produce and distribute their works more cheaply and efficiently.

There is arguably less respect and awareness of privacy and data protection compliance issues in the P2P creation environment. These new content creators, groups and websites can also collect, store and process large amounts of personal data. They equally need to be considered in terms of the concerns which arise for larger social networks and how to protect personal data.

See Sears Holdings Management Corp, File No 082 3099 (Federal Trade Commission 4 June 2009), as referred to in Gindin, *op. cit*, 5.

86 It may also be partly recognised in the USA. In the USA it appears that there is sometimes a recognition of higher obligations for sensitive personal data, eg FTC in the Sears investigation. See Sears Holdings Management Corp, File No 082 3099 (Federal Trade Commission 4 June 2009), as referred to in Gindin, *op. cit*, 5.

87 Article 8(1) Directive 95/46/EC of the European Parliament and of the Council of 24 October 1995 on the protection of individuals with regard to the processing of personal data and on the free movement of such data.

88 Article 8(2).

89 G Lastowska, "User-Generated Content and Virtual Worlds" (2007–2008) (10) *Vanderbilt Journal of Entertainment and Technology Law* 893 at 899.

90 Y Benkler, *The Wealth of Networks: How Social Production Transforms Markets and Freedom*, (New Haven: Yale University Press, 2006) 126–127, referred to in G Lastowska, "User-Generated Content and Virtual Worlds" (2007–2008) (10) *Vanderbilt Journal of Entertainment and Technology Law* 893 at 899.

Knowledge, Education

Some studies show that consumers are impulsive and do not appreciate the legal consequences of online activities.[91] There are also studies showing that consumers may not understand or pay sufficient attention to online notices.[92] Users may unwitting have their personal data used in a way which they may not have intended. There was a complaint to the UK ICO that Facebook did not allow users to delete their personal data. It appears that Facebook originally only permitted users to suspend, not delete, their profiles.[93] The right to have one's personal data deleted is one of the rights contained in the data protection regime.[94] The deletion issue is one of the concerns referred to in the audit of Facebook by the Irish Data Protection Commissioner.[95] The Data Protection Commissioner re-audit report[96] as well as other commentary make clear that websites must delete a user's personal data and personal profile if they decide to leave the website. The Data Protection Commissioner also required that more transparency be introduced.[97] In addition, the facial recognition feature was required to be turned off in the EU by the Data Protection Commissioner.[98]

Properly informing users and properly configuring consent options to the different possibilities on a website can often be easily achieved. Yet opt-in consents are less popular with marketers (ie individuals must positively indicate that they opt in and consent to particular processing of their personal data, as opposed to a website assuming and deeming such consent to exist unless the individuals deliberately indicate that they opt out). "Social Networking [web]sites often do not trouble their users with having to tick boxes or review privacy options, but it is vital to protect individuals' privacy".[99] As indicated above, the Irish Data Protection Commissioner requires that Facebook implement greater transparency measures.[100] This might apply to other websites too. Improved online-reporting, online abuse reporting-tools and behind-the-scenes procedures, protocols and personnel could contribute to a safer internet. It equally contributes to brand responsibility, and competitive advantage.

---

91 See SE Gindin, "Nobody Reads Your Privacy Policy or Online Contract? Lessons Learned and Questions Raised by the FTC's Action Against Sears" (2009) (8) *Northwestern Journal of Technology and Intellectual Property* 1 at 7, 21–23.

92 Gindin, *op. cit*, 9.

93 A Brown and L Pownall, "Facebook Data Concerns," *Society of Computers and Law*, 1 February 2008, available at http://www.scl.org/site.aspx?i=ed1035. Also, A Brown, "Facebook Data Concerns," *Society of Computers and Law*, 1 February 2008, available at www.scl.org/site.aspx?i=ed1035.

94 See section 6 Irish Data Protection Act 1988 as amended by the Data Protection (Amendment) Act 2003; and section 2(7) Irish Data Protection Act 1988 as amended by the Data Protection (Amendment) Act 2003.

95 See announcements at http://dataprotection.ie/docs/Home/4.htm.

96 See *Facebook Ireland Limited, Report of Re-Audit*, Irish Data Protection Commissioner, 21 September 2012, available at www.dataprotection.ie.

97 *ibid.*

98 *ibid.*

99 Brown and Pownall, *op. cit.*

100 See *Facebook Ireland Limited, Report of Re-Audit*, Irish Data Protection Commissioner, 21 September 2012, available at www.dataprotection.ie.

Mobile and Wireless Internet

Personal data, internet and social networking usage now also occur on handheld and mobile devices, giving rise to additional issues. In one survey half of consumers voiced concern over business use of mobile tech devices.[101] Personal privacy concerns are not reduced just because a mobile device is more user and travel friendly. Neither are data protection compliance obligations reduced. Arguably, they are greater because significantly more personal data can be collected, eg personal location data, and over periods that were not previously open to data collection by fixed or wired internet access. New concerns can also be evident, such as the ease of taking photographs of third parties, with or without their knowledge. This was even before Google Glass. This is a significant new issue to consider. In addition to new data collections by social networks and related websites, we also have to consider new data collection by other new technologies, such as wireless tags placed on products, such as RFID tags. The EU Article 29 Working Party has begun to consider some of these mobile and wireless issues.[102] The US Federal Trade Commission (FTC) also refers to RFID issues.[103] Overall, the significant increase in social networking undertaken on mobile devices will mean that particular attention will have to be devoted to privacy and data protection mobile issues in future.

Children

Many people would consider online abuse and the dangers facing children online via social networks to be one of the foremost concerns for society. Is it desirable for children (and teenagers) to use the internet and social networks in an unprotected and unsafe manner? However, as ever, the devil is in the detail.

The younger people are, the more concerned we should be about what forms of online social networks and websites they should be visiting. UK Prime Minister David Cameron has described some forms as being "vile." Should some be desirable, and others less so? Separately, should others never at all be available to children? The difficulty is in making sure children and adults in positions of influence are aware themselves of these concerns and act accordingly. Regulation, self-regulation, tools, reporting, investigation, procedures, etc also play a large part in ensuring child protection.

One of the bedrocks of data protection is that organisations need to implement compliance and protection measures that are proportionate to the risks involved. Given the scale of online abuse and the scale of reports being made (where certain tools are present or easily accessible), and that cyberbullying and suicide are

101 Sophos, "Half of Consumers Voice Security Concerns Regarding Business Use of Mobile Devices," Sophos Press Release, 20 April 2010, available at www.sophos.com/en-us/press-office/press-releases/2011/04/mobile-devices-security.

102 Article 29 Working Party, Opinion 02/2012 on Facial Recognition in Online and Mobile Services; Opinion 13/2011 on Geolocation Services on Smart Mobile Devices; Opinion 9/2011 on the Revised Industry Proposal for a Privacy and Data Protection Impact Assessment Framework for RFID Applications; all available at http://ec.europa.eu/justice/data-protection/article-29/documentation/opinion-recommendation/index_en.htm.

103 See www.ftc.gov.

sometimes real consequences of the dark side of the internet, are the tools presently available really proportionate to the risks? Perhaps like a rolling organic process, there will be no one static solution.

Given the risks, what is an adequate level of reporting personnel (assuming adequate tools and adequate processes were in place)? Is there a need for a specific minimum level of personnel per the size of the website/per the number of (active) users of a website/per the volume and number of complaints being received? Is this an area that requires more attention from the data protection authorities and policy makers? There is also potential scope for industry, international representative and standards-setting organisations.

Certain websites disclose how many intellectual property and copyright infringement report complaints they receive. There is less transparency in relation to online abuse and other reports. As much as the public are presently shocked at the level of online abuse and suicide, would they be even more shocked if there was full transparency on the number, categorisation and processing of online abuse reports being made? The Irish parliamentary Committee on Transport and Communications cyberbullying report recommends that online abuse reporting statistical data be furnished to the Data Protection Commissioner.[104]

A further gap in our knowledge, and which is equally important for data protection authorities, policymakers as well as the public, relates to having sufficient information to be able to compare the existence, level and sophistication of online abuse, online abuse reporting tools, online abuse processing and online abuse resolution between various websites.

A significant part of the impetus for self-regulation among social networks, and formal regulation, stems from the data protection regime. At what age can children give their consent to the collection and processing of their personal data? What is the minimum age for becoming a registered member of particular social networks? Are there specific privacy statement rules applicable to children and younger persons, as opposed to adults? What laws on online abuse, data protection and child protection are desirable in terms of protecting children (and teenagers) online, especially when they are engaged in social networking? Are existing law sufficient? Are existing laws utilised? What additional responsibilities do schools, parents, social networks and related websites and policymakers have?

In terms of dealing with sexual predators, and in particular convicted sexual predators with known predispositions towards children, what can parents, schools, social networks and other parties do? To what extent is it legally permissible to regulate or mandate that a social network or related website, a school, a library, etc, must filter internet traffic or must ban certain persons (eg convicted paedophiles) from using particular websites, such as named social networks, or indeed ban someone from using the internet entirely? In terms of piracy and intellectual property, various blocking orders have been granted by the UK and Irish High Courts, in particular

---

[104] Oireachtas Committee on Transport and Communications, *Addressing the Growth of Social Media and Tackling Cyberbullying*, 18 July 2013.

that internet service providers (ISPs) block access to Pirate Bay.[105] What rights, and competing rights, exist?

These issues have yet to be fully ventilated before superior courts.[106] Some of these issues may also have to be considered in the light of the constitutional referendum in Ireland to provide for greater recognition of childrens' rights in the Irish constitution.[107] It is interesting that none of the discussion leading up to or since the referendum sought to consider the interaction and potential influence of the amendment in the area of social networking. This may have to be considered in future.

Some of the less contentious areas of regulation/soft regulation in Europe in relation to children online were initiated and promoted from Ireland.[108] This relates to internet hotlines in Europe. If an internet user comes across a website or message that raises child concerns, they can report the matter to a central "hotline" telephone number or email for investigation.[109] The contact details are available at Hotline.ie. The international organisation of hotlines is Inhope.org. The US contact point is CyberTipLine.org.

As important as child safety issues are, other child issues also arise. One of these relates to the extent to which social networks (and indeed other websites) can legitimately ask for unnecessary personal information from children in order to create a marketing profile and to target them for targeted advertising of products and services—sometimes from that website and sometimes from third-party entities. Is it fair? Is it transparent? Is it lawful? To what extent can children be expected to understand what is happening and what they are being asked to consent to? Does the current data protection regime match and deal with what is happening in practice?

Arguably children (and teenagers) have a greater need to be able to enforce their current right to delete (in the EU Data Protection Directive 1995) and their right to

---

105 See, for example, *EMI Records Ltd & Ors v British Sky Broadcasting Ltd & Ors* [2013] EWHC 379 (Ch) (28 February 2013); *Twentieth Century Fox Film Corporation & Anor v Newzbin Ltd* [2010] EWHC 608 (Ch); *Twentieth Century Fox Film Corp & Ors v British Telecommunications Plc* [2011] EWHC 1981 (Ch) (28 July 2011); *Twentieth Century Fox Film Corporation & Ors v British Telecommunications Plc* [2011] EWHC 2714 (Ch) (26 October 2011). AG Cruz Villalon in ECJ/CJEU case *UPC v Constantin Film* also confirms blocking measures. Case C-314/12 13 November 2013. Also note *Sabam* cases.

106 Note, however, the separate litigation in relation to internet copyright infringement in the Irish cases of *Irma v Eircom* and *IRMA v UPC*; and the ECJ case of *Sabam v Tiscali/Scarlet* (*Scarlet Extended SA v Société Belge des Auteurs, Compositeurs et Editeurs SCRL* (SABAM) Case C-70/10). The Irish Data Protection Commissioner also considered the Eircom three-strikes deal with the music industry. See *EMI Records (Ireland) Ltd & Ors v The Data Protection Commissioner & Anor* [2012] IEHC 264 (27 June 2012); *EMI Records (Ireland) Ltd & ors v The Data Protection Commissioner* [2013] IESC 34 (3 July 2013).

107 See, for example, Office for the Minister of Children at www.dcya.gov.ie/viewtxt.asp?fn=%2Fdocuments%2Flegislation%2FconstRef.htm. Also C O'Brien, "Minister Insists Children's Rights Referendum to Go Ahead Next Year," *Irish Times* 19 December 2011; and *Rights-Based Child Law: The Case for Reform*, A Report by the Law Society's Law Reform Commission, March 2006; Referendum Ireland website, available at http://www.referendum.ie/.

108 Particularly by Cormac Callanan of Aconite Internet Solutions.

109 On hotline reporting of suspicious content relating to children in Ireland see, for example, www.hotline.ie, www.inhope.org and www.internetsafety.ie.

forget/delete in the proposed EU Data Protection Regulation.[110] They have a longer life expectancy and more opportunities to regret in relation to information online which may adversely affect them later in life. They are also the "internet generation" whom are placing more and more personal data online, without necessarily being fully appraised of the dangers and consequences both presently and later in life.

Apart from being asked to furnish personal information which will be useful for advertising and direct marketing (eg at the time of signing up for membership), it is also possible that the child's actual activities online can be tracked and monitored. This data can also be incorporated into a marketing profile in relation to the child. These "preferences" can then be used to direct or "target" even more specific advertising, marketing and services to the child. Hence the terms "targeted marketing" and "behavioural targeted marketing".[111] As with other areas of the internet, debate arises in relation to what is appropriate regulation and self-regulation.

The current data protection regime (with the amended EU ePrivacy Directive) and the proposed EU Data Protection Regulation) have significant changes in relation to children, in particular transparency, cookies, consent and the ability to delete and forget. In addition, the proposed EU Data Protection Regulation explicitly refers to children in the data protection regime for the first time.[112] It also defines a child by reference to age for the first time in data protection, by specifying a child as being under 18 years of age.[113] This could have a significant impact on social networking, given that so many users of social networks and related websites are currently below that age. This is understood to be the subject of discussion and possible amendment as the Regulation moves through the legislative process.

Social Networks

Social networking and related websites are used for many legitimate purposes. However, such websites "contain a virtual treasure trove of personal information".[114] As a result, "[p]erils await on all sides".[115] The popularity of social networks opens the door to misuse and abuse of personal data, such as:

- online abuse, including cyberbullying;
- blackmail;
- threats of rape, violence, murder;
- trolling;
- revenge porn[116];
- misuse of personal data of social networking users;

---

110 Proposed EU Data Protection Regulation, available at http://ec.europa.eu/justice/data-protection/document/review2012/com_2012_11_en.pdf.

111 These can be applied to adults also. See references to Phorm, tracking and marketing in later chapter(s).

112 Proposed Data Protection Regulation, available at http://ec.europa.eu/justice/data-protection/document/review2012/com_2012_11_en.pdf.

113 *ibid*, see definitions.

114 Nelson, *et al*, *op. cit*, 21.

115 *ibid*,1.

116 Uploading intimate pictures and videos of ex partners as an act of revenge or to embarrass them.

- collecting personal data without transparency, knowledge or consent;
- identity theft;
- cyber stalking[117];
- child solicitation, grooming and predation[118];
- undesirable employer vetting and monitoring[119];
- unwanted direct marketing;
- evidence gathering;
- behavioural advertising[120];
- spamming (unwanted and unsolicited electronic direct marketing);
- malicious software such as botnets, trojans, malware, viruses;
- use of personal photographs for other people's products and services, such as dating websites or pornographic websites.[121] In one instance a man found a picture of his wife on a singles advert on Facebook after it was copied from her Facebook profile.[122]

Social networking "makes traditional protection mechanisms and means of controlling privacy outdated in many respects".[123] While it may seem strange, many users do not avail of the privacy control settings available.[124] Policymakers as well as social networks need to appraise users of the need to avail of current privacy settings and of ongoing changes to protection measures. The Irish Data Protection Commissioner has required greater transparency by Facebook in relation to one of the areas examined in the audit report.[125] However, there are many other areas where transparency can be improved across various websites.

Security online is an ever important issue. Pictures and personal details from closed private social networking profiles have been used in attempts to blackmail individuals.[126] The recent UK Leveson Inquiry Report also highlights the illicit trade in personal data as well as personal data being used for blackmail purposes.[127]

---

117 For example, M Baer, "Cyberstalking and the Internet Landscape We Have Constructed" (2010) *Virginia Journal of Law & Technology* 153.

118 See, for example, Nelson, *et al*, *op. cit*, 23 *et seq*.

119 DB Garrie, M Duffy-Lewis, R Wong and RL Gillespie, "Data Protection: The Challenges Facing Social Networking" (2009–2010) (131) *International Law & Management Review* 127 at 128.

120 See M Hilderbrandt and S Gutwirth, *Profiling the European Citizen* (Springer Science, 2007), referred to in Garrie *et al*, above.

121 Nelson, *et al*, *op. cit*, 2 and references therein.

122 *ibid*, above at 2, and footnote10 at 2.

123 D Findlay, "Tag! Now You're 'It.' What Photographs on Social Networking Sites Mean for the Fourth Amendment" (2008) (10) *North Carolina Journal of Law & Technology* 171 at 175.

124 A Lenhart and M Madded, "Teens, Privacy & Online Social Networks" (2007) (ii) *Pew Internet & American Life Project*, http://pewinternet.org/pdfs/PIP_Teens_Privacy_SNS_Report_Final.pdf, as referred to in D Findlay, "Tag! Now You're 'It.' What Photographs on Social Networking Sites Mean for the Fourth Amendment" (2008) (10) *North Carolina Journal of Law & Technology* 171 at 182.

125 See *Facebook Ireland Limited, Report of Re-Audit*, Irish Data Protection Commissioner, 21 September 2012, available at www.dataprotection.ie.

126 Giving the example of a blackmail attempt on Miss New Jersey 2007, A Jenner, "NJ Miss in a Fix Over Her Pics," *New York Post*, 6 July 2007, 5, referred to in Nelson *et al.*, *op. cit*, 21.

127 UK Leveson Inquiry. *An Inquiry into the Culture, Practices and Ethics of the Press: Report, The Right Honourable Lord Justice Leveson*, November 2012. Available at http://www.official-documents.gov.uk/document/hc1213/hc07/0780/0780.asp. Also see the main inquiry website at http://www.levesoninquiry.org.uk/.

A Scottish teenager, Daniel Perry, is also reported to have committed suicide as a result of online blackmail threats.

There is a general lack of awareness and expertise in relation to what can happen to one's personal data once posted online. Many people are still unaware that their social networking content can be used against them. In *Cedric D v Stacia W*, for example, a father lost custody of his child after the court viewed his MySpace profile, suggesting that his lifestyle was not in the best interest of the child.[128]

In addition, the use of direct and indirect profiling of personal data and the online activities of individuals for targeted marketing needs careful consideration, and arguably more transparency.

Google Street View

Street View was launched in the US in March 2009.[129] This online facility contains real video images of thousands of real street-level images of cities and neighbourhoods. You and your house, garden, car, neighbour, etc can all be available for anyone to watch online. Daft.ie and other property websites now regularly use Google Maps and Google Street View. So too do Fáilte Ireland, Chambers Ireland and the Arts Council. The head of Google in Ireland, Mr. John Herlihy, said that Street View is "the best form of advertising this country will ever enjoy".[130] Critics say that it is Orwellian and infringes privacy and data protection rights.[131] There are numerous examples of concern from the images and details made available on social networks and related websites – sometimes without a person knowing. Burglars are able to gather intelligence in relation to properties they wish to break into, such as when people are on vacation or what lies behind a house. Street View has shown people receiving parking tickets, people being arrested, a women who moved from an estranged partner being filmed, a man leaving a sex shop, a man urinating, and other embarrassing and arguably intrusive incidents.[132]

While there are certain mechanisms to object, this is after the materials have gone live. In Germany, however, people had an opportunity to object prior to Street View going live. Apparently, 244,000 Germans objected and requested that certain location data and images in relation to them be blocked or made unrecognisable prior to being made available online.[133] This is the first country where people had this option. Up until the German roll-out, people had to opt out after the images went live. In Ireland as elsewhere, the Data Protection Commissioner over a number of years has been

---

128 *Cedric D v Stacia* W No 1 CA-JV 07-0056, 2007 WL 5515319, at *4 (Arizona Court Appeal 20 September 2007), referred to in HI Parness, "Toward 'Social Networking Law?" (March-April 2009) *Landslide* at 13, 16, and Nelson *et al.*, *op. cit*, 22.

129 D Flynn, "Right Up Your Street, Google's New Map Tool Has Caused Controversy, But It Could Be a Gift to House-Hunters," *Sunday Times* property supplement, 5 April 2009.

130 "Street View, 'the Best Advertising' Tool for Ireland," *Metro* 1 October 2010. Also, P Newenham and A Healy, "Google Street View Goes Live," *Irish Times*, 30 September 2010, available at www.irishtimes.com/newspaper/breaking/2010/0930/breaking41.html.

131 *ibid.*

132 *ibid.*

133 DW-World.DE, "More Than 244,000 Opt Out of Google Street View in Germany," 21 October 2010, available at www.dw-world.de/dw/article/0,,6133854,00.html.

engaging in raising public awareness as to the data protection regime and the rights, as well as in relation to specific problems and risks as they arise. Arguably more needs to be done in this regard. However, enhanced education and appreciation for data protection may not be limited to just the public (and organisations). Lord Justice Leveson was not shy in saying that more appreciation may be required at judicial level (in the UK).[134] The data protection regime provides rights to individual data subjects, including judicial remedies. Chapter III of the EU Data Protection Directive 1995 relates to "Judicial Remedies, Liability and Sanctions". Within Chapter III Article 22 relates to "Remedies" and states that individuals have "a judicial remedy for any breach of the rights guaranteed him [or her] by the national law applicable to the [data] processing in question."

Separately, Google, in capturing and recording the data and pictures for the Street View service, was apparently also recording a variety of other data. In particular, it is meant to have captured data from users in relation to their Wi-Fi networks. Google says that the data were collected in error.[135] Investigations have arisen in various jurisdictions as a result of these disclosures and Google has also been requested to hand over the data[136] or delete it. Google has also been fined €100,000 in France for the breach.[137]

At the time that these particular data collections became public knowledge, many data protection authorities investigated and/or queried Google. Google indicated that the Street View personal data collections occurred inadvertently and also that it was not aware that such collection could or would occur. Many data protection authorities accepted such assurances from Google. Indeed, Lord Justice Leveson in his recent report also refers to this.[138]

Google or Google personnel may have known that such data collections could occur at the initial design and roll-out of the Street View service. The US Federal Trade Commission (FTC) fined Google for the data breach, obstruction and the refusal of certain personnel to provide evidence to it. The FTC fine was for $25,000. The FTC states:

> "When European data protection authorities investigated Google's Wi-Fi data collection efforts in 2010, the Company initially denied collecting payload data. On May 14 2010, however, Google publicly acknowledged that it had been 'collecting samples of payload data from open (ie non password-protected) WiFi networks' but stated that it likely collected only

[134] UK Leveson Inquiry. *An Inquiry into the Culture, Practices and Ethics of the Press: Report, The Right Honourable Lord Justice Leveson*, November 2012. Available at http://www.official-documents.gov.uk/document/hc1213/hc07/0780/0780.asp. Also see the main inquiry website at http://www.levesoninquiry.org.uk/.

[135] See, for example, "Google Admits Collecting Wi-Fi Data Through Street View Cars," last accessed on 30 April 2011. Also "BBC, "Google is 'Close' to Handing Over German Wi-Fi Data," 3 June 2010, available at www.bbc.co.uk/news/10227854.

[136] See, for example, BBC, "Google is 'Close' to Handing Over German Wi-Fi Data," 3 June 2010, available at www.bbc.co.uk/news/10227854.

[137] See P Sayer, "France Fines Google for Street View Collection of Wi-Fi Data," *Mac World*, 21 March 2011, available at www.macworld.com/article/158671/2011/03/google_streetview.html.

[138] UK Leveson Inquiry. *An Inquiry into the Culture, Practices and Ethics of the Press: Report, The Right Honourable Lord Justice Leveson*, November 2012. Available at http://www.official-documents.gov.uk/document/hc1213/hc07/0780/0780.asp. Also see the main inquiry website at http://www.levesoninquiry.org.uk/.

fragmented data. Google traced the collection of payload data to code that was 'mistakenly' included in its Wi-Fi data collection software. On October 22 2010, Google acknowledged for the first time that 'in some instances entire emails and URLs were captured, as well as passwords.' And finally, as described below, the Company provided evidence to the Federal Communications Commission (Commission) showing that the data collection [redacted by FTC].

Upon learning that Google had collected payload data, the Commission began examining whether Google's conduct violated provisions of the [US] Communications Act of 1934, as amended (Communications Act or Act). Based on that initial review, in November 2010 the Commission's Enforcement Bureau (Bureau) issued a Letter of Inquiry (LOI) that launched an official investigation into whether Google's data collection practices violated Section 705(a) of the Act. The record developed in this investigation includes Google's written responses to questions from the Bureau, copies of relevant documents, and publicly available information. In addition, Bureau staff interviewed six individuals – five Google employees and an employee of Stroz Friedberg, a consulting firm Google retained to conduct forensic analysis of its Wi-Fi data collection software code. The Bureau also issued a subpoena to take the deposition of the Google engineer (Engineer Doe) who developed the software code that Google used to collect and store payload data. Through counsel, however, Engineer Doe invoked his Fifth Amendment right against self-incrimination and declined to testify.

For many months, Google deliberately impeded and delayed the Bureau's investigation by failing to respond to requests for material information and to provide certifications and verifications of its responses. In this Notice of Apparent Liability for Forfeiture (NAL), we find that Google apparently wilfully and repeatedly violated Commission orders to produce certain information and documents that the Commission required for its investigation. Based on our review of the facts and circumstances before us, we find that Google, which holds Commission licenses, is apparently liable for a forfeiture penalty of $25,000 for its noncompliance with Bureau information and document requests".[139]

Google Buzz

A Google social networking endeavour ran into data protection and privacy problems as it was preconfigured with a ready-made list of friends, based on a person's most frequently used emails. Privacy interest groups both in the US and the EU indicated that they would be pursuing official complaints and litigating if necessary.[140] It was argued that individuals should be able to choose their own network of friends, not have them pre-chosen for them. Google has since launched Google+.

Cloud

The Cloud brings many advantages. However, the Edward Snowden revelations

[139] Federal Trade Commission (FTC) decision, 13 April 2012, available at http://transition.fcc.gov/Daily_Releases/Daily_Business/2012/db0416/DA-12-592A1.pdf.

[140] K Lillington, "Privacy Fears Ruin the Buzz About New Gmail Service," *Irish Times*, 19 February 2010; D Rushe, "Evil Let Loose After Google Breaches Email Privacy," *Sunday Times*, 21 February 2010; "Facebook and Google Buzz Hit With Class Action Lawsuits Over Privacy Issues," *Law Librarian Blog*, 19 February 2010, available at http://lawprofessors.typepad.com/law_librarian_blog/2010/02/facebook-and-google-buzz-hit-with-class-action-lawsuits-over-privacy-issues.html; M Erwin, "Google Facing Legal Action Over Privacy on New Buzz," *Metro Herald*, 18 February 2010; "Google Buzz Social Network in Legal Row Over Privacy," *Mail Online*, 20 February 2010, available at www.dailymail.co.uk/sciencetech/article-1251678/Google-Buzz-row-privacy.html; and also "Google Buzz Prompts Legal Action by US Woman," *Daily Telegraph*, 30 April 2011, available at www.telegraph.co.uk/technology/google/7264993/Google-Buzz-prompts-legal-action-by-US-woman.html.

regarding government surveillance and access to the databases of internet companies and to internet traffic has raised concerns of potential Cloud users in relation to US Cloud service providers. Even US commentators are suggesting that such companies face difficulties as compared to their non-US based competitors as a result of the concerns raised by Snowden. For example, there were calls for South American and EU-based Cloud services, which do not rely on US services or servers.

There are many issues with new Cloud internet technologies apart from those now raised by Snowden's revelations. Some of the Cloud legal issues include:

- data protection;
- confidentiality;
- database rights;
- copyright;
- MiFID/SYNC (financial sector, where applicable) rules[141];
- security issues;
- evidence;
- discovery;
- forensics.

Other issues include a variety of concerns that arise with outsourcing services and activities.[142]

Cloud computing is achieving increasing industry and literature attention. Pre-Snowden, it seemed reasonably assured of being an industry success. The World Privacy Forum also reports on Cloud issues in *Privacy in the Clouds: Risks to Privacy and Confidentiality from Cloud Computing*, as does the European Network and Information Security Agency's *Cloud Computing – Benefits, Risks and Recommendations for Information Security*. However, there is a line of literature which is concerned with the issues raised, the most important of which appear to be security and privacy. DeVere asks if Cloud computing is the privacy storm on the horizon.[143] The Snowden episode will heighten those concerns.

The Irish Data Protection Commissioner also published guidance[144] in relation to Cloud computing and data protection in Ireland. It builds on work of the EU Article 29 Working Party Opinion on Cloud computing[145] and guidance produced by the

---

141 A Joint, E Baker and E Eccles, "Hey, You, Get Off That Cloud?" (2009) (270) *Computer Law & Security Review* 270.

142 R Smith, "Head in a Cloud," *Law Society Gazette*, December 2010, 24.

143 AC DeVere, "Cloud Computing: Privacy Storm on the Horizon?" (2010) *Albany Law Journal Science & Technology* 365. Note also, P Lanois, "Caught in the Clouds: The Web 2.0, Cloud Computing, and Privacy?" (2010) *Northwestern Journal of Technology and Intellectual Property* 29; IR Kattan, "Cloudy Privacy Protections: Why the Stored Communications Acts Fails to Protect the Privacy of Communications Stored in the Cloud" (2010–2011) *Vanderbilt Journal of Entertainment & Technology Law* 617; FM Pinguelo and BW Muller, "Avoid the Rainy Day: Survey of US Cloud Computing Caselaw" (2011) *Boston College Intellectual Property & Technology Forum*, available at www.bciptf.org; C Soghoian, "Caught in the Cloud: Privacy, Encryption, and Government Back Doors in the Web 2.0 Era" (2010) *Journal on Telecommunication an High Technology Law* 359.

144 Irish Data Protection Commissioner, cloud guidance, available at http://dataprotection.ie/viewdoc.asp?DocID=1221&m=f.

145 EU Article 29 Working Party Opinion 5/2012 of 1 July 2012.

National Standards Authority of Ireland (NSAI)/Irish Internet Association (IIA).[146] The European Network and Information Security Agency (ENISA) has also provided Cloud guidance.[147] (Also see Chapter 17 by Andrew Harbison below).

Location Data

One of the new second-generation internet (Web 2.0) issues centres on technology's ability to find and disclose a person's physical location. "The ability to know where someone is at all times, or to make your own whereabouts publicly known via a social network is fraught with potential privacy issues."[148] The issues arising with geolocation-based services are increasing as GPS (Global Positioning System/ Services, ie a system of satellites used for tracking the position of devices, vehicles and people), triangulation, data sharing, wireless are all rolled out.[149] It is recognised that current laws are inadequate in relation to, or ignore, issues of location data and geolocation by internet websites (and others).[150] The question arises, some might suggest, of whether websites (and others) really need to know the real-time location of everyone to provide the main service contracted for. Some may query whether it is proportionate or necessary.

Consider also, for example, the increasing use by employers and organisations of social networking to monitor employee activity, including the location of their employees. It is often taken for granted that there are no employee privacy issues with the real-time location of taxi drivers, couriers, delivery people, etc. Should every employer know exactly where their employee is located simply because they are using a company car, company laptop, smartphone or other device, and regardless of the importance of the employee's job level and job function? How should the employer's business interest be balanced against the employee's privacy interests?[151] One of the starting points to considering this question, and in beginning the assessment of data protection compliance, is to identify what the claimed justification or business case is in any given instance of geolocation monitoring.

The Canadian Supreme Court has recognised that employees have zones of privacy and expectations of privacy and data protection, which includes internet use and

---

146 See www.nsai.ie and www.iia.ie.

147 Available at http://www.enisa.europa.eu/?came_from=http%253A//www.enisa.europa.eu/activities/application-security/cloud-computing/introduction-to-cloud-computing%253Fsearchterm%253Dcloud.

148 "We know Where You Live: Privacy Implications ..." *Dataonomy*, 12 January 2010.

149 The original GPS was US-based. There is an interesting literature as regards other nations seeking to develop their own GPSs in order to have access to a system not controlled by the US. This includes Europe and its Galileo GPS. This may also have a Snowden impact.

150 KF Kind, "Personal Jurisdiction, Internet Commerce, and Privacy: The Pervasive Legal Consequences of Modern Geolocation Technologies" (2011) *Albany Law Journal of Science & Technology* 61 at 63. There are, of course, certain advantages to technical geolocation, such as being able to restrict certain content to jurisdictions where it is assumed to be legal, and restrict its access to countries where it is understood not to be. This would apply to alcohol, certain medicines, gambling and sex-related products or services. See *ibid*, 89 *et seq*.

151 Rosenberg, "Location Surveillance by GPS: Balancing an Employer's Business Interest with Employee Privacy" (2010) *Washington Journal of Law, Technology and Arts* 143.

browsing history.[152] The Irish Data Protection Commissioner and the EU Article 29 Working Party also recognise the legitimate expectations of employees in relation to their privacy and data protection rights.

Apple came under scrutiny and indeed pressure when researchers discovered that its iPhone products were recording location data on its users via the device's location.[153] Indeed, iPhone location data may already have been used forensically by the police.[154] Other issues include stalking and burglary. For example, burglars can monitor social networking websites to see when someone is on vacation or out of their house. Separately, websites such as Google Earth and Google Street View have also assisted burglars in planning their crimes. Location data and geolocation services are evolving themselves. However, technologies such as Google Maps mean that it is possible for previously non-geographical services to incorporate location data, maps, etc into their services.[155]

Some might argue that greater formality is required around the use of location-based services, such as an industry/sector codes of practice or regulation.[156] The Irish Data Protection Commissioner quite early on in the development of location-based services issued a guidance note on some of these issues.[157] As these issues become more evident, we may have to consider new rules and/or laws on data protection.

The EU Article 29 Working Party has also issued an Opinion in relation to location data, namely, Opinion 5/2005 on the Use of Locations Data with a View to Providing Value-Added Services.[158] It also issued an Opinion in relation to geolocation services on smart mobile devices.[159] This is obviously an area where further guidance will be required, given the increasing amount of activities and services which continue to be rolled out on mobile devices, all of which involve personal data.

Conclusion

While privacy and data protection face many threats,[160] the ones arising from the internet are most pronounced. Protecting "personal data represents one of recent

---

152 *R v Cole*, Supreme Court Canada 2012 SCC 53, available at http://scc.lexum.org/decisia-scc-csc/scc-csc/scc-csc/en/item/12615/index.do.

153 See, for example, "Apple Under Pressure Over iPhone Location Tracking," *Daily Telegraph*, www.telegraph.co.uk/technology/apple/8466357/Apple-under-pressure-over-iPhon; B Johnson, "Researcher: iPhone Location Data Already Used by Cops," available at www.gigaom.com/2011/04/21/researcher-iphone-loaction-data-already-used-by-cops/.

154 Johnson, "Researcher: iPhone Location Data Already Used by Cops" *op. cit.*

155 See, for instance, M Burdon, "Privacy Invasive Geo-Mashups: Privacy 2.0 and the Limits of First Generation Information Privacy Laws" (2010) *University of Illinois Journal of Law, Technology and Policy* 1.

156 Johnson, "Researcher: iPhone Location Data Already Used by Cops," *op. cit.*

157 "Guidance Note for Entities Considering the use of Bluetooth Technology for Direct Marketing Purposes", Irish Data Protection Commissioner, available at www.dataprotection.ie/docs/Guidance_Note_for_Entities_Considering_the_use_of_Bluetooth_/903.htm.

158 Available at http://ec.europa.eu/justice/policies/privacy/workinggroup/wpdocs/index_en.htm#new_technologies.

159 Opinion 13/2011 on Geolocation Services on Smart Mobile Devices, available at http://ec.europa.eu/justice/policies/privacy/workinggroup/wpdocs/index_en.htm#new_technologies.

160 In 2006 there were meant to be 4.2 million (official) CCTV cameras in the UK, yet there is no

most emerging legal issues … the privacy and the discretion of individuals are challenged by various new means of data collection and communications."[161] The issue is also "serious … because of the volume of users at risk from posting their content, without intervention by the [social networking websites]."[162]

As the expanding tapestry of the new generation of internet unfurls, and we begin to appreciate the full extent of the issues, we realise how complex it is to deal with them and how easily outdated our current generation of data protections laws and regulations actually are. That is not to suggest that current data protection laws do not apply and are not relevant. Of course they are. When we ask if personal space, privacy and informational data protection are respected on the internet, it is difficult to be completely affirmative. One of the issues facing policymakers, is how to update the data protection regime in order to respect personal privacy in the new internet environment, and in a manner which maintains commercial imperatives and facilitates technological development. Privacy and data protection must be reconsidered in light of new social networking technologies and the concerns they create.[163]

The proposed EU Data Protection Regulation is perhaps a start along the road of addressing the current host of issues, and the issues which will arise in future. Social networks and related websites also have a very important role to play, as do individuals, peers, parents, schools, etc.

---

explicit UK law of privacy. See D Flint, "Computers and Internet" (December 2006) *Business Law Review* 292 at 294.

161 R Polock, "Aims, Methods and Achievements in European Data Protection" (November 2009) (23) *International Review of Law, Computers & Technology* 179.

162 BL Mann, "Social Networking Websites – A Concentration of Impersonation, Denigration, Sexual Aggressive Solicitation, Cyber-Bullying or Happy Slapping Videos" (2009) (17) *International Journal of Law & Information Technology* 252, references omitted.

163 See DC Davis, "MySpace Isn't Your Space: Expanding the Fair Credit Reporting Act to Ensure Accountability and Fairness in Employer Searches of Online Social Networking Services" (2006–2007) (XVI) *Kansas Journal of Law and Public Policy* 237 at 240.

Chapter 4

PRIVACY AND DATA PROTECTION

Headline of Issues

- A new era for data protection
- Less traditional divisions
- Modern privacy expectations
- Modern privacy in court
- Public spaces
- Advertising

Introduction

Social networking and second-generation internet are increasing the pressure on personal information, privacy and the control of information relating to individuals. What is also new is that once personal details are revealed electronically, it is difficult to take this information back. Further still, and in apparent conflict with concepts such as the right to have incorrect information corrected, it may not always be possible to have all incorrect internet information corrected.

A New Era for Data Protection

There are many "privacy challenges raised by … [the] information society … global village"[1] and social networking in particular.[2] People have always been concerned with their personal space and informational privacy. This was even before modern formulations of what privacy means in a legal context.[3] These concerns are now emphasised in real time. "The popular usage of these [social networking] websites greatly impacts user privacy."[4] Do new privacy concerns demand new responses?[5]

---

1 Y Poullet, "Data Protection Legislation: What Is At Stake for Our Society and Democracy?" (2009) (25) *Computer Law & Security Review* 211.

2 U Munukutla-Parker, "Unsolicited Commercial Email, Privacy Concerns Relating to Social Network Services, Online Protection of Children, and Cyberbullying" (2006) (2) *I/S: A Journal of Law and Policy* 627 at 633–634.

3 The first modern formulation of a right or tort of privacy is seen in SD Warren and LD Brandeis, "The Right to Privacy" (1890) *Harvard Law Review* 193. For a more modern nuance see, for example, PS Abril, "Recasting Privacy Torts in a Spaceless World" (2007) *Harvard Journal of Law and Technology* 1.

4 DH Montes, "Living Our Lives Online: The Privacy Implications of Online Social Networking" (2010) (5) *I/S: A Journal of Law and Policy* 507.

5 See Miller, "The Facebook Frontier: Responding to the Changing Face of Privacy on the Internet" (2008–2009) *Kentucky Law Journal* 541 at 551–553.

Grimmelmann refers to the new era of social networking privacy issues. He states that:

> "Facebook knows an immense amount about its users. A fully filled-out Facebook profile contains about forty pieces of recognizably personal information, including name; birthday; political and religious views; online and offline contact information; gender, sexual preference, and relationship status; favourite books, movies, and so on; educational and employment history; and, of course, picture. Facebook then offers multiple tools for users to search out and add potential contacts. By the time you're done, Facebook has a reasonably comprehensive snapshot both of who you are and of whom you know."[6]

This is even outdated to the extent that there are now more than 40 data sets, fields or categories of personal data collected, held and processed by Facebook. The Europe Versus Facebook organisation claims to have identified many more.[7] Indeed, the Irish Data Protection Commissioner in his audit and re-audit of Facebook identified certain data that were not being made available to users when they utilised the online tool for data access requests.[8]

However, the:

> "profiles and links are only the beginning. Consider again the features and Applications described above. Each of them serves as a conduit for information-sharing:
>
> - Wall posts can contain information about the poster (one contact who posted on my Wall mentioned an upcoming trip to Pisa), about the postee (another asked about my beard), or about both (a third mentioned a course we'd taken together in college).
> - If I Poke you, it indicates that I'm online, and I'm thinking about you.
> - The payment infrastructure required by Gifts provides stronger links between a profile and offline identities; choosing one Gift over another (eg a 'Get Well' balloon rather than a lipstick kiss or a dreidel) has a meaning that at least one other person understands, as does the personalized message accompanying it.
> - If I upload and tag a Photo of you, it documents what you look like and someplace that you've been. It also documents that I know you and permits a reasonable inference that I was the photographer.
> - Each game of Lexulous you play gives some hints about your vocabulary. Playing a hundred games of Lexulous also says something different about your personality than having a Level 8 Zombie does.
> - Your list of Causes tells others what principles are meaningful to you.
> - Quiz Creator may not necessarily say much about the people who write quizzes, but the whole point of answering a quiz is to reveal things about your knowledge, beliefs, and preferences."[9]

Courts (at least in the US) have yet to address constitutional privacy rights in the context of social networks.[10] The balance between privacy and online services is not yet settled.[11] This is the case in the US and Europe.

---

6 J Grimmelmann, "Saving Facebook" (2009) (94) *Iowa Law Review* 1137 at 1149.

7 Europe Vs Facebook, available at http://europe-v-facebook.org/EN/en.html.

8 See *Facebook Ireland Limited, Report of Audit*, Irish Data Protection Commissioner, 21 December 2011, available at www.dataprotection.ie; and *Facebook Ireland Limited, Report of Re-Audit*, Irish Data Protection Commissioner, 21 September 2012, available at www.dataprotection.ie.

9 Grimmelmann, *op. cit.* at 1149–1150.

10 LL Baughman, "Friend Request or Foe? Confirming the Misuse of Internet and Social Networking Sites By Domestic Violence Perpetrators" (2010) (19) *Widener Law Journal* 933 at 963–964.

11 See discussion also in CM Gagnier, "On Privacy: Liberty in the Digital Revolution" (2010–2011) *Journal of High Technology Law* 229.

The Supreme Court in Canada has recognised that employees have rights of privacy and expectations of privacy and data protection at work, which includes internet use and internet browsing history.[12] The Irish Data Protection Commissioner and the EU Article 29 Working Party also recognise the legitimate expectations of employees in relation to their privacy and data protection rights.

Poullet[13] refers to two specific aspects of privacy interests relevant to social networking. The first is the right to seclusion. The second is the right to participate fully in society. Some worry that users appear to "misunderstand the privacy risks"[14] and terms of use/terms of service (TOS) of social networks. Garrie, Duffy-Lewis, Wong and Gillespie also pose the important question: "what level of privacy should be expected and required within the social networking environment?"[15] Nelson, Simek and Foltin ask "Privacy, What Privacy?"[16] Klosek also describes the increasing threats to privacy in the post-9/11 environment.[17] What information data are circulated about us?[18] We know some but certainly not all of the ever-increasing amounts of information being held in ever expanding numbers of electronic databases and locations.[19] There is an increasing tension in the traditional dividing line between private life and space and public space.[20] It is in this context that EU policymakers are pushing for enhanced privacy and data protection rules. It is also important that data protection and data protection rights be considered on an ongoing basis as new uses of personal data and new technological issues arise.

Frequently with technologies, and the rapid pace of the roll-out of services based on new technologies, the law is left behind and becomes merely reactionary.[21] This is particularly so with the internet. Examples include the peer-to-peer (P2P) music file-sharing wars; the film file-sharing wars; online contract formation and the original lack of specific legal regulations; electronic signatures; the misuse of personal data found online; personal data collected electronically and online; data loss; data theft; and the new issue of online abuse, including cyberbullying.

However, on occasion, technology can also provide a solution. When Facebook was faced with tens of thousands of data access requests simultaneously, as well as complaints and an audit investigation from the Irish Data Protection Commissioner, it decided to create a technological solution. It allocated technology engineering resources to develop an online tool to deal with access requests and to make (certain)

---

12 *R v Cole*, Supreme Court Canada 2012 SCC 53, available at http://scc.lexum.org/decisia-scc-csc/scc-csc/scc-csc/en/item/12615/index.do.

13 Poullet, *op. cit*, 211.

14 Grimmelmann, *op. cit*, at 1160.

15 Garrie *et al.*

16 Nelson, Simek and Foltin, "The Legal Implications of Social Networking," *Regent University Law Review*, (2009-2010) 1-34, at 20.

17 J Klosek, *The War on Privacy* (Praeger: London, 2007).

18 Poullet, *op. cit*, 211.

19 *ibid*, 211–121.

20 *ibid*, 213.

21 One example where it is not the case is the increasingly developed concept of "privacy by design". This is the concept of (requiring) new products and services to incorporate a privacy and data protection due-diligence analysis at the design phase, the aim of which would be to re-engineer the product or service to being privacy friendly and data protection compliant. The aim is to reduce the need for correction and reactionary firefighting once each data protection breach event occurs. See Chapter 32.

of the personal data it held in relation to users available to them. The tool developed is significant in demonstrating that social networks and related websites can provide clever solutions when they decide to. More recently, service providers are seeking to use technology to address child pornography and trolling abuse.

Employee privacy issues in the context of social networking are increasingly being considered both under the US Fourth Amendment[22] and the technology, computer and internet context.[23] Employers argue that they have countervailing interests which must also be balanced.[24] More complex issues then arise in relation to when employees work on their home computers.[25] This too is a concern. Employers should be careful too, when considering the possibility of monitoring and/or examining their employees' internet and social networking activities. For example, are employers entitled to vet potential (and current) employees based on their social networking profiles/activities?

In addition, employees are increasingly bringing their own technology devices into the work environment, with and without permission, some of which may come to store work-related data. There are enhanced risks and policy decisions for employers. Some of this has resulted in what are becoming known as "bring your own device" (BYOD) policies,[26] in addition to corporate internet and communications usage policies.

Electronic discovery is also an issue.[27] Personal data may sometimes be revealed through the litigation discovery process. Are social networking profiles and communications discoverable? The current US federal rules in relation to e-discovery do not properly encompass social networking issues, and there are likely to be many complex and expensive cases involved in addressing these issues.[28]

Importantly, data protection stands separate from litigation discovery. It is possible for a litigant to make a data access request separate from the actual formal litigation, and that request must be complied with. This was further confirmed in the *Dublin Bus* case.[29]

Government agencies and bodies have an increasing presence on social networks. This development is sometimes known as "Government 2.0". However, befriending such official agencies can sometimes bring dangers. Without resisting or being

22 Generally, relating to search and seizure. Available at www.usconstitution.net/const.html#Am4. Also, JP Semitsu, "From Facebook to Mug Shot: How the Death of Social Networking Privacy Rights Revolutionized Online Government Surveillance" (2011) *Pace Law Review* 291.

23 See Blank, *op. cit*, 511–514.

24 *ibid*, 497.

25 *ibid*, 516.

26 R Jones, "BYOD Policy" *Computers and Law* 1 August 2012; I Wimbush, "BYOD in Law Firms" *Computers and Law* 3 June 2013.

27 P Lambert, "The Search for Elusive Electrons: Getting a Sense for Electronic Evidence" (2001) (1:1) *Judicial Studies Institute Journal* 23; JD Frieden and LM Murray, "The Admissibility of Electronic Evidence Under the Federal Rules of Evidence" (2010–2011) *Richmond Journal of Law and Technology* 1.

28 Blank, *op. cit*, 497.

29 *Dublin Bus v Data Protection Commissioner* (2012) IEHC 339, 8 September 2012, available at http://www.bailii.org/cgi-bin/markup.cgi?doc=/ie/cases/IEHC/2012/H339.html&query=dublin+and+bus&method=boolean.

restricted, it may be difficult for an official entity not to capture and share the details with other agencies, such as the police and Revenue. By becoming online "friends" with one government agency, there can be a risk of greater government surveillance via the website in question,[30] in relation to individuals' location, activities as well as in relation to their official dealings.

Traditional Divisions Breaking Down

The dividing lines between what was "historically private information"[31] and public information[32] is under some strain. The same is the case with the work space and the home private life of employees.

Equally, old divisions and concepts do not always fit well in the internet age. One commentator states:

> "Courts have struggled to analogize the scenarios presented by cyberspace to considerations typically involved in determining traditional privacy expectations. Even before the explosions of social networking and the accompanying photograph-posting phenomena, courts had recognized that '[t]he advent of the electronic age and … the development of desktop computers … go beyond the established categories of constitutional doctrine. Analogies to other physical objects, such as dressers or file cabinets, do not often inform the situation we now face as judges when applying search and seizure law'".[33]

Expectations for Privacy in Modern Settings

Findlay states:

> "[g]iven such staggering new social dynamics, novel legal questions emerge regarding what privacy expectations exist in the social conscience of today's technologically hip world as well as whether traditional privacy formulations and the guarantees of the Fourth Amendment are adequately equipped to protect those expectations".[34]

In terms of the US at least, some authors have indicated that courts are unwilling to recognise reasonable expectations of privacy if an individual has posted material online without seeking to restrict or protect it.[35] They refer to the US case of Cynthia

---

30 See generally DK Citron, "Fulfilling Government 2.0's Promise with Robust Privacy Protections" (2010) (78) *George Washington Law Review* 822. Generally note also JS Schacter, "Digitally Democratizing Congress? Technology and Political Accountability" (2009) (89) *Boston University Law Review* 641.

31 D Findlay, "2Tag! Now You're 'It.' What Photographs on Social Networking Sites Mean for the Fourth Amendment" (2008) (10) *North Carolina Journal of Law & Technology* 171 at 192.

32 The Fourth Amendment prohibits illegal search and seizure of evidence. The line of US cases beginning with *Katz v United States* referring to the Fourth Amendment posit that once there is a subjective expectation of privacy and one which is reasonable, law enforcement authorities must a warrant to conduct a search; see Findlay, *op. cit*, at 186 and references therein. *Katz v United States* 398 US 347 (1967).

33 *United States v Walster* 275 F3d 981, 986 (10th Cir 2001), referred to in Findlay, *op. cit*, at 187–189.

34 Findlay, *op. cit*, 171. See also Semitsu, *op. cit*, 291.

35 Nelson *et al.*, *op. cit*, 21.

Moreno.[36] She posted comments about how much she hated her town. These were then published in a local newspaper. She and her family ultimately had to move after death threats, online abuse and gun shots. However, when she sued the newspaper, the court found against her, as her claim for privacy breach lacked private, non-public facts. There were no restrictions on publishing what was available online.[37]

In *Pennsylvania v Protetto* the court held that there was no privacy expectation in relation to sexually explicit emails sent to an underage person, as emails can be forwarded on to others.[38] This might seem a controversial decision as it relates to private correspondence, not public posts. A certain level of caution is needed when considering certain US cases in the EU.

A further level of complication arises where privacy expectations may "operate at different levels, owing to the varying levels of publicity which are possible."[39] It may be that in light of social networking "general conceptions of what is considered 'private' may also require expansion."[40]

The Supreme Court of Canada has recognised that employees have rights and expectations of privacy and data protection while they are at work. This includes their internet use and internet browsing history.[41] The Irish Data Protection Commissioner and the EU Article 29 Working Party equally recognise the legitimate expectations of employees in relation to their privacy and data protection rights. One could expect a similar position from other data protection authorities.

Privacy and data protection law are considered more developed in Canada and the EU than in the US. While there are certain laws in the US, they are on a piecemeal basis from state to state or limited to a small number of specific issues at a federal level. One example of this is the protection enacted for privacy and data protection relating to individuals' video rentals. This was enacted after a Judge's video rental history was disclosed at the time of his nomination hearings for the US Supreme Court.[42] Another relates to children eg COPPA.[43] New laws are developing.

Court Interpretations of Privacy in Modern Settings

The courts are said to be inconsistently interpreting and dealing with subjective and objective expectations of privacy[44] in the social networking age. There is a debate as to whether there can still be a reasonable expectation of privacy once a person

36 See *ibid.*

37 See *ibid*, referring to *Moreno v Hanford Sentinel Inc* 91 California Reporter 3d 858 (California Court Appeal 2009).

38 *Commonwealth v Protetto* 771 A2d 823–832 (Pa Super Court 2001), referred to in Nelson *et al.*, *op. cit*, at 22.

39 Findlay, *op. cit*, at 187.

40 *Smith v Md* 442 US 735, 743 (1979) and *Katz v United States* 389 US 347, 351 (1967), each as referred to in Findlay, *op. cit*, at 187.

41 *R v Cole* Supreme Court Canada 2012 SCC 53, available at http://scc.lexum.org/decisia-scc-csc/scc-csc/scc-csc/en/item/12615/index.do.

42 Video Privacy Protection Act of 1988 (18 USC § 2710 (2002).

43 US Children's Online Privacy Protection Act.

44 Findlay, *op. cit*, at 187.

posts a comment online regardless of context — and whether there can be private spaces on the internet, such as privacy and friends-restricted social networking, which do give rise to reasonable expectations of privacy. The US case of *Smith v Md* is an example of the former, while the case of *Katz* could be viewed as illustrating the latter.[45]

The issue is said to be "unsettled" in the US and particularly where photographs are posted on social networks by a third party.[46] The *Katz* case, if applied to social networking and posted photographs, asks whether the individual "knowingly expose[d] [the posted photograph] to the public".[47] Obviously, it is difficult to suggest that this is the case where a third party posts photographs of an individual without his or her knowledge or consent. Indeed, we might also ask whether a similar problem arises in the case of a third party tagging (ie labelling) an online social network photograph of a person.

These issues are potentially significantly more complicated when we consider the content of the photographs. The nature of the material may raise very different real expectations of privacy, eg family, romantic or children. This may be quite different than for a photograph in a public event or clearly public setting. The content and setting can lead to different subjective expectations of privacy.[48] More complicated is the position where two people may be in the same photograph but one may have (more) privacy concerns than the other eg a young child. This could include the child even of a celebrity taken in public.[49]

Even where a party posts a photograph of themselves, it is still possible to reasonably expect that privacy and data protection parameters will apply.[50] They may, for example, have restricted viewing access to only a few people.

In litigation "[o]nline profiles cannot be written off as mere entertainment or as simply the modern method to communicate, when they have proven useful in finding otherwise unattainable evidence of criminal behaviour."[51] The battle for social networking content in litigation is only likely to increase the strain on privacy and traditional lines of division and privacy expectations. While some materials may be relevant in a given instance, how should courts guard against general fishing expeditions into social networks? The number of contested cases will increase.

The Concept of Privacy

Privacy is widely viewed and understood as a fundamental human right[52] and is

---

45 *Smith v Md* 442 US 735, 743 (1979), and *Katz v United States* 389 US 347, 351 (1967), each as referred to in Findlay, *op. cit*, at 187.

46 *ibid.*

47 Findlay, *op. cit*, at 189–190.

48 See *ibid*, 190.

49 One celebrity who took a case to prevent photographs of their children being published was Harry Pottrer author JK Rowling. See *Murray v Big Pictures (UK) Ltd* [2008] EWCA Civ 446 (07 May 2008).

50 *ibid*, 190–191.

51 Montes, *op. cit*, at 527.

52 *Report of the Working Group on Privacy* (Department of Justice Equality and Law Reform, Dublin, 2006) at 8.

recognised by the Irish Constitution.[53] The seminal work in the privacy arena by Warren and Brandeis describes privacy as the "right to be let alone."[54] Their article was prompted by a fear that the technology of the day, a combination of photography and newspapers, would lead to "what is whispered in the closet ... [being] ... proclaimed from the house-tops".[55]

However, privacy is not a unified concept. Solove describes the term privacy as "an umbrella term relating to a wide and disparate group of related things".[56] Privacy can be divided into categories, for example, informational, spatial and decisional privacy.[57]

Informational privacy relates to an individual's entitlement to control the dissemination of information about themselves.[58] This includes control of all information that can be protected, depending on circumstance, from one's name to inherently private information, with medical history being a classic example.[59] Some commentators view this as the main concern of data protection laws. Edwards describes how data protection "protects what is known very generally as *informational privacy*."[60] Data protection laws also exist to protect freedom from surveillance and the interception of communications.[61] This may have added significant fallout as a consequence of the Snowden NSA revelations.

Spatial privacy relates to two distinct concepts. The first is the concept of territorial privacy most commonly related to one's home. This is reinforced with the protection afforded by "the inviolability of the dwelling".[62] Territorial privacy also extends outside one's home from a place of work or business[63] to hotel rooms.[64] The second concept is that of personal privacy. This relates to an individual's own personal space, in particular one's own body.[65] From there, it extends outwards. In light

53 There is no express constitutional provision relating to an individual's right to privacy. Article 40.3 of the Irish Constitution 1937, however, posits a guarantee by the State to defend and vindicate the personal rights of the citizen, and the Irish courts have determined that a right to privacy is implicit in that provision. The right to privacy is an unenumerated (or unspecified) personal right recognised by the Constitution. The constitutional right to individual privacy was successfully invoked before the High Court in *Kennedy and Arnold v Ireland* [1987] IR 587 in the context of telephone-tapping.

54 S Warren and L Brandeis, "The Right to Privacy" (1890) (4) *Harvard Law Review* 195.

55 *ibid.*

56 D Solove, "A Taxonomy of Privacy" (2006) (154) *University of Pennsylvania Law Review* 477 at 485.

57 H Delany and E Carolan, *The Right to Privacy* (Thomson Round Hall: Dublin, 2008), pp 20 and 41–56. See also *Report on Privacy: Surveillance and the Interception of Communications* LRC 57-1998, (Law Reform Commission, Dublin, 1998); *For Your Information: Australian Privacy Law and Practice*, ALRC 108 (Australian Law Reform Commission, Dublin, 2008).

58 Delany and Carolan, *op. cit*, pp 22 and 55.

59 The Irish Data Protection Connissioner is examining the apparent leaking of patient details regarding the reported case of the first legal abortion in Ireland, following a referendum in 2013. See, for example, F O'Cionnaith, "Watchdog Contacts Hospital Over Privacy Fears" *Irish Examiner* 28 August 2013.

60 L Edwards and C Waedle ed, *Law and the Internet* (Hart Publishing: Oxford, 2009), 445.

61 *Report of the Working Group on Privacy* (Department of Justice Equality and Law Reform, Dublin, 2006), 13.

62 Constitution of Ireland 1937, Article 40.5.

63 Delany and Carolan, *op. cit*, 46.

64 *ibid*, 48.

65 *Re a Ward of Court* [1996] 2 IR 79.

of the *Von Hannover* case, the concept of personal space includes an expectation of personal privacy even in public.[66] One might consider spatial privacy and the arrival of wireless internet and peer to peer, and in particular how retail outlets, discos, etc may wish to text and email a person who comes within proximity of their shop, club, etc.

The third category, decisional privacy, relates to an individual's right to autonomy, the freedom and right to make one's own decisions. Traditionally this category protected an individual from intrusion by the state.[67] So, for example in *McGee v Attorney General* marital privacy ensured that the state could not interfere in decisions on the use of contraception.[68] Delany and Carolan state that it seems reasonable to suggest that the right to decisional privacy may extend, for example, to prevent interference with one's choice of literature.[69] One could consider the implications of monitoring, behavioural advertising based on one's past internet and email communications and the extent to which one's decisions and decisional privacy may be impacted.

Each of these categories goes to the core of privacy and to the core of the individual. They are, as Henchy J described in the Irish Supreme Court, that "secluded area" we all require for the expression of individual personality.[70] Protection of this secluded area promotes breathing space for our "thoughts, sentiments and emotions",[71] providing a freedom and autonomy that fosters creative experimentation, self-fulfilment and participation in society.

Cases

The constitutional protection of privacy has extended over time to include non-state intrusion of one's privacy, as demonstrated in the Irish cases of *Sinnott v Nationalist and Leinster Times, Carlow*[72] and *Herrity v Associated Newspapers*.[73] The *Sinnott* case involved the publication of a photograph in which Mr Sinnott's private parts were accidently exposed during a football match. Damages were awarded for the breach of the constitutional right to privacy.[74] The photograph was printed in a local newspaper.[75]

An individual can be protected against unwarranted intrusion into their private space regardless of whether the intrusion results in sensitive details being discovered or

---

66 *Von Hannover v Germany* 59320/00 [2004] ECHR 294 (24 June, 2004); (2005) 40 EHRR 1.

67 *Re a Ward of Court (No. 2)* [1996] 2 IR 79 at 169; see also Hogan and Whyte, *JM Kelly: The Irish Constitution* (LexisNexis Butterworths, Dublin, 2003) at 1445; and Delany and Carolan, *op. cit*, 13.

68 *McGee v Attorney General* [1974] IR 284.

69 Delany and Carolan, *op. cit*, 41.

70 *Norris v Attorney General* [1984] IR 36 at 72.

71 Warren and Brandeis, *op. cit*, 198.

72 As reported "Appeal Against GAA Player Award Lost," *Irish Times*, 27 January 2007, at 4.

73 *Herrity v Associated Newspapers* [2009] 1 IR 316.

74 "Court Increases Payout to GAA Player Over Photo," *Irish Times*, 31 July 2008, at 4.

75 The photograph passed through all stages of the publication process from image selection to final production without being deemed unsuitable for publication.

made public.[76] In *Herrity v Associated Newspapers,*[77] a husband used a private investigator to intercept telephone conversations between his wife and a local priest. Transcripts of the calls were published. The court decided that there was a breach of the wife's right to privacy, and relied on the unlawful "illegal phone tap" used and awarded damages of €90,000.[78]

In a further case which settled, it is understood that an amount was paid by a newspaper which published details from private and intimate letters sent to a person in prison.

The Advertising Standards Authority (ASA) of Ireland upheld a complaint in relation to Nokia adverts which were seen to be encouraging people to take mobile photographs of strangers. It stated that "an individual may not appreciate their photograph being taken and then being posted on a social network online without their permission or knowledge. [The Complaints Committee of the ASA] considered that the advertisement had not been prepared with a sense of responsibility to consumers and they upheld the complaint".[79]

Conclusion

There is, however, no general right to privacy in Irish statute as yet. It is difficult, therefore, for courts considering cases involving privacy and internet activities.

[76] In *Kennedy and Arnold v Ireland* [1987] IR 587 at 593 Hamilton P. states that "[t]he dignity and freedom of an individual in a democratic society cannot be ensured if his communications of a private nature … are deliberately, consciously and unjustifiably intruded upon and interfered with." He goes on to emphasise the words "deliberately, consciously and unjustifiably" "because an individual must accept the risk of accidental interference with his communications and the fact that in certain circumstances the exigencies of the common good may require and justify such intrusion and interference."

[77] *Herrity v Associated Newspapers* [2009] 1 IR 316.

[78] *ibid.*

[79] Complaint Reference 15266, Bulletin 11/2, Batch No. 198, available at www.asai.ie/complaint_view.asp?CID=813&BID=40.

Chapter 5

EARLY TO CURRENT DATA PROTECTION

Headline of Issues

- The data protection regime
- The EU Data Protection Directive
- Definitions and meanings underpinning data protection regime
- Lawful data processing
- Data protection/quality principles
- Legitimate processing criteria/conditions
- General personal data
- Sensitive personal data
- Outdated data protection
- New EU measures proposed

Introduction

Social networking presents one of the biggest issues of discussion for the data protection regime. The data protection regime requires fairness, transparency and accountability in terms the collection and use of personal data.[1] Data subjects are also provided with a series of rights.[2] These do not, however, neatly reflect the social networking world. Current data protection laws are suggested as "sorely inadequate" to the issues posed by social networking.[3] This is because the current generation of data protection laws was generally drafted in a pre-social-networking world. Therefore, they are often inevitably inadequate in addressing the specific issues posed by social networking and the second-generation internet (Web 2.0). They are equally inadequate in providing certainty and assurance to websites. Data protection rules do however apply.

In terms of appreciating the problems, and considering solutions, we must first look at the current data protection legal regime. EU data protection law is primarily set

1 In terms of general internet and governing organisation accountability issues, see for instance RH Weber, "Accountability in the Internet of Things" (2011) (27) *Computer Law & Security Review* 133.

2 See Articles 10 (information to be given to data subject at time of data collection), 12 (access right) and 14 (right to object), EU Directive 95/46/EC of the European Parliament and of the Council of 24 October 1995 on the Protection of Individuals with regard to the Processing of Personal Data and on the Free Movement of such Data.

3 DB Garrie, M Duffy-Lewis, R Wong and RL Gillespie, "Data Protection: The Challenges Facing Social Networking" (2009–2010) (131) *International Law & Management Review* 127, at 128 and 141.

out in the Data Protection Directive 1995[4] and national implementing legislation. The Irish data protection regime is governed by the Data Protection Act 1988[5] and Data Protection (Amendment) Act 2003.[6] The 2003 Act implements the EU Data Protection Directive 1995. UK data protection was governed originally by the Data Protection Act 1984 and now by the Data Protection Act 1998.[7] There is a second EU data protection law: originally the Telecomms Data Protection Directive,[8] later replaced with the ePrivacy Data Protection Directive (ePrivacy Directive).[9] The starting point for understanding the data protection regime is described below.

The Data Protection Directive

The European Commission promoted two data protection directives, the general Data Protection Directive 1995[10] and the Telecoms Data Protection Directive[11] (later replaced by the ePrivacy Directive[12]). The Data Protection Directive 1995 was adopted formally on 24 October 1995.

---

4 The full title is EU Directive 95/46/EC of the EU European Parliament and of the Council of 24 October 1995 on the Protection of Individuals with regard to the Processing of Personal Data and on the Free Movement of such Data.

5 The Irish 1988 Data Protection Act implements the Council of Europe [COE] Convention for the Protection of Individuals with Regard to Automatic Processing of Personal Data 1986, and hence was in place before the EU Data Protection Directive 1995. The origin of data protection lies with the OECD Council Recommendation of 23 February 1980; the Guidelines on the Protection of Privacy and Transborder Flows of Personal Data; and the Council of Europe Convention for the Protection of Individuals with Regard to Automatic Processing of Personal Data 1986.

6 Enacted, in part, to implement parts of the EU Directive 95/46/EC of the European Parliament and of the Council of 24 October 1995 on the protection of individuals with regard to the processing of personal data and on the free movement of such data not implemented in the previous Irish 1988 Data Protection Act which implemented the COE 1986 Convention. The EU Data Protection Directive 1995 was required to be implemented in Ireland by 24 October 1995, which deadline was missed. Ultimately it was implemented in the Data Protection (Amendment) Act 2003.

7 Generally see S Rogerson, "Privacy and the New Data Protection Act," *Centre for Computing and Social Responsibility*, available at http://www.ccsr.cse.dmu.ac.uk/resources/general/ethicol/Ecv9no6.html.

8 EU Directive 97/66/EC of the European Parliament and of the Council of 15 December 1997 concerning the processing of personal data and the protection of privacy in the telecommunications sector (now replaced by the ePrivacy Directive).

9 EU Directive 2002/58 concerning the processing of personal data and the protection of privacy in the electronic communications sector. This has since been amended with the introduction of Directive 2009/136/EC of 25 November 2009 amending Directive 2002/22/EC on universal service and users' rights relating to electronic communications networks and services, Directive 2002/58/EC concerning the processing of personal data and the protection of privacy in the electronic communications sector and Regulation (EC) No 2006/2004 on cooperation between national authorities responsible for the enforcement of consumer protection laws.

10 EU Directive 95/46/EC of the European Parliament and of the Council of 24 October 1995 on the Protection of Individuals with regard to the Processing of Personal Data and on the Free Movement of such Data.

11 EU Directive 97/66/EC of the European Parliament and of the Council of 15 December 1997 concerning the Processing of Personal Data and the Protection of Privacy in the Telecommunications Sector. This has since been replaced with the ePrivacy Directive (Directive 2002/58).

12 EU Directive 2002/58 concerning the processing of personal data and the protection of privacy in the electronic communications sector. This has since been amended with the introduction of Directive 2009/136/EC of 25 November 2009 amending Directive 2002/22/EC on universal

The objective of the EU Data Protection Directive 1995 is to protect the fundamental rights and freedoms of natural persons, in particular the right to privacy with respect to the processing of personal data.[13] It applies to the processing of personal data wholly or partly by automatic means and to the processing otherwise than by automatic means of personal data that form part of a filing system.[14] Chapter II (General Rules on the Lawfulness of the Processing of Personal Data) of the EU Data Protection Directive 1995 makes specific provision for:

- principles in relation to data quality (also known as the data protection principles);
- criteria for making data processing legitimate (the legal processing criteria or conditions);
- special categories of processing (sensitive personal data);
- information to be given to data subjects;
- data subjects right of access to data;
- exemptions and restrictions;
- the data subjects right to object;
- confidentiality and security of processing;
- notification.[15]

Definitions in Data Protection Directive

The EU Data Protection Directive 1995 contains and is governed by a number of key data protection definitions. It is necessary to understand these in order to appreciate the mechanics of the data protection regime. These definitions include the following.

> "Personal data" means any information relating to an identified or identifiable natural person (ie data subject). An identifiable person is one who can be identified, directly or indirectly,

---

service and users' rights relating to electronic communications networks and services, Directive 2002/58/EC concerning the processing of personal data and the protection of privacy in the electronic communications sector and Regulation (EC) No 2006/2004 on cooperation between national authorities responsible for the enforcement of consumer protection laws.

13 See Article 1.1.

14 Chapter I (General Provisions) of the EU Directive 95/46/EC of the European Parliament and of the Council of 24 October 1995 on the protection of individuals with regard to the processing of personal data and on the free movement of such data sets out the objective of the Directive; the key definitions, the Directive's scope and specifics. Directive 95/46/EC of the European Parliament and of the Council of 24 October 1995 on the Protection of Individuals with regard to the Processing of Personal Data and on the Free Movement of such Data.

15 Chapter III (Judicial Remedies, Liability and Sanctions) of the EU Data Protection Directive 1995 deals with remedies, liability and sanctions. Chapter IV (Transfer of Personal Data to Third Countries) sets out the principles for dealing with the transfer of personal data to third countries outside the EU (known as trans-border data flows) and the exceptions that might apply. Chapter V (Codes of Conduct) makes general provision requiring Member States to promote codes of conduct. Chapter VI (Supervisory Authority and Working Party on the Protection of Individuals with Regard to the Processing of Personal Data) deals with the supervisory authorities that Member States are required to establish for monitoring the application of the Directive. It also establishes a Working Party to be composed of representatives of the supervisory authorities designated by each Member State and which has advisory status and acts independently. (EU Article 29 Working Party.) Chapter VII (Community Implementing Measures) provides that the EU Commission shall be assisted by a committee composed of representatives of the Member States and chaired by the representative of the Commission.

> in particular by reference to an identification number or to one or more factors specific to his or her physical, physiological, mental, economic, cultural or social identity.[16]
>
> "Processing of personal data" (processing) means any operation or set of operations which is performed upon personal data, whether or not by automatic means, such as connection, recording, organisation, storage, adaptation or alteration, retrieval, consultation, use, disclosure by transmission, dissemination or otherwise making available, alignment or combination, blocking, erasure or destruction.[17]
>
> "Data controller" (or "controller" in the Directive) means the natural or legal person, public authority, agency or any other party which alone or jointly with others determines the purposes and means of the processing of personal data; where the purposes and means of processing are determined by national or Community laws and regulations, the controller or the specific criteria for his nomination to be designated by national or Community law.[18]
>
> "Data processor" (or "processor" in the Directive) means a natural or legal person, public authority, agency or any other party which processes personal data on behalf of the controller.[19]

Throughout the EU Data Protection Directive 1995 there are requirements relating to obtaining the consent of the individual data subject, and distinctions are made between unambiguous consent and "explicit" consent.[20] The "data subject's consent" is defined to mean any freely given specific and informed indication of wishes by which the data subject signifies his or her agreement to personal data relating to him or her being processed.[21]

There is no uniform data protection law in the US, which instead seeks in a limited number of instances to regulate the third-party use of individuals' personal data in specific sectors, eg video rentals. However, the US Federal Trade Commission (FTC) does refer to a definition relating to private or personal data, namely, "information about children and adolescents, medical information, financial information and account numbers, social security numbers, sexual orientation information, government-issued identifiers, and precise geographic location".[22] The FTC in this respect operates under a consumer protection mandate, as opposed to a direct

---

16 Article 2(a), Directive 95/46/EC of the European Parliament and of the Council of 24 October 1995 on the Protection of Individuals with regard to the Processing of Personal Data and on the Free Movement of such Data.

17 EU Directive 95/46, Article 2(b).

18 EU Directive 95/46, Article 2(d).

19 EU Directive 95/46, Article 2(e). Other definitions include "third party", which means any natural or legal person, public authority, agency or any other body other than that data subject, the controller, the processor and the persons who, under the direct authority of the controller or the processor, are authorised to process the data (Article 2(f)); and "recipient", which means a natural or legal person, public authority, agency or any other person to whom data are disclosed, whether a third party or not; however, authorities which may receive data in the framework of a particular inquiry shall not be regarded as recipients (Article 2(f)).

20 See, for example, criteria for making data processing legitimate (Article 7); processing of special cases of data (Article 8; sensitive personal data); and transfer of personal data abroad (Article 26), also known as trans-border data flows (TBDFs).

21 Article 2(h) Directive 95/46/EC of the European Parliament and of the Council of 24 October 1995 on the Protection of Individuals with regard to the Processing of Personal Data and on the Free Movement of such Data.

22 See SE Gindin, "Nobody Reads Your Privacy Policy or Online Contract? Lessons Learned and Questions Raised by the FTC's Action Against Sears" (2009) (8) *Northwestern Journal of Technology and Intellectual Property* 1 at 28.

privacy or data protection mandate, as would be the case in the EU. There have also been calls for a more uniform general privacy or data protection law in the US[23] not dissimilar to the European model. The US does have a growing number of specific state laws relating to particular data and information issues. There is, for example, a growing number of data breach notification laws.

Lawful Data Processing

The EU Data Protection Directive 1995 sets out data quality criteria or principles[24] that must be complied with. These act as a precondition to lawful data processing.

It also specifies lawful or legitimate processing conditions that must be complied with.[25] These also act as a precondition.

It imposes requirements for the processing of special or sensitive categories of personal data.[26] Certain information must be given in cases where data have been collected directly from the data subject and in cases where data have not been obtained from the data subject.[27] There are requirements with regard to the security of processing of personal data.[28] The EU Data Protection Directive 1995 imposes obligations with regard to the transfer of personal data to third countries. It also has provisions addressing other issues.[29]

Data Quality Principles and Data Protection Principles

Article 6 of the EU Data Protection Directive 1995 contains some of the most important fundamental provisions of the data protection regime. It sets out the data quality principles that data controllers must comply with and that act on a precondition basis to lawful data processing.[30] Personal data must be:

---

23 TL Balaban, "Comprehensive Data Privacy Legislation: Why Now is the Time" (2009) *Case Western Reserve Journal of Law, Technology & the Internet* 1.

24 Article 6.

25 Article 7. The original Irish 1988 Data Protection Act obliged data controllers to comply with the data protection principles specified in section 2 of the Act, now expanded into the data quality principles. The seventh data protection principle, namely the requirement to take appropriate security measures, also apply to data processors.

26 Article 8.

27 Articles 10 and 11. These are built on the concept of fair obtaining and processing.

28 Article 17.

29 These include: processing of personal data and freedom of expression; exceptions and restrictions; confidentiality; notification and registration; judicial remedies, liability and sanctions; codes of conduct; supervisory authority and Working Party; EU Community implementations measures; national law applicable; and transitional provisions.

30 In Ireland these are based on the data protection principles in the Data Protection Act 1988 as amended by the Data Protection (Amendment) Act 2003. A data controller, under the Data Protection Act 1988 as amended by the Data Protection (Amendment) Act 2003, must comply with the data protection principles regarding personal data held, namely, the data or information constituting the data must be obtained and processed fairly; the data must be accurate and, when necessary, kept up to date; the data must be kept only for one or more specified and lawful purposes; the data must not be used or disclosed in a manner incompatible with the purpose or those purposes; the data must be adequate, relevant and not excessive in relation to the purpose or purposes; the data must be kept for no longer than is necessary for the purpose or those purposes; and appropriate security measures shall be taken against unauthorised access to, or alteration, disclosure or destruction of, the data and against their accidental loss or destruction.

- processed fairly and lawfully;
- collected for specified, explicit and legitimate purposes, and not further processed in any way incompatible with those purposes[31];
- adequate, relevant and not excessive in relation to the purposes for which they are connected and/or further processed;
- accurate and, where necessary, kept up to date. Every reasonable step must be taken to ensure that data which are inaccurate or incomplete, having regards to the purposes for which they were collected or for which they are further processed, are erased or rectified;
- kept in a form that permits identification of data subjects for no longer than is necessary for the purposes for which the data were collected or for which they are further processed. Member States must lay down appropriate safeguards for personal data stored for longer periods for historical, statistical or scientific use.

There are, therefore, requirements of fairness and proportionality of processing. The first data protection principle requires that personal data must be processed fairly and lawfully.[32] The seventh data protection principle requires that appropriate technical and organisational security measures must be taken to prevent unauthorised or unlawful processing or accidental loss or destruction of personal data.[33] The eight data protection principle states that personal data must not be transferred to a country outside the EEA unless that country ensures adequate levels of data protection.[34]

There is also a principle of proportionality, in particular that only so much data should be collected and processed as is necessary for the purpose. Proportionality is also referred to variously in relation to data protection rules.[35] The issue of proportionality has also been referred to by the Court of Justice of the European Union (CJEU, previously ECJ).[36] This proportionality principle also arises in relation to specific issues within data protection, such as health and biometrics.[37]

Criteria for Making Data Processing Legitimate

Article 7 of the EU Data Protection Directive 1995 contains the requirement of legitimising data processing. Personal data must be processed only if specific conditions are met. These conditions act as further preconditions to lawful data

---

A data processor must comply with the data protection principle in relation to the security of the personal data processed by it.

31 Further processing of data for historical, statistical or scientific purposes shall not be considered as incompatible provided that EU Member States provide appropriate safeguards.

32 s 2(1) Data Protection Act 1988 as amended by the Data Protection (Amendment) Act 2003.

33 *ibid*, s 2(1).

34 *ibid*, s 2(1).

35 See for example, *Opinion 1/2008 on Data Protection Issues Related to Search Engines*, Article 29 Working Party, 4 April 2008, at 13–15.

36 *Lindqvist v Sweden*, ECJ, Case No. c-101/01, 6 November 2003, at 92, paras 88–90.

37 See Article 6 Directive 95/46/EC of the European Parliament and of the Council of 24 October 1995 on the protection of individuals with regard to the processing of personal data and on the free movement of such data [1995] OJ L281/31; Y Liu, "The Principle of Proportionality in Biometrics: Case Studies from Norway" (2009) (25) *Computer Law & Security Review* 237; I Brown, "Data Protection: The New Technical and Political Environment," *Society of Computers and Law*, available at www.scl.org/site.aspx?i=ed14331.

processing. Personal data may be processed only if one of the following conditions is satisfied:

- The data subject has unambiguously given his or her consent;
- The processing is necessary for performance of a contract to which the data subject is party or in order to take steps at the request of the data subject prior to entering into a contract;
- The processing is necessary for compliance with a legal obligation to which the data controller is subject;
- The processing is necessary to protect vital interests of the data subject;
- The processing is necessary for the performance of a task carried out in the public interest, or in exercise of official authority vested in the data controller, or in a third party to whom the data are disclosed;
- The processing is necessary for the purposes of the legitimate interests pursued by the data controller or by the third party or parties to whom the data are disclosed, except where these interests are overwritten by the data subject's fundamental rights and freedoms.

Processing Special Categories of Personal Data (Sensitive Personal Data)

Article 8 of the EU Data Protection Directive 1995 provides that, subject to specific exceptions, certain categories of personal data must not be processed.[38] These categories are personal data relating to racial or ethnic origin, political opinions, religious or philosophical beliefs, trade union membership, and processing of data concerning sex life.[39] These sensitive categories of personal data may be processed only where one of the following specific exceptions apply:

- The data subject has given his or her explicit consent to the processing;
- The processing is necessary to carry out the obligations and specific rights of the data controller in the field of employment law insofar as it is authorised by national law providing for adequate safeguards;
- The processing is necessary to protect vital interests of the data subject or of a person where the data subject is physically or legally incapable of giving their consent;
- The processing is carried out in the course of legitimate activities with appropriate guarantees by non-profit-type bodies where the processing relates solely to their members or persons who have regular contract with them, and the data are not disclosed to a third party without the consent of the data subject;
- The processing relates to data that are manifestly made public by the

[38] Under the 1988 Data Protection Act the data protection principles applied regardless of the nature of the data in question. In other words, there are no categories of personal data that were subjected to particular treatment. Under the 1988 Data Protection Act the concept of sensitive categories of personal data was really only relevant in the context of whether or not a data controller would be required to register.

[39] Article 8(1) Directive 95/46/EC of the European Parliament and of the Council of 24 October 1995 on the Protection of Individuals with regard to the Processing of Personal Data and on the Free Movement of such Data.

data subject or are necessary for the establishment, exercise or defence of legal claims.[40]

Certain Information Must be Given to Individuals

Articles 10 and 11 of the Data Protection Directive 1995 require that certain minimum information must be given to data subjects in two specific circumstances: where the data are collected directly from the data subject[41] and where the data are not obtained from the data subject and where the data controller records the data or envisages disclosures of such data to a third party.[42] There is, therefore, directly collected data and indirectly obtained data.

The information that must be provided for *directly* collected data is:

- the identity of the data controller;
- the purposes of the processing for which the data are intended;
- any further information such as,
  (a) the recipients or categories of recipients of data;
  (b) whether replies to questions are obligatory or voluntary, as well as the possible consequences of failure to apply; and
  (c) the existence of right of access to and the right to rectify the data concerning them,

  in so far as such further information is necessary, having regard to the specific circumstances in which the data are collected, to guarantee fair processing in respect of the data subject.[43]

In terms of the Irish data protection audit investigation of Facebook, part of the complaints related to data collection and possible processing activities in relation to data that individual users have not been advised is actually being collected.[44] If they are not advised that it is being collected, the query arises as to how they could then have consented to its use and processing in relation to them. This is a problem not unique to one website however.

40 There is also an exemption where processing is required for the purposes of preventative medicine, medical diagnosis and similar circumstances where the processing is done by health professionals. See Article 9(3) EU Directive 95/46/EC of the European Parliament and of the Council of 24 October 1995 on the Protection of Individuals with regard to the Processing of Personal Data and on the Free Movement of such Data. Special provisions are made with regards to data relating to offences, criminal convictions or security measures. Such processing may be carried out only under the control of official authority and if suitable specific safeguards exist. Article 8(5), EU Data Protection Directive 1995. A complete register of criminal convictions may be kept only under the controller on official authority. It is open to Member States to provide that data relating to administration sanctions or judgments in civil cases shall also be processed on control of official authority. Member States may determine the conditions under which a national identification number or any other identifier of general application may be processed. Article 8(5), EU Data Protection Directive 1995.

41 Article 10 EU Directive 95/46/EC of the European Parliament and of the Council of 24 October 1995 on the Protection of Individuals with regard to the Processing of Personal Data and on the Free Movement of such Data.

42 Article 11.

43 Article 10.

44 See generally announcements and documents at http://dataprotection.ie/docs/Home/4.htm.

With *indirectly* obtained data, the information is broadly the same, with two exceptions:

- In the second bullet, the reference to "for which data are intended" is not included;
- In the third bullet, information such as the categories of data concerned have to be included.[45]

In the case of indirectly obtained data, information has to be given either at the time of undertaking the recording of personal data or, if a disclosure to a third party is envisaged, no later than at the time when the data are first disclosed, except where the data subject already has this data.[46]

Data Protection Meets Social Networking: Users

The EU Data Protection Directive 1995 was enacted before the social networking and the second-generation internet (Web 2.0) era and its ensuing issues.[47] There is, therefore, no explicit reference to social networking in the EU Data Protection Directive 1995. A further difficulty is that there is no explicit reference to children in the EU Data Protection Directive 1995, a frequent user population of social networks. These issues were simply not contemplated.

In terms of users' own social networking processing activity, this may be argued to fall within the household data-processing exemption, in that users are acting personally and at home. [48] It is also questionable to what extent individuals could comply with data protection obligations as a data controller.[49] For example, social networking users could face difficulties in relation to obtaining consent to post personal data relating third parties (including friends) on their own profile pages and also on the social networking profile pages of other people.[50] There is no explicit obligation to obtain consent or to inform the third-party data subjects in the context of social networking. However, this is an issue separate from social networks complying with the data protection regime and respecting informational privacy.

The social networks and related websites (as data controllers) and the users of social networks (as data subjects) each fall within the definitions of the EU Data Protection Directive 1995. Each is subject to the provisions of the EU Data Protection Directive 1995.[51] When individuals have their personal data posted online or otherwise processed online, including by a third-party, they qualify as data subjects under the EU Data Protection Directive 1995.

---

45 Article 11.

46 Article 11(1).

47 Garrie *et al.*, *op. cit.*

48 See commentary at "Social Networking Sites: Article 29 Working Party Opinion," *Society of Computers and Law* 22 June 2009, available at www.scl.org/site.aspx?i=ne12245.

49 Garrie *et al.*, *op. cit*, at 131–133.

50 See *ibid.*

51 *ibid*, 131.

However, the activities encompassed within social networking are beyond the contemplation of the EU Data Protection Directive 1995, and hence difficulties arise.

In addition, users will frequently post (ie upload), tag (ie label) or comment on photographs of third parties on their own profile pages and on third-party profile pages. This also can be without transparency, fairness or consent. However, the EU Data Protection Directive 1995 does not say anything explicitly in terms of the obligations on users posting photographs, nor on the rights of those included in the photographs.

Some of the EU Data Protection Directive 1995 general obligations relate to fair and lawful processing, prior information requirements, the data protection principles and the legitimate processing grounds. One requirement, for example, could require individual social networking users to obtain the consent of their "friends" in advance. There is, however, some divergence on the view that individual users who post on social networks are data controllers. The UK Information Commissioner, for instance, is referred to as being of this view.[52] A separate view may be that the recreational and journalistic purposes exemptions in the EU Data Protection Directive 1995 may apply to individual users.[53] Importantly, however, while there are certain exemptions in relation to journalism in the data protection regime, there are no such exemptions as regards social networks or related websites. Lord Justice Leveson in his UK report has been critical of the overbroad and unanticipated effects of the implementation of the data protection journalism exemption in the UK.[54] The report goes on to suggest specific amendments curtailing the exemption and raising the possibility of UK law being incompatible with or an incorrect implementation of the EU Data Protection Directive 1995.[55] While there may be political disagreement (at the time of writing at least) in relation to other aspects of the report, it appears that Prime Minister Cameron and Deputy Prime Minister Clegg are in full agreement on implementing the data protection changes.[56] These issues may, to some extent, have been overtaken by the official EU grouping known as EU Article 29 Working Party (WP29). It issued an Opinion in relation to social networking.[57] While the Opinion is useful and influential in terms of how national data protection authorities, eg the Irish Data Protection Commissioner, will interpret the EU Data Protection Directive 1995, it is not law and does not update the EU Data Protection Directive 1995. In addition, Garrie, Duffy-Lewis, Wong and Gillespie feel that while the Opinion clarifies certain matters (eg the Article 3.2 exemption in the EU Data Protection Directive 1995, which may benefit individual users), the exemptions may need to be expanded to refer to non-commercial uses.[58]

---

52 Referred to *ibid*, 140.

53 Referred to *ibid*, 140.

54 UK Leveson Inquiry. *An Inquiry into the Culture, Practices and Ethics of the Press: Report, The Right Honourable Lord Justice Leveson*, November 2012. Available at http://www.official-documents.gov.uk/document/hc1213/hc07/0780/0780.asp. Also see the main inquiry website at http://www.levesoninquiry.org.uk/.

55 *ibid.*

56 A Travis and O Bowcott, "Leveson Data Protection Proposals Unite Cameron and Clegg In Concern," *Guardian*, 30 November 2012, available at http://www.guardian.co.uk/media/2012/nov/30/leveson-data-protection-proposals-concern.

57 A29WP. Opinion 5/2009 on Online Social Networking. WP 163. Adopted on 12 June 2009.

58 Garrie *et al.*, *op. cit*, 151–152.

Some specific problems which Garrie, Duffy-Lewis, Wong and Gillespie feel arise for the EU Data Protection Directive 1995 are posed in the following questions:

1 "Would it be fair or practical to hold individuals who post information and photographs about friends and family to the strict requirements of 'data controllers' under the [EU Data Protection Directive 1995]?
2 Should the obligations and consequences for individuals be the same at all times as those for organisations?
3 Should a new category be created for individual data controllers with obligations adjusted accordingly? Would such a category be feasible?
4 Would application of the [EU Data Protection Directive 1995] to [social networking service] users stifle social networking because individuals would not want to go through the trouble of understanding and complying with [EU Data Protection Directive 1995] provisions? Conversely, would application of the [EU Data Protection Directive 1995] have a positive effect – a heightened awareness of user responsibilities in a user-generated environment?"[59]

The EU Data Protection Directive 1995 exemptions again were not drafted with social networking in mind.[60]

Data Protection Meets Social Networking

Graham and Andersen state:

> "Major social-networking [web]sites generally make efforts to comply with the [1995 Directive] and other relevant legislation. Their principle mechanisms for compliance are,
> - obtaining the consent of all users for the use of their personal data at the point of account opening;
> - having a detailed privacy policy setting out how the data will be used;
> - applying privacy settings which allow users to restrict who can view their data; and
> - ensuring security of the data on the website to prevent unauthorised access (ie access by those not permitted through a person's privacy settings)."[61]

Certain social networks or related websites located outside the EEA may argue that it is not required to comply with the EU data protection regime. They may say that they are located abroad and or its servers are located abroad.[62] However, it must still comply with the EU data protection regime once it has entities within the EU and or deals with EU citizens' personal data and or utilises equipment within the EU.[63]

---

59 *ibid*, 134.

60 *ibid*, 142.

61 N Graham and H Anderson, "Are Individuals Waking Up to the Privacy Implications of Social Networking Sites?" (2010) (3) *European Intellectual Property Review* 99.

62 Viviane Reding, the EU Justice Commissioner, stated at a conference that a "US-based social network company that has millions of active users in Europe needs to comply with EU rules. There should be no exceptions for third countries' service providers controlling our citizens' data"; referred to in "Social Networks Will Face Tighter Privacy Rule," *Financial Times* 16 March 2011, available at www.ft.com/cms/s/2/8519c882-500c-11e0-9ad1-00144feab49a.html#axzz1YyWrRdLH. See also, for example, L Philips, "EU to Force Social Network Sites to Enhance Privacy, 'Right to be Forgotten' Would Ensure Users of Facebook and Other Sites Could Completely Erase Personal Data," *Guardian*, 16 March 2011.

63 See EU Data Protection Directive 1995.

EU Commission, Data Protection and the Future

EU Commission Recognises Outdated Data Protection Regime

The EU Commission has recognised that there are problems with the inadequacy of the data protection regime in dealing with the issues of social networking, etc. The EU Data Protection Directive 1995 and ePrivacy Directive "are intended to deal with the problems of processing, as we understood them in 1995."[64] Therefore, even in temporal terms, it is outdated. Social networking and new communications technologies bring "new risks to privacy".[65] These are not catered for in the EU Data Protection Directive 1995. Indeed, we should not be overly surprised, as social networking was not contemplated at that time.

EU Commission and the Future

The EU Commission recognises that there are many new issues for data protection. It states that "rapid technological developments and globalisation have profoundly changed the world around us, and brought new challenges for the protection of personal data."[66] It specifically acknowledges and refers to social networking and Cloud computing.[67] It also states generally that the "risks to privacy and the protection of personal data associated with online activity are increasing."[68] The "ways of collecting personal data have become increasingly elaborated and less easily detectable."[69]

The EU Commission refers to the need for enhancing the control by users over their own personal data:

> "Two important preconditions for ensuring that individuals enjoy a high level of data protection are the limitation of the data controllers' processing in relation to its purposes (principle of data minimisation) and the retention by data subjects of an effective control over their own data. Article 8(2) of the Charter[[70]] states that 'everyone has the right of access to data which has been collected concerning [them], and the right to have it rectified.' Individuals should always be able to access, rectify, delete or block their data, unless there are legitimate reasons, provided by law, for preventing this. These rights already exist in the current legal framework. However, the way in which these rights can be exercised is not harmonised, and therefore exercising them is actually easier in some Member States than in others. Moreover, this has become particularly challenging in the online environment, where data are often retained without the person concerned being informed and/or having given his or her agreement to it.
>
> The example of online social networking is particularly relevant here, as it presents significant challenges to the individual's effective control over his/her personal data. The

---

64 Y Poullet, "Data Protection Legislation: What Is At Stake for Our Society and Democracy?" (2009) (25) *Computer Law & Security Review* 211 at 216.

65 *ibid*, 216.

66 Communications from the Commission to the European Parliament, the Council, the Economic and Social Committee of the Regions, A Comprehensive Approach on Personal Data Protection in the European Union, 4 November 2010, COM (2010) 609 Final, 2.

67 *ibid.*

68 *ibid.*

69 *ibid.*

70 The EU Charter also refers to the protection of personal data. Article 8 of the EU Charter of Fundamental Rights of the European Union provides that everyone has the right to the protection of personal data. Everyone has the right of access to data which has been collected and which relates to them. Individuals also have the right to have such data rectified.

> [EU] Commission has received various queries from individuals who have not always been able to retrieve personal data from online websites, such as their pictures, and who have therefore been impeded in exercising their rights of access, rectification and deletion.
> Such rights should therefore be made more explicit, clarified and possibly strengthened".[71]

In terms of specific action, therefore, the Commission will:

> "examine ways of:
> - strengthening the principle of data minimisation;
> - improving the ... exercise of the rights of access, rectification, erasure or blocking of data (eg by introducing deadlines for responding to individuals' requests, by allowing the exercise of rights by electronic means or by providing that right of access should be ensured free of charge as a principle);
> - clarifying the ... 'right to be forgotten', ie the right of individuals to have their data no longer processed and deleted when they are no longer needed for legitimate purposes. This is the case, for example, when processing is based on the person's consent and when he or she withdraws consent or when the storage period has expired;
> - complementing the rights of data subjects by ensuring 'data portability', ie providing the explicit right for an individual to withdraw his/her own data (eg his/her photos or a list of friends) from an application or service so that the withdrawn data can be transferred into another application or service, as far as technically feasible, without hindrance from the data controllers".[72]

Raising awareness is a key area highlighted by the EU Commission for enhancing the data protection regime.[73] In addition, the EU Commission will "examine ways of clarifying and strengthening the rules on consent."[74] The responsibility of data controllers will also be reviewed to see how they can be enhanced.[75] One example of this may be imposing mandatory data protection "impact assessments" in relation to proposed implementations of processing in specific areas.[76] Some of the possible examples referred to include sensitive personal data, profiling, and using specific technologies.[77]

The EU Commission recognises the increasingly global dimensions to data protection and data protection issues.[78] It intends to address and consider further measures in relation to international transfers of personal data (known as trans-border data flows) and the promotion of "universal principles" (including technical measures and standards).[79] Separately, the Snowden revelations are putting pressure on the continuance of the US-EU safe harbor arrangement for transfers of personal data.

---

71 Communications from the Commission to the European Parliament, the Council, the Economic and Social Committee of the Regions, A Comprehensive Approach on Personal Data Protection in the European Union, 4 November 2010, COM (2010) 609 Final, 7.

72 Communications from the Commission to the European Parliament, the Council, the Economic and Social Committee of the Regions, A Comprehensive Approach on Personal Data Protection in the European Union, 4 November 2010, COM (2010) 609 Final, 8.

73 *ibid* 8.

74 *ibid* 9.

75 *ibid* 11.

76 *ibid* 12.

77 *ibid.*

78 *ibid* 15.

79 *ibid* 15–17.

Conclusion

It is understood that the data protection regime in Europe is going to be overhauled, in part to meet the new needs of protecting personal data in the era of social networking and second-generation internet. It is also understood that this will be implemented via a Regulation, which would be directly applicable, thus circumventing the need for follow-on laws in each EU Member State. No official final version is available at the time of writing. However, the needs and concerns for new modern data protection are well canvassed. Some of these issues are also apparent in the next level of interpretation and implementation of the data protection regime in the EU, as referred to in the following chapter. The proposed EU Regulation has now been published and is subject to the legistative process, debate and amendment. Recent developments have increased its importance.

Chapter 6

INTERIM DATA PROTECTION

Headline of Issues

- Outdated data protection regime
- Useful opinions pending a full review and updating of EU law
- Interim data protection
- EU Article 29 Working Party
- Opinion on social networking
- Opinion on search engines
- The future of privacy opinion document

Introduction

The EU Data Protection Directive 1995[1] is outdated in certain respects when it comes to dealing with the issues arising with social networking and internet communications technologies. While there are proposals being considered in terms of updating the EU data protection regime, there is no exact timeframe for new or updated laws. It also remains to be seen how successful these may be.

While the current law is outdated, there has been some attempt in the meantime to fill the gaps, such as opinions, guidelines and interpretations of how data protection should apply to new issues. These come from interested bodies and authorities. The International Working Group on Data Protection in Telecommunications published guidelines in March 2008 in relation to social networking.[2] Another example is pronouncements from the EU data protection group known as the EU Article 29 Working Party (WP29).

The EU Article 29 Working Party is an important and influential body in relation to data protection problems and the development of the interpretation of the data protection legal regime. It is established pursuant to Article 29 of the EU Data Protection Directive 1995.[3] The working party comprises representatives of the Data Protection Commissioners/Authorities of each EU Member State. Therefore, when it publishes opinions in relation to particular data protection issues, they tend

1 Article 10 Directive 95/46/EC of the European Parliament and of the Council of 24 October 1995 on the Protection of Individuals with regard to the Processing of Personal Data and on the Free Movement of such Data.

2 Available at http://www.datenschutz-berlin.de/content/europa-international/international-working-group-on-data-protection-in-telecommunications-iwgdpt/working-papers-and-common-positions-adopted-by-the-working-group.

3 The body in it documentation describes itself as follows: the Working Party was set up under Article 29 of Directive 95/46/EC. It is an independent European advisory body on data protection and privacy. Its tasks are described in Article 30 of Directive 95/46/EC and Article 15 of Directive 2002/58/EC.

to be influential in terms of how each Member State interprets and implements the existing data protection laws. The EU Article 29 Working Party has issued individual guidance in relation children, search engines, social networking, smart borders, Apps, facial recognition, data breaches, Cloud computing and the data protection purpose limitation principle.

While not legal or binding, these are influential in the absence of any express reference to these issues in the EU Data Protection Directive 1995, both for national data protection offices and for social networks. The Working Party is comprised of members from national data protection authorities. Furthermore, the national data protection authorites seek to follow the Working Party Opinions.

As influential as they may sometimes be, such opinions, pronouncements, etc are not the law, nor do they change the text of current laws. Having said that, they may still be influential in terms of the direction of future legal changes. They can also be influential in relation to how EU data protection authorities may interpret the current data protection legal regime.

WP29: Opinion 5/2009 on Social Networking

The EU Article 29 Working Party refers to the issue of social network services (SNS) in its Opinion 5/2009 on Online Social Networking in 2009.[4] It notes that the:

> "dissemination and use of information available on SNS for other secondary, unintended purposes is of key concern to the [EU] Article 29 Working Party. Robust security and privacy-friendly default settings are advocated throughout the Opinion as the ideal starting point with regard to all services on offer. Access to profile information emerges as a key area of concern. Topics such as the processing of sensitive data and images, advertising and direct marketing on SNS and data retention issues are also addressed".[5]

It formulates some key recommendations, which it summarises as follows:

> "Key recommendations focus on the obligations of SNS providers to conform with the Data Protection Directive and to uphold and strengthen the rights of users. Of paramount importance, SNS providers should inform users of their identity from the outset and outline all the different purposes for which they process personal data. Particular care should be taken by SNS providers with regard to the processing of the personal data of minors. The Opinion recommends that users should only upload pictures or information about other individuals, with the individual's consent and considers that SNS also have a duty to advise users regarding the privacy rights of others."[6]

It defines SNS as "online communication … which enable individuals to join or create networks of like-minded users. In the legal sense, social networks are information society services, as defined in Article 1 paragraph 2 of Directive 98/34/EC as amended by Directive 98/48/EC."[7] SNS share certain characteristics, namely:

---

4 WP29, Opinion 5/2009 on Online Social Networking, WP 163. Adopted on 12 June 2009.

5 WP29, Opinion 5/2009 on Online Social Networking, 3.

6 *ibid.*

7 *ibid*, 4.

- "users are invited to provide personal data for the purpose of generating a description of themselves or 'profile';
- SNS also provide tools which allow users to post their own material (user-generated content such as a photograph or a diary entry, music or video clip or links to other sites);
- 'social networking' is enabled using tools which provide a list of contacts for each user, and with which users can interact".[8]

Concern is expressed in terms of how SNS providers organise and tailor their advertising to users.[9] "[EU] users ... have a legitimate expectation that the personal data they disclose will be processed according to European and national data protection and privacy legislation".[10]

Even though many social networks may originate outside the EU, the Opinion makes clear that the "provisions of the Data Protection Directive [1995] apply to SNS providers in most cases, even if their headquarters are located outside of the EEA".[11] Interestingly, one of the reasons for the Irish Data Protection Commissioner's review audit of Facebook is that its legal headquarters (outside the US and Canada) is in Dublin.

Separate from this, EU data protection law applies so long as it is EU citizens' personal data being processed and or so long as there is an entity in the EU or equipment is used in the EU.

The Opinion also considers access to profile information and states that "SNS should ensure privacy-friendly and free of charge default settings are in place restricting access to self-selected contacts".[12]

Security is recognised as a key concern. The Opinion states as follows:

> "Secure processing of information is a key element of trust in SNS. Controllers must take the appropriate technical and organisational measures, 'both at the time of the design of the processing system and at the time of the processing itself' to maintain security and prevent unauthorised processing, taking into account the risks represented by the processing and the nature of the data.
>
> An important element of the privacy settings is the access to personal data published in a profile. If there are no restrictions to such access, third parties may link all kinds of intimate details regarding the users, either as a member of the SNS or via search engines. However, only a minority of users signing up to a service will make any changes to default settings. Therefore, SNS should offer privacy-friendly default settings which allow users to freely and specifically consent to any access to their profile's content that is beyond their self-selected contacts in order to reduce the risk of unlawful processing by third parties. Restricted access profiles should not be discoverable by internal search engines, including the facility to search by parameters such as age or location. Decisions to extend access may not be implicit, for example with an 'opt-out' provided by the controller of the SNS".[13]

The Opinion also refers to the data protection prior information requirements:

---

8 *ibid*, 4–5.
9 *ibid*, 5.
10 *ibid*, 5.
11 *ibid*, 5.
12 *ibid*, 6.
13 *ibid*, 7. References omitted.

"SNS providers should inform users of their identity and the different purposes for which they process personal data according to the provisions laid out in Article 10 of the [EU Data Protection Directive 1995] including, but not limited to,

- usage of the data for direct marketing purposes;
- possible sharing of the data with specified categories of third parties;
- an overview on profiles: their creation and chief data sources;
- the use of sensitive data.

The [EU Article 29 Working Party] recommends that,

- SNS providers provide adequate warnings to users about the privacy risks to themselves and to others when they upload information on the SNS;
- SNS users should also be reminded that uploading information about other individuals may impinge upon their privacy and data protection rights;
- SNS users should be advised by SNS that if they wish to upload pictures or information about other individuals, this should be done with the individual's consent".[14]

If sensitive personal data are collected, the SNS provider requires explicit consent from the individual, and must set out the profile forms in such circumstances as to make clear that the sensitive data fields are not compulsory.[15]

The issue of non-members' personal data is considered. For example:

"Many SNS allow users to contribute data about other people, such as adding a name to a picture, rating a person, listing the 'people I have met/want to meet' at events. This tagging may also identify non-members. However, the processing of such data about non-members by the SNS may only be performed if one of the criteria laid down in Article 7 of the Data Protection Directive is fulfilled.

In addition, the creation of pre-built profiles of non-members through the aggregation of data that is independently contributed by SNS users, including relationship data inferred from uploaded address books, lacks a legal basis.

Even if the SNS had the means to contact the non-user and inform this non-user about the existence of personal data relating to him/her, a possible email invitation to join the SNS in order to access these personal data would violate the prohibition laid down in Article 13.4 of the ePrivacy Directive on the sending of unsolicited electronic messages for direct marketing purposes".[16]

There is a growing issue in relation to increasing access by third-party developers and social networks and related websites to the SNS user database. The Opinion provides that if this is to occur and is permitted, such access such be "layered access … [and] most limited".[17]

Direct marketing is of course a large issue. The Opinion, therefore, addresses this concern when it states that:

"Direct marketing is an essential part of the SNS business model; different marketing models can be used by SNS. Nevertheless, marketing using users' personal data should comply with relevant provisions of both Data Protection and ePrivacy Directive.

Contextual marketing is tailored to the content that is viewed or accessed by the user. *Segmented marketing* consists in serving advertisements to targeted groups of users;

---

14 *ibid*, 7. References omitted.

15 *ibid*, 8.

16 WP29, Opinion 5/2009 on Online Social Networking, Article 29 Data Protection Working Party, 01189/09EN, WP 163. Adopted on 12 June 2009, at 8.

17 *ibid*, 9. The Opinion also refers to Application Programming Interface (API) issues.

a user is placed in a group according to the information he has directly communicated to the SNS.

Finally, *behavioural marketing* selects the advertisements based on the observation and analysis of the users' activity over time. These techniques may be subject to different legal requirements, depending on the applicable legal grounds and the characteristics of the techniques used. The Working Party recommends not using sensitive data in behavioural advertising models, unless all legal requirements are met.

Whatever model or combination of models is used, advertisements can either be served directly by the SNS (the SNS provider acts here as a broker) or by a third party advertiser. In the first case, personal data of the users do not need to be disclosed to third parties. In the second case however, the third party advertiser might process personal data about the users eg if it processes the IP address of the user and a cookie that was placed on the user's computer."[18]

The Opinion also refers to retention issues[19] as well as user rights issues.[20] In addition, it refers to the growing concerns in relation to children and minors.[21]

The conclusion of the Opinion sets out the following:

"Applicability of EC Directives

1 The Data Protection Directive generally applies to the processing of personal data by SNS, even when their headquarters are outside of the EEA.
2 SNS providers are considered data controllers under the Data Protection Directive.
3 Application providers might be considered data controllers under the Data Protection Directive.
4 Users are considered data subjects vis-à-vis the processing of their data by SNS.
5 Processing of personal data by users in most cases falls within the household exemption. There are instances where the activities of a user are not covered by this exemption.
6 SNS fall outside of the scope of the definition of electronic communication service and therefore the Data Retention Directive does not apply to SNS.

Obligations of SNS

7 SNS should inform users of their identity, and provide comprehensive and clear information about the purposes and different ways in which they intend to process personal data.
8 SNS should offer privacy-friendly default settings.
9 SNS should provide information and adequate warning to users about privacy risks when they upload data onto the SNS.
10 [*sic, 10 missing in original*]
11 Users should be advised by SNS that pictures or information about other individuals, should only be uploaded with the individual's consent.
12 At a minimum, the homepage of SNS should contain a link to a complaint facility, covering data protection issues, for both members and non-members.
13 Marketing activity must comply with the rules laid down in the Data Protection and ePrivacy Directives.
14 SNS must set maximum periods to retain data on inactive users. Abandoned accounts must be deleted.
15 With regard to minors, SNS should take appropriate action to limit the risks.

Rights of Users

16 Both members and non-members of SNS have the rights of data subjects if applicable, according to the provisions of Article 10–14 of the Data Protection Directive.

18 *ibid*, 9–10. Original emphasis. References omitted.
19 *ibid*, 10.
20 *ibid*, 11.
21 *ibid*, 10–11.

17 Both members and non-members should have access to an easy-to-use complaint handling procedure set up by the SNS.
18 Users should, in general, be allowed to adopt a pseudonym."[22]

WP29: Opinion 1/2008 on Search Engines

The EU Article 29 Working Party also issued an Opinion in 2008 in relation to the development of search engine websites and services,[23] Opinion 1/2008 on Data Protection Issues Related to Search Engines, adopted on 4 April 2008. It focuses on how search engine websites should comply with the data protection regime.

The Opinion notes the example of where AOL in 2006 published the online searches of 650,000 people in redacted (edited) format.[24] It was meant to contain anonymous data. Yet the published materials contained sufficient information to reveal the identities of some of the users.[25]

The EU Article 29 Working Party Opinion notes that search engines — in their role as service providers — do not sufficiently explain "the nature and purpose of their operations to the users".[26]

The Opinion also refers to search engines as content providers, again expressing concerns, particularly in relation to profiling, information that can be uploaded and linked, access by third parties, and incorrect, incomplete or excessive data.[27]

It was also recognised that frequently the main business model of search engines is advertising.[28] They also process a large variety of data types, including log files, IP address and cookies,[29] in addition to personal data they collect at the membership sign-up stage.

In terms of privacy and data protection rights, the Opinion reiterates the fundamental right of respect to one's private life. It states that the "extensive collection and storage of search histories of individuals in a directly or indirectly identifiable form invokes the protection under Article 8 of the European Charter of Fundamental Rights."[30] In addition, an:

---

22 *ibid*, 12–13. No number 10 in original.
23 See commentary at "Social Networking Sites: Article 29 Working Party Opinion," *Society of Computers and Law*, 22 June 2009, available at www.scl.org/site.aspx?i=ne12245.
24 WP29, Opinion 1/2008 on Data Protection Issues Related to Search Engines, WP 148, 4 April 2008, at n3 at 4.
25 *ibid.*
26 *ibid*, 4–5.
27 *ibid*, 5.
28 *ibid*, 5–6.
29 *ibid*, 6–7, and in the appendix to the Opinion. It refers to cookies as follows: "[u]ser cookies are provided by the search engine and stored on the user's computer. The content of the cookies varies from one search engine provider to another. Cookies deployed by search engines typically contain information about the user's operating system and browser, and a unique identification number for each user account. They allow a more accurate identification of the user than an IP address"; *ibid*, 7.
30 *ibid*, 7.

"individual's search history contains a footprint of that person's interests, relations, and intentions. These data can be subsequently used both for commercial purposes and as a result of requests and fishing operations and/or data mining by law enforcement authorities or national security services."[31]

The Opinion refers to the EU Data Protection Directive 1995.[32] Recital 2 of the EU Data Protection Directive 1995 states that:

"data-processing systems are designed to serve man; whereas they must, whatever the nationality or residence of natural persons, respect their fundamental rights and freedoms, notably the right to privacy, and contribute to economic and social progress, trade expansion and the well-being of individuals".

It is then noted that:

"[s]earch engines play a crucial role as a first point of contact to access information freely on the internet. Such free access to information is essential to build one's personal opinion in our democracy. Therefore, Article 11 of the European Charter of Fundamental Rights is of special relevance because it provides that 'information should be accessible without any surveillance by public authorities, as part of freedom of expression and information'".[33]

It adds:

"An individual's search history is personal data if the individual to which it relates, is identifiable. Though IP addresses in the most cases are not directly identifiable by search engines, identification can be achieved by a third party. Internet access providers hold IP address data. Law enforcement and national security authorities can gain access to these data and in some Member States private parties have gained access also through civil litigation. Thus, in most cases – including cases with dynamic IP address allocation – the necessary data will be available to identify the user(s) of any IP address".[34]

A previous EU Article 29 Working Party document[35] states that "unless the Internet Service Provider [ISP] is in a position to distinguish with absolute certainty that the data correspond to users that cannot be identified, it will have to treat all IP information as personal data, to be on the safe side."[36] The present Opinion states that "[t]hese considerations will apply equally to search engine operators."[37]

The Opinion continues in relation to cookies (a form of tracking and recording software used by many websites):

"When a cookie contains a unique user ID, this ID is clearly personal. The use of persistent cookies or similar devices with a unique user ID allows tracking of users of a certain computer even when dynamic IP addresses are used. The behavioural data that is generated through the use of these devices allows focusing even more on the personal characteristics of the individual concerned. This is in line with the fundamental logic of the dominant business model".[38]

---

31 *ibid*, 7.
32 *ibid*, 8.
33 *ibid*, 8.
34 *ibid*, 8.
35 WP29, Opinion 4/2007 on the Concept of Personal Data, WP 136, 20 June, 2007.
36 Referred to WP29, Opinion 1/2008 on Data Protection Issues Related to Search Engines, WP 148, 4 April, 2008, at 8.
37 *ibid*.
38 *ibid*, 9.

A search engine is also a data controller according to the Opinion.[39]

As there is a growing concern as to which privacy laws apply to different social networking, there is reference in the Opinion to national law issues.[40] After analysis, the opinion states that the "combined effect of Articles 4(1)(a) and 4(1)(c) of the [EU Data Protection Directive 1995] is that its provisions apply to the processing of personal data by search engine providers in many cases, even where their headquarters are outside the EEA."[41] From the search engine provider's perspective, it will have to comply with multiple national data protection laws.[42] There is, however, an increasing argument that the EU data protection regime is becoming the default standard for best practice data protection compliance internationally.

The Opinion states that Article 5(3) (cookies and spyware) and Article 13 (unsolicited communications) of the ePrivacy Directive can also be applicable.[43]

Additional obligations can arise, for example, where a search engine may also be engaging in value-added services.[44] This also applies in the case of (additional) caching activities,[45] ie temporary transit storage.

The Opinion discusses the lawful purpose for processing (arising under Article 6 of the EU Data Protection Directive 1995), and identifies the main justification referred to by search engines.[46] The Opinion then states:

> "Generally, search engine providers fail to provide a comprehensive overview of the different specified, explicit and legitimate purposes for which they process personal data. Firstly, some purposes, such as 'improvement of the service' or 'the offering of personalised advertising' are too broadly defined to offer an appropriate framework to judge the legitimacy of the purpose. Secondly, because many search engine providers mention many different purposes for the processing, it is not clear to what extent data are reprocessed for another purpose that is incompatible with the purpose for which they were originally collected.
>
> The collection and processing of personal data may be based on one or more legitimate grounds. There are three grounds which search engine providers may appeal to for different purposes."[47]

There is some recognition, however, that some issues can or should be solved by the industry itself.[48]

The Opinion makes the following conclusions:

- "The [EU Data Protection Directive 1995] generally applies to the processing of personal data by search engines, even where their headquarters are outside the EEA;

---

39 *ibid.*

40 *ibid.* It refers to Article 9 Directive 95/46/EC of the European Parliament and of the Council of 24 October 1995 on the protection of individuals with regard to the processing of personal data and on the free movement of such data [1995] OJ L281/31.

41 *ibid*, 11.

42 *ibid.*

43 *ibid*, 12.

44 *ibid*, 14.

45 *ibid*, 15.

46 *ibid*, 15–16.

47 *ibid*, 16.

48 *ibid*, 19.

- Non-EEA based search engine providers should inform their users about the conditions in which they must comply with the [EU Data Protection Directive 1995], whether by establishment or by the use of equipment;
- The Data Retention Directive (2006/24/EC) does not apply to internet search engines;
- Search engines may only process personal data for legitimate purposes and the amount of data had to be relevant and not excessive in respect of the various purposes to be achieved;
- Search engine providers must delete or anonymise (in an irreversible and efficient way) personal data once they are no longer necessary for the purpose for which they were collected. The [EU Article 29 Working Party] calls for the development of appropriate anonymisation schemes by search engine providers;
- Retention periods should be minimised and be proportionate to each purpose put forward by search engine providers. In view of the initial explanations given by search engine providers on the possible purposes for collecting personal data, the [EU Article 29 Working Party] does not see a basis for a retention period beyond 6 months. However, national legislation may require earlier deletion of personal data. In case search engine providers retain personal data longer than 6 months, they must demonstrate comprehensively that it is strictly necessary for the service. In any case, the information about the data retention period chosen by search engine providers should be easily accessible from their homepage;
- While search engine providers inevitably collect some personal data about the users of their services, such as their IP address, resulting from standard HTTP traffic, it is not necessary to collect additional personal data from individual users in order to be able to perform the service of delivering search results and advertisements;
- If search engine providers use cookies, their lifetime should be no longer than demonstrably necessary. Similarly to web cookies, flash cookies should only be installed if transparent information is provided about the purpose for which they are installed and how to access, edit and delete this information;
- Search engine providers must give users clear and intelligible information about their identity and location and about the data they intend to collect, store or transmit, as well as the purpose for which they are collected;
- Enrichment of user profiles with data not provided by the users themselves is to be based on the consent of the users;
- If search engine providers provide means to retain the individual search history, they should make sure they have the consent of the user;
- Search engines should respect website editor opt-outs indicating that the website should not be crawled and indexed or included in the search engines' caches;
- When search engine providers provide a cache, in which personal data are being made available for longer than the original publication, they must respect the right of data subjects to have excessive and inaccurate data removed from their cache;
- Search engine providers that specialise in the creation of value added operations, such as profiles of natural persons (so called 'people search engines') and facial recognition software on images must have a legitimate ground for processing, such as consent, and meet all other requirements of the [EU Data Protection Directive 1995], such as the obligation to guarantee the quality of data and fairness of processing;
- Users of search engine services have the right to access, inspect and correct if necessary, according to Article 12 of the [EU Data Protection Directive 1995], all their personal data, including their profiles and search history;
- Cross-correlation of data originating from different services belonging to the search engine provider may only be performed if consent has been granted by the user for that specific service".[49]

Profiling techniques use statistical models using snippets of information on users collected from multiple sources stored in databases to try to predict the behaviour of individuals.[50] The means by which social networks, search engines and others may obtain and collect personal data, particularly in real time, is ever more sophisticated.

---

49 *ibid*, 24–26. Bullets numbered in original.

50 Poullet refers to profiling technique issues; see Y Poullet, "Data Protection Legislation: What

It is difficult to keep track of, and is often beyond the contemplation or understanding of many individual users.

WP29: Future of Privacy

The *Future of Privacy* document,[51] which was co-authored by the EU Article 29 Working Party, refers to some of the main challenges to privacy and data protection. It refers, for example, to globalisation and the present legal framework:

> "22 Under EU law, data protection is a fundamental right, protected under Article 8 of the Charter of Fundamental Rights of the European Union … In other parts of the world, the need for data protection is widely recognised but not necessarily with the status of a fundamental right.
>
> 23 The EU and its Member States should guarantee this fundamental right for everybody … In a globalised world, this means that individuals can claim protection also if their data are processed outside the European Union.
>
> 24 [EU Data Protection Directive 1995] has addressed this need for protection in … Article 4. The directive is applicable to data processing anywhere, and therefore also outside the EU (a) when the controller is established in the EU, and (b) when the controller is established outside the EU but uses equipment in the EU.
>
> 25 In addition, Article 25 and 26 of [EU Data Protection Directive 1995] include a specific regime for the transfer of personal data to third countries. The basic rule of Article 25 is that transfer is only allowed to third countries that ensure an adequate level of protection. Article 26 … derogations [include] … Bindings Corporate Rules (BCRs) and Standard Contractual Clauses implement this provision".[52]

The *Future of Privacy* document refers to applicable law.[53] It states:

> "26 The exact scope of [EU Data Protection Directive 1995] however is not sufficiently clear. It is not always clear whether EU law is applicable, which Member State law is applicable, and what would be the law(s) applicable in case of multiple establishments of a multinational in different Member States. Article 4 … determining when the directive is applicable to data processing, leaves room for different interpretation.
>
> 27 Moreover, there are situations which fall outside the scope of … the directive. This is the case where non-EU established [data] controllers direct their activities to EU residents which result in the collection and further processing of personal data. For example, … on-line vendors and the like using specific advertisement with local flavour, websites that directly target EU citizens (by using local languages, etc). If they do so without using equipment in the EU, then [EU Data Protection Directive 1995] does not apply.
>
> 28 At the moment, the [EU] Article 29 Working Party is writing an opinion on the concept of applicable law. The [EU] Article 29 Working Party envisages advising the European Commission on this topic in the course of the upcoming year. This advice might include further recommendations for a future legal framework".[54]

Is At Stake for Our Society and Democracy?" (2009) (25) *Computer Law & Security Review* 211, at 214.

51 WP29, The Future of Privacy, Joint Contribution to the Consultation of the European Commission on the Legal Framework for the Fundamental Right to Protection of Personal Data, Article 29 Data Protection Working Party, Working Party on Police and Justice, WP 168, Adopted 1 December 2009.

52 *ibid.*

53 *ibid.*

54 *ibid.*

The need for international standards (and the Madrid Resolution[55]) is also pointed to in the Future of Privacy document.[56]

> "29 Global standards regarding data protection are becoming indispensable. Global standards would also facilitate transborder data flows which, due to globalisation, are becoming the rule rather than the exception. As long as global standards do not exist, diversity will remain. Transborder data flows have to be facilitated whilst, at the same time, ensuring a high level of protection of personal data when they are transferred to and processed in third countries.
>
> 30 The 'Madrid Resolution,' a Joint Proposal on International Standards for the Protection of Privacy which has been adopted by the International Conference of Data Protection and Privacy Commissioners on 6 November 2009, deserves support. The Joint Proposal contains a draft of a global standard and brings together all the approaches possible in the protection of personal data and privacy, integrating legislation from five continents. It includes a series of principles, rights and obligations that should be the basis for data protection in any legal system all over the world, and demonstrates that global standards providing an adequate level of data protection are feasible in due course."[57]

The EU Commission is called upon to:

> "take initiatives towards the further development of international global standards regarding the protection of personal data with a view to promote an international framework for data protection and therefore facilitate transborder data flow while ensuring an adequate level of protection of data subjects. These initiatives should include investigating the feasibility of a binding international framework.
>
> In the absence of global standards, to promote the development of data protection legislation providing an adequate level of protection, and the foundation of independent DPAs [ie Data Protection Authorities], in countries outside the European Union. The basic principles for data protection, as laid down in the 'Madrid Resolution,' should be the universal basis for such legislation.
>
> These specific tasks of the Commission should be … in the future legal framework".[58]

In addition, it refers to improving the adequacy of decisions:

> "32. Ever more processing operations of personal data take place in a globalised environment. Ensuring the free flow of personal data, while guaranteeing the level of protection of individuals' rights, is an increasing demand. Thus, it is necessary to redesign the adequacy process:
>
> - Defining more precisely the criteria for reaching the legal status of 'adequacy', paying due attention to the approach of the [EU] Article 29 Working Party and various other approaches to data protection around the world, and especially to the rights and principles laid down in the Joint Proposal of International Standards on the Protection of Privacy.
> - Streamlining the procedures for the analysis of the legal regimes of third countries in order to take more decisions on the adequate level of protection.
>
> The future legal framework should specify these issues."[59]

It also refers to international agreements:

---

[55] The Madrid Privacy Declaration, Global Privacy Standards for a Global World, 3 November 2009, available at http://thepublicvoice.org/madrid-declaration/.

[56] WP29, The Future of Privacy, Joint Contribution to the Consultation of the European Commission on the Legal Framework for the Fundamental Right to Protection of Personal Data, Article 29 Data Protection Working Party, Working Party on Police and Justice, WP 168, Adopted 1 December 2009.

[57] *ibid.*

[58] *ibid.*

[59] *ibid.*

"33. Note has been taken of the activities of the EU-USA High Level Contact Group on information sharing and privacy and personal data protection. These activities might lead to a transatlantic agreement with common principles for privacy and data protection applicable to the exchange of information with the United States for the fight against terrorism and serious transnational crime.

34. International agreements are appropriate instruments for the protection of personal data in a global context, provided that the level of protection afforded is at least equivalent to the global standards mentioned above, that every individual has an easy and effective redress, including judicial redress, and that specific safeguards are included relating to the purpose for which the personal data will be used.

35. Under those conditions the foreseen transatlantic agreement could serve as a model for exchange with other third countries and for other purposes. The future legal framework could mention the conditions for agreements with third countries.

36. Furthermore, the EU should encourage the cooperation between international data protection authorities, for example on a transatlantic level. Such cooperation is a successful means to promote data protection outside the EU."[60]

The Future of Privacy Opinion document also refers to Binding Corporate Rules exceptions to trans-border data transfers and accountability. It states:

"37. The processing of data outside the EU can also be protected by Binding Corporate Rules (BCRs), international codes of conduct for multinationals, allowing for the worldwide transfer within a multinational corporation. BCRs have been introduced by the [EU] Article 29 Working Party in 2003. Both DPAs and multinationals are of the opinion that BCRs are a good means to facilitate international data flows whilst guaranteeing the protection of personal data. However, Directive 95/46/EC did not expressly take account of BCRs. As a result the process for adoption of BCRs, which is based on Article 26(2) of [EU Data Protection Directive 1995], requires the approval of all Member States concerned by a BCR. As a result, assessing and approving BCRs takes a long time. The [EU] Article 29 Working Party has devoted considerable effort to promote and facilitate the use and the approval of BCRs within the current legal framework. In order to improve the process, so far, nineteen DPAs have agreed to a procedure on the approval of BCRs called 'Mutual Recognition.'

38. Against this background a provision on BCRs should be further reinforced and included in the new legal framework, which would serve several purposes:

- Recognising BCRs as appropriate tool to provide adequate safeguards.
- Defining the main substantive and procedural elements of BCRs, following the [EU] Article 29 Working Party Opinions on the subject.

39. Moreover … a new provision could be included in the new legislative framework pursuant to which data controllers would remain accountable and responsible for the protection of personal data for which they are controllers, even in the case the data have been transferred to other controllers outside the EU …

…

40. … Often, when one thinks of 'globalisation,' one thinks of business. However, increasingly processing operations of personal data take place in a globalised world. Even though the individual often lives a local life, he can more and more be found on line where his data are processed globally. Globalisation … is linked to technology ..., the position of the data subject ..., data controller ..., DPAs/[EU] Article 29 Working Party … and law enforcement ...".[61]

Conclusion

While it is recognised that the data protection regime is somewhat out of date, and while the opinions of the EU Article 29 Working Party are not legal or binding, they are useful. They are important because they are more recent and timely than the

---

[60] *ibid.*

[61] *ibid.*

EU Data Protection Directive 1995. The EU Article 29 Working Party does address some of the specific social networking concerns that arise. They also make specific recommendations and highlight particular issues of concern for the consideration of the Commission in its review and proposals for future legislation. It helps to focus the Commission's endeavours on the many important social networking issues.

PART III: SOCIAL NETWORKS

CHAPTER 7

USER GENERATED CONTENT

Prof Dr Peggy Valcke, Marieke Lenaerts, Aleksandra Kuczerawy*
ICRI KU Leuven – iMinds

HEADLINE OF ISSUES

- Author, editor and publisher
- User generated content
- Liability models
- Radion, television, websites

INTRODUCTION

Since its arrival in 2005, user generated content (UGC) has grown explosively. This vast new trend that allows users to play an active role in the publication of content creates many great opportunities. However, it also opens doors for malicious intent. The difficulties to combat illegal or otherwise harmful material constitute major challenges for the further development of UGC.

In a complicated system involving many different actors, who does one address when illegal or harmful material is found online? Who can be held liable for damage? This chapter aims to discuss the conceptual framework for legal liability for UGC, by examining normative definitions and underlying rationales of existing liability models and by comparing the roles of traditional actors in the information value chain, on the one hand, and new intermediaries, on the other hand.[1] It aspires to formulate some assessments in view of a clearer definition of the scope of legal liability of new UGC intermediaries for illegal and harmful content disseminated via their websites.

USER GENERATED CONTENT

The term "User-Generated Content" or UGC appeared for the first time around 2005. Since then, UGC is playing an increasingly important role in the media landscape. Today, it is a booming business. The widespread broadband technology and high-quality electronic material at everybody's reach have stimulated the user to become an active participant in Web 2.0.

Defining UGC is a difficult task, since there is no widely accepted official definition.

---

[1] This chapter forms an update of our article previously published as: P Valcke & M Lenaerts. "Who's Author, Editor and Publisher in User-Generated Content? Applying Traditional Media Concepts to UGC Providers", (2010) (24:1) *International Review of Law, Computers & Technology* 119-131.

Generally, UGC is understood very broadly to include all content put online by users, whether it was created by them or not.[2]

UGC exists in many forms. Traditional forms include blogs (eg Blogger), wikis (like Wikipedia), multimedia sharing services for photographs (such as Flickr), videos (eg YouTube or Dailymotion), podcasts (such as Odeo) and tags. More recent are the social and professional networking websites (like Facebook and LinkedIn) and the virtual worlds (eg Secondlife). New types of services and variations on existing services keep appearing every day, such as for talent search (eg SellaBand), mobile specific services (like ShoZu) and social bookmarking websites (including Mister Wong). Some governments are even starting to use UGC websites as a way of communicating with their citizens (such as FixMyStreet). UGC can be text-based, graphic-based, audio, video or mixed. It can also include video games and virtual objects.[3]

As a result of the constant appearance of new web applications and the evolution of technology, UGC is permanently changing. This evolving and multifaceted character of UGC increases the difficulty to formulate a time-proof definition and to regulate it appropriately.

The growth of UGC has been explosive since 2005. The Flickr photograph sharing website, for instance, grew to over 518 million of shared photographs in 2012. The number of YouTube visitors increased until over 1 billion each month and the number of blogs kept growing steadily from 40 million to 180 million. The percentage of active internet users watching videos online increased from 30% to over 80% between 2005 and 2012. The number of users engaged in microblogging increased from 14% in 2009 to 42% in 2012 and those reading blogs online increased from 53% to 76%. Every minute, seventy two hours of video are uploaded to YouTube.[4]

The arrival of UGC is part of a broader evolution in the internet world. UGC is a phenomenon of Web 2.0 (the *read-write web*), in opposition to Web 1.0 (the *read only web*). Where Web 1.0 consisted of a one-way traffic from producers of content to a mostly passive public, Web 2.0 involves a broad interaction between traditional content producers on the one hand, and more active users, who are participating, commenting and also generating content themselves on the other hand. This has created a whole new collective intelligence to which all can add. This evolution and the appearance of UGC have many positive consequences. UGC leads to a better understanding and cooperation between people and organisations. Besides that, it plays a major role in the democratisation of the news process, by providing very diverse additional sources of information. UGC also represents an additional

2 It is worthwhile to note the difference between UGC and "user created content", which is limited to content that was actually created by users, requiring a certain amount of creative effort, outside of professional routines and practices (OECD Report: Participative Web and User-Created Content, 2007).

3 In their study carried out in 2008 for the European Commission on *User-Created-Content: Supporting a participative Information Society*, IDATE, TNO and IViR found that photographs were at that moment the most popular form of UGC, followed by video material and text; http://www.ivir.nl/publications/helberger/User_created_content.pdf.

4 Sources: Technorati, Flickr, YouTube, NM Incite, Alexa, Comscore, internetworldstats.com; McCann, Power to the People – Social Media Tracker Wave 3 (March 2008), The Business of Social – Social Tracker Wave 6 (2012) and Google (2009). Numbers are approximate.

control of the mainstream media. It facilitates social networking. Finally, it favors the growth of user autonomy and encourages cultural diversity.

But, on the other hand, the participative and uncontrolled character of UGC also holds dangers. UGC opens doors to hate speech, privacy invasions, intellectual property infringements, defamation, pornography and child pornography and other undesirable content such as suicide websites and newsgroups, websites encouraging eating disorders such as anorexia, violent or shocking images or insults to religious groups. Combating such illegal or undesirable content is difficult because the author is often hard to find. But when the author is unknown, who is responsible for such content? Under which circumstances can you address the messenger to claim for damages? And is the UGC website provider a mere "messenger" or does he fulfill a more active role? In the new context of Web 2.0, we have to ask ourselves who takes up the role as author, the editor and the publisher of content published online. A more fundamental question is whether we can still use these traditional concepts at all to define legal liability for UGC. The answer to these questions is crucial, both for victims of [online abuse,] illegal or harmful content and for the alleged infringer, but also for the website providers, whose service provision and business model heavily depend on what is legally required from them. To what extent can these websites be held responsible for the lawfulness of UGC and the activities of users on their websites (eg that users observe copyright law, data protection law or the rules on harmful content)?

This chapter will explore the conceptual framework for defining the scope of legal liability of new UGC intermediaries for illegal and harmful content disseminated via their websites. The existing liability models in media law will be examined and compared to the special features of UGC. We will start by presenting the dichotomy between the publisher and the hosting model that was put forward as the main distinction in the 2008 study by IDATE, TNO and IViR on *User-Created-Content: Supporting a Participative Information Society*.[5] We will then further unravel these models (arguing that there is actually no single publishing model, given the significant differences between print media and audiovisual media in terms of liability regimes), and take a more detailed look at normative definitions and underlying rationales of liability rules for print publications, radio and television broadcasting and internet intermediaries. Finally, we will formulate preliminary thoughts on where to place UGC within these frameworks.

Existing Liability Models

The Dichotomy Between the Publisher and the Hosting Model

In their study on User-Created-Content for the European Commission, IDATE, TNO and IViR, distinguish between two models of legal liability for third party content:

- On the one hand, they discuss the *publisher model,* which originates in media law and covers both print media and broadcasting media. Under this model, the full liability for the content that is disseminated is laid

---

5 See above, footnote 3.

on the publisher, independently if the content is his own or third party content. The underlying rationale is to protect the public's interest in the quality and lawfulness of media content;

- On the other hand, they analyse the *hosting model*, which relates to telecommunications law and is a model of liability exemption for certain technical services (including hosting services). Unlike in the publisher-model, liability for third party content in the hosting-model is the exception, not the rule. This can be explained by the difference in policy considerations: in telecommunications, the seemingless functioning of communications networks, net neutrality, universal carrier obligations and protection of users' privacy and communications secrecy are paramount. This is, in particular, reflected in the [limited] liability exemption foreseen in the eCommerce Directive *(infra)* for hosting services for illegal or harmful content posted by users; this exemption covers both criminal and civil liability as well as direct and indirect liability.

According to the study, UGC website providers *"do not fit well into either of the two models. The majority of UCC [websites] act in a grey zone between the provision of technical and content-related activities"*. In other words, they are situated exactly in between these two models, none of them being applicable. This intermediary position gives rise to difficult questions regarding their responsibility for third party content, which are part of an ongoing broader discussion of the rights and obligations of information intermediaries, such as ISPs, search engines, EPGs, web fora, etc.

As the study rightly points out, the various options to deal with different kinds of information intermediaries basically boil down to the following three: should we a) subject them to full publisher-style prior-publication monitoring obligations, b) to neutrality with regard to the content transmitted, with limited post-publication policing duties or is there c) a need for a new, specifically tailored approach?

In order to make an informed decision, it is important to understand where the different models came from and what is lying behind the existing normative definitions (such as "editor", "publisher", "broadcaster", or "host"). Therefore, in the following, we will take a closer look at the various liability rules as they exist in Belgian law and which are three-fold, rather than two-fold. The regulation of liability for print publications (books, newspapers and magazines), on the one hand, and for broadcasting (radio and television), on the other hand, will be studied as examples of the publisher model. The liability of internet intermediaries is regulated following the hosting model.

Liability for Print Publications

In Belgium, liability for print publications is regulated by a "cascade" system laid down in the Belgian Constitution of 1831. Article 25, al. 2, of the Belgian Constitution provides:

> *"When the author is known and resident in Belgium, neither the editor/publisher, nor the printer, nor the distributor can be prosecuted."*

Hence, for a press crime, in principle only the author can be held liable. This includes both criminal and civil liability. Only when the author is unknown, the other actors in the production chain can be held liable, in the following order: the editor or publisher, the printer and finally, the bookstore or kiosk.

This rule forms an essential part of the constitutional protection of the press freedom, which yields immunity against censorship from the State. It is linked to Article 25, al. 1, of the Constitution, which explicitly prohibits preventive censorship for the print press, on the one hand, and Article 150 of the Constitution, which provides that *a people's jury,* the "Assisenhof" and not the regular criminal courts, will decide on press crimes (except when racism or xenophobia is alleged), on the other hand. These provisions reflect the – at that time – prevailing view on the relation between the State and the media: above all, the State had a duty of abstention and had to be prevented from taking any *ex ante* measures which would result in public censorship of print publications. The repressive system that is anchored in the Constitution implies that, only when freedom of expression is abused during the exercise of that freedom, and a press crime is committed, *a posteriori* sanctions can be imposed; not by the State or by any public institution, but only by the citizens themselves. On top of that, the cascade system aims to shield the individual journalist from possible private censorship from the editor or the publisher. In order to keep the actors further down the production process from censoring publications that might be considered dangerous or risky, the law exempts them from liability, insofar the author is known and resident in Belgium.

However, in previous years, the constitutional cascade system has found itself regularly undermined by more recent provisions of law, or by a strict interpretation by courts.

- The cascade system only applies to "press crimes". According to the Constitution, a press crime is a regular crime committed by means of the press. In case law and legal doctrine, four criteria have been put forward to define the term more precisely. A press crime is (1) the expression of an opinion (2) by means of print, (3) distributed towards the public and (4) punishable by law. The expression of an opinion is interpreted narrowly, excluding the reporting of mere factual information. The condition of punishableness requires an explicit law prohibiting the specific act. Further, the text has to be circulated under people who did not have a previous connection with the author; a mere public exhibition of one copy or mailing to a limited list of people does not suffice. Finally, press crimes only concern printed texts. Photographs or images do not fall under the scope of the constitutional cascade system, since in case law they are still considered not to express an opinion. Radio and television broadcasting, as well as digital information channels like CD's or DVD's, are also obviously excluded as they do not offer information in printed form;[6]
- In case of general tort, the editor or publisher, the printer, or the distributor can still be held liable;
- The editor and publisher can also separately be held liable for the layout,

[6] P Martens, *Mediarecht voor journalisten*, 2005, Garant, 17, 26-27.

the titles and subtitles or pictures with comments they added [Court of First Instance Brussels, 25 April 2000, *Auteurs & Media* 2000, p 466];

- In principle, in Belgian labour law, an employee can only be held liable for fraud or for a severe fault during the exercise of his employment contract. For a light fault he only incurs liability when it happens on a regular basis. Otherwise, it is the employer who entirely carries the liability for damages caused by his employees. In the past, courts have applied this regulation to journalists, which led to the editor or the publisher being liable for regular light faults of their journalists. However, the Belgian Constitutional Court, considering there would be a real risk of censorship, has ruled on 22 March 2006 that this provision does not apply to journalists, even though they might have an employment contract. Only the journalist is liable for his content. According to the Court, labour law cannot change constitutional law; deciding otherwise would mean a violation of Article 25 of the Constitution [Constitutional Court, 22 March 2006, discussed in E. Brewaeys, "Recente rechtspraak van het Arbitragehof over persvrijheid", *Rechtskundig Weekblad* 2006-07, pp 1342-1347].

Recently, this "erosion" of the constitutional cascade system has been countered by the fact that the Belgian courts (up to the Court of Cassation) have qualified online publications as "press crimes". One example is a judgment of 13 February 2007, in which the Mons Criminal Court ruled that the notion "press" should be interpreted broadly because of the evolution of technology. It considered that since internet forums have become commonly used channels for the transmission of information and opinions, punishable comments on a website should be qualified as press crimes. In this case, however, the Court stressed that the same punishable information was later also published in a regular newspaper. In the appeal decision, rendered on 14 May 2008 by the Mons Court of Appeal, the extensive interpretation of the notion of "press crime" was confirmed, this time without a reference to the posterior publication in the printed press. The Court of Appeal ruled that, given the evolution of technology, a punishable writing published on the internet is analogous with punishable content in print publications. Therefore, it should be qualified as a press crime in the sense of article 150 of the Constitution. Several other decisions have applied a similar reasoning, which was ultimately confirmed by the highest court, the Court of Cassation, in two judgments of 6 March 2012.[7] This has resulted in a "revival" of the constitutional cascade system for press crimes.

Liability for Radio and Television Broadcasting

Media laws often establish an objective liability of the broadcaster for all content disseminated through its radio and television channels. The broadcasting laws of

[7] Criminal Court Mons, 13 February 2007, note D Voorhoof, "Is de Publicatie van een Strafbare Meningsuiting via Internet een Drukpersmisdrijf?", *Auteurs&Media* 2007, 178; Court of Appeal Mons, 14 May 2008, note Q Van Enis, "Le Délit de Presse sur Internet: la Cohérence et Rien de Plus?", *Journal des* Tribunaux 2009, 47-50. See also Criminal Court Brussels, 22 December 1999, *Auteurs&Media* 2000, 134; Court of Appeal Brussels, 27 June 2000, *Auteurs & Media* 2001, 142; Court of Appeal Antwerp, 9 February 2006, *Auteurs & Media* 2006, 204; Court of Cassation, 6 March 2012, *Auteurs & Media* 2012, 253.

the Communities in Belgium,[8] for instance, put the editorial responsibility on the broadcaster. This responsibility exists independently from the possibility for the broadcaster of actually reviewing or controlling the content. In November 2004, the CSA (*Conseil Supérieur de l'Audiovisuel*) ruled that the objective liability of the broadcaster is distinct from the personal liability of those who express themselves in the programmes. It can be invoked for all content containing incitements to hatred, discrimination or violence. Even if the broadcaster, *in casu* the RTBF, had no intention of discriminating, the mere fact that the programme contained such content was sufficient for the broadcaster to incur responsibility. Hence, the only question to be examined is whether the content is discriminating or not [*Conseil Supérieur de l'Audiovisuel*, 10 November 2004, *Auteurs&Media*, 2005/2, p 171-173].

It is worthwhile to note that, besides this objective legal liability of the broadcaster, the author or producer can still incur civil or criminal liability under general law.

The reason why broadcasting laws have traditionally focused on the broadcaster (and not the creator or producer of the programmes) as the main responsibility for the content disseminated, becomes clear when looking at the underlying rationale for the initial broadcasting regulations. Due to the scarcity, pervasiveness and immediacy of the medium, broadcasters were attributed an important social responsibility; in return for the use of spectrum, they were made subject to detailed broadcasting regulations and programme obligations. The State was considered to have an increased duty of care to preserve freedom of expression in this sector, and more specifically, to provide for regulations striking an appropriate balance between the broadcaster's communication freedom and the need to protect consumers from harmful content disseminated through this medium. This regulatory tradition contrasts heavily with the "hands-off" approach in print media. The system of objective liability in broadcasting has to be seen in the light of this different regulatory tradition in the audiovisual sector, where it was found to be the most protective of the public interest.

However, the recent advent of on-demand (or non-linear) services has also led to a blurring or an "erosion" of this system. A new actor, the provider of the website for on-demand audiovisual content (usually IPTV or cable, but to a growing extent also the internet and mobile networks), has introduced himself into the production chain and challenges the traditional concept of editorial responsibility. Does the editorial responsibility still entirely lie on the content provider (the broadcaster),

8 Since the first state reform in Belgium in 1970-1971, radio and television broadcasting fall under the competence of the Flemish, French and German speaking (cultural) Communities. This competence includes not only content-related aspects, but also organizational, economic and technical aspects (such as the attribution of frequency licences). All three Communities have consequently adopted their own broadcasting laws over the last three decades, which have been amended several times. The federal state has only remained competent to regulate the bi-lingual broadcasting activities in the area of Brussels Capital. The broadcasting rules that are currently applicable in Flanders (and which cover also on-demand audiovisual services) can be found in the new "*Mediadecreet*" of 2009: "*Decreet betreffende radio-omroep en televisie van 27 maart 2009*", published in the *Belgisch Staatsblad* of 30 April 2009 and amended by the "Decreet" of 24 July 2009. In the French Community, broadcasting (in the broad sense) is regulated by the "*Décret sur les services de médias audiovisuals du 27 février 2003*" and the "*Décret portant statut de la Radio-Télévision belge de la Communauté francaise (RTBF) du 14 juillet 1997*", specifically applicable to the RTBF (the public broadcaster of the French Community).

or does it lie on the provider of on-demand services (the website provider)? Or is there a shared responsibility?

The editorial task of the broadcaster works through a system of channel licensing. Channel operations involve a range of discrete activities, such as the commissioning, acquiring and scheduling of programming, the reviewing of programme compliance for consistency with the broadcasting law, the selling of advertising, including the scheduling and the sale of airtime, the playout and presentation of the programme and advertising content into a linear stream, including the provision of on-air programme links and warnings.

Yet, the provision of on-demand services also involves a range of discrete activities, such as the commissioning and acquisition of programming, the review of programmes for content characteristics for the purposes of packaging and labeling, the packaging of programming into Electronic Programme Guide categories, the design and execution of user interfaces for content information and the content control. In such a way, the provision of on-demand services also involves a certain amount of intellectual activity on the content. Discussions have arisen on the notion "editorial responsibility" in the context of the implementation of the Audiovisual Media Services Directive [Directive 2007/65/EC of the European Parliament and of the Council of 11 December 2007 amending Council Directive 89/552/EEC on the coordination of certain provisions laid down by law, regulation or administrative action in Member States concerning the pursuit of television broadcasting activities, *Official Journal* L332/27, 18 December 2007], and media regulators are currently grappling with the interpretation of 'media service provider' in the context of on-demand programme services.[9] The growing offer of non-linear services by IPTV, cable, internet or mobile providers indeed raises questions on where the effective control over the content lies and challenges the concept of objective liability of the broadcaster.[10] Moreover, the fact that website providers are more often than the content providers within the geographic reach of media regulators makes it tempting, from the perspective of effective enforcement, to hold them accountable for the content distributed.

Liability for Online Content

The liability of internet intermediaries has been regulated on the European level

9 R Craufurd Smith. "Determining Regulatory Competence for Audiovisual Media Services in the European Union" (2011) (3) *Journal of Media Law* 263-285; P Valcke, K Lefever & J Ausloos "Audiovisual Media Services 3.0: (Re)Defining the Scope of European Broadcasting Law in a Converging and Connected Media Environment" in Donders, Karen, Pauwels, Caroline & Loisen, Jan, *Handbook on European Media Policy,* Palgrave (in press 2013).

10 S Nikoltchev (ed.), W Schulz and S Heilmann, *Iris Special: Editorial Responsibility*, Strasbourg, European Audiovisual Observatory, 2008. See also M Ariño, "AVMS Implementation in the UK", Lecture in the IES Spring Series "Rethinking European Media and Communications Policy" at VUB, Brussels, 19 March 2008, who points to the fact that ATVOD members (ie the British Association for Television on Demand) include IPTV platform providers, such as BT and Tiscali (www.atvod.co.uk/).

according to the "hosting model" by the eCommerce Directive.[11] This Directive was transposed in Belgian law in the E-Commerce Act.[12]

The liability of intermediary service providers (ISPs) is discussed in Articles 18 to 21 of the Belgian E-Commerce Act, which follow closely the wording of the Articles 12 to 15 of the eCommerce Directive. In accordance with the Directive, the Act establishes a difference between "mere conduit", "caching" and "hosting" of information. *Mere conduit* consists of the transmission in a communication network of information provided by a recipient of the service, or the provision of access to a communication network. This may include an automatic, intermediate and transient storage of the information transmitted, but only in so far as this takes place for the sole purpose of carrying out the transmission in the communication network, and provided that the information is not stored for any period longer than is reasonably necessary for the transmission (Article 18). The *caching* of information involves a slightly bigger role for the ISP. It concerns the automatic, intermediate and temporary storage of information provided by a recipient of the service, for the sole purpose of making more efficient the information's onward transmission to other recipients, upon their request. Again, in essence, it consists of the transmission in a communication network of information provided by a recipient of the service (Article 19). Finally, *hosting* consists of the sole storage of information provided by a recipient of the service and at its request (Article 20).

The Directive and consistently, the E-Commerce Act, establish a limitation of liability for ISPs providing these services, under certain conditions. The rules for hosting services might be applicable to certain websites for UGC whose activities are limited to providing technical access and storage services.[13]

According to Article 20 of the E-Commerce Act, ISPs providing hosting services cannot be held liable for the information stored at the request of a recipient of the service as long as the following conditions are fulfilled:

- The provider does not have actual knowledge of any illegal activity or information, nor is aware of facts or circumstances from which the illegal activity or information is apparent;
- When the provider should obtain such knowledge, he acts expeditiously to remove or to disable access to the information.

Moreover, Article 21 of the E-Commerce Act prohibits Member States to impose general monitoring obligations on ISPs that provide mere conduit, caching or hosting services. Nor are the ISPs obliged to actively seek facts or circumstances indicating illegal activities.

---

11 EU Directive 2000/31/EC of the European Parliament and of the Council of 8 June 2000 on certain legal aspects of information society services, in particular electronic commerce, in the Internal Market (Directive on electronic commerce), *Official Journal* L178/1, 17 July 2000.

12 Wet van 11 maart 2003 betreffende bepaalde juridische aspecten van de diensten van de informatiemaatschappij, *Belgisch Staatsblad* 17 March 2003.

13 On this topic see also G Somers and J Dumortier, ICRI-IBBT, KULeuven, "Juridische aspecten van Web 2.0 – online informatie en aansprakelijkheid (content aggregation, content locating en user generated content)", *Cahier du Juriste*, 2/2009, 48-50, 55-56.

The background of this liability exemption for ISPs forms not only free trade, investment and internal market considerations, but also, just as for print publications and broadcasting regulations, the protection of the freedom of expression. Imposing a great risk of legal liability on the ISPs' shoulders would create an incentive for them to heavily censor the information passing through their storage services.[14] Moreover, these merely technical providers are, in principle, not involved with the content of the information transmitted. Only when it comes to their knowledge that illegal or damageable content is made available through the services they provide, it is justified to make them liable.

However, the practical application of this exemption of liability proves difficult. The assessment of the provider's actual knowledge of illegal or damaging content on its website is not easy to make. Further, the rapidity of his reaction is hard to assess since it is impossible to determine the precise moment in which he has obtained knowledge of it. Also, the meaning of the word "expeditiously" was not further defined by the legislator.

The delimitation of internet actors who can potentially benefit from the safe havens of these articles is not totally clear either. To be a host in the sense of Article 20 of the Belgian E-Commerce Act, is it necessary for an ISP to technically host the information on its own servers, or does this also include the case where the provider of an online website uses the services of a third person to technically stock the content?[15] Also, should UGC website providers be seen as a modern version of hosting providers, or are they more than that (given the fact that, in some cases, their role is more important than the mere technical storage)? The role UGC website providers play in the dissemination of content varies from case to case. Some read or edit UGC before publishing it (eg Ohmynews). Some monitor *ex ante* and label UGC before putting it online (eg Dailymotion in its specific programme "Motionmakers"). Some monitor content only *ex post* and take it down upon flagging by users. Some invite particular types of content. Some conclude licensing contracts with professional content producers and some even present UGC as part of their own content (eg Last.fm). The different types of UGC and the different grades of involvement of the website provider make it impossible to formulate a general statement on the application of Article 20 of the Belgian Act, and, in the same sense, of Article 14 of the eCommerce Directive, to UGC website providers.

Due to the development of the Web 2.0, these provisions are also subject to "erosion". First, some Member States have broadened the liability exemption by introducing similar rules for hyperlinks and/or search engines. In this way they wish to create incentives for investment and innovation and enhance the development of e-commerce by providing additional legal clarity for service providers. The

---

14 B Frydman and I Rorive, "Regulating Internet Content through Intermediaries in Europe and the USA" (2002) (23:1) *Zeitschrift für Rechtssoziologie* 41-59.

15 For a discussion on the term "host" (*hébergeur*) see: E Montero, "Les Responsabilités Liées au Web 2.0", *Revue du droit des technologies de l'information*, no 32/2008, 368-373. Crucial for the qualification as a hosting service is the fact that the content was provided by the user and transmitted or stocked at his request. Where in the web 1.0 this was understood in a purely technical way (hosting was the activity of materially stocking third party's content on his server), in the web 2.0 "hosting" is understood in a functional way (it can comprise all forms of stocking, including on someone else's server).

Commission has welcomed these initiatives, because they are in line with the Internal Market objective to ensure the provision of basic intermediary services. However, they create differences in the Member States' regulations of liability for internet content and give rise to inconsistency in the scope of application of each of the exemptions. For example, Spain and Portugal have opted for the hosting model for both search engines and hyperlinks, whereas Austria and Liechtenstein chose the mere conduit model for search engines and the hosting model for hyperlinks (First Report of the Commission on the application of the eCommerce Directive).

Secondly, since the wording of the legislator remains rather vague, case law plays an important role in the interpretation and concrete application of the law. The recent case law from across the EU forms a good example of the contradictory views of judges in real-life cases.

In some cases, the liability of the author is extended to the website provider. In a decision rendered in summary proceedings of 22 June 2007, the Paris TGI qualified Myspace as an editor, because it reasoned that the concrete activities of the provider went beyond those of a host. *In casu*, Myspace imposed presentation structures on its users and foresaw publicity spaces on the users' individual pages, of which it economically benefitted at each page visit. A similar reasoning was applied in the Tiscali case of 7 June 2006 by the Paris Court of Appeal.[16]

In other cases, the liability exemptions of a host are applied to the website provider. In the Lafesse/Dailymotion case, the Paris TGI qualified Dailymotion as a host (*hébergeur*) and not as an editor, since it is not involved in the choice of content. In this case the activities of Dailymotion were considered to be of a purely technical nature. However, being qualified as a host does not necessarily remove all responsibility. In another case involving Dailymotion a few months later, the Paris TGI ruled that although Dailymotion acted as a host, in this case it played a more active role on the content and it has to take on responsibility for that. It points out that the Directive does not install a total exoneration of liability, but only a restriction of liability limited to the cases where the provider "*does not have actual knowledge of illegal activity or information and, as regards claims for damages, is not aware of facts or circumstances from which the illegal activity or information is apparent*". In the Zadig/Google case of 19 October 2007 a similar reasoning was applied, where Google was qualified as a host and found its civil liability engaged because of failing to prohibit the posting of copyright infringing material.[17]

Similar inconsistencies can be found in UK jurisprudence. In *Bunt v Tilley* [2007] 1 WLR 1243 the issue at stake was whether internet service providers (ISPs) who were not alleged to have hosted any website relevant to the claims could be liable simply in respect of defamatory material communicated via the services they provided. According to judge Eady J to be held responsible there must be *knowing involvement in the process of publication of the relevant words*. It was therefore

---

[16] TGI Paris summary proceedings, 22 June 2007, *Lafesse/Myspace*; and Court of Appeal Paris, 7 June 2006, *Tiscali*, available from www.legalis.net.

[17] TGI Paris, 15 April 2008, *Lafesse/Dailymotion*; TGI Paris, 13 July 2007, *Nord Ouest Production/Dailymotion*; and TGI Paris, 19 October 2007, *Google Inc./Zadig Productions*, available from www.legalis.net.

held that an ISP which performs no more than a passive role in facilitating postings on the internet cannot be deemed to be a publisher at common law.

A similar reasoning was applied in *Metropolitan International Schools Ltd v Designtechnica Corpn* [2011] 1 WLR 1743. This case concerned defamatory comments which, having been posted on a website, appeared as a "snippet" of information when an internet search was carried out under the claimant's name on Google Inc's search engine. A mental element, as defined in *Bunt v Tilley*, was required to hold a person responsible for publishing of defamatory statements. As to the position of Google after it had been informed of the defamatory content, a distinction was made between removing offensive content by a search engine and someone hosting a website. As a result, the judge ruled that Google cannot be held liable on the basis of authorisation, approval or acquiescence.

In *Tamiz v Google Inc* [2013] EWCA Civ 68 (14 February 2013), a question was asked about qualification of the role of the service provider with regard to an anonymous comment on its blogging service (Blogger.com). In the first instance the High Court of Justice found Google not to be a publisher of the words complained of, whether before it was notified of the complaint or after such notification. Instead, Google's position was described as a "purely passive" platform provider. As such, Google "*was not required to take any positive step, technically, in the process of continuing the accessibility of the offending material.*"[18] The Court of Appeal, however, held that Google may be deemed a "publisher" of (and held liable for) defamatory user-generated content appearing in blogs hosted by Google [particularly][19] after being notified of the content's defamatory nature.[20] [Injunctions can occur regardless of liability issues.[21]]

Where Do UGC Websites Fit In?

When comparing the three chains of actors, active in print publications, in broadcasting and in internet content, we can generally establish three types of activities. First there is the act of *creating* the information. This is followed by the intellectual act of *selecting* within this information, *aggregating* it and *publishing* it. The final step is the technical act of *distributing* the information or providing *access* to it.

In print publications, the *source of the information* is the author or journalist. In broadcasting, it is the producer and in internet content it is the content producer, either professional or amateur. The *intellectual act of selecting and publishing* is done by

---

18 See also *Bunt v Tilley* [2007] 1 WLR 1243.

19 Editor addition.

20 See also *Trkulja v Google Inc LLC & Anor (No 5)* [2012] VSC 533 (12 November 2012), and *Trkulja v Yahoo! Inc LLC & Anor* [2012] VSC 88 (15 March 2012). In both cases in Australia, Google and Yahoo were considered publishers for defamatory content returned as a result to a search query about an individual. In both cases it was considered that providers of the search services were involved in the act of innocent dissemination, similar to those of newsagents or libraries. Their liability for these acts, however, has only been recognized from the moment they received complaints about the content, on which they did not act. See also *A v Google New Zealand Ltd* [2012] NZHC 2352.

21 Editor addition.

the editor and/or publisher in print publications, by the broadcaster in broadcasting and by the information service providers in internet content. The *technical act of distributing or providing access* is done by the printer and the bookstore or kiosk in print publications, by the network operator and the provider of consumer devices (such as decoders) in broadcasting and by access providers, network operators and providers of consumer devices for internet content.

Although the function of the actors performing these three activities is similar in each media type, the regulation of liability is different.

In print publications the liability lies (in Belgium) in principle on the author, but may, in some circumstances and by way of exception, also involve the editor and publisher (eg when the author is unknown). In broadcasting, legal liability traditionally focuses on the broadcaster, but is recently expanding towards the distributor or website provider. For internet content, the content producer is in principle responsible for his content, but very often access providers are sued in his place.

So, where do UGC websites fit in? In order to answer this question, we should start looking at which of the three activities mentioned above they perform. Since UGC website providers are not the source of the information themselves, the question is basically whether they perform the intellectual act of selecting and publishing or whether they act as technical intermediaries who merely host or provide access. The difference in responsibility lies in the intellectual or technical character of the intervention. Where the *intellectual* act of editing and publishing involves a value judgment on the content which justifies legal liability, the purely *technical* act of hosting information and making it available to the public does not involve liability for the content. Is a UGC website provider an editor or a publisher, who makes content available in such a form that it can be disseminated towards the public under his responsibility? Or is he a mere host, who makes third party content available, at their initiative, through technical services?

There is no uniform answer to this question. The intellectual or technical character of the UGC website owner's activities should be determined on a case by case basis, dependent on a range of criteria. From the existing case law we can however derive that there is actually no consensus about what constitute significant criteria[22]:

- The concrete activities of the website provider. In the Dailymotion case of 13 July 2007 [TGI Paris, 13 July 2007, *Nord Ouest Production/ Dailymotion*, available from www.legalis.net], the Paris TGI ruled that although the activities of Dailymotion are in principle only technical, it cannot be denied that the website provider plays a more active role regarding the content and that it is aware that illegal material is posted. Dailymotion is condemned to pay damages because of the presence of an intentional element;
- The imposition of a frame-based structure or format. In the Myspace case of 22 June 2007 [TGI Paris summary proceedings, 22 June 2007,

[22] See also E Montero, "Les Responsabilités Liées au Web 2.0", *op cit*, p 373-379; N Jondet, "The Silver Lining in Dailymotion's Copyright Cloud", 19 April 2008, available from www.juriscom.net.

Lafesse/Myspace, available from www.legalis.net] it was decided that imposing presentation structures on the users increases the involvement of the website provider. However, a few months later, the same court ruled in Google/Zadig Productions that offering users an architecture and the technical means to classify content cannot justify a qualification as an editor, since the content is furnished by the users themselves[23];
- The business model. Since the Paris Court of Appeal qualified Tiscali as an editor because of putting publicity announcements on the users' personal pages, the presence of publicity on the website can be of importance [Court of Appeal Paris, 7 June 2006, *Tiscali*]. In the Myspace case of 22 June 2007, the fact that the website provider was making money with the user's content manifestly added to his qualification as an editor. However, in the Dailymotion case of 15 April 2008, the Paris TGI ruled that the commercialisation of publicity spaces cannot justify a qualification as an editor;
- A website provider can be qualified as a host for some activities and an editor for others. For example, Dailymotion created the "Motionmaker" programme to explicitly promote creators of content and their UGC. Dailymotion actively participates by selecting the creators and reviewing and validating the content, a process in which it has an absolute discretion. The terms of the programme state explicitly that "*upon validation, Dailymotion will become the publisher and not merely the host [of the "Creative Content"]*".[24] However, for the content published on the website, outside of this specific program, Dailymotion is considered a hoster and benefits of the limitation of liability from the eCommerce Directive;
- The mental element. In the UK a number of cases involving different types of ISPs was ruled on the basis of the existence of "*knowing involvement in the process of publication of the relevant words*". Such reasoning was used in *Bunt v Tilley* as well as *Metropolitan International Schools Ltd v Designtechnica Corpn* where the judge ruled that a passive ISP cannot be deemed to be a publisher. As a consequence, such ISP is also not required to "*take any positive step, technically, in the process of continuing the accessibility of the offending material*". This opinion, however, has been rejected in *Tamiz v Google* by the Court of Appeal, which ruled that ISP can be considered and held liable as a publisher for defamatory user-generated content [particularly] after being notified about such character of this content.

Not only the assessment of the degree of liability of each of the actors involved in the publication of UGC, but also the actual and efficient enforcement may prove

---

[23] TGI Paris, 19 October 2007, *Google Inc./Zadig Productions*, available from www.legalis.net. See also: TGI Paris summary proceedings, 26 March 2008, *Olivier Martinez/Bloobox Net*, available from www.juriscom.net; TGI Nanterre summary proceedings, 28 February 2008, *Olivier C./Eric D.*; and TGI Nanterre summary proceedings, 28 February 2008, *Olivier D./Aadsoft Com*, available from www.legalis.net. In these cases the platform providers were qualified as editors because of the presentation structure consisting of RSS links to other websites.

[24] N Jondet, "The Silver Lining in Dailymotion's Copyright Cloud", *op cit*. This is an application of the functional understanding of the term "hoster", *cf.* E Montero, "Les Responsabilités Liées au Web 2.0", *op cit*, p 368.

difficult. A key element in this enforcement is whether the real author is known or not. The first question is to what extent a website provider is obliged to identify the users active on its website. In case law the answer varies from an obligation to conserve the user's IP and email address to the more far-reaching obligation to also ask for his name, first name, domicile and phone number.[25] The second question is whether the website provider, knowing the real identity of the users on its website, is allowed or obliged to reveal it to the authorities. Both questions raise privacy issues which are not further explored here.

Conclusion

What can we learn from the analysis of the existing liability regime for print publications, broadcasting and internet content, for our initial question about the appropriate regulation of liability for UGC?

The publisher model, encompassing the closely related, but not identical regimes for print publications, on the one hand, and broadcasting channels, on the other hand, principally links legal liability to the production and editing of content. Legally liable are the author (at the origin of the content) or the broadcaster (carrying editorial responsibility). Could this be applied to UGC? It is true that also for *non-professional* content on the internet, the basic responsibility lies with the author. It is mainly the difficulty of identifying him, acting against him and enforcing judicial decisions on him that justifies the involvement of other actors in the value chain. Hence, applying the model for print publications as it exists in Belgium, starting from the presumption that the author is usually easily identifiable and imposing liability on the editor and publisher only when the author is not known and not resident in Belgium, on liability for UGC does not seem realistic. Nevertheless, a similar approach can be found in the recently passed Defamation Act in the UK, which offers protection to website operators for third parties' content, however, only when the identity of the author is readily available to the complainant.[26] The impact of this new legislation is yet to be seen as its implementation will largely depend on assisting, detailed regulations that are currently missing.

It should not be forgotten, however, that the activities of the website provider often also include intentional elements, creating a similarity with the editorial activities of a broadcaster. This means that the imposition of legal liability on the website provider could, to a certain extent, be based on the logic underlying the publisher model, more specifically the regime for broadcasting, namely the presence of editorial activities and editorial responsibility similar to those of a broadcaster.

What the print and hosting models have in common is the shared concern to shield the intermediaries (respectively editors and publishers, and internet providers) from [some] legal liability for third party content in the interest of freedom of expression

25 TGI Paris summary proceedings, 7 January 2009, *Lafesse/Youtube*, legalis.net; TGI Paris, 14 November 2008, *Lafesse/Youtube*, legalis.net; C George, "Web 2.0 and User-Generated Content: Legal Challenges in the New Frontier", *Journal of Information, Law and Technology*, http://go.warwick.ac.uk/jilt/2007_2/george_scerri.

26 See UK Defamation Act 2013, available at: http://www.legislation.gov.uk/ukpga/2013/26/contents/enacted.

(to avoid any form of private censorship). The hosting model therefore puts forward a conditional "safe haven", ie a liability exemption under certain circumstances, for hosting services, as provided for in the European eCommerce Directive and Belgian E-Commerce Act. However, it seems difficult to apply this rule in all situations to UGC website providers because of their wide variety and the impossibility to generally classify them as either hosts or editors. Still, depending on the case, UGC website providers may benefit from the safe havens of the E-Commerce Act when it can be assessed that they provide mere technical services without knowledge of the content. The assessment is done on a case-by-case basis by the courts, resulting in a problematic legal uncertainty.

The study of IDATE, TNO and IViR finds that:

> *"deciding about the extent to which information services can be required to monitor and "censor" third parties' material is a matter of finding the right balance between a number of important, often constitutionally protected interests and rights".*

On the one hand, public interest values, such as protection of minors and human dignity, plead for a far-reaching liability for third party content. The media have a social responsibility to protect against illegal and harmful material in view of consumer and citizen protection and the protection of the public legal order. Also, since it is practically impossible for injured parties to act against the real author, the efficiency of enforcement requires the involvement of intermediary actors.

But on the other hand, equally important constitutionally protected rights defend a limited liability for third party content. In the first place, freedom of expression would be severely compromised. Making UGC website owners liable for content disseminated through their website would involve a risk of excessive censorship by them out of fear for prosecution. There is also a concern of fairness towards the UGC website providers. Putting the whole issue of liability for illegal and harmful content on their shoulders would expose them to an excessive financial, technical and legal burden. It is often impossible for them to monitor all activities on their website, because of technical and financial reasons. Besides that, when their liability is invoked, the legal burden is even more heavy. Finally, there is the issue of privacy protection. Website owners might have to infringe privacy rules when revealing the identity of the real author of illegal or harmful content.

Finding the right balance between these contradictory interests is a difficult task, albeit a crucial one. A well-defined regulation on liability for UGC would improve legal certainty and increase the general feeling of safety on the internet. Several attempts to achieve it have been undertaken recently. A first example is the new Defamation Act in the UK which we mentioned before and which is considered to be a major upgrade to the previous UK's outdated and repressive libel laws. However, it is not entirely clear yet how its provisions will interact with the rules set by the eCommerce Directive. Secondly, the eCommerce Directive itself is currently under review with special attention being given to the issues of ISP's liability for third parties' content. Also, the European Commission's initiative on Notice-and-Action aims for more legal certainty and harmonisation by providing more detailed rules on removing illegal or harmful content from the Internet. In this initiative, the European Commission focused on transparency, effectiveness, proportionality and fundamental rights compliance of the Notice-and-Action procedures. Consultations with stakeholders were held in 2012 and their results are expected in the course of 2013. The exact impact of these initiatives on the liability for UGC remains to be seen and will certainly merit further publications on this topic.

Chapter 8

SOCIAL NETWORKING POLICIES

Headline of Issues

- Terms and conditions/terms of service (TOS)
- Privacy statements
- Settings
- Consent
- Changes
- Retention
- Awareness

Introduction

Consideration of data protection compliance by an online organisation often begins with an examination of its legal policies. These include its terms and conditions/terms of service (TOS), privacy notices and agreements. In relation to social networking, an examination of the website terms and conditions/TOS, sign-up and membership agreements (if present), and the privacy statements are necessary.[1]

A debate exists in relation to the effectiveness and validity of these types of terms. Legality and effectiveness can depend on the awareness of the user and how transparent the TOS, privacy statement, etc are. It may also depend on how user-friendly the TOS, technical tools and website settings are for users to examine and understand. Criticism sometimes arises also in relation to the existence, transparency and user-friendliness of how users can police their own personal data, profile, etc on a given website. Some websites have been criticised for their alleged lack of transparency and user-friendliness. Social networking websites have also been criticised for making unannounced changes. More recently some have been criticised in relation to allegedly collecting personal data without users' knowledge or consent.[2]

Terms and Conditions/Terms of Service (TOS)

The terms and conditions/terms of service (TOS) relate to the general legal provisions governing the website's legal relationship with its members, users, etc. Typically it

---

1 A privacy statement sets out and governs the practices of an organisation in relation to the personal data it collects, uses and processes online, whereas a privacy policy governs all of the organisation's data protection practices regardless of where the personal data is gathered from. The Irish Data Protection Commissioner distinguishes privacy statements; see Data Protection Commissioner, *Guidelines for the Contents and Use of Privacy Statements on Websites*, available at www.dataprotection.ie/docs/PrivStatements/290.htm.

2 See generally, http://dataprotection.ie/docs/Home/4.htm.

will also include disclaimers, warranties, limitations of warranties and limitations on liability.[3] Basically, websites will seek not to be liable for things that may go wrong. Some websites will, in addition, have a separate agreement for members to agree to, when signing up, which may have additional legal terms. All these may sometimes have particular provisions in relation to privacy and data protection.

Increasingly, websites will distinguish their general terms of trade/service from privacy issues by having separate documents containing particular provisions governing privacy and data protection, called a privacy statement. In the EU it is recognised that having a clear and separate privacy statement is a compliance obligation. As some websites can involve more enhanced amounts of personal data, there are claims for an enhanced obligation to maintain a transparent privacy statement, and even layered and transparent privacy notices.

In many instances while there are terms and conditions and a separate privacy statement, the terms and conditions will cross-refer and even link to the privacy statement. Sometimes, the terms will seek to deem that individuals are also consenting to the privacy statement, and what may be included in it, regardless of whether they see, read or appreciate it.

While electronic contracts and terms are increasingly binding and recognised, there is concern that these are inadequate to protect user privacy, especially in the context of social networking.[4] Some would argue that "government intervention is warranted".[5] Others argue in terms of self regulation. Yet others still may argue for a hybrid of co-regulation.

Privacy Statements

Data protection requires transparency and fairness. A website must contain a data privacy statement setting out the website's policy in relation to the following: whether it collects personal data from users; what data it collects from them; for what purposes it is being collected and held for; who the data controller entity collecting the personal data is (ie the social network); and what else may happen to the personal data, such as transfers and marketing. The Irish Data Protection Commissioner has also set out guidance in relation to the distinguishing features and requirements of a privacy statement—albeit not specifically in the context of social networks.[6] Most social networks do maintain privacy statements and seperate terms on their website.[7] However, one of the concerns is whether these are fair and transparent and whether they correctly refer to all the forms of personal data

3 In relation to internet and software terms and contracts generally see, for example, P Klinger and R Burnett, *Drafting and Negotiating IT Contracts* (Bloomsbury: London, 2012).

4 JS Livingston, "Invasion Contracts: The Privacy Implications of Terms of Use Agreements in the Online Social Media Setting" (2011) *Albany Law Journal of Science & Technology* 591 at 592 and *passim*.

5 *ibid*, 635.

6 See Irish Data Protection Commissioner, *Guidelines for the Contents and Use of Privacy Statements on Websites*, available at www.dataprotection.ie/docs/PrivStatements/290.htm.

7 See comments in relation to same by JC Breen, "YouTube or YouLose: Can YouTube Survive a Copyright Infringement Lawsuit?" (2007) (16) *Texas Intellectual Property Law Journal* 151 at 157–158.

actually being collected, and all the uses of the personal data. It is also important for users to appraise themselves of what is contained within a privacy statement on social networks (as well as other websites) and the implications for them and their personal data. Parents and schools also have their role too.

As individual users access, and re-access, social networks through a variety of routes, there is an argument that privacy statements alone may not be sufficient. The Federal Trade Commission (FTC) in the US, for example, has indicated in relation to (targeted) behavioural advertising that a layered or two-tier-type privacy notice may be required. This may include: (1) a brief privacy notice and (2) a link to a longer more detailed privacy notice.[8] Increasingly, privacy statements and privacy notices need to be segmented and layered throughout the points of use and interaction with the website. Privacy and date protection information should be available to users at all stages of use of the website.

Indeed, contrast the importance many websites give to their terms, TOS, conditions, disclaimers and limitations. Often users are forced to click agree, and sometimes forced to open or actually read or scroll through the terms/TOS document. Sometimes, websites may not attach the same rigour or importance to privacy statements as they do with contract and term/TOS issues.

General website data protection compliance includes maintaining an adequate privacy statement. Not every website is yet fully complaint. The Irish Data Protection Commissioner in one review of commercial and official websites, found that a significant number did not have a privacy statement.[9] In many instances where there was a privacy statement, the privacy statement was found to be inadequate.[10] A review in Israel has similar findings of non-compliance.[11]

Small Print

One of the criticisms of websites, including social networking websites, is that the sign-up agreements, terms and conditions/TOS and privacy statements are in small print, legalese and not very user-friendly. In some instances, they may be hard to find. In other examples, they may be legally complex and difficult for users to understand.

Some people may be concerned that the full details of what is actually happening to their personal data are not (clearly) referred to in the policy documents. Arguments are made for more transparency, more layers of privacy notices and statements, and more direct user control of their personal data. Even large organisations and webistes can sometimes be found to be not fully compliant.

---

8 See SE Gindin, "Nobody Reads Your Privacy Policy or Online Contract? Lessons Learned and Questions Raised by the FTC's Action Against Sears" (2009) (8) *Northwestern Journal of Technology and Intellectual Property* 1 at 5, and n11 and n 12 at 5.

9 DPC website audits undertaken in 2005 and 2006. See Data Protection Commissioner, *Annual Report 2005*; Data Protection Commissioner, *Annual Report 2006*, at 6.

10 Data Protection Commissioner, *Annual Report 2006*, at 6.

11 M Birnhack and N Elkin-Koren, "Does Law Matter Online? Empirical Evidence on Privacy Law Compliance" (2010–2011) *Michigan Telecommunications & Technology Law Review* 337.

One FTC action suggests that online companies need to make explicit the systems, functionality and terms likely to influence the consumer in making any decision to purchase or participate.[12] It can be inadequate to bury the provisions in relation to privacy and personal data in the main terms or TOS document.[13] It has been argued that inadequate privacy terms may be unenforceable.[14] As always, the devil is in the detail of the terms or privacy statement. It is no use having a privacy statement if it is not transparent, available, prominent and drafted in an understandable and user-friendly manner.

One law professor argues that the courts should declare certain social network terms and conditions void and "unconscionable".[15] The Irish Data Protection Commissioner appears to be more practical in its audit investigations in terms of pointing to recommended best practice changes, and a policy of ongoing general review.[16] Certain changes can also be made obligatory.

One FTC Commissioner has stated:

> "Initially, privacy policies seemed like a good idea. But in practice, they often leave a lot to be desired. In many cases, consumers don't notice, read, or understand the privacy policies. They are often posted inconspicuously via a link at the very bottom of the [web]site's homepage – and filled with fine-print legalese and technotalk. A recent study submitted as a comment for this Town Hall examined privacy policies of Fortune 500 companies and found that they were essentially incomprehensible for the majority of internet users".[17]

Privacy statements should be more transparent and user-friendly in order to be easily understood.

Too Much Data

Websites are often criticised for seeking to obtain irrelevant or excessive personal data from users of the website. Of course this can happen for other organistaions also. Frequently, more personal data than is strictly necessary in relation to a particular service or transaction is sought from the user. This can be to use the data for profiling, advertising or marketing purposes.

The data protection principles state that the personal data collected should be adequate, relevant and not excessive in relation to the (primary) purposes for which the data are collected or further processed.[18] From a data protection perspective

---

12 *Sears Holdings Management Corp*, File No 082 3099 (Federal Trade Commission 4 June 2009), as referred to in Gindin, *op. cit*, 5.

13 *ibid.*

14 Gindin, *op. cit*, 5.

15 S Hetcher, "User-Generated Content and the Future of Copyright: Part One-Investiture of Ownership, Vanderbilt" (2008) (10) *Journal of Entertainment and Technology Law* 863.

16 See documents at http://dataprotection.ie/docs/Home/4.htm.

17 J Liebowitz, "Commissioner, Federal Trade Commission, Remarks at the FTC Town Hall Meeting on 'Behavioural Advertising: Tracking, Targeting & Technology,'" 4 (1 November, 2007) available at http://ftc.gov/speeches/liebowitz/07103ehavior.pdf, as referred to in Gindin, *op. cit*, at 21.

18 Article 6(1)(c) Directive 95/46/EC of the European Parliament and of the Council of 24 October

as well as a user friendly perspective, social networks should be as transparent as possible in identifying any intended primary and secondary purposes.

Technical Privacy Settings

Social networks offer "varying degrees of privacy controls to allow users to restrict access to their profiles".[19] Technical privacy settings on certain websites allow users to control who is able to see their social networking profile and the information they post or upload to their personal profile. Originally, many people may not have appreciated or understood the privacy settings. Hence, many did not properly avail of them.[20] Users may be becoming more familiar with the issues, and with the privacy settings. However, many argue that there is still a need for more transparent information and awareness of privacy issues. For example, a user may ulitise the privacy settings today, but if the processes, settings and data activities change next week, there can be a need for the user to update their settings. Some may argue, therefore, that any significant changes should be notified to users, so that they are made aware of the need to review and update their privacy preference settings. Users also need to be educated in relation to new technical privacy settings. Social networking users need to be able to protect and ring-fence their own personal information, in addition to balanced safeguards. Obviously, additional issues arise in terms of younger users.

Even when an individual actively uses privacy setting tools, it can be possible for a friend to simply copy and paste comments, photographs and materials that the individual has posted. That means that the privacy settings can be entirely circumvented. In effect, "your privacy settings are all for nought".[21]

It is also pointed out that even when one utilises the website privacy settings, "by default, information can be seen by any of your friends and anyone in your networks".[22] Some networks can also reveal personal details city-wide and state-wide.[23] The issue of "groups" which users can join is an issue in addition to the issues involved in becoming so called "friends" online with other people.

Consent

Social networks can be argued to need consent for the processing of users' personal

---

1995 on the protection of individuals with regard to the processing of personal data and on the free movement of such data [1995] OJ L281/31.

19 I Byrnside, "Six Clicks of Separation: The Legal Ramifications of Employers Using Social Networking Sites to Research Applicants" (2008) (10) *Vanderbilt Journal of Entertainment and Technology Law* 445 at 454.

20 See S Nelson, J Simek and J Foltin, "The Legal Implications of Social Networking" (2009–2010) (22) *Regent Law Review* 1 at 2 and references therein.

21 *ibid.*

22 MJ O'Connor, "School Speech in the Internet Age: Do Students Shed Their Rights When They Pick Up a Mouse?" (2009) (11) *University of Pennsylvania Journal of Constitutional Law* 459, at 478.

23 *ibid.*

data.[24] The data protection principles[25] and the data protection legitimate processing conditions[26] must be complied with. One of the legitimate processing conditions is user consent eg consent for the social networking data processing activity.

On occasion, consent may not have been obtained at all. In other examples, consent may exist for a primary activity but not for a secondary activity ancillary to the main purpose. For example, a website may refer to a specified activity or purpose, eg the website service (Purpose 1). It may legitimately obtain a user/member's consent for that data collection and processing. The website may be engaged in additional activities without notifying users and obtaining user consent. It may decide to use the personal details collected for additional Purposes 2 and 3. Without consent and fair and transparent data processing, there may arguably be no legitimate or legal authority for using personal data in relation to Purposes 2 and 3. This is increasingly a contentious area.[27]

Consent is generally required in relation to all data protection purposes and activities. This is particularly so for non-transparent and non-notified data-processing activities.

As noted by one commentator, while referring to official guidance:

> "If Web site operators wish to change their use of personal data they may not simply change their privacy statement. If you wish to change the way you use personal information you must obtain the individual's consent. Therefore, you must explain what you wish to do with the information and wait for the individual to indicate positively that he or she agrees. Not responding to an email message does not amount to consent. An example of where this could occur would be if an individual has agreed to marketing activity but the Web site extends the types of products that it sells, so for example, it may have started out selling books but now wishes to market financial services. As the products are not related, it is unlikely that the Web site operator could rely on the original consent by the individual and it would need to seek new consent. The significant issue is the customer's expectations of what the information will be used for. Depending on how much the new use differs from reasonable expectations, customers should be asked to opt in rather than opt out.
>
> If a Web based company merges or is taken over, it will need to let individuals know that the merger is taking place. There may be a problem with disclosure if it has previously reassured individuals that it will not disclose their personal information, in which case a specific consent will be needed. However, generally a new owner will in effect take over the existing business and the personal information will be used in the same way as before."[28]

Default Settings

There are many instances where a social network decides to change a setting or functionality to allow maximum visibility online of individual users' personal data.

---

24 Originally, this was interpreted and being a part of the fair processing provisions under the first data protection principle, see Article 6(1)(a) Directive 95/46/EC of the European Parliament and of the Council of 24 October 1995 on the protection of individuals with regard to the processing of personal data and on the free movement of such data [1995] OJ L281/31.

25 See Article 6, Directive 95/46.

26 See Article 7, Directive 95/46.

27 It also features in the Irish Data Protection Commissioner's review audit of Facebook. See documents at http://dataprotection.ie/docs/Home/4.htm.

28 H Hart, "Collecting Personal Information Using Web Sites," *Society of Computers and Law*, 2 July 2007, available at www.scl.org/site.aspx?i=ed979.

Many website default settings may also be set to obtain as much personal data as possible or to deem consent in relation to as many activities and purposes as possible. This commercial imperative is not unique to social networks. Particular concerns are raised where the information is for non-essential activities. Frequently, this will be for advertising or marketing purposes. Revealing as much profile and personal data to as many people as possible can also increase the website's traffic and other activities. Another example may be that default settings require that as many personal details as possible are revealed publically.[29] This might include, for example, revealing users' personal details on a social network in internet search engines.[30] It might also mean revealing a personal profile, or parts of a profile, to users outside a person's immediate circle of friends. Therefore, even if the user selects certain privacy settings, the website default settings may operate beyond the users' intentions or expectations. Some of these problems have been described as follows:

> "many social-networking [web]sites have very wide terms of use as to how they can use their customers' data. Are these terms of use reasonable? [Web]sites need to ensure that their use of such data is 'fair and lawful' as well as obtaining user content. It is arguable that some of the extremely wide licences to use the personal data are not fair because they are disproportionately wide but this has not been tested".[31]

However, while websites may provide a privacy setting and some technological protections, they are not a single silver bullet solving all concerns. This is particularly so where defaults override the privacy preferences and settings previously selected by the user.

One commentator highlights some such concerns:

> "After having read the 'privacy settings' of Facebook or other social networks and understood the restrictions on the flow of information about us to our close friends we think we control our internet profile. A quick read of the 'privacy notices' on these sites will end our illusions. Advertising we receive because we are a friend of so and so, that we are supposed be interested in too, keeping our personal information on file after we have cancelled our contract; these are examples of how in fact we do not master the personal data out there about us."[32]

Unilateral Changes

Some social networks have also been criticised for making technical, practice or policy changes that have an impact on personal data and users without being transparent or without alerting their users in advance. Unless users are notified in advance, some may ask how are they to know that important changes affecting them are proposed or are imminent?

Depending on the particular changes, new activities may be undertaken without the knowledge or consent of users. This can involve, for example, new purposes on the website, new marketing activities, cross-selling/cross-marketing, revealing or

---

29 Graham and Anderson, *op. cit*, 99.
30 *ibid*, 99.
31 *ibid.*
32 Y Poullet, "Data Protection Legislation: What Is At Stake for Our Society and Democracy?" (2009) (25) *Computer Law & Security Review* 211 at 214.

sharing new categories of personal data or even sharing users' personal data with third parties or the public.

One issue is that there may be no proper consent obtained. Also, there may be no opportunity for users to change or enhance their privacy settings once they are informed of the proposed changes. Easy opt-out options may not exist.

Facebook has sought to alter the practice of asking users to vote on the making general changes to its privacy policy.[33] The Irish Data Protection Commissioner asked for a delay, as well as certain changes.[34] Any such changes would affect millions of users, given that such a decision has an impact on Facebook users throughout the EU and elsewhere (outside the US and Canada).

Retention Periods

Generally, personal data should be held by a data controller only for as long as reasonably necessary for the particular use or purpose consented to.[35] However, from a marketing perspective it may appear useful to have as much profiling personal data as possible and for as long as possible. The period for which an organisation stores personal data can be referred to as the personal data retention period.[36] The longer the period, the more likely it is that privacy advocates will argue that it is being kept longer than is lawful, proportionate and necessary. The data protection principles state that personal data collected by data controllers should not be stored longer than is necessary in relation to the purpose for which it was originally collected.[37]

Some websites were indicated to be seeking to keep user data in perpetuity.[38] Google reduced its data retention period to 18–34 months, and subsequently again to nine months.[39] In Ireland, the Data Protection Commissioner has said that generally the maximum period of retention of personal data should be 12 months from the time

33 C Albanesius, "Privacy Groups Slam Facebook Plan to Ditch User Voting, More," *PCMag*, 27 November 2012, available at http://www.pcmag.com/article2/0,2817,2412525,00.asp.

34 P Flanagan, "Data Protection Group Seeking Change to Facebook Privacy Policy," *Irish Independent*, 29 November 2012, available at http://www.independent.ie/business/technology/data-protection-group-seeking-change-to-facebook-privacy-policy-3309757.html.

35 Or otherwise legitimised. See Article 6(1)(e) Directive 95/46/EC of the European Parliament and of the Council of 24 October 1995 on the protection of individuals with regard to the processing of personal data and on the free movement of such data [1995] OJ L281/31.

36 This is to be distinguished from "data retention" in the telecoms sector. Telecoms companies can be obliged to retain certain electronic and telecoms traffic data for a legally specified period. This is a contentious and as yet unresolved area. See, for example, various articles by Irish Times journalist Karlin Lillington (and her blog), DigitalRightsIreland.ie and TJMcIntyre.com. The most contentious issues in relation to telecoms data retention are privacy issues and the often perceived overlong period of the retention requirements. TJ McIntyre, "Data Retention in Ireland: Privacy, Policy and Proportionality" (2008) *Computer Law and Security Report* 326.

37 See, for example, Article 6(e) of the 1995 Data Protection Directive.

38 Graham and Anderson, *op. cit.*

39 *ibid*, 100.

of the last user transaction or activity.[40] These issues were also referred to in the Data Protection Commissioner's first review audit of Facebook.[41]

Are Privacy Statements Successful?

Some commentators have asked whether website terms of use/terms of service (TOC) and privacy statements actually protect the public. Graham and Anderson say that:

> "[O]ne of the key ways that social-networking sites comply with the DPA is by having terms of use and privacy policies on their websites. Users are required to accept these terms when first registering on the [web]site. However, do such terms protect the public in line with their expectations? How aware are users of the details of these terms? How many users actually read and understand the terms? Many users may be surprised by the scope of rights granted to the [web]sites under these terms and what they do not cover."[42]

They continue as follows:

> "The licences for use of user information granted to social-networking [web]sites are generally very wide. It is not unusual to see a licence as broad as saying that by posting information on a [web]site, a person may grant the [web]site a perpetual and irrevocable licence for the [web]site to use, copy, display or distribute your information in any way which the [web]site requires, including a right to sub-license such rights. Such wide rights are almost akin to ownership. It leaves the user with very little control over how their data may be used by the relevant social-networking [web]site or any third party to whom it sub-licenses. If, as is commonly the case, there is no express restriction on the purposes for which the social-networking [web]site can use the content, this leaves it open for the data to be used for commercial exploitation. Although such marketing or commercial exploitation of data is currently not the policy of most social-networking [web]sites, such as Facebook, the rights are often sufficiently wide to give them the power to carry out such activity in the future if they wished. With the growing commercialisation of social-networking [web] sites, the pressure to 'own' the users and use their data for commercial purposes is likely to increase."[43]

In addition:

> "Social-networking [web]sites often retain a right to unilaterally amend their terms of use at any time. This is standard practice for websites who make services available to a large proportion of the public. It gives them the flexibility to alter their business model and terms of business without needing to contact and agree terms with each user. However, such a right can undermine any long-term reassurance as to how the content may be used.
>
> One of the most successful growth areas for social-networking [web]sites has been the development and proliferation of platform applications on the [web]sites. These are applications developed by third parties which allow users to play games, share information and even give gifts to their friends. The applications often involve an exchange of data but they are operated by third parties, not the social-networking [web]sites themselves. When signing up for a new application, users are often agreeing to allow the third-party application provider to access the users' data as part of the service. Facebook requires these third parties to enter into contractual obligations to respect users' privacy before allowing the platform applications onto the website and takes general technical security measures,

---

40 Irish DPC Case Study 13/2008 refers to the retention of personal data obtained online, and refers specifically to an appropriate limit of 12 months. DPC Case Study 4/2001 held that previously used credit card details could not be used for future transactions.

41 See documents at http://dataprotection.ie/docs/Home/4.htm.

42 Graham and Anderson, *op. cit*, 100. Reference omitted.

43 *ibid.*

> but does not guarantee the compliance of the third parties. The user effectively enters into a contract with the third party directly. However, following the report by the Canadian Privacy Commissioner, Facebook has announced changes to its website to ensure that third-party applications do not access personal data unless they have the express consent of the individuals."[44]

This is an area that deserves more research. Which privacy statements are best at maintaining transparency and an appropriate level of protection for privacy of personal data, while allowing appropriate commercial developments? A further area of research relates to finding which privacy protection tools are most effective and user-friendly.

Security

There is a general obligation on social networks, and other data controllers, to implement appropriate technical and organisational security to protect personal data.[45] This includes protection against accidental disclosure as well as hacking. The UK government disclosures of health and social details are an example of the former,[46] while the Sony PlayStation hacking breach is an example of the later.[47]

There have also been a number of disputes and cases in relation to such security and related issues. In Canada, a complaint was upheld by the Privacy Commissioner that Facebook did not have adequate safeguards for preventing unauthorised access to personal data by third-party developers.[48] In another instance, Facebook is understood to have been investigated in New York for not dealing with parental complaints in relation to inappropriate and sexually explicit material.[49]

There is a trend of increasing fines and penalties for data breaches. This includes the US. In the UK, the Leveson Inquiry Report has recommended increased fines and criminal offences for breach of the data protection regime.[50] The UK Information

44 *ibid.*

45 See Article 17 Directive 95/46/EC of the European Parliament and of the Council of 24 October 1995 on the protection of individuals with regard to the processing of personal data and on the free movement of such data [1995] OJ L281/31.

46 "Data Lost by Revenue and Customs," stating that "HM Revenue and Customs (HMRC) Has Lost Computer Disks Containing Confidential Details of 25 Million Child Benefit Recipients," *BBC News*, 21 November 2007, available at http://news.bbc.co.uk/2/hi/7103911.stm.

47 K Stuart and C Arthur, "PlayStation Network Hack, Why it Took Sony Seven Days to Tell the World," *Guardian*, 27 April 2011, available at http://www.guardian.co.uk/technology/gamesblog/2011/apr/27/playstation-network-hack-sony.

48 E Denham, *Report of Findings into the Complaint Filed by the Canadian Internet Policy and Public Interest Center (CIPPIC) Against Facebook, Inc. Under the PIPPEDA*, Office of the Privacy Commissioner of Canada (2009), www.priv.gc.ca/cf-dc/2009/2009_008_0716_e.pdf, referred to by DB Garrie, M Duffy-Lewis, R Wong and RL Gillespie, "Data Protection: The Challenges Facing Social Networking" (2009–2010) (131) *International Law & Management Review* 127 at 137.

49 J Spector, "Cuomo Launches Probe of Facebook," J News (Westchester County NY) 25 September 2007, at 1B, referred to in Nelson *et al.*, *op. cit*, 24.

50 UK Leveson Inquiry. *An Inquiry into the Culture, Practices and Ethics of the Press: Report, The Right Honourable Lord Justice Leveson*, November 2012. Available at http://www.official-documents.gov.uk/document/hc1213/hc07/0780/0780.asp. Also see the main inquiry website at http://www.levesoninquiry.org.uk/.

Commissioner (ICO) (the equivalent of the Irish Data Protection Commissioner) is reported as welcoming the opportunity to enhance the penalties available.[51] It appears that Prime Minister Cameron and Deputy Prime Minister Clegg are in agreement to implement these data protection changes.[52] The UK ICO also favours prison terms for data breaches.

The UK ICO has also imposed a number of significant fines recently in relation to data loss. These include fining Greater Manchester Police £150,000, a charity £70,000 (Norwood Ravenswood), a health authority £70,000 (Aneurin Bevan Health Board), Midlothian Council £140,000, a hospital £375,000 (Brighton and Sussex University Hospitals NHS Trust), and a medical entity £225,000 (Belfast Health and Social Care Trust).[53] A spam text marketing firm was fined £440,000.[54] A local authority was fined £60,000 for sending a child-related report to the wrong person.[55] The ICO also imposed a £50,000 fine for inaccurate storage of financial personal data.[56]

Tagging

Tagging or labelling social networking photographs also raises privacy and data protection issues. By way of example, Facebook changed its photograph tagging (labelling) system. The previous position was that the original uploader of the photograph was responsible for tagging. This was amended to allow any permitted viewers to tag[57] any photograph that they could access. "Thus, the subject is fully exposed to unrestrained potential invasions of privacy — including the prying eyes of law enforcement — until he or she received the notifying email"[58] that he or she had already been tagged.

If someone objects to a third-party photograph of them being posted, Facebook says that he or she should contact the original poster to request its removal, but

---

51 A Travis and O Bowcott, "Leveson Data Protection Proposals Unite Cameron and Clegg In Concern," *Guardian*, 30 November 2012, available at http://www.guardian.co.uk/media/2012/nov/30/leveson-data-protection-proposals-concern.

52 *ibid.*

53 A Deighton, "ICO Fines Police and Charity for Data Breaches," Lexology, 29 October 2012, available at http://www.lexology.com/library/detail.aspx?g=7adda7a8-ba0c-4404-adba-1e6121b0824a; S Evans, "Huge Increase in ICO Fines for Data Breaches," *Computer Business Review*, 13 August 2012, available at http://www.cbronline.com/news/huge-increase-in-ico-fines-for-data-breaches-130812; "Data Breaches 10 Times Worse, Sau ICO Figures," BBC, 30 August 2012, available at http://www.bbc.co.uk/news/technology-19424197.

54 "Spam Texters Fines Nearly Half a Million Pounds as ICO Cracks Down on Illegal Marketing Industry," ICO, 28 November 2012, available at http://www.ico.gov.uk/news/latest_news/2012/spam-texters-fined-nearly-half-a-million-pounds-28112012.aspx.

55 "Plymouth City Council Fined £60,000 for Sending Child Neglect Report to the Wrong Person," 22 November 2012, ICO, available at http://www.ico.gov.uk/news/latest_news/2012/plymouth-city-council-fined-60000-for-sending-child-neglect-report-to-wrong-person-22112012.aspx.

56 "Prudential Fined £50,000 for Customer Account Confusion," ICO, 6 November 2012, available at http://www.ico.gov.uk/news/latest_news/2012/prudential-fined-50000-for-customer-account-confusion-06112012.aspx.

57 See D Findlay, "Tag! Now You're 'It.' What Photographs on Social Networking Sites Mean for the Fourth Amendment" (2008) (10) *North Carolina Journal of Law & Technology* 171 at 182 n48.

58 *ibid*, 184.

will not get involved itself.[59] Tagging is also referred to in the Irish Data Protection Commissioner's audit review of Facebook[60] and in the re-audit report.

Tagging is an example of how nuanced data protection policies should be. A user may be agreeable to certain activities, but be more restrained in terms of what, if any, photographs they want to be tagged and available in online.

User Awareness

Users all too frequently ignore or forget the significance of website terms and privacy statements.[61] Mann states:

> "[S]omething must be done to alert users to the risks. Documented evidence of computer users ignoring privacy policies and terms of use, in a [social network] is no excuse for acts of omission by the user. Scare tactics that work for habitual drunk drivers may be needed for habitual [social network] users acting *actus reus*, such as television commercials showing users in jail and others who have lost their job as a result of the UGC they generated in a [social network]".[62]

Terms/Privacy Statement Considerations

In relation to the policy considerations of different terms and privacy statement models, Grimmelmann states:

> "Some privacy scholars, companies, and regulators support an informed choice model of online privacy. On this view, government shouldn't regulate any specific privacy standards; instead, it should make sure that companies clearly tell consumers what will be done with their personal information. Armed with good information, consumers will make good choices. The traditional focus of this approach is the privacy policy; if a [web]site's privacy policy is clear and honest, its users will know what they're getting into and will approve of the consequences.
>
> An examination of Facebook's privacy policy shows that the informed choice model is completely unrealistic. Everything the model knows is wrong; there's no room in it for the social dynamics of how people actually make privacy-affecting decisions. Facebook's beautifully drafted privacy policy ought to be Exhibit A for informed choice: it bears a TRUSTe seal and contains reassuring statements such as 'We share your information with third parties only in limited circumstances' and 'Facebook takes appropriate precautions to protect our users' information.' Nonetheless, Facebook users don't read it, don't understand it, don't rely on it and certainly aren't protected by it. It's a beautiful irrelevancy. In the first place, most people don't read privacy policies, and even those users who do read them generally don't understand them. Facebook users are no exception. A 2001 poll found that only three percent of the people surveyed claimed to read privacy policies carefully 'most of the time,' and a 2007 poll found that thirty-one percent claimed to do so. Studies have also found that although the consumers surveyed claimed to care about privacy and to look to see whether [web]sites had privacy policies, large majorities of them were badly misinformed about what those policies actually said. A 2006 survey of Facebook users found that seventy-seven percent had never read its privacy policy and that large majorities had

59 *ibid*, 185.

60 See documentation at http://dataprotection.ie/docs/Home/4.htm.

61 BL Mann, "Social Networking Websites – A Concentration of Impersonation, Denigration, Sexual Aggressive Solicitation, Cyber-Bullying or Happy Slapping Videos" (2009) (17) *International Journal of Law & Information Technology* 252 at 256.

62 *ibid*, 252.

> mistaken beliefs about how Facebook collected and shared personal information. Even the twenty-three percent who claimed to have read the policy were no more likely to understand what it allowed. Between the lawyerly caution, the weasel words, the commingling of many standard terms with the occasional surprising one, the legally mandated warnings and disclaimers, and the legalese, most privacy policies have a painfully low signal-to-noise ratio.
>
> If its users did read Facebook's privacy policy closely – and even more counterfactually, if they understood it – they'd know that it doesn't restrict Facebook's activities in any genuinely significant ways ..."[63]

The privacy group Electronic Frontier Foundation (EFF) refers to "Facebook's Eroding Privacy Policy: A Timeline".[64] The associated commentary states that there has been a growing "shift away from privacy" through gradual changes to its privacy terms.[65] This can refer to a number of parties.

One commentator referring to the Facebook privacy statement states that:

> "Facebook's privacy statement, for example, includes the following statements so as to inform its users of the purposes for which it will process their data:
>
> — profile information is used primarily to be presented back to and edited by the user when the service is accessed and to be presented to others permitted to view that information by the user's privacy settings;
> — Facebook uses information (which has been anonymised) to pass to third parties, eg to calculate how many people in a network like a particular band and for direct marketing;
> — Facebook uses information about the user that it may obtain from other sources, eg newspapers and internet blogs to supplement the Facebook profile;
> — Facebook retains information so that a user can return to view prior messages and that when information is updated a back up copy of the prior version is usually kept for a reasonable period of time to enable reversion to the prior version of that information; and
> — even after removal, copies of user content may remain viewable in cached and archived pages or if other users have copied or stored your user content.
>
> As to when this information must be provided, the Information Commissioner has issued specific guidance to website operators in connection with the collection of personal information for use on websites. This makes it clear that it is not enough to simply say, 'click here to see our privacy statement.' There must be a description of how the data will be used wherever personal information is collected. Help in putting together a privacy statement can be obtained easily from the Organisation for Economic Cooperation and Development website, which has a privacy policy generator."[66]

Perhaps in response to such criticism, Facebook is reported to indicate that it is making its privacy settings more user-friendly and simpler.[67] Further changes are also meant to be agreed and in process pursuant to the Irish Data Protection Commissioner's initial audit review.[68]

In relation to the Facebook privacy statement, one commentator also writes:

---

63 J Grimmelmann, "Saving Facebook" (2009) (94) *Iowa Law Review* 1137 at 1181–1182.

64 See Electronic Frontier Foundation, "Facebook's Eroding Privacy Policy: A Timeline," available at www.eff.org/deeplinks/2010/04/facebook-timeline/.

65 *ibid.*

66 A Brown, "Facebook Data Concerns," *Society of Computers and Law*, 1 February 2008, available at www.scl.org/site.aspx?i=ed1035.

67 "Facebook to Simplify Privacy Tools," *Irish Times*, 24 May 2010, available at www.irishtimes.com/newspaper/breaking/2010/0524/breaking45.html?via=rel.

58 See documents at http://dataprotection.ie/docs/Home/4.htm.

> "Facebook requires users to agree to its privacy policy and Terms of Use when they first register. Members must agree to these provisions when they initially create a member profile. Assent to the agreement is indicated by checking a box with a link to the privacy policy. The Facebook privacy policy states:
>
> > 'You post User Content ... on the [web][s]ite at your own risk. Although we allow you to set privacy options that limit access to your pages, please be aware that nc security measures are perfect or impenetrable. We cannot control the actions of other Users with whom you may choose to share your pages and information. Therefore, we cannot and do not guarantee that User Content you post on the [web][s]ite will not be viewed by unauthorized persons. We are not responsible for circumvention of any privacy settings or security measures contained on the [web][s]ite. You understand and acknowledge that, even after removal, copies of User Content may remain viewable in cached and archived pages or if other Users have copied or stored your User Content'".[69]

The Facebook privacy statement provides that user information might be made public. It states:

> "When you use Facebook, certain information you post or share with third parties (eg a friend or someone in your network), such as personal information, comments, messages, photos, videos, Marketplace listings or other information, may be shared with other users in accordance with the privacy settings you select. All such sharing of information is done at your own risk. Please keep in mind that if you disclose personal information in your profile or when posting comments, messages, photos, videos, Marketplace listings or other items, this information may become publicly available."[70]

The privacy statement indicates that any information members provide may become "publicly available".[71] The privacy policy also notes, "[y]our name, network names, and profile picture thumbnail will be available in search results across the Facebook network and those limited pieces of information may be made available to third party search engines."[72]

Facebook Changes

Facebook has changed its privacy setting and functionality sometimes without notice to users. It also began automatically linking users to websites in which some of their personal details may have indicated they had an interest, but without informing users or obtaining consent. It also started allowing third parties to obtain access to users' details and to start offering services to them, and sometimes importing some of their personal details and preferences onto third-party services.[73]

One commentator refers to the Facebook changes as follows:

> "In an attempt to enhance its ability to generate advertising profits, Facebook recently tweaked the traditional advertising model, generating widespread user protest in the process. Its offense? Instead of merely tracking user activity on its own website and delivering ads to each user relevant to their web activity, Facebook went two steps further: (1) it started

69 Y Hashemi, "Facebook's Privacy Policy and Its Third Party Partnerships: Lucrativity and Liability" (2009) (15) *Bolton University Journal of Science and Technology Law* 140 at 149.
70 Referred to in Hashemi, *op. cit*, 149.
71 *ibid*, 149.
72 *ibid*, 149.
73 See "Facebook to Simplify Privacy Tools," *Irish Times*, 24 May 2010, available at www.irishtimes.com/newspaper/breaking/2010/0524/breaking45.html?via=rel.

> delivering ads to a user's 'friends,' with the user's name, photos, and endorsements attached; and (2) it started tracking user activities on third-party websites, announcing these activities to the user's friends, and delivering ads relevant to those activities".[74]

In 2007 Facebook announced three new changes, namely Public Search, Social Ads and Beacon.[75] The public search change is described as follows:

> "After the public search change, all users were automatically included in the public search listings, but users can opt-out of the public listings, after the fact, via Facebook's individualized privacy settings page. Although Facebook's privacy policy has not been amended to cover the implications of public searches, the … policy … state[d], 'Please keep in mind that if you disclose personal information in your profile or when posting comments, messages, photos, videos, Marketplace listings or other items, this information may become publicly available'".[76]

There were over 700,000 user protests to the making available of Facebook profile data to the general public.[77]

Given its size, it is perhaps not surprising that the issue of website changes in relation to privacy is frequently controversial with Facebook. Referring to Facebook changes, Graham and Anderson describes the following:

> "in February 2009, Facebook faced a storm of controversy when it attempted to change these provisions. Without any publicity, Facebook changed its terms of use to delete the section set out above. Contractually there was no barrier to Facebook doing this as it has the right to unilaterally amend its user terms at any time and users automatically accept the revised terms by their continued use.
>
> The significance of the change is that with the relevant wording deleted, it would give Facebook the right to continue using a user's data even where they have left the [web] site. The licence granted to Facebook is 'irrevocable' and 'perpetual' which means that without wording saying expressly that the licence expires, the licence would continue indefinitely even if the account were closed or the content purportedly removed from the [web]site by the user.
>
> Since Facebook is not required to highlight any changes it makes, this change, at first, went unnoticed. However, a journalist working for the *Consumerist* in the United States noticed the change and alerted the wider public. More than 38,000 users joined a user group on Facebook protesting at the change and it also received wide-scale news coverage and comments from blogs and internet [web]sites. The Electronic Privacy Information Center threatened to make a formal complaint to the Federal Trade Commission if the change was not reversed. At first Mark Zuckerberg, CEO of Facebook explained that there was nothing sinister about the change. He said the intention was simply to clarify the terms and that it was necessary in order to allow content to remain on other people's pages, for example posted on people's walls or in their inboxes, following termination of the account. He also tried to reassure the public that Facebook took privacy seriously and that Facebook, 'wouldn't share [it] in a way you wouldn't want.' As a result of this mounting pressure, Facebook reinserted the deleted wording. The concern centred on Facebook's scope of rights. Although Facebook's point about content on other people's pages is valid, it has wider implications. Under its terms, Facebook has the right to, 'use, copy, publicly perform, publicly display reformat, translate, excerpt … and distribute' the content. This is a wider right than what is required to allow the data to remain on Facebook where it sits on someone else's pages."[78]

---

74 Hashemi, *op. cit*, 141.

75 *ibid*, 142. Also A Morganstern, "In the Spotlight: Social Network Advertising and the Right of Publicity" (2008) *Intellectual Property Law Bulletin* 181.

76 *ibid*, 143–144.

77 *ibid*, 143–145. Also Graham and Anderson, *op. cit*, 99.

78 Graham and Anderson, *op. cit*, 100. Reference omitted.

It is sometimes questioned whether users are likely or willing to go to a separate section of a website to look at a privacy statement and terms.[79] There is a legitimate argument for social networks to be as user-friendly and privacy-friendly as possible. If terms and privacy statements are buried on a website, they are going to be argued to be not user friendly or transparent.

Facebook and Advertising

The social ads change is described as follows:

> "On November 7, 2007, Facebook announced on its blog that it was introducing what it called 'an entirely new advertising solution for Facebook' – Social Ads. Social ads display relevant advertisements related to actions that users have taken on the site. The announcement specified that the new Social Ads product would result in three main changes for Facebook users: (1) it would give users a way to connect with 'products, businesses, bands, celebrities and more'; (2) ads would become 'more relevant and more meaningful' to users; and (3) users would have the options to share actions they take on third-party websites with their Facebook friends. Facebook assured users that advertisers never have access to who is seeing their ads, personal information about users, or the social actions that accompany their ads. This announcement was only published in the Facebook blog, though in accordance with Facebook policy, no announcements were sent to users' personal email addresses."[80]

One of the issues is also the extent to which it shares or discloses personal data from its users with third parties, whether advertisers or applications service providers and developers.[81]

Facebook Beacon

The Facebook advertising privacy controversy relates to its roll-out of a notification and advertising programme called Beacon. Facebook Beacon is described as follows:

> "On November 7, 2007, Facebook also announced the introduction of its new 'Beacon' product on the Facebook blog. Beacon tracks user actions on third-party websites that are partnered with Facebook ('Affiliate Websites') and shares these actions with a user's friends through the News Feed in the form of news stories. The announcement assured users that Affiliate Websites will always notify users of any stories they want to send to the Facebook News Feed and that users will have two opportunities to opt out of the story: both on the Affiliate Website and on Facebook. As was the case with Social Ads, Facebook did not email the Beacon announcement to its users, nor did it take any other additional measures to notify its users of the new product".[82]

There were significant objections and concerns raised when Facebook launched its Beacon project. This advertising application notified users of Facebook when their friends bought products and services, with the aim of creating additional revenue

---

79 See Mann, *op. cit*, 253.
80 Hashemi, *op. cit*, 144.
81 *ibid*, 140.
82 *ibid*, 144.

from advertising and additional sales. There was an "outcry"[83] and "uprising"[84] over privacy concerns once the unannounced project was launched live.

Over 50,000 users signed a petition objecting to the activities being promoted by Beacon.[85] Other organisations also launched complaints to the FTC.[86] Users objected to advertising, the lack of opt-in consent, the difficulty in opting out on the website, etc.[87]

Ultimately, the growing criticism led Mark Zuckerberg to post an apology on 5 December 2007 for the way in which Beacon was launched and confirming that it was being changed to opt-in only.[88] However, the *Washington Post* criticised that many of the privacy concerns were still not addressed even after this change.[89]

Facebook has been criticised as follows:

> "It is particularly troubling, and even unprecedented, that Beacon tracks [even] logged-off Facebook members (including those who have opted-out of having Facebook include stories about their activities on affiliate websites in the News Feed), former members, and even non-members, without providing any notice".[90]

Facebook also amended its privacy statement on 6 December 2007 to include information in relation to Facebook Beacon:

> "Facebook Beacon is a means of sharing actions you have taken on third party [web]sites, such as when you make a purchase or post a review, with your friends on Facebook. In order to provide you as a Facebook user with clear disclosure of the activity information being collected on third party sites and potentially shared with your friends on Facebook, we collect certain information from that [web]site and present it to you after you have completed an action on that [web]site. You have the choice to have Facebook discard that information, or to share it with your friends."[91]

It also indicates that Facebook Beacon may track the activities of Facebook users who are not logged in Facebook users, and even non-Facebook users:

> "Like many other websites that interact with third party [web]sites, we may receive some information even if you are logged out from Facebook, or that pertains to non-Facebook users, from those [web]sites in conjunction with the technical operation of the system. In cases where Facebook receives information on users that are not logged in, or on non-Facebook users, we do not attempt to associate it with individual Facebook accounts and will discard it".[92]

---

83 G Lastowska, "User-Generated Content and Virtual Worlds" (2007–2008) (10) *Vanderbilt Journal of Entertainment and Technology Law* 893 at 896–897.

84 Mann, *op. cit*, at 254.

85 A Brown and L Pownall, "Facebook Data Concerns," *Society of Computers and Law*, 1 February 2008, available at www.scl.org/site.aspx?i=ed1035.

86 Hashemi, *op. cit*, at 146.

87 *ibid*, 146.

88 Referred to in Hashemi, *ibid*, 147.

89 JC Perez and N Gohring, "Facebook Partners Quiet on Beacon Fallout," *Washington Post* 11 December, 2007, available at http://washingtonpost.com/wp-dyn/content/article/2007/12/11/AR2007121100723.html. Referred to in Hashemi, *op. cit*, 147–148.

90 Hashemi, *op. cit*, at 149.

91 Referred to *ibid*, 149.

92 Referred to *ibid*, 149.

In addition, it has been said:

> "Although Facebook claims that it discards information gathered about non-Facebook users, it does not share the fact that it is gathering this information from non-users, who may not even know that Facebook even exists."[93]

Facebook has sought to settle a class action relating to Beacon complaints, for $20m.[94]

Personal Data After Leaving a Social Network

The use of personal data after leaving or termination of one's relationship with a social network[95] is an increasingly contentious issue. Some individuals have complained that even after they leave, Facebook retains their personal data. It has also been complained that it was not possible to formally terminate one's account with Facebook, as the most one could do was to suspend one's account. The issue of deletion is referred to in the Irish Data Protection Commissioner's Facebook audit review.[96] Deletion is now meant to be possible.

Borders

The extent to which laws between jurisdictions may differ does not assist in ensuring uniform or user-friendly policies on data protection. So, regardless of any given legal rules in relation to social networking and data protection, the international and cross-jurisdictional nature of data use in practice can make effective enforcement more difficult.

There are a few (but growing) occasions when US legislation is dedicated to specific data protection privacy issues. One of these relates to videos, after one infamous incident, namely, the video rentals of a Judge. Another is the California Online Privacy Protection Act, although it is weak in terms of the detail of the privacy policy that websites should have.[97] Data breach, and data breach reporting rules, are also increasing across the US.

Conclusion

If a user suspends their account, or permanently leaves a social network, one issue is whether all of their pictures (and pictures in which they are tagged) also permanently

---

93 *ibid*, 149.

94 *McCall v Facebook*, United States Court of Appeals for the Ninth Circuit, 29 September 2012, available at http://www.ca9.uscourts.gov/datastore/opinions/2012/09/20/10-16380.pdf. Also see T Peters, "Facebook Ordered to Pay $20m for Using Member 'Likes' as Endorsements for Adverts," *Irish Examiner*, 28 August 2013.

95 See Graham and Anderson, *op. cit*, 100–101.

96 See documents at http://dataprotection.ie/docs/Home/4.htm.

97 Hashemi, *op. cit*, at 154.

deleted and detagged[98] The Facebook complaints to the Irish Data Protection Commissioner include a complaint in relation to photographs on Facebook. It has been argued that there is an increasing trend for more transparent privacy statements online.[99] There are also calls for shorter, more user-friendly terms and privacy statements.[100] As yet, there is no single solution but the debate is continuing.

---

98 See generally A Brown, "Facebook Data Concerns," *Society of Computers and Law*, 1 February 2008, available at www.scl.org/site.aspx?i=ed1035.

99 Gindin, *op. cit*, 5.

100 *ibid.*

Chapter 9

ADVERTISING AND MARKETING

Headline of Issues

- Advertising
- Targeted behavioural marketing
- Definitions
- UK change
- US
- EU Article 29 Working Party

Introduction

Online targeted advertising is one of the newest issues regarding online privacy and data protection. This is the case in the EU and the US. It arises due to cookies and new monitoring software technologies that allow commercial advertisers to become more and more knowledgeable of what users are doing and their preferences, and thus to direct ever more targeted marketing materials to users. Users and interested parties have raised concerns that some users' communications, searches, key words and online activities are being monitored and recorded to assist advertisers in profiling and in targeting specific advertising materials to users.

While the issue of "monitoring" has proved controversial in and of itself, the nature of the roll-out of new profiling technologies has raised the criticism.[1] This is because trials and the roll-out of some of the new technologies have occurred without users being made aware of the existence of the activity. The exact nature of how the technology works is also less transparent than many feel is required. Targeted behavioural advertising has also raised the attention of data protection regulators.

Definitions of Targeted Behavioural Marketing

What is targeted behavioural advertising? The EU Article 29 Working Party (WP29) defines behavioural advertising:

> "based on the ... behaviour of individuals over time. Behavioural advertising seeks to study the characteristics of [user] actions (repeated [web]site visits, interactions, keywords, online content production, etc) in order to develop a specific profile and thus provide data subjects with advertisements tailored to match their inferred interests".[2]

---

1 See Phorm references later.

2 WP29, Opinion 2/2010 on Online Behavioural Advertising, WP 171, Adopted on 22 June 2010, at 4.

The US Federal Trade Commission (FTC) defines behavioural advertising as:

> "the tracking of a consumer's online activities over time — including the searches the consumer has conducted, the web pages visited, and the content viewed — in order to deliver advertising targeted to the individual consumer's interests".[3]

Berger refers to it as:

> "the emerging practice of collecting information about consumers' behaviour and using that information to customise an advertisement or other service for the consumer."[4]

The companies behind the technology of behavioural advertising suggest that the data connected is anonymous and does not identify individuals. However,

> "researchers, using surprisingly little additional information, have been successful in identifying individuals in data containing so-called anonymised or non-personally identifiable information".[5]

There are also reports that advertisers are now using and combining such data with other data sets of personally identifiable information (PII).[6]

UK Change of Position

The UK Information Commissioner Office (ICO) initially issued a statement that supported a behavioural adverting regime which required users opting-in to such services. Some form of positive consent would be initially required. However, subsequently the UK ICO apparently removed the statement from its website.[7]

US: FTC Principles

The FTC became concerned with behavioural advertising, and revised its guidelines in 2009.[8] It sets out four principles to be adhered to in relation to targeted behavioural advertising:

- transparency and consumer control;
- reasonable security and limited data retention for consumer data;
- affirmative express consent for material changes to existing privacy promises;

---

3 Federal Trade Commission, FTC Staff Report: Self-Regulatory Principles for Online Behavioural Advertising 42 (2009), available at http://ftc.gov/os/2009/02/P085400behavadreport.pdf, as referred to in Gindin, *op. cit*, at 6. It is noted that the US regime under the FTC is referred to as a self-regulatory system, not a formal legal statute obligation, see DD Berger, "Balancing Consumer Privacy with Behavioural Targeting" (2010–2011) *Santa Clara Computer & High Technology Law Journal* 3 and 43–48.

4 *ibid*.

5 Gindin, *op. cit*, at 30.

6 *ibid*, 8.

7 "Has the ICO Swung Behind Opt-outs in Behavioural Advertising?" *Society of Computers and Law* 20 March 2009, available at www.scl.org/site.aspx?i=ne11257.

8 Gindin, *op. cit*, 31.

- affirmative express consent to (or prohibition against) using sensitive data for behavioural advertising.[9]

Self-Regulation

Perhaps in light of the concerns with behavioural advertising, some of the associated industry-led organisations were involved in an attempt at self-regulation. The Internet Advertising Bureau issued Good Practice Principles in relation to behavioural advertising.[10] Some literature also refers to these efforts in terms of "self governing online communities".[11] This can include website moderation. Some have also argued for greater self-regulation even in the context of social networking and sexual predators.[12] Generally, industry favours self-regulation in relation to certain issues, where it involves less onerous costs and obligations on websites.

WP29: Opinion 2/2010 on Online Behavioural Advertising

The EU Article 29 Working Party has referred to the growing concern in relation to behavioural advertising. It issued Opinion 2/2010 on Online Behavioural Advertising.[13] Targeted behavioural advertising and cookies, (tracking software) located on the users' equipment, are referred to in the Opinion.[14]

It also refers to another form of targeted behavioural advertising that relies on examining the user's internet search traffic, known as deep packet inspection.[15] This requires cooperation between a number of parties. The Opinion notes that this technology was "tested" but that the EU Article 29 Working Party is "not aware" of any current use of this technology in the EU.[16] However, it states that:

> "the application of this technology raises serious legal issues beyond the processing of personal data, regardless of the purpose for which the data are being used. The analysis of this advertising technology falls outside the scope of this Opinion".[17]

If it is found that this technology (or similar technology) is used, currently or in the future, the EU Article 29 Working Party may have to issue a separate Opinion.

---

9 *ibid*, 31–32.

10 "Online Behavioural Advertising: IAB Good Practice Principles," *Society for Computers and Law*, 4 March 2009, available at www.scl.org/site.aspx?i=ne10776. The IAB is available at http://m.iabuk.net/1056/349/2775.

11 S-L Chen, "Self-Governing Online Communities in Web 2.0: Privacy, Anonymity and Accountability in Wikipedia" (2010) *Albany Law Journal of Science & Technology* 421. Also see N Suzor, "The Role of the Rule of Law in Virtual Communities" (2010) *Berkeley Technology Law Journal* 1817.

12 See S Van Der Heide, "Social Networking and Sexual Predators: the Case for Self-Regulation" (2008) *Hastings Communications/Entertainment Law Journal* 173.

13 WP29, Opinion 2/2010 on Online Behavioural Advertising, WP 171, Adopted on 22 June 2010.

14 See *ibid*, para 2.1, at 6–7.

15 *ibid.*

16 *ibid.*

17 *ibid.*

It refers to substantive scope of application of the EU Data Protection Directive 1995 and the processing of personal data. It states:

> "If as a result of placing and retrieving information through the cookie or similar device, the information collected can be considered personal data then, in addition to Article 5(3), [Data Protection Directive 1995] will also apply.
>
> The [EU Article 29 Working Party] notes that the behavioural advertising methods described in this Opinion often entail the processing of personal data as defined by Article 2 of [Data Protection Directive 1995] ... This is due to various reasons: i) behavioural advertising normally involves the collection of IP addresses and the processing of unique identifiers (through the cookie). The use of such devices with a unique identifier allows the tracking of users of a specific computer even when dynamic IP addresses are used ... such devices enable data subjects to be 'singled out', even if their real names are not known. ii) ... the information collected in the context of behavioural advertising relates to, (ie is about) a person's characteristics or behaviour and it is used to influence that particular person ... profiles [can] be linked at any moment with directly identifiable information provided by the data subject, such as registration related information. Other scenarios that can lead to identifiability are mergers, data losses and the increasing availability on the internet of personal data in combination with IP addresses".

It comments on the interplay between the Data Protection and ePrivacy Directives.

> "If both Directives apply, a relevant question is to determine the applicable provisions of each Directive ... Recital 10 of the ePrivacy Directive states that [Data Protection Directive 1995] applies, 'to all matters concerning protection of fundamental rights and freedoms which are not specifically covered by the provisions of this Directive, including the obligations on the controller and the rights of individuals.'
>
> ... Article 5(3) of the ePrivacy Directive which deals with informed consent will be directly applicable. The [Data Protection Directive 1995] will be fully applicable except for the provisions that are specifically addressed in the ePrivacy Directive, which mainly correspond to Article 7 of [the Data Protection Directive 1995] on the legal grounds for data processing. The remaining provisions of [Data Protection Directive 1995] including the principles regarding data quality, the data subject's rights (such as access, erasure, right to object), confidentiality and security of the processing and international data transfers will be fully applicable".

Network Providers/Ad Network Providers

The Opinion refers to roles and responsibilities of the different players,

> "[a]s described above, behavioural advertising involves various players, including ad network providers, publishers and advertisers. It can be important to assess the role they play in order to establish their obligations under current data protection legislation." [18]

In this regard, it refers to ad network providers:

> "the obligations [of] Article 5(3) of the ePrivacy Directive apply to those who place cookies and/or retrieve information from cookies already stored in the data subjects' terminal equipment ... irrelevant whether ... a data controller or a data processor ... the obligation to obtain informed consent [rests] upon ad network providers.
>
> ... when behavioural advertising entails the processing of personal data, ad network providers also play the role of data controller ... additional obligations [setm] from ... [Data Protection Directive 1995] will be applicable. Ad network providers have complete control over the purposes and means of the processing.

[18] *ibid*, 8–12.

They 'rent' space from publishers' web sites to place adverts; they set and/read cookie related information and, in most cases, collect the IP address and possible other data that the browser may reveal. Further, the ad network providers use the information gathered on internet users' surfing behaviour to build profiles and to select and deliver the ads ... [based on the] profile ... they clearly act as data controllers".[19]

PUBLISHERS

The Opinion also refers to publishers:

"Publishers ... rent out space on their websites for ad networks to place adverts. They set up their web sites in a way that visitors' browsers are automatically redirected to the webpage of the ad network provider (which will then send a cookie and serve tailored advertising). This raises the question about their responsibility [re] data processing.

... whether a publisher [is] a joint controller with the ad network provider will depend on the conditions of collaboration between [them] ... [EU Article 29 Working Party] notes that in a typical scenario where ad network providers serve tailored advertising, publishers contribute to it by setting up their web sites in such a way that when a user visits a publisher's web site, his/her browser is automatically redirected to the webpage of the ad network provider. In doing so, the user's browser will transmit his/her IP address to the ad network provider which will proceed to send the cookie and tailored advertising. In this scenario, it is important to note that publishers do not transfer the IP address of the visitor to the ad network provider. Instead, it is the visitor's browser that automatically transfers such information to the ad network provider ... the publisher triggers the transfer of the IP address, which is the first necessary step that will allow the subsequent processing, carried out by the ad network provider for ... serving tailored advertising. Thus, even if, technically the data transfer of the IP address is carried out by the browser of the individual who visits the publisher web site, it is not the individual who triggers the transfer. The individual only intended to visit the publisher's web site. He did not intend to visit the ad network provider's web site ...

... publishers have a certain responsibility for the data processing ... the publishers' responsibility covers the first stage, ie the initial part of the data processing, namely the transfer of the IP address that takes place when individuals visit their web sites. This is because the publishers facilitate such transfer and co-determine the purposes for which it is carried out, ie to serve visitors with tailored adverting. In sum, for these reasons, publishers will have some responsibility as data controllers for these actions. This responsibility cannot, however, require compliance with the bulk of the obligations contained in the Directives.

... Publishers do not hold personal information; so obviously, it would not make sense to apply some of the obligations of the Directive such as the right of access. However, ... the obligation to inform individuals of the data processing is fully applicable to publishers.

In addition ... publishers will be joint controllers if they collect and transmit personal data regarding their visitors such as name, address, age, location, etc to the ad network provider. To the extent that publishers act as data controllers they are bound by the obligations ... [of Data Protection Directive 1995] regarding the part of the data processing under their control ...

In sum, publishers should be aware that by entering into contracts with ad networks with the consequence that personal data of their visitors are available to ad network providers, they take some responsibility towards their visitors. The breadth of their responsibility, including the extent to which they become data controllers should be analysed on a case by case basis depending on the particular conditions of collaboration with ad network providers, as reflected in the service agreements. Accordingly, the service agreements between publishers and ad network providers should set up the roles and responsibilities of both parties in the light of their collaboration, as described in the agreement".[20]

---

19 *ibid*, 8–12.

20 *ibid*, 8–12.

Advertisers

In relation to advertisers, the Opinion states:

> "When a data subject clicks through on an ad and visits the advertisers' website, the advertiser can track which campaign resulted in the click-through. If the advertiser captures the targeting information (eg certain demographic data such as 'young mothers' or an interest group such as 'extreme sports fan') and combines it with the data subject's onsite surfing behaviour or registration data, then the advertiser is an independent data controller for this part of the data processing".[21]

In addition, it refers to the obligation to obtain prior informed consent.

> "The general rule contained in the first paragraph of Article 5(3) requires Member States to:
>
> 'ensure that the storing of information, or the gaining of access to information already stored, in the terminal equipment of a subscriber or user is only allowed on condition that the subscriber or user concerned has given his or her consent, having been provided with clear and comprehensive information, in accordance with [Data Protection Directive 1995], *inter alia* about the purposes of the processing.' This article was changed when the ePrivacy Directive was amended in 2009. The changes ... reinforce the need for users' informed prior consent ...
>
> 4.1 The obligation to obtain data subjects' prior consent to engage in behavioural advertising. Pursuant to Article 5(3), an ad network provider who wishes to store or gain access to information stored in a user's terminal equipment is allowed to do so if: i) it has provided the user with clear and comprehensive information in accordance with [Data Protection Directive 1995], *inter alia*, about the purposes of the processing and; ii) it has obtained the user's consent to the storage of or access to information on his or her terminal equipment, after having provided the information requested under i).
>
> It follows ... that: i) consent must be obtained before the cookie is placed and/or information stored in the user's terminal equipment is collected, which is usually referred to as prior consent and ii) informed consent can only be obtained if prior information about the sending and purposes of the cookie has been given to the user ... for consent to be valid whatever the circumstances in which it is given, it must be freely given, specific and constitute an informed indication of the data subject's wishes. Consent must be obtained before the personal data are collected, as a necessary measure to ensure that data subjects can fully appreciate that they are consenting and what they are consenting to. Furthermore, consent must be revocable."[22]

Browser Settings

The Opinion then refers to consent obtained by the way of browser settings.

> "Publishers and ad network providers engaged in behavioural advertising place tracking cookies in a data subject's terminal equipment when the data subject accesses a website that is part of the ad network. This happens unless the user's browser is set to reject cookies. In practice, once the cookie is placed and the data subject is browsing the web page where the ad has been served, he or she is put in a position to learn about the cookies and how to set the browser in order to control cookies. This is done by publishers and ad network providers. These controllers usually provide information in their general terms and conditions and/or privacy policies about third party cookies used for behavioural advertising. The information may include the basic uses/purposes of such cookies and how they can be avoided by setting the browser. However, this practice does not [satisfy] Article 5(3), particularly [as] amended

---

21 *ibid*, 8–12.

22 *ibid*, 12–19.

... which places emphasis on providing prior information and obtaining prior consent (prior to the starting of the processing).

Recital 66 of the amended ePrivacy Directive indicates that the user's consent may be expressed by using the appropriate settings of a browser or other application, 'where it is technically possible and effective, in accordance with ... Directive 95/46/EC.'".[23]

It gives three reasons for this, set out below:

"First, based on the definition and requirements for valid consent ex Article 2(h) of Directive 95/46/EC, generally speaking data subjects cannot be deemed to have consented simply because they acquired/used a browser or other application which by default enables the collection and processing of their information. Average data subjects are not aware of the tracking of their online behaviour, the purposes of the tracking, etc. They are not always aware of how to use browser settings to reject cookies, even if this is included in privacy policies. It is a fallacy to deem that on a general basis data subject inaction (he/she has not set the browser to refuse cookies) provides a clear and unambiguous indication of his/her wishes.[24]

Second, for browsers settings to be able to deliver informed consent, it should not be possible to 'bypass' the choice made by the user in setting the browser.[25]

Finally, consent by browser setting to receive cookies in bulk implies that users will accept future processing, possibly without any knowledge of the purposes or uses of the cookie. Consent in bulk for any future processing without knowing the circumstances surrounding the processing cannot be valid consent".[26]

It makes the following conclusion:

"Therefore, in order for browsers or any other application to be able to 'deliver' valid consent, they must overcome the above problems. Effectively, this means that:

(a) Browsers or other applications which by default reject 3rd party cookies and which require the data subject to engage in an affirmative action to accept both the setting of and continued transmission of information contained in cookies by specific web sites may be able to deliver valid and effective consent. By contrast, if the browser settings were predetermined to accept all cookies, such consent would not comply with Article 5(3) insofar as, in general, such consent cannot constitute a true indication of the data subject wishes. Such consent would neither be specific nor prior (to the processing). Whereas a given data subject could indeed have decided to keep the settings to accept all 3rd party cookies, it would not be realistic for ad network providers to assume that the vast majority of data subjects who have their browsers 'set' to accept cookies, effectively exercised this choice;

(b) Browsers, together or in combination with other information tools, including the cooperation of ad network providers and publishers, should convey clear, comprehensive and fully visible information in order to ensure that consent is fully informed. To meet the requirements of Directive 95/46/EC browsers should convey, on behalf of the ad network provider, the relevant information about the purposes of the cookies and the further processing".[27]

It states also:

"generic warnings without explicit references to the ad network which is placing the cookie are unsatisfactory.

The [EU] Article 29 Working Party is of the view that unless the above requirements are

---

23 *ibid*, 12–19.

24 *ibid*, 12–19.

25 *ibid*, 12–19.

26 *ibid*, 12–19.

27 *ibid*, 12–19.

met, providing information and, to some extent, facilitating the user's ability to reject cookies (by explaining how this can be done) cannot generally be deemed as informed consent ex Article 5(3) of the ePrivacy Directive and also in light of Article 2(h) of Directive 95/46/EC.

Given the importance that browser settings play in ensuring that data subjects effectively give their consent to the storage of cookies and the processing of their information, it seems of paramount importance for browsers to be provided with default privacy-protective settings. In other words, to be provided with the setting of 'non-acceptance and non-transmission of third party cookies.' To complement this and to make it more effective, the browsers should require users to go through a privacy wizard when they first install or update the browser and provide for an easy way of exercising choice during use."[28]

Opt-Outs

The Opinion also refers to consent and the exercise of opt-out options. It states:

"Ad network providers increasingly offer 'opt-out' mechanisms enabling users to opt-out from receiving targeted advertising. By relying on this mechanism, the data subject must go to the website of the ad network provider/s and indicate to the ad network provider/s that they wish to opt-out from being tracked for the purposes of being served targeted advertisements ...

Such cookie-based opt-out mechanisms are welcome ... However, such opt-out mechanisms do not in principle deliver data subjects' consent. .... First, ... users lack the basic understanding of the collection of any data, its uses, how the technology works and more importantly how and where to opt-out ... very few people exercise the opt-out option, not because they have made an informed decision to accept behavioural advertising, but rather because they do not realise that by not using the opt out, they are in fact accepting ....Second, consent means active participation of the data subject prior to the collection and processing of data. The opt-out mechanism often refers to a 'non' reaction of the data subject after such processing has already started ... This does not meet the requirements for legally effective consent."[29]

Opt-In

The Opinion states that prior opt-in consent mechanisms are better suited to achieve informed consent. It states:

"prior opt-in mechanisms, which require an affirmative data subject's action to indicate consent before the cookie is sent to the data subject, are more in line with Article 5(3) ... 'implicit consent does not always lead to unambiguous consent (as required by Article 7 (a) of the Directive) ....'

... [EU Article 29 Working Party] recommended the use of specific messages: 'In the case of cookies, the user should be informed when a cookie is intended to be received, stored or sent ... The message should specify, in generally understandable language, which information is intended to be stored in the cookie, for what purpose as well as the period of validity of the cookie.' After having received such information, the data subject should be offered the possibility to indicate whether he/she wants to be profiled for the purposes of behavioural advertising.

... in accordance with Recital 25 of the ePrivacy Directive ('the right to refuse (cookies) may be offered once for the use of various devices to be installed on the user's terminal equipment ... during subsequent connections'), users' acceptance of a cookie could be understood to be valid not only for the sending of the cookie but also for subsequent collection of data arising from such a cookie. In other words, the consent obtained to place

28 *ibid*, 12–19.

29 *ibid*, 12–19.

the cookie and use the information to send targeting advertising would cover subsequent 'readings' of the cookie that take place every time the user visits a website partner of the ad network provider which initially placed the cookie.

However, taking into account that i) this practice would mean that individuals accept to be monitored 'once forever,' and, ii) individuals might simply 'forget' that, for example, a year ago, they agreed to be monitored; [the EU Article 29 Working Party] considers that some safeguards should be implemented. In particular, [the EU Article 29 Working Party] proposes three courses of action".[30]

These are:

"First, to limit the scope of the consent in terms of time. Consent to be monitored should not be 'forever' but it should be valid for a limited period of time, for example, to one year. After this period, ad network providers would need to obtain a new consent. This could be achieved if cookies had a limited lifespan after they have been placed in the user's terminal equipment (and the expiry date should not be prolonged).

Second, the risks outlined above would be further mitigated with additional information practices, further addressed below under Section 4.2.1.

Third, freely given consent can always be revoked. Data subjects should be offered the possibility to easily revoke their consent to being monitored for the purposes of serving behavioural advertising. In this regard, the need to provide clear information about this possibility and how to exercise it is essential (see below under Section 4.2)".[31]

Children and Informed Consent

The Opinion refers to children and obtaining informed consent to collect and process children's personal data. It states:

"Opinion 2/2009 [of EU Article 29 Working Party] addressed the protection of personal data of children .... The problems related to obtaining informed consent are further emphasized as far as children are concerned. In addition to the requirements described above (and below) for consent to be valid, in some cases children's consent must be provided by their parents or other legal representatives. In the case in point this means that ad network providers would need to provide notice to parents about the collection and the use of children's information and obtain their consent before collecting and further using their information for the purposes of engaging in behavioural targeting of children ....ad network providers should not offer interest categories intended to serve behavioural advertising or influence children."[32]

Information and Targeted Behavioural Advertising

The Opinion refers to the obligation to provide users with information in relation to the context of targeted behavioural advertising. It states:

"Transparency is a key condition for individuals to be able to consent to the collection and further processing of their data ... users may not know or understand the technology that supports behavioural advertising or even that such types of advertising are being targeted at them. It is therefore of paramount importance to ensure that sufficient and effective information is provided in a way that will reach internet users. Only if data subjects are informed, will they be in a position to exercise their choices.

30 *ibid*, 12–19.

31 *ibid*, 12–19.

32 *ibid*, 12–19.

4.2.1 Which information must be provided and by whom?
Article 5(3) states that the user must be provided with information, 'in accordance with Directive 95/46/EC, *inter alia* about the purposes of the processing.' Article 10 of [Data Protection Directive 1995] deals with the provision of this information.

... data subjects should informed, *inter alia*, about the identity of the advertising network provider and the purposes of the processing. The data subject should be clearly informed that the cookie will allow the advertising provider to collect information about visits to other websites, the advertisements they have been shown, which ones they have clicked on, timing etc.

... Recital 25 of the ePrivacy Directive requires notices to be provided in a 'clear and comprehensive' manner. Statements such as 'advertisers and other third parties may also use their own cookies or action tags' are clearly not sufficient.

... Recital 25 requires [this information] to be 'as user friendly as possible.' ... providing a minimum of information directly on the screen, interactively, easily visible and understandable, would be the most effective way to comply with this principle. It is important for information to be easily accessible and highly visible. This essential information may not be hidden in general terms and conditions and/or privacy statements.

... it essential for ad network providers to find ways to inform individuals periodically that the monitoring is taking place. Unless data subjects are given clear and unambiguous reminders, by easy means, of the monitoring, it is quite likely that after a certain period of time, they may no longer be aware that it is still taking place and that they consented to it."[33]

Information Provider

The Opinion also refers to who should provide the information:

"should it be provided by the publisher or by the ad network provider or both? The outcome should be that data subjects receive easily accessible and highly visible information ... the cooperation of both ad network providers and publishers seem essential.

... the obligation to provide the necessary information and obtain data subjects' consent ultimately lies with the entity that sends and reads the cookie. In most cases, this is the ad network provider. When publishers are joint-controllers, for example in those cases where they transfer directly identifiable information to ad network providers, they are also bound by the obligation to provide information to data subjects about the data processing.

In addition, ... publishers share with ad network providers certain responsibility for the data processing that happens in the context of serving behavioural advertising ... this responsibility covers the first stage of the processing, ie the transfer of the IP address to ad network providers that takes place when individuals visit their web sites and are re-directed to the ad network provider web site.

... publishers have certain obligations vis-à-vis data subjects that stem mainly from the [Data Protection Directive 1995] ... publishers are bound by the obligation to provide information to data subjects about the data processing that takes place as a result of the re-directing of their browser and also about the purposes for which the information will be used later on by ad network providers. The information should refer not only to the transfer of IP address for the purposes of displaying acts but also to further data processing carried out by the ad network providers, including the setting up of cookies."[34]

Special Categories of Data

The Opinion continues in relation to other data protection obligations under the EU Data Protection Directive 1995. It states:

---

[33] *ibid*, 12–19.
[34] *ibid*, 12–19.

> "In addition to Article 5(3), data controllers must ensure compliance with all the obligations that arise from [Data Protection Directive 1995] that do not overlap with Article 5(3) among others, they must ensure:
>
> 5.1. Obligations regarding special categories of data
> Data revealing racial or ethnic origin, political opinions, religious or philosophical beliefs, trade-union membership or data concerning health or sex life is considered sensitive ex Article 8 of [Data Protection Directive 1995]. [There are] serious risks to infringe the personal data of individuals if this type of information is used for the purposes of serving behavioural advertising. Any possible targeting of data subjects based on sensitive information opens the possibility of [online] abuse. Furthermore, given the sensitivity of such information and the possible awkward situations which may arise if individuals receive advertising that reveals, for example, sexual preferences or political activity, offering/using interest categories that would reveal sensitive data should be discouraged.
>
> However, if nevertheless, ad network providers offer and use interest categories that reveal sensitive information, they must comply with Article 8 of [Data Protection Directive 1995]. For example, if an ad network provider processes individual behaviour in order to 'place him/her' in an interest category indicating a particular sexual preference they would be processing sensitive data under Article 8 of [Data Protection Directive 1995]. This Article prohibits the processing of sensitive data except in certain, specific circumstances. In this context, the only available legal ground that would legitimize the data processing would be explicit, separate prior opt-in consent ex Article 8(2)(a). The requirement for a separate, affirmative prior indication of the data subjects' agreement means that in no case would an opt-out consent mechanism meet the requirement of the law. It also means that such consent could not be obtained through browser settings. To lawfully collect and process this type of information, ad network providers would have to set up mechanisms to obtain explicit prior consent, separate from other consent obtained for processing in general."[35]

Data Quality

It also refers to data quality, ie how the personal data must be secured and maintained. It states:

> "5.2 Compliance with the principles relating to data quality
> Article 6 of [Data Protection Directive 1995] sets forth various principles which must be respected by the data controller. In this context, the following are particularly relevant:
>
> > ... profiles collected and used for behavioural advertising could potentially be used for purposes other than advertising ... [eg] the development of new services whose nature is as yet undecided.
>
> However, the above is conditioned to the compliance of Article 6(1)(b) setting forth the *purpose limitation principle*. This principle prohibits the processing of personal data which is not compatible with the purposes that legitimised the initial collection. In other words, incompatible secondary uses of the information collected and stored for behavioural advertising would contradict Art 6(b) of [Data Protection Directive 1995]. For example, if ad networks form part of a group of companies that provide multiple services, in principle the ad network can not use the data collected for behavioural advertising for such other services (unless it can be demonstrated that the purposes are compatible). For the same reasons, ad networks can not enrich the information gathered for the purposes of behavioural advertisement with other information.
>
> If ad network providers want to use information gathered for behavioural advertisement for secondary, incompatible purposes, for example across services, they need additional legal grounds to do so ex Article 7 of [Data Protection Directive 1995]. Hence, they will need to inform data subjects and, in most cases, obtain their consent ex Article 7(a).
>
> Article 6(1)(e) requires data to be deleted when it is no longer necessary for the purpose for which the data were collected (retention principle). Compliance with this principle

[35] *ibid*, 19–21.

requires limiting the storage of information. Accordingly, companies must specify and respect express timeframes under which data will be retained.

... information about users' behaviour has to be eliminated if it is no longer needed for the development of a profile. Indefinite or overly long retention periods contradict Article 6(1)(e) of the Directive ...If/when an individual ask for a deletion of his/her profile or if he/she exercises his/her right to withdraw the consent, these actions require the ad network provider to erase or delete promptly the data subject's information insofar as the ad network provider ceases to have the necessary legal grounds (ie the consent) allowing the processing".[36]

It also refers to individual data subjects' rights. It states:

"Data controllers should enable individuals concerned by the processing to exercise their rights of access, rectification, erasure and to object as laid out in Articles 12 and 14 of [Data Protection Directive 1995]".[37]

Security

The Opinion also refers to other obligations such as security. It states:

"Article 17 of the Directive imposes the obligation upon data controllers and processors to apply technical and organisational measures to protect personal data against accidental or unlawful destruction loss, disclosure, and other forms of unlawful processing. Compliance with the security obligations will require ad network providers to implement state of the art technical and organisational measures to ensure the security and confidentiality of the information.

Pursuant to Article 18 of [Data Protection Directive 1995], data controllers may have to *notify the processing* of personal data to data protection authorities, unless they are exempt. Accordingly, if applicable under national law, ad network provides must notify the data processing. In addition, if the data is transferred outside the EU, for example, to servers located in third countries, ad network providers must ensure compliance with the provisions on transfers of personal data to third countries (Art 25 and 26 [Data Protection Directive 1995])".[38]

Recommendations

The Opinion makes the following recommendations in relation to applicable laws:

"• The EU legal framework for the use of cookies is primarily laid down in Article 5(3) of the ePrivacy Directive.

- Article 5(3) applies whenever 'information' such as a cookie is stored or retrieved from the terminal equipment of an internet user. It is not a prerequisite that this information is personal data.
- In addition, [Data Protection Directive 1995] applies to matters not specifically covered by the ePrivacy Directive whenever personal data are processed. Behavioural advertising is based on the use of identifiers that enable the creation of very detailed user's profiles which, in most cases, will be deemed personal data.

...

Roles and responsibilities

---

36 *ibid*, 19–21 (original emphasis).

37 *ibid*, 19–21.

38 *ibid*, 19–21 (original emphasis).

- Ad network providers are bound by the obligations of Article 5(3) of the ePrivacy Directive insofar as they place cookies and/or retrieve information from cookies already stored in the data subjects' terminal equipment. They are also data controllers insofar as they determine the purposes and the essential means of the processing of data.
- Publishers have certain data controller related responsibilities regarding the processing that takes place in the first phase of the processing, ie, when by virtue of the way they set up their web sites they trigger the transfer of the IP address to ad network providers (which enable the further processing). Such responsibility entails some, limited data protection obligations (see below). In addition, when/if publishers transfer directly identifiable personal data to ad network providers themselves, they will be deemed joint controllers".[39]

It refers to obligations and rights and recommends as follows:

"Regarding ad network providers:

- Article 5(3) of the ePrivacy Directive which sets up an obligation to obtain prior informed consent applies to ad network providers;
- Browser settings may only deliver consent in very limited circumstances. Notably, if browsers are set up by default to reject all cookies (having the browser set to such an option) and the user has changed the settings to affirmatively accept cookies, for which he has been fully informed about the name of the data controller, the processing its goals and the data that is collected. Therefore, the browser must either alone or in combination with other means effectively convey clear, comprehensive and fully visible information about the processing;
- Ad network providers should encourage and work with browser manufacturers/developers to implement privacy by design in browsers;
- Cookie-based opt-out mechanisms in general do not constitute an adequate mechanism to obtain informed user consent. In most cases user's consent is implied if they do not opt out. However, in practice, very few people exercise the opt-out option, not because they have made an informed decision to accept behavioural advertising, but rather because they do not realise that the processing is taking place, much less how to exercise the opt out;
- Ad network providers should swiftly move away from opt-out mechanisms and create prior opt-in mechanisms. Mechanisms to deliver informed, valid consent should require an affirmative action by the data subject indicating his/her willingness to receive cookies and the subsequent monitoring of their surfing behaviour for the purposes of sending him tailored advertising;
- In accordance with Recital 25 of the ePrivacy Directive, a users' acceptance to receive a cookie could also entail his/her acceptance for the subsequent readings of the cookie, and hence for the monitoring of his/her internet browsing. It would not be necessary to request consent for each reading of the cookie. However, to ensure that data subjects remain aware of the monitoring over time, ad network providers should: i) limit in time the scope of the consent; ii) offer the possibility to easily revoke their consent to being monitored for the purposes of serving behavioural advertising and iii) create a symbol or other tools which should be visible in all the web sites where the monitoring takes place (the website partners of the ad network provider). This symbol would not only remind individuals of the monitoring but also help them to control whether they want to continue being monitored or wish to revoke their consent;
- Network providers should ensure compliance with the obligations that arise from [Data Protection Directive 1995] which do not directly overlap with Article 5(3), namely, the purpose limitation principle, and security obligations;
- In addition, the ad network providers should enable individuals to exercise their rights of access and rectification and erasure. [The EU Article 29 Working Party] welcomes the practice of some ad network providers to offer data subjects the possibility to access and modify the interest categories in which they have been classified;
- Ad network providers should implement retention policies which ensure that information collected each time that a cookie is read is automatically deleted after a justified period of time (necessary for the purposes of the processing). This also

[39] *ibid*, 22–24.

applies for alternative tracking technologies used for behavioural advertising such as JavaScript installed in the user's browser environment".[40]

In relation to ad network providers and publishers it makes a number of recommendations:

- "Providing highly visible information is a precondition for consent to be valid. Mentioning the practice of behavioural advertising in general terms and conditions and/or privacy policies can never suffice. In this regard and taking into account the average low level of knowledge about the practice of behavioural advertising, efforts should be applied to change this situation;
- Ad network providers/publishers must provide information to users in compliance with Article 10 of [Data Protection Directive 1995]. In practical terms, they should ensure that individuals are told, at a minimum, who (ie which entity) is responsible for serving the cookie and collecting the related information. In addition, they should be informed in simple ways that (a) the cookie will be used to create profiles; (b) what type of information will be collected to build such profiles; (c) the fact that the profiles will be used to deliver targeted advertising and (d) the fact that the cookie will enable the user's identification across multiple web sites;
- Network providers/publishers should provide the information directly on the screen, interactively, if needed, through layered notices. In any event it should be easily accessible and highly visible;
- Icons placed on the publisher's website, around advertising, with links to additional information, are good examples. The [EU] Article 29 Working Party urges the network providers/ publisher industry to be creative in this area".[41]

Cookies and Data Protection Commissioner

The Irish Data Protection Commissioner's website states the following in relation to cookies and consent on websites:

> "where it is technically possible and effective, such consent could be given by the use of appropriate browser settings, as long as reliance is not placed on the default settings. In order to meet the legal requirements, such settings would require, as a minimum, clear communication to the user as to what he/she is being asked to consent to and a means of giving or refusing consent to any information being stored or retrieved. It is particularly important that the requirements are met where so called 'third party' or 'tracking' cookies are involved – such as when advertising networks collect information about websites visited by users in order to better target advertising.
>
> For non-third party cookie usage in the Irish market we would be satisfied with a prominent notice giving information on cookie use on the homepage with an ability to click through to make informed choices.
>
> If a website is localised to other markets in the EU, a 'pop-up screen' asking the user to provide consent can be used to ensure compliance. However, there are other ways to obtain consent, such as the following,
>
> - A static information banner on top of a website requesting the user's consent to set some cookies, with a hyperlink to a privacy statement with a more detailed explanation about the different controllers and the purposes of the processing (eg www.ico.gov.uk);
> - A splash screen on entering the website explaining what cookies will be set by what parties if the user consents;
> - A default setting prohibiting the transfer of data to external parties, requiring a user to click to indicate consent for tracking purposes;

[40] *ibid*, 22–24.
[41] *ibid*, 22–24.

- A default setting in browsers that would prevent the collection of behavioural data

Information that is necessary to facilitate the transmission of a communication, or information that is strictly necessary to provide an information society service explicitly requested by the user, is not subject to this requirement. If a cookie is strictly necessary to facilitate a transaction requested by the user – for example, storage of items in a shopping cart on an online website – advance consent will not be required. This will generally be the case where the cookie is stored only for as long as the 'session' is live and will be deleted at the end of the session. Information on such use should be readily available to the user of a website."[42]

Conclusion

The various opinions coming from the EU Article 29 Working Party are important in and of themselves. They provide guidance to national data protection authority regulators as well as commercial organisations on how they should interpret and operate in compliance with the data protection regime. However, the data protection regime and the internet are evolving. While many areas are left unaddressed in the EU Data Protection Directive 1995, including social networks, children, etc, the opinion guides from the EU Article 29 Working Party act as helpful interim measures (albeit not of a formal legal nature). Finally, they may also serve to assist the EU Commission in developing the next generation of data protection law in the EU and other countries, in particular the proposed new Regulation. Indeed, from an Irish and UK perspective, it may be that the various pieces of guidance from the EU Article 29 Working Party assist the Irish Data Protection Commissioner, ICO and others in dealing with important internet issues.

42 "My Website Uses Cookies, What Do I Need to Consider?" in *Topical Data Protection Issues*, Irish Data Protection Commissioner, available at http://www.dataprotection.ie/docs/Topical_Data_Protection_Issues/1241.htm.

Chapter 10

BEACON SETTLEMENT

Cáit Brennan

Headline of Issues

- Beacon
- Beacon settlement
- Social networking data
- Advertising
- Opt-in/opt-out
- Breach
- Fines
- Future issues and roles

Social Networking Sites – A Spaghetti Junction with Nowhere to Hide?

Social networking sites are a fantastic tool for community-building and social change, but simultaneously a minefield of privacy issues.[1] With so much information about people readily available online today, it is vital that correct legislation is in place to protect an individual's personal data. Privacy policies are usually defined when signing up to social networking and other websites, though more often than not they are ticked as read and understood without the users' having read them at all, in their enthusiasm to join up. However, these privacy policies define how the site is allowed to use members' data. The use of this data may not always be in line with data protection legislation. As online social networks are rapidly evolving, it is important to ensure that personal data are protected, and that use of this data by the site is clearly explained to the members. This is not always the case.

This chapter reviews the class-action case taken in the US against Facebook in relation to the use of the marketing tool known as Beacon and whether the penalty imposed was a penalty at all. The enforcement of penalties on social networking companies for breaches of data protection is discussed. The ongoing issues of privacy on social networks are discussed, in particular the issue of consent, which seems to be largely ignored by social networking companies. Looking to the future, the new career area of privacy professionals arising from the need for companies to address their data protection issues seems to be the only hope of grasping back some form of adherence to regulations. This, together with widespread enforcement of the law by Data Protection Commissioners and legislators worldwide may eventually make social networking websites a safer place.

---

[1] M Shiels, "Facebook Violates Privacy Laws," BBC, 31 May 2008, available at http://news.bbc.co.uk/go/pr/fr/-/2/hi/technology/7428833.stm.

What is Facebook (If You Are Not One of the Billion Members Who Already Know) and What is Beacon?

Facebook is an online social networking website set up in the US in 2004 where people who sign up can upload personal information on an individual profile and share information with other members.[2] In June 2010 Facebook had 500 million users, becoming the second most visited site in the world after Google and debates on privacy issues were already ongoing.[3] As of October 2012, Facebook had 1 billion monthly active users, 81 percent of whom are outside the US and Canada.[4]

In November 2007, Facebook introduced Beacon. Beacon was a partnership with 44 websites. Users logged onto Facebook automatically had a notification posted regarding their activities on these websites. For example, if members purchased a video from a website that was one of the 44 connected websites through Beacon, their Facebook profiles would be updated with details of what they had purchased on the connected website.[5] The concept of the program was akin to a beacon of light that would shine on the members' activities, thus highlighting to their friends what websites they were visiting and purchasing goods from. This would be an endorsement form of advertising, where friends would see the website being used by another member and therefore be encouraged to purchase goods from that website. It was a bit like word of mouth, except online (and everyone in the user's social circle heard about it immediately). The creator of Facebook, Mark Zuckerberg, said that the goal of Beacon was to build a simple product to let people share information across websites with friends.[6] He did not mention the more obvious intention, to introduce more advertising to the website and thereby more income. Facebook was arguably sailing perilously close to the limits of digital decency.[7]

Opting in? Don't Bother – Facebook Did it for You

Beacon did not require Facebook members to opt in. Users were automatically deemed as opted into the service unless they specifically opted out. Furthermore, the opt-out option appeared only in the lower right-hand corner of the screen of the connected website for about 10 seconds, and then automatically disappeared.[8] So user consent was the default setting.[9] Users had to remove their default consent from every Beacon-partnered website, and notification of new companies joining Beacon

---

2 *Lane v Facebook* 2012 WL 4125857 (CA9 (Cal)), 6.

3 M Lebert, *Booknology: The eBook* (1971–2010) 29 http://www.gutenberg.org/catalog/world/readfile?fk_files=1942909&pageno=29.

4 newsroom.fb.com/content/default.aspx?NewsAreaId=22.

5 K Kane, "Balancing Anonymity, Popularity, & Micro-celebrity: the Crossroads of Social Networking and Privacy" (2012) (20(2)) *Albany Law Journal of Science & Technology* 327, 336.

6 A Klaassen, "Why Lying, Not Beacon, Was Facebook's Biggest Blunder" (2007) (78(49)) *Advertising Age* 20.

7 M Cole, "Social Aspects of Social Networking" (2009) (29) *International Journal of Information Management* 248.

8 Kane, *op. cit*, 337

9 A Morgenstern, "In the Spotlight: Social Network Advertising and the Right of Publicity" (2007–8) (12) *Intellectual Property Law Bulletin* 181, 184.

was not passed on to Facebook users.[10] Many users felt that Beacon fundamentally violated their privacy and disliked the lack of clear consent.[11] Many users purchased gifts and had the surprise element ruined by public notification of their purchases.[12] One participating company, Overstock.com, decided to stop running the program until it became an "opt-in" option for users.[13] On 11 November 2007, Facebook changed the program to opt-in and on 5 December 2007 a permanent opt-out option was provided for users. [14] The Beacon program was discontinued by Facebook shortly after.[15]

Opting out – Facebook Opted out of Beacon and Ended up in Court

A group of 19 plaintiffs filed a class action against Facebook claiming that Facebook had violated members' privacy rights by gathering and sharing information about their online activities without consent.[16] Facebook agreed as part of the settlement to pay $9.5 million.[17] Approximately $6.5 million was to be used to set up a charity organisation that would fund and sponsor programmes to educate users regarding online privacy issues.[18] The remainder was to cover legal fees.[19]

Facebook identified 3,663,651 class members following a district court order.[20] Facebook then had to inform all class members of the settlement and give them adequate time to consider, in case they wanted to opt out or object. Facebook emailed class members and posted a notice of the settlement in the "Updates" section of relevant accounts.[21] A notice was also published in the US newspaper US Today.[22] 108 class members opted out and four filed objections.[23]

The settlement was appealed, but the original decision was upheld. Two judges (Judge Proctor Hug and Judge William Fletcher) agreed to the settlement. One dissenting judge (Judge Kleinfield) maintained that the settlement twisted the class action into a device that deprived victims of solutions to wrong-doings, while benefiting both those responsible for the wrongdoing and the lawyers who are supposed to represent the class.[24] However, the settlement was agreed as being fair, reasonable and adequate. [25] The two assenting judges perceived as unremarkable that Facebook retained active control over how the $6.5 million funds are used to ensure

---

10 *ibid.*
11 *ibid.*
12 *ibid.*
13 Hashemi, *op. cit*, 146.
14 *ibid.*
15 *Lane v Facebook* 2012 WL 4125857 (CA9 (Cal)), 7.
16 *ibid.*
17 *ibid.*
18 *ibid*, 3.
19 *ibid*, 7.
20 *ibid.*
21 *ibid*, 8.
22 *ibid.*
23 *ibid.*
24 D Kravets, "Facebook's $9.5 Million 'Beacon' Settlement Approved," http://www.wired.com/threatlevel/2012/09/beacon-settlement-approved/.
25 *ibid.*

that Facebook is not harmed as a result.[26] A month earlier in San Francisco, Judge Richard Seeborg disallowed a similar settlement related to Facebook's "Sponsored Stories" program, as he was concerned that the terms of the settlement were picked out of the air.[27] The deal included payment of $10 million to attorneys and donation of $10 million to charity. Interestingly, Judge Seeborg was the same district judge who approved the Beacon settlement.[28]

Who Are the Class Members Anyway?

The definition of class members changed during the course of the settlement, according to Judge Kleinfield, who filed a lengthy dissenting opinion.[29] The complaint challenged only the opt-out programme that was in place for the first few weeks after the launch of Beacon. It did not include the opt-in option, which Facebook then switched to after receiving many complaints. However, in the settlement, the class was not certified, which left Facebook free, when ordered later to define the class, to classify members and include all those affected during the entire life of the Beacon program on Facebook.[30] This incorporated approximately 3.6 million people and could be perceived as a clever device to deny as many people as possible the opportunity to litigate against Facebook or any Beacon-partnered companies with regard to Beacon.[31] Possible collusion of attorneys is also suggested. Kleinfield maintained that collusion is far more likely before certification, and much more likely if the class is expanded as part of the settlement.[32] The case report continues to describe a "clear sailing" agreement on attorneys' fees, in other words, an agreement to not oppose huge legal fees, where the defendants' pay-out is the same regardless of legal fees, inducing the plaintiffs' counsel to concede.[33]

The final court endorsement of the $20m settlement was approved by US District Judge Richard Seeborg. The settlement is reported as requiring Facebook to make modifications to enable greater user control in relation to their personal data.[34]

Charity Begins at Home

$6.5 million of funds from the Beacon settlement was directed to set up a trust fund which would allocate grants to organisations researching online privacy in a bid to improve protection of website users' data.[35] The charity's board of directors consisted of three members, one of whom was Facebook's director of public policy.[36] Privacy groups argued that a Facebook director should not be on the board of the

26 *ibid.*
27 *ibid.*
28 *ibid.*
29 *Lane v Facebook* 2012 WL 4125857 (CA9 (Cal)), 18.
30 *ibid.*
31 *ibid.*
32 *ibid*, 16.
33 *ibid*, 17.
34 See T Peters, "Facebook Ordered to Pay $20m for Using Member 'Likes' as Endorsements for Adverts" *Irish Times* 28 August 2013.
35 *ibid.*
36 *ibid.*

trust fund, and were also dissatisfied that the plaintiffs received no compensation for the breach of their privacy as a result of the Beacon program.[37] The judges who upheld the appeal agreed that the settlement was fair, reasonable and adequate by way of *cy pres* remedy and that defendants often insist on concessions in exchange for monetary payments and can be expected to structure the settlement in a way that least harms their interests.[38] Kleinfield, the senior circuit judge, disagreed and commented that there was nothing to stop Facebook and class counsel from running the charity in such a manner as to serve their own interests and use the funds to pay whomsoever they chose.[39] So funds supposedly to be used to protect the plaintiffs were actually being directed and controlled by the defendant. It is reasonable to assume that the defendant will first and foremost act in its own best interest (in line with company policy) rather than in the interest of the class members.

Other Facebook Investigations

In 2010 the Wall Street Journal investigated Facebook and found that the top 10 applications used on Facebook, including Farmville, Mafia Wars and Texas Hold'em, gave information identifying users (UIDs) to advertising and internet-tracking companies.[40] Facebook accused the press of exaggerating the incident and said the information given out was unintentional.[41] Facebook's policies state that developers cannot share user information to advertising companies or data brokers, and that private user data cannot be accessed without explicit user consent.[42] So this sharing of data was apparently in breach of Facebook's own policy, even for users with the most secure settings. In view of this, it is not just Beacon that has caused privacy issues.

Do You Consent? The European Perspective

The EU Data Protective Directive 1995 defines the data subject's consent as any freely given specific and informed indication of his or her wishes by which the data subject signifies his or her agreement to personal data relating to him being processed.[43] Section II Article 7 of this Directive defines the criteria for making data processing legitimate. The first requirement on the list is that data can be processed only if the data subject has unambiguously given his or her consent.[44] The opt-out option given by Facebook in the US in relation to Beacon-partnered websites could not really be defined as unambiguous.

On 6 March 2012, The District Court of Berlin in Germany ruled against Facebook

---

37 "Facebook Forced into Privacy Business" (2010) *March Computer Fraud and Security* 1, 2.
38 *Lane v Facebook* 2012 WL 4125857 (CA9 (Cal)), 10.
39 *ibid*, 18.
40 "Facebook Admits 'Inadvertent' Privacy Breach," 18 October 2010, *Daily Telegraph* http://www.telegraph.co.uk/technology/facebook/8070513/Facebook-admits-inadvertent-privacy-breach.html.
41 *ibid.*
42 *ibid.*
43 Directive 95/46/EC [1995] OJ L281/31, Article 2(h).
44 Directive 95/46/EC, Article 7(1).

in relation to data protection issues arising in relation to its "Find friends" function, its terms and conditions and its privacy policy.[45] Restrictions were imposed on Facebook for users in Germany, prohibiting Facebook from unlawfully contacting or marketing to consumers who have not previously given consent to use of their email addresses.[46] In the "Find friends" program, Facebook sent an email to everyone in a member's email contact list asking them to join Facebook via their association with the current member. This resulted in people receiving emails asking them to join Facebook, even if they had never heard of it. It amounted to Facebook sending advertisements to people who had not consented to their email addresses being used. It was proposed that Facebook violated the German Protection against Unfair Competition Act and the German Federal Data Protection Act.[47] Under this court ruling, Facebook can no longer use the "Find friends" function in Germany. A list of restrictions to the Facebook terms and conditions allowed were also put in place. This includes a ban on Facebook using any intellectual property content (eg photographs) posted by German users, using names and profile pictures to connect with commercial or sponsored content, and certain methods of notification of changes to Facebook's terms and conditions.[48] A fine was also imposed.[49] It is clear from this ruling that Facebook was not acting in line with German data protection law and, in particular, was not obtaining user consent prior to using a person's email address for advertising purposes.

The Irish Data Protection Commissioner received a record number of complaints in 2011, the increase largely due to people concerned about the security of their personal data.[50] During the audit of Facebook carried out by the Data Protection Commissioner, Facebook clearly stated that it does not share user information with advertisers without user permission. Facebook's Data Use Policy provides: "We do not share any of your information with advertisers (unless, of course, you give us permission)."[51] This is apparently at odds with Facebook's use of Beacon in the US, where Facebook assumed consent and shared information unless the user happened to spot the small opt-out box while it was on display for all of 10 seconds. This information allowed Beacon-partnered companies to advertise their names and products via the user's news feed while no prior consent was given by Facebook users.

Is Consent Still Required if the Person's Details Are Fake?

In August 2012, Facebook admitted to having 83 million fake users on its social networking website.[52] Facebook shared this information with the US Securities and

45 *Federal Association of Consumer Organizations and Consumer Groups v Facebook Ireland Limited* 2012 16 O 551 /10.

46 *ibid.*

47 *ibid.*

48 *ibid.*

49 *ibid.*

50 E Edwards, "Data Protection Commissioner Sees 48 per cent Surge in Number of Complaints," *Irish Times*, 1 May 2012, online edition.

51 Facebook Ireland Ltd. Data Protection Commissioner's Audit Report December 2011, 55.

52 "Facebook Admits It Has More Than 83 Million 'Fake' Users" (2012) *Digital Journal* http://digitaljournal.com/article/329944.

Exchange Commission (SEC).[53] Given that 8.7 percent of Facebook users have fake accounts, surely consent from these fake users is invalid? This is irrelevant as 91.3 percent of users have valid accounts, and it is Facebook's responsibility to ensure adequate privacy to all users. It does raise the question, though, of the validity of consent from a fake account.

Facebook – Criticised in Canada

Facebook also received complaints in 2008 from a privacy group in Canada, claiming that it was in breach of the Canadian Personal Information Protection and Electronic Documents Act (Pipeda).[54] The Canadian Internet Policy and Public Interest Clinic filed a complaint with the Canadian Privacy Commissioner claiming 22 breaches of privacy law.[55] The complaint relates to information being collected and shared by Facebook without users' consent.[56] Users are not informed of how their information is being used, and data are not deleted after accounts are closed.[57] A large number of Canadian users are aged between 14 and 25.[58] Many do not properly understand website privacy settings nor of the consequences of their personal data being shared.[59] If a survey of Facebook members was carried out, it would be interesting to see what percentage of users understand their privacy settings, regardless of age.

China's Data Protection Regulations

The stated objective of the Chinese Computer Information Network and Internet Security, Protection and Management Regulations[60] is to enhance the security and protection of computer information networks and the internet in China.[61] Article 7 of the Regulations forbids individuals or organisations from using the internet to violate the freedom and privacy of network users.[62] Examples of such violation activities include the use of web-based technologies to spy on internet users and the unauthorised collection of confidential data belonging to an internet user, for example data that can be used to find out the internet user's identity, address, telephone number, billing, payment information and other services accessed by the user on the internet.[63]

Facebook has been banned in China since 2009.[64] China has its own social networking website called Wei-bo, which is a mixture of Twitter and Facebook.[65] If

---

53 *ibid.*

54 M Shiels, "Facebook Violates Privacy Laws," BBC, 31 May 2008, available at http://news.bbc.co.uk/go/pr/fr/-/2/hi/technology/7428833.stm.

55 *ibid.*

56 *ibid.*

57 *ibid.*

58 *ibid.*

59 *ibid.*

60 U Jerome Orji, "An Analysis of China's Regulatory Response to Cybersecurity," (2012) 1, 4.

61 *ibid.*

62 *ibid.*

63 *ibid.*

64 J Hempel, "Facebook's China Problem" (2012) (66(5)) *Fortune* 103.

65 *ibid.*

Facebook ever does get into the Chinese market, it would have to abide by China's strict regulations.

Sensitive Personal Data – How Can Facebook Tell?

What is interesting to consider further in relation to the EU Directive is the issue of processing sensitive personal data. According to the EU Data Protection Directive 1995, personal data revealing racial or ethnic origin, political opinions, religious or philosophical beliefs, trade union membership, and the processing of data concerning health or sex life is classified as sensitive personal data.[66] Beacon had no screening process in place to check whether the data being shared could have been classified as sensitive personal data. For example, if a Facebook user's online purchase of a book on homosexual health issues was broadcast to all the user's friends via Beacon, this information could be seen as data concerning health or sex life. The Directive requires that for this type of data, the data subject must have given his or her explicit consent. However, under Beacon, there was no control over whether the data processed fell under the category of sensitive personal data.

So What Are New Members Signing up to?

Facebook is a public space, much like a public road.[67] In November 2012, Facebook launched a revamped sign-up process for new users, which deals with privacy concerns including default settings; sharing permissions; policies on data access; rules about applications, games, third-party websites, advertisements and photograph tags; and how Facebook finds friends and connections.[68] This follows recommendations made during the audit of Facebook by the Irish Data Protection Commissioner. While Facebook is gearing up processes to improve privacy for users, one wonders if changes could be made earlier. It already has over a billion users already signed up using the original privacy settings.[69] These users have already agreed to the original privacy policy and will have to look this up all over again.

Other companies are also upgrading their privacy tools. Google Chrome's upgrade to version 23 includes the long-awaited easily accessed "Do not track" tool.[70] A new drop-down menu on the page icon tells the user how many cookies a page has set and how many are blocked by Chrome (if any).[71] In addition, there is a link to delete cookies and, most importantly, block any domains users do not want tracking them.[72] Interestingly, the tool is disabled by default.[73] Similar to Facebook's original

66 Directive 95/46/EC [1995] OJ L281/31, Article 8.

67 D Kelleher, "Social Networking, Privacy and the Future of News" (2011) (1) *The Irish Jurist* 191.

68 H Tsukayama, "Facebook Release Privacy Guide for New Users," *Washington Post*, 2 November 2012, http://www.washingtonpost.com/business/technology/Facebook-rele…sers/2012/11/02/de6cecd8-2522-11e2-9313-3c7f59038d93_print.html.

69 *ibid.*

70 S Gilbertson, "Google Chrome Adds 'Do Not Track' Privacy Tools" http://www.webmonkey.com/2012/11/chrome-23-skidoos-out-of-beta/.

71 *ibid.*

72 *ibid.*

73 *ibid.*

privacy default settings, which resulted in easily accessible accounts, the path of least protection seems to be the common denominator adopted by these companies currently.

Time to Fine – Who's First?

This lack of proactiveness on the part of social networking companies is getting them in trouble, though. More organisations are being found guilty, and fined, over breaches in relation to personal data. In the UK, public-sector organisations were fined over £2 million in 18 months as a result of poor handling of personal data.[74] In addition, Stoke-on-Trent city council was recently fined £120,000 for a second offence involving data on a child custody case where data were emailed over an unencrypted, insecure network to the wrong person.[75] Given that this council had previously been fined over data protection non-compliances, this shows a culture where compliance to data protection laws is non-existent, and staff are dangerously unaware of their responsibilities in this area. It seems the private sector is equally at fault. Recently in the UK, the Information Commissioner's Office (ICO) fined pensions and insurance company Prudential £50,000 for incorrect handling of personal data and failure to keep data records up to date and accurate.[76] Records of two customers with the same name, surname and date of birth were mixed up, resulting in retirement funds being placed in the wrong person's account.[77] It took three years to resolve the situation despite Prudential's being alerted to the issue numerous times.[78] The head of enforcement at the ICO said this case should serve as a warning that data records must be kept accurate and up to date in order to comply with legislation.[79] This demonstrates that the ICO is enforcing other aspects of non-compliance, not just data loss. It also demonstrates again the lack of awareness of data protection at staff level in organisations. There is frequently an ignorance of the seriousness of the issues at hand. Training programmes on how to comply with data protection legislation are urgently needed in many organisations.

On 8 August 2012 the District Court for the Northern District of California in the US fined Google $22.5 million as a result of action brought by the Federal Trade Commission (FTC).[80] The FTC claimed that Google got around Apple's Safari internet browser to enable tracking of user activity via third-party cookies.[81] This is the largest fine imposed as a result of FTC action.[82] On 16 November 2012, a federal judge in San Francisco approved the fine.[83] Google has agreed to remove

74 "UK Public Sector Tops £2M in Data Handling Fines," http://www.infosecurity-magazine.com/view/29157/uk-public-sector-tops-2m-in-data-handling-fines.

75 *ibid.*

76 D Worth, "ICO Fines Prudential £50,000 for Database Mix Up", http://www.v3.co.uk/print_article/v3-uk/news/2222690/ico-fines-prudential-gdp50-000-for-database-mix-up.

77 *ibid.*

78 *ibid.*

79 *ibid.*

80 CM Assam, "United States: Privacy - Google Agrees to Pay USD 22.5m Penalty, Largest FTC Fine for Violation of an Order" (2012) (7(8)) *World Communications Regulation Report* 20.

81 *ibid.*

82 *ibid.*

83 "Google's Civil Penalty of $22.5 Million Now Confirmed" http://www.privacylaws.com/Publications/enews/International-E-news/Dates/2012/11/Google-fined-225-million/.

all the relevant cookies from computers by February 2014.[84] There were calls for a larger fine, but the judge's opinion was that the fine imposed was "fair, adequate and reasonable".[85] A similar comment was made by the judges who agreed to the Beacon settlement. It is felt that this fine is an example of the increased importance attached to personal data. However, large as it may seem, it is still a drop in the ocean for huge global entities such as Google or Facebook. The proposed EU Data Protection Regulation may vastly change this.

Are Governments in Compliance?

In Germany, a law passed in 2006 allows personal data to be collected on terror suspects by police and intelligence agencies.[86] Germany's Constitutional Court was also called to examine this law for compliance with the constitution.[87] The definition of "supporters of supporters" of violence/terror is arguably vague, and could include unsuspecting innocent bystanders who happen to come into contact with terror suspects.[88] Not only is personal data collected on such individuals without their knowledge or consent, but such data also include information on religious beliefs, which fall into the category of sensitive personal data. Such data are subject to extra stringent compliance measures according to EU data protection law. The question of consent again arises here, specifically with regard to sensitive personal data where explicit consent should be attained. As the data are shared with 38 agencies, the transfer of sensitive personal data also comes into play here.[89] It will be interesting to see what the outcome of this investigation brings.

In New Zealand, a recent poll showed that 60 percent of people do not trust the government to protect their personal data.[90] This follows major public-sector privacy breaches in 2012, including by Accident Compensation Corporation (ACC) and Ministry of Social Development (MSD).[91] The Data Commissioner noted that government agencies need to develop a culture of respect for privacy in addition to putting policies and practices in place to ensure personal data are adequately protected throughout the organisation.[92] The Data Commissioner received 1,142 complaints in 2012, an increase on the 968 complaints received the previous year.[93] The Snowden revelations are set to increase government and security agency attention.

84 *ibid.*

85 *ibid.*

86 "German Court Checks Anti-terror Data Retention Laws", http://www.dw.de/german-court-checks-anti-terror-data-retention-laws/a-16359509.

87 *ibid.*The case was argued in November 2013. Similar cases are coming to be argued in various courts throughout Europe.

88 *ibid.*

89 *ibid.*

90 *Privacy Commissioner's Annual Report 2012 – The Year of the Data Breach: Media release*, 28 November 2012, http://privacy.org.nz/privacy-commissioner-s-annual-report-2012-the-year-of-the-data-breach-media-release/.

91 *ibid.*

92 *ibid.*

93 *ibid.*

The Birth of a New Profession – Privacy

The requirement by law for companies and public-sector organisations alike to comply with data protection legislation has created a new profession, namely that of privacy managers and privacy related positions. A recent advertisement for a privacy manager placed by Vodafone defined the following responsibilities: implementing and maintaining the company's privacy risk management system; provision of materials for internal training and development programmes, area meetings and internal conferences; responding to internal and external complaints related to breach of data protection and legal requirements; dealing with queries; and supporting the development, skills and knowledge of privacy team members.[94] Privacy teams are fast becoming a key requirement in organisations where personal data are being collected, stored and/or processed.

It is interesting to note that when the advertisement webpage appears, a box also appears at the top of the page telling the viewer that the website uses cookies to store information on the user's computer.[95] It is further explained that some cookies are required and others help improve user experience.[96] Regarding consent, the next sentence tells the viewer that by using the website, the viewer consents to the placement of these cookies.[97] Eventhough the website is that of the International Association of Privacy Professionals, it is queried whether it is fully ensuring that users are made somewhat aware of how their personal data are being actually used.

The International Association of Privacy Professionals, which was founded in 2000 and has over 10,000 members in 70 countries, aids in the definition of the privacy profession and provides support and improvements via certification, networking and education.[98] The association is seeking nominations for a range of privacy advisory boards, including the Canadian Advisory Board, European Advisory Board, IAPP Board of Directors, Certification Advisory Board, Publications Advisory Board, Education Advisory Board and INSIDE 1 to 1: Privacy Advisory Board.[99]

This body of professionals will seek to maintain a standard of data protection via training, awareness and ensuring compliance to data protection legislation in both the private and public sectors. Perhaps it will shine some light at the end of the tunnel. However, unless key online players buy into compliance voluntarily, the online world and particularly the social networking world will remain a very public place where data can be taken and used by third parties without anyone even being aware it is happening.

---

94 "Privacy Manager, Vodafone, Newbury, Berkshire, UK," https://www.privacyassociation.org/resource_center/privacy_manager_vodafone_newbury_berkshire_uk.

95 *ibid.*

96 *ibid.*

97 *ibid.*

98 https://www.privacyassociation.org/about_iapp.

99 "Join an IAPP Advisory Board," https://www.privacyassociation.org/community/join_an_iapp_advis…ce=EuropeDigest&utm_campaign=AdvisoryBoards.

The Future – Where Does Privacy on Social Networks Go from Here?

The Facebook Beacon settlement is a key example of how online social networking companies can sometimes put profits before privacy. Both Facebook and all the companies that signed up to Beacon apparently saw nothing wrong with sharing people's personal data without any form of what could be considered as informed consent. This also demonstrates a lack of awareness of data protection responsibilities on the part of the corporations that signed up to the Beacon tool with Facebook. Blockbusters' participation in Beacon also arguably violated the Video Privacy Protection Act.[100]

The monetary settlement made in the Facebook Beacon case was small given the seriousness of the issue and the likelihood of its being held as a precedent for a whole new world of such issues. It seems disturbing that one-third was to pay attorneys and the remainder to set up a charity run by a Facebook executive and two others. It seems the legal profession (with Facebook) rewarded themselves well and seemed to forget about the victims ie the 3.6 million class members. These members not only got no money but also lost the right to litigate in future for similar and even identical products brought out by Facebook, particularly in light of the class being expanded as part of the settlement. All things considered, it is fair to ask: who really won this case? Facebook's profits reaped from use of the Beacon program apparently well outweighed the $9.5 million dollars paid out to settle this action. It seems Facebook came out on top after all.

It is very unusual for a US judge to be so outspoken when filing a dissenting opinion, particularly for such a high-profile case. Circuit Court Judge Kleinfield filed a lengthy and articulate dissenting opinion outlining why the Facebook Beacon settlement was unfair. Judge Kleinfield was over-ruled. However, this issue is not going away. Facebook and similar online networkings are gaining popularity and becoming part of everyday life, as indeed they already are for over 1 billion active users of Facebook. Does opting into Facebook mean opting out of privacy in relation to all online transactions? By signing in to these websites, are users giving an infinite consent to use of their personal data placed on Facebook? From this settlement, it seems so, in the US at any rate.

The EU offers better data protection by way of the Directive in place, particularly following the Irish Data Protection Commissioner's audit of Facebook in 2011 and the recommendations that followed. However, as advertising is the means by which Facebook makes a profit, and thereby its means to survive as a corporate entity, it is something users will have to balance in return for receiving a free social networking service. The outcome of the Beacon settlement is very much in favour of both Facebook and their advertising partner companies. The collection and use of personal data for advertising seems to be, in effect, the price for using Facebook. Privacy often takes a back seat. While enforcement is starting to gain some momentum, the law is playing catch-up with the social networking industry that arguably acts on occassion without proper consideration of privacy rights of the consumer.

[100] J Grimmelmann, "Privacy as Product Safety" (2009–2012) (19) *Widener Law Journal* 793, 809.

Is There a Solution in Sight?

It is possible to envisage the current situation improving if adequate training is undertaken across the online industry and strict enforcement of data protection regulations enacted. Regular audits of such companies, for example, every three years, could be of greater assurance to users. However, this is not currently possible given the limited resources of Irish Data Protection Commissioner's office.

The Irish Data Protection Commissioner's audit of Facebook is a huge body of work and took several years to complete. It is a good start, and avoids relying solely on court cases to upgrade data protection procedures in such online organisations. The UK Information Commissioner (ICO) has warned of the resources required to enforce fully the proposed EU regulations.[101] The explosion of technological advances has proved a challenge for legislation, often written before the present-day constant stream of online interaction was even envisaged.

For now, the only way to limit the unauthorised flow of data seems to be the substantial fines handed down by courts for privacy breaches — that is, until legislation catches up with technology. The draft of the new EU Data Protection Regulation lists a maximum penalty of 2 percent of worldwide annual turnover; however, it is suggested that this could be up to 5 percent.[102] Even when the law does catch up, it may take many more substantial fines for privacy breaches, and perhaps even custodial sentences for directors, before social networking and other organisations sit up and take action.

---

101 "Get Involved in Forming New Data Rules, Says Information Commissioner," *ComputerWeekly.com*, 2012.

102 A Winton and N Cohen, "The General Data Protection Regulation As It Applies to Online Advertising, E-commerce and Social Media" (2012) (18(4)) *Computer and Telecommunications Law Review*, 97.

CHAPTER 11

EUROPE AGAINST FACEBOOK

Europe Against Facebook and Max Schrem

HEADLINE OF ISSUES

- Facebook
- Irish Data Protection Commissioner
- Reports
- Complaints

COMPLAINT 01: "POKES"

The December Report quotes the complaint and brings forward FB-I's argument that the retention of more than two year old pokes is necessary to prevent "cyber bullying". In our meeting with Facebook Ireland (FB-I) in Vienna it was added that they have to be kept for "all sorts of reasons", but FB-I was unable to tell us the exact purposes for which they are processed. In a follow-up letter by Richard Allen (FB-I) he also added that FB-I is using the deleted information "for other purposes in connection with bringing the ... service to the users". The letter refers to the clause of FB-I's policy that allows for any kind of processing:

> "We use the information we receive about you in connection with the services and features we provide to you and other users, like your friends, our partners, the advertisers that purchase ads on the site, and the developers that build the games, applications, and websites you use."

We were unable to find any solid consequence as to how FB-I changed its system concerning old pokes in the September 2012 report. In our direct talks we were not informed about how FB-I has changed or was intending to change the processing of "Pokes".

Neither the Irish Data Protection Acts, nor Data Protection Directive 1995 allow mass storage of data without the consent of the data subject and for the mere possibility to prevent the rights of a user in a rather hypothetical situation ("cyber bullying via pokes").

While it is true that cyber bullying happens on facebook.com, like anywhere else on the internet, there are other solutions (eg by "blocking" the user) than keeping every little bit of information about every user. Otherwise most of the data protection legislation would be redundant, since all information could be possibly used for some hypothetical legal case.

In addition we want to mention, that the recipient (so the hypothetical victim of "poke bullying" situation) in this situation has deleted these pokes. If the victim eg wants to press charges because of "poke harassment" he/she can simply not delete the pokes.

- The only substantial counterclaim of FB-I why pokes are kept for an indefinite time ("poke harassment") is surely creative, but legally absurd.

The fact that FB-I has stored information, without a legitimate purpose and without a justification, without proper information and for an indefinite time constitutes a clear breach of the provisions of the Irish Data Protection Acts (DPA) and the Data Protection Directive 1995 as described in our Complaint 01 from 18 August 2011.

- We ask the Irish Office of the Data Protection Commissioner (ODPC) to investigate how "Pokes" are treated by FB-I after the complaint was launched and disclose all information that FB-I has delivered on this issue;
- We ask the ODPC to ensure that this illegal processing of data is not conducted further and all old "poke" data is deleted;
- If no other arguments, evidence or files are before the ODPC, we are now reassured that FB-I has been in breach of the law and that our complaint was therefore fully justified;
- To show that a breach of the Irish law is not without consequences, to prevent other companies in Ireland and the EU to breach the law as well and to show that international companies are not above the law we hope that the DPC will impose a substantial penalty.

Complaint 02: "Shadow Profiles"

After researching the findings in both reports and the technical analysis, we came to the conclusion, that despite FB-I's claim not to hold "shadow profiles", there are far reaching data sets about users and non-users that are invisible to the data subject (which we have called "shadow profiles"). This can also be seen on a daily basis when invisible data is "surfacing" eg as "friend suggestions" or when things that are only related in the background are eg "grouped" on facebook.com. This "shadow data" enables FB-I to know much more about users than what they deliberately shared or exchanged via facebook.com. When submitting the initial complaint we were unable to further specify the issue, but we are now able to do so:

As an example we want to submit the graphic below. It combines Max Schrems' friend list with the friend lists' of his friends. The result is a "web" that shows certain groups of friends. This (simple) graphic in connection with basic information about the friends allows eg to determine that he was serving his community service as an ET at the Red Cross instead of serving at the military (1), was a member of an NGO (2), stayed in a Muslim country for a longer time (3) or went to certain Universities and Schools (4). Other information (eg health, sexual orientation or political views) can be determined in the same way.

This is a very basic graphic, only using friend lists. In reality there are additional "hidden" connections to many more users (eg by searches, imports, address books, click data) and every dot is not only a name, but again a whole Facebook profile.

In addition to these profiles and connections, hidden click data, advertisement information or data from social plugins can be added to every dot.

The result is what is known as "big data": After prices for processing and data storage dropped, companies have departed from a purpose based processing of data, but are instead deploying "web" systems that are able to connect seemingly unrelated data of millions of users with each other ("correlations"). For doing so the "visible" data is connected with "invisible" data that might serve another purpose (eg protocols, IPs, friend finder data, administrative data, data of others). This allows for profiling on people that have never really shared anything on facebook.com, or are not even a member. This practice seems to be the background of what we called "shadow profiles" in the initial complaint. In essence, data that the user did not knowingly share or is not visible is processed in a way that a profile can be derived that is much bigger than what is visible for the user.

In the section on advertisement in the report from December 2011, FB-I only seems to mention the most basic possibilities to target ads. There is no word on more sophisticated functions as described above, even though such techniques are "state of the art" and are knowingly deployed by most internet giants. It seems like FB-I has only disclosed the types of data processing that are very obvious and reasonable. When considering the exact wording of such statements, it become clear that they are all written in a way which also allows for other processing:

> "For example, FB-I stated that if a user mentioned a car in a status update and also "liked" something related to cars, FB-I might target ads to the user at a potential car buyer". (Report, Page 45)

This does not say, that FB-I does not use other, less obvious, information to target ads, promote their service or suggest "friends".

The audit and the technical report cover so far only the small fraction of this form of processing that was deployed by FB-I to "friend suggestion", but did not elaborate the overall problem of "shadow profiles" and data processing by FB-I that is not solely based on the information that users have deliberately shared on Facebook.com. Our Complaint 02 clearly names the "friend suggests" as only one of many possible results of these extensive profiles.

- We cannot elaborate further, because of the lack of evidence, arguments and files in relation to this complaint;
- Therefore, we ask the ODPC to investigate if and how such processing of data takes place and disclose all information that FB-I has delivered on this issue and investigate further to determine if the complaint is justified or not and get back to us with the results;
- Currently we have no reason to believe that our initial complaint is not justified, given the doubts above.

Complaint 03: "Tagging"

We welcome that FB-I has introduced the option to preapprove "tags" before they are publically shown. At the same time this is just a first step in the right direction, since users have to actively opt-out from automatic publication of tags that other users can place at any time. It takes many steps to deactivate the automatic tagging mechanism (8 clicks). Compared to the other options in the relevant pop-up FB-I requires users to go down one more level into the menu, by having a second pop-up that is only accessible through a text link, instead of a button (like the rest of the option). The wording is also confusing, since users have to choose "enabled" to prevent the automatic publication of tags.

This change to the previous system only changes the initial visibility of tags (in pictures or postings). It does not, however, allow disabling tagging itself. It does also not change the removal of tags. FB-I still keeps all "removed" tags.

- The new system allows to prevent automatic publication of tags (a step in the right direction);
- The system is in fact an "opt-out" from automatic publication and is well hidden;
- There is no change in relation to the removal of tags and the fact that FB-I keeps even the "removed" tags.

The ODPC has changed its position from the first report towards the review: While in the first report it has claimed that there must be a possibility to fully turn off tags, it has changed its position without any material argument that was any new:

> "Taking account of the various tools available to users to manage Tags and to delete them if they so wish we are not requiring an ability to prevent Tagging at this time." (Review, page 48)

Only some numbers from the US that indicate that only some people remove tags seemed to be new evidence. We cannot understand why the ODPC has changes its position.

- We hereby ask the ODPC to explain this change of position;
- If any arguments, files or evidence was not disclosed in relation to this change we hereby ask the ODPC to deliver such documents.

The reports are not covering all the issues of your initial complaints, especially the question how there could possibly be an *informed* and *specific* consent by the data subject to the postings, if the data subject does not even know which kind of picture or posting he/she got connected to, was not covered.

The law does not allow to process data based on "consent", but without any affirmative action by the data subject, just because people may say "no" later. The report is also missing another point: The law applies to "visible" but also "invisible" data. Even when people remove the tags, FB-I still keeps the information. It is just not visible anymore, but can still be used to track users or serve "relevant ads". Even just the fact that the information is kept constitutes "processing" of personal data.

- There is no affirmative action that can possibly constitute "specific" and "informed" consent;

- The data is processed even after the "removal", therefore FB-I does not even provide an "opt-out";
- Also tags that had to be "reviewed" are kept after they are removed;
- We hereby ask the ODPC to produce or disclose evidence, files and counterarguments in connection with the initial complaint. Currently we see ourselves reassured that the original complaint was fully justified.

Currently there is only one solution which we would understand to be fully compliant with the law. This solution is by the way the standard procedure with "invitations" or "adding" people in just about all other systems we know of and should be deployed with tags, groups, events and other "objects" that data subjects get connected to by others:

> Step 1: A third party can establish a link between a data subject and an object; This link stays invisible until there is an action by the data subject;
>
> Step 2: The user gets a notice to "accept" or "remove" it;
>
> Step 3: Removed links are deleted, users may get the option to "stay disconnected" (the removal is then stored).

Accepted links are turning into a visible link (eg a tag, group membership or RSVP) and may be processed further by FB-I (eg for serving ads).

Additional systems like limiting the users that can establish links, deleting links if no action by the user is taken within a reasonable time, or "block" lists could further enhance the system.

- This solution is a standard practice and the only known system that is compliant with the law.

Complaint 05: "Deleted Postings"

According to the December Report, FB-I has claimed that the deleted posts were only visible because they were still within the deletion period of 90 days. In fact FB-I says that Max Schrems has deleted these postings at approximately 12 days before the "access request". We are uncertain if FB-I refers to the production of the file (which would be July 11th 2011) or the filing of the access request (which would be June 2nd 2011).

We also miss a stringent explanation of why only some postings were available, while most postings were not in the file. Were the other undeleted postings not disclosed, or were other postings deleted?

- Therefore, we are asking the ODPC to disclose the exact reaction by FB-I to in relation to this complaint, as well as possible evidence that was delivered in relation to this complaint;
- We ask the ODPC to let FB-I explain how they were able to come up with

the exact number of "approximately 12 days" and how they calculated this exact number of days;
- We also want to get a stringent explanation how only certain postings ended up in the file.

Either way the claim seems to be false. I have repeatedly used a Firefox Plug-In, called "iMacros", which has automatically deleted all postings on my wall, as well as other Facebook data like my messages. A short video that shows how this works can be found on YouTube.

I have run the plug-in for the first time during the year 2010 or even before that and the last time during the first half a year of 2011. I can recall this because this was before and during my studies abroad.

While I cannot recall the exact times, I hereby assure that I have deleted all of my Facebook "wall" repeatedly and way before the 90 day period that FB-I claims.

- We ask the ODPC to get solid proof which would support FB-I's claim that the postings were deleted only 12 days before the filing of the access request or before the production of the data file which "Facebook Inc." (the US parent of FB-I) has sent to Max Schrems;
- The postings that were found in the data set were dating back to 2008 and 2009. This means that they must have been deleted when Max Schrems has used the automatic script for the very first time in 2010. This would have been way before the 90 days and would surely include postings from 2008 and 2009. The claim by FB-I seems to be false and misleading;
- In essence we are asking the ODPC to investigate the exact circumstances and get back to us with the exact arguments and solid evidence for FB-I's counterarguments;
- Currently we have no reason to believe that Complaint 05 is not justified, given the doubts above.

Complaint 06: "Posting on other Users' Pages"

We are happy to see that FB-I has made great progress in respect to this complaint by implementing a system where data subjects can see the audience of another users' page they comment on. The report points out the functions and we have nothing further to add at this point.

- FB-I has changed towards a model that we suggested in the initial complaint;
- Therefore, we have no doubt that our initial complaint was justified.

FB-I's new solution also has a drawback that we have pointed out in previous exchange with the ODPC: Data subjects can only consent in an "informed" and "specific" way. The main information that data subjects will consider before posting is the audience of a posting. FB-I displays the audience set by the owner of the page, but it also allows users to change eg from "friends only" to "public". It is a cornerstone of facebook.com to make people believe that they exchange among their friends and that it is not public if one user posts on another users' page. Only thorough this system FB-I gets users to open up under their real name in a way they would never do on a public blog or discussion forum.

This is undermined since the "owner" of the page (*mind: FB-I currently claims to be the controller of facebook.com*) can switch the postings from "friends" to "public". Making any comment viewable and searchable for anyone in the world. This is the assessment of the ODPC:

> "This Office has considered this issue in detail (...) and is inclined to the view that if a Facebook user chooses to post on another Facebook user's page that they do not do so with an expectation that the post will be either private or restricted to an audience that they are comfortable with." (Second Report, Page 49).

We cannot share this position, since it was the core idea and supported by the ODPC that users should get this information in order to make informed decisions. It is not stringent to now claim that users do not post data with the expectation that this post will only be shown to a restricted audience.

The ODPC further noted:

> "If a user has a concern about the audience for a post they make or that the audience might be subsequently expanded from say "friends only" to "public" then there is a simple solution available to them and that is not to post on other user's pages". (Second Report, Page 49).

This argument has nothing to do with the law. If this argument is consequently deployed we could shred the whole proceeding against FB-I, since in the end all users have the option not to use the service. It is the essence of data protection law to allow people to use new technology and be able to trust it.

- We cannot share the view of the ODPC in this respect and think our initial complaint is justified;
- We hereby ask the ODPC to disclose all documents that relate to this complaint;
- In addition we urgently ask the ODPC to name the provision of the Irish Data Protection Act from which it has derived this "simple solution", since we were unable to find it.

Complaint 07: "Messages"

The reports and technical analysis are helpful to get a broader insight of how FB-I processes deleted messages. At the same time there are certain inconsistencies of the technical report with the facts we found. For example the report suggests that once a user has deleted his "outbox", it is not possible to find corresponding messages in the "inboxes" of the hundreds of recipients:

> "Another alternative would be to scan all other cells in Titan [FB-I's storage system] to determine whether any other references to the attachment are left. This would remove the advantage of the fact that there is no association between cells." (Technical Report in the "Review", page 51)

We want to stress that FB-I was able to deliver all messages that were deleted when supplying Max Schrems with the response to the initial access request (there were about 300 pages of "deleted" messages). FB-I has claimed that these messages were not deleted because it was in the "inbox" of other users, as we have anticipated in the initial complaint. This fact demonstrate that FB-I is capable of retrieving all deleted messages of a particular users, even when he/she deleted at the copies that were stored in the original section of the system.

- FB-I is able to retrieve all deleted messages from the system, no matter where they are stored.

FB-I has further argued that messages are fully deleted when all data subjects that have been part of the conversation have deleted the message. We cannot see any facts or material arguments that would support this claim in the reports or the technical analysis.

- We could not find any fact based evidence that messages

Their Individual Copy of the Message

FB-I claimed that it is not processing the content of a message. There has not been any fact based evidence supporting this claim. There are facts that indicate that FB-I uses non-content data of personal messages and recently FB-I has said that it also scans the content for different filters and an alert system aiming at child predators. The technical analysis of the report only says that *"a full, detailed review of the operation of the private messaging system is beyond the scope of this audit"*.

There is also no provision in FB-I's privacy policy that would hinder FB-I from processing the content of messages for any purpose (like eg advertisement or friend suggestions). The difference between content and other message data is not reflected in the policy. To the contrary "messages" are listed in the general section about "information we receive about you". All this data is only governed by one provision in the policy which allows for any practically operation:

> "We use the information we receive about you in connection with the services and features we provide to you and other users like your friends, our partners, the advertisers that purchase ads on the site, and the developers that build the games, applications, and websites you use".

- There is no fact based evidence of the extent of processing of the content of messages;
- FB-I's own privacy policy does not limit the use of content of messages for specific purposes;
- There is fact based evidence that non-content data is not used.

The Material Claim

Independent from these factual problems the reports have not dealt with the material claim in the initial complaints which is in essence that the system itself might work reasonable in respect to each detail of the operation, but that the overall result of the processing is excessive given the purpose.

Deletion Process

FB-I generates endless amounts of personal, private chat messages that can factually not be deleted. All users that have communicated via facebook.com have to "delete" every single conversation, which takes 6 clicks from the start page. If a user would want to delete all his/her copies if would take hours. There is no way for "mass deletion" and FB-I does not automatically "delete" old chats, like every other chat system we are aware of. The merger between "chats" and "messages" has further lead to a system where every little exchange is treated like highly relevant personal mail. This does not reflect the users' reality and is an exceptional approach that cannot be seen anywhere in the world.

- It is practically impossible for users to delete all their messages with reasonable efforts;
- There is no standard deletion and no option for mass deletion.

Comparison to Email and Chat Programs

If this is compared to emails we want to stress, that emails do not work in a similar fashion, since the "inbox" and "outbox" of the different users are spread out all over the personal computers of every individual user or maybe situated at their provider (webmail). If a user deletes his set of emails it is factually impossible to find the corresponding emails in the outbox or inbox of the other recipients because no one can reconstruct the communication and is therefore unable to know about the other recipients. This is totally different on facebook.com as the data set of Max Schrems has demonstrated. In addition normal software (like "Outlook") on a users' computer makes the user archive or delete old messages and offers many options to get rid of old emails.

In comparison to systems that are closer to what a user expects from a "chat" like the one offered on facebook.com it is more than obvious that all these services delete chats within a very short period of a couple of hours or days. There is never an endless storage of all private messages in a central location.

- FB-I's chat system can in no way be compared to other systems that offer similar functionality, since these systems do not allow to centrally retrieve old, deleted messages.

Government Access

In addition FB-I is legally obliged to disclose such information upon orders by authorities from all over the EU or the US. In addition FB-I also allows authorities of other countries to get copies of this highly personal communication. In the US where the servers are situated, there is not even a constitutional right to privacy when messages are stored on a central system. This legal way to access such data has to be taken into consideration when assessing the risk of privacy violations.

Surveillance by Design

In summary we are looking at a system that might not be intentionally aimed at getting users into this position, but does in fact generate endless amounts of junk data (= old chats) that can practically not be deleted by the individual users, since it can always be retrieved through the counterparts of the copies. The system that FB-I has generated does not follow the idea of "privacy by design" but could rather be described as (possibly unintentional) "surveillance by design".

The law does not only cover intentional threats to the right to data protection of the individual, but is mainly covering systematic problems that bear a tremendous factual risk of a breach of the right to privacy of data subjects. This is the preventative character of the law, which must clearly be triggered by this system and the risks that we mentioned above.

Facebook.com was initially designed as a student project, but since it has become a standard form of communication and for some the main form of communication, a design that is in fact making every single message centrally retrievable, independent from the deletion by the user cannot be in line with the principles set out in Section 2 DPA and Article 6 of the Data Protection Directive 1995.

- Therefore, we have every reason to believe that our initial complaint it fully justified;
- We ask the ODPC to disclose all files, evidence and arguments on this complaint and make FB-I produce a material counterargument;
- We would not sport a penalty, since we believe this happened without any negligence by FB-I.

COMPLAINT 08: "PRIVACY POLICY AND CONSENT"

Privacy Policy

Old Policy

Since we have filed our initial complaints in August 2011, FB-I has changed its privacy policy twice (!) and there is a third change on the way. We want to point at WP187 and the original complaints concerning the level and form of information, which especially very complex systems have to be accompanied with (see WP187 page 21).

The claims FB-I has submitted to the ODCP concerning the old policy seem not stringent to us. The report has only cited claims by FB-I that our claims are wrong, but the report does not deliver any material arguments by FB-I. From the current level of information we cannot see that any material counterarguments were brought forward concerning our initial complaints.

Because of the limited information we got through the report, we cannot really respond to the counterarguments to what we have brought forward concerning the content of the old privacy policy. But we understand the ODPC's findings in the report of December 2011 to be very much supporting our view and see nothing that would be contrary to the claims in our initial complaint.

- We ask the ODPC to disclose all arguments, evidence and files in relation to FB-I's counterarguments. We face total absence of material counterarguments by FB-I;
- We are still of the view that FB-I's old policy could not constitute a valid legal basis for the processing of our data under the DPA and Data Protection Directive 1995;
- If there are no other arguments than the ones named above, we are of the view that our complaint was justified in relation to the previous policy.

New Policy

We very much welcome that FB-I now has a single document and stopped linking to hundreds of other pages in its policy. At the same time the new policy is still of extreme length, extremely vague and impossible to understand for a normal user. After working with this policy for almost a year, it is still not possible for the members of our group to exactly say what FB-I does or does not do with users' data, based on this policy.

We believe that there are ways to limit the length of the policy to a couple of pages, if FB-I puts some effort into it. Currently it seems that FB-I rather puts a lot of effort in a lengthy policy in order to deter users from reading and understanding it.

We welcome the approach of "inline" consent for every function. We have ourselves suggested to get specific consent every time a user uses a new tool for the first time, since it is impossible for a user to understand "facebook.com" after signing up for the first time. This point was also made by ODPC in the first report. While this helps to constitute a valid and meaningful act of consent, there must be a document in the end that specifies in one place what certain actions that are done "inline" mean and what consequences they have. This has in the end to be done in a privacy policy, which might be separated into "modules" for the different functions of Facebook.com a user has activated.

The first report by the ODPC of December 2011 has to our view outlined many important things concerning the current policy. We especially want to point at the findings on pages 39 to 41. When looking at the changes by FB-I and the review, we had to find that not much of these findings were in the end implemented. The change in the policy is in the end just a minor "face lift" that in fact mainly deprives users of rights and allows FB-I to process data in an even broader way. The new policy has not led to any limitation of FB-I's use of data.

We are still of the view that, while the new policy has at least shrunk to one single document, it is still not a valid basis for the processing by FB-I. This is not only because of the vague, unclear and lengthy style, but also because many provisions seem to be in violation of the DPA and Data Protection Directive 1995. We have summarised some issues as examples why we are still of the opinion that this cannot be the basis for a valid consent:

a. We believe FB-I has to clearly say or list what they do with our data. While FB-I elaborates over pages about where they get data and how export or display it to users they are not saying very much about what happens in the "black box".
Currently the only sentence that generally controls the use of user data is the following:

> "We use the information we receive about you in connection with the services and features we provide to you and other users [like your friends, our partners, the advertisers that purchase ads on the site, and the developers that build the games, applications, and websites you use]."

This sentence splits into two segments:

The first segment defines a purpose which embraces all "services and features" FB-I provides. If this segment is inverted it says that FB-I is only *prohibited* from using data in relation to services and features it does *not* at all provide. In plain English this translated segment says,

> "We may use your data for everything, except of things we don't do."

The second segment defines the people in relation to which FB-I may use personal data. This segment limits FB-I's use of personal data in relation to "*you and other users*". These other users are then specified by giving examples *("like")* which amount to everyone FB-I has any contract or business with. Given the fact that FB-I has about 1 billion users and millions of additional partners, cooperate users or advertisers and we currently have a little more than 2 billion internet users, this is again a meaningless definition and translates to,

> "We may use your data in relation to everyone we interact with (half of the internet)."

This is maybe the most abstract (and therefore the most unlimited) purpose ever written into a privacy policy. It can impossible be a "specific and informed" consent. This is rather a text book example of blanket consent: Practically any set of operation can be done under this provision. Such a statement is totally contrary to the law and any legal opinion we know, including WP187, pages 19f.

On top of this, the policy also claims that users consent to future developments of facebook.com. So users are supposedly giving a "specific and informed" consent to processing that does not even exist:

> "Granting us this permission not only allows us to provide Facebook as it exists today, but it also allows us to provide you with innovative features and services we develop in the future that use the information we receive about you in new ways."

There is no way that consent to an unclear and non-existing future form of processing personal data can in any way be informed or specific. This allows FB-I to do practically everything, since the limitation to process data only in relation to "services and features" as examined above can be widened any time by FB-I's decision to engage in new "services and features".

b. FB-I has to work towards a "module" policy system that allows to get an overview over the process and then consent to it. FB-I works in this direction by implementing "in line" consent, but this is currently a fractioned system, which mainly leads to confusion, not informed consent.

c. FB-I has to implement an "Opt-In" instead of an "Opt-Out" system for all data use and all features (eg face recognition, applications or tags). Now new options are automatically activated without notice. Users should be able to make an informed decision. This is also in line with the findings of the ODPC in the first report and WP187 of the EU Article 29 Working Party. See also Complaint 16 below.

d. FB-I has to precisely say which personal data it stores. Currently there are only very vague and general claims (eg "We receive information about you from your friends and others").

Clear information could be delivered through a continuously updated list of all data categories and subcategories that are stored about a user. FB-I should also explain the purpose for keeping the information. It has to be clear and easy to understand what is generally captured by FB-I's services.

e. FB-I has to clarify who is responsible (the "controller") for what part of FB-I. We oppose that users FB-I now claims that it is the controller for personal pages, messages and pictures. FB-I has put a provision into the new policy saying it is the (sole?) controller, but at the same time FB-I makes public statements to the contrary (see "General Remarks 3: Controller" above).

f. FB-I has to use clear and understandable language. We think that FB-I's usage of vague wording (eg "like", "may" or "could") is not appropriate for a specific and informed consent.

g. FB-I has to rewrite the information on "cookies". FB-I should clearly say which kind of cookies (eg HTTP or Flash), with which content and for what exact purpose they are using. The current section is full of general statements: "We use technologies like cookies ... to provide and understand a range of products and services".

h. FB-I has to delete all data the users have previously "removed" or "deleted". It seems like the deleted data we have discovered in 2011 is still on FB-I's servers and only data that was deleted after the changes are in fact deleted.

i. After it was discovered that "deleted" information was still kept by FB-I they simply relabeled the buttons to "hide", in order to prevent people from effectively deleting data, this cannot be the proper reaction. It usually takes extra effort to really delete information (hidden sub menus) and intends to deter users form deleting data. We believe FB-I has to have "delete" as a standard option to allow user control and in order to allow users to withdraw previous consent.

j. FB-I has to implement functions that allow users to "mass delete" data. Such as a function to delete all data of a certain category and all data that is older than a certain date. This allows users to efficiently get rid of old "junk data" if the users wishes so.

The reports' approach of highlighting "per item" deletion makes it practically impossible for users to delete more than just individual pieces of data. If a user wants to delete eg all old data on a timeline they would sit for hours to click on every item for at least three times to get rid of it.

This in fact undermines the possibility to withdraw consent for the processing of data: Users are only able to delete the whole account, or little bits of data, there is nothing between these two extremes. It is state of the art with all other "cloud" systems to allow for mass deletion.

k. FB-I has to list specific data retention criteria that make it clear to users how long which information is held by FB-I. Currently FB-I just says that it may keep old information as *"long as necessary"*, which is a mere restatement of Section 2(1)(c)(iv) DPA, but not an adequate information about FB-I's actual practice. The ODPC has asked FB-I to provide a clear retention policy; we are missing such a clear statement by FB-I up to this very day.

In a video Erin Egan (Facebook Inc.'s "Chief Privacy Officer) was trying to explain retention periods, but only said that she "*thinks*" FB-I was talking about 180 days (see video on YouTube at 19:04), but this is about as much as we were able to find out in relation to exact retention periods.

Such non-information about exact retention periods is unacceptable and does not allow for a specific and informed consent.

l. FB-I has to take back the change that allows them to keep users' information after users have deleted their accounts. FB-I goes even further on this in the recently proposed third version of the new policy.

It used to be that FB-I said it deleted all information when you delete an account, this was changed with the new policy. FB-I does at the same time not disclose which information is kept after deletion of an account and how long such information is kept. We ask the ODPC to find out which data is kept, the purpose for this and the legal basis for such processing. This provision also seems to be in conflict with the withdrawal of consent and the idea that data which is used on the bases of consent should not be processed on another basis when consent was withdrawn (see WP187).

m. FB-I has to take into account that it cannot effectively enforce its policies in relation to external developers. As the investigations of the ODPC have shown FB-I cannot even ensure that developers have some sort of privacy policy, not to mention the other obligations of an external provider of applications. FB-I cannot rely on agreements with external contractors, if they are impossible to police and enforce in reality. FB-I points at agreements that are not worth the paper they are written on. FB-I should close these holes in the legal framework and find other solutions that might mean that only developers that are certified, checked or at least personally identified can get a hold of users' data (see also "Complaint 13 - Applications").

n. We believe FB-I has to take back the change that makes the user responsible for getting back the data from applications or other third parties. The old policy said developers are obliged to delete all user data as soon as the user deleted the application, which was in line with the EU laws and the Safe harbor agreement.

Under the new policy the user has to specifically ask the application provider to delete such data. The deletion of an application is a clear and explicit act that constitutes a withdrawal of consent, previous consent cannot be a basis for further processing.

o. We believe FB-I has to limit the use of users' data for advertisement and other purposes to certain data categories. Currently FB-I can use any of the users' data for advertisement (eg private messages, sexual preferences, interactions with friends or what others post and share). The new policy restates this. While FB-I is, according to the reports, claiming that it is in fact not processing all data categories for all purposes the privacy policy does not reflect this and needs to be adapted in a way that this is reflected.

p. FB-I has to take back the changes that limit the scope of the "show my social actions in FB-I Ads" options. Under the old policy users could turn this function off, the new policy limits the scope of the opt-out.

q. FB-I has to disclose which data categories are used for determining users' personal interests. Currently it is unclear how FB-I finds out users' interests for targeted advertisement if the information is not posted by the user (see also Complaint 02 – Shadow Profiles).

r. FB-I works mainly with examples to explain their processing. Most of these examples seem reasonable (eg if users say they "like" cars, they get ads on cars), but the general provisions also allow for other processing that might not be that reasonable an acceptable for users. We believe that FB-I has to highlight processing that cannot be reasonably expected, instead of rather obvious processing.

As said before, the issues listed above are only some examples. In general FB-I's privacy policy is a lengthy document, that has endless vague and general provisions, that allow endless leeway. A data subject cannot predict what FB-I is, or is not doing with its data after reading this document.

FB-I sometimes claimed that the policy has to be "flexible" to allow for new services without changing the policy every time. In fact FB-I currently proposes the fourth policy since we have filed our initial complaints, despite having a very "flexible" policy. So this argument seems to lack any substance.

FB-I does provide some examples that substitute these general rules which allows for some insights, but as they are not an exhaustive description of FB-I's operations, this can therefore only constitute informed and specific consent for these specific operation.

Overall we believe that FB-I has to draft a totally new policy. We suggest there is one section for the core features and additional sections for additional features that users consent to opting into such features. FB-I should prompt users about any major updates and thereby get explicit and informed consent whenever new features are introduced. Such a system would be in line with the law as well as WP187 and WP163. Such an approach would surely be supported by NGOs, DPCs and users and would constitute real "best practice".

- We ask the ODPC to get a clear statement on who is the controller of every operation on facebook.com and what FB-I means when saying the users' data "belongs" to the user, when they are at the same time not letting the user be the controller over "their" data;
- We ask the ODPC to disclose all arguments, evidence and files in relation to FB-I's counterarguments concerning the new and old privacy policies;
- We ask the ODPC to have FB-I produce a list of all data categories and explain the exact, specific purposes for which this data is uses (see also "Complaint 10 – Access Requests");
- We ask the ODPC to review FB-I's new privacy policy in line with the claims listed above;
- Given the issues brought forward above, we are sure that Complaint 08 is justified in relation to the new policy as well.

Consent

Old Sign-Up Process

We welcome that the ODPC has made FB-I change its sign-up process towards a new system that gets much closer to what we have outlined in our initial complaint. At the same time the report does not say one word about the millions of users that have signed up to facebook.com before this change was made. There is no mentioning about the validity of the consent for former users. If the ODPC is saying that the form of consent that FB-I obtained previously is not satisfactory, there is no stringent way around that fact that this means that users that signed up previously have not given a valid consent. We are still of the view, that FB-I does currently not have a valid consent by users that signed up before this change. Mind, that this still allows FB-I to operate under other provisions of the DPA and Data Protection Directive 1995 (eg performance a contract).

FB-I is cited repeatedly in the report form December 2011 to claim that the ongoing use of facebook.com would constitute informed, specific and unambiguous consent to the (old or new) policy. We are again pointing to WP187, which is clearly saying that the sole use of a page (or online game) does not constitute unambiguous consent to a far reaching privacy policy (see WP187, page 23).

- In substance FB-I deployed arguments we cannot share. We are still of the view that there has been no valid act of consent. FB-I would have to ask all existing users for a new and valid consent;
- If there are no other arguments than the ones named above, we are of the view that our complaint was justified in relation to the act of consent under the old sign-up process.

New Sign-Up Process

We welcome the improvements, but the new page is still not really emphasising that there is some act of consent to a privacy policy. The relevant text has grown by only 1 pixel from 7 to 8 pixels, making it again the smallest text on the page. All other text is at least 50% bigger (13 pixels).

We still question if this small link can really constitute an informed, unambiguous and specific consent, given the large amount of very problematic and complicated data processing FB-I engages in. The solution is surely a step ahead, but "best practice" would be at least a check box, which is seen to be necessary for any form of consent in many member states. The reports did also not take into account the fact that facebook.com has become a standard form of communication and that a consent to a monopoly is hardly "free". This view was also shared by the EU Article 29 Working Party in WP187:

> "Considering the importance that some social networks have acquired, some categories of users (such as teenagers) will accept the receipt of behavioral advertising in order to avoid the risk of being partially excluded from social interactions."

- The relative size of the text was practically not improved, there is no "check-box" and the consent to the usage of data is not separated from consent to the civil law terms;
- The new sign-up page is a step in the right direction, but hardly in line with the law and for sure not "best practice";
- The ODPC did not touch on how "free" consent on facebook.com really is. FB-I did bring forward any counterarguments. We ask the ODPC to produce and disclose such documents.

Improved Information for New Users

We welcome that new users get additional information. At the same time new users are still not "walked" through the settings, but there is only one of many links to this information, which appears on the "Welcome Page". The four steps are not taking into account all the different settings FB-I offers, but only show some settings that are already well known to many users. Every picture constitutes of a picture and only one or two sentences:

1. "You can pick and choose the audience for the things you post on your timeline — like share your school publicly, but only let friends see your photos. You can also hide the things other people post to your timeline";
2. "Tagging is an easy way to let people know when they're in photos*. A tag creates a link to the person's timeline and may share your post with their friends";
3. "You can control who can send you friend requests in your How You Connect settings";
4. "Control who can access what, including what info your friends and others can bring with them in the apps and websites they use."

We are wondering how these 107 words (of which 14 words are only promoting a tool) can constitute proper information about a highly complex system with more than 170 possible options (counted by the "*New York Times*" in 2010). Many options are not explained at all. There is eg no mentioning that users can totally turn off "apps" or "personalized ads" or the options for the access by search engines.

- The additional information that is provided is another small step into the right direction, but surely not the giant leap towards an informed consent by all users;

- We still believe that only a system where users get a quick information when they first use a function compared with "privacy friendly" default settings can combined constitute a specific, informed an unambiguous consent.

Complaint 09: "Face Recognition"

We very much welcome the deactivation of the automatic biometric facial recognition tool (called "tag suggest" by FB-I). The tool was clearly not in line with the DPA and Data Protection Directive 1995. This was very clearly stated in WP163 issues by the EU Article 29 Working Party. The procedure has shown to our understanding, that there must be unambiguous, informed and specific consent for additional processing like the facial recognition. This cannot be obtained by inactivity of the user or by an "opt-out" system (see also WP187, page 35). We hope the ODPC is moving towards this - European - understanding in relation to other complaints as well (eg Complaint 16 – "Opt Out").

What is at the same time disturbing is that the ODPC has in the relating statements more or less said that an unambiguous consent is not really necessary under the law, but more a consequence of pressure from other European DPCs and somewhat inspired by the ODPC's "best practice" approach.

We also want stress that the ODPC has not dealt with the other provisions of the Irish DPA and the Data Protection Directive 1995 that are necessary to make this form of data processing legitimate. The EU Article 29 Working Party has clearly stated that even a valid consent does not allow the controller to waive other principles of data protection law (see eg WP187 page 34). Especially the requirement to be non-excessive seems to be relevant in the relation to FB-I's facial recognition tool. The ODPC has not at all elaborated the question whether it is proportionate to generate biometrical data of 1 billion users only in order to avoid a couple of clicks for a user that wants to tag someone. It is is not excessive, we wonder what is?

Even though the first attempt by FB-I to get the tool "approved" by a notice on facebook.com seems to be obsolete after the Re-Audit, we still want to quickly point to the wording and the way FB-I has implemented this mechanism.

Despite the fact that the message was only displayed three times and the user was further enrolled with the facial recognition tool if he/she was not interacting with it (see above) the wording not allowing for an "informed" consent. There is no word on "facial recognition" or "biometrics". By the wording FB-I only uses the information that someone is "tagged" (so the tag information itself) to group pictures. In reality FB-I uses their faces (*not the tags*) to do so. The wording of the button ("Okay, Got It") does not give the impression that the user has a choice, but that this is just an information. Further information and an option to turn the feature off, could only be found in the second or third layer of the menu. Color, pictures of friends and vague wording was also used to deter users from opting-out. All together is a prime example how there would never be a valid consent, even if the user clicked on "Okay, Got it".

We are waiting to see how the new system will be designed that only recognises faces of users that have previously consented. From a logical side it seems to be necessary to recognise people first before it can be checked if they have consented to facial recognition. This seems also to be unclear in the current situation: How does FB-I guarantee that a photo of a data subject living in the EU that is eg uploaded in South America is not processed by the facial recognition tool? Given the experiences mentioned above will also have to see how FB-I is exactly getting a valid consent when redeploying this tool in the EU/EEA.

"EU" and "EEA" are also the key words for the last remark we want to make: According to the reports the ODPC is responsible for all processing of "Facebook Ireland Ltd", so all operations of facebook.com outside of the US and Canada.

The DPA and Data Protection Directive 1995 do not distinguish between the data of "EU data subjects" and the data of other people. It is, therefore, not stringent, that FB-I was only made to comply with the legal requirements for users' within the EU/EEA. The right to data protection is not only a human right (in opposition to "citizens' rights") but we are also bound to protect the right to data protection of users' outside of the EU/EEA according to international law. Any user from associated countries (like eg Switzerland) will hardly understand why the ODPC did not enforce their fundamental rights.

- We welcome the new approach, but believe that the ODPC has to ensure that an unambiguous, specific and informed consent is necessary under the law (not just under a "best practice" approach);
- We ask the ODPC to figure out how FB-I is currently distinguishing between users form the EU/EEA and other users and how FB-I is intending to do so between users that have and have not consented to facial recognition;
- We ask the ODPC to also elaborate over the other principles that govern processing of data;
- We are making the ODPC aware that it is responsible for all users outside of the US/Canada and that all these users have the same rights under EU (and Irish) law.

Complaint 10: "Access Requests"

One of the most "prominent" complaints was the complaint dealing with the right to access and FB-I's non-compliance with the initial access request by Max Schrems that was sent to FB-I on June 2nd 2011. Given the fact of its prominence and that more than 40,000 people have made access requests as well we would have expected that this issue would be prioritised and investigated in an especially transparent and detailed way. Instead we had to find that the exact opposite seemed to have happened, which is also supported by the facts we had to find when looking at the current "solution" to access requests.

The ODPC's Reports and Investigation

Despite the fact that the "access requests" were a point of great public discussion with more than 40,000 users directly affected and about 1,000 complaints at the ODPC there is very little information that can be derived from the reports.

The report claims that the 40,000 requests were a massive issue for FB-I and that this *"would place a strain on the ability of any organisation to provide personal data within 40 days"*. In this relation we want to mention that 40,000 requests at a user base of about 900 Million users means that only 0.004% (!) of Facebook's user base has made an access request. This is equivalent to a single request at a data controller with 22,500 customers.

If this is seen as "too much", FB-I should not have waived the right to ask for €6.35, which would surly have limited the amount of people that made requests to only the ones that really wanted to get access. It seems hypocritical to first tear down the only limitation to then complain about an "extreme" number of requests. We believe that FB-I was simply unable or unwilling to additionally process the payments by thousands of users and therefore waived the fee in its very own interest.

- Access Requests by (only) 0.004% of the overall user base is not exceptional;
- FB-I has added to getting more requests by waiving the fee of € 6.35.

While the report was repeating the law, saying that there is no exception form the 40 days deadline under Section 4 DPA, the ODPC has in fact simply "waived" the law for FB-I. By doing so it has deprived 40,000 data subjects, including us, of their right to access within a reasonable time. Also other controllers in the EU will have a hard time understanding why the law applies to everyone but FB-I.

As communicated to the ODPC before, we are deeply disturbed that the law was simply "waived" for a tech giant. If laws are simply waived for some, this questions core values of the democratic system. This could be interpreted that the "rule of law" is not of relevance for the ODPC.

- The ODPC has illegally "waived" a statutory obligation of FB-I and allowed it to break the law.

The first report states that "a significant proportion of the audit was ... focused on establishing the extent of personal data held by FB-I and whether any of the limited exemptions contained within the Data Protection Acts could be validly claimed by FB-I." While the ODPC seemed to have worked through the list in our complaint ("10 – Access Request"), the ODPC has not made any evidence, argumentation or legal analysis public. We have no possibility to independently verify the final results (which is in fact just a tiny list). Neither the factual basis (eg a list of all data FB-I holds) neither the legal argumentation (eg which data is not "personal data") was disclosed.

- Therefore, we ask the ODPC hereby to disclose evidence, arguments and files in relation to the existence and legal qualification of (personal) data on FB-I's systems;

- We hereby ask the ODPC to disclose in detail the methodology that led to the ODPC's finding, how the fact finding was conducted and explain the legal analysis which led to the published results.

As a user it is practically impossible to know about all the data categories that a controller holds, therefore, the user is dependent on the investigations of the authorities to ensure that all data is disclosed. We have submitted a list of examples that should have triggered reasonable doubt about FB-I's compliance with the law. At the same time there are no facts that would indicate that the ODPC has looked for data categories beyond the list we have submitted.

The ODPC has let us know that is has taken account of the 19 data categories we have listed in our initial complaint. We have repeatedly pointed out that this was *not* an exhaustive list of data categories and that we expected the ODPC to investigate into other data as well. We have even offered to submit a second list of data categories that we have collected after the initial complaints. The ODPC has not gotten back to us on this proposal. We currently have evidence of about 20 more categories.

During our talks with FB-I in Vienna, the representatives of FB-I have declared that the 19 categories we listed were exactly the only 19 categories FB-I did so far not disclose. Given the fact that the list was only an educated guess, it would be an incredible miracle if we would have made a "100% hit".

In a "live session" FB-I's Chief Privacy Officer, Erin Egan has indirectly stated that FB-I does currently not deliver all personal data through its self-service tools (see YouTube at 21:50):

> "I know people might say: 'Oh why aren't you giving us access to more'. But think about how much we are giving access to – I think it is a terrific tool and we are constantly working. You know it's not easy!"

Therefore, we do not believe that the ODPC has found all data categories. We are sure that the data categories listed on pages 64-65 of the first report do not represent all personal data held by FB-I. The list of these categories is also only naming the "headlines" of the categories. It is unclear which exact data fields or sub-categories are included under these headline. The report lists eg "photos", but there are also IPs, Dates, EXIF data or tags attached to pictures these sub-categories are not listed in the report.

- There is evidence that the list of data, published in the ODPC's reports, is incomplete;
- We hereby ask the ODPC to disclose the methodology and evidence used to derive this list.

The ODPC has repeatedly said that is has worked together with FB-I very closely and checked on the implementation and functioning of the "self-service approach" taken by FB-I.

Given the obvious flaws that we discovered and described below (see section "C. Self-Service Approach" below) we are wondering how the ODPC could overlook these issues. It seems like the ODPC has never investigated and cross-checked on the factual implementation by FB-I. If these most obvious issues were not effectively discovered, we are very much worrying about the quality of the investigation into other issues (eg the investigation on other, so far non-disclosed data categories).

- How could the ODPC overlook that the "tools" where in fact not working properly?
- How can the ODPC guarantee that other questions of fact were properly examined if even such basic problems were not discovered by it?

Facebook's Credibility Relating to Access Requests

Given this record there is no reason why we would possibly believe the current claims by FB-I that it discloses all information. After misusing the trust of users it is now upon FB-I to demonstrate by the use of solid evidence that every little bit of information that falls under the right to access is disclosed.

- There is no reason to believe claims by FB-I on the existence of certain data categories without solid proof, given this history of false claims and deliberate lies;
- We hereby ask the ODPC to disclose all evidence, arguments and files that were produced in relation to the existence of data categories on FB-I's servers and the question whether they constitute "personal data" or not.

"Self-Service" Approach

FB-I has taken a very "*different*" approach in relation to the response to access requests. Instead of supplying the users' with a copy of the raw data, which is the standard procedure, the ODPC has given FB-I excessive amounts of time (more than one year, instead of 40 days under the law) to develop "self-service tools" that should allow users to access all data that is covered by the right to access. We have been very critical of this approach, since these tools replaced the standard response.

We would not have criticized this approach as an "additional" feature for users that do not want to go through the trouble of making a formal request and want to avoid the Irish "access request fee" of €6.35, but we cannot see how such a tool can replace a formal response to an access request.

In relation to the timeframe FB-I has added the last bits (EFIX data) to the tool in October 2012, so more than a year after the initial complaints, about 1.5 years after the initial requests and 4 months after the July 2012 deadline that was agreed on in the first report, which was published in December 2011.

Download Tool(s) – Access

We are not opposing a "download tool" as an additional or alternative option for users to get their data in an unbureaucratic way and without costs. The tool is very hard to find: On "account setting" page FB-I has not placed a link in line with other text, but in a gray small (8 pixel) text at the bottom of the page.

In addition we had to find that the "juicy" information is hidden in the "extended download tool" that can only be found when clicking on a tiny link below the main "download tool". The link is only in the 10th (!) line of text below the main tool. This separation seems to have no other purpose than to massively hinder users to get the more problematic data in the "extended download tool".

FB-I has even moved data that was previously available in the normal "download tool" to the "extended download tool". It leaves us with the impression that FB-I is ashamed of all the data it collects instead of working towards full transparency.

Especially inexperienced or older data subjects might not be able to find and operate these self-service tools. Users have to make a request through the help page, they get an email back, have to find the tiny links, request the archive, download the ZIP file, extract the HTML files and open them). We (europe-v-facebook.org) had to explain to hundreds users how to go through this in the last year!

- The download tools are designed to make it especially hard for users to get certain data;
- There is no reasonable explanation why FB-I separates the same function into two separate tools, of which one is very well hidden;
- FB-I clearly tries to fool users by making them believe that the "normal" download tool is all data it holds about them;
- Even the "normal" download tool is only accessible through a tiny link.

Download Tool(s) – Content

We have found many inconstancies when the downloaded data was compared with the "raw data" we have received previously. When comparing all three "raw" data sets with the results of today's data sets, we were missing (among other data) much of the "meta data" associated with the users' data.

In fact there was "meta data" to just about every piece of information in the raw data sets. This starts with user IDs, that are by definition "personal data" and associated with just about every action a user takes, goes on with exact IP addresses, URLs, dates and times, Object IDs and many other forms of meta data, that constitute "personal data", as you can see in the picture on the left, which shows when users are "active".

Deleted messages, a category of data that is especially problematic (see Complaint 07), are not at all included in the download tool(s). There is no doubt that FB-I holds such information in a form that constitutes personal data. The first report only lists "inbox messages". We were unable to find any word on why messages that were deleted, but still held by FB-I should not fall under the right to access.

We also had to experience that data was not showing up in the download file: As one example the "Alternative Name" category was empty in the file, even though it was visible in the "account settings". This means that also the categories that should be displayed are obviously missing in practice.

In addition we have to stress, that the download tool(s) are a form of derivative data from the original raw data set. This allows for easy manipulation or technical bugs, which in the end undermines the right to access by users. We would have never been able to uncover the misconduct by FB-I without access to the raw data sets. We therefore believe that FB-I has a vital interest not to deliver the raw data.

- The "download tool(s)" are still not delivering all data that is "personal data";
- Even categories FB-I has agreed on including are not showing up in practice;
- Much data is missing if compared to the "raw data" we got previously;
- Deleted messages are personal data that fall under the right to access;
- Given the fact that in such obvious cased like the meta data, or deleted data FB-I is not including all data, we have to reasonably suspect that other data is still undisclosed;
- We ask the ODPC to explain why deleted messages are not included in the download tool;
- Did the ODPD find other deleted data categories that are now not included?
- We ask the ODPC to ensure that users, which are willing to pay the access fee and go through the trouble of a formal access request, get a 1:1 copy of the raw data, as it is common practice.

Activity Log

According to FB-I the access to 18 data categories should be possible through the "activity log". In fact this tool does not live up to the promises of FB-I and even less to the DPA and the Data Protection Directive 1995.

The most obvious problem is, that massive amounts of data are simply missing in the "activity log". Some categories like "pages visited" are not showing up at all. Other data seems to only show up on a random basis, with declining chances the further one goes back in time: For demonstration we have collected two very obvious examples, both were taken from the account of Max Schrems on November 6 2012.

As a very obvious sign that the "activity log" is incomplete we experienced that the further one goes back in time, the less postings can be found. Interestingly there are certain dates shown, but no "activity" that would actually constitute the personal data. In the case of the account of Max Schrems, there are only dates (and no activities or other personal data) for the time before 2010. The account is active since the June 8 2008, so the initial 1.5 years (of about 4 years) are totally missing.

This means that FB-I does currently not give full access to the 18 data categories, despite claims that this data can be retrieved through the "activity log". The data must be stored - otherwise there should not be any "lonely dates" without any accompanying information in the "activity log".

- FB-I holds personal data but does display them in the "activity log";
- The 18 data categories in the "activity log" are not properly made available to users.

After we found this very obvious problem quite stunning, we have checked for more recent postings in the years after 2010. With a couple more clicks we soon discovered that also more recent data is simply missing. The first randomly picked comment was dated December 27 2010 (so about one year after the total non-functioning of the "activity log"). When we scrolled to that data in the "activity log" there was not even a "lonely date" displayed. Reloading the page and clicking on "December 2010" or repeated scrolling (which makes the log load) did not change the result.

In a similar way there were no entries for postings on other peoples' walls, for videos,

- There was no reference whatsoever to the comment on another users' pictures, postings on other peoples pages or videos despite FB-I claiming that this data is delivered through the "activity log".

An additional problem is that users have to click on every month of every year and then scroll up and down for minutes until the whole "activity log" is finally loaded. This procedure takes (depending on internet traffic and the speed of the users' browser) a couple of minutes to 10 minutes of constant clicking, scrolling and waiting.

Inexperienced users have no chance to get all data with a couple of clicks, since many months do not show all the data at first, but need reloading or clicking on "show more" links. The standard setting is also set to show only "posts and apps", only after changing this setting to "all", the other data is (possibly) shown. This is another obstacle for the data subjects' right to get all data.

If the data subject has finally gotten the "activity log" to load everything that's possible there is another major problem: The data is not disclosed in a tangible format.

In contrast to the "download tool(s)" there is no way of downloading the data that is contained in the activity log. Given the fact that the right to access is also a basis for other complaints this is a massive draw back. A user might only be able to take hundreds of screenshots, or print the entire page, which does in fact get corrupted when printed on a normal page. Only more experienced users will find ways to get a copy of the "activity log".

In summary FB-I does still not deliver a solid data set through the "activity log", this is 1 year and 6 months after the initial access request which was filed with FB-I on June 2nd 2011. FB-I has had more than 13 times as long as the DPA allows FB-I to take to deliver a full, correct and all-embracing response to an access request, but still the result is simply not there.

In addition we have to stress, that the activity log is a form of derivative data from the raw data set, which allows for excessive manipulation or technical bugs, which in the end limit the data the users can access.

- FB-I received about 1.5 years since the initial requests to develop the "activity log", still FB-I is not delivering the data it is pledging to disclose through it. The tool is either full of obvious "bugs" that FB-I simply does not care about or FB-I is deliberately not disclosing all data through it;
- Given the fact that in such obvious cases like demonstrated on the previous pages FB-I is not including all data, we have to reasonably suspect that other data is still undisclosed;
- The data has to be delivered without obstacles in a raw format and in a tangible format;
- We ask the ODPC to ensure that users, which are willing to pay the access fee and go through the trouble of a formal access request, get a 1:1 copy of the raw data, as it is common practice;
- Given the extensive time FB-I was given and the poor result, we have to conclude that the "activity log" is an obvious disaster.

Other "Hiding Places" of Personal Data

According to the first report "Credit Cards", "Linked Accounts", "Privacy Settings" and the "Vanity URL" are again neither included in the various download tools nor the activity log, but in other placed all over facebook.com. This makes it again harder to for a user to get a full overview over what FB-I holds about them. Except from the credit card information (which is especially sensitive) this separation seems to have no other purpose than to hinder users to get a full overview of their data.

- It is unacceptable to send the data subjects on a "treasure hunt" all over a webpage to collect every little bit of information themselves, after going through the trouble of making a formal access request.

Purposes, Recipient and Sources

As we have pointed out previously, FB-I does not give data subjects relevant information in relation to the sources, recipients and purposes for each and every kind or bit of information. Currently FB-I sends out an automatic email in response to access requests that simply refers to the privacy policy.

If data subjects want to know the specific purpose for a data category they will only find the following statement in the section 'how we use the information': *"We use the information we receive about you in connection with the services and features we provide to you and other users".*

These "other users" are further specified only naming some examples: "like your friends, our partners, the advertisers that purchase ads on the site, and the developers that build the games, applications, and websites you use." *Mind:* These are only examples and *not* an exhaustive list.

In essence the "purpose" that FB-I claims is "everything we might do", not only in relation to the specific user, but also in relation to one billion other users, companies that have a page on facebook.com, the advertisement industry, developers, other controllers and any partner.

As said before this is likely the most abstract and general purpose in the history of data protection litigation. There would be no factual difference if FB-I would simply say: "Anything that our company does, or will do, ourselves or that might be done by anyone that we engage with."

In direct talks with FB-I it eg claimed that certain data is used "for security and other important purposes". When we inquired about these "other important purposes" FB-I has told us that they cannot disclose them because of either trade secrets, or "because you might be able to use them against FB-I".

In this relation we want to stress, that there is no exception from the right to access that FB-I could possibly claim in order to not have to disclose the specific purpose of every operation.

The right to access is not worth the paper it is written on, if this additional information to the raw data is missing. It is impossible to determine if some form of processing personal data is allowed eg under Sections 2 and 2A DPA or Article 6 and 7 Data Protection Directive 95.

- We hereby ask the ODPC how a data subject should determine if certain personal data is still "relevant" for the purpose, only used for the specific "purpose" or obtained "fairly", if the only information that FB-I delivers is that they use the information for "other important purposes" or "in connection with the service"?
- We hereby ask the ODPC to ensure that FB-I produces a fact based, all embracing description of the purposes of every category of personal data they hold about us and delivers them to us as soon as possible, since this is a crucial basis for all other complaints and therefore necessary to make our "best possible case".

Summary – Self-Service Approach

Following what we have uncovered above it must be clear to everyone reading this section that FB-I does still not react to access requests adequately, despite the fact that they had about 1.5 years, since the initial requests to respond to them. The tools are not functioning adequately.

FB-I makes it especially hard for users to access their data by spreading it out into different tools that are well hidden or take major afford to load, like the activity log. The data is currently spread out over different tools, pages and subpages. FB-I does not "deliver" the data, but lets the user go on a lengthy "treasure hunt" which is unlikely to be much of a great "evening entertainment" for most users. Instead this is clearly intending to distract users from getting all data. For inexperienced and average users it is currently impossible to download all data with reasonable efforts.

Many data fields that constitute "personal data" are missing in the various tools and pages that FB-I directs users to. Some data is simply not included (eg meta data or deleted messages), other data is "randomly" not accessible.

FB-I does not allow users to get a 1:1 copy of the raw data, but only gives users derivative data. This does not allow uncovering misconduct by FB-I, which is one of the ideas behind the right to access. We would have never been able to file the 22 complaints without access to raw data.

- The ODPC has allowed FB-I to take about 1.5 years to respond to the initial access request in a correct way, instead of 40 days under the Irish DPA. This is more than 13 times (!) the legal time limit under the Irish statute, but FB-I is still not delivering the necessary data to its users;
- FB-I has taken substantial efforts to deter users from getting their data, by hosting a "treasure hunt" for personal data. This results in a situation where average users are unable to get access;
- The "raw data" is not delivered, much of the data is clearly missing, the tools are not properly functioning and additional information under section 10 DPA are still not disclosed;
- Overall the "self-service" approach cannot substitute a traditional response to an access request and does not make FB-I complaint requests under section 10 DPA.

Non-User Access Requests

We also want to mention FB-I's reaction to access requests by non-users. Currently FB-I allows to make an access request via email through the address "datarequests@fb.com".

Even though this constituted a legally binding access request, FB-I responds with an automatic email, talking about how users (not non-users) can access their data. In fact the only thing FB-I seems to do is sending a standard text back to whatever email address was used to contact this email.

As an alternative non-users can go to facebook.com (which makes them subject to FB-I's user tracking) and submit different information to an online form. After many reports we got from non-users we have filled out this form with various information from existing non-users and with false information. No matter what we did, there was always the same result:

Even when we used email addresses that have never existed, we got the information that FB-I holds "the email address" and the "date where you were invited to join Facebook". This shows again, that FB-I is not taking access requests serious, is not even checking on the mere existence of the data it is holding about non-users.

- In summary FB-I is not giving a material response to access requests by non-users, but "spams" data subjects with standard emails, independent from the individual situation of the user;
- This is another obvious breach of FB-I's obligation under the DPC and Directive 95/46/EG to respect the right to access by data subjects and shows FB-I's ignorance towards the rights of data subjects.

Summary – Access Requests

Facebook

In summary we could hardly believe the extremely dilettantish attempt by FB-I to comply with the right to access. After 1.5 years from the initial access requests FB-I has not been delivering a full, tangible, solid and somewhat valid response to our initial access requests. FB-I has not implemented a procedure that would possibly be compliant with section 10 DPA and Article 12 Data Protection Directive 1995. It is obvious that FB-I was unable to demonstrate that we got all the data it is holding about us.

The wording of Data Protection Directive 1995 and the Irish Data Protection Acts are clearly indicating that the controller has to "deliver" the data and "supply" the data subject with the information after an initial access request. This wording clearly means an active ("push") delivery of the information. Users have no duty to go "treasure hunting" all over a webpage to get the data. Compared to a paper file this would equally mean that a controller has complied with the right to access by only giving a key to the files that are spread all over an archive. We would be able to accept if there is one file, that users can download and are directed to, but the right to access cannot be validly turned into a "right to hunt for data" without departing from the wording of the Irish Data Protection Acts and Data Protection Directive 1995.

In addition we want to mention that we have never directly gotten any email or communication that would have invited us to use the new tools that were developed. The last email Max Schrems got directly in relation to his initial complaint is an email from 28 October 2011, saying that all data was disclosed and that FB-I is not giving out further data.

ODPC

The ODPC has not only "waived" the legal deadline of 40 days for FB-I, but has also factually "waived" the duty to disclose the recipients, sources and purposes for the individual data categories. This is extremely problematic in relation to the rule of law.

The ODPC has also managed to overlook the most basic problems in relation to the systems FB-I has deployed. This is raising serious questions about the ODPC's technical and practical capability to analyze, investigate and research complex systems like facebook.com. While we are aware that the ODPC does not have the necessary personal and resources to investigate every line of code, we are stunned that it has not discovered the most obvious flaws of FB-I's "self-service tools". It only takes a couple of minutes of scrolling around and cross-checking to demonstrate that these tools are not functioning. If the ODPC was not able to discover such issues that are visible for every average user, it will be very hard to trust that more complex issues were investigated properly.

Without a copy of the raw data it would have been impossible to make the initial complaint. By not making FB-I produce a copy of the raw data the ODPC has massively limited our ability to make our case.

- We want to highlight that the ODPC has "waived" FB-I's duty to respond to access requests;
- Even though FB-I got about 1.5 years to respond to the initial requests, which is more than 13 times (!) the legal time limit under the Irish statute the response is still not adequate;
- We highlight that the ODPC is overdue to enforce our right to access as soon as possible;
- We ask for a 1:1 copy of all raw data FB-I holds about us to be delivered as soon as possible. This is necessary as a basis for all other complaints;
- In addition we ask the ODPC to have FB-I produce a list of all data categories and data fields FB-I processes and an explanation about the source, recipients and exact and specific purpose for all data categories;
- We ask the ODPC to disclose the methodology, evidence, files and arguments in relation to the complaint concerning the right to access;
- We are reassured that our initial complaint was completely justified. FB-I did clearly not deliver all personal data within the legal deadline of 40 days;
- To show that a breach of the Irish law in such obvious cases is not without consequences, to prevent other companies to ignore the law as well and to show that international companies are not above the law we think that the DPC should impose a substantial penalty.

Complaint 11: "Deleted Tags"

Please refer to what we have brought forward above in the section on "Complaint 03 – Tags".

We want to mention that currently it seems like "removing" tags in postings does not work. We have tried to remove tags in postings in different profiles, on different computers and by using different browsers. There was only one result: Nothing happened, when clicking "remove tag".

Therefore, we were unable to assess if "removed" tags in postings are kept by FB-I. At the same time it was possible to remove tags in pictures, and we found that these tags are still kept by FB-I, without notice.

- In fact the removal of tags in postings is not working

As outlined in the section on "Complaint 03 – Tags" we cannot see any major improvement, there seems to be no counterargument that we did not already anticipated in the initial complaint. FB-I is still not allowing users to remove information that was posted by others. There is also nothing in the reports that talk about FB-I's usage of the data besides preventing re-invitations. This data may also be used for targeting ads, "friend suggestions" or other data processing by FB-I.

- We hereby ask the ODPC to disclose all arguments, files and evidence in relation to this complaint;
- Currently we have no reason to believe that our initial complaint was not

justified, rather we are of the view that the facts and the legal analysis were correct.

Complaint 12: "Data Security"

As outlined in the initial complaint, the complaint is mainly based on the provisions of FB-I's terms. In this relation we have the feeling that the ODPC's investigation has revieled what we have suspected. The first report has made clear that FB-I was not really following "best practice" in this respect, which is shown by these statements:

> "We were somewhat concerned that the provisioning tools in place for ensuring that staff were authorized to only access user data on a strictly necessary basis were not as role specific as we would have wished to see." or "Many policies and procedures that are in operation are not formally documented. The absence of these documented policies and procedures means that it is difficult to assess the audit trail data stored by Facebook within the context of their information security policy."

- From the findings in the report we are satisfied that the complaint was justified.

At the same time we were wondering which exact methodology the ODPC and the external expert have deployed. Some statements in the report only relied on submissions by FB-I but did not independently verify compliance;

> "The majority of the controls described by Facebook appear to be effective."

Some statements in the report seem to suggest, that just by the fact that breaches were not all over the media, there is no reason to doubt or investigate into actual compliance:

> "If large-scale, frequent data breaches were taking place on Facebook's corporate networks, it is believed that this would be widely reported, particularly considering Facebook's global profile. Since this is not the case, the information security controls in Facebook appear to be preventing these types of incidents."

- According to this logic every atomic power plant is "safe", as long as it has not turned into another Chernobyl - a claim that can be made, but does not seem to be very helpful.

This is especially questionable if we look at hackers, data dealers and other criminal (or illegal) activity: These people are usually working in secret and will not broadcast their hack into Facebook on CNN.

FB-I (or its parent) has recently started a campaign to pay hackers that were able to access their systems (see CNN.com). It would eg be more relevant to have FB-I disclose the awards and reports that FB-I got through this campaign, in order to get a solid understanding of how well FB-I is sticking to its obligations under the law, than just looking at the media.

In this relation we also want to mention that it was possible for "Open Data City", a German company for data visualisation to "scrap" the friend lists of more than 200 profiles, which were friends with Max Schrems. The information was used to generate eg the graphic that can be seen above at "Complaint 02 – Shadow Profiles". This demonstrates that it is possible to scrap substantial data if only individual users are targeted (eg by private investigators).

Other cases (with wider media coverage, see eg this American report on YouTube) was eg "lovely-faces.com" which was mentioned in the initial complaint. In this case artists were able to scrap about one million profile pictures of FB-I's users.

Another wonderful example is "profileengine.com" that has scrapped millions of profiles from facebook.com, including profiles that were set to be "private" and not to be open to search engines. The website claims to be a "public social network" and that the DPC of New Zealand has approved of it, because the relevant information was "public" when scraped (see profileengine.com/help).

There are profiles of different members of our group, like this one of Max Schrems: profileengine.com/#/people/10869930/max.schrems. Profiles of other members of our group show even more data publicly (see eg profileengine.com/#/people/17052974/andreas.kezer).

When we were searching the web for news, we soon found many other stories about scrapping and other forms of security breaches on facebook.com. Even the first report names another incident where pictures were accessible on the internet (see page 109). So overall we look at everything but a "clean record" when looking at FB-I's data security history.

- There have been (widely reported) cases of successful scrapping and circumventing of FB-I's security systems;
- It seems to be questionable, if only the fact that there has not been permanent coverage about data breaches and scrapping constitutes solid evidence that FB-I ensures adequate safety for users;
- Therefore we ask the ODPC to disclose, as far as possible without risking the security of FB-I's operations, all evidence, arguments and files in relation to the security of facebook.com;
- We also ask the ODPC to explain the methodology that was deployed to deliver the ODPC's finding in relation to FB-I's security systems.

Complaint 13: "Applications"

Changes

We welcomed the thorough investigation by the ODPC into third party apps, we especially thought that the insight on the possibility to "trade" tokens to be very interesting and problematic.

We want to remark that, despite the rather clear language on the side of the ODPC, there were no material changes by FB-I. The only step that seems to have derived from our initial complaints seem to be that FB-I wants to deploy a system that checks if there is a life link to a privacy policy, but so this still seems to be developed from what we could read in the review. We also welcome the possibility to select the audience for posting by an app that the ODPC has pushed for.

On the other hand we had to observe that FB-I has taken a big step back in user information and getting a clear, informed and unambiguous consent when changing to its new "app center". While we thought that the previous system made it rather clear that "something happens", the new system is a step backwards to a system that does not make it clear that the users' data is now transferred out of facebook.com and that this might be critical. We doubt that all users understand this procedure und the new setting. While the old system (see below) was titled "Request for Permission" and was clearly indicating that the user grants something by using buttons labeled "Allow" and "Don't Allow", the new version does not use such wording.

In the example on the left, there is no headline and the button is simply called "Visit Website" and is not indicating to grant anything.

If these two versions are looked at a little closer and "side-by-side" it is easy to see that the essence of the agreement was moved into subtext or totally deleted. As an example "basic info" was describes as also including the whole friends list of a user, while this can now only be seen if a user "hovers" over the little question mark. The information on what other allowances cover was totally removed. The text was changed from a black, bold and central information to a small, grey text on the side.

Overall this is clearly a step back: The new system reminds us of the "sign up" process (see complaint 08) before FB-I improved this process. We have eg already seen a headline like "your basic info" as fraudulent when this also includes friends' data, but when this information is now even hidden behind a tiny grey question mark, we have no reason to think that the initial complaint is not still justified.

- The new system is a step backwards and reminds us of the old sign up process;
- We hereby ask the ODPC to get arguments about (1) why this was changed and (2) if there are statistics on how many users have aborted the process before and after the change.

Consent by Third Parties

The main issue we brought up was the problem that users can forward personal data of all their friends to an external application, without any notice or even consent of the data subject. FB-I has simply claimed in this respect during our talks in Vienna that the other users consented for the data subject. This would be a legal miracle, since making legal arrangements without getting the power by the subject of these arrangements is impossible ever since the Roman law. Unless FB-I would be able to underpin this miracle with solid arguments we are currently not willing to accept this explanation.

Another approach that FB-I might take is claiming that by consenting to the policy and not turning off the "platform" option (again: this is an opt-out that users are not actively informed about) this would constitute consent. The problem is, however, that the user would be blankly consenting to a form of processing of any controller for any purpose and under any policy. Such a form of consent is under no way legally binding and would never be in line with the law that requires an *informed*, *specific* and *unambiguous* consent.

- There is no way that FB-I gets valid consent from a third party to forward personal data to a third party, without any knowledge or information of the data subject.

Arrangement with Third Parties

It is a core principle of Data Protection Directive 1995 that data must be contained in a legal sphere where the right to data protection is factually enforceable. As the ODPC has rightfully outlined in the report it is insufficient for FB-I to claim that by posting some terms on their page this would factually ensure compliance. To further develop this problem we also want to point to the content of these requirements do not fully ensure compliance with European law. The privacy policies of applications are often not even remotely defining the basics. In addition, an "app developer" can stay totally anonymous by using a fake account. FB-I can currently only "turn off" such apps, but has no way to prevent developers form uploading new apps or even pursuit breaches of the law.

While users might be able to consent to having their own data transferred out of a solid legal sphere (if they are controllers of their page/timeline) this is unacceptable for third party data. Only where developers are identified, are situated in an "adequate" country or are bound by an agreement that ensures factual legal consequences when breached, FB-I could possibly allow access to third party data.

- We ask the ODPC to disclose all arguments, files and evidence;
- FB-I has to stop forwarding third party data to "apps" outside of a solid legal framework;
- We have no reason to think that our initial complaint is not fully justified.

COMPLAINT 14: "DELETED FRIENDS"

The reports did not exactly deal with the complaint and the substance of it. FB-I has indicated in the first report and also in our direct talks in Vienna, that "deleted friends" are only used to prevent these users to be suggested to the person again. Removed friends can at the same time send another invitation any time. Only when users have additionally "blocked" the person this is not possible.

While this small "benefit" of now suggesting removed users to be added again, this purpose does not seem to be proportionate that previous friends are kept for an indefinite time. It also would not really harm any user if previous friends show up once in a while, in fact FB-I constantly shows people in the "people you might know" section that users mainly do not want to be friends with.

Independent from this question of law, we also found a new phenomenon.

While FB-I claimed in the report and in our talks in Vienna that it was only using the "deleted friends" to not suggest the same person again, we found that FB-I was in fact processing this information further to suggest the friends of the deleted friend to a person.

To show this we have opened a new profile. This profile was friends with a real user (Max Schrems). Both profiles were used to be able to make some screenshots. After this the friendship was deleted. Following the deletion FB-I was still suggesting Max Schrems' friends to the test profile.

- FB-I has made false statements to the ODPC about the use of "deleted" friends;
- FB-I uses "deleted" for other purposes than just not suggesting deleted friends;
- We ask the ODPC to deliver all arguments, evidence and files in relation to this complaint;
- We have no reason to believe that our initial complaint would not be justified. To the contrary we think that given the fact that FB-I uses this information further they are fully correct.

Complaint 15: "Excessive Processing of Data"

The reports did not analyze the exact claim in our complaint, but just remotely touched on it. There is only one excerpt from the counterargument by FB-I that made it into the first report:

> "FB-I, inter alia, pointed to the worldwide popularity of the platform and contended that the fact that Facebook processes the data of a very large number of people does not in itself mean that that processing is excessive. Furthermore, FB-I noted that processing is excessive where it was unnecessary, not simply where it justifiably involved a large amount of personal data." (First Report, Page72)

In this statement FB-I misses the point. The initial complaint has never said that the fact that FB-I runs a popular service is by itself excessive. The second argument, that only "unnecessary" processing of personal data would be "excessive", is totally ignoring the wording of Section 2(1)(c)(iii) Irish Data Protection Acts and Article 6 of Data Protection Directive 1995. The fact that processing must be "necessary" in relation to the purpose is already enshrined in Section 2(1)(c)(i) since it has to be obtained for one purpose, data that is not necessary is by definition not allowed to be processed. The additional rule that it should also not be "excessive" in relation to the purpose means that the data processing should (even when within the purpose) not be disproportionate.

Often times a purpose can be served in many different ways. As long as every step of the process is necessary to get a certain result, it is generally within the principles of the law. But at the same time the same purpose might be able to be served through less intensive, narrower, leaner processing. In other cases there is simply a disproportion by the large, intense and broad processing of endless amount of personal data for a purpose. As an example FB-I might be able to predict even better what users are interested in by having 100 times the amount of information it already has. It might be even better with 1 million times the amount of data. It might become even better when cross referencing this with the same amounts of other people and so on ... all this processing is "necessary" if you want to deliver even better results, but at some point it is excessive given the purpose of selling ads better.

If FB-I holds thousands of pages of data and uses all this information for any operation of FB-I, partners, developers and so on. We believe that the level of limitless processing is reaching a level that is "excessive". Given the practically limitless purpose, the endless options to cross reference data, the massive amounts of data that FB-I is getting and generating about users and the fact that much of this data is not directly visible (see complaint 02), we have to ask FB-I: If this form of "big data" is not excessive, what is?

As outlined in the initial complaint FB-I would need to limit the data that is available for a specific purpose (eg only use certain data – meaning certain types or timespans) and FB-I has to enable users to "recycle" old junk data by allowing for mass deletion (this was eg introduced by FB-I for the "search history" in the activity log, but not for any other type of data). The same though was also used by the ODPC when discussion about advertisement (report, page 41) - in the end this is about proportionality.

- We ask the ODPC to disclose all arguments, files and evidence that was produced;
- We currently see no reason why this complaint would not be justified, but are open for counterarguments and evidence that proof the contrary.

Complaint 16: "Opt-Out"

The first part of the complaint addressed the sign up process. This has be changed in a way that was surely a step in the right direction (see also Complaint 08 above) – especially the problem that users had to enter data without any knowledge of the policy and the settings seem to be solved.

- FB-I has changed the sign-up process towards a system that is closer to the law;
- Therefore we understand that our complaint was justified in this respect.

On the other hand FB-I still uses the most privacy-unfriendly settings as default settings, there seems to be no change whatsoever during the last year. This is not in line with WP187 and WP163. The reports do not explain how FB-I's "best practice" approach can be contrary to very clear and the most basic recommendations by the EU Article 29 Working Party that it has published exactly in relation to default settings of social networking sites:

> "(...) Because of the uncertainty as to whether the lack of action is meant to signify consent, not clicking may not be considered unambiguous consent." (WP187, Page 24)

The ODPC also took the view in the first report that the current approach by FB-I was not satisfactory and that there must be a meaningful change to the current opt-out approach:

> "This Office has no difficulty with FB-I expressing its position as to what it believes a person should select to gain the greatest experience from the site but we do not accept that the current approach is reflecting the appropriate balance for Facebook users. By extension it is clearly the case that the process also needs to be adjusted for current users to take account of this approach. This Office therefore recommends that FB-I undertake a thorough re-evaluation of the process by which it empowers its users both new and current to make meaningful choices about how they control the use of their personal information." (First Report, December 2011, page 40)

Other than the new "information" (four pages and 104 words) that is presented to new users, there seems to be no substantial change by FB-I (see more details above at Complaints 08).

The reports did not cover the claim that FB-I deters users from choosing more privacy friendly settings, other than citing a counterclaim by FB-I that does not deliver any material arguments. It is still a long and tiring work to go through countless pages, subpages, pop-ups and deactivate one check box after the other, which leads in fact to users just giving up on it.

The report has also asked FB-I for settings on an "per item basis". This already exists on most pages, but turns out not to be very privacy friendly. Users can only change individual settings or delete individual items of information. When users eg do not want applications to get any data and express this wish thorough the form above, they have to uncheck 17 (!) check boxes.

Currently it is also factually impossible to delete all old "post", old "messages" or participation in old "events". By making it technically impossible for users to express their wishes in a common form, FB-I ensures that it is harvesting more and more data, without any realistic chance of users to mitigate this.

We suspect that this is planned in a "big data" strategy (see above, complaint 02 "Shadow Profile"). Any other provider of cloud services (eg web mail, video pages or online office software) allows for mass deletion or mass manipulation of the users' data - everyone, but Facebook.

- FB-I has not changed the default settings, even though there is a very clear interpretation of Directive 95/46/EG through WP187 and WP163 that make an "opt-out" system necessary;
- The ODPC has quite clearly said that there must be substantial changes, but we cannot see them;
- We hereby ask the ODPC to make FB-I produce an explanation why it only allows for "per item" manipulation of users' settings and forward this explanation to us;
- We hereby ask the ODPC to disclose all evidence, arguments and files in relation to these issues and tell us if there were any other changes agreed with FB-I;
- Given the view that is expressed in WP187 and WP163 and the ODPC's elaboration we have no doubt that our complaint was justified.

In fact FB-I has even departed from the legal requirement to offer "Opt-In" function further by "adding" checked boxes for users whenever FB-I changes something about its system. When users have gone through the trouble of unchecking all the boxes, FB-I simply added new boxes that were again checked, instead of respecting the clear whish of the users that has unchecked all boxes.

This is not only problematic in relation to the "unambiguous consent" by the data subject, but there is no way that this could be seen as a form of "fair" processing of users' data.

- FB-I has even departed further from the goal of an "unambiguous" consent, by not only "adding" new boxes, but also "adding" the users' consent, even if users have clearly indicated their wishes by unchecking every single box;
- We ask the ODPC to inquire about this behavior at FB-I and get back to us with the results.

COMPLAINT 17: "LIKE BUTTON"

The reports have dealt excessively with social plugins and we welcome the steps in the right direction that derived from it (like eg FB-I's pledge to delete the last bit of the IP addressed).

On a factual level the reports and the technical analysis did not deliver any substantial new outcomes. The information that is transferred between a users' computer and FB-I when social plugins are loaded was already discovered before our initial complaints. We also believed that the website, that uses social plugins through an iframe, does not get direct access to the users' data. There has not been further information about what data constitutes (potential) personal data and what does not.

- FB-I does not at all contest that is does generate personal data about users that visit websites off facebook.com when they load (not interact) a social plugin. This information is stored for 90 days;
- It has yet to be checked if also non-users can be tracked in a personal way (eg by connecting the browser cookie with a person). We ask the ODPC to investigate on this or disclose all information that would clarify this question.

Purpose

After repeatedly reading all documents from the ODPC we can only see that FB-I has claimed "that it has not designed its systems to track users and non-users browsing activity" (first report, page 82).

In FB-I's submission from July 2012 they say that "The Report Audit has confirmed that (a) FB-I did not use the data it received when logged-in users visited sites with social plugins for advertising purposes, and (b) FB-I only used such data for the purposes of bug-fixing and analysis of social plugin performance."

During our talks in Vienna, FB-I said that the data is used to (a) find bugs, (b) check on the success of a like button and (c) to generate statistics for the page owner. The last purpose (statistics for web pages) cannot be found in the documents of the audit. Therefore, we have to assume that the audit failed to list all purposes FB-I uses the data for. In addition the "security" argument was also deployed in a letter sent to us by Richard Allen, which would constitute another purpose not listed in the two reports.

A limitation of purposes is also not reflected in the privacy policy of FB-I: In its policy FB-I does have special provisions concerning the purpose of social plugin data. The section on social plugins does in no way limit the use of such data, instead it is covered by the core provision for all data it receives, which says that,

> "We use the information we receive about you in connection with the services and features we provide to you and other users like your friends, our partners, the advertisers that purchase ads on the site, and the developers that build the games, applications, and websites you use."

The technical analysis shows an attempt to look into the "black box" by randomly clicking pages. This attempt could have delivered compelling results, which it did not. But just by the absence of obvious relations between webpages that where visited and ads, we cannot conclude that the data is not used in any other or more complex way. Targeting systems are very complex and might not deliver obvious results after browsing different pages for a couple of minutes or even an hour. This was also concluded in the report, which only says that such obvious relations could not be found, but does not say that their non-existence is a fact. In this relation we also want to draw the attention to the first and second test on page 184 of the first report: There was no reaction by the system of FB-I no matter if users have just loaded or interacted with like buttons in relation to "parenting/childcare", while there was a relation in later tests concerning "motorbikes", "Harley Davidson" and "Cisco". If there would be a 1:1 relation, such difference would not occur.

The technical report also says that all accounts were brand new and did not have friends. FB-I has pointed out repeatedly that there might be multiple factors (eg posting something and liking something else) that triggers the advertisement system. Only browsing pages would surely be considered a weak indicator of users' interests compared to "likes" of products and postings about certain topics.

Overall we have to conclude that there are indications for the exact purpose, but no solid evidence for what exact purposes FB-I uses the "social plugin" data exactly. The purposes named in the reports do not match up with the purposes we were given by FB-I.

- While there might be a factual limitation of the purposes which FB-I uses the data for, it is allowing itself to use such information for any purpose under its policy;
- There is so far no solid evidence that FB-I only uses such information to "fix bugs", "analysis of social plugin performance". In our talks it was eg also claimed to be used to "generate statistics for the page owner" or for "security purposes". Therefore, the reports are clearly incomplete;

- We ask the ODPC to get a list of all operations that are done using "social plugin" data;
- We ask the ODPC to disclose all evidence, arguments and files that were produced in relation to this issue.

Consent

FB-I says that it has consent for the generation of such data through the privacy policy. The question at stake is not if there could be some act of consent to a policy that explains this behavior, but if this consent can be "*informed*" and "*specific*":

A user cannot predict which pages have a "social plugin" before loading the page. The core of a *specific* consent is, that a data subject cannot give blanket consent to any operation. Data subjects will usually feel very different about tracking on a news page, political page, one concerning health, sexual orientation, religion or a porn page (we have submitted examples of such use in the initial complaint).

When FB-I says that by signing up to facebook.com data subjects have allowed it to track users anywhere on the web, no matter of the content, time and purpose, FB-I ignores that consent must be *informed* and *specific*. This is not the case and there is currently no counterargument by FB-I. This is in essence also the view that was shared by other DPCs in Europe, like the German "ULD".

The reports and documents also do not take into account the other reasons we have submitted in the initial complaint that make the form of processing illegitimate. We especially want to stress that it does not elaborate more privacy friendly approaches (eg the "two click" solution) that would constitute a more privacy friendly alternative that has to be taken to fulfill Section 2(1)(c)(iii) DPA.

- We ask the ODPC to disclose all evidence, arguments and files that were produced in relation to this issue and ask the ODCP to get the other necessary facts and counterarguments from FB-I;
- Currently we have no reason to believe that our initial complaints were not justified, especially given the fact that the ODPC has forced FB-I to make multiple changes.

Complaint 19: "Picture Privacy Settings"

The report and the technical analysis did not bring forward any new facts or arguments that were not already known in the initial complaints. Our guess that one part of the URL functions as a key against attacks was verified and seems to be effective against external attacks, but this was not the point.

The reports did not elaborate about the legal questions that were brought forward in our complaint. Most notably the question whether it is adequate to allow users to only control the "password" (being the URL) to the picture, while telling the users that they can control the audience of the picture itself.

FB-I's security concept works like a hotel room that is opened via a code. The code is not changed when new guests arrive, allowing former guests to get into their former rooms. This problem was not touched.

- We ask the ODPC to produce or disclose files and arguments in relation to this complaint;
- We currently have no doubt that our initial complains were justified.

Complaint 20: "Deleted Pictures"

We welcome that FB-I has pledged to delete pictures that are delivered through "Akamai". In our talks in Vienna FB-I told us that 90% of the pictures will be deleted "in minutes", while it may take up to 45 (!) days to really delete pictures on the servers, this was not reflected in the reports.

This sounded great, but in reality we were not able to see a material change in deletion periods when testing random pictures. The deleted pictures were deleted after 4-7 days (!), none were gone earlier.

- We were unable to see any material change;
- We ask the ODPC to disclose any documents that would allow us to assess FB-I's response.

The report has not at all covered the issue that Akamai is a US company, but not on the Safe Harbor. We have not received any arguments, evidence or files that indicate that the use of an external processor was covered under the law.

- We ask the ODPC to produce or disclose such evidence, as well as any other files, evidence or arguments in relation to this complaint;
- Given the facts above, we have no doubt that our initial complains were justified.

Complaint 22: "New Policy"

The report does not talk about the essence of the complaint and does not provide any counterarguments by FB-I. The report referred to an agreement between "Facebook Inc." (the US parent company of "Facebook Ireland Ltd") and the US Federal Trade Commission, as a reason why it did not deal with our complaint in the report. We understand that this agreement from November 29 2011 was meant: http://ftc.gov/os/caselist/0923184/111129facebookagree.pdf

This agreement has nothing to do with our complaints against FB-I, since the ODPC and FB-I is of the opinion that FB-I operates independently from "Facebook Inc" as a separate controller for all users outside of the US and Canada. Agreements with the US parent company are not automatically covering foreign subsidiaries that do not even cater to US consumers.

- We ask the ODPC to deliver FB-I's response to the complaint, so that we can assess if the complaint is still justified;
- We ask the ODPC to disclose all evidence, arguments and files that refer to this issue.

There is by definition no informed, specific and unambiguous consent to a policy that a user is not even aware of. FB-I has deployed different arguments during the change of the privacy policy this spring that were all rather absurd. Some of them were eg that "the media is informing the users anyways" or that they have placed "ads" on facebook.com to inform people about it. None of these actions guarantee that users are first of all aware and secondly agreeing to changes.

FB-I has previously pointed at its great option for users to even vote on any change of privacy policies when more than 7,000 users demand it. When our group has tested this pledge, by getting about 45,000 people to ask FB-I to make certain changes, it has conducted a vote, but was hiding it in such a way that just 0.038% of its worldwide users have voted. The turnout of 86.9% against the vote was simply ignored.

To our understanding FB-I has not even managed to conduct the change in the privacy policy under its very own provisions, which can only be read in a way that a "real" vote has to be conducted. But it can be even less in line with the law, to simply change the essence of what users have given their unambiguous, informed and specific consent to. This would totally undermine the essence of the "informed consent" in the law.

- Currently we have no doubt that our initial complaint was and is justified.

Chapter 12

FACEBOOK AUDIT

Donnacha O'Sullivan

Headline of Issues

- Facebook
- Data Protection Commissioner
- Complaints
- Audit
- Europe v Facebook
- Data Protection and Facebook
- Audit assessment and impact
- Criticisms

Introduction

> "Technology is neither good nor bad, nor is it neutral….Technology's interaction with the social ecology is such that tech developments frequently have environmental, social and human consequences that go far beyond the immediate purposes of the technical devices and practices themselves".[1]

Since its inception in 1988[2] the Office of the Irish Data Protection Commissioner (ODPC) has grown in importance with leaps and bounds. It seems highly unlikely that at its inception, those involved would have foreseen the current climate for personal data collection and its relationship with social networking.

Of course in the world of social networking there is one behemoth that over shadows other services, not only in terms of members, but the sheer amount of data that it has the opportunity to collect on society. From Judges[3] to students,[4] terrorists[5] to grandparents[6] and spiritual leaders[7] every section of society is represented. The

---

1 M Kranzburg, "Technology and History: Kransburg's Laws" *Technology and Culture* (July 1986)(27) 544 545.

2 Irish Data Protection Act 1988.

3 C Cray, "The Too Friendly Judge? Social Networks and The Bench," *Judicature* (2009-2010) (93) 236.

4 JL Behrens, "About Facebook: Change at the Social Networking Juggernaut Creates New Opportunities for Law Library Outreach," *American Association of Law Libraries Spectrum* (2007-2008) 14.

5 G Weimann, "Terror on Facebook, Twitter, and Youtube," *Brown Journal of World Affairs* (2009-2010)(16) 45.

6 M Warman "One in Seven Grandparents on Facebook" *Telegraph*, http://www.telegraph.co.uk/technology/facebook/8589986/One-in-seven-grandparents-on-Facebook.html, 26 November 2012.

7 Alastair Jamieson Pope to go on Facebook as Vatican Embraces Online Technology, http://www.telegraph.co.uk/news/religion/5354026/Pope-to-go-on-Facebook-as-Vatican-embraces-online-technology.html.

proverbial elephant in the room is of course Facebook, the social networking phenomenon which one in every seven people on the planet is a member of.[8] From humble beginnings in 2004 (a mere one million members)[9], Facebook has seen exponential growth to the point where it is now a publicly traded company with over one billion monthly users.[10] Facebook opened offices in Dublin in February 2009[11] and subsequently became subject to the rules of European data protection law.

Article 8 of the EU Charter of Fundamental Rights states that "[e]veryone has the right to the protection of personal data concerning him or her"[12] and that "[s]uch data must be processed fairly for specified purposes and on the basis of the consent of the person concerned"[13] and finally "[e]veryone has the right of *access* to data which has been collected concerning him or her, and the right to have it rectified".[14]

This chapter provides an overview of the reasons for the audit, discuss some of the issues raised in the report made by the Irish Data Protection Commissioner and look at the effects of these findings. It will also assess the recommendations of the report and examine whether or not they are a viable model for the international stage. The current state of the law regarding this area will be discussed as will the issue of whether or not it is adequate enough to protect the rights of Facebook users in the EU.

Background to the Audit: "Europe v Facebook"

One of the catalysts for the Irish Data Protection Commissioners audit was a complaint it received on 18 August 2011 from a group called "Europe versus Facebook".[15] EVF is an Austrian based group and their complaints relate to how Facebook gathers, handles and uses the personal data of its members.[16] Their website contains excellent links to the relevant source material relating to their claims and individual PDFs of all twenty two complaints lodged with the Data Protection Commissioner between 18 August and 22 September 2011.[17] These complaints were varied and related to many aspects of the site ranging from one complaint noting that "pokes" on Facebook are kept in the users data set even after the user has removed them,[18] to even more serious allegations about the inadequacies of the company's privacy policy for users.[19] EVF states that "The privacy policy is vague,

8 The Associated Press, "Number of Active Users at Facebook Over the Years," http://finance.yahoo.com/news/number-active-users-facebook-over-years-214600186--finance.html.

9 *ibid.*

10 *ibid.*

11 Facebook Press Release, "Facebook establishes Dublin office and appoints Colm Long as Director of Online Operations," <http://www.glandore.ie/files/Facebook%20Announcement.pdf> accessed 6 December 2012.

12 Charter Of Fundamental Human Rights (2000/C 364/01) Article 8.1.

13 *ibid,* Article 8.2.

14 *ibid.*

15 Herinafter "EVF"

16 Europe vs Facebook, *Press Information* 2012 (2).

17 Europe vs Facebook, "Legal Procedure Against Facebook Ireland Limited," available online at http://www.europe-v-facebook.org/EN/Complaints/complaints.html.

18 Europe vs Facebook, *Complaint against Facebook Ireland Ltd – 01 "Pokes"* 2011, 2.

19 Europe vs Facebook, *Complaint against Facebook Ireland Ltd – 08 "Consent and Privacy Policy"* 2011, 2.

unclear and contradictory. If European and Irish standards are applied, the consent to the privacy policy is not valid".[20]

Nina and Boers applaud EVF and their tactics stating that "the strength of the user lies in the network itself. Strength – as it were- in numbers".[21] Another example of user revolt can be found in the case of LinkedIn whereby users revolted against the company sharing their information with third-party advertisers.[22]

This was not the first time that Facebook has had its privacy policy been the subject of third party scrutiny. The Office of the Canadian Data Protection Commissioner,[23] the US Federal Trade Commission[24] and the German Data Protection Commissioner[25] have all examined Facebook's privacy policy in the past and raised similar issues as those raised by EVF. The much publicised Beacon case[26] had previously brought to light Facebook's inadequacies regarding data protection. Here Facebook began publicising the products bought by its members via online retailers such as Amazon and Blockbuster by way of an application it launched called Beacon. The class action was settled out of court for $9.5 million and approved recently.[27]

This concern with privacy regarding advancements in technology or shifts in how we communicate is not a trend confined to the present. In 1890 Warren and Bardeis wrote "The Right to Privacy"[28] which was intended to address the increase in the numbers of newspapers, cameras and other technological advancements. They too felt that the innovation in the technology of their day was to be of concern to the concept of privacy. They stated "Recent inventions and business methods call attention to the next step which must be taken for the protection of the person, and for securing to the individual what Judge Cooley calls the right 'to be let alone'. Instantaneous photographs and newspaper enterprise have invaded the sacred precincts of private and domestic life; and numerous mechanical devices threaten to make good the prediction that 'what is whispered in the closet shall be proclaimed from the house-tops.'"[29] With the benefit of hindsight these words seem almost prophetic and they mirror the same concerns of groups like EVF.

---

20 Europe vs Facebook, "Legal Procedure Against Facebook Ireland Limited," available online at http://www.europe-v-facebook.org/EN/Complaints/complaints.html.

21 Ñusta Nina and Raoul Boers, "Disliking the Like User Policy-Change and Perception of the Internet as a Democratic Medium," (BOBCATSSS 2012 20th International Conference on Information Science Amsterdam, January 2012).

22 J Guynn, "How to Opt Out of LinkedIn Sharing your Data with Third Parties' *Los Angeles Times* (Los Angeles, 10 August 2011).

23 Office of the Privacy Commissioner of Canada, *Annual Report to Parliament 2011*, 42.

24 Federal Trade Commission, "Facebook Must Obtain Consumers' Consent Before Sharing Their Information Beyond Established Privacy Settings," http://www.ftc.gov/opa/2012/08/facebook.shtm.

25 M Vermuelen, "Another Data Protection Authority Says Facebooks Facial Recognition Feature Violates European Data Protection La," (Privacy International, 10 August 2011) https://www.privacyinternational.org/blog/another-data-protection-authority-says-facebooks-facial-recognition-feature-violates-european accessed> 04 December 2012

26 *Lane v Facebook* 2012 WL 4125857 United States Court Of Appeals Ninth Circuit

27 D Kravets, "Facebook's $9.5 Million 'Beacon' Settlement Approved," 21 September 2012 http://www.wired.com/threatlevel/2012/09/beacon-settlement-approved/.

28 Warren and Bardeis, "The Right To Privacy" *Harvard Law Review* (1890)(4) 193.

29 *ibid.*

Academics seem to have a mixed view of Facebook's attitude towards privacy and its attempts to protect users. Matecki applauded its privacy policies written clarity, noting that it "is written in clear, plain English. Facebook discloses the fact that they use information in profiles to solicit third party advertisements, and does not attempt to hide this practice behind confusing legalese".[30] However, she also notes that "Facebook's privacy policy is extremely lengthy, accessible only from a small link towards the bottom of the page, and thus users may not be likely to make the effort to seek out, fully read, or comprehend its often vaguely worded provisions".[31]

While some have heavily criticised its Facial Recognition features,[32] Chander has applauded its usefulness in actually protecting a user's account from unauthorised access.[33]

"From Pokes to Privacy": The Issue of Data Protection and Facebook

In total the Irish Data Protection Commissioner examined Facebook Ireland under a total of seventeen headings.[34] These Seventeen Headings are, in order: Privacy Policy, Advertising, Access Requests, Retention, Cookies, Third Party Apps, Disclosure to Third Parties, Facial Recognition, Data Security, Deletion of Accounts, Friend Finder, Tagging, Posting to other Profiles, Facebook Credits, Pseudonymous Profiles, Abuse Reporting and Compliance Management/Governance.

Most of the complaints lodged by EVF informed the headings under which Facebook Ireland would be audited. For the purposes of this discussion we will only focus on a few of these complaints and examine closely those which are deemed to be the leading issues regarding Facebook Ireland (FB-I). At this point it should be noted that the recommendations made in the audit were not legally binding and were merely guidelines as to how Facebook could meet EU data protection standards. As was stated in the report: "The recommendations in the Report do not carry an implication that FB-I's current practices are not in compliance with Irish data protection law. Neither do they represent formal decisions of the Commissioner on the complaints submitted to him as the Audit was led by me under "authority".[35]

The Irish Data Protection Commissioner noted that while auditing Facebook it was necessary to examine the company's responsibilities in two distinct areas:

---

30 L Matecki, "Next Steps for Protecting Youth Privacy Rights in the Social Networking Era," (2010) (5:1) *Northwestern Journal of Law & Social Policy* 369, 392.

31 *ibid.*

32 Article 29 Working Party, Opinion 02/2012 on Facial Recognition in Online and Mobile Services, (22 March 2012), http://ec.europa.eu/justice/data-protection/article-29/documentation/opinion-recommendation/files/2012/wp192_en.pdf.

33 A Chander, "Who Rules Facebookistan?" (2011-2012) (90) *North Carolina Law Review* 1807, 1849.

34 These Seventeen Headings are, in order: Privacy Policy, Advertising, Access Requests, Retention, Cookies, Third Party Apps, Disclosure to Third Parties, Facial Recognition, Data Security, Deletion of Accounts, Friend Finder, Tagging, Posting to other Profiles, Facebook Credits, Pseudonymous Profiles, Abuse Reporting and Compliance Management/Governance.

35 Data Protection Commissioner, *Facebook Ireland Ltd: Report of Audit* (ODPC-2011).

i. Does Facebook provide users with appropriate privacy controls to users and adequate information on how to utilise these controls effectively?[36]
ii. The extent to which Facebook uses personal data of users to target advertising towards them.[37]

It also examined the privacy governance structure within Facebook.[38] The Office of the Irish Data Protection Commissioner audited Facebook Ireland with these guidelines in mind and made a number of recommendations to the company. They would then review the report in July 2012 and examine the extent to which Facebook had addressed the recommendations made by their office.

The "Facebook Ireland Ltd Report of Re-Audit"[39] would be issued on 21 September 2012 and would outline areas where Facebook had successfully implemented the recommendations and areas where the changes recommended had not been successfully implemented. In a statement by the ODPC they stated that they were satisfied by the attempts of Facebook to address the issues raised in the first report. They were particularly pleased with a number of changes made by Facebook. The ODPC were particularly pleased with: "The provision of better transparency for the user in how their data is handled, the provision of increased user control over settings, the implementation of clear retention periods for the deletion of personal data or an enhanced ability for the user to delete items and the enhancement of the user's right to have ready access to their personal data and the capacity of FB-I to ensure rigorous assessment of compliance with Irish and EU data protection requirements".[40]

"From Here to There": An Assessment of the Impact of the Audit

As a result of the Audit Facebook made substantial changes to its services and this greatly affected the users of the site.

Users now receive much more detail about the data that Facebook collects on them when they request a data report from the site.[41] In the Audit Report the ODPC said that the right for an individual to access personal data held by a data controller established in the EU is a basic right enshrined in the EU Data Protection Directive 1995.

Section 3 of the Data Protection Act states:

> "An individual who believes that a person keeps personal data shall, if he so requests the person in writing –
> (a) be informed by the person whether he keeps any such data, and
> (b) if he does, be given by the person a description of the data and the purposes for

---

36 *ibid*, 4.
37 *ibid*.
38 *ibid*, 143.
39 Data Protection Commissioner, *Facebook Ireland Ltd Report of Re-Audit* (ODPC-2012).
40 Office of the Data Protection Commissioner, "Report of Review of Facebook Ireland's Implementation of Audit Recommendations Published – Facebook Turns Off Tag Suggest in the E," http://dataprotection.ie/viewdoc.asp?DocID=1233&m=f.
41 Data Protection Commissioner, *Facebook Ireland Ltd Report of Re-Audit* (ODPC-2012) 21.

which they are kept, as soon as may be and in any event not more than 21 days after the request has been given or sent to him".[42]

Section 4 of the Data Protection Act states:

"Subject to the provisions of this Act, an individual shall, if he or she so requests a data controller by notice in writing:

be informed by the data controller whether the data processed by or on behalf of the data controller include personal data relating to the individual,... as soon as may be and in any event not more than 40 days after compliance by the individual with the provisions of this section and, where any of the information is expressed in terms that are not intelligible to the average person without explanation, the information shall be accompanied by an explanation of those terms".[43]

In response to this Facebook made the data available without the user having to make a formal access request. Personal data is available to members in four ways:

- Through their own account;
- Through their activity log;
- Through a download tool which provides additional data that users are typically interested in;
- Through an expanded archive which gives large amounts of extra personal data that most users are not seeking to access.[44]

The ODPC were satisfied that since this implementation of policy, all users are now receiving access to their personal data held by Facebook. Subsequently they felt that Facebook is now fully compliant with s 3 and s 4 of the Data Protection Acts.[45]

In a more visible and public move Facebook switched off its Facial Recognition Tagging feature in line with a recommendation in the audit,[46] a move that was surely welcomed greatly by the EU Article 29 Working Party group[47] amongst others.

In its report the ODPC noted that "when a user uploads a photo album, photos containing the same person are automatically grouped together by Facebook. Facebook then suggests names for friends in some of these groups in order to help save the user time creating and sharing albums."

The ODPC found that Facebook should have handled the implementation of this feature in a more appropriate manner and recommended that Facebook take more appropriate steps from a best practices perspective to ensure the consent collected from users to this feature can be relied upon.[48] Facebook agreed to provide an additional form of notification for the tag suggest:

---

42 Data Protection Act 2003 s 3.

43 Data Protection Act 2003 s 4.

44 Data Protection Commissioner, *Facebook Ireland Ltd Report of Re-Audit* (ODPC-2012) 21.

45 *ibid*, 22.

46 *ibid*, 37.

47 Article 29 Working Party, Opinion 02/2012 on Facial Recognition in Online and Mobile Services, (22 March 2012), http://ec.europa.eu/justice/data-protection/article-29/documentation/opinion-recommendation/files/2012/wp192_en.pdf.

48 Data Protection Commissioner, *Facebook Ireland Ltd Report of Re-Audit* (ODPC-2012) 37.

- Each user was given prominent notice of the new feature on their home page at least three times;
- The notice provided a link to more detailed information;
- The method of disabling the feature was modified to further simplify it.

Subsequently the EU Article 29 Working Party released its opinion in the area of Facial Recognition and Biometric data and the ODPC recommended that Facebook comply with the recommendations made in this report.[49] As Facebook were in the process of complying with these recommendations the German Data Protection Commissioner reopened an action they had taken against Facebook regarding the Facial Recognition feature. In light of this Facebook decided to deactivate the feature until they could find a way to fully implement the policy in a manner that would satisfy all the concerns raised by various groups relating to the technology. Not only did they deactivate the service in Germany but it was turned off all across Europe a move which was welcomed by EVF.[50]

When new users sign up there is a substantial tutorial on how to utilise Facebook's privacy features and a thorough explanation of the tools available to users. Facebook have also introduced a privacy blog which will highlight and educate users on issues regarding their privacy and have also created open forums with users to discuss privacy issues.[51]

However the changes outlined above (and many more besides) were not sufficient to satisfy EVF. They recently stated their unhappiness with the results of the report:

> "After a detailed analysis of the 'audit' documents it became clear that the authority has taken very important first steps, but that it has not always delivered accurate and correct result ... A non-binding audit might not need such accuracy, but we expect that the authority goes into every detail when deciding about our complaints. In some cases we also had to wonder if the authority has really checked Facebook's claims, or if they have blindly trusted Facebook".[52]

They have also committed to taking a case against Facebook Ireland before the Irish courts arguing that Facebook does not meet the data protection standards of Irish or European Law. "We will ask the Irish authority again to deliver all necessary files and evidence. So far we were not allowed to even see the counterarguments by Facebook. After this we will ask for a formal, legally binding decision on all 22 complaints".[53]

There is no doubt that the audit had a direct impact on European users as Facebook had to change its services across Europe as a result of the audit. There is also a

---

49 Article 29 Working Party, Opinion 02/2012 on Facial Recognition in Online and Mobile Services, (22 March 2012), http://ec.europa.eu/justice/data-protection/article-29/documentation/opinion-recommendation/files/2012/wp192_en.pdf.

50 Europe v Facebook, "*Response to 'Audit' by the Irish Office of the Data Protection Commissioner on Facebook Ireland Ltd,*" 4 December 2012, 44.

51 *Facebook Site Governance,* Responding to Your Feedback , https://www.facebook.com/notes/facebook-site-governance/responding-to-your-feedback/10152321231735 30.

52 Irish Data Protection Authority was Unable to Resolve Privacy Dispute. Austrian Students are Preparing to Fight "Facebook" in Courts. Press Release 4 December 2012.

53 *ibid.*

possibility of change on a global scale if Facebook decides to implement the changes to the site worldwide in order to ensure uniformity in its services. Similarly it may indirectly force US companies developing applications for Facebook to conform to higher data protection standards in order to operate their services within Facebook in Europe.

"The Future of Facebook and Data Protection" Criticisms

There is no doubt that the audit did raise the levels of privacy afforded to users of Facebook and improved and implemented tools that users can utilise to enforce their privacy rights on the site. The ODPC were particularly happy with a number of changes made by Facebook, specifically:

- The provision of better transparency for the user in how their data is handled;
- The provision of increased user control over settings;
- The implementation of clear retention periods for the deletion of personal data or an enhanced ability for the user to delete items;
- The enhancement of the user's right to have ready access to their personal data and the capacity of FB-I to ensure rigorous assessment of compliance with Irish and EU data protection requirements.[54]

The Commissioner stated:

> "I am satisfied that the Review has demonstrated a clear and ongoing commitment on the part of FB-I to comply with its data protection responsibilities by way of implementation or progress towards implementation of the recommendations in the Audit Report. I am particularly encouraged in relation to the approach it has decided to adopt on the tag suggest/facial recognition feature by in fact agreeing to go beyond our initial recommendations, in light of developments since then, in order to achieve best practice. This feature has already been turned off for new users in the EU and templates for existing users will be deleted by 15 October, pending agreement with my Office on the most appropriate means of collecting user consent. By doing so it is sending a clear signal of its wish to demonstrate its commitment to best practice in data protection compliance".[55]

However, the issue is far from closed and both Facebook and the ODPC[56] recognise that their relationship and dealings with one another will be on going and ever evolving as Facebook continues to operate and change. It is also clear that ongoing engagement with the company will be necessary as it continues to bring forward new ways of serving advertising to users and retaining users on the site. The value of such engagement to identify and deal with any data protection concerns prior to launch of new products and services is fully accepted by FB-I.[57]

A major flaw in the new privacy policy of Facebook is the completion of the Privacy

---

54 Office of the Data Protection Commissioner, "Report of Review of Facebook Ireland's Implementation of Audit Recommendations Published – Facebook Turns Off Tag Suggest in the EU," http://dataprotection.ie/viewdoc.asp?DocID=1233&m=f.

55 *ibid.*

56 *ibid.*

57 *ibid.*

tutorial which is optional and can be bypassed. Although this will be of great use to the new users, should they choose to take the tutorial, it offers little in the way of education for the existing users. It should be considered that all users who when agreeing to the new changes in the privacy policy, should be mandatorily made to complete the privacy tutorial. This would offer great value to both data subjects and Facebook as a data controller. Users would not be able to plead ignorance towards their rights on the site and would also be fully informed and educated on the privacy settings available to them on the site.

However, the blame is not to be laid solely at the feet of Facebook. While Levine argues that the law has not kept pace with technology,[58] Witte credits part of the blame to the legal system itself, concluding that some of these problems arise due to the laws ability to react quickly and resolve disputes.[59] Kane notes that the legal system is "struggling to adjust to both the permanence and pervasiveness of information transfers via social networking sites".[60] One solution to this problem which will be discussed is Grimmelmann's theory that social networking services should have the same standards applied to their services as product safety liability.[61] Chander proposes that this may not be such a bad thing as it forces lawmakers to strengthen and improve their laws.[62] This could be considered a means to provide for the agile, creative and effective responses that Stoddart calls for in Canadian legislation:

> "Protecting privacy in this rapidly transforming online landscape demands agile, creative and effective responses. The reality is, however, that we have a situation where legislative amendments wind their way through the Parliamentary process at a glacial pace in comparison to the rate at which the world is changing. A dispute over a point of law can take several years to resolve through the courts. It is not realistic to anticipate dramatic change in how the wheels of the legal and Parliamentary systems move in the foreseeable future. Therefore, it is incumbent upon us to think about how we can make existing laws work".[63]

Perhaps this "creative, effective and agile response" call from Stoddart is already in place in the EU. Another aspect of the issue that should be considered is the wording of Article 8:

1. Everyone has the right to the protection of personal data concerning him or her;
2. Such data must be processed fairly for specified purposes and on the basis of the consent of the person concerned or some other legitimate basis laid down by law; Everyone has the right of access to data which has been collected concerning him or her, and the right to have it rectified;

---

58 D Levine, "Facebook and Social Networks the Governments Newest Playground for Information and The Laws That Haven't Quite Kept Pace" (33) (3) *Hastings Communications & Law Journal* 485.

59 DS Witte, "Your Opponent Does Not Need a Friend Request to See Your Page: Social Networking Sites and Electronic Discovery," (2010) (41) *McGeorge Law Review* 891.

60 B Kane, "Balancing Anonymity, Popularity and Micro-Celebrity: The Crossroads of Social Networking and Privacy," (2010) (20:2) *Albany Law Journal* 329, 331.

61 J Grimmelmann, "Privacy vs Product Safety," (2010) (19) *Widener Law Review Journal* 793.

62 A Chander, "Facebookistan," (2011-2012) (90) *North Carolina Law Review* 1807, 1851.

63 J Stoddart, "Privacy in the Era of Social Networks Legal Obligations of Social Media Sites," (2011) (74) *Saskatchewan Law Review* 263, 270.

3. Compliance with these rules shall be subject to control by an independent authority.[64]

As we can see within Article 8 there is a certain amount of ambiguity. This ambiguity is highly necessary in order for this particular piece of legislation to be effective. Kane notes that existing legal procedures, laws and decision-making are designed to address conventional and predictable legal issues however social networking and all of its evolutions do not follow the rules of convention.[65] Therefore, the loose, almost vague wording of Article 8 would seem apt. It can be interpreted to apply to unforeseen changes that may arise from technological advancement but still have some of the rigidity of legislation.

Conclusions

In conclusion, the audit of Facebook by the ODPC can be viewed as a success. It is important to remember that that the recommendations made in the audit were not legally binding and were merely guidelines as to how Facebook could meet EU data protection standards. When viewed in this light, the audit can be seen to be a success for a number of parties.

The ODPC managed to achieve a number of changes to Facebook's policies. The most significant of these changes are:

- A mechanism for users to convey an informed choice for how their information is used and shared on the site including in relation to Third Party Apps;
- A broad update to the Data Use Policy/Privacy Policy to take account of recommendations as to where the information provided to users could be further improved;
- Transparency and control for users via the provision of all personal data held to them on request and as part of their everyday interaction with the site;
- The deletion of information held on users and non-users via what are known as social plugins and more generally the deletion of data held from user interactions with the site.
- Increased transparency and controls for the use of personal data for advertising;
- A switch off of the controversial Facial Recognition system across Europe.

Facebook users as data subjects also benefited from the audit as they had the methods used to protect their fundamental rights examined thoroughly. In a similar vein due to the changes made by Facebook on foot of the report it is now easier for users of the site to help protect their personal data on Facebook. This was achieved by the simplification of privacy settings, tutorials available online for users to utilise these settings effectively, a comprehensive means of retrieving all personal data kept by

[64] Charter Of Fundamental Human Rights (2000/C 364/01), Article 8.

[65] B Kane, "Balancing Anonymity, Popularity and Micro-Celebrity: The Crossroads of Social Networking and Privac" (2010) (20:2) *Albany Law Journal* 329, 362.

Facebook and the deletion of data held by third party apps. While all these benefits may not have been felt by worldwide Facebook users the potential for users outside the EU to share in the benefits of such changes is there. Facebook may decide to implement these policies across all of its services for the sake of harmonisation.

Facebook itself also benefitted from the audit. The audit basically consisted of the ODPC explaining to Facebook where they were failing to meet specific standards of European Data Protection law without Facebook having fear of legal sanctions. In essence it was a yellow card for Facebook, allowing them to go back and revisit the services of the website and asses where they needed to change aspects of their product to comply with European law. As Facebook is now a publicly traded company this would surely have been a concern of shareholders.

In summation, the audit was a success in many eyes and somewhat underwhelming to others, especially EVF. At the time of writing the changes implemented seem apt and suitable but this begs the question for how long will they remain so? Commissioner Hawkes said the review is "no more than an assessment at a point in time"[66] and new developments in advertising and services will continue to "throw up challenges"[67] for both FB-I and the Irish Data Protection Commissioner.

---

66 S O'Carroll, "Data Protection Commissioner Satisfied with Facebook Ireland", 21 September 2012, http://businessetc.thejournal.ie/data-protection-commissioner-satisfied-with-facebook-ireland-604429-Sep2012/.

67 *ibid.*

Chapter 13

LAWS RE-PHORMED?

Damien McCallig

Headline of Issues

- Phorm
- Phorm test
- Constitutional privacy issues
- Statutes
- Cookies
- Data protection compliance
- Interception
- Criminal
- Civil

Introduction

> "In general, a fact about ourselves is someone's business if there is a specific social relationship between us which entitles them to know. We are often free to choose whether or not to enter into such relationships, and those who want to maintain as much privacy as possible will enter them only reluctantly."[1]

The words of James Rachels have a strong resonance with the basis of the right to privacy in Irish law. Privacy is an aspect of one's social existence.[2] It has at its core the recognition of the values of freedom, individuality and autonomy.[3] Irish constitutional law has accepted a conception of privacy as a sophisticated relational right securing and protecting one's "dignity and autonomy as a socially situated individual".[4]

Irish law recognises that the lives of individuals and their communities are "integrated".[5] The freedom to integrate and participate "in the spread of ideas and in the creation of meanings" helps individuals to grow and develop into mature participants in society, and this consequently helps to shape positively communities

---

1 J Rachels, "Why Privacy is Important" (1975) (4:4) *Philosophy and Public Affairs* 323 at 331.

2 *Report on Privacy: Surveillance and the Interception of Communications*, Law Reform Commission, LRC 57-1998 (Government Publications, Dublin, 1998) at para 1.13: "[P]rivacy is more than a tool for protecting the seclusion of the individual. It is an organising principle of civil society."

3 Henchy J in *Norris v Attorney General* [1984] IR 36 at 71 recognised that privacy was a "complex of rights, varying in nature, purpose and range, each necessarily a facet of the citizen's core of individuality within the constitutional order."

4 H Delany and E Carolan, *The Right to Privacy* (Thomson Round Hall, Dublin, 2008) at 37.

5 R Dworkin, "Liberal Community" (1989) (77) *California Law Review* 479 at 491.

and wider society.[6] As we are social beings, maintaining privacy becomes an on going balancing exercise between individual and social values.

The digital age and associated technologies greatly expand the possibilities for individual participation in society. They make possible interaction in forms and on a scale previously unthinkable. But the digital age and its associated technology have made data "collection and processing extraordinarily efficient."[7] New methods of monetising internet traffic and tapping into the incredibly rich click-stream of online activity mean that surveillance has become big business online.[8] Online behavioural advertising is a business model that is primarily based on the surveillance of a user's online activities. One company, Phorm,[9] has received much media attention due to methods of delivering online behavioural advertising.[10]

Legal analysis to date on the Phorm business model is focused on English law and has concluded that it encroaches on individual privacy, contravenes data protection law and could even constitute criminal computer intrusion or interception.[11] This chapter assesses the Phorm business model from an Irish perspective. What if an Irish internet service provider (ISP) was to deploy the Phorm system secretly in Ireland? Identifying the legal issues that result provides a type of stress test of Irish privacy and data protection laws. Does the relationship between internet subscribers and their website or service provider entitle an associated advertiser to use facts about a subscriber in order to target online advertising?

It is an opportune time to undertake this Phorm test, particularly in light of the ePrivacy Directive[12] and the proposed EU Data Protection Regulation.

This chapter begins by introducing the concept of online behavioural advertising and goes on to describe how the Phorm business model works. It then introduces the key elements of Irish privacy law, both constitutional and statutory, that are applicable to the phenomenon of online behavioural advertising. Next it evaluates and analyses whether the Phorm model is in compliance with Irish law. The Phorm

---

6 J Balkin, "Digital Speech and Democratic Culture: A Theory of Freedom of Expression for the Information Society" (2004) (79) *New York University Law Review* 1 at 4.

7 L Lessig, *Code: Version 2.0* (Basic Books, New York, 2006) at 22.

8 R Picker, "Online Advertising, Identity and Privacy," *University of Chicago Law and Economics*, Olin Working Paper No. 475 (29 June 2009) at 6.

9 See www.phorm.com/about_us/index.html.

10 B Johnson, "Outrage as New Phorm Trial Begins," *Guardian*, 30 September 2008. However, on 8 April 2011 the Crown Prosecution Service (CPS) decided not to consent to a request from an individual to begin a prosecution of BT Group Plc and Phorm Inc. The CPS invoked section 4.2 of the Code for Crown Prosecutors in deciding that "a prosecution would not be in the public interest" in this case, available at www.cps.gov.uk/news/press_releases/116_11/index.html.

11 See N Bohm, "The Phorm "Webwise" System – a Legal Analysis," 23 April 2008, available at www.fipr.org/080423phormlegal.pdf; and S Deane-Johns, "Behavioural Targeting of Internet Advertising" (2009) (20(2)) *Computers and Law* 22; and L Edwards and C Waedle ed, *Law and the Internet* (Hart Publishing, Oxford, 2009) at 533–537 and 542.

12 Directive 2009/136/EC of the European Parliament and of the Council of 25 November 2009 amending Directive 2002/22/EC on universal service and users' rights relating to electronic communications networks and services, Directive 2002/58/EC concerning the processing of personal data and the protection of privacy in the electronic communications sector and Regulation (EC) No 2006/2004 on cooperation between national authorities responsible for the enforcement of consumer protection laws [2009] OJ L337/11.

test highlights a number of weaknesses and inconsistencies in the current Irish legal framework. Most notable are the issues relating to consent for both the processing of personal data and the processing of cookies, and what constitutes personal data in Irish law following the *EMI v Eircom*[13] judgment.

Online Behavioural Advertising: Context and Emergence

The concept of targeting advertising is not a new one. The goal of effective advertising is to match buyers with sellers. Advertising is costly and in most circumstances it passes many sets of eyes before making a match. John Wanamaker is attributed with the saying that "[h]alf the money I spend on advertising is wasted; the trouble is I don't know which half."[14] This saying now over a century old still holds true for much of the advertising one sees today. Look to the advertisements on television, in newspapers, and on the billboards one passes every day: what percentage, if any, of those paid advertisements successfully matches a buyer to a seller?

Online behavioural advertising offers the promise of greatly increasing the efficiency of each euro spent. Online behavioural advertising is the process of displaying advertisements to an online subscriber based on data about that subscriber's internet browsing activity. It involves setting a cookie[15] to the subscriber's browser or hard drive or both, in order to track the subscriber's activity on a website.[16] The cookie acts as a unique identifier for the subscriber. It can also collect data about the subscriber's activity on a website.[17]

The use of behavioural advertising is seen as a "commercial pot of gold" in the advertising and marketing industry.[18] ISPs have begun to link up with advertisement delivery providers to try to capture the potential of the information flows to and from their subscribers. Companies such as NebuAd[19] and Phorm[20] have emerged in attempting to partner with ISPs. The potential earnings are significant: it is estimated that British Telecom (BT) alone could have earned £87 million pounds per year from a deal with Phorm.[21]

ISPs in the United Kingdom carried out secret trials in order to investigate the possibility of deploying the Phorm system for online behavioural advertising.[22] The

13 *EMI v Eircom* [2010] IEHC 108.

14 See "John Wanamaker (1838–1922)", in *The Advertising Century*, available online at http://adage.com/century/people006.html; also quoted by R Picker, "Online Advertising, Identity and Privacy," *University of Chicago Law and Economics*, Olin Working Paper No. 475 (29 June 2009) at 28.

15 "Cookies are small text files which reside on the local hard disk of the computer, or terminal equipment of, a subscriber and contain a limited amount of profile information about that subscriber," in Edwards and Waedle, *op. cit*, 512.

16 Deane-Johns, *op. cit*, 22.

17 *ibid.*

18 Edwards and Waedle, *op. cit*, 531.

19 P Ohm, "The Rise and Fall of Invasive ISP Surveillance" (2009) *University of Illinois Law Review* 1417 at 1434.

20 See www.phorm.com/about_us/index.html.

21 Ohm, *op. cit*, 1434.

22 B Johnson, "Outrage as New Phorm Trial Begins," *Guardian*, 30 September 2008.

European Commission subsequently referred the United Kingdom to the European Court of Justice for not fully implementing EU rules on the confidentiality of electronic communications following complaints about how the UK authorities had dealt with concerns about the secret Phorm trials.[23]

Phorm may be implemented in Brazil, with five ISPs having reportedly signed deals.[24] The American equivalent, NebuAd, had previously signed agreements to partner with ISP Charter Communications; however, in the face of mounting criticism and threatened legal action, Charter abandoned plans with NebuAd.[25]

What is Phorm and How Does it Work?

Phorm describes itself as "a global personalisation technology company that makes content and advertising more relevant."[26] The following paragraphs summarise Clayton's analysis of the Phorm system and how it operates.[27] He describes the basic concept behind the Phorm model as intercepting or taking "a copy of the traffic that passes between an end-subscriber and a website".[28] This allows Phorm to inspect the traffic and content in order to understand the types of websites visited in order to target advertisements at subscribers.[29]

This is carried out with the assistance of a subscriber's ISP. When subscribers request a target website, their browsers are sent http redirects — electronic notices designed to inform the subscriber's browser that a website has moved — which redirect the subscriber's browser to a Phorm-run website in order to fool the subscriber's computer into accepting a package from Phorm that includes the target webpage and a Phorm cookie that pretends to come from the subscriber's intended target website.[30] The Phorm cookie will contain the 24-digit unique identifier (UID), which enables Phorm to identify and profile a subscriber.[31] Phorm states that the UID is used solely "to distinguish between subscribers, not to identify them".[32]

Phorm does not inspect all web traffic; it ignores a number of file type extensions, for example for images.[33] Traffic will also be ignored from a list of webmail websites[34] and the system does not view any information on secure websites (ie HTTPS websites).[35] Phorm also state that prior to any analysis, it excludes: "strings of

---

23 European Commission Press Release, "Digital Agenda: Commission Refers UK to Court Over Privacy and Personal Data Protection," IP/10/1215 Brussels, 30 September 2010.
24 M Palmer, "Phorm Wins Ad-tracking Deals in Brazil," *The Financial Times*, 26 March 2010.
25 Ohm, *op. cit*, 1434.
26 See www.phorm.com/about_us/index.html.
27 R Clayton, "The Phorm 'Webwise' System," 18 May 2008; available at www.cl.cam.ac.uk/~rnc1/080518-phorm.pdf.
28 *ibid*, para 1.
29 *ibid*.
30 *ibid*, paras 14 – 24; and Ohm, *op. cit*.
31 Clayton, *op. cit*, paras 5, 20 and 34; and see *Phorm* presentation "How Phorm Technology Works", available at www.phorm.com/technology/index.html.
32 www.phorm.com/technology/delivering_personalisation.html.
33 Clayton, *op. cit*, para 35.
34 *ibid*, para 38.
35 Available at Technology and Privacy section of FAQs at www.phorm.com/faq.html.

numbers longer than three digits to ensure that we do not collect credit card numbers, phone numbers, National Insurance or other potentially private information such as names or email addresses."[36] It also ignores <input> fields on a webpage; these are fields used to fill in a form on a webpage.[37]

Each copied page that remains is broken down into the individual words that appear on it. The system ignores words containing "@" as possible email address, words following Mr and Mrs as possible names, and other noise words, including *and*, *but*, and *or*.[38] The remaining words are ranked by frequency and a summary of the top 10 keywords that appear on the webpage is retained as a representation of the page visited by the subscriber's UID.

The frequency ranking is carried out by the "profiler", which has access to a subscriber's UID and IP address, and is controlled by the ISP. These results are sent to another machine known as an "anonymiser", which is also ISP controlled, and a record is then issued to the "channel server", which is Phorm controlled.

The channel server receives a record that includes the URL, search terms, UID and keywords that are then matched against channels. The Phorm channel server saves a record against the UID of the channel and date-stamp.[39] These records are held for six months.[40] Therefore, a subscriber's profile as matched against his or her UID will contain all channels and associated date-stamps for a rolling six-month period.

Targeted online behavioural advertisements are served, based on the profile of channels created against the UID.[41] When a subscriber visits a webpage of a participating website, the subscriber's browser will fetch an advertisement from Phorm and display it.[42] The subscriber's browser in the request for the image will include the UID. The UID will be passed through the "anonymiser" on to the "channel server" and serve the appropriate advertisement based on a real-time auction between advertisers and other predefined serving rules.[43]

Scope and Application of the Constitutional Privacy Right

Privacy is widely viewed and understood as a fundamental human right,[44] and is

---

36 *ibid.*

37 Clayton, *op. cit*, para 47.

38 *ibid*, para 48.

39 *ibid*, para 58.

40 *ibid*, para 61.

41 *ibid.* Channels can either be predefined or automatically generated, both being subject to review and approval by Phorm. No channels will be created which relate to advertisements for "adult material, for anything medical, or for alcohol, tobacco, gambling or politics."

42 *ibid*, para 63.

43 *ibid*, paras 69 and 70. The predefined rules include rules on advertisement conflicts or clashes, for example advertisements served on a website will not promote a direct competitor, and a "frequency cap" that prevents a subscriber from receiving the same advertisement on a repeated basis.

44 *Report of the Working Group on Privacy* (Department of Justice Equality and Law Reform, Dublin, 2006) at 8.

recognised by the Irish Constitution.[45] The seminal work in the privacy arena by Warren and Brandeis describes privacy as the "right to be let alone".[46] Their article was prompted by a fear that the technology of the day, a combination of photography and newspapers, would lead to "what is whispered in the closet … [being] … proclaimed from the house-tops".[47]

However, privacy is not a unified concept. Solove describes the term privacy as "an umbrella term relating to a wide and disparate group of related things".[48] Commentators divide privacy into categories, most commonly: informational, spatial and decisional privacy.[49] These categories follow along the lines discussed by the Law Reform Commission in Ireland[50] and the more recent report of the Australian Law Reform Commission on this area.[51]

Informational privacy is the archetypal category. It relates to an individual's entitlement to control the dissemination of information about oneself.[52] This includes control of all information that can be protected, depending on circumstance, from one's name to inherently private information, with medical history being a classic example. Some commentators view this as the main concern of data protection laws. Edwards states that data protection "protects what is known very generally as *informational privacy*".[53] However, data protection laws also exist to protect freedom from surveillance and the interception of communications.[54]

Spatial privacy relates to two distinct concepts. The first is the concept of territorial privacy most commonly related to one's home. This is reinforced with the protection afforded by "the inviolability of the dwelling".[55] Territorial privacy also extends outside one's home from a place of work or business[56] to hotel rooms.[57] The second concept is that of personal privacy. This relates to an individual's own personal space, in particular one's own body.[58] From there, it extends outwards. In light of

45 There is no express constitutional provision relating to an individual's right to privacy. Article 40.3 of the Irish Constitution 1937, however, posits a guarantee by the State to defend and vindicate the personal rights of the citizen, and the Irish courts have determined that, a right to privacy is implicit in that provision. The right to privacy is an unenumerated (or unspecified) personal right recognised by the Constitution. The constitutional right to individual privacy was successfully invoked before the High Court in *Kennedy and Arnold v Ireland* [1987] IR 587 in the context of telephone-tapping.

46 S Warren and L Brandeis, "The Right to Privacy" (1890) (4) *Harvard Law Review* 195 at 195.

47 *ibid.*

48 D Solove, "A Taxonomy of Privacy" (2006) (154) *University of Pennsylvania Law Review* 477 at 485.

49 Delany and Carolan, *op. cit*, 20 and 41–56.

50 *Report on Privacy: Surveillance and the Interception of Communications*, Law Reform Commission, LRC 57-1998 (Government Publications: Dublin, 1998).

51 *For Your Information: Australian Privacy Law and Practice*, Australian Law Reform Commission, ALRC 108 (Sydney, 2008).

52 Delany and Carolan, *op. cit*, 22 and 55.

53 Edwards and Waedle, *op. cit*, 445.

54 *Report of the Working Group on Privacy* (Department of Justice Equality and Law Reform, Dublin, 2006) at 13.

55 Constitution of Ireland 1937, Article 40.5.

56 Delany and Carolan, *op. cit*, 46.

57 *ibid*, 48.

58 *Re a Ward of Court* [1996] 2 IR 79.

the *Von Hannover* case, the concept of personal space now includes an expectation of personal privacy even in public.[59]

The third category, decisional privacy, relates to an individual's right to autonomy, the freedom and right to make one's own decisions. Traditionally this category protected an individual from intrusion by the state.[60] So, for example in *McGee v Attorney General* marital privacy ensured that the state could not interfere in decisions on the use of contraception.[61] Delany and Carolan state that it seems reasonable to suggest that the right to decisional privacy may extend, for example, to prevent interference with one's choice of literature.[62]

Each of these categories goes to the core of privacy and to the core of the individual. They are, as Henchy J described in the Irish Supreme Court, that "secluded area" we all require for the expression of individual personality.[63] Protection of this secluded area promotes breathing space for our "thoughts, sentiments and emotions",[64] providing a freedom and autonomy that foster creative experimentation, self-fulfilment and participation in society.

The constitutional protection of privacy has extended over time to include non-state intrusion of one's privacy, as demonstrated in *Sinnott v Nationalist and Leinster Times, Carlow*[65] and *Herrity v Associated Newspapers*.[66] The *Sinnott* case involved the negligent publication of a photograph in which Mr Sinnott's private parts were accidently exposed during a football match. Budd J in the appeal to the Irish High Court awarded damages of €11,000 for the breach of Mr Sinnott's constitutional right to privacy.[67] It is easy to understand both the injury to Mr Sinnott's dignity and the invasion of privacy suffered by having an image of such an inherently private part of one's body printed in a local newspaper due to negligence of those involved in the publication process.[68]

But the protection of privacy provided by the Constitution is essentially information-neutral. The information or matters protected do not need to be inherently private or be of a particularly sensitive nature. The act of intrusion into one's private space can also amount to a breach of privacy. An individual is protected against unwarranted intrusion into his or her private space regardless of whether the intrusion results in sensitive details being discovered or made public.[69] The methods employed to obtain

59 *Von Hannover v Germany* 59320/00 [2004] ECHR 294 (24 June, 2004); (2005) 40 EHRR 1.
60 *Re a Ward of Court (No. 2)* [1996] 2 IR 79 at 169; see also Hogan and Whyte, *JM Kelly: The Irish Constitution* (Lexis Nexis Butterworths, Dublin, 2003) at 1445; and Delany and Carolan, *op. cit*, 13.
61 *McGee v Attorney General* [1974] IR 284.
62 Delany and Carolan, *op. cit*, 41.
63 *Norris v Attorney General* [1984] IR 36 at 72.
64 Warren and Brandeis, *op. cit*, 198.
65 As reported in "Appeal Against GAA Player Award Lost," *Irish Times*, 27 January 2007, at 4.
66 *Herrity v Associated Newspapers* [2009] 1 IR 316.
67 M Carolan, "Court Increases Payout to GAA Player Over Photo," *Irish Times*, 31 July 2008, at 4.
68 The photograph passed through all stages of the publication process from image selection to final production without being deemed unsuitable for publication.
69 In *Kennedy and Arnold v Ireland* [1987] IR 587 at 593 Hamilton P. states that "[t]he dignity and freedom of an individual in a democratic society cannot be ensured if his communications of a private nature, …, are deliberately, consciously and unjustifiably intruded upon and interfered

the information and subsequent use of that information may amount to a breach of the constitutional right to privacy.

This was the case in *Herrity v Associated Newspapers*,[70] where an estranged husband hired a private investigator to intercept telephone conversations between his wife and a local priest. The husband threatened to publish the telephone conversations if his wife refused to sign over the family home to him. She refused, and transcripts of the intercepted telephone calls were published. The court, in finding a breach of the wife's right to privacy, was heavily reliant on the unlawful method employed in order to obtain information, by use of an "illegal phone tap", and awarded damages totalling €90,000.[71]

Both of these elements of privacy—protection of information and freedom from unwarranted intrusion—must be balanced with other rights and ultimately in the Irish context with the common good.[72] The problem posed for Irish law is how these elements of privacy are affected by technology that is becoming increasingly pervasive and invasive.

Online behavioural advertising, as explained above, creates records of online activity, consumption and intellectual exploration. Without appropriate consent from an internet subscriber, this clearly invades informational privacy. By peering into subscribers' personal space, it also invades their spatial and decisional privacy. If they know they are being watched, will they visit that website? Will they download that song or purchase that book? More fundamentally, will they search for the content online in the first place?

Balkin questions whether online subscribers are being nudged into fragmented markets of consumer interest.[73] There are two risks inherent in this practice. First, subscribers are being influenced by a bombardment of information and behavioural advertisements that will ultimately limit their intellectual exploration, by narrowing their field of vision.[74] Secondly, will knowing they are under surveillance further limit the desire for intellectual exploration? This is the so-called chilling effect.[75]

Elkin-Koren summarises it well, describing technology's ability in defining and controlling information availability ultimately to influence subscribers' positions, concepts and ideas.[76] This is reiterated by Cohen:

---

with." He goes on to emphasise the words "deliberately, consciously and unjustifiably" "because an individual must accept the risk of accidental interference with his communications and the fact that in certain circumstances the exigencies of the common good may require and justify such intrusion and interference."

70 *Herrity v Associated Newspapers* [2009] 1 IR 316.

71 *ibid.*

72 *Kennedy and Arnold v Ireland* [1987] IR 587 at 592.

73 Balkin, *op. cit*, 22.

74 J Cohen, "Privacy, Ideology, and Technology: A Response to Jeffry Rosen" (2000–2001) *Georgetown Law Journal* 2029–89.

75 J Cohen, "DRM and Privacy" (2003) (18) *Berkley Technology Law Journal* 575 at 576.

76 N Elkin-Koren, "Let the Crawlers Crawl: On Virtual Gatekeepers and the Right to Exclude Indexing" (2000–2001) (26) *University of Dayton Law Review* 179 at 185.

> "We may think what we please, but we respond to the information that we are shown ... Over time, this dynamic constructs and modifies habits, preferences, and beliefs".[77]

Relevant Statutory Provisions

There is no general right to privacy legislated for in Irish law. However, a variety of primary and secondary legislation creates specific privacy rights and obligations relevant to the issue of online behavioural advertising. The subset of Irish privacy law that deals with data protection is rooted in and influenced by European law. The EU Data Protection Directive 1995[78] and Privacy and Electronic Communications Directive,[79] together with their transposing legislation, provide statutory protection for invasion of at least some of the interests reflected in the constitutional right to privacy.[80]

The Irish Data Protection Act 1988 as amended by the Data Protection (Amendment) Act 2003[81] (collectively DPA) regulates the collection, processing, keeping and disclosure of "data relating to a living individual who is or can be identified either from the data or from the data in conjunction with other information that is in, or is likely to come into, the possession of the data controller."[82]

Irish Statutory Instruments No 535 of 2003[83] and No 526 of 2008[84] implement the Privacy and Electronic Communications Directive. These regulate *inter alia* confidentiality, including the interception of electronic communications and the use of cookies on electronic communications networks. The law on interception of communications is also informed by the Postal and Telecommunications Services Act 1983, the Interception of Postal Packets and Electronic Communications Messages Act 1993 and the DPA.

As the Phorm test will also consider the methods employed to obtain the data that is used to profile internet subscribers, the statutory provisions relating to unlawful and unauthorised surveillance are also relevant. This brings into focus the provisions relating to the unlawful use of a computer and to creating a false instrument in the

---

77 Cohen, "Privacy, Ideology, and Technology," *op. cit*, 2029.

78 Directive 95/46/EC of the European Parliament and of the Council of 24 October 1995 on the protection of individuals with regard to the processing of personal data and on the free movement of such data [1995] OJ L281/31.

79 Directive 2002/58/EC of the European Parliament and of the Council of 12 July 2002 concerning the processing of personal data and the protection of privacy in the electronic communications sector (Directive on privacy and electronic communications) [2002] OJ L201/37.

80 *Report of the Working Group on Privacy* (Department of Justice Equality and Law Reform, Dublin, 2006) at 23.

81 The Data Protection Act 1988 as amended by the Data Protection (Amendment) Act 2003, also referred to as the Data Protection Act 1988 as amended by the Data Protection (Amendment) Act 2003.

82 Data Protection Act 1988 as amended by the Data Protection (Amendment) Act 2003 at section 1(1).

83 European Communities (Electronic Communications Networks and Services) (Data Protection and Privacy) Regulations 2003 (SI No 535 of 2003).

84 European Communities (Electronic Communications Networks and Services) (Data Protection and Privacy) (Amendment) Regulations 2008 (SI No 526 of 2008).

Irish Criminal Justice (Theft and Fraud Offences) Act 2001,[85] the unauthorised access to data provision in the Criminal Damage Act 1991[86] and the offence of harassment in the Non-Fatal Offences Against the Person Act 1997.[87]

Compliance with the Cookie Regulations

The Privacy and Electronic Communications Directive 2002/58/EC requires that Member States ensure privacy and confidentiality on electronic communications networks. Recital 24 of the Directive states that:

> "Terminal equipment of users of electronic communications networks and any information stored on such equipment are part of the private sphere of the users requiring protection under the European Convention for the Protection of Human Rights and Fundamental Freedoms."[88]

This recognises that the terminal equipment of a user is an inherently private zone and that a reasonable expectation to privacy exists for a user in their terminal equipment. Recital 24 goes on to describe that certain devices can enter the terminal equipment of a subscriber or user without his or her knowledge in order "to store hidden information or to trace the activities of the user and may seriously intrude upon the privacy of these users."[89]

Recital 25 then provides that devices, such as cookies, can be intended for a legitimate purpose and therefore their use should be allowed, on condition that users are provided with clear and precise information about the purposes of cookies, so as to ensure that users are made aware of information being placed on their terminal equipment. The recital goes on to state that users should have the opportunity to refuse to have a cookie stored on their terminal equipment.[90]

This is implemented in Ireland by the European Communities (Electronic Communications Networks and Services) (Data Protection and Privacy) Regulations, SI No 535 of 2003, as amended by SI No 526 of 2008. Regulation 5(1) provides that an electronic communications network will not be used to "store information, or to gain access to information stored in the terminal equipment of a subscriber or user"[91] unless they are provided with clear and comprehensive information in accordance with the Data Protection Acts, which is both prominently displayed and easily accessible, and includes, without limitation, the purpose of the processing,

---

85 Sections 9 and 25 respectively of the Criminal Justice (Theft and Fraud Offences) Act 2001.

86 Section 5 of the Criminal Damage Act 1991.

87 Section 10 of the Non-Fatal Offences Against the Person Act, 1997.

88 Recital 24 of Directive 2002/58/EC of the European Parliament and of the Council of 12 July 2002 concerning the processing of personal data and the protection of privacy in the electronic communications sector (Directive on privacy and electronic communications) [2002] OJ L201/37.

89 Recital 24, Directive 2002/58.

90 Recital 25.

91 Regulation 5(1) of the European Communities (Electronic Communications Networks and Services) (Data Protection and Privacy) Regulations (SI No 535 of 2003), as amended by SI No 526 of 2008.

and the subscriber is offered by the data controller the right to refuse to consent to that use.[92]

These regulations cover the use of "cookies" as operated by the Phorm system. The specious cookie, used by Phorm, does not meet any of the possible exceptions to this regulation, as it is unnecessary either to facilitate the transmission of a communication or to provide an information society service on the explicit request of the subscriber or user.[93]

The Phorm business model as trialled in the UK did not seek the consent of subscribers or users. Edwards and Hatcher claim that Phorm has made it clear to the Information Commissioner's Office (ICO) in the United Kingdom that it does not intend to collect "explicit positive consent from the user" but would give the user opportunities to opt out.[94]

However, it was not clear whether the European and Irish regulations required actual prior consent for the placing of a cookie on a subscriber or user's terminal equipment. The answer, it appeared, could be both yes and no. The regulations relating to cookies apply to "information" that is stored, or stored and accessed, on the terminal equipment of a user or subscriber. Where this information does not qualify as personal data under the DPA, a statement in a privacy policy describing the purpose of the processing, coupled with the option for the subscriber or user to opt out, would be adequate to meet the requirement under the regulations.

However, should the information stored, or stored and accessed, be personal data or sensitive personal data, the requirements for consent and fair processing applicable under the DPA apply. The EU Article 29 Working Party[95] (WP29) state that it is widely believed that online behavioural advertising methods often require the processing of personal data.[96] The specifics relating to Phorm and whether the information processed is personal data or sensitive personal data are analysed elsewhere in this chapter.

Without the prior consent to process the "personal data" of the subscriber, and utilising information stored and accessed in a cookie, Regulation 5(1) will be contravened and the Data Protection Commissioner can enforce the regulation or issue directions as per Regulations 17 and 19.[97] It should also be noted that any person who suffers loss or damage as a result of a contravention of any of the requirements of the Regulations shall be entitled to damages.[98]

---

92 Regulation 5(2).

93 Regulation 5(2).

94 Edwards and Waedle, *op. cit*, 535.

95 The WP29 is the independent European Union advisory body on data protection and privacy. WP29 has been established by Article 29 of Directive 95/46/EC. Its tasks are laid down in Article 30 of Directive 95/46/EC and in Article 15 of Directive 2002/58/EC.

96 Article 29 Data Protection Working Party, *Opinion 2/2010 on Online Behavioural Advertising* – WP171, (22 June 2010) at 9.

97 Regulations 17 and 19 of the European Communities (Electronic Communications Networks and Services) (Data Protection and Privacy) Regulations (SI No 535 of 2003), as amended by (SI No 526 of 2008).

98 *ibid*, Regulation 16.

The cookie regulations are currently under review by the Irish Department of Communications, Energy and Natural Resources as part of the wider "Consultation on Draft Regulations on the Telecoms Regulatory Reform Package."[99] The consultation documents include a proposed draft regulation—European Communities (Electronic Communications Networks and Services) (Privacy and Electronic Communications) Regulations 2011[100]—which would transpose the ePrivacy Directive 2009/136/EC and amend the Irish law on cookies.[101]

The ePrivacy Directive amends the text of the cookie regulations by reinforcing the need for prior consent by clearly requiring "that the subscriber or user concerned has given his or her consent" before cookies are stored.[102] The need for prior consent is also achieved by changing to the past tense the main information requirements of the regulation; replacing "are provided with clear and comprehensive information" with "having been provided with clear and comprehensive information".[103] These changes are copied almost word for word into the proposed draft regulation included in the consultation process.

The other major changes contained in the ePrivacy Directive concern the possible use of browser settings or other technological means to convey the user's consent and the aspiration to make the process of consent and the methods of providing information as user-friendly as possible.[104]

These changes have been incorporated into the draft of the proposed regulation.[105] With respect to obtaining consent through browser settings, the EU Article 29 Working Party has pointed out that this is not "an exception" to the regulations but a reminder that consent can be given in different ways, provided it is technically possible and effective.[106] In most cases the default for browser settings is to accept cookies.[107] Some suppliers of internet browsers are beginning to embrace the concept that not all users want their browser to facilitate tracking of their online behaviour by default. Both Microsoft and Mozilla are reported to be trying implementing a

---

99 Details on the consultation are available at http://www.dcenr.gov.ie/Communications/Communications+Policy/Consultations/Consultation+on+Draft+Regulations+on+Telecoms+Regulatory+Reform+Package.htm; the closing date for submissions/observations was 15 April 2011. [update?]

100 A copy of the specific draft regulation is available at http://www.dcenr.gov.ie/NR/rdonlyres/90781A17-354D-46CD-A444-06093BB4EDD7/0/2011_0303DraftofPrivacyRegs.doc.

101 Directive 2009/136/EC of the European Parliament and of the Council of 25 November 2009 amending Directive 2002/22/EC on universal service and users' rights relating to electronic communications networks and services, Directive 2002/58/EC concerning the processing of personal data and the protection of privacy in the electronic communications sector and Regulation (EC) No 2006/2004 on cooperation between national authorities responsible for the enforcement of consumer protection laws [2009] OJ L337/11.

102 Article 5(3), Directive 2009/136.

103 Article 5(3).

104 Recital 66.

105 Draft European Communities (Electronic Communications Networks and Services) (Privacy and Electronic Communications) Regulations 2011 at Regulation 5(4).

106 Article 29 Data Protection Working Party, *Opinion 2/2010 on Online Behavioural Advertising* – WP171 (22 June 2010) at 13.

107 *ibid*, 14.

"do not track tool" on their internet browsers in order to give users more control.[108] They are however meeting objections from the wider advertising industry.

From the wording of the proposed regulation, browser settings can be used to indicate consent of a subscriber or user, provided the subscriber or user has been given prior information regarding the purposes of the processing of the information stored in the cookie. Whether Phorm is processing personal data or sensitive personal data remains relevant. If the Irish Data Protection Acts are engaged by the information, the prior informed consent of the subscriber or user is required. This is increased to prior *explicit* informed consent if sensitive personal data are being processed. The view of the EU Article 29 Working Party is very clear: that inaction by a subscriber or user cannot be equated with informed consent.[109]

Another aspect of consent for the storing or storing and access to cookies is the requirement for providing information to a subscriber or user. The draft of the proposed regulation states:

> "It shall not be sufficient to solely provide the required information to the subscriber or user within a statement of terms and conditions or a privacy policy."[110]

This is an additional requirement on those web-based businesses that wish to have their cookies accepted by a subscriber or user. What additional method (other than in the terms and conditions or privacy policy) of providing information will be acceptable? Will another written method be acceptable? Will audio, video or iconography be sufficient? Will subscribers or users be required to indicate that they have been provided with the information in more than one format or method?

It is essential that the information must not be hidden in terms and conditions or privacy policies, so as to ensure that the subscriber or user can find the information more easily and provide informed consent. However, the feasibility of clearly and comprehensively explaining without limitation how behavioural advertisers collect, profile and process information through interactive on-screen pop-up windows or through icons will prove extremely challenging.

For a good practical example of the issues involved in providing information to online users in a user-friendly way, one can look to Bilton's article in the New York Times analysing Facebook's privacy policy, and highlighting that it was 5,830 words long and contained 170 options for users.[111] However, as the draft of the proposed regulation is currently worded, the requirement is to provide clear and comprehensive information in a user-friendly format in addition to that provided through terms and conditions or a privacy policy.

---

108 N Wingfield and J Angwin, "Microsoft Adds Do-Not-Track Tool to Browser," *Wall Street Journal*, 15 March 2011, available at http://online.wsj.com/article/SB10001424052748703363904576200981919667762.html.

109 Article 29 Data Protection Working Party, *Opinion 2/2010 on Online Behavioural Advertising* – WP171 (22 June 2010) at 14.

110 Draft European Communities (Electronic Communications Networks and Services)(Privacy and Electronic Communications) Regulations 2011 at Regulation 5(4).

111 N Bilton, "Price of Facebook Privacy? Start Clicking," *New York Times*, 12 May 2010, available at www.nytimes.com/2010/05/13/technology/personaltech/13basics.html?_r=1.

Compliance with the Data Protection Act

Central to the lawful operation of the Phorm business model in Ireland is whether Phorm, in profiling users or subscribers for online behavioural advertising, process personal data. Under the Irish Data Protection Acts it is lawful to process personal data only if the data subject — in the case of the Phorm system the user or subscriber — has given consent to the processing[112] or if the processing is necessary[113], on contractual, pre-contractual or legal grounds, or to prevent an injury or other damage to the data subject.[114]

It is also probable that Phorm processes "sensitive personal data".[115] The definition of sensitive personal data includes information on racial or ethnic origin, the political opinions or religious or philosophical beliefs, health or sex life, and the commission or alleged commission of any offence or proceedings in any court.[116] In order to process sensitive personal data the "explicit consent" of the data subject is required. For both personal data and sensitive personal data the data protection principles must be complied with in order to make processing legitimate.[117]

The Irish Data Protection Acts define personal data as "data relating to a living individual who is or can be identified either from the data or from the data in conjunction with other information that is in, or is likely to come into, the possession of the data controller".[118] According to the EU Article 29 Working Party, the interpretation of personal data is based on the building blocks of:

- "any information
- relating to
- an identified or identifiable
- natural [living] person".[119]

This is consistent with the definition and interpretation as outlined by the European Court of Justice in the *Bodil Lindqvist*[120] case and was thought to be the basis of interpretation the Irish courts would follow.[121] However, in a recent judgment by Charleton J in *EMI v Eircom*[122] a rather narrow interpretation of personal data was employed. This case addressed whether a settlement that was reached between record companies including EMI and Eircom (an Irish ISP), arising out of earlier litigation, was compatible with the Irish Data Protection Acts . The settlement provided for a

---

112 Data Protection Act 1988 as amended by the Data Protection (Amendment) Act 2003 at subsection 2A(1)(a).

113 Subsections 2(A)1(b)-2A(1)(d).

114 D Kelleher, *Privacy and Data Protection Law in Ireland* (Tottel Publishing: Dublin, 2006) at 223–238.

115 Data Protection Act 1988 as amended by the Data Protection (Amendment) Act 2003 at section 1(1).

116 *ibid.*

117 Kelleher, *op. cit*, 157–170.

118 *ibid.*

119 *Opinion 4/2007 on the concept of personal data – WP136*, Article 29 Data Protection Working Party, (20 June 2007) at 6.

120 Case C-101/01 *Bodil Lindqvist* [2003] ECR I-12971.

121 Kelleher, *op. cit*, 134–144.

122 *EMI v Eircom* [2010] IEHC 108.

three-strike approach to dealing with copyright infringement by Eircom's internet subscribers.[123]

Under the terms of the settlement, the record companies will inform Eircom that a particular IP address is involved in copyright infringement. Eircom can identify individual subscribers from IP addresses. Upon the third such notification of infringement relating to an individual subscriber, Eircom will disconnect the internet service for that subscriber.[124] The implementation of the settlement raised *inter alia* the issue of whether the data comprising IP addresses, in the hands of the record companies and taking account of the purpose for which they are collected, constitute personal data.[125]

In addressing this issue, the court placed great emphasis on the facts in question and asserted that neither EMI nor the other plaintiffs (various record companies) have any interest in personally identifying any living person who is infringing their copyright by means of the settlement they had reached. They merely sought the disconnection of the IP addresses.

The court also stated that the only legal means to identify the individuals is through a costly court action,[126] through a *Norwich Pharmacal* order.[127] This reference to legal means in assessing whether personal data are processed appears to eliminate the need for one of the data controller's duties, namely data security and the duty to "protect from unlawful forms of processing."[128] This analysis also seems to run contrary to the judge's (Charleton J) own *dictum* that "[a]n Act should never be split up into its constituent pieces and then analysed as if each were disconnected from the broader purpose that constitutes the legislation."[129]

Charleton J appears to be creating an additional exception to the definition of personal data. By interpreting the word "likely" in the definition of personal data as meaning "probable", by accepting the intention of the parties not to identify a living person and by considering the possible cost associated with obtaining other information to effect identification, he arguably limits the likelihood of identification and possibly narrows the meaning of personal data in Irish law. This appears to be at odds with one of the objectives of the data protection directives, namely, to protect the fundamental rights and freedoms of natural persons and in particular their right to privacy, with regard to the processing of personal data. This may also conflict with the recognition of data protection, as a treaty right, under Article 16 of the Treaty for the Functioning of the European Union (Lisbon Treaty).

The Directives and transposing legislation have already built into them a "substantial

---

123 *ibid*, para 9.
124 *ibid.*
125 *ibid*, para 16.
126 *ibid*, para 25.
127 *EMI v Eircom* [2005] 4 IR 148.
128 Data Protection Act 1988 as amended by the Data Protection (Amendment) Act 2003 at Section 2C.
129 *EMI v Eircom* [2010] IEHC 108 at para 22.

degree of flexibility"[130] so as to strike the appropriate balance between protection of the data subject's rights and the legitimate interests of data controllers, third parties and the public interest which may be present.[131]

With respect to the Phorm business model, the process of frequency ranking as carried out by the "profiler" and described earlier in this chapter collects, stores and processes the UID (contained in the cookie), IP address, URL, search terms, keywords and date-stamp for each specific user or subscriber. This would be considered the processing of personal data under a broad interpretation of the Irish Data Protection Acts.

As Phorm's efforts not to process certain potentially sensitive information such as names or email addresses are not coextensive with the categories of information designating sensitive personal data, the data they are processing could also be considered sensitive personal data under the Irish Data Protection Acts. This is difficult to argue in the abstract, however, if one looks to the *Bodil Lindqvist* case, where the fact that an "individual has injured her foot" was adequate to meet the threshold of sensitive personal data under the Data Protection Directive 1995.[132]

The EU Article 29 Working Party states that in the hands of a third party involved in behavioural advertising the combination of IP address and cookie appears to be capable of falling within the definition of personal data.[133] Phorm would claim that its process of aggregation and anonymisation renders the identification of a subscriber impossible. However, AOL user number 4417749 was able to be identified by the *New York Times* to identify Thelma Arnold based and the data in relation to her online searches even though the data was meant to be anonymous.[134] The identification of the individuals behind apparently anonymous data can no longer be seen as impossible. Ohm has written persuasively on the disruptive impact that the failure of so-called anonymisation has on the assumptions underpinning the development and application of privacy laws.[135]

Ohm also makes a strong argument that technology has created the ability to link freely available data in public databases — he describes this as the richness of outside information—which, when combined with information such as an IP address or search terms, freely and easily provide for the identification of individuals.[136] The reliance by the Irish High Court on the cost involved, in what was claimed to be the only legal means of identifying a living individual from an IP address, appears to ignore the current technological realities.

Furthermore, under the narrow interpretation of personal data in Irish law a claim

---

[130] Article 29 Data Protection Working Party, *Opinion 4/2007 on the Concept of Personal Data,* WP136, (20 June, 2007) at 6.

[131] *ibid.*

[132] Case C-101/01 *Bodil Lindqvist* [2003] ECR I-12971 at paragraph 51.

[133] Article 29 Data Protection Working Party, *Opinion 5/2009 on Social Online Networking*, WP 163 (12 June 2009) at 10.

[134] P Ohm, *op. cit*, 1456.

[135] P Ohm, "Broken Promises of Privacy: Responding to the Surprising Failure of Anonymization" (2010) (57) *UCLA Law Review* 1701.

[136] *ibid*, 1774.

by Phorm that it has no intention of identifying a living individual may keep it outside the definition of a data controller processing personal data. However, it is obvious that the information collected by Phorm relates to an individual and that the information is subsequently used in order to influence that individual through targeted advertising. Such a claim by Phorm appears indefensible.

Another reality is that the ISP has in its possession names and addresses of subscribers. They are in a contractual relationship with Phorm. This contract enables the online behavioural advertising to take place. Both the ISP and Phorm process this information across the "profiler", "anonymiser" and "channel server," as outlined above in this chapter, and the data processed "in conjunction with" data held by the ISP would meet a literal interpretation of the definition of personal data under the Irish Data Protection Acts.[137] Therefore, as it processes personal data, Phorm is a data controller, as they "either alone or with others, control the contents and use of personal data."[138]

Falling within the definition of personal data requires the consent of the data subject. The Irish Data Protection Acts do not offer a definition of consent. Kelleher advises that one look to the Data Protection Directive 1995, which provides that data must not be processed unless consent is unambiguous, freely given, specific and informed.[139] The EU Article 29 Working Party claims that the data subjects must fully understand what they are consenting to; they must be made aware of what will happen to their data if they decide to consent to it being processed.[140]

The EU Article 29 Working Party opinion detailed above remains relevant and makes it very clear that inaction by a subscriber or user cannot be equated with informed consent.[141] Therefore, prior, fully informed consent provided by an opt-in mechanism will be required. It seems likely that the consent threshold required under the proposed cookie regulations also described above will become the standard for online behavioural advertising models. In any event, according to Kelleher, the burden of proof will fall on the data controller — Phorm — to prove that the consent was valid.[142]

There appears, however, to be a discrepancy emerging in the regulation of personal data in Irish law. A greater degree of certainty will now be provided under the proposed cookie regulations regarding the clarity, comprehensiveness and user-friendly manner in which the data subject is provided with information regarding the processing of his information. No such explicit legal requirement exists in Irish law

---

137 Data Protection Act 1988 as amended by the Data Protection (Amendment) Act 2003 at Section 1(1).

138 *ibid.* This is also consistent with the Article 29 Working Party opinion as *Phorm* are the legal person, "which alone or jointly with others determines the purposes and means of the processing of personal data"; see *Opinion 1/2010 on the Concepts of "Controller" and "Processor,"* Article 29 Data Protection Working Party, WP 169 (16 February 2010) at 7 and 23.

139 Kelleher, *op. cit*, 210.

140 Article 29 Data Protection Working Party, *The Future of Privacy: Joint Contribution to the Consultation of the European Commission on the Legal Framework for the Fundamental Right to Protection of Personal Data*, WP168 (1 December 2009) at 17.

141 Article 29 Data Protection Working Party, *Opinion 2/2010 on Online Behavioural Advertising* – WP171 (22 June 2010) at 14.

142 Kelleher, *op. cit*, 221.

regarding the information to be provided with respect to the processing of personal data where the use of cookies does not form part of the process.

Interception of Communications

The Irish law on the interception of communications is regulated by section 98(1) of the Postal and Telecommunications Services Act 1983, as amended by the Postal and Telecommunications Services (Amendment) Act 1999:

> "a person who … intercepts or attempts to intercept … telecommunications messages being transmitted by a licensed operator [which includes an ISP as an authorised undertaking, as designated by Comreg[143]] … shall be guilty of an offence".[144]

An offence is also committed by "using information from an intercepted message".[145] The Phorm model of redirecting a subscriber's browser from the target webpage falls under interception defined as "acquiring the substance or purport of any telecommunications message without the agreement"[146] of the sender and the recipient.[147] This requires that both subscriber and webpage publisher would have to agree to the interception of the communication between them, something that is missing from the proposed Phorm business model. The subsequent use of that information in profiling subscribers would therefore also amount to an offence under the 1983 Act as amended.

Criminal Provisions

Clayton in his analysis has been critical of Phorm and states that they "forge cookies", an action which is "clearly illegal" under British law.[148] Other commentators have also raised the use of cookies by online advertisers, with Siebecker claiming that there is a very strong case that online advertisers trespass on our computers by using cookie technology.[149] Hansell, in his blog BITS published by the New York Times, describes as "parasite cookies" the method employed by Phorm.[150] Do the forging of cookies or any other aspects of the Phorm business model contravene the Irish criminal code?

---

143 *ibid*, 447; and D Kelleher and K Murray, *Information Technology Law in Ireland* (Tottel Publishing: Dublin, 2007) at 365.

144 s 98(1) of the Postal and Telecommunications Services Act 1983 as amended by the Postal and Telecommunications Services (Amendment) Act 1999.

145 s 98(1)(f).

146 s 98(5).

147 *ibid.*

148 R Clayton, "The Phorm 'Webwise' System," 18 May 2008, available at http://www.cl.cam.ac.uk/~rnc1/080518-phorm.pdf. It should be noted that on 8 April 2011 the Crown Prosecution Service decided not to consent to a request to begin a prosecution for the alleged unlawful interception of internet browsing data against BT Group Plc or Phorm Inc, available at www.cps.gov.uk/news/press_releases/116_11/index.html.

149 M Siebecker, "Cookies and the Common Law: Are Internet Advertisers Trespassing on Our Computers?" (2003) (76) *Southern California Law Review* 893 at 952.

150 S Hansell, "Phorm's All-Seeing Parasite Cookie," 7 April 2008, available at http://bits.blogs.nytimes.com/2008/04/07/phorms-all-seeing-parasite-cookie/.

In Ireland under section 9 of the Criminal Justice (Theft and Fraud Offences) Act 2001 the unlawful use of a computer is an offence, where a person dishonestly operates or causes to be operated a computer within the State with the intention of making a gain for himself or another.[151] Under Section 25 of the same Act an offence of creating a false instrument arises if it is done with the intention that it shall be used to induce another person to accept it as genuine and, by reason of so accepting it, to do some act—in this case to track and profile a subscriber online.[152] Under both these provisions, the cookie forging could be deemed to be a criminal offence. The Criminal Damage Act 1991 creates an offence of unauthorised access to a computer and it is also an offence to damage data.[153] The forging of a cookie could constitute damage to data under this Act. As pointed out by McIntyre the Irish legislature created "an offence which is remarkably broad and applies not just to 'damage' in the ordinary sense of the word but to any modification of any information stored on a computer."[154]

Another possibility is that Phorm, if it does not have the consent of the subscriber, may commit the offence of harassment as defined in section 10 of the Non-Fatal Offences Against the Person Act 1997.[155] The offence is committed where a person without lawful authority is persistently following, watching, pestering, besetting or communicating with a subscriber.

The harasser must by his or her actions, either "intentionally or recklessly, seriously interfere" with the subscriber's privacy and the conduct must be "without lawful or authority or reasonable excuse".[156] As demonstrated above, the informational, spatial and decisional privacy of a subscriber would be violated by the surveillance, profiling and subsequent targeting of advertising operated without the consent of the subscriber.

Civil Remedy

As the right to privacy is protected by the Irish Constitution, an invasion of privacy in an unlawful manner would open Phorm to the potential of damages. This can be seen in the reasoning of Dunne J in *Herrity v Associated Newspapers*, where the method used to obtain the information was central to the finding of an invasion of privacy and the subsequent award of damages.[157] The damages consisted of €60,000 assessed in relation to ordinary and aggravated damages for the conscious and deliberate invasion of privacy and a further €30,000 punitive damages assessed for the subsequent use of the unlawfully obtained telephone transcripts.[158]

---

[151] Criminal Justice (Theft and Fraud Offences) Act 2001 at section 9.
[152] Section 25.
[153] Criminal Damage Act 1991 at section 5.
[154] TJ McIntyre, "Computer Crime in Ireland: A Critical Assessment of the Substantive Law" (2005) (15(1)) *Irish Criminal Law Journal* 13 at 14.
[155] Non-Fatal Offences Against the Person Act 1997 at section 10.
[156] Subsection 10(2)(a).
[157] *Herrity v Associated Newspapers* [2009] 1 IR 316.
[158] *ibid*, 347.

Conclusion

The modern online integration of individuals and society must be informed by the accepted concept that individuals enjoy an entitlement to respect for their privacy. Irish law treads a fine line in reconciling the needs of the individual and society through its data protection and privacy laws. The balance achieved in protecting individuals from encroachment allows a freedom for personal exploration and growth and the possibility to decide when to open the boundaries of the self.

Issues regarding the indeterminacy of law, and the contextual and conceptual difficulties in providing a prescriptive legal definition of what encroaches on an individual's privacy, are best surmounted by placing the individual in control. Individual control should be limited only by important social or collective considerations in the public interest. This is particularly so when it comes to informational privacy. The right to privacy in Irish law is at all times balanced with the exigencies of the common good.[159] Consent of the individual, either express or implied, enables protection of the dignity and freedom of the individual.[160]

As Carolan states, it is the individual who is "entitled to assess the level of risk of public exposure which he is willing to take. It is for him to decide when to draw his curtains and when to leave them open."[161] Carolan was analysing the impact of 24-hour surveillance off-line.[162] This principle is also applicable to an individual's online life.

The Phorm test highlights that the Irish Data Protection Acts and associated secondary legislation require further clarity and consistency regarding consent. The cookie regulations provide a greater likelihood that online subscribers encountering cookies will be provided with more adequate and user-friendly information in order to provide their informed consent to the processing of their personal data than counterparts who do not encounter cookies.[163]

The cookie regulations provide a solid platform to place the user or subscriber in control of when and how facts about their online behaviour become someone else's business. The challenges posed by the regulations in providing clear and comprehensive information on the collection and processing of information and presenting this in a user-friendly manner to users or subscribers will require imaginative solutions from web-based businesses.

Irish law also needs to recognise that digital technology means that freely available public information can easily be combined with seemingly innocuous or trivial data to identify individuals. The narrow interpretation of personal data provided

---

159 Delany and Carolan, *op. cit*, 58.

160 *ibid*, 37 and 214–244.

161 E Carolan, "Stars of Citizen CCTV: Video Surveillance and the Right to Privacy in Public Places" (2006) (13(1)) *Dublin University Law Journal* 326 at 334.

162 *ibid.*

163 The information requirements contained in the draft cookie regulations will also apply to a subscriber or user who encounters other technical methods that seek to store or store and access information on his or her terminal equipment.

by the judgment in *EMI v Eircom*[164] arguably does not (appropriately) address this reality. In order to ensure that only those who obtain subscriber or user consent can lawfully exploit personal facts, information and other details of one's online behaviour and activity, the application of Irish privacy law must keep pace with technological developments.

Since the publication of an earlier version of this chapter in *Communications Law*,[165] the Irish Minister for Communications, Energy and Natural Resources, on 1 July 2011, transposed the "cookie regulations" into law.[166] On the date the new regulations came into force the Irish Office of the Data Protection Commissioner also published a guidance note on *Data Protection in the Electronic Communications Sector*, which included guidance on the "cookie regulations".[167]

The new regulations mirror the draft proposals in most aspects. Regulation 5(3) describes the requirement for "clear and comprehensive information" that is "prominently displayed and easily accessible," as well as the requirement for prior subscriber or user consent. As advised by the Irish Data Protection Commissioner, the regulations "do not prescribe how the information is to be provided or consent is to be obtained, other than this should be as user friendly as possible."[168]

However, a number of changes from the draft regulations are noteworthy. The draft regulations had expressly provided that:

> "[i]t shall not be sufficient to solely provide the required information to the subscriber or user within a statement of terms and conditions or a privacy policy".[169]

This was not included in Regulation 5(4) which was signed into law. According to the Department of Communications, Energy and Natural Resources the proposed wording "went beyond the scope of the Directive and it was therefore removed from the final Regulations."[170]

With respect to the use of "appropriate browser settings" to indicate subscriber or user consent, this is now permitted where it is "technically possible and effective".[171] However, the Irish Data Protection Commissioner, in his guidance note, advises that most settings currently available on the main browsers do not appear to be

---

164 *EMI v Eircom* [2010] IEHC 108.

165 D McCallig, "Online Behavioural Advertising: Are Irish Privacy Laws in Need of 're-Phorm'?" (2011) 16 *Communications Law* 60.

166 European Communities (Electronic Communications Networks and Services) (Privacy and Electronic Communications) Regulations (SI No 336 of 2011).

167 Office of the Data Protection Commissioner, *Guidance Note on Data Protection in the Electronic Communications Sector*, available at http://www.dataprotection.ie/documents/guidance/Electronic_Communications_Guidance.pdf.

168 *ibid*, section 6.

169 *Draft* - European Communities (Electronic Communications Networks and Services)(Privacy and Electronic Communications) Regulations 2011 at Regulation 5(4); this is discussed in the main article.

170 Email from Communications Policy Division, Department of Communications, Energy and Natural Resources to author (13 October 2011).

171 European Communities (Electronic Communications Networks and Services) (Privacy and Electronic Communications) Regulations (SI No 336 of 2011) at Regulation 5(4).

sufficient in themselves to meet the legal obligations.[172] The definition of "subscriber" contained in the draft "cookie regulation" was removed as it is already contained in the framework Regulations (SI No 333 of 2011).[173]

Compliance with the Regulations by Irish websites appears to have been very poor, with one survey, carried out in May 2012, reporting a 2 percent rate of compliance.[174] The Office of the Irish Data Protection Commissioner, in December 2012, began a process of contacting websites in order to seek information on the steps that they have taken to comply with the Regulations. The 80 websites, which were chosen at random as a representative sample, include those of government departments, airlines, banks, print and broadcast media, universities and many well-known commercial enterprises.[175]

The website operators had 21 days to respond to the Data Protection Commissioner to demonstrate how compliance with the regulations is achieved. If compliance is not yet achieved, website operators are required to provide,

> "... an explanation setting out why it has not been possible to comply by now, a clear timescale for when compliance will be achieved, and details of specifically what work is being done to make that happen".[176]

The Office of the Irish Data Protection Commissioner confirmed that where website operators fail to engage with the process or fail to meet the requirements of the Regulations, it will take enforcement action. Action of this type by the Data Protection Commissioner is likely to promote greater levels of compliance in Ireland during 2013.

The European Commission case against the United Kingdom, discussed above, has been closed. The infringement procedure followed the secret trials by Phorm and ISPs, and cited the failure of the UK properly to implement rules on privacy in electronic communications. The EU Commission accepts that the UK has since correctly implemented the rules.[177]

With respect to the online behavioural advertisers mentioned earlier in the chapter, Phorm has since signed deals and begun serving targeted advertising with ISPs in Romania (Romtelecom) and Turkey (TTNET). However, in Romania, the Data

---

172 Office of the Data Protection Commissioner, *Guidance Note on Data Protection in the Electronic Communications Sector*, at section 6, available at http://www.dataprotection.ie/documents/guidance/Electronic_Communications_Guidance.pdf.

173 European Communities (Electronic Communications Networks and Services) (Framework) Regulations 2011 (SI No 333 of 2011) at Regulation 2(1).

174 Espion Group, "White Paper: EU Cookie Directive - A User-Driven Assessment of Online Compliance in the UK and Ireland", available upon request from http://www.espiongroup.com/information-governance/request/709.

175 A full list of the 80 websites targeted is available at http://dataprotection.ie/viewdoc.asp?m=f&fn=/documents/press/listwwebsites.htm.

176 See letter from the Office of the Data Protection Commissioner to website operators, December 2012, available at http://dataprotection.ie/viewdoc.asp?m=f&fn=/documents/press/letterissued.htm.

177 Commission (EU), Press Release: "Digital Agenda: Commission Closes Infringement Case After UK Correctly Implements EU Rules on Privacy in Electronic Communications," IP/12/60 (26 January 2012).

Protection Authority held that both Phorm and the ISP contravened data protection law and the targeting system is currently not in use. The ISP (Romtelecom) has since challenged this decision in the Romanian courts.[178] Efforts by Phorm to develop in Brazil and South Korea are also reported to have been unsuccessful.[179]

Finally, as a result of a class action taken against it, which claimed various invasions of privacy, NebuAd has had its assets assigned to creditors as part of a $2.409 million settlement approved by the courts in December 2011.[180]

---

178 Letter from Autoritatea Nationala de Supreveghere a Prelucrarii Daelor cu Catacter Personal (Romania) to Keith Mallen, 31 October 2012.

179 P Bernal, "Phorm – A Chapter Closes?," (28 January 2012) available at http://paulbernal.wordpress.com/2012/01/28/phorm-a-chapter-closes/.

180 *Valentine v NebuAd*, ND Cal, Case No 08-05113 (Henderson J, 19 December 2011).

Chapter 14

DATA BREACHES

Headline of Issues

- Breaches of data protection
- Loss of personal data
- Threats to maintaining personal data
- Social networks and data security
- Data security
- Notification of loss and breach

Introduction

Many organisations, both official and private, have suffered data security and data protection breaches. Some examples involve the organisation directly losing particular personal data sets, such as losing laptops or media storage devices. Other examples involve the security of the organisation being breached by third parties, eg hackers in deliberate attacks. While the later electronic threats have always been an issue, they are increasing in frequency. The increasing scale and regularity of these breaches is alarming and is now increasingly recognised as an important official policy concern.

Breaches, Data Loss and Threats

Over the last number of years there have been some breath-taking examples of data loss and data breach. In some single instances, the personal data of millions of users or customers has been put at risk. This has involved commercial entities such as banks and utilities, and also official agencies from health to revenue agencies. These breach instances can involve general personal data as well as sensitive personal data.

There are now attacks not just on particular websites or organisations, but also on infrastructure-related companies such as computer security firms RSA and Comodo and also Google in China.[1] These are entities that provide technology infrastructure and security to others. Defence and security-related entities are also attacked by hackers, despite the perception that these would be more secure.[2]

---

1 D O'Brien, "Web Security Breaches Show Better Solutions Are Necessary," *Irish Times*, 25 March 2011.

2 E Pilkington, "Hackers Expose Defence and Intelligence Officials in US and UK, Security Breach by 'Hactivists' Reveal Email Addresses of 221 British Military Staff and 242 Nato Officials," *Guardian*, 8 January 2012.

Social Networks

On occasion regulators also warn social networks to enhance their privacy security and privacy practices, even in the US which is perceived as having less data protection laws than in the EU.[3] For example:

> "US lawmakers told Facebook today they were concerned about changes in its privacy policy that would allow personal information to be viewed by more than friends, and options on other websites that would allow third parties to save information about Facebook users and friends."[4]

The Irish Data Protection Commissioner also requested Facebook to delay proposed changes to its privacy policies.[5] There was after the audit by the Data Protection Commissioner.[6]

Social networks, as well as other data controllers, have to be constantly on guard against security attacks and security lapses.[7] They also share the same obligation as other organisations in terms of implementing appropriate security measures.

The importance of security in social networks is important in a number of respects. Social networks now collect and store personal data in relation to billions of users. This crosses both general and sensitive personal data. While users may be uploading comments, materials, photographs, etc, they frequently would not expect that some — or all — of their personal details would be freely available on the internet for anyone to access.

In addition, a significant number of social networking users are children and young people. Many view this type of personal data as deserving particular sensitivity and protection above that of adult personal data. Indeed, children raise personal physical safety as well as psychological safety issues.

There is a proportionality requirement in data protection, which requires that only so much personal data as are legitimately required in relation to a stated processing purpose need to be collected. Equally, proportionality applies to data protection security measures. The same level of security protections proportionate and applicable to a bank is not needed for a corner grocery store. A window-cleaning company does not necessarily need the same level of security as may be needed for a doctor or hospital dealing with sensitive medical data.

---

3 See "Facebook Told to Tighten Privacy," *Irish Times*, 27 April 2010, available at www.irishtimes.com/newspaper/breaing/2010/0427/breaking72.html?via=rel.

4 See *ibid.*

5 P Flanagan, "Data Protection Group Seeking Change to Facebook Privacy Policy," *Irish Independent*, 29 November 2012, available at http://www.independent.ie/business/technology/data-protection-group-seeking-change-to-facebook-privacy-policy-3309757.html.

6 See *Facebook Ireland Limited, Report of Audit*, Data Protection Commissioner, 21 December 2011, available at www.dataprotection.ie; and *Facebook Ireland Limited, Report of Re-Audit*, Data Protection Commissioner, 21 September 2012, available at www.dataprotecticn.ie.

7 See, for example, story in relation to Facebook security issues and upgrades, "Facebook Rolls Out Tighter Security," *Irish Times*, 14 May 2010, available at www.irishtimes.com/enwspaper/breaking/2010/0510/breaking30.html?via=rel.

One can argue, therefore, that stronger and more proportionate security measures need to be applied to social networks than many other organisations and websites, given:

- the scale of membership and users;
- the vast quantities of different types of personal data collected;
- that sensitive personal data as well as general personal data are involved;
- that visual as well as text-based content is involved; and
- that children's personal data are a significant category of the user database.

UK

There are numerous examples of data breaches in the UK. In November 2007, for example, an official body lost the personal details of 25 million UK citizens.[8] Personal details of 84,000 UK prisoners were also lost on an unencrypted memory stick device.[9] The UK government terminated its contract with a company as a result of one data-loss incident.[10] In addition, it announced a review of all official contracts in order to ensure that there were adequate policies dealing with data protection, security and data loss issues.[11]

Ireland

Ireland also has a growing number of data breaches. Laptops with customer data were stolen from Bord Gáis, involving the personal data of 75,000 customers.[12] Ten laptops were also stolen from the Revenue Commissioners, albeit later recovered.[13] Trinity College had to apologise for a breach whereby a file containing student and staff names, addresses, identifications and emails was inadvertently available on the college network.[14] What is most surprising is the length of the breach. The material was available apparently from August 2009 to March 2011.[15] Insurance companies also breached data protection rules when employees inappropriately looked at claims histories of families, friends and well-known personalities, as well as quoting polices after reviewing an industry claims database.[16] The breach involving Loyalty Build is reported as involving over 1 million users. This highlights security obligations as well as storing personal data longer than may have been necessary.

---

8 Referred to in, for example, JA Cannataci and JPM Bonnici, "The UK 2007 – 2008 Data Protection Fiasco: Moving on From Bad Policy and Bad Law?" (March–July 2009) (23) *International Review of Law Computers and Technology* 47.

9 See A Rigby, "Government Review of Data Processing Contracts," *Society of Computers and Law*, 10 September 2008, available at www.scl.org/site.aspx?i=ed1099.

10 The contract with PA Consulting was reported as being terminated on 10 September 2008, as referred to in Rigby, *op. cit.*

11 *ibid.*

12 See Bord Gáis, "Statement from Bord Gáis Energy on Laptop Theft," 17 June 2009, available at http://www.bordgaisenergy.ie/news/?d=20090617.

13 "Revenue's 10 Laptops Recovered," *Irish Times*, 12 February 2011.

14 University correspondence dated 29 April 2011. Copy with author.

15 *ibid.*

16 See D Labanyi, "Insurers Breached Data Rules," *Irish Times*, 27 April 2011, available at http://irishtimes.com/newspaper/breaking/2011/0427/breaking11.html.

Ultimately, large-scale prosecutions are expected in Ireland[17] as well as other countries. This potentially includes social networks in the event of breach (both of security and data protection compliance obligations).

CONSEQUENCES

The consequences of loss or breach can include loss of users, damage, lawsuits, adverse publicity and investigation from the Irish Data Protection Commissioner, the Information Commissioner's Office (ICO) in the UK, the Federal Trade Commission (FTC), etc.

While there have been some cases in the US in terms of data loss and damage, there are relatively few in the EU.[18] This is set to change given the increasing level of losses and breaches, both in terms of claims for damage and or official penalties imposed.

Sometimes different rights can clash, for example, data protection and privacy rights can on occasion conflict with copyright.[19] This can relate to service disclosures regarding users, to online tracking, injunctions and litigation.[20]

There are also suggestions that the presentation of the data protection regime, especially to industry, be reformulated into a business case for data protection rights.[21] This includes privacy by design (PbD).[22]

DATA SECURITY OBLIGATIONS: DPA

The data security obligations apply to social networks as they do to other data controllers. These are contained in the Irish Data Protection Acts (and representative data protection laws in each of the EU nations). Primarily, it states that those collecting and processing personal data must take:

> "appropriate security measures shall be taken against unauthorised access to, or unauthorised alteration, disclosure or destruction of, the data, in particular where the processing involves the transmission of data over a network, and against all other unlawful forms of processing".[23]

---

17 Referred to in Cannataci and Bonnici, *op. cit*, 52. In relation to loss claims generally arising from data loss, see for example Rigby, "Government Review of Data Processing Contracts," *op. cit*; and A Rigby, "Terminating the PA Consulting Contract," *Society of Computers and Law*, 31 October 2008, available at www.scl.org/site.aspx?i=ed1110. Also see R Preston-Jones, "Civil Liability for Mass Data Loss: Lessons from the USA," *Society for Computers and Law* February/March 2010 at 21.

18 Preston-Jones, *op. cit*, 21.

19 OB Vincents, "When Rights Clash Online: The Tracking of P2P Copyright Infringements Vs the EC Personal Data Directive" (2007) (16) *International Journal of Law and Information Technology* 270.

20 *ibid.*

21 "Privacy Protection: Discussion Document on the Business Case," *Society for Computers and Law*, 26 August 2009, available at www.scl.org/site.aspx?i=ne12800. It also refers to Privacy by Design (PbD).

22 *ibid.*

23 s 2(1)(d), Data Protection Act 1988 as amended by the Data Protection (Amendment) Act 2003.

Section 2C states that, in determining what are appropriate security measures, in particular where the processing involves the transmission of data over a network, a data controller may have regard to the state of technological development and the cost of implementing the measures, and shall ensure that the measures provide a level of security appropriate to:

- the harm that might result from unauthorised or unlawful processing, accidental or unlawful destruction or accidental loss of, or damage to, the data concerned; and
- the nature of the data concerned.[24]

Data controllers must take all reasonable steps to ensure that persons employed by them, and other persons at the place of work concerned, are aware of and comply with the relevant security measures.[25]

Data Breach/Loss Notofication Rules

Certain jurisdictions are now introducing or considering specific rules obliging employers and other data controllers to report any instance of data security breach to the relevant regulator. Sometimes the users also have to be notified, for example so that they may take their own security precautions in the event of loss or breach by the organisation. This may include changing PINs, passwords, etc. Some examples include reporting laws in New York and California.[26] The US Department of Health and Human Services has also made proposals that certain loss and breaches in relation to health personal data must be notified within one hour.[27] There are proposals in relation to data loss and breach notification obligations in the proposed EU Data Protection Regulation.

The Irish Data Protection Commissioner has also issued a code of practice, dated 29 July 2011, whereby incidents of personal data loss or breach by organisations should be notified to the Data Protection Commissioner.[28]

The code is entitled Personal Data Security Breach Code of Practice. It reiterates:

> "The Data Protection Acts 1988 and 2003 impose obligations on data controllers to process personal data entrusted to them in a manner that respects the rights of data subjects to have their data processed fairly (Section 2(1)). Data controllers are under a specific obligation to take appropriate measures to protect the security of such data (Section 2(1)(d))".[29]

---

24 s 2C as amended by the Data Protection (Amendment) Act 2003.

25 s 2C as amended by the Data Protection (Amendment) Act 2003.

26 Each as referred to in T Smith, "New York State Information Security Breach and Notification Act: State breach Notification Requirement" (2010) *Albany Law Journal of Science and Technology* 399.

27 J Roman, "One Hour to Report Breach: Possible? HSS Proposal Could Impact Health Data Exchanges" *GovInfoSecurity*, 19 August 2013, available at www.govinfosecurity.com/one-hour-to-report-breach-possible-a-5999.

28 *Personal Data Security Breach Code of Practice*, Data Protection Commissioner. Available at http://www.dataprotection.ie/docs/7/7/10_-_Data_Security_Breach_Code_of_Practice/1082.htm.

29 *ibid.*

The Irish Data Protection Commissioner states that the Code of Practice is to address incidents where "personal data has been put at risk of unauthorised disclosure, loss, destruction or alteration".[30] In such incidents, the focus of the Data Protection Commissioner will be "on the rights of the affected data subjects in relation to the processing of their personal data".[31]

In the event of a data loss, or potential loss, incident:

> "the data controller must give immediate consideration to informing those affected. Such information permits data subjects to consider the consequences for each of them individually and to take appropriate measures. In appropriate cases, data controllers should also notify organisations that may be in a position to assist in protecting data subjects including, where relevant, An Garda Síochána, financial institutions etc".[32]

Advice is given in relation incidents where the data lost may be protected by encryption technology:

> "If the data concerned is protected by technological measures such as to make it unintelligible to any person who is not authorised to access it, the data controller may conclude that there is no risk to the data and therefore no need to inform data subjects. Such a conclusion would only be justified where the technological measures (such as encryption) were of a high standard".[33]

Outsourced data processors must immediately report any incidents to the data controller[34]:

> "[a]ll incidents in which personal data has been put at risk should be reported to the Office of the Data Protection Commissioner as soon as the data controller becomes aware of the incident, except when the full extent and consequences of the incident has been reported without delay directly to the affected data subject(s) *and* it affects no more than 100 data subjects *and* it does not include sensitive personal data or personal data of a financial nature. In case of doubt – in particular any doubt related to the adequacy of technological risk-mitigation measures – the data controller should report the incident to the Office of the Data Protection Commissioner".[35]

Contact should be made "within two working days of becoming aware of the incident" and "outlining the circumstances surrounding the incident".[36] There are also obligations in terms of maintaining reports, etc.[37] The Commissioner may then investigate the incident and issue recommendations, as well as enforcement proceedings if necessary.[38]

---

30 *ibid.*
31 *ibid.*
32 *ibid.*
33 *ibid.*
34 *ibid.*
35 *ibid.* Original emphasis.
36 *ibid.*
37 *ibid.*
38 *ibid.*

Recent UK Penalties

The UK ICO has imposed a number of significant fines recently in relation to data loss in the UK, eg:

- A police force £150,000 (Greater Manchester Police);
- A charity £70,000 (Norwood Ravenswood);
- A health authority £70,000 (Aneurin Bevan Health Board);
- A council £140,000 (Midlothian Council);
- A hospital £375,000 (Brighton and Sussex University Hospitals NHS Trust);
- A medical entity £225,000 (Belfast Health and Social Care Trust).[39]

A spam text marketing firm was fined £440,000.[40] A local authority was fined £60,000 for sending a child-related report to the wrong person.[41]

Prudential was fined £50,000 for inaccurate records when it mixed up the account data of customers.[42]

Leveson

More recently still, the UK Leveson Inquiry Report has recommended a more robust approach to implementing (and understanding) the data protection regime, including criticising the UK Information Commissioner (ICO) for not being more proactive in policing the data protection regime.[43] The report also highlights the needs for a greater appreciation of the data protection regime, in particular at judicial level.[44] This may also be the case in Ireland.

---

39 A Deighton, "ICO Fines Police and Charity for Data Breaches," Lexology, 29 October 2012, available at http://www.lexology.com/library/detail.aspx?g=7adda7a8-ba0c-4404-adba-1e6121b0824a; S Evans, "Huge Increase in ICO Fines for Data Breaches," *Computer Business Review*, 13 August 2012, available at http://www.cbronline.com/news/huge-increase-in-ico-fines-for-data-breaches-130812; "Data Breaches 10 Times Worse, Say ICO Figures," BBC, 30 August 2012, available at http://www.bbc.co.uk/news/technology-19424197.

40 "Spam Texters Fines Nearly Half a Million Pounds as ICO Cracks Down on Illegal Marketing Industry," ICO, 28 November 2012, available at http://www.ico.gov.uk/news/latest_news/2012/spam-texters-fined-nearly-half-a-million-pounds-28112012.aspx.

41 "Plymouth City Council Fined £60,000 for Sending Child Neglect Report to the Wrong Person," 22 November 2012, ICO, available at http://www.ico.gov.uk/news/latest_news/2012/plymouth-city-council-fined-60000-for-sending-child-neglect-report-to-wrong-person-22112012.aspx.

42 "Prudential Fined £50,000 for Customer Account Confusion," ICO, 6 November 2012, available at http://www.ico.gov.uk/news/latest_news/2012/prudential-fined-50000-for-customer-account-confusion-06112012.aspx.

43 UK Leveson Inquiry. *An Inquiry into the Culture, Practices and Ethics of the Press: Report, The Right Honourable Lord Justice Leveson*, November 2012. Available at http://www.official-documents.gov.uk/document/hc1213/hc07/0780/0780.asp. Also see the main inquiry website at http://www.levesoninquiry.org.uk/.

44 *ibid.*

Criminal and Custodial Sentences for Breach

The Leveson Report also recommends legal amendment to introduce custodial sentences in the UK for breach of the data protection regime.[45] This recommendation has been welcomed by the ICO.[46] Importantly, there appears to be full political support for this.[47]

Conclusion

Given the nature of the activities of social networks there will inevitable be increased scrutiny of the security measures employed. Where these prove to be inadequate, the potential for liability arises. It is hoped that social networks will assess the risk and proportionality of social networks prior to an event of serious data loss or data breach.

---

45 *ibid.*

46 A Travis and O Bowcott, "Leveson Data Protection Proposals Unite Cameron and Clegg In Concern," *Guardian*, 30 November 2012, available at http://www.guardian.co.uk/media/2012/nov/30/leveson-data-protection-proposals-concern.

47 *ibid.*

CHAPTER 15

TAGGING

HEADLINE OF ISSUES

- Posts
- Third party
- Tagging
- Taking down
- Detagging
- Updates
- Rights

INTRODUCTION

There is an ever-increasing ease in the ability to post and label photographs and videos on social networks. From the website and user perspective, these can increase the richness and compelling nature of the social network. The social networks are not the only parties trying to increase the willingness of users to post their personal and friend videos and photographs. Commercial organisations such as television programmes and stations solicit video footage[1] and photographs from viewers, eg storm footage. They also seek to have users post them to the organisation's social network pages and websites. The volume of user photographic and video footage uploaded to social networks is increasing exponentially.

Whether photographs are taken at home,[2] at work, at a sporting or social event, or anywhere outdoors, they can all feature in social networking posts. Depending on the contents, they can all be sensitive, embarrassing or even worse.

These images can also be described and labelled. This is sometimes known as "tagging" or "tagging the photograph". The "tag" usually includes the names of the people in the photograph. There can be numerous tags in any given photograph, one for any number of individuals in the photograph.

PERSONAL POSTINGS

In terms of privacy and data protection, one issue is that these photographs and videos contain personal pictures and or descriptions of the user. Only a few short years ago, people would have been reluctant to place their images online. Once uploaded, these

---

1 See generally, D Flint, "Computers and Internet," *Business Law Review*, December 2006, 292 at 293.

2 D Findlay, "Tag! Now You're 'It.' What Photographs on Social Networking Sites Mean for the Fourth Amendment" (2008) (10) *North Carolina Journal of Law & Technology* 171 at 200.

images can in certain circumstances be available to the whole world. It can be quite complicated to restrict access, even if one wishes to avail of technical restrictions and privacy settings, as may be available on a given social network.

Third-Party Postings

A further complicating issue is that frequently photographs or images posted on a social network contain images of third parties other than the person taking or posting the photograph. These can be the friends, acquaintances, work colleagues, etc of the user posting the images. They can also be complete strangers. Any of these parties may be concerned that their images are being placed online. Some may of course consent. However, others may not. There is also the separate issue of whether they know that their images are being posted by the user. Assuming that they are not happy to have their images posted online, even to a social network where certain privacy setting may have been employed, what rights does the person have? These issues are only now coming to be considered.

Taking Down Third-Party Images

In the first instance, one could ask the user who posted their image to take it down. This may work, but does not guarantee that the image has not already been viewed and even copied by many users and friends of the original poster. They might also look to the terms and conditions/terms of service (TOS) and privacy statement of the social network to see if they have any rights, or if there is a defined policy as to what happens in an instance like this. In terms of data protection, they can argue that they have not consented to their image being posted online, and demand that it be taken down.

Tagging Increases

Tagging is the technical ability to tag and identify people in photographs on social networks.

Photographs of people can be uploaded, copied, distributed and shared more easily online than ever before. This can be with and without consent, and with and without knowledge.

This becomes an issue not merely because of the advent of social networks, but of the ever-increased adaptability of photographic and mobile devices. The ease of taking such photographs and from almost any location, increases the risk for individuals. Now images can be taken on Google Glass. Frequently, the subject of the photographs can be unaware that the photographs were taken, and also that they have been posted. It is also easier today for an individual to be caught in a group photograph — with or without their knowledge. Any of these photographs can appear on social networks.

Tagging facilities allow friends to tag and identify one another in their posted photographs. One can also be tagged and identified in third-party photographs. One implication is that while you may have certain privacy settings, if a friend tags you, this information or the photograph may then become visible to people outside your friends group. A person's privacy setting may thus be circumvented.

The publication of social networking photographs online has been used in various cases of discipline and expulsion by schools and universities regarding their students.[3] Social networking photographs have been used in custody cases, eg photographs of drinking in one party's house.[4] A personal injury claimant lost her case after being cross-examined with her MySpace photographs.[5]

The use of photographs on social networks "challenge[s] existing notions of privacy expectations within the confines of [for example] the [US] Fourth Amendment and government searches and seizures".[6]

Detagging

While many issues arise as a consequence of tagging, one of the solutions is the technical ability to detag. Generally, users may decide to detag themselves, or users can be requested to detag or even take down a photograph if someone objects.

As to whether a social network will detag upon complaint will depend on the social network in question, eg if the poster will not detag when requested.

There is an evolving solution of the user having to obtain consent initially from third parties in order to tag them in the first instance. This introduces the elements of consent and also advance transparency to third parties who may be contained in a user's photographs. It remains to be seen, however, what will happen to the many millions of images already posted and tagged without consent.

A further issue to be resolved is that not all persons who are included in images and videos placed on social networks are actually members of the particular social network. While this might mean that their consent would never be forthcoming for a new tag request, and thus their image perhaps should not be uploaded or tagged without their knowledge and consent. There may also be differences in how a social network treats posting and tagging photographs. Again, the issue of the millions of tags and photographs to date remains a consideration.

---

3 See Findlay and references therein; Findlay, *op. cit*, 172; including MJ Hodge, "The Fourth Amendment and Privacy Issues on the 'New' Internet: Facebook.com and MySpace.com" (2006) *S Ill University Law Journal* 95.

4 *NP v JP* 2008 Del Fam Lexis 45 (Del Fam Ct Jan 30 June 2008), as referred to in Findlay, *op. cit*, 178.

5 *Oldham v Jackson* and *Smith Excavation Inc* No 06-CVS-642 (Chatham County Super Ct June 11 2008), and also G Loranger, "MySpace Photographs Used Against North Carolina Injury Plaintiff," *NC Law Weekly*, 30 June 2008, at 1, each as referred to in Findlay, *op. cit*, 178.

6 Findlay, *op. cit*, 175. Also see JP Semitsu, "From Facebook to Mug Shot: How the Death of Social Networking Privacy Rights Revolutionized Online Government Surveillance" (2011) *Pace Law Review* 291.

Status Updates

A further issue is the interface of "update" applications and tagging applications. If one is tagged in a photograph or a third party is tagged in one of your photographs, this action and a copy of the photograph may become notified and or visible to a group wider than your immediate friend list. Other people can be notified of the tagging. There is also an example of a case where social networking "invites" to an event were introduced in court.[7]

Facebook

Facebook changed its photograph tagging system in 2012. The previous position was that the original uploader of the photograph was responsible for tagging. This was amended to allow any permitted viewers to tag[8] any photograph that they could access. "Thus, the subject is fully exposed to unrestrained potential invasions of privacy – including the prying eyes of law enforcement – until he or she received the notifying email"[9] that they had already been tagged.

If someone objects to a third-party photograph of them being posted, Facebook said only that they should contact the original poster and request them to remove it, but will not get involved itself.[10]

Since then, however, more user controls allow a user to change defaults and specify that a third party needs their consent first before being able to tag them in a photograph. The user must specify this in advance.

Interim Audit Review

The Irish Data Protection Commissioner undertook a privacy and data protection audit review of Facebook in 2011 and 2012. One of the issues of contention is tagging.[11]

The Irish Data Protection Commissioner's interim or first *Report conclusion and best practice recommendation* regarding the tagging issue states that there does not appear to be a compelling case as to why individual members cannot decide to prevent tagging of them once they fully understand the potential loss of control and prior notification that comes with it. Facebook initially responded that it will examine the broader implications of this recommendation.

---

7 *State v Tonelli* 2008 Iowa Sup Lexis 88 (Iowa 10 June 2008), as referred to in Findlay, *op. cit*, 177.
8 See Findlay, *op. cit*, 182, n48.
9 *ibid*, 184.
10 *ibid*, 185.
11 See documentation at http://dataprotection.ie/docs/Home/4.htm.

Re-Audit Review

The Irish Data Protection Commissioner notes that there are in this regard certain tools available. The Re-Audit Report states that it assumes users will be able to use the tools to prevent and delete tagging if they wish to.[12] It is unclear, however, if there was an assessment of how user-friendly and transparent the tools actually are, in particular for younger users.

This issue also crosses with facial recognition software and automated suggested tagging on the basis of facial recognition. The Irish Data Protection Commissioner demanded that this feature be turned off.[13] It since has been turned off in the EU. However, towards the end of 2013, there are some reports that facial recognition may still be favoured by the social network.

Conclusion

These are current issues of concern. While technical solutions like detagging and advance consent provide some comfort for new and further images, they are by no means a complete solution. Not everyone is a member of a social network, or the particular social network where their image is posted or tagged. It is unclear if all photographs containing third parties will require advance consent such as a tag consent. There may be potential technical difficulties. Social networking polices, technical solutions as well as their privacy statement may well differ from website to website, but more importantly from one legal jurisdiction to the next. Therefore, the rights that may be applicable in terms of consent, takedowns and detagging may depend on whether the individual and the social network is located in the EU or elsewhere.

---

12 See *Facebook Ireland Limited, Report of Re-Audit*, Data Protection Commissioner, 21 September 2012, available at www.dataprotection.ie, at 10 and 36–39.

13 *ibid*, 8–9, and 47–48.

PART IV: SOCIAL NETWORKING AND EVIDENTIAL ISSUES

Chapter 16

EVIDENTIAL ISSUES

Headline of Issues

- Electronic evidence
- Social networking materials as evidence
- Civil evidence
- Criminal evidence
- Discovery
- Preservation of evidence
- Cases
- Statutory Instrument 93 of 2009 (Discovery)
- eDiscovery Ireland
- Best Practice Ireland Guide

Introduction

Online and electronic communications are often no longer a secondary means of communication,[1] but rather the primary means. It is inevitable that social networking will increasingly be looked at in terms of providing electronic evidence and electronic discovery. This presents new issues and considerations. "[T]he law provides little guidance on how we should deal with some of the newest sources of evidence ... social networking [web]sites".[2] How the law adapts to electronic evidence obtained from social networking remains to be fully seen, although there are examples of it already being used. Questions, however, remain as to if and when it should be used. These have yet to be fully contested and considered in superior courts.

Some authors feel that detailed familiarity with social network evidence issues is now a requirement for all lawyers. "It should now be a matter of professional competence for attorneys to take the time to investigate social networking [web]sites. You must pan for gold where the vein lies — and today, the mother lode is often online".[3] In addition, "law enforcement, school administrators, opposing legal counsel, and even community vigilantes are actively seeking out"[4] social networking — both instances of obtaining information and evidence.

---

1 D Flint, "Computers and Internet," *Business Law Review*, December 2006, 292.

2 DS Witte, "Your Opponent Does Not Need a Friend Request to See Your Page: Social Networking Sites and Electronic Discovery" (2010) (41) *McGeorge Law Review* 891.

3 S Nelson, J Simek and J Foltin, "The Legal Implications of Social Networking" (2009–2010) (22) *Regent Law Review* 1 at 14.

4 D Findlay, "Tag! Now You're 'It.' What Photographs on Social Networking Sites Mean for the Fourth Amendment" (2008) (10) *North Carolina Journal of Law & Technology* 171 at 198.

New Uses and Sources of Electronic Evidence

Electronic evidence increasingly relies on information obtained from social networks. Divorce, separations and family law cases, for example, increasingly use social networking information. This includes social networking page profiles, comment postings, and photographs and activity on social networks, dating websites, etc. There are many instances where social networking activity can reveal evidence of infidelity, for example.[5]

Certain pertinent evidence can be easily evident when the opposing parties are direct friends on a social network. However, there are also examples of incriminating details being found out indirectly, when the two parties are not direct friends on a particular social network. In one instance, a wife was able to get access to the incriminating Facebook profile through her friend's access.[6] In some instances now, the first thing to occur in new divorce cases, may be respective searches of the social networking profiles.[7]

There are additional sources of such evidence in addition to social networks. These include activity on online communities[8] and discussion boards. In addition, instant messaging communications can also provide electronic evidence, albeit more difficult to produce. In addition to revealing new smoking guns for litigation, social networking might actually be the trigger for litigation. It is clear, however, that social networking content is increasingly being sought after in the discovery process and discovery requests,[9] and is often perceived (rightly or wrongly) as being fully available.[10] Many cases will come to test this.

Individual and Organisational Liability Issues

Individuals themselves also face significant personal liability issues when they stray beyond the boundaries of what is reasonably permissible — even when they feel they are anonymous. Examples include trolling, defamation and harassment.

Social networking presents many potential problems for employers and organisations, some of which include accessing pornography, sending sexually related or harassing

5 See, for example, "Ride the Lightening, Social Networks: An Avalanche of Evidence," http://ridethelightening.senseient.com/2009/03/social-networks-an-avalanche-of -evidence.html , referred to in Nelson *et al.*, *op. cit*, 13.

6 *ibid.*

7 Nelson *et al.*, *op. cit*, 13.

8 Highlighted by TZ Zarsky, "Law and Online Social Networks: Mapping the Challenges and Promises of User-generated Information Flows" (2008) (18) *Fordham Intellectual Property Media & Entertainment Law Journal* 741 at 742.

9 RA Ward, "Discovering Facebook: Social Network Subpoenas and the Stored Communications Act" (2011) *Harvard Journal of Law & Technology* 563. C Calvert, "Fighting Words in the Era of Texts, IMS and Emails: Can a Disparaged Doctrine be Resuscitated to Punish Cyber-Bullies?" (2010–2011) *DePaul Journal of Art, Technology & IP Law* 1.

10 EE North, "Facebook Isn't Your Space Anymore: Discovery of Social Networking Websites" (2010) *Kansas Law Review* 1279.

messages, gambling, theft of trade secrets and intellectual property rights.[11] Criminal law liability issues also arise.[12]

There are significant potential liability issues for organisations in relation to what their employees post and upload on their own personal pages, blogs and discussion fora. This will increasingly be an issue in employment disputes and court cases.

Aaron Bland states that "[e]mployees' use of computers now commonly expands the work place well beyond the office walls."[13] However, data protection laws restrict the extent to which employers can monitor or otherwise utilise employees' email, internet and social networking content. (This is despite the widespread availability of software for employee monitoring[14] (where permitted)). This is increasingly an issue of contention. There is also a perception that US law may permit more employee monitoring than may be permitted elsewhere.

Social networking electronic evidence can arise in both civil cases and criminal cases. These are highlighted below.

Evidence

Civil Evidence

The permanence of electronic evidence continues to escape many people. Even President Obama advises users (especially younger users) to "be careful about what you post on Facebook, because in the YouTube age whatever you do, it will be pulled up again later somewhere in your life".[15] Colonel Oliver North was also partly undone with electronic evidence.

Increasingly, civil litigation relies on electronic evidence. Employee litigation might just as easily seek out employee computers, hard drives[16] and electronic devices as social networking content when looking for incriminating evidence.

The Irish Electronic Commerce Act 2000 provides for the equivalence of electronic documents, signatures, etc. In addition, the new electronic discovery rules provide new mechanisms and procedures in relation to electronic discovery in Ireland. These are referred to in SI No 93 of 2009.[17] Electronic data or electronically stored

---

11 A Blank, "On the Precipe of E-Discovery: Can Litigants Obtain Employee Social Networking Web Site Information Through Employers?" (2010) (18) *CommLaw Conspectus* 487 at 491.

12 *ibid.*

13 *ibid*, 494.

14 *ibid*,499.

15 In North, *op. cit*, 1287.

16 Blank, *op. cit*, 501–503. Personal diaries have been discoverable; see *Ramsay v Bailey* 531 F2d 706, 707 (5th Circuit 1976). Referred to in North, *op. cit*, 1280.

17 SI No 93 of 2009: Rules of the Superior Courts (Discovery) 2009. Note also P Lambert, "The Search for Elusive Electrons: Getting a Sense for Electronic Evidence" (2001) (1:1) *Judicial Studies Institute Journal* 23; and Law Reform Commission, Consultation Paper, *Documentary and Electronic Evidence*, LRC CP 57 – 2009 (Government Publications, Dublin, 2009).

information (ESI) became a distinct set of discoverable documents under US discovery rules from 2006.[18]

There are increasing numbers of electronic evidence cases relating to social networking. One recent example in Ireland is *Net Affinity v Conaghan and Avvio*.[19] This involved, *inter alia*, data claimed by the employer on electronic devices in the possession of the leaving employee. Injunctions restraining the employee leaving, and the new employer that the employee was moving to, were granted. Various materials were also handed back to the employer containing confidential materials. Non-compete injunctions were also imposed.

A Canadian court in March 2009 permitted access and cross-examination in relation to a plaintiff's Facebook profile.[20] The court stated that it was "reasonable to infer that his social networking [web]site likely contains some content relevant to the issue of how [the plaintiff] has been able to lead his life since the accident."[21]

A US woman lost a child custody case after her boyfriend's sexually explicit comments were revealed on his MySpace profile.[22]

A US husband was also undermined in a case when his MySpace profile described him as "single and looking".[23] A related issue which arises is whether it is ethical for the lawyer to attempt to directly or indirectly bypass an individual's social networking privacy settings by getting someone to befriend the party so as to gain access to their social networking profile information.[24] This is an issue which does not appear to have been considered in great detail as of yet.

A further issue also arises. Intermediary social networks are increasingly subject to applications to court for orders to identify users,[25] following on from their online activities. Ryanair is just one recent example.

Criminal Evidence

Nothwithstanding the NSA-Snowden revelations, law enforcement authorities

---

18 Rule 34, Federal Rules of Civil Procedure (1970). Referred to in North, *op. cit*, 1281. Also see JD Frieden and LM Murray, "The Admissibility of Electronic Evidence Under the Federal Rules of Evidence" (2010–2011) *Richmond Journal of Law and Technology* 1.

19 *Net Affinity v Conaghan and Avvio* IEHC 2011/1574. Dunne J. Interim and Interlocutory injunctions granted against leaving-employee and new employer poaching customer. Available at http://www.bailii.org/ie/cases/IEHC/2011/H160.html.

20 T Remtulla, "Canada: Facebook Not So Private? Ontario Court Finds Facebook Profile Discoverable," *Mondaq*, 23 March 2009, www.mondaq.com/article.asp?articleid=76332, referred to in Nelson *et al.*, *op. cit*, 11–12.

21 *ibid.*

22 V Jaksic, "Litigation Clues Are Found on Facebook," *National Law Journal* (New York City), 15 October 2007, 1, referred to in Nelson *et al.*, *op. cit*, at 12.

23 *ibid.*

24 See Nelson *et al.*, *op. cit*, 11 at 15.

25 Blank, *op. cit*, 504–506. Note also EP Stedman, "MySpace, But Whose Responsibility? Liability of Social-Networking Websites When Offline Sexual Assault of Minors Follows Online Interaction" (2007) (14) *Villanova Sports & Entertainment Law Journal* 363 at 377–394.

increasingly rely on social networking searches.[26] The police are also utilising the information posted on social networks, in terms of gathering intelligence, investigations and using this information as evidence at trial. It can also be used at sentencing hearings. The police see many benefits to reviewing social networking profiles.[27] However, Wells cautions against invasive police use of the internet and social networking. Such privacy-invasive police techniques will "prove costly, oppressive, and foster a dangerous disrespect for privacy in the digital age".[28] "Aggressive" police tactics will rebound and have negative consequences.[29] The police may also be doing so without warrant and any express legal authority, and the question arises as to whether such access violates the right to privacy[30] and data protection. The lawfulness of certain NSA activities, if reports are correct, have also been queried by Eric Schmidt of Google.

There are already cases in the UK and Ireland that utilise email evidence.[31] However, this is still often a new consideration in litigation here. Some examples from elsewhere are referred to below.

In a US fatal drink driving case a defendant may have had her sentence escalated to a custodial sentence after the judge referred to her MySpace photographs, which revealed her in alcohol-related poses, the implication being that these were taken after the drink-driving incident.[32] The judge said that she had not learned her lesson and had shown no remorse.[33]

In a US drink-driving injury case, the defendant was alleged to have received a higher custodial sentence after a photograph of him wearing a prison uniform emblazoned with the words "Jail Bird" at a party were posted by a friend on Facebook, and later revealed in court.[34]

At a US sentencing hearing a person who tried to portray himself as peaceful was met with pictures and comments of himself on MySpace with a gun.[35]

---

26 D Findlay, "Tag! Now You're 'It.' What Photographs on Social Networking Sites Mean for the Fourth Amendment" (2008) (10) *North Carolina Journal of Law & Technology* 171 at 179.

27 DH Montes, "Living Our Lives Online: The Privacy Implications of Online Social Networking" (2010) (5) *I/S: A Journal of Law and Policy* 507 at 526–528.

28 PA Wells, "Shrinking the Internet" (2010) (5) *New York University Journal of Law & Liberty* 531 at 532.

29 *ibid*, 567–568. See also MJ Hodge, "The Fourth Amendment and Privacy Issues on the 'New' Internet: Facebook.com and MySpace.com" (2006) *Southern Illinois University Law Journal* 95.

30 Findlay, *op. cit*, 174.

31 See for example S Hickey, "Ex-Bank Workers Appeal Dismissal for 'Porn' Emails," *Irish Independent*, 20 January 2011.

32 *ibid*. The case was of Jessica Binkerd.

33 *ibid*.

34 "Drinking, Driving, and Facebook Don't Mix," *CBS News*, 18 July 2008, available at http://cbsnews.com/stories/2008/07/18/tech/main4272846.html, referred to in Nelson *et al.*, *op. cit*, 12. This was the case of Joshua Lipton. Also Associated Press, "Unrepentant on Facebook? Expect Jail Time," CNN, 18 July 2008, available at http://cnn.com/2008/crime/07/18/facebook.evidence.ap/index.html, as referred to in Findlay, *op. cit*, 177.

35 E Perez, "Getting Booked by Facebook," *Milwaukee Journal Sentinel*, 3 October 2007, at 9A, available at http://redorbit.com/news/technology/1087625/getting_booked_by_facebook/index.html, referred to in Nelson *et al.*, *op. cit*, 13.

It has also been stated that MySpace pages on which a person had gang tattoo photographs may have partly contributed to the defendant in a US case receiving a death sentence.[36] In one Seattle case, a personal injury claim settled without trial after the defence was able to produce a CD of photographs downloaded from the plaintiff's Facebook and MySpace profile photogaraphs showing him snowboarding and jumping[37] after the disputed injury. A group of Virgin airline employees were fired after posting comments about the company on Facebook.[38] More recently in Ireland, there have been a number of instances of employees as well as students being disciplined in relation to posts on social networks and related websites. The airline Ryanair has also been involved in a number of employee related disputes where it has sought orders in relation to Norwich electronic evidence regarding the identity of posters of comments online as well as discipling employees in relation to particular comments. It has also successfully sued a German blogger in Ireland.

One developing area is the use of social networking to assist criminals. They may, for example, find out through online postings that a person is on holiday and that his or her house is therefore vacant. In one research study it was found that in one year in the UK there were over 100,000 reported crimes with a connection to Facebook.[39]

Material on social networks is also increasingly being used in relation to selecting jury members in the US. For example, finding information on which to challenge prospective jurors.[40] There are also contentious issues in the UK. Jurors have been sentenced for comments and other activities online regarding cases they have been involved in. This includes custodial sentences for jurors and trolls.

Records

There is debate as to whether social networking can or should be permissible evidence. Some people consider tweets, emails and text messages to be no different from correspondence.[41] In one sense that is correct. The Electronic Commerce Act

---

36 J Gormley, "MySpace and Facebook Becoming Evidence in Court," CBS, 3 February 2009, available at http://cbs11tv.com/local/MySpace.Facebook.Evidence.2.926231.html, referred to in Nelson, *et al.*, *op. cit*, 13.

37 Referred to in North, *op. cit*, 1279.

38 S Thiel, "Virgin Atlantic Fires 13 Cabin Crew Following Facebook Comments," *Bloomberg*, 1 November 2008, available at www.bloomberg.com/apps/news?pid=newsarchive&sid=aObNS7eFKlUY. Referred to in North, *op. cit*, 1287. This may not have been fully tested in court.

39 "More Than 7,000 Associated Crimes Since January – UK Investigation," *TheJournal.ie*, 20 December 2010, available at www.thejournal.ie. Also S Boggan, "Facebook: As Offences Linked to Social Networking Sites Increase 7,000%, the Terrifying Truth About Criminals Targeting Your Home," *Daily Mail*, available at www.daily mail.co.uk, last accessed on 21 December 2010.

40 J Kay, "Social Networking Sites Help Vet Jurors," *The National Law Journal*, 13 August 2008, available at http://law.com/jst/legaltechnology/pubArticleLT.jsp?id=1202423725315&rss=ltn, referring to *US v Hassoun* No 0:04-cr-60001 (SD Fla 2006), as referred to in Findlay, *op. cit*, 178.

41 SD Nelson and JD Simek, "Capturing Quicksilver: Records Management for Blogs, Twittering and Social Networks" (June 2009) *Wyoming Law* 1, available at www.wyomingbar.org/pdf/barjournal/barjournal/articles/Twitter.pdf, referred to in Nelson *et al.*, *op. cit*, 16.

2000[42] in Ireland, for example, provides for the equivalence and non-discrimination between electronic documents, writing, etc and traditional hardcopy versions.

Can an employee's tweets, for example, amount to a company record for evidence purposes, record-keeping requirements and ESI electronic evidence preservation purposes? What is a "record"? What is a company's resource? Is there a BYOD policy? These issues remain unsettled.[43] The management, legal and record keeping requirements/implications of social networking, and the scale of the implications, create a "Goliath-sized headache".[44] The technologies are not settled; they are ever fluid and ever expanding. In addition, there can be multiple postings from various authors.[45] "Your opponents will have trolled the Web for data. Can you claim ignorance? Must you produce ... off-site communications by your employees? Can you afford not to know about Web 2.0 data? These are questions that are giving CEOs (and their lawyers) recurring nightmares".[46]

The opportunities for a company or its employee to say something that is incriminating or creates legal implications have increased significantly. Defamation and product liability are just two examples. Separately, certain organisations or industry sectors have record-keeping requirements. These are more onerous than before in terms of the scale of the data, their locations, complexity and availability, and when they are required. Equally, the extent to which organisations can control or minimise their risk is made more difficult. Cloud issues may create further headaches to consider.

Discovery

Information on social networks can be electronic evidence or ESI as it is referred to in the US.[47] Social networks provide new and "fertile ground"[48] for relevant discovery of electronic information and materials. However, there are few cases in the US dealing with social networking and discovery,[49] and even fewer in Ireland and the UK.

Thomas discusses the question of whether social networks can or should be discoverable:

> "The case law regarding email and text messaging could be equally applicable to the use of Facebook accounts with privacy settings in place in the private employment context. If there is a question as to whether the information on a social networking [web]site may be

---

42 This Act implements the Electronic Signatures Directive (1999/93/EC) and in part, the Electronic Commerce Directive (2000/31/EC).

43 Nelson *et al.*, *op. cit*, 16. Also references therein, namely, Nelson and Simek, *op. cit*, 16, and T Baldas, "Beware: Your 'Tweet' on Twitter Could Be Trouble," *National Law Journal* (New York City), 22 December 2008 at 6.

44 Nelson *et al.*, *op. cit*, 16.

45 *ibid*, 19.

46 Nelson *et al.*, *op. cit*, 20, references omitted.

47 Witte, *op. cit*, 892.

48 *ibid*, 893. In relation to US federal rule changes note, for example, A Peck, "The December 2006 Federal Rules Amendments Governing Electronic Discovery" (2008) *PLI/Lit* 783; Blank, *op. cit*, 487.

49 L Thomas, "Social Networking in the Workplace: Are Private Employers Prepared to Comply with Discovery Requests for Posts and Tweets?" (2010) (63) *SMU Law Review* 1373 at 1383.

discoverable, by analogy to third-party providers of emails and text messaging, it appears that the information on such [web]sites would be discoverable in civil litigation. Though a private employer does not pay for access to a Facebook account, the account is hosted by a third party and could be used for both business and personal use. Thus, applying the principles from *Rozell v Ross-Hoist*, a judge would have discretion to limit production of the information posted to a Facebook account to the extent of the parties' initial disclosures. The use of a social networking [web]site at work thus would not give the defendants or plaintiffs free reign to discover anything and everything posted on the [web]site when privacy controls are in place on the account. Allowing discovery of a Facebook profile just because a party has an account would create the situation where counsel would just be fishing for information on the [web]site without any basis. Moreover, considering the networks and numerous friends that a person has on the [web]site, it is economically unfeasible to require production of every posting, email, or conversation on the [web]site for an extended period, because sorting through the information would take too much time to justify the value of the information. It is for this very reason that a request for production from such social networking [web]sites may be used strategically against a party to drive up the cost of discovery and push the case toward settlement. Also, because companies are not likely to have encountered numerous requests for production regarding the [web]sites and are unfamiliar with them, it is likely that such requests can be used to distract the party from the real issues of the case, in addition to driving up the costs of discovery.

If a party to a suit has a Facebook account or a Twitter account, a court would be likely to find that such an account is in the possession, custody, or control of the party and, as such, that a party would need to produce relevant information from the [web]site under Rule 34 based on the user agreements in place with Facebook and Twitter. An additional concern is the ability to procure the information for discovery purposes. A recent virtual roundtable by Symantec addressed the problems with obtaining a record of the information from Facebook or Twitter in a useable, understandable format. When users view their profile page on Facebook, it appears to them to be a consolidated page with all information in one place. However, when such user content is archived, information is located in different databases and does not appear in the same format as it appears on a Facebook page Thus, to pull all the information together and decipher how a page appeared takes more time than if the information on a page at any given time were stored as a discrete package of information, like a Word document or an email. This will likely create the biggest e-discovery hassle with respect to compliance with discovery requests.

Another consideration is the Stored Communications Act and the degree that the Act may affect the ability of a party to a suit to obtain information from a third-party provider. It appears that Rule 45 subpoenas issued to third-party providers have limitations that Rule 34 requests for production can overcome. Thus, in the initial interrogatories stage a party should question whether relevant information is present on a Facebook or Twitter page and request that the opposing party produce the information under Rule 34. By going through the party itself to obtain the information, the issues with consent and the Stored Communications Act may be avoided if the information is from the party's own profiles".[50]

Thomas then refers to social networking in the context of employment:

"Considering the problems that may arise with the use of social networking in the workplace, private employers and their counsel must consider the benefits and the costs associated with the use of such [web]sites in the workplace. Twitter and Facebook market to employers that they can use the [web]sites to connect with their clients or consumers. But the legal implications of the use of such [web]sites and the need to preserve the [web]sites in the anticipation of litigation may lead to headaches for employers, their IT groups, and their counsel. As such, employers who decide to use social networking [web]sites for marketing purposes, for internal communications, or for communications with their clients need to take steps to ensure that if the information is ever needed for discovery, they are well-prepared. The first decision to be made by employers is whether to allow their employees the use of social networking during business hours while at work. The use of social networking in the workplace may be beneficial but may also be problematic due to a loss of productivity in the workplace, the potential for theft of data, liability for the contents of the [web]sites in

50 *ibid*, 1394–1395. Internal references omitted.

> lawsuits, and damage to the employer's image. Due to these risks, many companies have banned the use of Facebook and Twitter in the workplace, including certain investment banks and law firms. Some employers that do not completely ban the use of Facebook have taken a middle-ground approach to the posting of information on the [web]site. For example, ESPN prohibits its employees from posting onto Facebook or Twitter any content related to sports without its permission. The Associated Press takes an even stronger approach and requires its employees to monitor what they and their friends say on Facebook, and to delete certain posts on their Facebook pages. Assuming that employers allow social networking in the workplace, certain steps can be taken to minimize their risk, both with respect to the company's fan page and the employees' personal profiles".[51]

The UK case of *Hays Recruitment v Mark Irons* in 2008 granted an order requiring the leaving employee to disclose his contact friend list on LinkedIn, as the first employer felt that its client list had been taken to populate the employees list for the new competing company. The US case of *Ledbetter v Wal-Mart Stores Inc* held that social networks are discoverable once the other side believed there is evidential material.[52] There appears no direct reported case pronouncing that social network content *per se* can be discoverable evidence in Ireland.[53]

Social Networking Evidential Issues

How relevant are social networks in terms of discovery?[54] Marsico suggests that social networks are becoming the new evidential fingerprints of the 21st century.[55] Discovery issues generally[56] become more complex with online activity. The scope of discovery[57] in "normal" litigation is expanding because of social networking content. In addition, it should be noted that the discovery of social networking materials is more complex as it involves third-party social networks.[58]

Third-party discovery even normally is a complex policy issue in litigation. The issue of third-party access/discovery of employer/employee social networking content is set to become a hotly contested area in litigation.[59]

Podolny also raises the interesting point that social networking "friends" (who can be real friends or otherwise) can also become adversaries in litigation.[60] This raises interesting issues in terms of discovery and access to materials that may be sought to be relied on.

The EU Article 29 Working Party refers to cross-border discovery issues in civil

---

51 *ibid.*

52 *Ledbetter v Wal-Mart Stores Inc* No 06-cv-01958-WYD_MJW, 2009 WL 1067018, at *2 (D Colorada 21 April 2009). Referred to in North, *op. cit*, 1279. See also Thomas, *op. cit*, 1391.

53 Emails and telephone records, however, quite regularly appear in cases here.

54 Blank, *op. cit*, 497–498.

55 E Marsico, "Social Networking Websites: Are MySpace and Facebook the Fingerprints of the Twenty-First Century?" (2010) *Widener Law Journal* 967.

56 Blank, *op. cit*, 495–496.

57 *ibid*, 496–497.

58 *ibid*, 503–504.

59 *ibid* at 497.

60 R Podolny, "When 'Friends' Become Adversaries: Litigation in the Age of Facebook" (2009) *Manitoba Law Journal* 391.

litigation.[61] Social networking enhances the potential for disputes that include cross-border content issues.

There are also a growing number of examples where proceedings, notice of proceedings and court orders have been served electronically by email and even to the social networking pages of individuals.[62]

The internet is no longer restrained and wired. Modern mobile and handheld devices are still proliferating and invariably it is also possible to access the internet and websites through these devices. This includes Facebook, Google+ and other social networks. Various content, comments, photographs, histories, etc can also be maintained on these devices. It is natural, therefore, that mobile electronic discovery is also an evolving area.[63] A note of caution is deserved. A litigator should not be blinkered into thinking that mobile telephones and handheld network telecommunications devices are the only mobile and storage devices that may contain pertinent electronic evidence. Other examples include Sim cards, data storage cards, photographic storage devices, disks, USB keys, etc.

Publicity is always a consideration in litigation, and internet news and social networks have increased the potential for publicity. A related sub-issue is that of pre-trial publicity and prejudicial pre-trial publicity in particular.[64] Internet news and social networks increase the potential chance of these issues arising.

Preservation of Evidence

Electronic evidence can be easily created. In some instances it can be easily deleted or altered, too. In litigation, therefore, there can be a duty to preserve[65] and prevent the spoliation[66] of electronic evidence.

In relation to e-discovery generally, it is noted that:

> "In the seminal e-discovery cases of *Zubulake v UBS Warburg LLC*, best known for the judge's 'costshifting' analysis factors, the court held that the duty to preserve evidence attaches, at the latest, on the date an action is filed. In Zubulake IV, Judge Scheindlin wrote

---

61 See Working Document 1/2009 on Pre-Trial Discovery for Cross Border Civil Litigation, Article 29 Data Protection Working Party, 00339/09/EN, WP 158, Adopted on 11 February 2009.

62 RA Ward, "Discovering Facebook: Social Network Subpoenas and the Stored Communications Act" (2011) *Harvard Journal of Law & Technology* 563; AL Shulz, "Superpoked and Served: Service of Process Via Social Networking Sites" (2009) *University of Richmond Law Review* 1497; MM Dan, "Social Networking Sites: A Reasonable Calculated Method to Effect Service of Process" (2010) *Case Western Reserve Journal of Law, Technology & the Internet* 184; RJ Hedges, KN Rashbaum and AC Losey, "Electronic Service of Process at Home and Abroad: Allowing Domestic Electronic Service of Process in the Federal Courts" (2010) *The Federal Courts Law Review* 55.

63 See, for example, DB Garrie and YM Griver, "Mobile Messaging and Electronic Discovery" (2009) *Loyola Law and Technology Annual* 95.

64 See generally M Mastromauro, "Pre-trial Prejudice 2.0: How YouTube Generated News Coverage is Set to Complicate the Concepts of Pre-trial Prejudice Doctrine and Endanger Sixth Amendments Fair Trial Rights" (2010) *Journal of High Technology Law* 289.

65 See Witte, *op. cit*, 895.

66 See Thomas, *op. cit*, 1384–1385. Generally, in relation to the US, note Frieden and Murray, *op. cit*, 1.

> that this duty may attach 'at the time that litigation [is] reasonably anticipated' if a party has reason to suspect a pending suit".[67]

The reference to cost shifting refers, in part, to the fact that dealing with e-discovery can become a very costly exercise.[68] Some cases even settle on the basis not of the merits on either side, but rather on the basis of the anticipated costs of the electronic discovery.

Issues such as preservation might best be considered in advance where possible, as opposed to reacting to an instant contentious situation. In either instance, various internal departmental expertise will be required from management, legal, HR, marketing, etc, as well as appropriate external expertise.[69]

Discovery and Privacy

Many discovery and privacy issues arise. For example:

> "The convergence of social-networking [web]sites and litigation presents a host of complex questions implicating user privacy. This Comment addresses three issues in particular. First, how can a court determine whether there is relevant information contained within a party's private social-networking profiles beyond relying on the requesting party's good-faith assertions? Second, a user who implements Facebook's privacy settings may have a higher expectation of privacy than a user who grants unfettered access to hundreds or even thousands of 'friends,' and users may expect more privacy with regard to some types of information. How can these expectations be measured for objectivity or reasonableness? Third, the complex interconnectedness of social networking [web]sites presents difficult questions surrounding the expectation of privacy in relevant content posted by third parties. When a user is tagged in a third party's photo and that photo is relevant, is the photo discoverable?"[70]

In relation to the US, Thomas states:

> "From a discovery standpoint, employees' use of social networking for business purposes will greatly increase the realm of discoverable information that a company has to control, and as such, modifications to data retention procedures must be made. If litigation is anticipated, a company and its counsel should issue a litigation hold that encompasses information posted on social networking [web]sites – no information should be deleted from the employer's page, the employee's business pages, or archives thereof. As mentioned in Zubulake, a litigation hold does not end the counsel's duty of preservation. The litigation hold with respect to the information on social networking [web]sites must be reissued periodically to make sure that employees are aware of their obligations. In addition, employers and counsel must request the information from social networking [web]sites or gain access to it from employees who likely have relevant information and be particularly explicit with those employees' obligations of preservation. To save time, employers may also request that employees locally archive their social networking [web]site pages to ensure that the data is not lost. There is a caveat with this approach – the stronger the data retention policy, the more data there will be to mine in the event of a discovery request. Companies should be mindful that a policy should be implemented but should also be cautious that in the

---

67 Rule 34, Federal Rules of Civil Procedure (1970). Referred to in North, *op. cit*, 1282.

68 Note, for example, "E-Disclosure - Controlling Costs and Reducing Risks," *Society of Computers and Law*, 18 September 2013.

69 Consider, for example, K Grandhi, "The Discovery Within: Employing E-Discovery Coordinators fro Management of Electronic Discovery Processes in Federal and State Cases" (2011) *Temple Journal of Science, Technology & Environmental Law* 1.

70 North, *op. cit*, 1290.

event of litigation, spoliation does not occur that results in discovery sanctions. Ultimately, companies should be educated about media their employees are using to collaborate with each other, contact clients, conduct business, and should work with their IT groups to formulate retention and archiving policies that are suited for their specific business needs."[71]

US Cases

A US case law commentary states as follows:

"The most complete discussion by an American court on this problem appears in *Mackelprang v Fidelity National Title Agency of Nevada, Inc.* In Mackelprang, the court denied the defendant's motion to compel the plaintiff in a sexual harassment lawsuit to consent to the release of her private MySpace messages. The defendant employer initially issued a subpoena to MySpace to learn the profile information and identity behind two accounts that it suspected belonged to the former employee. The employer alleged that the former employee set up dual identities on MySpace, with one account listing her as single with no interest in children and the other listing her as married with six children. The employer believed the plaintiff used the first account to send emails of a sexual nature to colleagues she accused of sexual harassment. MySpace produced some 'public' information associated with the account, but it declined to provide any private messages absent a search warrant or a letter of consent from the account holder. The company complied with the defendant's subpoena duces tecum by providing a spreadsheet that confirmed the plaintiff as the user for two accounts on the [web]site. In other cases, MySpace has declined to provide substantive user content in response to subpoenas. In its motion to compel the plaintiff to consent to a release of her MySpace communications, the defendant argued that the private messages could contain evidence that the plaintiff exchanged consensual, sexually charged emails with members of the [web]site. The court agreed with the plaintiff that the request amounted to a 'fishing expedition' that 'would allow Defendants to cast too wide a net for any information that might be relevant and discoverable' and could result in discovery of irrelevant private communications.

But the court invited a more narrowly tailored request, noting that the 'proper method' would be to serve the plaintiff with 'limited requests for production of relevant email communications[,]' including MySpace 'private messages that contain information regarding her sexual harassment allegations in this lawsuit or which discuss her alleged emotional distress and the cause(s) thereof.' The court invited the defendant to provide 'some basis, beyond mere speculation, to support a reasonable belief that Plaintiff engaged in sexually [sic] email communications on her Myspace.com accounts with former coemployees' to warrant reconsideration of the motion. The court denied the defendant's motion without prejudice, leaving the door open for more targeted discovery.

Two recent trial orders involving suits against schools demonstrate the wide usage of Facebook among young people and the potential for relevance to litigation. The procedure followed in *Bass v Miss Porter's School* illustrates a 'best practice' for handling Facebook discovery requests. In Bass, the defendant school requested production of any text messages or Facebook content related to the teasing and taunting of the plaintiff, a student at the school, or any content related to communications involving the student's allegations. The student, who had since lost access to her Facebook account, served a subpoena on Facebook to obtain content from her former profile to comply with the school's request. When Facebook agreed to provide 'reasonably available data' spanning the pertinent time period, the judge ordered the student to provide any responsive documents to the school and the entire set of documents 'to the Court for in camera review ... distinguishing the subset of documents provided to Defendants.' The student provided approximately one hundred pages of content in response to the school's request, and she provided 'more than 750 pages of wall postings, messages, and pictures' to the court, which represented Facebook's complete production in response to the subpoena. The court determined that there was 'no meaningful distinction' between the documents the student provided to the school and those provided for in camera review. The court ordered that the entire set of documents be made available to the school because relevance was 'more in the eye of the

71 Thomas, *op. cit*, 1398–1401. Internal references omitted.

beholder than subject to strict legal demarcations,' and the student could not unilaterally determine which documents might be 'reasonably calculated to lead to the discovery of admissible evidence.'

In *TV v Union Township Board of Education*, a middle school student sued her school for emotional distress resulting from a sexual assault allegedly perpetrated by another student on school grounds. The school attempted discovery of the plaintiff's private Facebook and MySpace pages to show evidence of her mental state before and after the incident. The student moved for a protective order for her private profile information, citing privacy rights and undue burden. The trial judge granted the protective order 'barring the defendants from seeking or obtaining any discovery or information' from the plaintiff's online profiles. The court left the door open for later discovery if the school could make a particularized showing of relevance.

The Bass court's creative solution to the defendant's discovery request indicates both fidelity to the liberal discovery regime under the Federal Rules and an open-mindedness about the potential relevance of social-networking information. By way of contrast under similar facts, the state trial court in T.V. required an up-front showing of relevance by the requesting party. The Bass approach of serving a subpoena on the social-networking [web] site and requiring in camera review of all supplied documents removes the possibility that a responding party will selectively remove damaging photos or status updates from the discoverable documents. This approach also permits a responding party to file protective orders for certain documents after they are provided by the social-networking [web]site but before they are given to the requesting party. It is sufficiently flexible to ensure that all relevant social networking content is discovered while creating a safety valve to prevent especially private or prejudicial information from being discovered".[72]

Canadian Cases

There are also Canadian cases, described in one review as follows:

"One of the most thorough discussions appears in *Leduc v Roman*, a recent Canadian personal injury case. In Leduc, the plaintiff claimed damages for physical and mental injuries sustained after a traffic accident with the defendant. The defendant moved for production of the entire contents of the plaintiff's private Facebook profile on the basis of a single, publicly accessible profile photo and identifying information on the plaintiff's public Facebook page. After a lower court denied the request, the appellate court reversed in part, reasoning that the private profile 'likely contain[ed] some content relevant to the issue of how Mr Leduc has been able to lead his life since the accident'".[73]

The court referred to cases which held that a Facebook profile can contain information relevant to the issues in a particular case:

"'Photographs of parties posted to their Facebook profiles have been admitted as evidence relevant to demonstrating a party's ability to engage in sports and other recreational activities where the plaintiff has put his enjoyment of life or ability to work in issue .... In one case the discovery of photographs of a party posted on a MySpace webpage formed the basis for a request to produce additional photographs not posted on the [web]site ....'

The Leduc court also considered the socialization purpose of Facebook, noting that 'Facebook is not used as a means by which account holders carry on monologues with themselves . . . [and] Facebook profiles are not designed to function as diaries.' The court aptly described the goal of social-networking [web]sites to 'enable users to construct personal networks or communities of 'friends' with whom they can share information about themselves, and on which 'friends' can post information about the user.' The court explained that Facebook profiles are 'data and information in electronic form' producible as 'documents' under the Rules of Civil Procedure,' and as such, should be disclosed when 'relevant to the allegations in the pleadings.' Perhaps most importantly, Leduc dismissed

---

72 North, *op. cit*, 1291–1293. Internal references omitted.

73 *ibid* at 1294–1295.

the idea that public and semi-private profile contents should be treated differently: 'A party who maintains a private, or limited access, Facebook profile stands in no different position than one who sets up a publicly-available profile. Both are obliged to identify and produce any postings that relate to any matter in issue in an action.'

Leduc correctly recognized that social-networking information provides a wealth of relevant information about a plaintiff's condition before and after an accident in the personal injury litigation context. But despite the court's characterization of the social purpose of Facebook, it had to tackle the issue of the plaintiff's expectation of privacy in some of the information. The Leduc court dismissed these concerns rather summarily, but other courts have struggled with the expectations of privacy in various forms of social-networking content".[74]

Statutory Instrument (SI No 93 of 2009)

Irish Statutory Instrument No 93 of 2009 relates to and provides for issues of electronic discovery in Ireland.[75] While not contemplated at the time, it potentially encompasses forms of electronic discovery where social networking content is relevant, necessary, discoverable and permissible.[76] Caselaw is awaited.

eDiscovery Ireland

One of the developments in this sector in Ireland has been the launch by Owen O'Connor of the now annual eDiscovery Ireland conference. It comprises a large number of headline speakers and break-out sessions from recognised experts in Ireland and internationally.

Best Practice Ireland Guide

A number of interested parties in the eDiscovery and forensic sector in Ireland have sought to deal with perceived issues and problems with the new Statutory Instrument regarding ediscovery (SI No 93 of 2009) in Ireland. They have drafted a best practice guide which, with judicial endorsement, is hoped to provide guidance to practitioners and indeed to the courts. It is entitled *Good Practice Guide to Electronic Discovery in Ireland* (16 April 2013).

Conclusion

While there are relevant provisions in the Irish Electronic Commerce Act 2000 and now in the electronic discovery rules, it is perhaps the activity of social networking and its interface with intellectual property and with the employment sphere that will also bring electronic evidence issues to the fore in Ireland. The forecast search for elusive electrons[77] is increasingly social.

---

74 *ibid* at 1294–1295.

75 Statutory Instrument 93 of 2009 Rules of the Superior Courts (Discovery) 2009.

76 Generally, see S Mason ed, *Electronic Evidence, Disclosure, Discovery & Admissibility* (Lexis Nexis Butterworths: London, 2012).

77 P Lambert, "The Search for Elusive Electrons: Getting a Sense for Electronic Evidence" (2001) (1) *Judicial Studies Institute Journal* 23–49. In terms of the US, see, for example, Frieden and Murray, *op. cit*, 1.

Chapter 17

CLOUD COMPUTING

Andrew Harbison

Headline of Issues

- Cloud Computing
- History
- Virtualisation
- Software as a Service (SaaS)
- Where we are and how did we get here

Introduction

While there is a lot in the literature surrounding cloud computing[1] that is erudite and engagingly written, much else is very technical and is full of the acronyms and mnemonics to which a lot of writers on technical subjects seem to be irresistibly drawn.

I have been teaching long enough to know that when explaining technical subjects it is a great deal easier to provide a good complicated explanation that a good simple one. But I have been given instructions that this chapter should try to explain the concepts and issues behind cloud computing without scaring, confusing or boring the reader — which may explain why this chapter has gone through as many drafts as it has.

I finally decided that, given those instructions, trying to explain cloud computing to a non-technical readership in the style I usually write technical articles was likely to cause me to scare, confuse and bore readers simultaneously. Instead, I am writing this in a manner to make it comprehensible to ordinary human beings who will probably have a computer on their office desk and another at home, but who might not be entirely clear on the difference between a router and a switch, and who probably have a healthy disinterest in what an Internet Protocol Address is.

So, in the next few pages I am going to try to set down what cloud computing is, and how we got to the point that a technical expert such as me feels the need to write an article about it. I will explain how and why it is different to conventional computing. I will finally provide my own opinion on the many advantages of cloud computing over "non-cloud" approaches and on the many disadvantages of the approach.

---

[1] Editor addition: note also the EU Article 29 Working Party Opinion 5/2012 on Cloud Computing; K Burden, "'Wandering Clouds' Emerging Trends in Cloud Services Contracts," *Society of Computer and Law*, 16 August 2013, available at www.scl.org.

Big Computers in Cold Rooms

Back in the early 1950s an internal management study at IBM, in one of the most spectacularly wrong statements ever written, predicted that total global market for computers was unlikely to ever be more than a dozen or so machines. Back then, however, this was not such an unrealistic a statement to make. Computers back in the '50s were huge and rather unreliable room-sized electro-mechanical devices with the processing power of a modern pocket calculator. They had many moving parts and tended to break down a lot. The reason why modern computer techies refer to computer failures as a "bugs" is because one of the first serious failures was caused by an actual bug — a moth that got caught in a relay in one of first machines.

The IBM study writer may not even have been aware that, at the very time he was writing, three scientists working for Bell Telephone, John Bardeen,[2] William Shockley and Walter Brattain, had come up with a little gadget: the Transistor. Transistors are switches made of silicon or some other "semi-conducting[3]" material that could replace the large and unreliable electrical relays which up to that point had been used in computers. The old relays had moving parts and would regularly break, jam, burn or get small insects stuck in them. Transistors were "solid-state" — they did the same job as relays, but had no moving parts. Better still, it turned out that transistors could be miniaturised down to a microscopic level. Even today they remain the key component in practically every silicon computer chip.

Fast-forward 20 years to the mid-1970s and there were, indeed, a lot of more computers on the planet, but they were still far from common. They were still big electronic machines, found in big air-conditioned rooms, tended by people with mathematics and engineering degrees. The computer rooms you see in 1960s and 1970s spy movies pretty accurately reflect what computer rooms looked like back then. Lots of noisy machines and spinning tapes, with piping in the background for the expensive fire suppression systems any sensible computer room designer would insist on installing.

Computers were still impractically expensive for anyone but the large companies, universities and governmental organisations that could afford the infrastructure to keep one of the big beasts alive. Anyone who had to connect to one of these "mainframe" computers[4] would do so over a terminal—a blinking monochrome screen with a keyboard attached. The device we now call the computer mouse was still nothing more than a good idea in the minds of a couple of engineers working in Palo Alto, California.

---

2 Bardeen, by the way, is one of the least remembered geniuses of the 20th century. He was the only person to win the Nobel Prize for Physics twice: in 1956, with Shockley and Brattain for the invention of the transistor, and again in 1972 for discovering superconductivity.

3 "Semi-conducting" means that if a low voltage is put across a material, it does not conduct electricity; but if a larger voltage is put across the same stuff, it will conduct electricity. This ability to be both an electrical insulator and an electrical conductor under different circumstances means that semiconducting materials such as Silicon, Germanium and Gallium Arsenide are ideal for use in electronic valves (called diodes) and electronic switches (called transistors).

4 Mainframe computers were so-called because all the computing electronics were organised on a main metal structure or frame, with other devices, such as data storage, printers and terminals connected to it with cables.

Fortunately, a number of young computer geniuses were starting to develop new technologies based around microprocessors; miniature computers made up of thousands of transistors that were originally developed for the Apollo space programme. There were a few of these young geniuses, but by far the most successful were Steve Wozniak and Steve Jobs. Wozniak was a superb engineer and an expert in designing computer circuit boards. Jobs, as everyone now knows, was a master at designing and selling attractive electronic products. Their invention, the Apple II personal computer, began the process of putting a computer on every office worker's desk.

Fast-forward another 15 years and things had changed again. By the early 1990s there was a computer on a lot of people's desks, but usually there were still a few big "server" computers in a computer room. The reason why was because it was quickly found that some functions—file management and data backup, and a new-fangled idea called electronic mail, were better managed from a central location on large computers. Managing and maintaining files spread out across people's workstations was just too difficult and inefficient.

More and more organisations began to have networks installed. Network cables were run thorough buildings, through the walls and under the floors. At one end of these wires usually sat people's workstation computers, although perhaps some of the more "techno-savvy" CEOs might have had one of the newly introduced and very expensive laptop computers. At the other end of the wire would still be a big, air-conditioned room, with a well-designed fire suppression system, full of whirring machines still tended by people with advanced science degrees.

Data did not get transferred between organisations very much. It was not easy to move data from one computer to another. (Partly why there was no data loss on the scale there is today.) Computers in different locations could talk to one another using sophisticated gadgets such as modems and frame relay switches but, like the big computers of 15 years before, these were only really available for big organisations. The rest of the world still relied on floppy disks and the postal service.

Fortunately, two things happened in 1991 that changed everything. First, in 1991 the US government started allowing the general public to use a widespread governmental computer network called the internet. This rather cleverly designed network was originally developed by the US Defense Department as a means for the survivors of a nuclear apocalypse to send messages to one another regardless of whatever parts of the world had been wiped out by atomic bombs. Later, when Armageddon failed to arrive, the network was handed over to a bunch of universities and academic institutions, which used it mostly for email and transferring files from one to another (email had been around for years before the general population started using it). Initially after the internet became generally available only businesses and other large organisations joined the universities on the internet. It took another invention to get everyone else interested in it.

CERN (La Centre Européenne de Recherce Nucléaire) is mostly known today for smashing nuclear particles into one another using the Large Hadron Collider and other exotic machines, but it has been an important centre for all kinds of physics and engineering research for years. Back in 1980 a young scientist at CERN called

Tim Berners-Lee developed a system called ENQUIRE that allowed researchers to share and update information easily. This system was based on the idea of hypertext and hyperlinks—pieces of text in documents which link to other documents where the linked text is described in more detail. Hypertext was a very big idea in 1980. After developing ENQUIRE Berners-Lee left CERN and worked with a company that manufactured computer networking equipment. He came back to CERN after a few years and, armed with everything he had learned about networking, realised that if you could combine the existing ENQUIRE system with parts of the internet you could come up with something really useful. He wrote a program he called a web-browser and developed a set of rules for other computers to send data to it, called the Hypertext Transfer Protocol (http). He admits, however, that he never really expected that this World Wide Web project of his would be quite as popular as it quickly became.

If we jump forward another 15 years, offices are very different again. Computers are now on everybody's desks, and in many of their homes. Indeed, Steve Jobs is about to have another very good idea, and very soon many people are going to have miniature computers in their pockets as well. The computers on people's desks are now a lot smaller, quicker and easier to use than they were 15 years before. Lots of people have laptops, probably more than have old-fashioned desktops. Practically every computer has access to the internet and to Tim Berners-Lee's World Wide Web. Most people have access to email—and very few companies do not provide it to employees.

Lots of people have electronic mail devices in their pockets, Blackberries and Palm Pilots. Many of these devices do not even have to be connected up to a wire. They can communicate wirelessly with one another, and with the mass of servers hidden in the organisations computer room.

Yes, the big air-conditioned room is still there. It still has a fire suppression system, although rather less lethal than 15 years earlier. Of course, there is no longer a single big box being tended by a few people with computer science degrees. There are many smaller streamlined-looking computers being tended by, if anything, even more people with computer science degrees.

There are file servers, mail servers, database servers, backup servers, proxy servers, Sharepoint servers, telephone servers, blackberry servers, DNS servers, SMS servers and many other servers beside. There are active directory controllers and primary domain controllers and any number of other controllers making sure that the mass of servers do not collapse together in a heap of logic. And really the only people who know how it all works are the IT technicians. So while on the office floor and in people's homes things have changed radically, inside the air-conditioned room … not so much.

Outside the Air-Conditioned Room

Of course, not everyone has a big air-conditioned room to let them connect up to the internet and use their computers. How does an ordinary computer user at home use the internet?

Most of them use the services of an internet service provider (ISP)—a Vodafone, an O2, a Verizon. These suppliers let them connect up to the internet, and may even give them some kind of private email service. Users can also sign on with other online mail services, such as Microsoft's Hotmail or Google's Gmail. They can do a lot of other things online, too. They can access their bank accounts online, they can even share documents online. An idea started developing in a lot of managers' minds: I seem to be able to work on my computers perfectly well at home without a big, air-conditioned room full of servers. Just how much do I really need that big air-conditioned room in my office?

In fact, organisations had been hiring time on computers outside their networks for years, practically since the birth of the internet.

The first such system widely used many non-technical readers may never have heard of. It is called the Domain Name System (DNS), and the devices on which it depends are called DNS servers. They are necessary because the computers connected to the internet do not actually recognise one another by their domain names but by a unique Internet Protocol address (always called an IP address), akin to an internet telephone number. IP addresses consist of 4 numbers, from 0 to 255, separated by dots, so that, for example, what you know as Google.com your computer knows as 173.194.70.102, and when you look for Facebook.com, your computer will actually go looking for 66.220.152.15 .

But how does your computer know that, for example, Youtube.com is 173.194.70.91 and Amazon.com is 72.21.214.128? The answer is that it looks them up on a DNS server.

A lot of larger companies maintained, and still maintain, their own DNS server, particularly if they had an intranet, a miniature World Wide Web accessible to people on their own internal networks. Smaller organisations often did not, however. Having a DNS server involved adding another expensive server to the air-conditioned room, and the money almost certainly could have been used more efficiently elsewhere. Furthermore, DNS servers have never needed to be very powerful computers, so that even the cheapest, lowest-specification server would be largely wasted operating as a DNS server.

Of course, these organisations still need some access to the DNS: otherwise, how will their staff find their way around on the internet, and how will their customers find them? The solution is that often that the ISPs that provide organisations their access to the internet will also provide them with a DNS service. Even companies that have their own DNS server will often pay a small amount to have one of their ISP's DNS servers act as a backup to their own. It is not expensive and, given the importance of DNS, it is a very sensible precaution.

Another such "online" function, used by organisation for years, is web-hosting: having an external company run the computers on which your organisation's website is loaded. There are a number of very good reasons why organisations "host out" their webservers. One of the most important of these reasons is security.

It is an unfortunate fact of the modern internet that hackers and similar computer criminals are a serious and apparently intractable problem. Such online irritants were preying on internet users even before the network was made generally available in the early 1990s, and ever since then the problem has been getting worse. Webservers are by far the favourite target for hackers and have been for years. A lot of hackers are little more than vandals and, of course, vandalism is a lot less fun if people do not see the damage that has been inflicted. Hence, webservers are ideal targets for internet vandalism. There is, however, a more fundamental reason hackers like attacking webservers: they are a lot easier to break into than practically any other type of computer.

Any experienced hacker (and I confess I am one) will tell you that the most difficult thing to do in a hack is to gain access, any access, to a computer. Once you have performed the (occasionally) difficult task of gaining first access to a computer, be it using a low-privilege guest or user account, it is usually far more straightforward to "escalate" your privileges to that of top level administrative or "root" user. Once you have "rooted" a computer in this way you can pretty much do what you like—and usually what you like to do, if you are a hacker, is find another computer on the same network you can hack.

Once you have found your way onto a network by breaking onto the first computer, it is usually relatively easy to find your way onto another and another until you find something really valuable.[5] The first step—gaining first access onto the first computer—is usually the hardest. Unless, of course, the first step is onto a webserver, in which case the step is often not very hard at all.

Webservers are intrinsically insecure. To download webpages from them, visiting web-browsers have to be given a degree of access to them. If you visit a webpage, you are made a guest on the webserver computer. Hence the hacker's biggest headache, gaining a foothold on the computer, is immediately solved. For this reason more than 80 percent of successful hacking attacks are made on webservers.

Any sensible IT manager is, therefore, reluctant to have one of these insecure "hacker-magnets" on their network if it is at all avoidable. Of course, if you are running an internet bank or some kind of big e-commerce operation, it *is* pretty much unavoidable. If, however, you are running a "brochure" website, telling people who you are and what you do and not really providing any kind of online service, there is no reason why your website server should be anywhere near any of the other computers on your network, or on your network at all. Also, because developing, running and securing websites is rather a specialised business even among IT persons, it is probably more convenient for most organisations to leave the running of your website to a company that does it for a living rather than paying the costs of doing it themselves on their own networks.

Another good reason to host out a website is that, like DNS servers, such websites do not usually require a very powerful computer to run them. A web-hoster might efficiently run the websites of a dozen clients off the same server without difficulty. Occasionally, however, this approach might also increase the efficiency of the

---

5 Hackers call this technique "enveloping".

hackers trying to deface the websites. A weakness in one webpage might lead to every website on the server being defaced.

The third service that has been regularly outsourced for years is electronic mail. I have already discussed the various web-mail services like Hotmail and Gmail, but there was another, more business-friendly way mail servers could be outsourced based on computers called POP[6] servers. Typically a small company would have their ISP collect any mails that would be sent in onto a POP server. This server would store the mails until a user logged in with a mail program—usually Microsoft Outlook Express, because that was included free on most Windows operating systems. As soon as the mail program logged into the POP server, the mails that had built up on the server since the last log in would be dumped down into the users' mail program and, usually, deleted from the server.

POP was not a perfect solution. Using it meant that emails were scattered across workstations throughout an organisation, which made organising them and backing them up rather difficult; but, in general for small organisations, these were minor nuisances compared with maintaining a rather expensive server and an even more expensive IT person to keep it running.

As time went on more services were outsourced. A lot of companies would pass their incoming mails through the servers of a spam-filtering company to keep the number of Viagra advertisements to a minimum. Some careful firms would back up key document stores to the servers of a disaster recovery provider in case their own computers were disabled or destroyed and they needed to re-establish services quickly.

One minor problem that arose from outsourcing IT services like this was that it made diagramming computer networks a little complicated. Any good IT manager will maintain tidy diagrams of their networks, with complex patterns of lines showing the network connections between the various servers, routers, switches, firewalls and other devices, with the IP addresses of each recorded under little pictures of each device. These diagrams would also show the network's external connections, usually a line on the edge of the diagram, with a little picture of a router or firewall device on one end of the line and, at the other end, a stylised picture of a cloud with the word "internet" underneath.

If you were looking at the diagram and asked the IT manager where the DNS server, or the webserver, or the POP mail server was, and these had been outsourced, all he could do would be to point at the edge of diagram and say that they were "in the cloud". The name stuck. Outsourced computer services were "in the cloud".

So as you can see, computing in the cloud—cloud computing—has actually been with us a very long time.

---

6 POP stands for "Post Office Protocol". Strictly speaking the standard method of setting up a POP server is the third version of this protocol called POP3, but practically everyone calls them POP servers.

Virtualisation: Many Computers, One Machine

It has already been mentioned that the machines in the air-conditioned rooms have changed radically, even if the room itself has not. But how much have they changed?

In the 1965 a computer scientist called Gordon E Moore postulated what is now called Moore's Law. In fact, he never saw it as some kind of physical law, more a general observation. He noticed that the capabilities of computers—their speed, their memory, etc—tended to double every 18 to 24 months. It was an accurate observation, and it has held true ever since Moore made it. The computer you buy today will generally be twice as powerful in every respect as the one you bought around two years ago. It will be twice as fast, have twice as much memory, and have twice as big a hard drive. The only thing that will not double is the size. All these performance characteristics will all double for a computer the same size or smaller.

It is now around 30 years since the release of the first IBM personal computer. That means there have been close to 20 of Gordon Moore's doublings in that time. This means that the modern desktop computer is around half a million times more powerful than the first PC, and the modern server computer is that many times more powerful than the first servers. The average person now carries around in their mobile telephone considerably more computing power than would have been found in the computer rooms of the largest corporations in 1980. In 1980 the total amount of stored digital data on the planet was less than 2 terabytes[7] (TB)—in other words, the amount stored on the hard drive of a single, new, workstation computer.

Now, we have already noted that some of the things modern server computers need to do actually do not require anything like the kind of computing power even the cheapest of those machines can deliver. DNS, web-hosting, even email servers do not need a very fast computer, even if email usually needs a very big hard drive. There are other functions on a computer network that do need a lot of resources, but not all the time. For example, most networks have a computer called a domain controller which makes sure that people are logging on to the network with the right passwords or other credentials, and assigns them the right permissions on the network once they have logged in. Now obviously, this computer gets very busy between 8:30 and 9:00 in the morning—in big organisations to the point that a backup domain controller computer is put in place to share the load. Of course, by 9:30 the backup domain controller is not needed anymore, but in conventional networks there is still a shiny, high-powered machine sitting there doing not very much for the next 23 hours until the next morning rush begins. It is not terribly cost-effective.

Most modern computers are so quick and so powerful that they could do the work

---

7 IT people use terms such as megabytes, gigabytes and terabytes to measure the data capacity of computer storage devices. Unfortunately, excessive use of these terms often leads the very same IT people to forget just how much data they are storing. A megabyte is equivalent to a million typed letters, numbers or other characters. A gigabyte is a billion characters and a terabyte a trillion. To put it in context, a gigabyte of computer storage can store roughly 10,000 emails and attachments. Twenty terabytes is enough to store the entire text content of the US Library of Congress. Printing one terabyte of data would require the felling, pulping and conversion to paper of around 50,000 large trees. It is a *lot* of data.

of half a dozen different servers. Which is why, increasingly, that is what they are made to do.

A lot of computer networks are now "virtualised". This means that a big computer is installed with an operating system, like Windows, as usual, but is then also installed with what is called virtualisation software. The best known of these software packages is called "VMWare". These virtualisation applications perfectly mimic a smaller, less powerful computer within the bigger one. These mimicked computers are called virtual machines.

So, for example, you could have a backup domain controller running on one virtual machine, a DNS server on another, a webserver on another and a mail server on another, and all four of these virtual machines could run at the same time on the same big computer. When the backup domain controller needs extra resources at 9:00 AM the virtualisation software will give them to it. A few minutes later the same resources can be given to another machine—probably the mail server as everyone checks their morning mails. It is a great way of sharing out resources and getting the most out of big, powerful, modern computers.

In fact, there is hardly any kind of server computer in use in modern organisations that cannot be virtualised to some degree. I suppose there is probably not much benefit in "virtualising" the data storage drives of big file and database servers. If they have to use huge swathes of computer storage, virtualising them is not going to provide any advantage. Indeed, it might even slow them down a little. Nevertheless, even with servers like that you can still virtualise the operating system of the file storage computer and the applications the computer uses to manage and search the files and databases.

The other great advantage of virtual machines is that you can set them up in a few minutes. It can take a couple of days to set up a physical computer correctly, by the time you have installed all the drivers[8] and other software and "hardened" it to make sure any passing hackers do not get into it. In comparison, setting up a virtual computer can take minutes. The virtual computers, you see, will "borrow" a lot of the parent computer's hardware, operating system software and settings, so these will not have to be set up a second time. Virtualised computers exist only as big files on their parent computers. To set up another computer of the same type, all you need to do is copy one of these big files.

Of course, I am rather oversimplifying this. Virtualisation software is extremely complex and is only easy to use because most of it is very well designed. At the core of any virtualisation application is a system called a "hypervisor" which constantly assigns memory, processor time, hard drive space, peripheral equipment and other resources from the parent computer to the various virtual computers on the basis of need. It also makes sure that none of the virtual machines starts absorbing too many resources. In the early days of virtual computing, system administrators were

---

[8] A driver program is one which the computer users to control a particular piece of equipment either in the computer or connected to it. So there will be driver programs for the monitors, keyboards and mouse; drivers for the hard drives, CD/DVD drive and USB keys; even drivers for the computer's processor and power supply.

reluctant to virtualise certain kinds of database servers, for example, because they could not be trusted not to grab large amounts of computing resources suddenly at the wrong time, disabling all the other virtual computers on the same physical machine. Nowadays, virtualisation software has developed to the point that they can usually keep even the greediest database server under tight control.

The fact that an IT firm can essentially "magic" a new server out of the air in minutes has greatly increased the number of things external IT services providers—"cloud providers"—can do for their customers. To give an example, I recently had to crack the passwords of a number of encrypted documents for use in a legal case. While there are a number of ways to speed up the process, cracking passwords on recent Microsoft Office documents essentially requires making hundreds of billions of guesses of what the right password for the document might be. It can take a long time, and the only way to speed up the process is to set up a few very fast computers working in parallel to share the task. I was able to buy computer time online from one of the big cloud computing providers. I logged onto their website, asked them to set up four high-speed multiprocessor virtual computers for me, and 15 minutes later was able to start cracking passwords. When the job was finished two or three weeks later, I was able to shut down the virtualised machines and ask the provider to send me a bill. I am quite sure that within a few minutes of my shutting down the virtual password cracking machines the same server computers had been reassigned to running someone else's databases, managing someone else's mail or some other task. My virtual password-cracking servers had been shut down to become static data files stored on a file server at the provider in case I ever need them again.

Doing things this way was not cheap—the bill for the computer time came to several thousand dollars—but it was a lot quicker and cheaper than buying four actual high-specification server computers, setting them up, networking them and running them in parallel. Going to a cloud provider saved me days of time in setup and probably weeks or even months of time getting the passwords cracked. While not many people need to do password cracking, this is still a good example of how virtualisation can make cloud computing a very attractive proposition. If, for example, you want to set up a webserver and database for a single marketing campaign, or you need to provide server capacity for group of consultants on a short-term job, or your business is very seasonal, it may be very practical to make use of cloud services. The fact that well-configured computers can be made available quickly on lease for the period you need them, and then can be disposed of as soon as they are no longer required, can be enormously convenient and cost effective. You can, I am sure, imagine any number of projects that might be possible where resources can essentially be turned on and turned off like that.

So What Can I Do with Cloud Computing? Stuff as a Service

Cloud services can be purchased in a number of different ways to meet a wide range of requirements. Sometimes an organisation just needs to have a server computer available to it for a time, to store documents or to act as a backup for the systems in place. In these circumstances the cloud provider typically provides only a high-capacity server with virtualisation software installed, with the networking equipment necessary for the organisation to connect to it with their own computers.

The organisation using the cloud service provides everything else—the operating systems for any virtual machines, the application software and the data. This approach is employed by organisations that do not want to invest in large amounts of hardware for various reasons, and prefer to lease the computing capacity they need from an external provider.

This approach to cloud computing, where computing hardware is hired online, is referred to as "Infrastructure as a Service" (IaaS). For reasons best known to the IT technicians who work in the field, practically every cloud computing model is referred to something "as a Service", so for example:

- Software as a Service (SaaS);
- Platform as a Service (PaaS);
- Storage as a Service (STaaS);
- Data as a Service (DaaS);
- Desktop as a Service (DaaS).

As you can see, they all have acronyms that (like many others in the IT field) confuse rather than simplify. There is not time here to set out all the various "as a Services" out there, but suffice to say that most cloud offerings fall into the three broad areas of "Infrastructure as a Service," "Platform as a Service" and "Software as a Service".

I have already discussed IaaS—in essence, it is large companies leasing space on their servers for other organisations to set up and run their own virtual machines.

In PaaS the company providing cloud services leases the customer rather more than mere hardware. They will also provide the virtual machines, fully loaded with running operating systems. They will also, typically, provide the more heavy-duty kinds of application software—database management systems and webservers most commonly. The cloud provider will also typically provide a level of support and maintenance on all these computers. When a company goes to a web-hosting company it is typically looking for webservers to be provided on a PaaS basis. The website itself—the software—will still be provided by the organisation buying the service rather than the cloud service provider, however.

There are a lot of other uses for PaaS. Many software companies use PaaS for development and releasing new versions. Some organisations use PaaS to maintain off-site databases to back up the websites they run (usually, also on a PaaS basis). Some PaaS services are becoming widely available. Dropbox, iCloud and other online data storage services can be seen as PaaS.

The most common form of cloud computing, however, is "Software as a Service" or SaaS. DNS servers Gmail, Hotmail and Yahoo mail are fairly classic examples of software as a service, as are POP email servers. The new online applications websites like Google Apps are SaaS as are, less prosaically, most online gaming websites. Electronic banking websites are, at this stage, longstanding examples of SaaS. In essence, anyone on the internet who allows you to log onto their computers and use the software on that computer to do something useful—like pay your bills, or write an email, or do your accounts, or kill some dragons—is providing Software as a Service. The possibilities are almost endless.

So Just How Useful is Cloud Computing?

Cloud computing provides a number of very attractive advantages to organisations. As we have seen already, it allows organisations to be flexible in the way they run their IT systems allowing them to add and remove computing capacity quickly as their requirements dictate. If extra computing capacity is needed at specific times during the day, week or year it can be added with minimal fuss (although not necessarily minimal cost).

Cloud computing can also provide greater reliability. If a server fails, a replacement can be put into service in a few hours, or even a few minutes. This gives organisations a resiliency most simply could not afford otherwise. As we have seen, some organisations already maintain backup systems in the cloud, so it is not so great a jump to have their main operations based there too.

Since cloud services are, essentially, independent of location, they can make mobile working a lot easier. The technology needed to connect up to a cloud provider from your office is very similar to that needed to connect up from your home, or your hotel room. Deciding to move your IT services to the cloud automatically gets you a long way towards enabling yourself to telecommute.

I would be incorrect, however, if I did not admit the biggest and most attractive reasons organisations move to the cloud is cost. Cloud computing is at least perceived to be a very efficient way of delivering computing services cheaply.

The reasons are fairly obvious. That big cold computer room is very expensive to maintain. Those racks of thundering computers consume a lot of expensive electricity, most of which is emitted as heat, heat which must then dissipated by air-conditioning systems that burn even more electricity. And all those servers do not run themselves. Any organisation with a reasonable amount of IT equipment needs IT people to look after them, and these are by no means cheap either.

Good IT people are hard to find. Although exact figures are difficult to find, it is thought that even in the depths of the recent recession unemployment among IT staff worldwide never got above around 5 percent. In Ireland, which suffered one of the most serious economic crises in the world, there was a persistent shortage of IT personnel throughout the crisis. The country was still granting immigration visas for IT staff even as the general rate of emigration went through the roof. For this reason, there are very good salaries in IT, and very good job opportunities too. This is excellent news for anyone of the "tech" persuasion, but not so good for those organisations that might need IT personnel simply to allow them operate.

It does not help that the roles organisations often need IT personnel for are not the kinds of jobs IT people want to do. Helpdesk operations,—sometimes referred to as "Helldesk" by the IT industry,—are an essential part of an efficiently functioning IT setup. The problem is that many good IT people hate doing helpdesk. It is a harsh thing to say, but people do not typically take jobs working in IT because they want to get out and meet other people. Consequently IT people who are good at helpdesk are quite rare personality types, and are therefore hard to find. Making things worse is that helpdesk operations are often quite complicated, so you need good IT people doing them, but these are the very people who will not want to do them and will, therefore, have to be royally remunerated if they are going to stay around in an organisation for any length of time. There is a saying in the IT community that anyone good enough at IT to do helpdesk well is too good at IT to be stuck in a helpdesk job.

An additional problem is that for most of the time IT people are not very busy. They really come into their own when things go wrong on the network, at which point they are very much needed. Hence, organisations will find themselves paying IT people a lot to sit around surfing the web, updating their Facebook pages, etc.

To a degree, cloud computing provides a solution to these issues. A lot of the helpdesk functions can be delegated to the cloud service provider. Obviously a lot of server problems can be solved only by an IT people working on the server. If the server is somewhere else, then the IT people fixing it is probably going to be somewhere else too. Hence a lot of salary, HR, overhead and other costs can be avoided by outsourcing IT provision to a cloud service provider.

Another cost issue, particularly for smaller organisations, is that annual expenditure on IT tends to vary widely over time. Servers will generally last around three to five years before they become too old and slow and need to be replaced. Some can last longer than this, but in general any organisation manager will start coming under pressure from their IT staff every five years to buy new equipment. Buying new equipment is, of course, expensive, and by some estimates the overall capital costs of buying new computers is only a third of the total costs. Setup, training and maintenance all consume substantial additional costs.

With a cloud service provider, all that has to be paid is a regular monthly or annual fee. It is the provider's problem to buy new equipment, to set it up and to run it. This means that the costs of IT can be far more efficiently budgeted. Furthermore, because cloud providers are typically much larger organisations than the organisations they sell services to, they will gain considerable economies of scale, scope and experience that might not be available directly to their clients. Of course, a lot of these economies will be reflected in profits on the cloud provider's balance sheet, but the hope of any cloud computing consumer will be that some of these cost savings will be passed on them.

One final cost-based advantage of cloud computing that is not always appreciated is that because organisations have to pay by the gigabyte for online storage they often become far more effective at managing the data that is stored on their information systems. Most organisations that maintain their IT in-house find themselves resorting to the "landfill" model of data management. Nobody ever deletes any file or email. The file servers and email servers keep filling up and up. When the servers start hitting their maximum capacity the IT team simply buys a new, bigger data storage system or adds some additional storage capacity onto an existing data storage server. After all, data storage capacity is cheap. You can now buy a couple of dozen terabytes of data storage (equivalent in size to the entire printed collection of the Library of Congress) for a few thousand euros.

The landfill approach causes problems, however. The first problem is creating backups for all of it. I know of one organisation that has long since stopped taking nightly backups of its email server. Why? Because there is so much data on it that the backup process takes two and a half days. Worse, this particular Augean stable of an email server is so packed with data that not even Hercules would touch it. There is no hope of the company ever having the time, resources or money to clean it out. But this, amazingly, is not the worst of it.

A bigger problem is what happens if you ever have to search through all of it. In the past this never really happened, but times have now changed. Your organisation can receive a Data Protection Data Access Request requiring you to find all references to an individual on your gigantic, ill-organised servers, for which you will receive the princely sum of €6.35. I have seen the actual costs of meeting such requests in large organisations exceed €10,000 per request, and they are becoming increasingly common. Worse still, what if an organisation gets into a legal dispute and has to provide legal discovery?

The Irish court rules changed in 2009, and organisations can now be required to provide electronic discovery to the other side in court cases. This can involve copying, searching and reviewing the entire contents of your information systems, and the more data that is on them, the more expensive it is going to be. In a recent case in Ireland a company defending itself found itself hit with over €8 million in discovery costs for the simple reason that it had held on to practically every document it had generated in the previous 20 years. A large proportion of them ended up having to be reviewed by a (willing) law firm for potential inclusion in the case.

Cloud computing can force organisations to think about the actual cost of having a lot of data in their possession. Granted, the cost per gigabyte stored is usually not all that high, but even getting organisations to ask "do we really need all this data" is a good start. In fact, most organisations do not need to hold onto anything like as much of their data as they actually do. Business records need to be held for quite a long time, but the other stuff of business, the day-to-day communications, can be dumped as soon as it is convenient. Indeed, data protection guidelines require organisations to get rid of personal data as soon as they are permitted to, and to keep that data up to date as far as possible. These rules, I believe, may become a great deal stricter than they are already are in the next number of years.

That being said, it is likely that Irish organisations will start taking data management seriously in the next few years anyway, but only because I foresee that a couple of them are going to be made examples of in the courts or by the Irish Data Protection Commissioner. There is nothing like someone else's misfortune to concentrate your mind. Fortunately for the partisans of cloud computing, the victims of these misfortunes are probably less likely to arise from those firms that have moved their IT to the cloud than from those still running an in-house data mountain.

The Big "But"

So why has everyone not moved their data to the cloud? The arguments I have just made are pretty persuasive, particularly to the people in organisations such as CEOs and CFOs, who have to pay for IT without being able to draw the job satisfaction an IT person might get from looking daily on rack after rack of rumbling high-specification computer servers in his very own air-conditioned computer room.

So, if cloud computing is so wonderful, why are not more people using it?

First, and most obviously, it is not for everyone. If you are running a large organisation with a large IT infrastructure, then cloud sourcing a large chunk of your IT infrastructure may simply be a more expensive way of going about things than putting in your own servers and hiring the IT staff to run them. If your IT infrastructure is big enough, you are going get the same kind of economies of scale and experience that the cloud providers will, so moving to the cloud will simply not save you any money.

The reason why organisations outsource their DNS, webservers, spam filtering, etc, is because these are activities that intrinsically have large economies of scale associated with them or, as in the case of web-hosting, provide other significant advantages (ie not allowing a back door into your network for the opportunists out there). These economies of scale are a lot less evident in other applications. Email hosting might be practical for a small firm, but for larger organisations it is probably just as practical to run an email server in-house. The bigger an organisation is, the more of a nuisance it is to run something like a POP server, which might scatter emails all over the network.

Another issue is "bandwidth"—your network connection needs to be fast enough to allow you to use the cloud properly. If your servers are located far away in an industrial estate, you will need a reasonably and reliably fast network connection to those servers so that will be able to use them. If you cannot connect to your servers, the cloud is really not going to be a great deal of use to you. Bandwidth can also catch you out in the event that you have to copy a lot of data off the cloud computers for any reason—to move it to another provider, for example, or to take copies for an investigation or for legal action.

Security is another issue. Remember we talked about a weakness in one website rendering every other website on the same server vulnerable? What if you change the word "website" for "email server" or "file server"? If you have your IT systems running as virtualised devices on the same physical server, or even the same network as another organisation's systems, security errors in those other systems may lead to problems in your own. That being said, email servers and files servers are typically a lot more secure than webservers, so the risk of being "infected" with someone else's security problems are a lot lower; but this is still a problem that does not exist when your own servers are behind your own walls. Similarly, if you do not control the parent computer, you really cannot be sure that some other virtual computer on the same system as your own machine will not suddenly decide to start devouring a lot of computing resources, causing your own virtual machines to suffer. As noted already, hypervisors are a lot better than they used to be, but none are 100 percent reliable.

You may also be dependent on the cloud supplier's IT staff and procedures to provide security on your data. Experience has shown that outsourcing providers simply do not value your data as much as you do. They cannot know what is important or sensitive, and therefore deal with it all equally and do not prioritise the really valuable stuff. As a consequence, in the US something like 50 percent of all data security breaches occur from the systems of outsourcers rather than organisations' own systems.

Another unfortunate fact of life is that the contracts that govern cloud computing services have a tendency to be written very much in the providers' favour. This can cause no end of problems if, for example, you want to do something with your data outside the scope of the contract. In the past I have had a lot of problems investigating data breaches from cloud systems: why would a cloud provider cooperate in an investigation that might end up getting them sued? I have also experienced difficulties, or at least a distinct lack of cooperation, in retrieving data from cloud providers for discovery in legal cases. Cloud providers make their money by running huge predictable data factories—they really are not set up to handle anything out of the ordinary, so any special requests from clients can genuinely be very disruptive to operations. Their reaction will, therefore, be to ignore any special requests in the hope they go away, deny the requests because they are outside the terms of the operations contract, or charge a lot of money to carry the request out.

Finally, the question that always seems to be missed in cloud contracts: what if your cloud provider goes out of business? As any new industry is born there is usually a huge growth in the number of providers delivering products in that area; think about the birth of the computer revolution (remember Amstrad, Sinclair, Commodore, Compaq, Gateway?) or the internet bubble of the last decade. Rapid growth is quickly followed by pretty remorseless Darwinian evolution as most of the players in the market get out-competed and go out of business. Many, of course, will be bought out by competitors, but others will go bust. What might happen if the company looking after your data goes to the wall? You can move a webserver or a DNS server in a couple of hours with only a little annoyance, but how quickly can you move a big email server, or a file server?

So, as you can see, for all the advantages of cloud computing, not everything is exactly joy and light.

The Caveats at the End

So where is cloud computing going? Fortunately, my remit in writing this chapter is does not include a requirement for prophecy.

However, if you want my own, relatively unqualified view, I think that, after a lot of analysis, organisations are likely to make an educated decision about whether or not to move some or all of their IT infrastructure to the cloud. Those that get the decision correct will prosper; those that do not, will not.

Although I risk sounding like the author of that IBM report back in 1950, I do not think there will be a mass migration to the cloud. On balance, I think that cloud services are better suited to individuals and smaller organisations than large ones for the simple reason that the economies to be gleaned from the cloud are higher for small organisations. I base this prediction on the not unreasonable grounds that, while it has relatively recently become fashionable, the "cloud" has actually been around since the internet was created, and smaller entities have always had more to gain from using it than larger ones.

I think a lot of the cloud providers are going to have to become a little more cooperative and flexible to their customers' requirement as a consequence. A one-size-fits-all approach is simply not going to work for a heterogeneous mix of organisations with different technology and support requirements. The cloud providers that best adapt to this will be the ones that ultimately succeed. Of course, some will say that there is more profit in making clients adapt to their own model; but ultimately the cloud providers that do that will do nothing more than place their own clients at a competitive disadvantage, and that is not an approach that is likely to bring long-term success.

Of course, I could always be wrong.

PART V: EMPLOYEES AND EDUCATION

Chapter 18

EMPLOYEES

Headline of Issues

- Existing employees
- Potential employees
- Risks
- On site
- Off site
- Employee social networking
- Employee profiles
- Defamation
- Harassment
- Monitoring and consent
- Restrictions, laws and cases
- Evidence, archives, records, spoilation

Introduction

Organisations can be held legally responsible for what their employees and agents do online.[1] This applies in the US as it does in Ireland and the UK. Caution is needed so that organisations and employees avoid, for example, creating legally binding unintended contracts while online.[2] Organisations also need to be careful that their employees do not engage in creating or distributing defamatory comments online, which can lead to the employer being held directly or contributorily liable for defamation. Many organisations will already be familiar with managing these risks and will have appropriate policies and procedures in place. Employers and organisations now need to be aware of social networking and how this can affect their liability. Policies will need to be updated and reviewed. Risks need to be monitored on an ongoing basis.

Employer Liability Issues

Employers and organisations need to understand social networking and react to it. They can be held legally responsible for what their employees and agents do online.[3] Risk management for organisations in relation to social networking is now

---

1 AJ Bojorquez and D Shores, "Open Government and the Net: Bringing Social Media into the Light" (2009–2010) (11) *Texas Tech Administrative Law Journal* 45 at 46.

2 *ibid*, 50. The article also refers to Florida Attorney General Opinion 9-19 (2009), which refers to a proposed official Facebook page, which if arranged would need to ensure all records were accessible, and all virtual meetings were open to the public. See *ibid*, 50 and n43 at 50.

3 *ibid*, 46.

"a major concern".[4] This is especially so when adverse comments are being made; when a corporate disaster or data loss strikes[5]; or when corporate resources are used disproportionately or inappropriately and against specific organisational policies.

Viruses, Etc

Employees accessing social networks can also expose the organisation to viruses and malicious software threats.[6] The means by which unscrupulous third parties seek to get access to, or damage, the computers and network of the employer or steal data are ever increasing.

Bandwidth and Resources

The use of social networks, whether authorised or unauthorised, can use up a large amount of bandwidth resources[7] and time resources of the organisation.

Some organisations block access to social networks, or alternatively restrict the hours of such access.[8] In the US, it has been suggested that employees generally will have no expectation of privacy in electronic communications transmitted through the employer's network systems.[9] Employers and organisations elsewhere need to be very cautious in adopting this approach. General monitoring of employees is not permissible under EU data protection laws, and the EU Article 29 Working Party has commented as such. Furthermore, it has been acknowledged by national data protection regulators that there can be expectations of privacy in certain contexts. That is to say nothing of what might be argued in terms of privacy and unenumerated privacy expectations under constitutional law eg Irish Constitution, etc.[10]

Defamation

Defamation[11] can occur when an employee states something online, or repeats a third-

4 Nelson *et al.*, *op. cit*, 34.

5 Generally see comments in M Boran, "A Tweet in Time Could Help Save Your Company, How do Firms Stay Afloat When Disaster Strikes and the Story Takes on a Life of its Own in Cyberspace?" *Irish Times*, 1 April 2011.

6 Bojorquez and Shores, *op. cit*, 65. Also note, for example, Miller, "The Facebook Frontier: Responding to the Changing Face of Privacy on the Internet" (2008–2009) *Kentucky Law Journal* 541 at 551–553.

7 See H Tarrant, "What Facebook Costs Business," *Moneyweb*, 16 August 2007, available at http://moneyweb.co.za/mw/en/page292671?oid=154231&sn=2009%20Detail, referred to in Bojorquez and Shores, *op. cit*, 65.

8 Bojorquez and Shores, *op. cit*, 66, and references therein.

9 *ibid*, 67. Note also case of *Pack v Wood County* No 6:08cv198 2009 US District Lexis 57103 (ED Texas 30 July 2009), referred to *ibid*, where the employee was held not to be able to restrict access to his communications on the employer systems.

10 See G Hogan and G Whyte, *The Irish Constitution* (Butterworths: Dublin, 1994), 746 and 755 for example.

11 KM Gurney, "MySpace, Your Reputation: A Call to Change Libel Laws for Juveniles Using Social Networking Sites" (2009) (82) *Temple Law Review* 241 at 249–250 and 254–256; AE Horton, "Beyond Control?: The Rise and Fall of Defamation Regulation on the Internet" (2009) (43) *Valparaiso University Law Review* 1265.

party comment that is untrue.[12] However, this can create liability for the organisation in a variety of circumstances. Those who author defamatory statements on social networks are liable and responsible for them under defamation law.[13] One example is where the statements are posted in the work environment, or even circulated in the work environment electronically, thus implicating the employer.

Traditionally the concerns related to email. However, employers and organisations need to consider whether they allow social networking by employees from the work venue generally. If they do, it is not inconsistent that someone would claim defamation against the employer as well as the irresponsible employee who may have said something alleged to be defamatory on a social network. This is particularly so where that employee, or other employees, regularly mention work issues on their social networking profile pages. Issues in relation to statements made on instant messaging available on social networks should not be discounted.

A separate example of concern arises where the employer uses content from employee and potential employee social networks that later transpires to be defamatory.[14] An organisation may, for example, have a publicity or recruitment campaign and decide to include employee comments from various sources, including social networking.

Horton states:

> "The increase in forums and the ability of internet users to publish information – through bulletin boards, chat rooms, and web journals, often referred to as blogs – has created a greater threat of damage to one's reputation on a much larger scale. Defamation, libel, and slander issues in cyberspace have all posed challenges for the law, and in order to better understand the legal issues, one must first understand how the information superhighway, and the growing cyber community, work".[15]

One of the issues with social networks is that statements are frequently posted anonymously or under a made-up user name.[16] This can create problems pursuing or dealing with a particular matter.

Records and Information

Social networking now also has an impact on data preservation and record retention obligations.[17] Organisations need to be aware of whether and how social network content may affect their data preservation and record retention obligations.[18] Also,

---

12 Generally, note the new Defamation Act 2009; M McGonagle, *Media Law* (Round Hall, Dublin, 2012); J Maher, *The Law of Defamation* (Round Hall, Dublin, 2011); E Carolan and A O'Neill, *Media Law in Ireland* (Bloomsbury, Dublin, 2010); B McMahon and W Binchy, *Law of Torts* (Tottel, Dublin, 2000).

13 Gurney, *op. cit*, 256.

14 I Byrnside, "Six Clicks of Separation: The Legal Ramifications of Employers Using Social Networking Sites to Research Applicants" (2008) (10) *Vanderbilt Journal of Entertainment and Technology Law* 445, at 468–469.

15 Horton, *op. cit*, 1277.

16 Gurney, *op. cit*, 256.

17 Bojorquez and Shores, *op. cit*, 46 and 50 *et seq*.

18 *ibid*, 46 and 50 *et seq*.

freedom of information (or public access in the US[19]) issues arise in relation to certain social networking content. Issues of public access (in the US[20]) and freedom of information might include certain social networking content.[21]

Employee Profiles

There is no specific law currently explicitly prohibiting the use by organisations of potential employees' social networking profiles.[22] However, other laws may be indirectly applicable, such as privacy, data protection, terms of use, terms of service, discrimination and defamation.[23] An organisation needs to consider the legal issues and impact carefully before undertaking equivalent search activities here in relation to potential employees.

Given that there is a greater reticence against blanket monitoring in the EU under the data protection regime, caution needs to employed by organisations in terms of regular searches of employees' online social networking, etc. Employers and organisations always need to bear in mind differences between the laws of different jurisdictions, and that a decision from one country may not automatically translate into another jurisdiction. Caution also needs to be maintained when considering decisions of lower-level courts. They may not always be applied by higher-level courts, regardless of jurisdiction.

A separate issue also arises in terms of employees' profiles. Employment-related websites mean that it is possible for an employer inadvertently to come across a profile that might relate to an existing employee. This "seeking work" profile might be posted directly by the individual or by an employment agent.

Similar problems may also arise with non-dedicated employment websites. Many general commercial profile websites exist, possibly the most prominent of which is LinkedIn. Individuals upload information and status reports on their academic or professional careers. It can be useful for an employee to advertise their skills on LinkedIn, especially if they are considering a new employment position. However, as LinkedIn, etc are often publicly available websites, the risk arises that their employer may also see the posts or comments. One example of this is the case of John Flexman, who claims to have been forced out of his job after the employer saw certain CV details on his LinkedIn profile page.[24] Employees (and indeed users generally) should always remember that the comments and materials they post online can come back and be used against them subsequently.[25]

---

19 *ibid*, 46.

20 *ibid*, 46.

21 Generally, see S Mason, *Electronic Evidence, Disclosure, Discovery & Admissibility* (Lexis Nexis Butterworths: London, 2012); Bojorquez and Shores, *op. cit*, 50.

22 See Byrnside, *op. cit*, 445; DH Montes, "Living Our Lives Online: The Privacy Implications of Online Social Networking" (2010) (5) *I/S: A Journal of Law and Policy* 507 at 524.

23 *ibid*, 524–525.

24 D Hare, "Construction Manager 'Forced Out' Over LinkedIn CV," *ConstructionWeekOnline.com*, 9 January 2012; C Williams, "Executive 'Forced Out of Job' Over LinkedIn CV," *Daily Telegraph*, 5 January 2012.

25 T Stretton, "Anything You Tweet or Post Can and Will be Used Against You," *Computers and Law*, Society of Computers and Law, 6 December 2011.

TELECOMMUTING

The advent of working from home and telecommuting also poses problems for employers. Once at home there is, even according to US commentators, a reasonable expectation of privacy at home.[26] That an employee is working from home during office hours does not mean the normal data protection policies and accepted employee rights are to be ignored. Neither should organisations assume that respect for privacy and data protection of employees disappears after business hours. While (certain) organisational policies and procedures may be argued to extend beyond the physical and temporal confines of the organisation, employees do not abandon their rights on leaving the employer's building. Some may argue that employee privacy and data protection rights are greater at such times. Complexities also arise in relation to mingling of personal data and employment data on the same computer device, as well as device-related issues (eg ownership, control, payment of bills for devices, authority to access, etc).

EMPLOYEES AND BLOGS

Blogs are frequently viewed by individuals as their personal websites. (Of course, they can be commercially or professionally focused also.) However, defamation can also arise in the event of employee blogs, official or otherwise. Some of the other dangers of blogs include employees disclosing confidential information, trade secrets or insider information. Privacy as well as intellectual property rights (IPRs) issues are also concerns.[27] Information on blog postings might be used in employee disciplinary actions (up to and including termination) and harassment cases, so employees should always be careful with what they say online, including on social networks. This is yet another area where organisations may feel the need to ban or restrict employees from using or accessing blogs.

Up to now many employers may have felt that there were no laws or regulations preventing them from looking at social networks in order to vet applicants.[28] In many instances there is no legal case determining a particular issue.[29] That does not mean that liability cannot arise. Employees as well as employers need to be particularly cautious until such time as the matter is decided in a higher-level court. Even in the US, commentators have raised potential issues of privacy, discrimination, fair credit reporting, violation of website terms and conditions, defamation, etc.[30] Social networking screening or vetting has also been described as a "nightmare" issue for individuals.[31]

Indeed, there are an increasing number of examples where sports clubs are banning, restricting and regulating professional athletes in relation to their social networking

---

26 Bojorquez and Shores, *op. cit*, 68.

27 G Lastowska, "User-Generated Content and Virtual Worlds" (2007–2008) (10) *Vanderbilt Journal of Entertainment and Technology Law* 893 at 897.

28 See Byrnside, *op. cit*, 458.

29 See *ibid*, 459 and references therein.

30 *ibid*, 445.

31 C Brandenberg, "The Newest Way to Screen Job Applicants: A Social Networker's Nightmare" (2007–2008) *Federal Communications Law Journal* 597.

activities. Recent examples include soccer players' use of Twitter. Regardless of what decisions may be taken by organisations, such decisions should be made available in a written and transparent manner to all employees. This includes detailing the company's position in relation to employee action, communications and devices that may be used off site, if this is permitted.

The extent to which employers may be able to regulate or ban blogs, social networking, etc by employees may ultimately depend on the nature of the specific relationship, the business activities, and how regulators and courts may interpret the data protection regime. However, one case suggests that a company may be able to prevent employees accessing blogs.[32] An organisation may feel, for example, that too much time is wasted online and decide to ban internet access, or restrict access to certain websites and online services. Certain colleges also ban social networking at exam time.

Where blogs are permitted, one issue facing an organisation is the extent to which it may want to or be obliged to maintain a record of employees' blogs.[33] This raises many issues.

Different issues will also arise in terms of organisations' own official blogs.[34] Some of the issues to be decided are the parameters, content, tone, subjects, etc on which employees are permitted to comment, and indeed which employees are permitted to post the blog.

Recruiters increasingly use social networking and mobile messaging to proactively engage and recruit new staff.[35] There are issues in terms of how they obtain contact details in the first instance, but also in terms of what personal data they collect and how they use, store it and disclose it.

Harassment

Harassment and sexual harassment in the workplace are regulated. Social networking is a new means for such harassment, including between employees or between former/estranged partners or spouses.[36] Both can take place in and from the work place, on work equipment and devices.

Harassment is prohibited in Ireland under s 10 of the Non-Fatal Offences Against the Person Act 1997.[37] The offence can be committed when a person without lawful authority is persistently following, watching, pestering, besetting or communicating

32 *Nicholas v Fletcher*, No 3:06-CV-00043 KKC 2007 WL 1035012, at 1, 9 (ED Ky 30 March 2007), referred to in Nelson *et al.*, *op. cit*, 17.

33 See Nelson *et al.*, *op. cit*, 16–17.

34 *ibid*, 12.

35 M Maher, "You've Got Messages: Modern Technology Recruiting Through Text-Messaging and the Intrusiveness of Facebook" (2007) *Texas Review of Entertainment & Sports Law* 125.

36 See LL Baughman, "Friend Request or Foe? Confirming the Misuse of Internet and Social Networking Sites By Domestic Violence Perpetrators" (2010) (19) *Widener Law Journal* 933 and examples therein.

37 Non-Fatal Offences Against the Person Act 1997 at s 10.

with a subscriber. The harassment may, either "intentionally or recklessly, seriously interfere" with the subscriber's privacy and the conduct must be "without lawful or authority or reasonable excuse."[38] Where a person harasses an employee or even a third party on the employer's network, and potentially on social networks, the employee and potentially the employer can have issues to answer. In addition, if the employee accesses someone else's emails, passwords, etc, legal issues can arise separately from the harassment offence.

Social networking, such as Facebook and Twitter, now means that sports stars and celebrities are more accessible to the general public. While sports stars may be able to promote themselves and their brand, for instance, it also opens them up to complaint or unfavourable direct comments from third parties, sometimes anonymously. Stephen Fry is a notable example of a celebrity leaving Twitter after third-party criticism on the website (albeit returning subsequently). So too presenter Ryan Tubridy. A 21-year-old was arrested in connection with allegedly racist statements made on Twitter about the soccer player and commentator Stan Collymore.[39] The UK has seen numerous arrests and charges in relation to online abuse (including rape and death threats).

Under s 9 of the Irish Criminal Justice (Theft and Fraud Offences) Act 2001 the unlawful use of a computer is an offence.[40] The Criminal Damage Act 1991 also creates an offence of unauthorised access to a computer and it is also an offence to damage data.[41] McIntyre states that the Irish legislation creates a "remarkably broad [offence] [regarding] 'damage' [and] modification of any information stored on a computer".[42]

As the right to privacy is protected by the Irish Constitution, an invasion of privacy in an unlawful manner could open the employer to potential damages. The case of *Herrity v Associated Newspapers* held that there was an invasion of privacy and awarded damages of €60,000 ordinary and aggravated and €30,000 punitive damages.[43] This related to the use of a transcript of an illegally recorded telephone conversation regarding private relations.

In the US there can be specific laws encompassing harassment. For example, section 33.07 of the Texas Penal Code makes it an offence where a person:

> "uses the name or persona of another person to create a web page or to post one or more messages on a commercial networking site: (1) without obtaining the other person's consent; and (2) with the intent to harm, defraud, intimidate or threaten any person".[44]

Under s 33.07(b) of the same Texas law it is a crime to:

---

38 *ibid* at s 10(2)(a).

39 "Newcastle Man Arrested Over Racist Tweets Sent to Stan Collymore," *Huffington Post*, 7 January 2012.

40 Criminal Justice (Theft and Fraud Offences) Act 2001 at s 9. S 25 of the Criminal Justice (Theft and Fraud Offences) Act 2001 creates an offence of creating a false instrument.

41 Criminal Damage Act 1991, s 5.

42 TJ McIntyre, "Computer Crime in Ireland: A Critical Assessment of the Substantive Law" (2005) (15(1)) *Irish Criminal Law Journal* 13 at 14.

43 *Herrity v Associated Newspapers* [2009] 1 IR 316 and 347.

44 Referred to in Bojorquez and Shores, *op. cit*, 68–69.

> "send an (electronic mail, instant message, text message, or similar communication that references ... identifying information belonging to any person: (1) without obtaining the person's consent; (2) with the intent to cause the recipient ... reasonably believe that the other person authorized ... the communication; and (3) with the intent to harm or defraud any person".[45]

It is also commented that "with every new technology, there are laws (ie privacy ... defamation, and copyright), social norms, and business practices that warrant thoughtful consideration and communication with public officials and employees."[46]

There have been various attempts at local and federal legislation in the US prohibiting online or cyber harassment.[47] Ireland does not have a law dealing explicitly with social networking or online harassment, whether by employees or others. There is also no UK law explicitly dealing with online harassment.[48] While there is a Protection from Harassment Act 1997, it is questioned how applicable this can be to internet harassment,[49] and hence social networking harassment. It is argued in the UK that "the current overall legislative framework is inaccessible, uncertain and thus inadequate to encompass activities in today's evolving age of online social networking".[50] Online harassment is wide and includes sending abusive, threatening or obscene email or messages (including via instant messaging or social networks); sending friend requests or "poking" on social networks; stalking on Second Life; impersonation (eg fake profiles); spamming; sending malicious email or email attachments; and subscribing a person to mailing lists, etc.[51] It can also include monitoring communications.[52] Indeed, interception offence issues also arise.

In terms of litigation of these issues, significant evidential issues arise in terms of obtaining and admissibility of such evidence in court.[53] These include authenticity, hearsay, best evidence rule, fraud and false information.[54] Some cases are illustrative of the expansion of harassment issues. In one example in Kent, a librarian was harassed when a Facebook group was set up called "[f]or those who hate the little fat library man".[55] Another UK case saw a man cleared of a harassment charge for sending friend request to an ex-girlfriend.[56] The House of Lords has previously held that a silent telephone call can amount to harassment.[57]

Perhaps non-internet-related laws may be used in relation to social networking

---

45 Bojorquez and Shores, *op. cit*, 69.

46 *ibid*, 69.

47 See various references and commentary in Montes, *op. cit*, 519–521.

48 N Geach and N Haralambous, "Regulating Harassment: Is The Law Fit for the Social Networking Age?" (2009) (73) *Journal of Criminal Law* 241.

49 *ibid.*

50 *ibid.*

51 Geach and Haralambous, *op. cit*, 242.

52 Baughman, *op. cit*, 940–941.

53 See, for example, *ibid*, 945–946.

54 *ibid*, 946–956.

55 "'Fat Library Man' Bullied Online," *BBC News*, 23 July 2007, available at http://news.bbc.co.uk/2/hi/uk_news/england/kent/6912409.stm, referred to in Geach and Haralambous, *op. cit*, 242.

56 P John, "Man Cleared of Facebook Harassment," *Birmingham Main*, 27 March 2008, referred to in Geach and Haralambous, *op. cit*, 243.

57 *R v Ireland* and *R v Burstow* [1998] AC 147, referred to in Geach and Haralambous, *op. cit*, 245.

harassment, namely in the UK, the Protection from Harassment Act 1997 (s 2), the UK Malicious Communications Act 1988 (s 1(1)) and the Communications Act 2003 (s 127).[58] The Public Order Act 1986 (s 5 and s 4A) could also "theoretically" apply.[59]

However, the range of activity, its severity and its effect vary considerably, and as with other laws that may now require greater nuancing (eg child criminals), cyber harassment and cyber stalking also require the right remedies for the right offence.[60]

Employee Monitoring

Some US commentators suggest that employers are permitted generally to monitor their employees' usage of telephones, emails, internet and work location (via CCTV).[61] In the US there appears to be a perception that it is legitimate for employers to monitor their employees' electronic activities, including social networking. For example, one article states: "checking the social networking [web]sites of potential employees could be wise, as an employer might get some sense of trouble brewing in the future: a lack of discretion, angry entries, a 'TMI' (too much information) proclivity, etc".[62]

However, there are differences between the US and the EU in terms of data protection and the rights of individual data subjects. EU data protection law does not permit the blanket monitoring of employee activities, including online and electronic communications usage (eg EU Article 29 Working Party). This would most likely include social networking. Note also the case of *Herrity v Associated Newspapers*, noted above, which awarded aggravated and punitive damages for invasion of privacy.[63]

Even in the US there are on occasion cases that support employees' rights of privacy from monitoring, even on employer devices. One example if the case of *Quon v Arch Wireless*.[64]

The Supreme Court in Canada has recognised that employees have rights of privacy, expectations of privacy and data protection at work, which includes internet use and internet browsing history.[65]

The Irish Data Protection Commissioner and the EU Article 29 Working Party also

58 Referred to in Geach and Haralambous, *op. cit*, 241.

59 *ibid*, 254.

60 M Baer, "Cyberstalking and the Internet Landscape We Have Constructed" (2010) *Virginia Journal of Law & Technology* 153. Also, C Calvert, "Fighting Words in the Era of Texts, IMS and Emails: Can a Disparaged Doctrine be Resuscitated to Punish Cyber-Bullies?" (2010–2011) *DePaul Journal of Art, Technology & IP Law* 1; JJ Exum, "Making the Punishment Fit the (Computer) Crime; Rebooting Notions of Possession for the Federal Sentencing of Child Pornography Offenses" (2009–2010) *Richmond Journal of Law & Technology* 1.

61 See for example, Bojorquez and Shores, *op. cit*, 67.

62 Nelson *et al.*, *op. cit*, 19.

63 *Herrity v Associated Newspapers* [2009] 1 IR 316 and 347.

64 *Quon v Arch Wireless* 529 F3d 892 (9th Cir 2008). This related to a public-sector employee.

65 *R v Cole* Supreme Court Canada 2012 SCC 53, available at http://scc.lexum.org/decisia-scc-csc/scc-csc/scc-csc/en/item/12615/index.do.

recognise the legitimate expectations of employees in relation to their privacy and data protection rights.

Public Organisations and Information Published

Many public organisations seek to make information available to the public on websites and increasingly on social networks. However, it is possible that too much information may be published or posted, or on occasion information that is private, privileged, confidential or otherwise restricted.[66]

There can also be specific rules and regulations pertaining to other issues affecting what may or may not be permitted officially on social networks.[67]

Difficulties can also arise in relation to distinguishing between which communications and postings are official and which are personal.[68] Some of the relevant factors may include: who prepared the materials; who has control and access; the specific nature of the material; whether it was used in the course of conducting government business; whether public funds were spent to create the material; the purpose of the material; and whether the government entity requires creation of the material.[69]

Social networks can be summarised as creating additional "administrative and legal headaches".[70] It is equally essential that public organisations are aware of the implications of social networking and implement appropriate policies and procedures to inform personnel of the correct protocols and to regulate such activity.[71]

Existing Employees

Organisations should have appropriate policies and contracts in place with their employees, which includes regulating their usage of social networking.[72] Given the recent advent of social networking, and indeed that many organisations remain unfamiliar with social networking, policies dedicated to social networking risks are in many instances absent. Frequently, larger organisations will be the first to implement appropriate and dedicated policies. One example is the *IBM Social Computing Guidelines: Blogs, Wikis, Social Networks, Virtual Worlds and Social Media*.[73] It should always be remembered that regardless of what the policies are, they always need to be reviewed regularly, at least annually.

---

66 See Bojorquez and Shores, *op. cit*, 50.
67 *ibid*, 50.
68 *ibid*, 54.
69 *ibid*, 54.
70 *ibid*, 65.
71 *ibid*, 65.
72 AR Levinson, "Industrial Justice: Privacy Protection for the Employed" (2009) (18) *Cornell Journal of Law and Public Policy* 609.
73 Available at http://www.ibm.com/blogs/zz/en/guidelines.html.

Potential Employees

While employers may be equally interested in everything to do with their potential employees as with their existing employees, there may in fact be less of a fair and legitimate entitlement to examine the online and social networking of such persons. Despite this, many employers, particularly in the US, regularly seek to vet potential employees' social networking activities. Social networking is, therefore, frequently contentious.[74] Potential employers go to the internet as part of their candidate selection and interview process. Caution, however, is required in the EU.

Individuals may be concerned that when they are applying for a job, the employer may take into account factors that are irrelevant or in breach of their data protection rights.[75] Job applicants have been refused employment when the prospective employer found out through their social networking that the person smoked cannabis.[76] Even Microsoft has indicated that such searches of social networking information is "fairly typical".[77]

The use of "social networking [web]sites for gathering applicant information raises several potential legal issues, including invasion of privacy, discrimination, violation of the Fair Credit Reporting Act [1970], violation of terms of service, and defamation ... this is an emerging area of law that is far from settled."[78]

The main problems with employer searches and decisions based on these searches are (1) inaccurate, irrelevant or indeed false information leading to unfair decisions, (2) illegal decisions being made by employers aided by lack of explicit regulation in this area, and (3) violation of legitimate expectations of privacy.[79]

Some claim that laws must be amended and updated to ensure adequate user protection against "unfair, illegal or arbitrary employment decisions".[80]

There is concern that employers may be influenced by the off-duty activities of employees and potential employees.[81] No easy solution exists, but employers and organisations should be proactive as new issues and risks arise, even when a specific issue does not appear to be explicitly referred to in the current legal regime.

In an ExecuNet survey, 75 percent of recruiters indicated that they used web searches

---

74 Brandenberg, *op. cit*, 597.

75 See RB Ecker, "Comment, To Catch a Thief: The Private Employer's Guide to Getting and Keeping an Honest Employee" (1994) (63) *UMKC Law Review* 251 at 255–261, referred to in Byrnside, *op. cit*, 452.

76 A Finder, "When A Risque Online Persona Undermines a Chance for a Job," *New York Times*, 11 June 2006, S 1, at 1, referred to in Nelson *et al.*, *op. cit*, 21.

77 Referred to Warren Ashton, Group Marketing Manager, Microsoft, in A Finder, "When a Risque Online Persona Undermines a Chance for a Job," *New York Times*, 11 June 2006, 1, referred to in I, Byrnside, above at 456.

78 Byrnside, *op. cit*, 445.

79 *ibid*, 237.

80 *ibid*.

81 SD Sugarman, "'Lifestyle' Discrimination in Employment" (2003) (24) *Berkeley Journal of Employment and Labour Law* 377, 378, 407, referred to in Byrnside, *op. cit*, 452.

to screen applicants.[82] One view is that once something is in the public domain, it is "fair game".[83] In addition, it can be argued to have been voluntarily posted online by the individual directly.[84] Some commentators even feel that this will be the case where an individual had restricted their privacy settings and a potential employer "hacks past" them.[85] This should be cautioned against in the EU.

Also:

> "Although employers have begun using social networking [web]sites to assist with hiring decisions, the potential legal ramifications of such a practice are unclear, to say the least. No case has been brought on the basis of such use of these social networking [web]sites. However, the increasing popularity of such [web]sites brings with it the potential for numerous legal problems to arise in this 'emerging area of law,' bolstering the chance that such a case may arise in the not-so-distant future".[86]

Employers rightly or wrongly "are increasingly checking the social networking profiles of their applicants and that those applicants may suffer as a result of the information they have posted on the Internet."[87]

Background checks in the US are indicated not to be illegal, "so long as employment decisions based on this information are consistent with 'business necessity' and do not have a disparate impact on a certain class of applicants."[88]

Some also argue that an employer's use of social networking information in relation to employees and applicants violates the website terms and conditions, which generally refer to personal non-commercial use.[89]

Identity

Regardless of whether or not employers are permitted to use social networks for vetting potential employees or existing employees, issues of identity and authenticity arise. While they may find a profile online, they have no guarantee in every instance that the profile they are viewing is that of the applicant/employee.[90] This also arises in relation to comments posted online. Employers may like to use such internet profiling because of the "wealth of information available from online social networking profiles to screen potential employees ... [and because it is] cost-effective ...".[91] There are many surveys where employers have confirmed that they use such

---

82 J Greenfoelds and D Haugh, "When What Happens on MySpace Doesn't Stay on MySpace," *Chicago Tribune*, 28 March 2006, at C1, referred to in Byrnside, *op. cit*, 456.

83 M Irvine, "When MySpace Becomes Everyone's Space," *Globe & Mail* (Toronto), 30 December 2006, at R12, referred to in Byrnside, *op. cit*, 461.

84 Byrnside, *op. cit*, 461–462.

85 *ibid*, 462.

86 *ibid*, 447–448.

87 *ibid*, 457.

88 *ibid*, 450.

89 *ibid*, 466–468.

90 *ibid*, 470.

91 Montes, *op. cit*, 521.

profile information, and also many documented examples of this happening.[92] This trend appears to be increasing, especially in the US.

Restrictions

These issues are not always explicitly referred to in the data protection regime, and hence need to be interpreted from the existing provisions by data protection regulators. The upcoming reform of the EU data protection regime may add some clarity, if not further specific regulation, in this area.

The US Credit Reporting Act is aimed at ensuring that decisions are made only on accurate and relevant information.[93] There are claims that the Credit Reporting Act should be expanded to cater properly for social networking and employment issues.[94] For example, minor amendments could ensure that information must be accurate but also that users of social networking are aware of the information being used in relation to them.[95]

In the US certain questions may be prohibited by, for example, the Title VII of the Civil Rights Act 1964 (prohibiting discrimination on the basis of race, colour, religion, nationality), the Age Discrimination in Employment Act 1967, and Titles I and V of the Americans with Disabilities Act 1990.[96] However, while there may be no:

> "direct discrimination or unlawful questioning based on the above, it is very difficult to prove or disprove that this information did not filter into an otherwise lawful decision to not employ, promote, etc, any particular person. Some feel that as yet there is 'no adequate protection' against such filtering scenarios."[97]

Title VII is the main federal statute relating to anti-discrimination, and prohibits employers from discriminating against applicants and employees based on race, colour, religion, sex or national origin.[98]

In order to maintain a claim of invasion of privacy, it is necessary to show that there was a reasonable expectation of privacy.[99] In the EU, data protection laws will apply.

Redress

If employers do something that they should not do and this has adverse consequences for an employee/potential employee, what sanction should arise? What redress or punishment is appropriate?[100]

---

92 *ibid*, 522–523.
93 Davis, *op. cit*, 240.
94 *ibid*, 237.
95 *ibid*, 241, 251–255.
96 Referred to in Montes, *op. cit*, 523.
97 *ibid*, 523.
98 *ibid*, 449.
99 *California v Greenwood* 486 US 35, 39–40 (1988), as referred to in Byrnside, *op. cit*, 452.
100 Issue raised in Byrnside, *op. cit*, 472.

Byrnside states:

> "Until a definitive judicial decision or legislative decree is announced that addressed these issues, it is safe for applicants to assume that at least some employers will be checking their social networking profiles. Therefore, applicants should operate under the assumption that potential employers will see everything they post on their profiles. With this in mind, it is important for applicants to use discretion in deciding in deciding what information to post on their social networking profiles and what information to leave out. If applicants insist on putting certain information on their social networking profiles, they should, at the very least, adjust the privacy settings to restrict access to their profiles".[101]

Individuals may face an "uphill battle" in attempting to prevent employers using their social networking information —even if "password protected".[102] Obviously, however, one consequence is damages. Also, an employer may not be able to discipline or dismiss an employee in a given instance due to its breach.

Using Social Networking for Business

Should a company permit employees to use social networks for business purposes? Such use might:

> "include[e] communications with clients and internal communications with coworkers. If employers allow access to social networking [web]sites or employees circumvent controls that limit their access, employees may be using the [web]sites to conduct the business of their employers or collaborate with colleagues. As such, the information that relates to the employment of the individual may be relevant to a potential suit. The policy that an employer takes with respect to the use of social networking must be specific and detailed but at the same time, cannot be so constraining that the purpose for using the [web]sites to reach clients, consumers, and colleagues is defeated.
>
> IBM has taken the reigns and developed guidelines specific to social computing. The company places some responsibility on its employees for monitoring what is said on social networking [web]sites and reporting conduct that strays from its guidelines. This would be an important part of any policy relating to social networking to ensure that the policy has an enforcement mechanism. Particularly unique to IBM's policy is the requirement that when employees discuss matters related to the company, employees have to identify themselves by name and their role at the company and make it clear that they are speaking for themselves and not on behalf of the company. In addition to this, the company requires employees who post to blogs to use a disclaimer that the views posted do not represent the company's views. The guidelines require employees to be thoughtful with respect to dispersing internal, confidential communications externally via social networking [web] sites. Also, the employee may not comment on the business performance of the company or affirm or deny rumors related to the company's business performance. The company makes users personally responsible for the information that is posted on these [web]sites and emphasizes that employees cannot alter previous posts without making it clear that the post has been altered. The policy also requires employees to be respectful with their postings and gently reminds employees not to let their social networking activities interfere with their work-related commitments and duties.
>
> In addition to the IBM guidelines, there are a few additional steps that employers can take with respect to an employee's use of social networking in the workplace that may avoid the problems associated with obtaining the information for litigation purposes and maintain a company's reputation on social networking [web]sites. First, like IBM has done, companies should make sure that they create a social networking policy that is specific and that employees are educated about the policy and the repercussions in the

---

[101] *ibid*, 473.
[102] *ibid*, 477.

> case of violations of the policy. The policy should also be enforced. An umbrella computer usage policy may not be sufficient to encompass the specific concerns related to social networking, especially if social networking is not mentioned. With respect to enforcement, the company should be consistent and actually follow its own policy guidelines for the policy to have any meaning.[[103]]
>
> In contrast to a general email policy that usually advises employees that their business email communications should not be considered private, social networking [web]sites are usually not viewed in this way because they are personal accounts. A step that employers could take is to require employees who would like to use social networking for business purposes to create a separate business account, based on their business email address, as a condition to use the [web]sites in the workplace and on the employer's equipment, including mobile phones, desktops, and laptops. In addition, the company could require that the employee link to the company's fan page or website on his own business page. The employees should also be made aware that the information they post on social networking [web]sites, their emails, and conversations may be discoverable. The employer should formulate a written agreement stating that in exchange for the employee's access and use of social networking in the workplace, the employee will grant consent for the disclosure of the information from his business profile page, including email, posts, notes, and all features of Facebook or Twitter used for communication purposes, in the event the information is needed for litigation or general auditing purposes. The policy must also make it clear that the employee has no expectation of privacy with respect to communications on social networking [web]sites made through the employee's business account, on the employer's computer network, or on the employer's hardware, including desktop computers, laptop computers, and mobile phones".[104]

Much will depend on the culture of the organisation and what is normally permitted and viewed as acceptable. However, when a particular policy is adopted, it is important to enforce it. If it is not consistently and fairly enforced, it can leave the employer open to claims that the policy does not apply or should not apply because other people were previously permitted to ignore the policy, or were not similarly disciplined.

Education

Education is also important. One author refers to education issues as follows:

> "In addition to implementing a detailed policy with respect to social networking, employees who use the [web]sites must be educated that the same rules that apply with respect to business conversations and communications apply to the use of social networking in the workplace. Though social networking users generally do not adhere to the rules of formality associated with business communications, it is imperative that employees are educated that communications for business purposes on social networking [web]sites should adhere to the same level of formality as email communications and other written communications for business purposes. Thus, employees should be mindful of what they say on such [web] sites and should be educated that what they say could lead to liability, not only for them but also for their employers."[105]

---

[103] Note, for example, N Lindquist, "You Can Send This But Not That: Creating and Enforcing Employer Email Policies Under Sections 7 and 8 of the National Labor Relations Act After Register Guard" (2009) *Shidler Journal of Law Communications and Technology* 15.

[104] L Thomas, "Social Networking in the Workplace: Are Private Employers Prepared to Comply with Discovery Requests for Posts and Tweets?" (2010) (63) *SMU Law Review* 1373 at 1398–1401. Internal references omitted.

[105] *ibid.*

Policy on Social Networks

When dealing with policy issues, organisations need to refer to:

> "the degree of privacy that the employee account should maintain at a minimum. It is unlikely that an employer would want their employees' profiles set to public so that an internet search would reveal information about the employer's business contacts and clients. Depending on the nature of the information and the business of the company, the employer must be explicit regarding what privacy settings the employees' profiles should maintain so that the employers and employees are protected from the unwanted viewing of business profiles on social networking [web]sites ... employees [need to be aware of the employer's social networking policy]".[106]

Contract Consent

Consent issues, as always, raise particular considerations:

> "By using a contract where the employee agrees to consent to disclosure of the information in exchange for use of social networking [web]sites at work for business purposes, a company will be able to ensure that it has the ability to access information so that it retains control of its employees' reluctant actions on social networking [web]sites. If a company decides to allow employees to communicate for business purposes on social networking [web]sites, it is imperative that the guidelines be clear with respect to what the employees can and cannot say on the [web]site, the employees' expectations of privacy regarding the communications, the employer's expectations of professionalism, and the penalties for failure to follow the guidelines. And once again, the policy should be enforced to have any merit."[107]

This is another issue which appears not to have reached a judicial decision as yet here.

Fan Pages

Other issues also arise as regards company fan pages. For example:

> "The creation of a company fan page may seem like an easy task, but the employer must consider whether the page can be archived or preserved in anticipation of litigation and who has access to the page to act as its administrator. The first issue to consider in creating a company's Facebook page or Twitter account is who is responsible for maintaining and monitoring the [web]site. It has been suggested that a separate email account should be created for all social networking [web]site endeavors and account information should be available to all 'stakeholders.' It is important that the company's Facebook page is viewed as a company-controlled page, rather than any kind of individual asset. As such, the company should limit who posts on these [web]sites as the face of the company. In addition, the individuals in charge of the page should monitor the postings and comments.
>
> An additional consideration regarding who should have access to the page is how to limit access once the employee is terminated or leaves employment. Suppose that an employee in charge of postings on a company's social networking page is fired. Assuming that person is the administrator of the company's Facebook page, that employee could still maintain access despite the fact that he is no longer with the company. Because the individual could post to the page and damage the company's reputation, there must be a limit in place to prevent such an occurrence. One source suggests that a company can create a profile page akin to a personal profile page. Once that page is created, a page for the company can be created

---

106 *ibid.*

107 *ibid.*

and additional administrators to the page can be added. These administrators can be readily changed so that when an employee who was in charge of the page leaves the company, he can be deleted as an administrator. Thus, when a company page is created, an employer must decide who will administer the social media [web]sites and transmit information from the company to the public and ensure that upon termination, the ability of the terminated employee to access the [web]sites as an administrator is prevented.

In addition, employees in charge of the [web]site should have clear guidelines as to what can and cannot be posted on the company's Facebook page. Also, it should be clear that the monitoring of social media and postings on such [web]sites are within the scope of employment of the individual and subject to any limitations and restrictions that the company imposes on such postings. There should be an approval process in place before a posting is made so that upper management in marketing has some oversight in the process. By doing so, the employer maintains a level of control over the postings such that it will be accountable for the content. Because the page should be viewed as a company-controlled asset, it is likely that a court would find that the [web]site is within the company's 'possession, custody, or control' and as such, information pertinent to suit must be disclosed to the opposing party and produced by the party in custody of the material. As mentioned previously, there are many problems with the way that social networking [web]sites are archived that could lead to problems in obtaining the information."

Spoilation Changes

Preserving electronic evidence is important. Thomas states:

> "There are a few steps that employers can take to make sure that they do not suffer spoliation sanctions for destruction of information relevant to suit on their social networking pages. First, if a company has a reasonable anticipation of litigation, it should issue a litigation hold and a preservation order and contact Facebook and Twitter to make sure they are aware of the preservation order. The preservation order should be specific, relate to the company page for a set period of time, and advise administrators not to delete the postings from the page. In addition to contacting Facebook and Twitter, the administrators of the [web]site for the company should be aware of the holds. Luckily, with Facebook, as long as posters and administrators have not deleted postings on a company's page, older posts can be seen with mere clicks on the company page. But, Facebook does not guarantee that such information will always be available by this method. With Twitter, however, there is approximately a one-and-a half-week window in which the tweets can be retrieved by searching for them using the search engine on Twitter, though they never disappear from a user's Twitter stream. Thus, once again, with a litigation hold, the administrators of a Twitter [web]site should not delete content from the Twitter page during the relevant time period to avoid the extra step of having to retrieve the information from Twitter itself".[108]

These issues of electronic evidence, maintaining and not damaging potential pertinent electronic evidence, and discovery and electronic discovery are extremely complex. Social networks that are outside the normal direct control of the employer or the organisation, and thus potentially add costs and additional issues to be confronted by employers.

The Sedona conference and Sedona rules are useful US guides to consider on this issue.[109]

---

[108] *ibid.*

[109] Sedona, available at https://thesedonaconference.org/.

Archives

Thomas states:

> "Companies that want to be extra cautious with their Facebook or Twitter pages may want to archive the pages themselves and save them locally. There are programs in circulation for archiving tweets that a company's IT department would be able to implement successfully, but this is a task for IT to undertake. The same archiving possibility' may exist for Facebook as well, and it is a good idea for IT to consider whether locally archiving a company's Facebook page would be a viable option. But once again, a company's IT group should formulate the policy regarding the archiving of such [web]sites after discussion with upper management and counsel".[110]

Employers and organisations need to consider normal archiving and destruction of electronic materials that might be required for litigation. Third-party discovery of social networks is itself a potential issue. The company's records may, for example, be pertinent where employees access social networks via the company's computer systems.

Conclusion

Some question whether introducing new laws or expanding regulation would actually solve the problems presented.[111] The issues and concerns for organisations and for employees in terms of privacy and data protection are difficult and complex. The advent of social networking, blogging and the like makes it ever more difficult to maintain traditional boundaries. Where these boundaries run, such as when the work day truly ends, and what employees may do as individuals online with expectations of privacy, will remain hotly debated, in practice, contracts and policies, as well as in litigation and new laws.

110 Thomas, *op. cit.* Note also, for example, DS Witte, "Your Opponent Does Not Need a Friend Request to See Your Page: Social Networking Sites and Electronic Discovery" (2010) *McGeorge Law Review* 891 at 895–897.

111 Montes, *op. cit*, 525.

Chapter 19

EDUCATIONAL INSTITUTIONS

Headline of Issues

- Concerns for schools, universities and parents
- Laws
- Policies
- Conflict of rights, safety, integrity, association, free speech
- Proportionate policy versus overreaction
- On/off-campus activity
- Teachers online

Introduction

Social network content and communications are beginning to be used as forms of evidence, as highlighted above. This includes both civil cases and criminal cases. Some of these themes are also continued below. We can consider, for instance, a school wishing to litigate in order to protect its computer system or pursue those who may damage its computer system.

However, in the educational sphere we also need to consider the expanding theme of social networking content and communications being used as evidence in what might be termed social evidence or social justice, that is, decisions based on evidence obtained from social networking that does not reach a court of law.

There is also the sometimes related but separate theme of information and content on social networks focusing on school or college relations and activities. Students can now "peer into their teachers' personal lives"[1] and create false personas and profiles falsely representing to be a particular student or teacher. Indeed, social networks have particularly focused on student users. When Facebook began, for example, it was restricted to users from university.

Concern for Schools, Universities and Parents

Schools

"[P]arents, teachers, and anyone else responsible for the care and safety of children should be aware of the potential dangers of the internet".[2] Parents and everyone

1 AW Estrada, "Saving Face From Facebook: Arriving at a Compromise Between Schools' Concerns With Teacher Social Networking and Teachers' First Amendment Rights" (2010) (32) *Thomas Jefferson Law Review* 283.

2 MJ O'Connor, "School Speech in the Internet Age: Do Students Shed Their Rights When They

in loco parentis[3] are legitimately concerned that students should not be presented with pornographic websites when they conduct innocent internet search requests. They are also concerned that adverts should not be appearing for medicines and sex websites when they are looking for education-related websites. Some of this may result in technical and organisational-type security measures. However, the need for both parents and educators to teach themselves about what children are doing online should never be underestimated.

Teachers

As indicated above, educator teaching and familiarity with technology and the activities of children, teenagers, etc are primary considerations. In addition, the actions and safeguards adopted by educators are also important. In reacting and in being proactive, however, educators also need to be conscious that balance is required. This is very often easy to forget. It is all too easy to overreact, too.

It is also possible to overreact in relation to teacher conduct. There are concerns that what teachers say or do online might conflict with their duties to the school, children, parents, etc. It is also recognised that teachers should not socially interact online with their pupils. This is a developing area and it is unclear what the attitudes of schools are here in relation to teachers' online contacts with children. How should a teacher react to a Facebook friend request from a student?

Some schools and legislators have even sought to restrict the *use by* teachers of social networking.[4] Is this proportionate? Is it an overreaction? Is it constitutional? Is there a right to use or have access to the internet? These are obvious issues for future litigation—on both sides of the Atlantic.

Teachers have also been disciplined for particular activities and posted comments online. Examples arise in Florida, Colorado, Tennessee and Massachusetts.[5] One teacher referred to a student as "retard" and was disciplined; a kindergarten teacher had a pornographic video on Facebook raising concerns; and another teacher referred to his or her drug use online.[6] A sports coach was dismissed for an intimate picture with her fiance. Many US schools deal with these issues in accordance with a district-wide school policy.[7] In terms of a proposed California rule regulating teachers' online social networking, one commentator suggests that "the proposed statute withstands constitutional scrutiny. California cannot rely on teachers' common sense alone to guard against irresponsible use of social networks. State action on the matter is imperative".[8] It remains to be seen how a superior court will decide these issues.

Pick Up a Mouse?" (2009) (11) *University of Pennsylvania Journal of Constitutional Law* 459 at 476.

3 DC Bechstrom, "Who's Looking at Your Facebook Profile? The Use of Student Conduct Codes to Censor College Students' Online Speech" (2008) (45) *Williamette Law Review* 261 at 279–280.

4 See Estrada, *op. cit*, 284, referring to HR 1314, 94th General Assembly, 2d Reg Sess (Mo 2008), among others.

5 *ibid*, 285–286 and references therein.

6 *ibid*, 285–286.

7 *ibid*, 287–289.

8 *ibid*, 311–312.

It also remains to be seen how these matters will develop at policy level in Ireland and the UK, and ultimately in contested cases.

However, while the concerns and implementing safety precautions are legitimate, there is growing concern that the rights of teachers may be overridden or ignored. For example, their rights to free speech (eg US First Amendment) could be infringed.[9] Other rights to be considered include "associational rights".[10] One can easily see how these differing standpoints could come into conflict here. Safety is not always a standalone issue, and on occasion must be balanced and proportionate in relation to other legitimate rights that can exist. Fulmer argues for teacher privacy rights, submitting that these are needed because there is so little redress available to teachers after the event where an error is made in accusing them.[11]

Conflicts between teacher rights, discovery, seizure and official policies are also issues of contention. For example, while there are instances of teachers acting inappropriately or having relationships with their students, and criminal proceedings issuing, the right of the school or college to use evidence of such activities seized or discovered on the teacher's mobile phone, laptop, etc. There is a "vacuum" and "uncertainty" regarding teachers' devices and their seizure, access, discovery and use by third parties such as the school.[12]

Universities

Some of these issues and concerns also exist in higher-level educational establishments. Universities need to consider, perhaps, the more advanced maturity of university students. The concerns arising from social networks do need to be carefully considered. For example:

> "[Universities] need guidance on how to appropriately deal with the issue to prevent situations in which students are unfairly punished. [School/university] officials have admitted to not knowing what students' speech rights are, and the current student speech jurisprudence is not easily applied to postings on MySpace and Facebook. However, the Supreme Court's reasoning in *Tinker*[13] provides a basis for articulating a standard specific to students' use of social networking [web]sites. Revising and modifying *Tinker* to factor into consideration the differences between public profiles results in a standard that both protects student speech rights and ensures that the [schools/universities] are able to maintain order and discipline. The final, and perhaps most important, step in this process is to communicate the standard to the [schools/universities], as well as to students and parents, who can then work together to eliminate the problem."[14]

As has been found by many employers when dealing with these issues, if appropriate and balanced policies do not exist, it is difficult to react in the most appropriate

---

9 See generally *ibid*, 283 and 289–297.

10 *ibid*, 283 and 297–303. Estrada also analyses a proposed law in California, namely, the California Education Code; *ibid*, 303–308.

11 EH Fulmer, "Privacy Expectations and Protections for Teachers in the Internet Age" (2010) *Duke Law & Technology Review*.

12 JO Oluwole, "Teacher Cell Phone Searches in Light of *Ontario v Quon*" (2010–2011) *Richmond Journal of Law and Technology* 1 at 2. Referring to *Ontario v Quon* 130 Supreme Court 2619 (2010).

13 *Tinker v Des Moines Independent Community School District* 393 US 503.

14 KD Williams, "Public Schools Vs MySpace: The Newest Challenge to Student Rights" (2008) (76) *University of Cincinnati Law Review* 707 at 730–731.

manner. The University of Minnesota Duluth, for example, had difficulties in dealing with students who posted racist social networking comments about another student when the policies were not as clear on the issue as they could be.[15] Twitter has also updated its policies after a number of online abuse incidents in the UK involving threats of rape and bombs.[16]

As difficult as these issues are, they are somewhat easier to deal with, and regulate at a policy level, when all the factual issues occur on campus (or at the school).

However, what happens when all the activity is out of hours and off premises? Universities in the US are reported to be expanding their conduct and discipline policies to encompass off-campus activities, potentially including activities online.[17] There have already been complaints made in relation to students' off-campus online comments.[18] Examples include the University of Central California, University of Illinois and Valdosta State University.[19]

However, this is still an area fraught with difficulty, and indeed some novelty. These are new issues and new technologies. There have been few cases dealing with these issues and few explicit references in statute laws to these matters. It has, therefore, been commented that because US "federal courts have remained fairly quiet on this emerging medium of speech, institutions of higher education are more able to continue disciplining students for off-campus cyberspeech that is thought to violate an institution's student conduct code".[20] The law remains "underdeveloped".[21] The comment continues that there may be the glimmer of a tentative recognition of greater respect for students' free speech and First Amendment rights — or at least university students.[22] There are three important US cases dealing with college students' free speech rights.[23] The extent to which off-campus student speech may be protected constitutionally may depend on the effect it has on campus.[24] Regard may also be had to reasonableness, interpretations, recipients of the comments, etc.[25]

It has been argued that public universities should be able to discipline students for crimes, and that this can include serious matters such as serious off-campus

15 T Strike, "One Law School's Experience in Creating a Social Networking Policy" (2010)(15) *AALL Spectrum* 24.

16 M Townsent and L Moon, *Guardian*, "Twitter Clamps Down on Abuse After Rape and Death Threats. Site Will Roll Out 'Report Abuse' Button as its Bosses Apologise to Women and Say: 'People Deserve to Feel Safe on Twitter'" 3 August 2013.

17 Bechstrom, *op. cit*, 262–263.

18 *ibid*, 261–262.

19 *ibid*, 263 and 261–263 in relation to the former.

20 *ibid*, 264.

21 *ibid*, 281. Refering to the US Supreme Court in *Tinker v Des Moines Independent Community School District* 393 US 503 (1969); *Bethal School District No 403 v Fraser* 478 US 675 (1986); *Hazelwood School District v Kuhlmeier* 484 US 260 (1988), referred to *ibid*, 281–287.

22 *ibid*, 281. Referring to the US Supreme Court in *Tinker v Des Moines Independent Community School District*, *Bethal School District No 403 v Fraser* and *Hazelwood School District v Kuhlmeier*, referred to *ibid*, 281–287.

23 *ibid*, 287–290, namely, *Healy v James* 408 IS 169 (1972); *Papish v Board of Curators of University of Missouri* 410 US 667 (1973); and *Rosenberger v University of Virginia* 515 US 819 (1995).

24 See *ibid*, 294, and cases referred to at 290–298.

25 See Bechstrom, *op. cit*, 302–303.

harassment, "such as [online] sexual harassment."[26] This poses questions, however. If no crime is prosecuted, the student would presumably remain innocent in relation to that accusation from a criminal-law perspective. Also, not every conceivable infringement that a college may be concerned with, or that a student, lecturer, etc may complain about, would amount to a criminal act as defined in statute.

This also ignores locus issues. One argument is that "colleges should not discipline students for their off-campus cyberspeech unless such speech presents a true threat or constitutes a crime ... institutions should also modify their student conduct codes accordingly".[27] Some would argue that colleges should not be able to discipline for any off-campus speech or activities.

There is a surprising effort to have college students and applicants disclose their social networking details to the university or faculty in question.[28] It is questioned how constitutional this may be,[29] and it is seen as an attack on freedom to associate.[30] Social networking may be argued to be an association or collection of associations.[31] Obviously, free-speech arguments also arise. There could also be a significant chilling effect on what students may be willing to say or post on their social networking profiles[32] if they fear that a university or applications committee may access their social network history. Proposals to allow university access to students and applicants' social network pages may well be reactive and disproportionate when there are other less restrictive mechanisms to deal with the issues.[33] It may also be unlawful. The solution ultimately needs to be nuanced,[34] proportionate and not indiscriminate in relation to the concerns posed. One could also suggest that there is at least some irony that such proposals are coming from supposedly liberal institutions.

There are legitimate concerns in relation to violence and hate speech[35] as well as harassment and sex-related activities. These are legitimate issues for universities to consider and also refer to appropriately in "[s]tudent conduct codes".[36] However, proportionality is needed, as well as respect for other rights and issues. Off-campus activity is one such issue. Non-statute criminal activity is another. Free speech and free association are significant issues also. These are complex issues, regardless of the legal jurisdiction. One US commentator describes the US situation as follows:

> "In *Tinker v Des Moines Independent Community School District*, the Supreme Court definitively established that students do not 'shed' their right to free speech 'at the [school/college] gate.' However, the Court also said that those rights must be 'applied in light of

---

26 *ibid*, n 20 at 265.
27 *ibid*, 310.
28 J Sabin, "Every Click You Make: How The Proposed Disclosure of Law Students' Online Identities Violates Their First Amendment Right to Free Association" (2008–2009) (17) *Journal of Law and Policy* 699 and 701–701.
29 *ibid*, 702.
30 *ibid*, 721.
31 *ibid*, 721–725.
32 *ibid*, 725–727.
33 *ibid*, 729–733.
34 *ibid*, 733.
35 Bechstrom, *op. cit*, 280–281.
36 *ibid*, 270–276.

the special characteristics of the [school/college] environment ....' Ever since, there has been debate over the exact boundaries of those rights".[37]

In addition:

"despite discussing student First Amendment rights in at least five significant cases (*Tinker*, *Fraser*, *Board of Education, Island Trees Union Free School District No 26 v Pico, Hazelwood, and Morse*), the Supreme Court has thus far only obliquely examined the extent to which the student speech doctrine extends beyond the physical boundaries of the school. Cut adrift without Supreme Court guidance, the lower courts and numerous commentators have attempted to divine the extent to which the [school/university] speech doctrine reaches off-campus conduct, but it is not clear if they have had any success. While I suspect the Court will eventually have to confront this issue head-on and I may therefore be adding my voice to a storm soon to be quelled, I will nevertheless make the attempt because it is an important component of an examination of school speech in the internet age.

The Supreme Court's only examination (if one can call it that) of the off-campus speech issue came recently in *Morse*, where it recognized 'some uncertainty at the outer boundaries as to when courts should apply school-speech precedents, but not on these facts.' Its determination was based on the fact that Morse's actions were directed towards the [school/university] and visible by its students. They took place across the street, during regular [school/university] hours, at an event sanctioned by the school and supervised by its staff. The Court concluded that 'Frederick cannot stand in the midst of his fellow students, during school hours, at a school-sanctioned activity and claim he is not at school'".[38]

A separate point appears to exist in terms of university researchers using social networks for data-mining purposes.[39] The extent to which such details may use or incorporate identifiable (whether alone or in conjunction with other data) personal data of users remains an issue of potential concern.

Student Awareness

In the US, schools are increasingly using social networking as a basis for disciplining their students - in particular, student athletes.[40] One example is the case of Jessica Schoch in 2006 in Ohio.[41] She appealed a school decision to expel her based on comments on her MySpace social networking profile. She was ultimately reinstated in school after free speech and First Amendment issues were argued.[42] Another student was suspended in Colorado based on comments he made on MySpace.[43] In California 20 students were suspended for viewing a MySpace post containing threats against another student.[44] Students in Ireland have also been disciplined for social networking comments.

---

37 MJ O'Connor, "School Speech in the Internet Age: Do Students Shed Their Rights When They Pick Up a Mouse?" (2009) (11) *University of Pennsylvania Journal of Constitutional Law* 459. References omitted.

38 *ibid*, 472–473. References omitted.

39 LB Solberg, "Data Mining on acebook: A Free Space for Researchers or an IRB Nightmare" (2010) *Journal of Law, Technology & Policy* 311. In relation to other social networking research possibilities see, for example, JL Behrens, "About Facebook. Change at the Social Networking Juggernaut Creates New Opportunities for Law Library Outreach" (April 2008) *AALL Spectrum* 14.

40 D Findlay, "Tag! Now You're 'It.' What Photographs on Social Networking Sites Mean for the Fourth Amendment" (2008) (10) *North Carolina Journal of Law & Technology* 171 at 179.

41 Referred to in Williams, *op. cit*, 707.

42 Referred to *ibid.*

43 Referred to *ibid.*

44 Referred to *ibid.*

Regardless of legality of statute laws and institutional policies to regulate and discipline some or all social networking activities, students need to be aware of the risks. There are dangers online in terms of strangers. Students need to be aware that it is always possible that what they say online may come to the attention of their school or university.

In years to come an employer or an employment agency may find that embarrassing comment or photograph from the past. As Perlmuter notes:

> "[F]riends can hurt your reputation as much as you can yourself: That embarrassing photo of you at a party, or that impolite quote you made about your department, can be an unguided missile wandering about cyberspace ready to shoot down your good name".[45]

Students need to be aware that once they say something online, it can spread quickly and far afield, as well as remaining there perhaps indefinitely.

Public Organisations

Social networks can create additional "administrative and legal headaches".[46] It is essential that public organisations are aware of the implications of social networking and implement appropriate policies and procedures to inform personnel of the correct protocols and to regulate such activity.[47]

Employee access to social networks can also expose the organisation to viruses and malicious software threats.[48]

Public organisations must also be cognisant of what they and their employees say and do online, which now includes social networks. Many public organisations pursue an interest in making information available to the public on websites and increasingly on social networks. However, it is possible that too much information may be published or posted, or information that is private, privileged, confidential or otherwise restricted.[49] There can also be specific rules and regulations pertaining to other issues, which affect what may be permitted officially on a social networks.[50]

One of the difficulties for such organisations is deciding what they must seek to regulate and how to achieve that in a prudent and proportionate manner.

Difficulties can also arise in relation to distinguishing between which communications and posts are official and which are personal.[51] Some of the relevant factors may include:

---

45 DD Perlmuter, "Facebooking Your Way Out of Tenure," *The Chronicle of Higher Education*, 3 July 2009, available at http://chrinicle.com.article/Facebooking-Your-Way-Out-of/46951, referred to in Montes, *op. cit*, 524.
46 Bojorquez and Shores, *op. cit*, 65.
47 *ibid.*
48 *ibid.*
49 See *ibid*, 50.
50 *ibid*, 50.
51 *ibid*, 54.

- who creates the materials;
- who has control and access;
- the specific nature of the material;
- whether it was used in the course of conducting government business;
- whether public funds were spent to create the material;
- the purpose of the material; and
- whether the government entity requires creation of the material.[52]

Appropriate and considered polices are necessary. If they are too strong, there is a risk that they may be successfully challenged. The other danger is that it may not be possible to act in the first instance when a problem arises if there is no, or no adequate, policy to deal with a situation.

Further caution is needed. While some US commentators suggest that employers are permitted generally to monitor their employees' usage of telephones, email, internet and work location (via computer or CCTV, for example),[53] this should be cautioned against in Europe and elsewhere. Blanket monitoring is not compatible with the EU data protection regime, unlike the situation in the US, where blanket monitoring by organisations appears to be more accepted.

Conclusion

Social networking creates many problems for individual students, parents and educational organisations in relation to the use of social networks. Some of these issues are new, but sometimes they bring old rights areas into the conflict once again, such as defamation, abuse, freedom of speech and association.

While educational organisations are rightly concerned, there is also a danger of going too far, in for example blanket monitoring, demanding access to the social networking pages of student applicants or seeking to regulate activities outside the educational environment—be that students or teachers. Caution may also be needed in that one solution may not always fit all; certainly, every US solution may not be an EU solution.

Separately, both students and teachers do need to be aware and prudent in relation to what they say and do online. In the sphere of education, perception can often be as much an issue as actuality.

52 *ibid*, 54.

53 See, for example, *ibid*, 67.

PART VI: PERSONAL ISSUES

CHAPTER 20

TRACKING THE TRACKERS

Gary Kovacs

HEADLINE OF ISSUES

- Internet use
- Browsing
- Monitoring use
- Tracking use
- Tracking the trackers
- Do not track

ONLINE TRACKING[1]

I do not know why, but I am continually amazed to think that two and a half billion of us around the world are connected to each other through the internet and that at any point in time more than 30 percent of the world's population can go online to learn, to create and to share. And the amount of time each of us is spending doing all of this is also continuing to go grow. A recent study showed that the young generation alone is spending over eight hours a day online. As the parent of a nine-year-old girl, that number seems awfully low.

But just as the internet has opened up the world for each and every one of us, it has also opened up each and every one of us to the world. And increasingly, the price we are being asked to pay for all of this connectedness is our privacy. Today, what many of us would love to believe is that the internet is a private place; it is not. And with every click of the mouse and every touch of the screen, we are like Hansel and Gretel leaving breadcrumbs of our personal information everywhere we travel through the digital woods. We are leaving our birthdays, our places of residence, our interests and preferences, our relationships, our financial histories, and on and on it goes.

Now do not get me wrong, I am not for one minute suggesting that sharing data is a bad thing. In fact, when I know the data that's being shared and I am asked explicitly for my consent, I want some sites to understand my habits. It helps them suggest books for me to read or movies for my family to watch or friends for us to connect with. But when I do not know and when I have not been asked, that's when the problem arises. It is a phenomenon on the internet today called behavioral tracking, and it is very big business.

[1] This is taken from a talk at the technology and ideas seminars on the Ted Talks website, "Tracking the Trackers," Gary Kovacs, March 2012, Longbeach, California, available at http://www.ted.com/talks/gary_kovacs_tracking_the_trackers.html.

In fact, there's an entire industry formed around following us through the digital woods and compiling a profile on each of us. And when all of that data is held, they can do almost whatever they want with it. This is an area today that has very few regulations and even fewer rules. Except for some of the recent announcements here in the United States and in Europe, it is an area of consumer protection that is almost entirely naked.

So let me expose this lurking industry a little bit further. The visualization you see forming behind me is called Collusion and it is an experimental browser add-on that you can install in your Firefox browser that helps you see where your Web data is going and who is tracking you. The red dots you see up there are sites that are behavioral tracking that I have not navigated to, but are following me. The blue dots are the sites that I have actually navigated directly to. And the gray dots are sites that are also tracking me, but I have no idea who they are. All of them are connected, as you can see, to form a picture of me on the Web. And this is my profile.

So let me go from an example to something very specific and personal. I installed Collusion in my own laptop two weeks ago and I let it follow me around for what was a pretty typical day. Now like most of you, I actually start my day going online and checking email. I then go to a news site, look for some headlines. And in this particular case I happened to like one of them on the merits of music literacy in schools and I shared it over a social network.

Our daughter then joined us at the breakfast table, and I asked her, "Is there an emphasis on music literacy in your school?" And she, of course, naturally as a nine-year-old, looked at me and said quizzically, "What's literacy?" So I sent her online, of course, to look it up. Now let me stop here. We are not even two bites into breakfast and there are already nearly 25 sites that are tracking me. I have navigated to a total of four.

So let me fast-forward through the rest of my day. I go to work, I check email, I log onto a few more social sites, I blog, I check more news reports, I share some of those news reports, I go look at some videos, pretty typical day - in this case, actually fairly pedantic - and at the end of the day, as my day winds down, look at my profile. The red dots have exploded. The gray dots have grown exponentially. All in all, there's over 150 sites that are now tracking my personal information, most all of them without my consent.

I look at this picture and it freaks me out. This is nothing. I am being stalked across the Web. And why is this happening? Pretty simple – it is huge business. The revenue of the top handful of companies in this space is over 39 billion dollars today. And as adults, we are certainly not alone. At the same time I installed my own Collusion profile, I installed one for my daughter. And on one single Saturday morning, over two hours on the internet, here is her Collusion profile.

This is a nine-year-old girl navigating to principally children's sites. I move from this, from freaked out to enraged. This is no longer me being a tech pioneer or a privacy advocate; this is me being a parent. Imagine in the physical world if somebody followed our children around with a camera and a notebook and recorded their every movement. I can tell you, there is not a person in this room that would sit idly by. We'd take action. It may not be good action, but we would take action. We cannot sit idly by here either. This is happening today.

Privacy is not an option, and it should not be the price we accept for just getting on the internet. Our voices matter and our actions matter even more.

Today we have launched Collusion. You can download it, install it in Firefox, to see who is tracking you across the Web and following you through the digital woods. Going forward, all of our voices need to be heard. Because what we do not know can actually hurt us. Because the memory of the internet is forever. We are being watched. It is now time for us to watch the watchers.

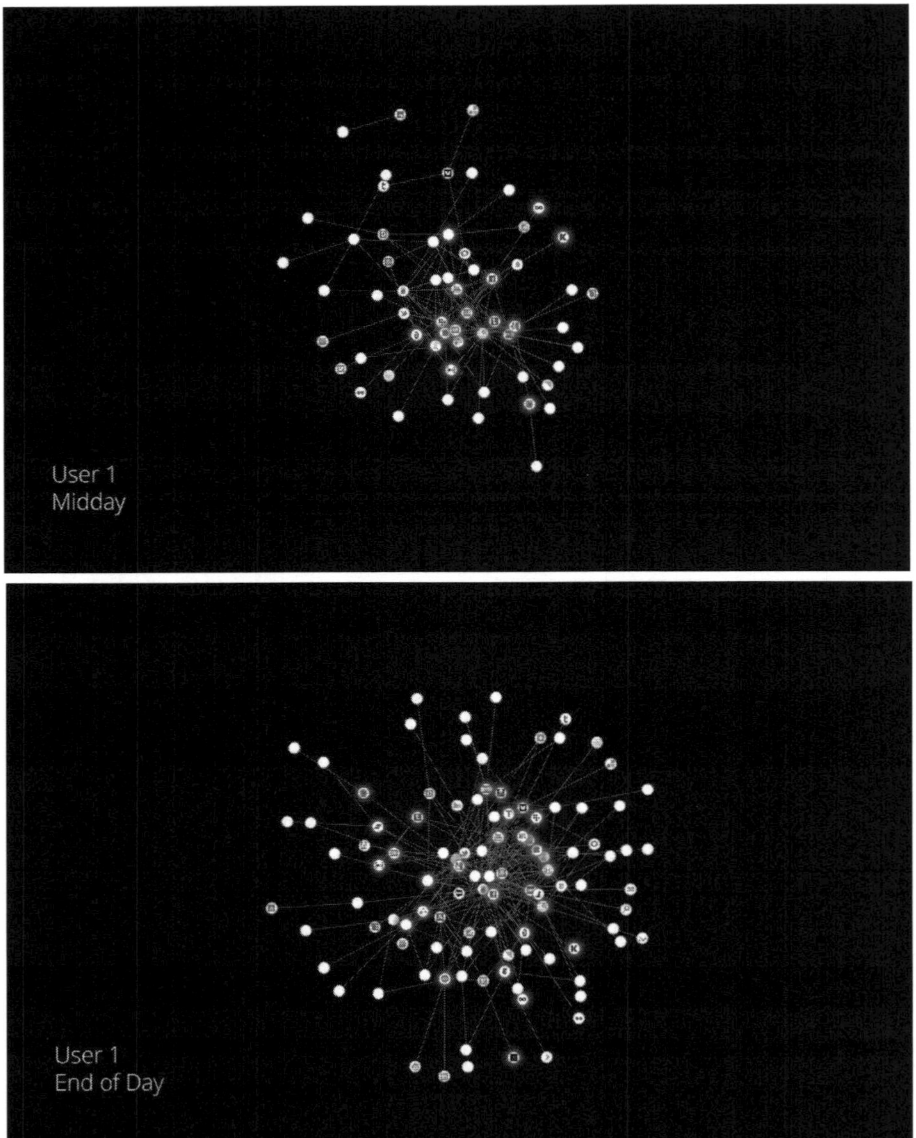
User 1
Midday
User 1
End of Day

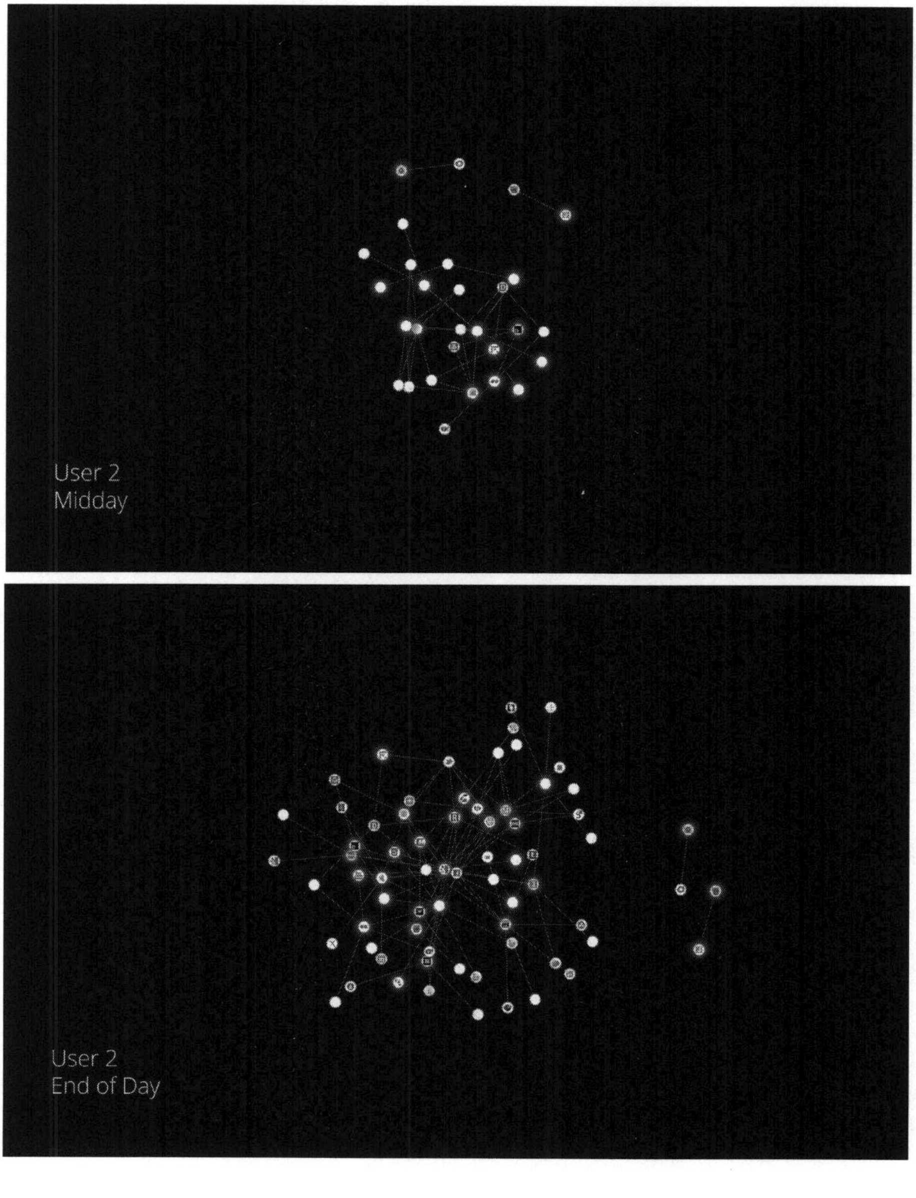
User 2
Midday
User 2
End of Day

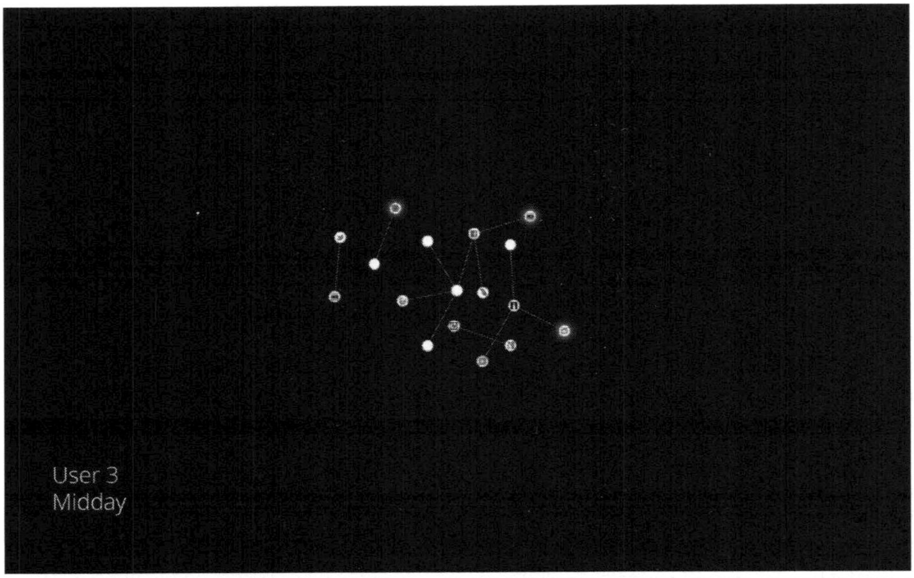
User 3
Midday

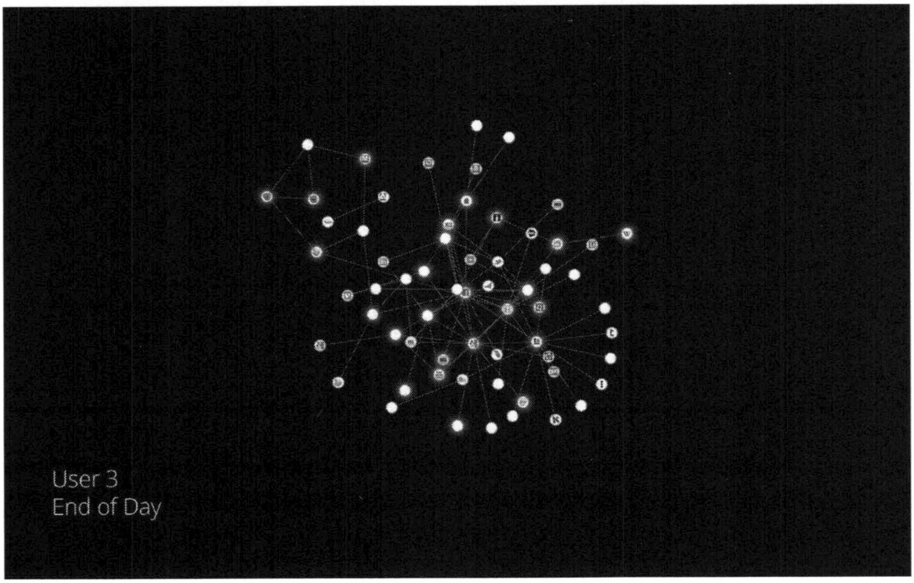
User 3
End of Day

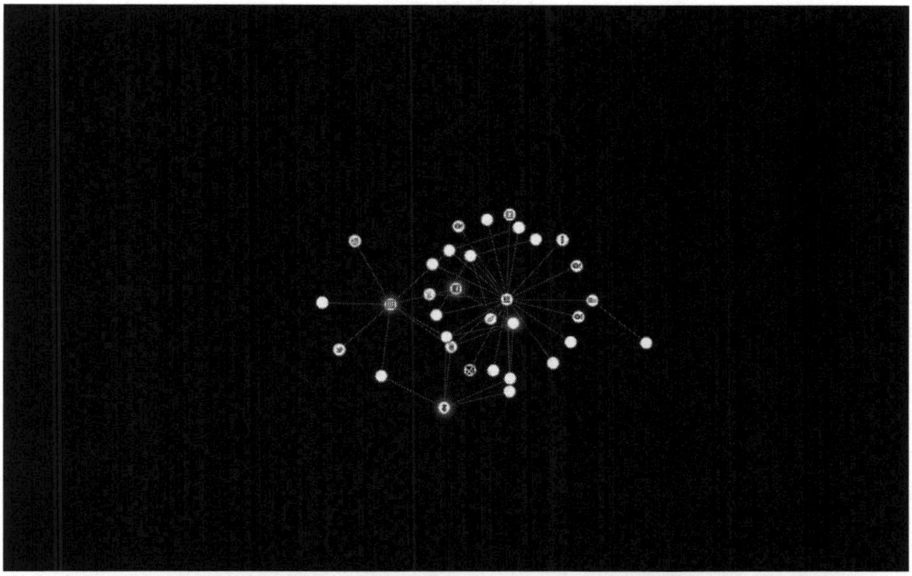

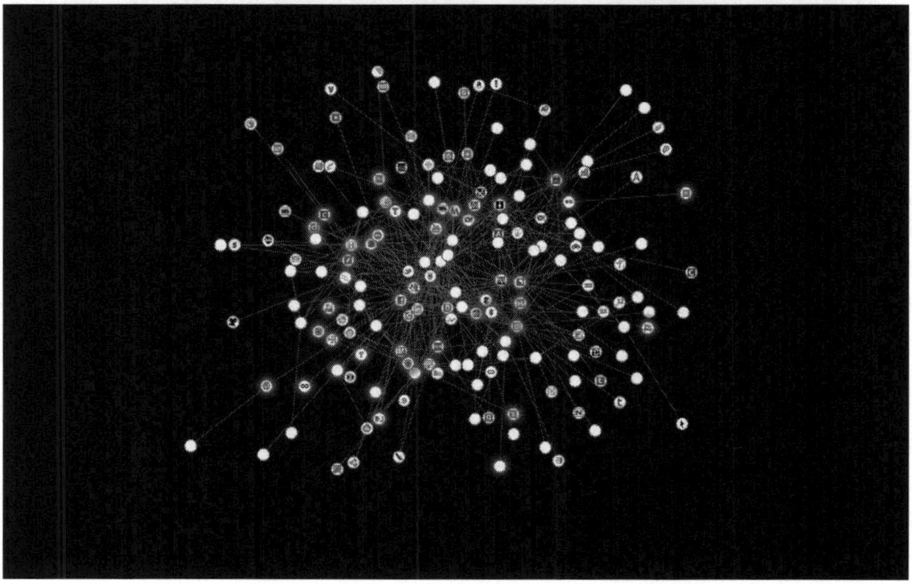

Chapter 21

PERSONAL RELATIONS

Headline of Issues

- Social networking, personal relations and personal data
- Stalking, etc
- Cases
- Laws
- Relationships
- Sexting
- Texting
- Virtual Cupid

Introduction

Some of the more contentious areas in relation to data protection and social networking relate to the issues of personal relationships. These are frequently hitting general news headlines.

Online Abuse, Bullying, Stalking, Harassment, Bullying and Grooming

The media and interest groups variously highlight the recognised difficulties of online abuse, bullying, stalking, harassment and most particularly sexual grooming of underage persons for purposes of sexual exploitation.

The issue of bullying and harassment is also frequently referred to in discussion. This can take a number of forms. A primary example perhaps relates to mobile and social networking bullying and harassment of teenagers or schoolchildren by their peers. It is not limited to children however. Bullying and harassment can also arise in the workplace among adults.

Many solutions are being suggested, some better than others, and even some unrealistic. Other issues have not yet been considered in great details. On occasion traditional laws and torts sometimes have to be reconsidered in relation to new technology-related activities.[1] Some people are also suggesting new laws, updated laws, self-regulation, co-regulation and even that no regulation is needed. There is clearly a complex social, technology, legal and policy discussion at play as better solutions are sought.

---

1 N Hoffman, "Battery 2.0: Upgrading Offensive Contact Battery to the Digital Age" (2010) *Case Western Reserve Journal of Law, Technology & the Internet* 61.

Relationships Fall Foul of Social Networking

Personal relationships are also a source of conflict as a result of social networking. Examples can be where a spouse or partner discovers infidelity through a social networking profile of their partner. One of the more nasty issues developing at the moment is what is known as revenge porn. This where an ex partner will upload sexual and intimate pictures from a relationship in an act of revenge. There have been calls to outlaw revenge porn.[2] There have also been instances where people may be blackmailed because an ex partner has sexual images of them.

Sexting Online Abuse

Unsolicited sexual comments via mobile devices and social networks is increasingly recognised as a problem. Solicited sexual comment is also perceived as a problem. This is sometimes now known as sexting.[3] One author describes it as the "digital exchange of sexually explicit images between teenagers using text messaging services on camera-equipped cell phones".[4] It is also described as the practice of posting or sending text messages or images that are sexually suggestive or even graphic, including nude or semi-nude photographs, whether via mobile phone or internet.[5] This raises potential online abuse, bullying, harassment, revenge porn, blackmail, unauthorised access to accounts, phone numbers, passwords and or personal data, any of which can also be in contravention of the data protection regime in addition to other specific offences. These issues can encompass both school, work and home environments.

Teenagers may be more sexually active now than heretofore. Teenagers in the US have been convicted of child-pornography-related offences and have been required to register as sex offenders.[6] The impact of social networking and mobile technologies are new relevant factors to be considered.

A Revenue employee was convicted in Ireland of sending sexual messages to his female supervisor, some of which indicated that he was threatening to rape and kill women.[7]

A lady was banned by a court in Texas from (1) using the internet; and (2) texting

---

2 See for example, A Steinbaugh, "Revenge Porn: The Fight Against the Net's Nastiest Corner" *Guardian*, 13 April 2013.

3 S Livingston, L Haddon, A Gorzig and K Olafsson, "Risks and Safety on the Internet: The Perspective of European Children. Full Findings," in *EU Kids Online* (LSE, London, 2011), 7. See reference at Social Networking, Age and Privacy, referred to in *EU Kids Online*, available at www2.lse.ac.uk/media@lse/research/EUKidsOnline/Home.aspx. See also www.eukidsonline.net.

4 EC Eraker, "Stemming Sexting: Sensible Legal Approaches to Teenagers' Exchange of Self-Produced Pornography" (2010) *Berkeley Technology Law Journal* 555.

5 C Arcabascio, "Sexting and Teenagers: OMG RU Going 2 Jail???" (2009–2010) *Richmond Journal of Law and Technology*," 1.

6 *ibid*, 556. Note also, Arcabascio, *op. cit*, 1.

7 "Meath Man to be Sentenced for Text Harassment," Breaking News, available at www.breakingnews.ie/ireland/meath-man-to-be-sentenced-for-text-harassment-503520.html, last accessed on 27 November 2012.

anyone other than a family member.[8] She was convicted in relation to sending a nude photograph of herself (she was aged 38) to a 16-year-old boy. The recipient was a friend of her son.

A German national was convicted in Ennis Circuit Court in Ireland for sending "chilling, disturbing and ominous" text messages and emails to a psychologist.[9] He received a three-year suspended sentence.

A particular concern is where the sexual communications are solicited or reciprocated between non-adults.[10] Can children, and consenting children, be held to the same liability as would an adult? Ethical , social and legal policy issues also arise.

However, one of the problems with many current laws is that they are arguably emotive and reactionary. Child pornography laws, for example, were generally drafted prior to social networking as we now know it. As such, current laws generally do not cater for the offenders being children and young persons themselves. Child pornography laws as well as sexting laws may require amendments to reflect this nuance.[11] Others have alternatively called for more restraint on the part of official prosecutors,[12] short of legal changes.

There is also increasing recognition that issues from the child's perspective may affect this discussion, for example, the child's or teenager's rights of free speech, freedom of expression or "right to sexual privacy"[13] (and now express constitutional rights in Ireland) in future. Pavia also makes the novel argument that sexting should be constitutionally protected privacy—but as part of the fundamental rights of parents.[14]

As more and more problem cases come to light, there will be increased discussion of the need for a right, or rights, to be forgotten and/or deleted.

Texting Online Abuse

A somewhat related issue is texting in vehicles while driving. This is increasingly

---

8 "Katy Mom Banned from Internet After 'Sexting' Son's Friend," *CBS Houston*, 14 November 2011, available at http://houston.cbslocal.com/2011/11/14/texas-housewife-banned-from-internet-over-sexting-sons-friend/; "Mother Banned from the Internet After Pleading Guilty to 'Sexting' 16 Year Old Son's Classmate Naked Pictures of Herself," *Daily Mail*, 14 November 2011.

9 G Deegan, "Man Sent 'Ominous' Texts to Psychologist," *Irish Times*, 24 February 2011, available at www.irishtimes.com/newspaper/ireland/2011/0224/1224290732379.html.

10 See *CC v Ireland*, Supreme Court, 23 May 2006, available at http://www.courts.ie/judgments.nsf/f69fbd31c73dda2580256cd400020877/877f6b6773b3dcee80257177003c6586?OpenDocument; *MD (a Minor) v Ireland*, Supreme Court, 14 April 2011. D McDonald, "Businessman in Challenge Over Underage Sex Law," *Irish Times*, 29 November 2011.

11 JL Barry, "The Child as Victim and Perpetrators: Laws Punishing Juvenile 'Sexting'" (2010–2011) *Vandenberg Journal of Entertainment & Technology Law* 129.

12 *ibid.*

13 See *ibid*, 166–171.

14 CJ Pavia, "Constitutional Protection of 'Sexting' in the Wake of *Lawrence*: The Right of Parents and Privacy" (2011) *Virginia Journal of Law & Technology* 1. Referring to *Lawrence v Texas* 539 US 558 (2003).

penalised. It may also amount to an offence of dangerous or unsafe driving. Texting while driving is now often expressly banned in road traffic safety legislation. For example, a British MP was sentenced for dangerous driving linked to texting while driving.[15] In another case, in Allen County in Indiana, a man was convicted in a road traffic case where his daughter was killed after his texting caused a car crash.[16]

Possibly, browsing or updating one's social networking profile while driving may now be included in texting offences depending on the specific technical definitions of the offences. In future there may be calls to create specific offences relating to the use of social networking while driving.[17] These will ultimately be debated in superior court cases.

There has also been argument that (certain) driving text bans may be unconstitutional.[18]

Virtually Speaking

Animated social networking is becoming increasingly popular and has raised numerous issues. Some activities are clearly legitimate, while others would clearly be illegal if they involved real videos or photographs. There are many grey areas in between.

One of the most popular examples of virtual characters in social networking is Second Life. It has been described as follows. It is a:

> "[V]irtual reality playground that also fits the definition of social networking website. Reporter Jason Farrell recently investigated child pornography in Second Life and discovered an area called 'Wonderland' that was used by child abusers where 'child-like' avatars were offering sex. Since Second Life is a user-created virtual environment, player interactions are not saved on the client computer. Home Secretary Jacquie Smith, in an interview with Farrell, said that she would be publishing a consultation paper to outlaw virtual imagery of child abuse used in virtual on-line worlds. Since then, Second Life owner-managers Linden Lab, Inc. has installed a verification system, and the experimenting with tracking players' interactions. Nevertheless British police are going undercover in Second Life to investigate depictions of adult-child sex to track down paedophiles".[19]

Offences, infringements or breach of privacy can arise with virtual activity or even virtual names. Issues of virtual harassment in virtual or created characters and created environments online will also need to be considered. For example,

---

15 Referred to in "British MP Sentenced for Driving Dangerously; Was Texting at the Time," *Media Law Prof Blog*, 25 February 2009, available at http://lawprofessors.typepad.com/media_law_prof_blog/2009/02/british-mp-sent.html.

16 "Man Sentenced in Texting While Driving Case," *HomeTownStations*, 29 March 2011, available at www.hometownstations.com/Global/story.asp?S=14341541.

17 Penalty points can be issued for texting while driving. Note *Survey of Mobile Phone Use by Car Drivers*, Road Safety Authority (RSA), September 2010, available at http://www.rsa.ie/Documents/Campaigns/Mobile%20Phone/Mobile%20Phone%20Survey%202009.pdf.

18 A Lazerow, "Near Impossible to Enforce at Best, Unconstitutional at Worst: the Consequences of Maryland's Text Messaging Ban on Drivers" (2010–2011) *Richmond Journal of Law and Technology* 1.

19 BL Mann, "Social Networking Websites – A Concentration of Impersonation, Denigration, Sexual Aggressive Solicitation, Cyber-Bullying or Happy Slapping Videos" (2009) (17) *International Journal of Law & Information Technology* 252, references omitted.

unauthorised access to accounts, passwords or merely leaving abusive or harassing messages, texts, etc, are issues that are already beginning to be encountered. Telecommunication companies (telcos), for example, have had to tighten up data protection and compliance procedures so as to ensure that only account holders are able to access account details.

Virtual pornography, or at least certain forms of it, has already been litigated and repeatedly tackled in the US. Virtual social networking and virtual characters will continue to present problems for law and data protection.

A difficulty also is the extent to which personal names, contacts, etc, can or should be revealed. Many people adopt pseudonyms. Social networks increasingly have to reveal these in civil and criminal cases pursuant to court orders. This is in part linked to the increase in online abuse. However, it is noted that there is increasing emphasis on the (in part) real name membership or posting policies of certain service providers such as Facebook, YouTube and the Huffington Post.

Hacking

Unauthorised access to accounts, passwords, etc, can involve the offence of hacking. It also on occasion does not need to involve someone who is extremely accomplished at computer programming. Some of the revelations in the UK phone hacking scandal and Leveson Inquiry[20] as to the manner of the hacking confirm this. Indeed, the Irish Data Protection Commissioner advised the public to change the generally known default password setting for their mobile phone voicemails.[21] Two Irish students are reported to have pleaded guilty to defacing the Fine Gael political party election website.[22] There have been reports of possible future charges against the students in addition to the Fine Gael incident.[23]

Conclusion

Personal relations and relationships can be some of the most personal and private aspects of peoples' lives. As people interact online more frequently it is inevitable that issues and threats informational privacy will arise. We are at a nexus where we begin to deal with, react and plan for these problem issues.

---

20 The Leveson inquiry, available at http://www.levesoninquiry.org.uk/.

21 "Commissioner Urges Public to Secure Their Mobile Phones," Data Protection Commissioner, 22 July 2011, available at http://dataprotection.ie/viewdoc.asp?DocID=1160&m=f.

22 M Tighe, "Student Hackers Face New Charges," *Sunday Times*, 28 August 2013.

23 *ibid.*

CHAPTER 22

SOCIAL NETWORKING AFTER DEATH

HEADLINE OF ISSUES

- Social networking profiles and pages remain after a person dies
- What happens to them?
- Do privacy and data protection rights still exist?
- Who owns or has a right to access and control over the social networking pages of those who have passed away?

INTRODUCTION

Everyone dies. What happens to the personal information on an individual's social networking page when someone dies? What happens to the social networking ghost, or as some computer commentators might say, the social networking "ghost in the machine"?

Do privacy and data protection rights extend beyond death? Up until relatively recently, most data protection practitioners would have said no. However, some comments on one EU Article 29 Working Party Opinion[1] raise for discussion the possibility that data protection should extend post mortem, at least in certain circumstances. The current consensus remains in favour of data protection ceasing upon death, but we may be entering a period where we will encounter a number of hard cases where "interests" exist post mortem and deserve "informational" protection. It may be that there will be an increasing case for the data protection regime to step in as the most appropriate legal mechanism to protect these interests.

In such an instance, there may be a need to re-interpret the EU Data Protection Directive 1995, or to expand it in the current EU data protection review. In other instances, such as the Irish Data Protection Acts, which is more explicitly restrictive in terms of accommodating post-mortem informational data protection, specific amendments may be required. The Irish Data Protection Acts refer explicitly to a "living individual", while the Data Protection Directive 1995 does not.[2]

---

1 Article 29 Working Party, *Article 29 Working Party Opinion 4/2007 on the Concept of Personal Data*, WP 136, at 22 – 23.

2 See definition of "personal data" in the Irish Data Protection Act 1988 as amended by the Data Protection (Amendment) Act 2003.

THE SOCIAL NETWORKING GHOST

We are becoming familiar with the growth and popularity of social networks. Some issues are immediately obvious; some come to light only over time. Now social networking is beginning to reveal one of the areas that may enhance calls for informational protection post mortem, and some may argue for having such protection on a regulatory footing. Again, the data protection regime may well be the most appropriate legal sphere for such explicit rights. In the interim, there may be increasing arguments to extend current definitions and interpretations of the data protection regime.

Billions of people have social networking profile pages containing a host of personal data in relation themselves personally and also their friends and family. However, as the timeline of social networking advances, increasing numbers of members inevitably pass away. Their personal data remains a lingering ghost in the social networking machine. This will become an increasingly important issue.

The question, therefore, arises as to who owns and controls social network profiles and personal data of deceased people.

According to interpretations of data protection laws up until now, personal data related to living individuals. Does that mean that personal data as defined in legislation automatically cease to be personal data once the data subject has passed away? Alternatively, does it mean that only the data protection rights of the dead individual cease to exist?

The main concern is that there is great personal interest in the informational ghost that remains on the system. While the individual data subject may be dead, he or she may have friends, partners, children and other family relations. They will obviously be concerned with—and interested in—what happens the ghost personal data. Indeed, let us not forget the person who has died. During their lifetime individuals may be concerned as to what happens to their personal data once they have died. These individuals may be few and far between as yet, but it is not difficult to anticipate that they may have certain wishes and intentions as to what should happen their data afterwards.

Notwithstanding that there may be difficulties in deciding which family member is the most appropriate person to control the data, the family arguably have many legitimate interests in gaining access to and control of the personal profile. They may wish to get access; post an announcement in case friends and acquaintances are unaware of the death; post a memorial or appreciation; delete the profile; or copy photographs or materials from the profile.

It must be acknowledged that the social networks are beginning to react. Some websites have a policy in place to begin addressing these ghost access issues. This is not universally the case, and even where there is a policy or notice on the website, it is not always transparent or available in a user-friendly manner.

What happens if the matter is not addressed or not addressed to the extent that the next of kin, etc, would like? What happens when there is a conflicting claim? What is the specific claim?

Indeed, a longstanding partner may also be greatly concerned as to what happens the social networking profile and information. This gets even more complicated when we consider married, estranged, separated, divorced, partner and same sex issues.

While the legal position may be uncertain, there is legitimate argument that data protection or other privacy laws are the more appropriate mechanism to address these emerging social networking ghost issues. That there may not be a policy in place with all social networks or that they are not, on occasion, user-friendly only emphasise this concern.

Indeed, there is a separate point to be made. Data protection rights and obligations frequently mean that data processing for new purposes, and new data transfers, will turn on how transparent and fair the new purposes and transfers may be. Would the data subjects reasonably expect or envisage the new activities at the time of their original consent to processing? If these concepts of reasonable and legitimate expectations are expanded to social networking ghost data, what would these people envisage would happen to their personal data after they pass away? Do social networks need to engage users with these issues while people are alive?

As indicated above, social networks and data protection laws may have to deal with competing claims of access. Is a son more entitled than a widow to access and control the deceased's social networking profile? What happens if one relative wants to delete but another wants to make a post on the social networking profile?

What happens in the case of difficult personal relationships such as estranged parties, mistress, wife, separated and divorced partners, etc? Courts may have to decide these issues in future.

In these and other instances, should people anticipate these problems, like they may do when they contemplate a will? Are social networks obliged to respect a preference made in a will in respect of what should happen to a profile after the person dies?

While succession law is well established,[3] it is an altogether different problem to decide whether social networking profiles are a recognised form of property, or some other recognised category which may legitimately be included in a traditional will.

Yet further difficulties arise. How will a dispute be adjudicated if the person specified in a will is not the natural next of kin, or is different from the person recognised by a social network in its policy?

These issues are far from resolved. Indeed, they are only just beginning to come into consideration in data protection and informational rights discussions. Soon these issues will be contested in courts.

---

3 In Ireland this is governed by the Succession Act 1965. UK succession law is governed by Administration of Estates Act 1925. (Note that other laws will also apply in terms of most questions of succession law and practice.)

The Health Analogy

While succession law may provide some analogies, as referred to above, we might also be able to look at the analogy with health personal data. While health data are recognised as the more important form of sensitive personal data, they are not referred to in the content of social networking or post-mortem data in data protection law. Yet, certain laws and policies in relation to health data may provide an analogy. Indeed, this is not a fanciful concern, as Google has proposed the online storage of certain health-related data in the Google Health and Health Vault services.[4]

The Access to Health Records Act 1990 in the UK refers to the regulation of access to medical data after a patient dies.[5] This relates mostly to disclosure by medical practitioners and medical institutions. These access issues can be quite complicated. An insurance company, for example, may make an access request where the individual previously expressed an objection to disclosure.[6] The next of kin might also object to such disclosure.[7] How is a doctor, hospital or nursing home meant to resolve these issues? The legal concept underlying the protection of the file is the common-law duty of confidentiality, which is stated to extend beyond the date of death.[8] The Irish Medical Counsel also refers to confidentiality obligations.[9] Confidentiality was examined in *Coco v AN Clark (Engineers) Limited*[10]; *House of Spring Gardens v Point Blank*[11]; and *Mahon v Post Publications*[12]; and in the UK in *Campbell v MGN 2.*[13] One factor to be considered is what detriment will be suffered if there is a disclosure of the data.[14] However, these authorities do not deal with the personal data of deceased persons.[15] New considerations arise.

The British Medical Association (BMA) also provides some guidance in relation to health data in its *Access to Health Records, Guidance for Health Professionals in the United Kingdom.*[16] The types of situations that may be specified are who may apply for access,[17] what happens where somebody lacks capacity[18] (as might a child who engages in social networking), etc. It states:

---

4 Referred to in J Caldarella, "Privacy and Security of Personal Heath Records Maintained by Online Health Services" (2010) *Alb Law Journal of Science & Technology* 203. Note also, LB Jacques, "Electronic Health Records and Respect for Patient Privacy: A Prescription for Compatibility" (2010–2011) *Vandenberg Journal of Entertainment & Technology Law* 441.

5 See "Data Protection After Death," Wessex Local Medical Committees, available at www.wessexlmcs.com/confidentiality_anda_data_protection_after_death.html.

6 *ibid.*

7 *ibid.*

8 *ibid.*

9 Medical Council, *Guide to Professional Conduct and Ethics for Registered Medical Practitioners*, 7th Edition 2009, Section 24 General Principles of Confidentiality, at 26–27.

10 *Coco v AN Clark (Engineers) Limited* [1969] FSR 415.

11 *House of Spring Gardens v Point Blank* [1984] IR 611.

12 *Mahon v Post Publications* [2007] IESC 15.

13 *Campbell v MGN* 2 WLR [2004] 1232.

14 AA Sheikh, "The Data Protection Acts 1988 and 2003, Some Implications for Public Health and Medical Research," *Health Research Board*, 84–85.

15 *ibid*, 85.

16 British Medical Association, Access to Health Records, Guidance for Health Professionals in the United Kingdom, December, 2008. Also see "Confidentiality," General Medical Council, available at www.gmc-uk.org/guidance/ethical_guidance/confidentiality.asp.

17 *ibid*, Section 4.1 Who May Apply For Access?, at 3.

18 *ibid*, Section 4.1.4, at 4.

"The ethical obligation to respect a patient's confidentiality extends beyond death. The Information Tribunal in England and Wales has also held that a duty of confidence attaches to the medical records of the deceased under section 41 of the Freedom of Information Act. The Freedom of Information Act in Scotland contains an exemption to the disclosure of medical records of the deceased patients. However, this duty of confidentiality needs to be balanced with other considerations, such as the interests of justice and of people close to the deceased person. Heath professionals should therefore counsel their patients about the possibility of disclosure after death and solicit views about disclosure where it is obvious that there may be some sensitivity. Such discussions should be recorded in the records".[19]

The BMA continues:

"Statutory rights of access are set out in the access to Health Records Act 1990 or Access to Health Records (Northern Ireland) Order 1993. The Access to Health Records Act 1990 covers manual health records made since 1 November 1991. In Northern Ireland the corresponding legislation, the Access to Health Records (Northern Ireland) Order 1993, covers manual records from 30 May 1994. Access must also be given to information recorded before these dates if this is necessary to make any later part of the records intelligible".[20]

It is also noted that the BMA refers to the practice whereby it was recommended not to reply to insurance company requests for certificates partly on the basis that the deceased person is no longer in a position to give informed consent.[21]

Of course, there are various business cases for access to medical records for research purposes, which can also be post mortem.[22] Generally, the Irish Data Protection Commissioner has issued guidance on health research, in its *Data Protection Guidelines on Research in the Health Sector*.[23] It states, *inter alia*:

"The Data Protection Acts require that where access to patient identifiable information is not accompanies by an explicit consent that it be undertaken for medical purposes and be undertaken by a health professional or a person who, in the circumstances, owes a duty of confidentiality to the data subject that is equivalent to that which would exist if that person were a health professional. The term health professional is defined in the appendix to this document and is intentionally broad to ensure all appropriate health professional can access patient data for medical purposes which also include research.

Questions as to whether a staff member, who is not a health professional and is to access patent identifiable information without consent, can be considered to owe an equivalent duty of confidentiality to the patient, need to be assessed on a case by case basis. As a general guide such persons would need to have a contractual duty of confidentiality that would carry an appropriate penalty would there be a breach of confidentiality".[24]

There is also proposed legislation in California to protect an individual's genetic health data.[25] Among other things, the proposed law seeks to ensure that there is

---

19 *ibid*, Section 5 Deceased Patients, at 8.

20 *ibid*, Section 5.1 "Are There Any Rights of Access to a Deceased Patient's Records?," at 8.

21 *ibid*, Annex 2.

22 A Withers, "Archiving and Storing Patients' Health Records After Death Can Help with Medial Research," Artlicles Online, 29 August 2010, available at http://articlesonlinedirectory.com.

23 Data Protection Commissioner, *Data Protection Guidelines on Research in the Health Sector*, available at http://dataprivacy.ie.

24 *ibid*, Section 2.8 "Persons Accessing Patient Identifiable Data," at 12.

25 T Ray, "Vermont, California Follow Massachusetts in Introducing Genetic Data Protection Bills," 9 March 2011, *Genome Web, Pharmacogenomics Reporter*, available at www.genomeweb.com/dxpgx/vermont-california-follow-massachusetts-introducing-genetic-data-protection-bill?utm_source=twitterfeed&utm_medium=twitter. In relation to the UK generally,

written consent before use; and that genetic data cannot be the basis of employment or housing discrimination (which would append to existing anti-discrimination law).[26] Another US bill, in Vermont, defines genetic data as forming "real property" and the "exclusive property" of the individual.[27] In addition, in recognition of the value of such data even post mortem, the proposed law provides that individuals can provide instructions in their will as to what should happen (or not happen) with their genetic data.[28] There is also the concept of primary and secondary uses in relation to medical and health data.[29] Can the next of kin decide what to do with the social networking profile data?

The question arises in Ireland, as elsewhere, as to if and what personal health data of deceased persons can be disclosed. One commentator suggests that this health data issue "is a complex area of law and it cannot be said that there exists a clear answer to the query."[30]

Personal Data

The EU Data Protection Directive 1995 defines personal data as:

> "any information relating to an identified or identifiable natural person ('data subject'); an identifiable person is one who can be identified, directly or indirectly, in particular by reference to an identification number or to one or more factors specific to his physical, physiological, mental, economic, cultural or social identity".[31]

However, the Irish Data Protection Acts defines personal data as data relating to a "living individual" who is or can be identified either from the data or from the data in conjunction with other information that is in, or is likely to come into, the possession of the data controller.[32]

In the UK personal data are defined as:

> "data which relate to a living individual who can be identified —
> (a) from those data, or
> (b) from those data and other information which is in the possession of, or is likely to come into the possession of, the data controller,
> and includes any expression of opinion about the individual and any indication of the intentions of the data controller or any other person in respect of the individual".[33]

The EU PRIVIREAL Project discusses what amounts to personal data, and states as follows:

---

see *Inside Information: Balancing Interest in the Use of Personal Genetic Information* (Human Genetics Commission, UK, 2002), in particular at 85–87, as referred to in Sheikh, *op. cit*, 81.

26 *ibid.*

27 *ibid.*

28 *ibid.*

29 Sheikh, *op. cit*, 76, referring to BMA Guidance on Secondary Uses of Patient Information, Ethics Department BMA, 2007, at 5.

30 Sheikh, 81 *et seq.*

31 Article 2.

32 S 2, Data Protection Act 1988 as amended by the Data Protection (Amendment) Act 2003.

33 Data Protection Act 1998 (as amended).

> "This is not a question of 'rights' for the dead. The central issue is whether the directive covers data that relates to a person who has dies. It concerns whether duties apply to the personal data that was obtained from living people who are now dead. Clearly, some of the duties of the Directive do not apply. It is not possible to inform the dead person about the processing of the data or to seek their consent for new processing. However, if the data was collected from the dead person when alive for specific purposes, do duties in relation to the processing of that data continue for those stated aims? Must the processing remain lawful and fair? Must the data be kept securely? Is the effect of the death of the data subject that of removing the data from the scope of the Directive. The implementation of the directive by Member States shows a variety of approaches to this area".[34]

The PRIVIREAL Project recommends that the EU Commission should seek to clarify whether or not the personal data of deceased persons fall within the definition of "personal data".[35]

EU WP29

The EU Article 29 Working Party has also refers to these issues in its Opinion 4/2007 on the Concept of Personal Data. It states:

> "Information relating to dead individuals is therefore in principle not to be considered as personal data subject to the rules of the Directive, as the dead are no longer natural persons in civil law. However, the data of the deceased may still indirectly receive some protection in certain cases.
>
> On the one hand, the data controller may not be in a position to ascertain whether the person to whom the data relate is still living or may be dead. Or even if he may do so, the information on the dead may be processed under the same regime as that on the living without distinction. As the data controller is subject to the data protection obligations imposed by the Directive as regards the data on living individuals, it will probably be easier for him in practice to process also the data on the dead in the way imposed by the data protection rules, rather than to separate the two sets of data. On the other hand, the information on dead individuals may also refer to living persons. For instance, the information that the dead Gaia suffered from haemophilia indicates that her son Titius also suffers from the same disease, as it is linked to a gene contained in the X-chromosome. Thus, where the information which is data on the dead can be considered to relate at the same time also to the living and be personal data subject to the Directive, the personal data of the deceased may indirectly enjoy the protection of data protection rules.
>
> Thirdly, information on deceased persons may be subject to specific protection granted by sets of rules other than data protection legislation, drawing the lines of what some call 'personalitas praeterita.' The obligation of confidentiality of medical staff does not end with the death of the patient. National legislation on the right to one's own image and honour may grant also protection to the memory of the dead".[36]

However, it adds that:

> "nothing prevents a Member State from extending the scope of the national legislation implementing the provisions of [Data Protection Directive 1995] to areas not included in the scope thereof provided that no other provision of Community law precludes it, as the

---

[34] Sheikh, *op. cit*, 81, referring to http://www.privireal.org/content/recommendations/#Refc, the PRIVIREAL Project, which is an EU body dedicated to examining the Directive 95/46/EC of the European Parliament and of the Council of 24 October 1995 on the protection of individuals with regard to the processing of personal data and on the free movement of such data in the context of the medial research issues.

[35] Sheikh, *op. cit*, 82.

[36] *Opinion 4/2007 on the Concept of Personal Data*, Article 29 Working Party, at 23.

> ECJ has recalled.[37] It is possible that some national legislator may decide to extend the provisions of national data protection law to some aspects concerning processing data on deceased persons, where a legitimate interest may justify it".[38]

UK

Some guidance on disclosures is also provided by the UK General Medical Council regarding disclosures after death, which include factors such as:

- whether the disclosure of information may cause distress to, or be of benefit to, the patient's partner or family;
- whether disclosure of information about the patient will in effect disclose information about the patient's family or other people;
- whether the information is already public knowledge or can be anonymised;
- the purpose of the disclosure.[39]

Ireland

It has been suggested that the Irish Data Protection Acts "are not applicable to the dead".[40] The Data Protection Directive 1995 also refers to "living individuals".

Sheikh, however, raises a separate point. "The protection of the Acts may arise in the case where there is joint personal data in relation to both the dead and a living person."[41]

While some rights are recognised in law as existing post mortem, other laws are less explicit, while others are clear in providing that rights are extinguished on death.

The Irish Civil Liability Act 1961 provides that causes of action can continue to the benefit of a person's estate where the person dies.[42]

An example of where rights cease on death is US defamation law.[43] A similar provision in the Civil Liability Act 1961 in Ireland provides that Irish defamation actions also cease on death.[44]

(Living) Third-Party Interests

One commentator concludes that for the moment it seems that that privacy interests do not survive death "except where disclosure of a certain type of information would cause distress to families if released. In these cases, it seems that such information

---

37 Judgment of the European Court of Justice C-101/2001 of 06/11/2003, Lindqvist, § 98.
38 Opinion 4/2007 on the Concept of Personal Data, Article 29 Working Party, at 23–24.
39 *Confidentiality: Protecting and Providing Information*, UK General Medical Council (April 2004), para 30, referred to in Sheikh, *op. cit*, 83.
40 Sheikh, *op. cit*, 82.
41 *ibid*, 82.
42 See s 7(1). As referred to in Sheikh, *op. cit*, 86.
43 Sheikh, *op. cit*, 86.
44 See s 7(1). As referred to *ibid*.

has been protected from disclosure as it may affect the privacy of the existing family."[45] There has been an example of a case where this was successfully argued.

In the US case of *New York Times Company v National Aeronautics and Space Administration*[46] (NASA) the families of astronauts on the fatal space shuttle Challenger were objecting to recordings of their deceased family members being released to the media. The media were requesting access to the black box recordings. The court stated:

> "the Challenger families' privacy interest in the tape in question outweighs the public interest such that release of the tape would constitute a clearly unwarranted invasion of the families' personal privacy".[47]

The media also requested access to photographs of a deceased legal counsel to President Clinton. The case, *National Archives and Records v Favish*,[48] held that

> "[t]he right to personal privacy is not confined ... to the 'right to control information about oneself.' ... To say that the concept of personal privacy must 'encompass' the individual's control of information about himself does not mean it cannot encompass other personal interests as well."[49]

The court also said: "In addition this well-established cultural tradition acknowledging a family's control over the body and death images of the deceased has long been recognised at common law."[50] The decision was upheld on appeal to the US Supreme Court.[51]

The comment is made in Ireland that:

> "[w]here aspects of the deceased may affect the living person by causing, especially family members, him/her harm, such connection has been recognised by the law of privacy and protected. Where private information about the deceased will affect the living individual and case him/her harm, the public interest in disclosure will be examined and disclosure may be prohibited if harm will be caused to the living individual".[52]

However, it is acknowledged that there is no law in Ireland equivalent to that in other jurisdictions on this issue.[53] Furthermore, the Irish Data Protection Acts are limited to living individuals.[54] "In the absence of relevant legislation, there exists only common law and ethical guidelines that might guide medical practitioners."[55] The data protection principles in the UK appear similar.

---

45 Sheikh, *op. cit*, 86.

46 *New York Times Company v National Aeronautics and Space Administration* 782 F Supp 628 (12 December 1991) (affirmed on appeal to the Supreme Court).

47 *ibid.*

48 *National Archives and Records v Favish*, United States Court of Appeals for the Ninth Circuit, 30 March 2004.

49 *ibid*, referred to in Sheikh, *op. cit*, 87.

50 *ibid.*

51 See *The Oyez Project, National Archives and Records Administration v Favish*, 541 U.S. 157 (2004) www.oyez.org/cases/2000-2009/2003/2003_02_954.

52 Sheikh, *op. cit*, 88.

53 *ibid.*

54 *ibid.*

55 *ibid.*

Ultimately, this is an issue which has yet to be properly dealt with in legislation, and may have to be dealt with an EU level. "While some of the national laws strictly define the personal data as only such that identify a living person, some of the laws including the harmonisation directive do not solve the problem and leave the question open."[56] The final version of the EU Data Protection Regulation is also awaited.

Conclusion

While the solutions and indeed full parameters of what should happen to the social networking personal data of deceased persons are far from clear, it is inevitable that this problem will have to be considered much more frequently. Certain comfort may come through self-regulation and self-administered social network policies. However, these policies will arguably not be able to deal with each and every data ghost problem that arises. Ultimately, some of the solutions may have to come from the data protection regime. In that regard, there may be increasing pressure to recognise that personal data as protected under the data protection regime needs to be reinterpreted or expanded post mortem. It will also need to be considered what interest or value is actually being protected. Data protection variously refers to privacy and fundamental rights, while the Constitution, constitutional (property) rights and succession law may refer to other interests. The concept and interests grounding expanded data protection need to be considered.

[56] R Polock, "Aims, Methods and Achievements in European Data Protection" (November 2009) (23) *International Review of Law, Computers & Technology* 179 at n16 at187.

Chapter 23

PROFILES IN PURGATORY

Claire Wallace

Headline of Issues

- Profiles of the deceased
- Right to privacy
- Right to privacy and data protection after death
- Lacuna in law
- Regulation/self-regulation
- Social networking settings, wills, online repositories

Introduction

> "The right to privacy should not be undermined merely because it has become easier and more profitable to break it in the virtual world."[1]

Three quarters of all Europeans believe that sharing personal information is an increasing part of modern life,[2] while six in 10 Europeans believe there is no alternative to disclosing personal information to purchase products and services.[3] We are sharing data like never before, through traditional avenues and, increasingly, online. Data protection legislation seeks to give data subjects control over the data they share. It recognises the value of personal data to the individual, giving data subjects the power to request access to,[4] rectification[5] or removal[6] of their personal data, while data controllers must comply with obligations including the maintenance of accurate data,[7] fair processing[8] and confidentiality.[9] Data protection legislation, however, is out dated and arguably no longer fit for purpose. The legislation did not envisage the pace at which data are currently being shared online and the difficulties that have arisen, for example, in identifying data controllers in the increasingly complex online arena. The prevalence of online providers based outside the EU, in particular social networks, engaged in processing personal data poses difficulties in

---

1 BEUC, *EU reassures consumers with new Data Protection strategy*, (BEUC Press Release, 4 November, 2010) accessed 8 August 2011, available at http://www.beuc.org/BEUCNoFrame/Docs/3/MMHODOHDDKCCOEBPNLCEMDJEPDWD9DBNC39DW3571KM/BEUC/docs/DLS/2010-00687-01-E.pdf.

2 TNS Opinion & Social, *Attitudes on Data Protection and Electronic Identity in the European Union,* (European Commission Special Eurobarometer 359, June 2011), accessed 8 August 2011, available at http://ec.europa.eu/public_opinion/archives/ebs/ebs_359_en.pdf, at 23.

3 *ibid*, 27.

4 S 4, Data Protection Act 1988, as amended by Data Protection (Amendment) Act 2003.

5 S 6, Data Protection Act 1988, as amended by Data Protection (Amendment) Act 2003.

6 *ibid.*

7 S 2, Data Protection Act 1988, as amended by Data Protection (Amendment) Act 2003.

8 *ibid.*

9 *ibid.*

terms of enforcement, and this has been acknowledged by the EU Commission.[10] The EU is in the process of overhauling data protection legislation with a view to updating and harmonising procedures.[11]

While we wait for reform, however, there is one lacuna of particular concern: once we die, our data becomes fair game. Personal data, even sensitive personal data, enjoy no protection under Irish data protection legislation once the data subject is deceased. The definition of "personal data" refers explicitly to a "living individual"[12]; therefore, all obligations on data controllers to treat personal data in accordance with the Irish Data Protection Acts are extinguished on the death of the data subject.[13] If you consider a situation whereby an individual passes away, they may leave behind a diary, or perhaps a locker containing private letters or photographs. The family or close friends of the deceased may wish to keep them for posterity, and choose the appropriate person to look after them, or indeed the deceased may have stipulated an intended recipient of personal effects in his or her will. The executor of the will is charged with distributing these items to the appropriate beneficiary, and there is no third-party involvement. It would seem unthinkable that the company that produced the blank diary, or indeed printed the letterhead, may feel it has a right to use and share the contents. Translate this to the online arena, and that unthinkable notion is closer to reality.

Social network profiles provide the prism through which the *modern* challenges brought about by the sharing of data can be addressed. The need for legislation is palpable in the context of social networking. A recent market analysis report has shown that there are more social network profiles than there are people on earth.[14] Social networking is increasing across all sectors of society, among both the very young[15] and the older members of society. A PEW Internet report found that social network usage by persons aged 50 to 65 grew by 88 percent between April 2009 and May 2010, while there was a 100 percent increase in usage by the people aged over 65.[16] An unfortunate side effect of the growth in the number of older users is the rise in the number of users passing away.[17] The "coming of age"[18] challenge for social networks, therefore, is how to deal with deceased users' profiles.

---

10 See V Reding, *Building Trust in Europe's Online Single Market: Speech at the American Chamber of Commerce to the EU* (Brussels, 22 June 2010).

11 V Reding, *The Reform of the EU Data Protection Directive: the Impact on Businesses* (Brussels, 18 May 2011).

12 Section1 Data Protection Act 1988 as amended by the Data Protection (Amendment) Act 2003.

13 Data Protection Commissioner, *Can I Access Personal Data in Relation to a Deceased Relative?*, available at www.dataprotection.ie/viewdoc.asp?DocID=628.

14 S Portet, "Social Network Accounts Outnumber People on Earth," *Silicon.com*, 1 April 2011, available at www.silicon.com/technology/mobile/2011/04/01/social-network-accounts-outnumber-people-on-earth-39747241/

15 72% of teens purportedly have a social network profile according to Internet Safety 101, *Social Network Statistics*, available at www.internetsafety101.org/Socialnetworkingstats.htm.

16 M Madden, *Older Adults and Social Media: Social Networking Use Among Those Ages 50 and Older Nearly Doubled Over the Past Year* (PEW Internet and American Life Project, 27 August 2010) at 2.

17 N Perlroth, "Facebook's Death Problem," *Forbes*, 14 March 2011, available at www.forbes.com/forbes/2011/0314/focus-1000-memories-wieden-kennedy-facebook-death-problem.html.

18 J Wortham, "As Facebook Users Die, Ghosts Reach Out," *New York Times*, 17 July 2010, available at www.nytimes.com/2010/07/18/technology/18death.html.

Social network profiles are potentially the most comprehensive record of an individual. Containing detailed information regarding a user's name, age, address, date of birth, religion, gender, marital status, phone number, educational and employment history, sexuality and indeed photographic images, a social network profile unquestionably contains personal data, the amount of which is dictated by the individual user. Social network profiles are becoming the go-to record of a deceased individual, by the media in particular. They are arguably a fundamental part of the historical record. While living, a person may remove his or her own profile; but some data relating to the user that is contained on another user's profile, eg a photograph, may remain.[19] When a user dies, however, there are no uniform rules for the treatment of profiles.[20]

Facebook, for example, takes no action without the express request of a member of the deceased user's immediate family to have the profile removed.[21] Alternatively, a family member or friend of the deceased user may request to have the user's profile memorialised.[22] A memorialised profile is essentially locked in time, no new friends may be added, it is not visible to the public, and only existing friends may post on the wall of the memorialised account.[23] By removing or memorialising a deceased user's profile, it prevents a situation whereby users receive "suggestions" from Facebook to reconnect with the deceased person, a feature which is intended to reconnect Facebook friends who have not made recent contact.[24] There are significant drawbacks to this procedure, however. First, automation is the "key to social media success",[25] and Facebook has no definitive way of knowing whether a user has passed away. In the absence of a connection to national birth and death registrars as suggested by Leftly, there is no way for Facebook to become aware of the death of a user automatically.[26] Even if such a connection was in place, the use of online aliases would pose problems and undoubtedly lead to incidences of mistaken identity. Secondly, the requirement that an online obituary or press article is provided in order to memorialise an account, or indeed a death certificate to have a profile removed, is not feasible in all circumstances. Other commentators have suggested that Facebook take a more practical approach and scan profiles for phrases such as "rest in peace" and "I miss you," which would then prompt an inspection by a Facebook staff member in order to determine whether the user has passed away.[27] This course of action would be open to obvious online abuse but may be the most realistic option, in conjunction with verification by a deceased user's designated relative or friend.

---

19 For example, Facebook, "Privacy: Deactivating, Deleting, and Memorializing Accounts," available at www.facebook.com/help/?page=842.

20 This author considers the procedures in place on both Facebook.com and Myspace.com. This author contacted Bebo about its procedures relating to deceased users, but no detail was provided.

21 See "Deceased Users – Special Requests," Facebook, available at www.facebook.com/help/contact.php?show_form=memorialize_special_requests.

22 See "Report a Deceased Person's Profile", Facebook, available at www.facebook.com/help/contact.php?show_form=deceased.

23 Facebook, "Memorialising Accounts," available at www.facebook.com/help/?page=842.

24 Wortham, *op. cit.*

25 *ibid.*

26 T Leftly, "The Ultimate Privacy Issue: Facebook Hassles Your Friends After Death," *Techi*, 18 July 2011, available at www.techi.com/2010/07/the-ultimate-privacy-issue-facebook-hassles-your-friends-after-death/.

27 *ibid.*

Myspace operates a similar procedure to Facebook, whereby a profile may be deleted or preserved on the request of a user's next of kin.[28] Next of kin may also request that specific content is deleted from the deceased user's profile, which is then reviewed by Myspace. Interestingly, Myspace offers a reminder that if a survivor has access to the email account of the deceased, they may retrieve the Myspace account password by clicking the "forgot password" link.[29] This displays a willingness to permit the next of kin of a deceased user to control the user's profile absent the involvement of the social network provider.

The competing interests at play in this debate, as ever, are the interests and expectations of the living user, surviving family and friends, and the public good. It is intended to address these concerns in turn with a view to highlighting the importance of both industry and legislative intervention in this area, before concluding that the data representative model is the most suitable resolution to this problem.[30]

To balance the interests of the deceased, the public, and survivors, living data subjects must be in a position to stipulate unequivocally how they wish their data to be treated posthumously. In order to achieve such a balance, this author advocates the creation of a framework to allow living data subjects to record their wishes, and the nomination of a "data representative" to enforce these directions after death. This mechanism would be set out in updated data protection legislation, placing an obligation on all Data Representatives to follow the directions of the data subject, save for exceptional circumstances in the public interest.

Analogous to testamentary wishes, however, these directions cannot be absolute.[31] Access requests by survivors other than the nominated data representative must be considered by a committee of the Office of the Irish Data Protection Commissioner as part of an expanded role under proposed data protection legislation, and the public interest in disclosure must be taken into account. This legislative model cannot stand alone, and requires the cooperation of social networks. Practical difficulties such as the provision of passwords and rapid growth in the volume of online data may require technological intervention, which will be discussed below. This proposal for reform is admittedly skeletal; practical examples must provide the flesh. The following discussion highlights the realities facing social network users, and the uncertainty surrounding such data after death.

Control and Expectations of the Living User

Unlike the circumstances surrounding medical records, for example, where patients

[28] See "How Can I Delete or Access a Deceased User's Profile?" *Myspace*, available at www.myspace.com/help.

[29] *ibid.*

[30] See C Wallace, "Protecting the Data of the Dead: An Analysis of the Treatment of the Data of Deceased Persons, with Particular Focus on Medical Records and Social Media Profiles" (2011) National University of Ireland Galway, LLM Law Technology and Governance.

[31] Under s 117 of the Succession Act, for example, the court may require that provision is made for the child of the testator if the court is of the opinion that the "testator has failed in his moral duty to make proper provision for the child in accordance with his means." The interests of the survivor may, therefore, supersede the wishes of the deceased.

may inform their medical practitioners of their wish to forbid or perhaps limit access to their health records after their death, thereby ethically binding them to secrecy, there is no equivalent procedure on social networks. There are no provisions made for user directions after death. Users may edit their privacy settings to limit access to their profiles during their lifetime, but there are no equivalent settings governing access after death.

In a recent Eurobarometer report, *Attitudes on Data Protection and Electronic Identity in the European Union*, for the EU Commission, results show that eight in 10 social network users who disclose personal information feel in control over the data they shared.[32] As discussed above, however, it is clear that all control over social network profiles is ceded to the social network providers in conjunction with the user's next of kin after death. Users currently have no control over personal data on social network profiles after death *within* the confines of social networks. This apparent user confidence is therefore misplaced.

Why is control given to next of kin? What interests do survivors have in social network profiles of deceased persons? McCallig points to the "opportunity to assimilate digital remains to enhance the memories and better understand the natural persons the dead formerly were while alive."[33] Conversely, relatives may find it disconcerting to see the profiles of deceased users remaining online, and may wish to avoid the sense of "coming back from the dead" that has been reported.[34] Social networks have placed a value on the wishes of the relatives of the deceased in their privacy policies, and the Canadian Internet Policy and Public Interest Clinic have surmised that "a reasonable person would not expect Facebook to continue to display a user's profile posthumously despite the user's family's wishes to the contrary."[35] The fact that survivors enjoy control over the social network data of deceased users after death is aligned to the proposed data representative model; but, critically, survivors are not currently bound to follow directions left by the living user. While the predominant reasons for upholding the wishes of a user's family after death is one of practicality and verification, is it worthy of assessing the role played by the wishes of the user themselves when they are alive, and the practicalities of fulfilling those wishes.

Right to be Forgotten, Free Speech and Maintaining Online Archives

McCallig notes that "in the offline world memories fade, paper trails are shredded and the connections to friends are often severed with time."[36] In the online world, however, personal data contained on social network profiles has the potential to last

[32] *European Union,* (European Commission Special Eurobarometer 359, June 2011), available at http://ec.europa.eu/public_opinion/archives/ebs/ebs_359_en.pdf, at127.

[33] D McCallig, "The Law of Digital Remains: Property and Persona in the Cloud" (2010) National University of Ireland Galway, LLM, Law Technology and Governance, at 9.

[34] Wortham, *op. cit.*

[35] Canadian Privacy Commissioner, *Report of Findings into the Complaint Filed by the Canadian Internet Policy and Public Interest Clinic (CIPPIC) against Facebook Inc. Under the Personal Information Protection and Electronic Documents Act* (16 July 2009) at 65.

[36] McCallig, *op. cit*, 2.

for eternity. There is a growing movement supporting the "right to be forgotten"[37] or indeed the "right to withdraw"[38] from social networks, which this author argues should extend after death.

Viviane Reding, Vice President of the European Commission, has been very vocal on the topic of controlling personal data. Reding identifies the very "power of data" which "requires us to be on our guard to ensure that web surfers' privacy rights are fully protected."[39] She highlights the need for clear obligations to respect privacy rights in order to ensure that online users are fully aware of the use to which their data are being put. Reding opines that the "data revolution is putting individuals centre stage when it comes to the 'management' of their personal data."[40] Users must be informed of their rights and the obligations of data controllers before consent can be given to use their personal data. Critically, focus is placed on the empowerment of users, to have confidence in the way in which their personal data are being treated online. This empowerment can extend past death through the directions given to data representatives under the proposed model. Central to this empowerment is consent, and its operation in practice. The EU Article 29 Working Party recently issued an opinion on the definition of consent which reaffirms the need for informed consent in the social network context for any use of a user's data.[41] Furthermore, the EU Article 29 Working Party encourages granularity while obtaining the consent of the user through the use of pop-up boxes. The use of a social network profile as a memorial is arguably not part of the initial purpose for which the profile was set up, nor is it necessary for the user to be able to use the social network. Therefore, additional consent would be required for such a purpose in order to conform to data protection principles. Without the consent of the data subject, the creation of a memorialised profile is an impermissible use of personal data. This discussion, however, remains theoretical and indeed futile, as data protection rights currently lapse on death. This dilemma may be solved by following the wishes of the deceased, who may or may not have stipulated that they wish their data representatives to remove their social network profiles.

The crux of the "right to be forgotten" is very simply that "internet users must have effective control over what they put online and be able to correct, withdraw or delete it at will."[42] The Social Network Bill of Rights drafted at the 2010 *Computers, Freedom and Privacy in a Networked Society* conference makes explicit reference to the "right to withdraw", referring to the right to "allow [a person] to delete [their] account and remove [their] data."[43] Matthew Newman, spokesman for Reding, clarified that all reference to your data should be removed when consent is withdrawn, and no remnants should remain on a "server somewhere".[44] Perhaps most ground-breaking of all in this debate, is Reding's insistence that the burden

---

37 See V Reding, *Building Trust in Europe's Online Single Market: Speech at the American Chamber of Commerce to the EU* (Brussels, 22 June 2010).

38 Danimor, "Introducing the Social Network User's Bill Of Rights," *Social Times*, 23 June 2010, available at http://socialtimes.com/introducing-the-social-network-users-bill-of-rights_b15728.

39 V Reding, *Building Trust in Europe's Online Single Market*, *op. cit*

40 *ibid.*

41 *Opinion 15/2011 on the Definition of Consent*, Article 29 Working Party, WP 187 (13 July 2011) at 19.

42 Reding, *Building Trust in Europe's Online Single Market*, *op. cit.*

43 Danimor, *op. cit*

44 S Olenski, "You Have the Right to Be Forgotten Online," *Social Media Today*, 24 March 2011,

of proof will be on a data controller to prove that it needs to keep the data.[45] It is very difficult to imagine an argument for retention of the social network profile data of a deceased user. This shift in thinking looks likely to manifest itself in default privacy settings of a higher standard, and the need for explicit permission for all gathering of data.[46] However, the very issue of retaining the social network profile of a deceased user without consent becomes irrelevant if living directions under the data representative model are outlined and followed after death.

The Spanish Data Protection Authority has been particularly supportive of the right to be forgotten, and has given in to the demands of 90 individuals demanding the removal of their data from the internet.[47] Google has challenged five of these cases in the Spanish National Court in 2011 alone, one of which involved a plastic surgeon wishing to remove content relating to a dispute with a former patient in which he was acquitted of any wrongdoing.[48] If users may successfully request the removal of data created by others, it would follow that a request to remove user-created content such as a social network profile would be similarly fulfilled.

The Spanish have been heavily criticised for their approach, with many commentators believing that removal of online content undermines the "integrity of the index"[49] and therefore the public good. The Library of Congress in the United States has emphasised the fragile nature of digital content, the dependence on the survival of compatible technologies and the need for active management to maintain archives.[50] The US has demonstrated a clear preference for a broader definition of freedom of information rather than the right to be forgotten.[51] Indeed, Mayes has gone as far as describing the right to be forgotten as an "emasculation of our power to act in the world" which degrades the very concept of rights.[52]

The right to be forgotten stirs up notions of censorship[53] and an interference with

---

available at http://socialmediatoday.com/steve-olenski/280649/you-have-right-be-forgotten-online.

45 L Phillips, "EU to Force Social Network Sites to Enhance Privacy," *Guardian*, 16 March 2011, accessed 8 August 2011, available at www.guardian.co.uk/media/2011/mar/16/eu-social-network-sites-privacy.

46 *ibid.* See also E Dou, "Internet Privacy and the 'Right To Be Forgotten,'" *Reuters*, 17 March 2011, available at http://us.mobile.reuters.com/article/technologyNews/idUSTRE72G48Z20110317.

47 E Flock, "Should We Have a Right to be Forgotten Online?" *Washington Post*, 20 April 2011, available at www.washingtonpost.com/blogs/blogpost/post/should-we-have-a-right-to-be-forgotten-online/2011/04/20/AF2iOPCE_blog.html.

48 K Cameron, "Google Opposing the 'Right To Be Forgotten,'" *Identity Blog*, 21 April 2011, available at www.identityblog.com/?p=1187.

49 *ibid.*

50 Library of Congress, "Why Digital Preservation is Important for Everyone," available at www.digitalpreservation.gov/videos/digipres/index.html, referred to in D McCallig, "The Law of Digital Remains: Property and Persona in the Cloud" (2010) National University of Ireland Galway, LL.M Law Technology and Governance at n.23.

51 Dou, *op. cit.*

52 T Mayes, "We Have No Right to Be Forgotten Online," *Guardian*, 18 March 2011, available at www.guardian.co.uk/commentisfree/libertycentral/2011/mar/18/forgotten-online-european-union-law-internet.

53 G Sterling, "Google Confronting Spain's 'Right to Be Forgotten,'" *Search Engine Land*, 8 March 2011, available at http://searchengineland.com/google-confronting-spains-right-to-be-forgotten-67440.

freedom of expression.[54] Reding, however, has countered this argument, explaining that the ability to remove our data online in fact promotes creativity. She argues that in order to "think freely, grow up, make mistakes, say silly things, experiment, be creative or pursue any other interest," individuals need space. [55] If our data are irretrievably out of our control once published online, creativity may be stifled. This argument is equally applicable to social network profiles. Users should be able to retain control over content published, encouraging imagination and freedom of speech, in the confidence that they are in charge of the destiny of such data. The proposed legislation fulfils this aim.

There are undoubtedly practical difficulties associated with deletion of online content.[56] Content can be copied and pasted and widely distributed.[57] These difficulties are brought into sharp focus in the context of deceased users, which will be discussed below. Regulators must draw on the experience of enforcing copyright, and the potential for the use of privacy enhancing technologies must be examined as part of the proposed model for reform. [58] As De Hert concedes, "even if the right to be forgotten would be a weak one in the final [data protection] legislation, it is a step forward to at least develop the concept of it."[59]

Social Network Settings, Wills and Online Repositories

The Assistant Privacy Commissioner of Canada published a report in 2009, responding to a complaint filed by the Canadian Internet Policy and Public Interest Clinic (CIPPIC) against Facebook.[60] The complaint contained specific reference to the treatment of the accounts of deceased users.[61] CIPPIC contended that Facebook should give users a clear opportunity to opt out of posthumous displays of their profiles.[62] In their preliminary report, the Assistant Privacy Commissioner stated that it was:

> "concerned that, by omitting to allow users to opt out of Facebook's future use of their personal information for purposes of memorializing their accounts, Facebook is in effect requiring them to consent to an unnecessary purpose as a condition of service".[63]

In the final report however, the Assistant Privacy Commissioner concluded that the use of a deceased user's account for memorialisation constitutes "an intended use of

54 D Desai, "Property, Persona, and Preservation" (2008) (81) *Temple Law Review* 67 at 93.

55 V Reding, *Building Trust in Europe's Online Single Market, op. cit.*

56 M Gibson, "Do You Have the 'Right To Be Forgotten' on the Internet?," *Time*, 21 March 2011, available at http://newsfeed.time.com/2011/03/21/do-you-have-the-right-to-be-forgotten-on-the-internet/.

57 J Aron, "A Right to be Forgotten Online? Forget It," *New Scientist*, 17 March 2011, available at www.newscientist.com/blogs/onepercent/2011/03/a-right-to-be-forgotten-forget.html.

58 *ibid.*

59 V Pop, "EU to Press for 'Right to Be Forgotten' Online," *EU Observer*, 4 November 2010, available at http://euobserver.com/9/31200.

60 Canadian Privacy Commissioner, *Report of Findings into the Complaint Filed by the Canadian Internet Policy and Public Interest Clinic (CIPPIC) against Facebook Inc. Under the Personal Information Protection and Electronic Documents Act* (16 July 2009).

61 *ibid*, 65.

62 *ibid.*

63 *ibid*, 68.

the user's personal information".[64] Notwithstanding that conclusion, however, the Assistant Privacy Commissioner recommended that Facebook should provide and notify users of a means to opt out of such use.[65] Facebook declined to implement such a procedure, making the following statement:

> "We still do not believe that retaining data for the purpose of allowing users to remember their friends constitutes another use under PIPEDA, and in any event users are perfectly capable of using other means to express their wishes in this area. We also believe that it would be inappropriate to create a standard for handling information in this case that would be at variance with existing legal norms for the disposition of estate property".[66]

Facebook clearly regard online social network profiles as material capable of inclusion on the term "estate property". This would imply that users could direct the destiny of their profiles by traditional means, ie in a will. In a practical sense, however, this simply means that the users' personal representatives would be bound to delete, memorialise or indeed leave untouched users' profiles after their death in accordance with the wishes of the deceased users rather than using their own judgment. This produces an identical result to the proposed data representative model. It may simply mean than a user's password is passed on to a specified individual, as discussed below, giving living users some level of control over the destiny of their social network profiles. In practice, however, if a user states in his will, or stipulates via the framework proposed in the reform model, that he wishes Mr X, his next-door neighbour, to have responsibility over his profile after death, neither Facebook nor Myspace would honour the requests of Mr X, as they have stated that requests for removal or memorialisation may be made only by next of kin or immediate family. There are practical difficulties with the implementation of the testamentary instructions of a user in the absence of a uniform procedure. This may be solved by supplying a data representative with official documentation from the Office of the Irish Data Protection Commissioner, confirming both the death of the user and the transfer of data control to the identified data representative. Central to the effectiveness of the model is the cooperation of social network, and recognition of the standing of the data representative in accordance with proposed legislation. Consultation with social network providers would therefore be crucial prior to the implementation of proposed legislation.

Alternatively, there is the option of the inclusion of an opt-out or opt-in section in the sign-up process to determine whether a user's profile is deleted or memorialised if Facebook is informed of his or her death, which would give users peace of mind that their personal data will be deleted or retained in accordance with their wishes. This does not solve the problem, however, as next of kin may not provide Facebook with the necessary death certificate or obituary in order to delete the account in accordance with users' wishes, as there is no statutory obligation to do so. Is it preferable in that case to remove the social network provider from the equation entirely and simply ensure that passwords are supplied to trusted individuals who delete or maintain a user's profile as directed?

On that point, Facebook noted the existence of private vendors who carry out services

---

64 *ibid.*
65 *ibid*, 69.
66 *ibid.*

pertaining to access to digital assets in the event of death. It is assumed that this reference is to the existence of providers such as Legacy Locker,[67] Entrustet[68] and Asset Lock,[69] which offer users the ability to direct how their digital information will be used.

These online repositories offer users the ability to store passwords and online account details in a password-protected account in the cloud. When setting up an account, the user must nominate "verifiers" who would have access to the user's death certificate when they pass away. Users then detail all their online assets, specifying the website, username and password of all online accounts held. Critically, the user identifies the intended beneficiary of each online account.[70] When the user dies, a verifier must contact the company to confirm the death before access is given to the user's data. These facilities do serve a valuable purpose in eliminating many of the problems identified thus far, as a user can choose the individual best suited to carry out their wishes and respect their privacy, and reliance is not necessarily placed on the next of kin. It is believed that the use of such repositories in conjunction with the Office of the Irish Data Protection Commissioner may represent the final piece of the puzzle. Instead of providing instructions concerning data in a will, which may be read by numerous individuals and become quickly out-dated, the data subject can log all details of their data, where it is held and how access can be gained, through the use of an online repository operated by the Data Protection Commissioner. Once the Data Protection Commissioner verifies the identity of the data representative, access may be given to that online repository. Notably, the issue of online aliases can also be overcome if all online accounts held by a data subject are registered with the online repository.

Alternatively, users could keep records of their data in a tangible safety repository to be given to the intended beneficiaries on their passing. However, companies that operate online repositories claim that the ease with which users can amend details and beneficiaries when new accounts are created, or indeed deleted, provides them with their unique selling point. McCallig notes that problems arise in the context of certain websites that prohibit transferability of accounts and retain the right to deny access to accounts once they are informed of the death of a user.[71] This problem is mitigated, however, by the difficulties facing online providers in confirming the death of a user.

Cooperation with all relevant stakeholders must take place before the introduction of proposed legislation, to ensure the effective implementation of the data representative scheme. Notwithstanding the transfer of passwords through an online repository, the cooperation of Facebook, for example, would still be required in order to memorialise a deceased user's account in accordance with his or her wishes.

---

67 http://legacylocker.com/.

68 www.entrustet.com/.

69 www.assetlock.net/.

70 For example, see http://legacylocker.com/features/beneficiaries.

71 See Yahoo, Terms of Service, available at http://info.yahoo.com/legal/uk/yahoo/utos-173.html, as referred to in McCallig, *op. cit*, 34.

Conclusion

> "We are a society strangely obsessed both with privacy and obtaining information.[72]" A balance must be struck both pre mortem and post mortem.

It is clear from the discussion above that existing procedures governing the social network data of the deceased are inconsistent and ineffective. Indeed, the pace and regularity with which changes are made to social network privacy settings and procedures may add to the uncertainty. Standardised mechanisms must be introduced to address the problem of "suggestions to reconnect" with deceased persons, and the difficulty in reliably ascertaining when a user has died. While social networks have amended aspects of their privacy settings in line with an increasing appetite for greater user control, the wishes of data subjects in relation to the treatment of their profiles after death have been ignored.[73] Technology is vital in closing this gap, and the utilisation of online repositories to their full potential may address the practical difficulties in implementing the wishes of data subjects after death.

The data of the deceased is vulnerable and must be protected.[74] The data representative model may not provide the answer to all these questions, but it may be the most effective solution available at the present time. Individuals must be proactive in protecting their data. The data representative model requires registration by data subjects in a manner akin to data controllers.[75] Data subjects are given the opportunity to create an up-to-date bank of their details, safe in the knowledge that the Irish Data Protection Commissioner oversees the system. Data representatives must be aware of their responsibilities and must assent to the nomination of the data subject. A monitoring system must be established to ensure data representatives comply with the directions of the data subject, potentially in the form of audits carried out by the committee of the Data Protection Commissioner. The critical hurdle to be overcome when protecting the data of the dead is the establishment of a procedure to inform the relevant persons of the death of the data subject. It is envisaged that the Data Protection Commissioner would have access to the register of deaths in order to fulfil this function and inform the relevant data representative, if appointed, of the commencement of their duties. The responsibility of informing the appropriate data controller of the death of the data subject and taking the specified action then lies with the data representative.

The extension of protection to the data of the deceased is clearly an enormous administrative task. This system may not work in practice, but its introduction on a trial basis should be contemplated. The need for such a system grows as

72 J Berg, "Grave Secrets: Legal and Ethical Analysis of Post Mortem Confidentiality" (2002) (34) *Connecticut Law Review* 81 at 122.

73 See C Cox, "Making It Easier to Share With Who You Want," *The Facebook Blog*, 23 August 2011, available at www.facebook.com/blog.php?post=10150251867797131. Changes to Facebook privacy settings have given users greater control over the sharing of posts and tagging, providing certainty in relation to the privacy of posts. No changes were made to the procedures governing profiles after death.

74 See Comment and Analysis, "Social Welfare Fraud," *Irish Times*, 4 August 2011, available at www.irishtimes.com/newspaper/opinion/2011/0804/1224301816589.html. Anecdotal evidence suggests that PPS numbers of deceased persons are being used to fraudulently claim social welfare benefits, as PPS numbers are not automatically extinguished upon death.

75 S 16, Data Protection Act 1988, as amended by the Data Protection (Amendment) Act 2003.

increased volumes of social network data are shared, through a variety of media. Data protection legislation must adapt, and must recognise the need to remedy the significant flaws in the current system.

Chapter 24

A CRITICAL APPROACH TO RIGHT TO BE FORGOTTEN

José M. Baño Fos

Headline of Issues

- Individuals quest to always be remembered
- A critical approach to the right to be forgotten
- EU Data Protection Directive 1995
- The questions raises by the Spanish Court
- The right to be forgotten: conceptual aspects
- The right to be forgotten: substantive issues
- Territorial aspects of the request
- Conclusions: the internet paradox

Introduction

The "right to be forgotten" is a very appealing term, some would say that even poetic, but ascertaining what it exactly means is certainly an ugly and obscure task. This is a task that the European Court of Justice (ECJ/CJEU) has been asked to carry out in the recent request for a preliminary ruling raised by the Spanish High Court (la "*Audiencia Nacional*") in the Mario Costeja case.

The case concerns the issue of whether an individual has right to ask a search engine to remove links to public and truthful information that, in his view, damages his reputation. In this chapter I examine the legal questions that the ECJ currently faces, analyzing the arguments in favor and against, as well as the consequences that might arise from them and, along the way, we take the opportunity to make some suggestions about the direction that legislative reform on the field of data protection could take in this regard.

In 1968, Andy Warhol coined the famous sentence "*In the future, everyone will be world-famous for 15 minutes*". His prophecy was, to a large extent, very accurate. Nowadays, the expansion of the information society and the internet allows trends and topics to become viral and spread through the entire world within seconds. Social networks empower citizens to be the editors of their own walls, their own "newspapers". Today, everybody has a better chance to get their 15 minutes of fame. However, even though you might be famous for only 15 minutes, you might be remembered for much longer than that.

It used to be the case that something written on a newspaper would soon fade in the shadows of history and be left to historians or bookworms. Currently, that is no longer the case, information posted on the internet remains on the internet forever.[1] In other words, events can become forgotten in the eyes of the majority but not for any individual with a minimum of interest and a good internet connection.[2] Whether this is a positive or a negative externality cannot be answered univocally, the truth is that the response will greatly vary depending on the person to whom the question is addressed.[3]

In the case that the ECJ is currently studying, Mr Costeja certainly thinks that this accessibility to information about his persona is a bad thing. Mr Costeja is a Spanish citizen who, at a given point in time, accrued some debts before the Spanish Social Security. As a result of these debts, a property belonging to him was auctioned and the auction announced on the printed version of a Spanish newspaper at the request of the Spanish Social Security. Years after, the newspaper decided to post its archives online and with them a little column in page 23 of the Monday newspaper of January 1998 became part of the World Wide Web.[4]

Sometime after, Mr Costeja realized that if he typed his name in Google, page 23 of that Monday newspaper would show up when clicking in one of the links that Google suggested could be a good fit for his query. He requested both Google and the newspaper to remove that information and to make it no longer available to the public.

Not surprisingly both parties refused, so Mr Costeja filed a complaint before the Spanish Data Protection Agency. The Agency saw Mr Costeja's complaint with sympathetic eyes and issued a decision which might have seemed very Solomonic to them at the time. The information should remain available on the newspaper's website but not on Google's search engine's. In other words, if you typed in Google Mr Costeja's name, the link to the newspaper should not be available. Nonetheless, a different thing would happen if a user went directly to the newspaper's website or if she used another search engine. How to implement this decision technically-speaking was something that the agency left for Google to decide.[5]

At first sight the reasoning of the Agency seems to strike a balance. This way the freedom of information was apparently protected — truthful information remained in the public arena - but it could be forgotten unless you knew in which newspaper to look for it or you had the time to go newspaper by newspaper looking for it.

---

1 As long as the webmaster (or the Courts) so wishes.

2 Some authors have phrased this phenomenon as the gradual shift from "the default of forgetting" towards the "default of remembering". J Ausloos, "The Right to be Forgotten, Worth Remembering", *Computer Law & Security Review*, (2012)(28) 143-152. See also V Mayer-Schönberger, *Delete: the Virtue of Forgetting in the Digital Age*, (Princeton University Press: Princeton, 2009).

3 J Zittrain, *The Future of the Internet and How to Stop It*, (Yale University Press: Yale, 2008) who argues that people should be entitled to a fresh start on the World Wide Net. See also J Ausloos, "The Right to be Forgotten, Worth Remembering", *Computer Law & Security Review*, (2012)(28) 143-152, on the benefits and disadvantages of such a right.

4 http://hemeroteca.lavanguardia.com/preview/1998/01/19/pagina-23/33842001/pdf.html

5 On the different cases pending before the Spanish Courts related to the behavior of the Spanish Data Protection Agency see Peter Fleischer, "The Right to be Forgotten", *seen from Spain* (5 September 2011).

However, this delicate balance seems to be easily challenged when you look at the bigger picture. What about the interests' of society as a whole to access the information? What about Google's freedoms of expression, enterprise and to provide services? How can a Spanish agency decide what worldwide users can see on the internet? Is this proportional? What precedents and (perverse) incentives does it create for publishers?[6]

Those seem some of the logical issues that Google raised in their appeal before the Spanish High Court. Given the nuances, the difficulty of these issues and the fact that data protection is governed by EU law (in particular the European Directive 95/46/ EC on Data Protection), it is not surprising that the Spanish High Court passed the "hot potato" to the European Court of Justice.

The Questions Raised by the Spanish High Court

Facing these facts, after Google's appeal of the Spanish Data Protection decision, the Spanish High Court submitted the following questions to the CJEU.[7] It states:

> "First, with regard to the territorial application of Directive 95/46/EC and, consequently, of the Spanish data-protection legislation:
>
> 1.1. must it be considered that an "establishment", within the meaning of Article 4(1)(a) of Directive 95/46/EC, exists when any one or more of the following circumstances arise:
>
> — when the undertaking providing the search engine sets up in a Member State an office or subsidiary for the purpose of promoting and selling advertising space on the search engine, which orientates its activity towards the inhabitants of that State,
>
> or
>
> — when the parent company designates a subsidiary located in that Member State as its representative and controller for two specific filing systems which relate to the data of customers who have contracted for advertising with that undertaking,
>
> or
>
> — when the office or subsidiary established in a Member State forwards to the parent company, located outside the European Union, requests and requirements addressed to it both by data subjects and by the authorities with responsibility for ensuring observation of the right to data protection, even where such collaboration is engaged in voluntarily?
>
> 1.2. Must Article 4(1)(c) of Directive 95/46/EC be interpreted as meaning that there is "use of equipment ... situated on the territory of that Member State" when a search engine uses crawlers or robots to locate and index information contained in web pages located on servers in that Member State
>
> or
>
> when it uses a domain name pertaining to a Member State and arranges for searches and the results thereof to be based on the language of that Member State?
>
> 1.3. Is it possible to regard as a use of equipment, in the terms of Article 4(1)(c) of Directive 95/46/EC, the temporary storage of the information indexed by internet search engines? If the answer to that question is affirmative, can it be considered that that connecting factor is present when the undertaking refuses to disclose the place where it stores those indexes, invoking reasons of competition?

---

6 We explore these issues in detail in the following sections.

7 C-131/12, *Google Spain, S.L., Google Inc. v Agencia Española de Protección de Datos, Mario Costeja González*, available at http://curia.europa.eu/juris/document/document.jsf?docid=123131&doclang=EN.

> 1.4. Regardless of the answers to the foregoing questions and particularly in the event that the Court of Justice of the European Union considers that the connecting factors referred to in Article 4 of the Directive are not present: must Directive 95/46/EC on data protection be applied, in the light of Article 8 of the European Charter of Fundamental Rights, in the Member State where the centre of gravity of the conflict is located and more effective protection of the rights of European Union citizens is possible?"

Secondly, as regards the activity of search engines as providers of content in relation to Directive 95/46/EC on data protection:

> "2.1. in relation to the activity of the search engine of the "Google" undertaking on the internet, as a provider of content, consisting in locating information published or included on the net by third parties, indexing it automatically, storing it temporarily and finally making it available to internet users according to a particular order of preference, when that information contains personal data of third parties, must an activity like the one described be interpreted as falling within the concept of "processing of ... data" used in Article 2(b) of Directive 95/46/EC?
>
> 2.2. If the answer to the foregoing question is affirmative, and once again in relation to an activity like the one described: must Article 2(d) of Directive 95/46/EC be interpreted as meaning that the undertaking managing the 'Google' search engine is to be regarded as the 'controller' of the personal data contained in the web pages that it indexes?
>
> 2.3. In the event that the answer to the foregoing question is affirmative, may the national data-control authority (in this case the Agencia Española de Protección de Datos - Spanish Data Protection Agency), protecting the rights embodied in Articles 12(b) and 14(a) of Directive 95/46/EC, directly impose on the search engine of the 'Google' undertaking a requirement that it withdraw from its indexes an item of information published by third parties, without addressing itself in advance or simultaneously to the owner of the web page on which that information is located?
>
> 2.4. In the event that the answer to the foregoing question is affirmative, would the obligation of search engines to protect those rights be excluded when the information that contains the personal data has been lawfully published by third parties and is kept on the web page from which it originates?"

Thirdly, regarding the scope of the right of erasure and/or the right to object, in relation to the "derecho al olvido" (the "right to be forgotten"), the following question is asked:

> "3.1. must it be considered that the rights to erasure and blocking of data, provided for in Article 12(b), and the right to object, provided for by Article 14(a), of Directive 95/46/EC, extend to enabling the data subject to address himself to search engines in order to prevent indexing of the information relating to him personally, published on third parties' web pages, invoking his wish that such information should not be known to internet users when he considers that it might be prejudicial to him or he wishes it to be consigned to oblivion, even though the information in question has been lawfully published by third parties?"

The questions raised are detailed, and considerably thought, and cover multiple and varying scenarios. Nonetheless, in our view from a conceptual point of view they can be summarized in three simple categories: conceptual, substantive and territorial, as follows:

- Is there a right to be forgotten in the Directive? (*Conceptual issues*);
- Is the Data Protection Directive applicable to a search when it supplies links to information posted on the internet in response to a query? And who should be responsible for protecting that right? (*Substantive issues*);
- If so, is the Data Protection Directive applicable to a search engine operating from California? (*Territorial issues*).

In what follows, we will provide a brief analysis of each of these questions.

The Right to be Forgotten: Conceptual Aspects

First of all, one needs to bear in mind that the concept "right to be forgotten" as such is not [editor note: explicitly] included anywhere in the EU Data Protection Directive 1995.[8] The term has been gaining momentum lately in the context of the discussions of the Data Protection Reform and the proposed EU Data Protection Regulation. If we look at this proposal and its explanatory works, the drafters seems to point in the direction of social networks and the like.

The Draft Regulation which is currently being debated at the European Parliament describes the right to be forgotten in the following terms:

> "Any person should have the right to have personal data concerning them rectified and a 'right to be forgotten' where the retention of such data is not in compliance with this Regulation. In particular, data subjects should have the right that their personal data are erased and no longer processed, where the data are no longer necessary in relation to the purposes for which the data are collected or otherwise processed, where data subjects have withdrawn their consent for processing or where they object to the processing of personal data concerning them or where the processing of their personal data otherwise does not comply with this Regulation. *This right is particularly relevant, when the data subject has given their consent as a child, when not being fully aware of the risks involved by the processing, and later wants to remove such personal data especially on the internet.* However, the further retention of the data should be allowed where it is necessary for historical, statistical and scientific research purposes, for reasons of public interest in the area of public health, for exercising the right of freedom of expression, when required by law or where there is a reason to restrict the processing of the data instead of erasing them".

As explained by some authors, the EU legal framework does not provide for a general "right to be forgotten"[9] even though some existing provisions in the data protection framework could be interpreted as diluted "right to be forgotten" provisions.[10] This is consistent with the views provided by Commissioner Redding who has been the force behind the draft Regulation. According to her:

> "Thirdly, the reform will give individuals better control over their own data. (...) *The new rules will provide for data portability. Another important way to give people control over their data: the right to be forgotten.* I want to explicitly clarify that people shall have the right – and not only the 'possibility' – to withdraw their consent to the processing of the personal data they have given out themselves. The internet has an almost unlimited search and memory capacity. So even tiny scraps of personal information can have a huge impact, even years after they were shared or made public. *The right to be forgotten will build on already existing rules to better cope with privacy risks online.* It is the individual who should be in the best position to protect the privacy of their data by choosing whether or not to provide it. It is therefore important to empower EU citizens, particularly teenagers, to be in control of their own identity online. By the way, 81% of German citizens are worried they are no more in control of their personal data!"[11]

---

8 Some authors argue that the intellectual roots of the right to be forgotten can be found in French law, which recognizes a *droit à l'oubli* – a right that allows a convicted criminal who has served his time to object to the publication of facts relating to his conviction. J Rosen, "The Right to Be Forgotten", *Stanford Law Review Online* (2012)(64) 88.

9 RH Weber, *The Right to Be Forgotten, More Than Pandora's Box*, "the term right to be forgotten has only recently been created" available at http://www.jipitec.eu/issues/jipitec-2-2-2011/3084/jipitec%202%20-%20a%20-%20weber.pdf.

10 J Ausloos, "The Right to be Forgotten, Worth Remembering", *Computer Law & Security Review*, (2012)(28) 143-152.

11 Viviane Reding Vice-President of the European Commission, EU Justice Commissioner,

In the examples provided by the European Commission, the right to be forgotten seems to presuppose, as some authors have pointed out, a contractual relationship. The concept is, therefore, not suitable to cope with privacy issues where personal data is (legally) obtained without the individual's consent.[12] Other scholars, however, take the view that the draft Regulation, as currently written supports a broader reading that could include up to three different categories of information (personal posts, re-posts and posts with personal information from a 3rd party)[13] highlighting the risks that this might entail for free speech on the internet.[14]

In my view, rather than focusing on the future draft Regulation, the appropriate question is *what does the directive currently grant?* The answer is quite clear: the Directive currently grants a right to rectification, erasure or blocking (under Article 12) and a right to object (under Article 14).

Article 12. Member States shall guarantee every data subject the right to obtain from the controller: (...) (b) as appropriate the rectification, erasure or blocking of data the processing of which does not comply with the provisions of this Directive, in particular because of the incomplete or inaccurate nature of the data.

Article 14. Member States shall grant the data subject the right: (a) at least in the cases referred to in Article 7(e) and (f), to object at any time on compelling legitimate grounds relating to his particular situation to the processing of data relating to him, save where otherwise provided by national legislation.

As some scholars have pointed out, these are the most important provisions with regard to the right to be forgotten. However, their scope application is heavily limited. Article 12 only applies when the processing does not comply with the provisions of the Directive, in particular because of the incomplete or inaccurate nature of the data. Article 14, on the other hand, is also restricted as it only requires Member States to provide a right to object in cases referred to in Articles 7(e) and 7(f) of the Data Protection Directive and if they are based on "compelling and legitimate grounds".[15] In other words, this means that Member States are not bound to grant this right where the data subject provided unambiguous consent, where the processing is necessary to perform a contract, *legal obligation* or to protect a vital interest.[16]

So in this context, whether there is a right to be forgotten – in other words a right that could legitimate Mr Costeja's requests – can be answered in two possible ways.

- No, there is no right to be forgotten on the Directive (literal interpretation);
- Yes, there is an implicit right (either a teleological interpretation or a wide interpretation of the right to erasure, blocking or objection).

"The EU Data Protection Reform 2012: Making Europe the Standard Setter for Modern Data Protection Rules in the Digital Age", Innovation Conference Digital, Life, Design Munich, 22 January 2012.

12 Ausloos, above.
13 P Fleischer, *Foggy Thinking About the Right to Oblivion*, (March 2011).
14 J Rosen, *The Right to Be Forgotten*, (64) *Stanford Law Review Online* 88.
15 Ausloos, above.
16 *ibid.*

In any event, the indisputable fact is that there is no explicit right with such a name in the Directive as opposed to the draft Regulation.

The Right to be Forgotten: Substantive Issues

Having said that, for the sake of the discussion, let's assume that there is such a right in the Directive, the logical question therefore should be who should be in charge of enforcing it: the newspaper, the search engine or both?

In order to answer this question, it is important to solve three questions:

- First, does the directive apply to search engines and/or webmasters?;
- Second, how do search engines and webmasters work? This is a crucial question since understanding the functioning of search engines will help us determine – from a technical point of way – the most cost-efficient (and thus proportional) ways of enforcing Mr Costeja's requests;
- Lastly, from the perspective of the European Court of Justice, we need to wonder what would be the logical consequences of imposing the obligations on both of them or only of them. How will they affect the social welfare of all internet users?

In his influential paper, the "Problem of Social Cost", Professor Coase argued:

> "If factors of production are thought of as rights, it becomes easier to understand that the right to do something which has a harmful effect (such as the creation of smoke, noise, smells, etc.) is also a factor of production. Just as we may use a piece of land in such a way as to prevent someone else from crossing it, or parking his car, or building his house upon it, so we may use it in such a way as to deny him a view or quiet or unpolluted air. The cost of exercising a right (of using a factor of production) is always the loss which is suffered elsewhere in consequence of the exercise of that right-the inability to cross land, to park a car, to build a house, to enjoy a view, to have peace and quiet or to breathe clean air. It would clearly be desirable if the only actions performed were those in which what was gained was worth more than what was lost. But *in choosing between social arrangements within the context of which individual decisions are made, we have to bear in mind that a change in the existing system which will lead to an improvement in some decisions may well lead to a worsening of others*".[17]

In what follows, we will try to look at the problem from this perspective of ensuring the maximization of total welfare. In this regard, we acknowledge that the approach towards personal data moves away from the more traditional "personal privacy" approach and towards the "commodity" approach advocated by some scholars.[18] However, this law and economics perspective seems to us not so different from the traditional EU principle of proportionality and the recognition that the right to

---

17 R Coase, "The Problem of Social Cost", (1960) (3) *Journal of Law and Economics*, a summary available at http://weber.ucsd.edu/~jlbroz/Courses/POLI200C/syllabus/Coase_social%20cost.pdf.

18 Ausloos, above. In this line, it seems very appropriate the famous quote by Gordon Gekko in the Francis Ford Coppola movie Wall-Street, "*the most valuable commodity I know of is information, don't you agree?*"

be forgotten might conflict with other fundamental rights such as the freedom of expression, freedom of information[19] or the freedom to provide services.

Controllers and Processors: the Addressees of the Data Protection Directive

Both Articles 12 and 14 set out obligations which are applicable only to the Member States and the "controllers". Therefore, even if one assumes that there is a right to be forgotten embedded either in Articles 12 or 14, it is necessary to determine who is the "controller" which will implement that right to be forgotten.

Article 2(d) of the Data Protection Directive reads "controller" shall mean the natural or legal person, public authority, agency or any other body which alone or jointly with others determines the purposes and means of the processing of personal data; where the purposes and means of processing are determined by national or Community laws or regulations, the controller or the specific criteria for his nomination may be designated by national or Community law.

To the observant reader, it will seem evident that one of the key elements in this wording is the sentence "determines the purposes and means of the processing of personal data".

In this regard, the EU Article 29 Working Party, a group of experts on Data Protection, has issued an expert opinion where it states the following:

> "…even if the capacity to 'determine' may arise from a specific attribution made by law, it would usually stem from an analysis of the factual elements or circumstances of the case: one should look at the specific processing operations in question and understand who determines them, *by replying in a first stage to the questions 'why is this processing taking place? Who initiated it?* Being a controller is primarily the consequence of the factual circumstance that an entity has chosen to process personal data for its own purposes. Indeed, a merely formal criterion would not be sufficient at least for two kinds of reasons: in some cases the formal appointment of a controller - laid down for example by law, in a contract or in a notification to the data protection authority - would just be lacking; in other cases, it may happen that the formal appointment would not reflect the reality, by formally entrusting the role of controller to a body which actually is not in the position to 'determine'".

It seems that looking at the natural sequence of the events, in the present case, the one who "initiated" the processing was the newspaper and not the search engine which just accessed information already available. This initial guess gets confirmed when we look at the functioning of search engines and we apply a simple law and economics approach to the issue.

This seems to be the view of the WP29, which in a specific Opinion concerning search engines pointed out that:

> "The Data Protection Directive does not contain a special reference to the processing of personal data by information society services that act as selection intermediaries. (….) The principle of proportionality requires that to the extent that a search engine provider acts purely as an intermediary, it should not be considered to be the principal controller with regard to the content related processing of personal data that is taking place. In this case the principal controllers of personal data are the information providers".

---

19 Ausloos, *ibid.*

In my opinion, the current wording of the Directive only allows for search engines to be considered controllers for the personal information of the users (cookies, etc). Whether the WP29's statement should be read as suggesting that search engines are not truly controllers but something akin to it with regards to the search results they provide is something which has been debated during the oral hearing of the Mario Costeja case at the ECJ. In our view, as AG Jääskinen pointed out during the oral hearing; this is fruitless debate since it would imply creating a concept that is not expressly acknowledged in the Directive.[20]

Technical Aspects of the Functioning of the Internet

The way web search engines work is by creating an index of the websites that are available on the internet. These pages are retrieved by a web crawler (sometimes also known as a spider); which is an automated web browser which follows every link on the site and access the information which is later deconstructed to create the index.

Because not every person that posts information on the internet wants it available through search engines, different tools have been developed to prevent search engines from accessing the information. One of these tools are the robot.txt protocols. As explained, in Google's website, robots.txt file restricts access to your website by search engine robots crawling the web. These bots are automated, and before they access pages of a site, they check to see if a robots.txt file exists that prevents them from accessing certain pages.[21]

In accordance with the principle of proportionality, which is one of the general principles of Community law, the lawfulness of the prohibition of an economic activity is subject to the condition that the prohibitory measures are appropriate and necessary in order to achieve the objectives legitimately pursued by the legislation in question, *it being understood that when there is a choice between several appropriate measures recourse must be had to the least onerous, and the disadvantages caused must not be disproportionate to the aims pursued.*[22]

From the perspective of simple cost analysis, it seems quite clear that the most economical mechanism to avoid personal information appearing on the internet is to impose that obligation on the original webmaster who first posted the information on the net. One could raise the opposite argument and contend that it might be very hard for webmasters to follow the path that the information has followed once posted (ie who else has re-posted that information). However, this is a fallacious argument since it implies that the webmaster was not available to determine ex-ante whether he wanted to have the information available to search engines. The webmaster can determine ex-ante the diffusion that the information can have on the internet. He is the one that can mitigate any damages with the minimum cost. Think for example of

20 When questioning the commission's reasoning in favor of imposing the obligation on the search engines and, in particular, the additional obligations that the Directive would impose on search engines if they were to be labeled as controllers in the terms of the Directive *"Do you mean, legally, that we have lightweight controllers with [fewer] obligations than others?"* M-Lex, "Google's duty to 'forget' individuals under scrutiny in EU Court" (26 February 2013).

21 Google Support available at http://support.google.com/webmasters/bin/answer.py?hl=eN&answer=156449.

22 C-331/88, *R v Minister of Agriculture*, ECR I-04023 (1990).

the opposite scenario, how many resources and time will a third party that just found the information need to devote in order to determine the legality and adequateness of the information? I will expand on this point in the next section.

Policy Considerations

Another approach towards the questions raised by the Spanish Courts is to look at it from a prospective perspective. In other words, what are the possible consequences of ruling in favor of considering that the Directive can be interpreted as containing a right to be forgotten to be enforced against search engines and not webmasters.

From our point view, there is a plausible argument that this could create a pervasive incentive on the webmasters to avoid any self-control over the information they post. If they believe that they will have a reasonable argument that their information was to be overseen by a third party, why worry then?

On the other hand, from the users' perspective this could also raise an incentive for individuals to use "pirate" search engines to find information. As we have explained before there are tools and protocols on the internet that prevent indexation, however, they function for as long as both sides —webmasters and search engines — respect them. The internet is currently experiencing the appearance of pirate search engines which do not respect these tools or protocols. Deleting the information from legally abiding search engines could prompt a raise in the use of pirate search engines.

In addition, even if we were to agree that there is a right to be forgotten in the Directive and that search engines should enforce it without risking an increase in potentially damaging information, two practical questions remain to be answered.

<u>First</u>, any obligation imposed by a Court on a search engine should be made binding to all search engines. This is the logical conclusion to avoid, on the one hand, forcing the individual to sue every search engine and, on the other hand, to provide a competitive advantage to less used search engines. If the user knows that information that used to be accessible through Google is no longer there, it seems logical to assume that he will start trying to use another search engine.

<u>Second</u>, how do we determine what information should be "forgotten"? We have to factor in that the information concerned is not illegal, it is lawful and truthful, and thus who should decide when does the information get forgotten? The individual, the search engine, the Courts…

- The Individual. From the perspective of the usefulness of the Web, it seems evident that as a society we cannot allow granting a blank check to every individual, otherwise we will risk creating a system of private censorship where the World Wide Web will only contain positive information about everyone[23];

---

[23] M-Lex, "Google's duty to 'forget' individuals under scrutiny in EU Court" (26 February 2013) "*Questions from several judges focused on whether the arguments put forward by the commission would undermine EU criticism of similar take-down measures sought by authoritarian regimes. Further, it raised the question of whether, for example, the Chinese*

- The Search Engine. If search engines are left to determine whether the information should be removed or not, they will have to build entire legal departments to deal with these requests since we cannot include personal considerations into a mathematical algorithm. However, even if so, is this really a feasible alternative?[24] In my opinion, this alternative is unrealistic and troubling for several reasons: first, the issue is not always a matter of obsolescence of the information therefore there might multiple border-line scenarios, secondly, as a result all - or most - these decisions would have to be ultimately reviewed by a Court as they are guided by personal considerations but, more importantly, what would be the legal basis for legitimately burdening search engines to conduct a review (even if preliminary) that most constitutions have left in the hands of the judiciary? How can one of the stakeholders involved decide as to the adequateness of the information?;
- The Courts (either directly or as an appeal against the search engine decision). This raises again two issues, whether we want to burden our judicial system with these cases and, most importantly, how can we determine the jurisdiction of our national Courts to rule on these cases that affect the internet and, therefore, have a clear beyond the boundaries of any country. This question is explored in the next section.

In my view, all these arguments support the conclusion that from a legal and policy approach any obligations arising from an alleged right to be forgotten need to be imposed on the webmasters.

Territorial Aspects of the Request

The territorial aspects of the case pending before the ECJ can be divided in two categories: (a) those concerning the application of the Directive, ie whether the Directive can apply to a search engine operating from outside the EU? And (b) those concerning the territorial effects of the Directive, ie can the Directive have effects over all internet users or only on users IP located in the EU?

The Territorial Application of the Directive

The Data Protection Directive was enacted in 1995, before the birth of Google. It was, therefore, quite difficult for the legislators to envision the changes that the new-born internet would cause to data protection in the following years. In fact, at the

---

government could make use of EU data protection authorities to seek the removal, globally, of references to dissidents".

24 This is the scenario that Judge, Egils Levits, raised at the oral hearing. According to M-Lex "Another judge, Egils Levits, pointed to a "dilemma" that would arise from a broad interpretation of Google's obligations. Under one scenario, Google's examination of removal requests would be "quasi-automatic", which would result in links being deleted on a simple request. This could result in millions of such requests, and "the internet would disappear, but we would live in a 'clean' internet world". The other option would be that each request was subject to a full judicial examination. "Google should then have a legal department of tens of thousands of lawyers to examine each request, and it would be necessary to hear the other side and with three instances, and several countries". M-Lex, "Google's duty to 'forget' individuals under scrutiny in EU Court", (26 February 2013).

time of the drafting of the Directive, the drafters' main concern was data contained in physical documents.[25] It is, therefore, not surprising that the territorial application of the Directive is built around the concept of establishment.

Article 4.1 sets out:

> "1. Each Member State shall apply the national provisions it adopts pursuant to this Directive to the processing of personal data where: (a) the processing is carried out in the context of the activities of an establishment of the controller on the territory of the Member State; when the same controller is established on the territory of several Member States, he must take the necessary measures to ensure that each of these establishments complies with the obligations laid down by the national law applicable".

As explained by the EU Article 29 Working Party in their Opinion 8/2010 on applicable law, the Directive does not however provide a clear definition of the term establishment. The strong emphasis put in the preamble of the Directive on "effective and real exercise of activity through stable arrangements" clearly echoes the "stable establishment" referred to by the Court of Justice at the time of the adoption of the Directive. Although it is not clear whether this and subsequent interpretations by the ECJ as regards the freedom of establishment under Article 50 TFEU could be fully applied to the situations covered by Article 4 of the Data Protection Directive, the interpretation of the Court in those cases can provide useful guidance when analyzing the wording of the Directive.

As explained by the Working Party, with regard to Article 4(1) a, the reference to an establishment means that the applicability of a Member State's law will be triggered by the location of an establishment of the controller in that Member State, and other Member States' laws could be triggered by the location of other establishments of that controller in those Member States. To trigger the application of the national law, the notion of the "context of activities" of the establishment is decisive. It implies that the establishment of the controller is involved in activities implying the processing of personal data, taking into consideration its degree of involvement in the processing activities, the nature of the activities and the need to guarantee effective data protection.

From this perspective, it seems difficult to conclude that a search engine whose servers are located outside one Member State the European Union has an establishment within that Member State when it has subsidiaries in that country that only perform marketing activities but are not involved in the functioning of the crawlers or the index.

The Directive foresees an alternative mechanism to "capture" a data processor, the means criteria. According to Article 4.1.c of the Directive "the controller is not established on Community territory and, for purposes of processing personal data makes use of equipment, automated or otherwise, situated on the territory of the said

[25] As explained by the Article 29 Working Party in their *Opinion 8/2010 on Applicable Law* "in the course of the discussion in European Parliament and in the Council of the EU, there was a shift from the criterion of the location of the file to the criterion of the establishment of the controller. The location of the means was identified as the second criterion when the controller is not established in the EU".

Member State, unless such equipment is used only for purposes of transit through the territory of the Community".

Again, the physical element is evident. The means shall be located within the Member States. In our view, a search engine cannot be said to be using means located in the EU when providing search engine services to users located in the EU. A different thing, however, would occur if we were talking about personal data concerning the search profile of users for marketing purposes. In this case, we would agree that the Directive is applicable.

The Extraterritorial Effects of the Directive

Put it blatantly, the issue here is how can a Data Protection agency of one single Member State decide what *worldwide users* can find and see on the internet? One could argue that information that is illegal in a country (for example for copyright infringement) is normally deleted from the internet and that the territorial effect is only an extension of that illegality effect. However, in the present case, the information is not illegal thus its deletion from the search engine is based on a balance of the different interests at stake which is to a large extent biased by cultural elements and not by international agreements.

In fact, from the press reports on the issues that were covered in the oral hearing held on in Luxembourg, this seems to be a concern for some of the Judges of the Grand Chamber which is currently confronted with the case.

According to M-Lex, during the oral hearing AG Jääskinen said the Commission's broad interpretation of the way the legislation is applied triggered another problem. "*If we accept this broad interpretation, wouldn't all third countries, including authoritarian regimes, have the legitimate claim of the scope of the application of their jurisdiction over Google, including demands for censorship*" "*If we require that for the EU there is some kind of universal jurisdiction, over a global scale, what arguments would we have that third countries shouldn't do the same?*" the AG continued.[26] According to the reports, Judge Lars Bay Larsen followed up and asked whether Google would be obliged to take away a link globally or only within the EU, the Commission answering that the effect would be worldwide.[27]

These are powerful and compelling questions that in my view justify a careful approach towards the present case. In fact, in my view they raise the need for an international agreement on the matter to acknowledge the fact that the internet is and can only be a global market, rather than policy making case law more appropriate for Common Law jurisdictions but not for the more civil law based approach of the ECJ.

Conclusions: The Internet Paradox

From the study above, we can conclude there is no right to be forgotten under the current Data Protection Directive. There is however a right to erasure that should

26 M-Lex, "Google's duty to 'forget' individuals under scrutiny in EU Court", (26 February 2013).
27 *ibid.*

be properly used and not misinterpreted. If information is public and truthful it should remain online as in those cases is hard to argue that the right to "private censorship" should prevail over the right to information. Obligations, if any, need to be imposed on webmasters.

It is true however that there is an urgent need to reform legal publication obligations to acknowledge the internet era and that, in any event, maybe we should start thinking about an international treaty on the use of internet and data protection. Something I reckon quite unlikely as there should be first a consensus about the "fundamental right" nature of the right to privacy and the right to be forgotten. Therefore, at the very least, in my view, a plausible temporary solution might be for publishers to adopt a code of safe practices as to the procedures and safeguards to be met when uploading their printed archives on-line.

There are some particulars features of the internet that make it very difficult to govern without specific rules designed to it. For example, it is quite a paradox that the fact that Mr Costeja brought these proceedings to be forgotten has only increased the information concerning him. Something that he might find not so bad considering that he has agreed to be interviewed and photographed by Spanish newspapers, radios and even on TV.[28] If he wins the case, is he going to sue Google and every newspaper for information related to the case? Will this article have to be kept in the shades of history not to offend Mr Costeja?

In sum, all these issues suggest that the ECJ should be very careful in providing an answer to the questions raised by the Spanish Courts and that, probably, the answer is that the task that the ECJ has been asked to fulfill belongs to the legislators and not to the judiciary.[29]

---

[28] See for example http://sociedad.elpais.com/sociedad/2013/03/21/actualidad/1363889407_114848.html.

[29] Editor Note: Since drafting, the Advocate General opinion has been issued, and which is in part favourable to the Google arguments. See Advocate General's Opinion in Case C-131/12 *Google Spain SL, Google Inc v Agencia Española de Protección de Datos*, Advocate General Jääskinen 25 June 2013, available at http://curia.europa.eu/jcms/upload/docs/application/pdf/2013-06/cp130077en.pdf. The full court decision is still awaited.

PART VII: CHILDREN AND SOCIAL NETWORKING

Chapter 25

CHILDREN AND SOCIAL NETWORKING

Headline of Issues

- Child concerns online and on social networks
- Current and developing issues
- Laws
- EU Article 29 Working Party
- Solutions, laws, self-regulation and technology
- Referendum in Ireland
- Cyberbullying offence
- Single oversight body

Introduction

The internet can be a dangerous place for children.[1] Some of the biggest concerns in relation to children are often online abuse (especially cyberbullying), online sexual solicitation and exposure to online sexual or pornographic content.[2] There is undoubtedly an increase in predatory risks with social networking, whereby sexual predators seek to make contact or profile children through social networks.[3] Social networks are said to "create an environment"[4] which assists sexual predators in communicating with children. A study compiled for Safer Internet Day found that 73 percent of children surveyed were afraid of being contacted by strangers online.[5] Policy makers have sometimes been criticised for acting slowly to address these problems.[6] The UK National Society for the Prevention of Cruelty to Children (NSPCC) in a 2013 survey found that one in five children have been the victims of cyberbullying, and also note that significant number of children under the age of 13 are members of social networks and relate websites.[7]

---

1 EP Stedman, "MySpace, But Whose Responsibility? Liability of Social-Networking Websites When Offline Sexual Assault of Minors Follows Online Interaction" (2007) (14) *Villanova Sports & Entertainment Law Journal* 363 at 372.

2 JS Groppe, "A Child's Playground or a Predator's Hunting Ground? – How to Protect Children on Internet Social Networking Sites" (2007) (16) *CommLaw Conspectus* 215 at 216.

3 Referred to in, for example, S Hetcher, "User-Generated Content and the Future of Copyright: Part One-Investiture of Ownership" (2008) (10) *Vanderbilt Journal of Entertainment and Technology Law* 863 at 869.

4 Stedman, *op. cit*, 364.

5 Referred to in A Healy, "73% of Children Fear Internet Strangers – Survey," *Irish Times*, 8 February 2010, available at http://irishtimes.com/newspaper/ireland/2010/0208/1224263954466.html. Survey total N=860 children in 37 schools aged 9–16. Survey published by the National Centre for Technology in education. EU Safer Internet Day occurs on 9 February each year.

6 Groppe, *op. cit*, 216.

7 "One in Five Children in UK Victim of Cyberbullying: Survey", *Times of India* 12 August 2013.

Child Concerns Online and on Social Networks

Reid refers to the issues of protecting children online:

> "The twenty-first century generation are the first to grow up completely immersed in the information technology age. They are growing up in an era of ubiquitous and pervasive, mobile computing and 24/7 online connectivity and communication. Their world is interactive, interconnected and instantaneous. They use information technology to play games, to learn about the world around them and for social interaction and to generally furthering their personal development through defining, refining and expressing their personal preferences. Thus, mobile information technology offers limitless opportunities but also many pitfalls for the unwary user, especially young adopters of the technology. Young people are naturally inquisitive and enthusiastic adopters of new technology, thus the trend of information technology use by children and young persons is likely to exponentially increase.
>
> The dangers that manifest themselves in children's and young people's use of online services are well-documented and can be conveniently grouped into three broad classifications: Content, Contract and Commerce. These dangers include, but are not limited to: sexual grooming and contact with strangers; exposure to pornography and other harmful content, such as hate [web]sites, pro-anorexia and pro-suicide [web]sites, cyber-bullying and harassment; advertising and increased financial pressure and online liability, for example misuse of intellectual property and publishing defamatory statements online, through the use of peer-2-peer services, social network [web]sites and the creation of user-generated content".[8]

However, despite the enhanced dangers for children and younger people, there is no additional protection in the EU Data Protection Directive 1995.[9] While protecting personal data, the Directive does not explicitly refer to or address children's personal data[10] or the risk of solicitation. In contrast, the US enacted the Child Online Privacy Protection Act 2000 (COPPA)[11] in order to address some of these issues.[12] In one case a company was fined $1 million for breaches when it collected children's personal data[13] in contravention of the Act. However, the effectiveness of the legislation has also been queried.[14] There is increasingly commentary, research and even acknowledgements from service providers that significant numbers of users are under the age of 13.

Further concerns relate to the social networks themselves, and in particular in

Also note U Schrott, "High Cybercrime Levels and Worrying Youth Cyber-bullying, Latest Irish Survey Shows" *ESET Ireland* 4 April 2013 available at http://blog.eset.ie/2013/04/04/high-cybercrime-levels-and-worrying-youth-cyber-bullying-latest-irish-survey-shows/.

8 AS Reid, "Online Protection of the Child Within Europe" (2009) (23) *International Review of Law Computers & Technology* 217.

9 *ibid*, 218

10 E Bartoli, "Children's Data Protection vs Marketing Companies" (March–July 2009) (23) *International Review of Law Computers & Technology* 35 at 36.

11 Children's Online Privacy Protection Act 15 USC S 6501(1) (2000).

12 DH Montes, "Living Our Lives Online: The Privacy Implications of Online Social Networking" (2010) (5) *I/S: A Journal of Law and Policy* 507 at 509 *et seq.*

13 Press Release, Federal Trade Commission, "Xanga.com to Pay $1 Million for Violating Children's Online Privacy Protection Rule" (7 September 2006) available at http://wwwftc.gov/opa/2006/09/xanga.sthm.

14 LA Matecki, "Update: COPPA is Ineffective Legislation! Next Steps for Protecting Youth Privacy Rights in the Social Networking Era" (2010) *Northwestern Journal of Law and Social Policy* 369. Generally, see also D Levine, "Facebook and Social Networks: the Government's Newest Playground for Information and the Laws that Haven't Quite Kept Pace" (2011) *Hastings Communications & Entertainment Law Journal* 481.

relation what responsibility they have or should have. Are they legally responsible for third-party actions and comments? Some would suggest they need to share at least some of the responsibility for child protection, including some liability. There are many policy reasons, however, for suggesting that they should not be. Indeed the most developed arguments in relation to intermediary and website liability relates to the European eCommerce Directive[15] and the US Digital Millennium Copyright Act.[16] These types of laws recognise that websites and intermediaries should have lesser liability in relation to third-party content transmitted on their services. Despite the copyright jurisprudence and intermediary defences, there have been some attempts to fix liability for child sex predators on social networks. For example, MySpace was sued, unsuccessfully, when a rapist was introduced to a child via its social network.[17] However, this area will continue to receive attention, given the controversial nature of the issues.[18]

Sexual Exploitation

Sexual exploitation facilitated by social networking is a grave concern, as is indicated above. Children can be befriended by third-party adults with less than innocent intentions. Sexual predators use social networking to make contact with children to profile children and even to make arrangements to meet children in actuality.

Harmful Content

A further issue is harmful content. Adults are concerned that children may access or have sexually related content both accidentally and otherwise. One problem is that harmful social networking content may or may not be illegal.[19] Criminal laws must always be drafted with certainty and specificity in mind. Therefore, that new technological problems may not always be covered sufficiently in criminal law. How should we define "harmful" content? There is significant disagreement as to what constitutes harmful content.[20] Problems also arise in defining "inappropriate" content and in dealing with it.[21]

Some of those contacted can be children who are deliberately targeted. Others, however, may be aimed generally at adults or adults and children. In some instances, children or young persons can deliberately or accidentally access particular inappropriate content.

---

15 EU Directive 2000/31/EC on Electronic Commerce.

16 Digital Millennium Copyright Act 1998. Note also US Communications Decency Act 1996.

17 *Doe v MySpace Inc* No D-1-GN-06-002209, 1 (District Court of Travis County Texas, filed 19 June 2006), as referred to in Stedman, *op. cit*, 364 and n8 at 364.

18 On defence issues generally, note for example, C Marsden, "Network Neutrality and Internet Service Provider Liability Regulation: Are the Wise Monkeys of Cyberspace Becoming tupid?" Global Policy (2011)(2(1)) 1-14.

19 Reid, *op. cit*, 220.

20 *ibid*, 221.

21 *ibid*. This also occurs in relation to video and film classification, despite attempts at consensus. See *ibid*. In *Dynamic Medien*, case C-244/06 [2008] ECR I-505, the ECJ held that Germany was able to restrict the import of games not bearing the German rating system ratings. Referred to *ibid*, 221. This led to the Audio Visual Directive ultimately, Directive 2007/65. See *ibid*, 212.

Cyberbullying

Cyberbullying is also a worrying concern.[22] "Cyberbullying is a form of online harassment that may be accomplished through the posting of cruel or even threatening messages online. Unlike cyber harassment or cyber stalking, which involves adults, cyberbullying involves minors on both sides of the harassment".[23] There is also the associated issue of text bullying, which can often go hand in hand with online bullying.

The Lori Drew case provides a graphic example. In this case an adult pretended to be a younger person and befriended an acquaintance of one of her children. She set up a false profile to contact the 13-year-old. This resulted in a stream of communications. A final message from the adult to the 13-year-old stated that "[t]he world would be a better place without you".[24] The 13-year-old soon afterwards hanged herself.[25] There is also the much publicised case of Phoebe Prince, an Irish girl being bullied in school when her family moved to the US. While some activity was physical, much centred on social networks, apparently even after she died.[26] There have been a number of convictions. Prime Minister Cameron has also pushed service providers to do more to deal with child pornography and separately commented upon "vile" cyberbullying websites.

Children and Advertising

In addition to harmful-type dangers, there are also what Reid refers to as the "commercial dangers",[27] such as advertising, marketing, spam, profiling and targeting. Children are particularly vulnerable to advertising, marketing and profiling. In addition, they are sometimes deliberately enticed with "free" games and tokens.[28] Sometimes:

> "children are ready to give away their personal data in exchange for a present illustrates the fact that children tend to consider their immediate interest rather than their long term interest. Children are not mature enough to have the skills to defend themselves against the dangers that the internet may present for privacy".[29]

Increased awareness and promotion of child safety issues online is welcome generally[30], including marketing and advertising profiling activities.

From a data protection perspective, queries arise in relation to if, and when, children are able to consent to particular online policies and terms and conditions, and then

---

22 U Munukutla-Parker, "Unsolicited Commercial Email, Privacy Concerns Relating to Social Network Services, Online Protection of Children, and Cyberbullying" (2006) (2) *I/S: A Journal of Law and Policy* 627 at 644–550.

23 *ibid*, 628.

24 Montes, *op. cit*, 513–519.

25 *ibid*.

26 A Drew, "Bully Writes 'Accomplished' on Phoebe Prince's Facebook Page on Day of Death," 2 April 2010, available at www.irishcentral.com/news/Bully-writes-accomplished-on-Phoebe-Princes-Facebook-page-on-day-of-death-89764722.html.

27 Reid, *op. cit*, 224.

28 Bartoli, *op. cit*, 35–36.

29 *ibid*, 37.

30 Groppe, *op. cit*, 242–248.

to the further collection of their preferences, activity histories, etc. What should the minimum sign-up age be for children on social networking? What responsibilities do social networks have? Should the responsibilities and the level of transparency and consent be higher for children on social networks than adults?

Children as well as adults can be the recipients of spam or unsolicited direct marketing communications. Spam or unsolicited commercial communications "refers to the dissemination of identical email advertisements to thousands or more recipients".[31] It is unsolicited, often involves and infringes data protection rights, and takes up considerable bandwidth. Children are less informed and less mature than adults. While greater care should be afforded in terms of advertising and marketing, where should the line be drawn? What should the obligations be?

These are difficult issues to address. The US Congress responded to the problem with the CAN-SPAM Act 2003, as have most US states with local legislation of one sort or another. It is enforced on a practical level by the Federal Trade Commission (FTC) and Department of Justice.[32] In Europe, the EU Data Protection Directive 1995 does not expressly refer to children. The EU data protection update Regulation does refer to children. It also remains to be seen if a recent constitutional referendum in Ireland may also affect these considerations, albeit not originally considered at the time of the referendum itself.

UK

The UK Information Commissioner (ICO) issued a good practice guide in relation to the taking of photographs in schools.[33] Social networking is not expressly addressed, but similar considerations could well be expanded or interpreted to encompass the use of social networking in and in relation to schools.

Some aspects of the above UK guide do appear to be relevant. Consider, for example, how easy it is to take photographs on a mobile telephone and post them on a social network. The guide refers to "videophones in schools" and states:

> "Schools can play a crucial role in setting out precautions for the use of MMS, audio and video recording where personal data referring to third parties are involved, without the data subjects' being aware of it. Schools should warn their students that unrestrained circulation of video recordings, audio recordings and digital pictures can result in serious infringements of the data subjects' right to privacy and personal data protection".[34]

It also states that the EU Data Protection Directive 1995 should be interpreted in line with children's rights and international children's law.[35] It concludes with the following statement:

---

31 Munukutla-Parker, *op. cit*, 627.

32 *ibid*, 629.

33 Information Commissioner, *Data Protection Good Practice Note: Taking Photographs in Schools*, 1 December 2005.

34 *Opinion 2/2009 on the Protection of Children's Personal Data (General Guidelines and the Special Case of Schools)*, Article 29 Data Protection Working Party, 398/09/EN, WP 160, Adopted on 11 February 2009 at 18.

35 *ibid*, 18–19.

> "The role of data protection authorities is four-fold: to educate and inform, especially children and authorities responsible for the well-being of young people; to influence policy makers to make the right decisions as regards children and privacy; to make controllers aware of their duties; and to use their powers against those who disregard legislation or do not adhere to codes of conduct or best practice in this area.
>
> An effective strategy, in this context, can be the formulation of agreements between DPAs, Ministries of Education and other responsible bodies, defining clear and practical terms of mutual cooperation in this area to foster the notion that data protection is a fundamental right.
>
> Children should be made aware, in particular, that they themselves must be the primary protectors of their personal data. According to this criterion, the gradual participation of children in the protection of their personal data (from consultation to decision) should be made effective. This is an area where the effectiveness of empowerment can be demonstrated".[36]

Hart discusses the UK Information Commissioner's good practice note on the collection of personal data by websites. He states:

> "The Note also deals with Web sites directed at children. It points out that Web sites that collect information from children must have stronger safeguards in place to ensure any processing is fair. Privacy notices must be appropriate to the child's level and should not exploit any lack of understanding. The language used should be clear and appropriate to the age group the Web site is aimed at. It will often be necessary to seek verifiable consent from a parent. A child is generally considered to be a person aged 16 or under, but there is a general requirement not to use information from children under 12 without first obtaining the permission of a parent or guardian. Parental consent must be verified. It will not usually be enough to ask children to confirm that their parents have agreed by using a mouse click. The ICO goes as far as to say that if parental consent is required but verifying the consent would involve a disproportionate effort then the proposed activity should not be carried out".[37]

The UK Direct Marketing Association[38] also has a Code of Practice for Commercial Communications to Children Online. While the Irish Direct Marketing Association has various separate guidelines, including in relation to data protection, email marketing, etc, there is apparently none yet dedicated to children.[39]

Ireland

The Irish Data Protection Commissioner has had to deal with complaints in relation to direct marketing to Irish school children.[40] He does not appear to have any specific guide dealing with data protection and children's social networking in relation schools. He does, however, have a guide in relation to biometrics in educational institutions.[41] There is also a special "tool" resource for schools.[42]

The Irish Data Protection Commissioner's website does state the following:

---

36 *ibid*, 20.

37 H Hart, "Collecting Personal Information Using Web Sites," *Society of Computers and Law*, 2 July 2007, available at www.scl.org/site.aspx?i=ed979.

38 At www.dma.org.uk.

39 Irish Direct Marketing Association, see guides at http://www.idma.ie/guidelines.html.

40 Case Study 10/2004, Bank of Ireland Marketing of 12 and 13 Year Old School Children, available at www.dataprotection.ie/docs/Case_study_10/04_-_Bank_of_Ireland_marketing_of_12_and_13_ye/269.htm.

41 *Biometrics in Schools, Colleges and Other Educational Institutions*, available at www.dataprotection.ie/viewdoc.asp?DocID=409&ad=1.

42 Available at www.dataprotection.ie/docs/Training_and_Public_Awareness/805.htm.

> "The data protection issues relate to consent (particularly if the person is under 14) for the processing of their information and the right of an individual to seek blocking of any personal data in relation to them that is incorrect or that was placed on the [web]site without their consent. This might be a picture of a teacher perhaps taken in a classroom context without their knowledge or factual statements that are false in relation to a person. The powers of the Office do not extend to material that is offensive, pornographic or just simply defamatory. However, such abuses require the same response on the part of the websites in question and that is an effective complaints mechanism that is appropriately staffed with trained personnel who can respond quickly to the issues raised".[43]

EU Article 29 Working Party Opinion 2/2009

Opinion 2/2009 of the EU Article 29 Working Party (WP29),[44] is one of the few official references to children and data protection. It is limited specifically to the uses of children's personal data in a school and educational setting, which it refers to as "school data".[45] One will recall that the Data Protection Directive 1995 does not explicitly refer to or acknowledge children's rights. It refers, however, to a separate EU initiative[46] from the EU Commission, *Towards an EU Strategy on the Rights of the Child.*

The Opinion also states in relation to the children's right to participate:

> "Children gradually become capable of contributing to decisions made about them. As they grow, they should participate more regularly about the exercise of their rights, including those relating to data protection.
>
> The first level of this right is the right to be consulted.
>
> This duty of consultation consists of taking into account – though not necessarily submitting to – the child's own opinions.
>
> But when children attain adequate capacity, their participation can increase, even resulting in a joint or autonomous decision.
>
> The right to participate can apply to various different matters, such as geolocation, use of children's images or others".[47]

The EU data protection regime, comprising the Data Protection Directive 1995 and ePrivacy Directive,[48] does not explicitly mention the privacy or data protection rights of the child.[49] While mentioned, it remains to be seen how this will be fully addressed in the proposed Data Protection Regulation.

In terms of fulfilling the privacy rights of children, the:

> "data protection needs of children must take into account two important aspects. These are, firstly, the varying levels of maturity which determine when children can start dealing

43 "1.6 Do Data Protection Requirements Apply to Material Placed on Social Networking Sites?," available at www.dataprotection.ie/viewdoc.asp?DocID=592.

44 *Opinion 2/2009 on the Protection of Children's Personal Data (General Guidelines and the Special Case of Schools)*, Article 29 Data Protection Working Party, 398/09/EN, WP 160, Adopted on 11 February 2009.

45 *ibid*, 2.

46 *ibid*.

47 *ibid*, 5.

48 Directive 2002/58/EC.

49 *Opinion 2/2009 on the Protection of Children's Personal Data (General Guidelines and the Special Case of Schools)*, Article 29 Data Protection Working Party, 398/09/EN, WP 160, Adopted on 11 February 2009, at 7.

> with their own data and, secondly, the extent to which representatives have the right to represent minors in cases where the disclosure of personal data would prejudice the best interests of the child. The following will deal with the question of how the existing rules of the Directive could best be applied to ensure that children's privacy is adequately and effectively protected".[50]

In terms of ensuring transparency and the right of data subjects to be informed (of data collection, data processing and the nature of the data itself), and in particular children and/or their representatives:

> "special emphasis should be put on giving layered notices based on the use of simple, concise and educational language that can be easily understood. A shorter notice should contain the basic information to be provided when collecting personal data either directly from the data subject or from a third party (Article 10 and 11). This should be accompanied by a more detailed notice, perhaps via a hyperlink, where all the relevant details are provided".[51]

These series of notices and "information must (always) be given to the legal representatives, and, after attaining adequate capacity, also to the child."[52]

However, one can envisage issues arising in relation to social networking and children's internet use. Indeed, it should be recalled that Opinion 2/2009 does not deal with social networking nor social networking of children.

The Opinion does, however, add that "[s]pecial requirements are applicable to information posted online".[53] It adds:

> "As the Working Party has noted in its recommendation about online data processing, it is fundamental for the notices to be posted at the right place and time – ie they should be shown directly on the screen, prior to collecting the information. As well as being a requirement under the Directive, this is especially important as a tool to raise children's awareness of the possible risks and dangers arising out of online activities. Indeed, it might be argued that in the online environment, unlike in the real world, this is the only opportunity for children to be apprised of such dangers".[54]

It is noted that Opinion 2/2009 is primarily in relation to the use of children's personal data *by* schools. It does not set out to address the concerns of children's social networking—whether at school, at home or elsewhere. Only subsequently does it say:

> "A special problem concerns the publication of school results on the internet, which is a convenient way of communicating them to the interested persons. The risks inherent in this mode of communication demand that access to the data should only be possible with special safeguards. This might be achieved by using a secure website, or personal passwords assigned to the legal representatives or, when they are already mature, to the children".[55]

The EU Article 19 Working Party recognises that children have a right to non-

---

[50] *ibid*, 5.
[51] *ibid*, 10.
[52] *ibid*, 10.
[53] *ibid*, 10.
[54] *ibid*, 10.
[55] *ibid*, 14.

surveillance via CCTV in the classroom (possibly [from teachers, supervisors or parents] online). It states:

> "in classrooms, where video surveillance can interfere not only with students' freedom of learning and of speech, but also with the freedom of teaching. The same applies to leisure areas, gymnasiums and dressing rooms, where surveillance can interfere with rights to privacy.
>
> These remarks are also based on the right to the development of the personality, which all children have. Indeed, their developing conception of their own freedom can become compromised if they assume from an early age that it is normal to be monitored by CCTV. This is all the more true if webcams or similar devices are used for distance monitoring of children during school time".[56]

In relation to school websites, it states:

> "A growing number of schools create websites targeted at students/pupils and their families, and those websites become the main tool for external communications. Schools should be aware that disseminating personal information warrants more stringent observance of fundamental data protection principles, in particular data minimisation and proportionality; additionally, it is recommended that restricted access mechanisms are implemented with a view to safeguarding the personal information in question (eg login via user ID and password)".[57]

In a related section dealing with children's photographs, it states:

> "Schools are often tempted to publish (in the press or on the internet) photos of their pupils. Special attention should be drawn to the publishing by schools of photos of their pupils on the internet. An evaluation should always be made of the kind of photo, the relevance of posting it, and its intended purpose. Children and their legal representatives should be made aware of the publication.
>
> If the school intends to post individual photographs of identified children, prior consent from parents or other legal representatives (or from the child, if already mature) should be obtained.
>
> In the case of collective photos, namely of schools events, and always in accordance with national legislation, schools might not require prior consent from the parents where the photographs do not permit easy identification of pupils. Nevertheless, in such cases schools must inform children, parents and legal representatives that the photograph is going to be taken and how it will be used.
>
> This will give them the opportunity to refuse to be included in the photograph".[58]

Children's social networking both in the school environment and generally can be considered further, particularly in light of recent tragic events.

Children: Consent and EU Article 29 Working Party Opinion 2/2010

The EU Article 29 Working Party refers to consent in relation to children, social networking and behavioural advertising. Its Opinion states:

> "Informed consent: children
> In Opinion 2/2009 the EU Article 29 Working Party has addressed the protection of personal data of children. The problems related to obtaining informed consent are further emphasized as far as children are concerned. In addition to the requirements described above (and below)

---

56 *ibid*, 16.
57 *ibid*, 17.
58 *ibid*, 17.

for consent to be valid, in some cases children's consent must be provided by their parents or other legal representatives. In the case in point this means that ad network providers would need to provide notice to parents about the collection and the use of children's information and obtain their consent before collecting and further using their information for the purposes of engaging in behavioural targeting of children.

In the light of the above and also taking into account the vulnerability of children, the EU Article 29 Working Party is of the view that ad network providers should not offer interest categories intended to serve behavioural advertising or influence children".[59]

Children: EU Article 29 Working Party Opinion 5/2009

The EU Article 29 Working Party Opinion 5/2009 on Online Social Networking refers to children, minors and social networking. It sets out the environmental context and the options available. It states:

"A large proportion of SNS services [social networking services] are utilised by children/minors. The Working Party's Opinion WP147 focused on the application of data protection principles in the school and educational environment. The Opinion emphasised the need for taking into account the best interest of the child as also set out in the UN Convention on the Rights of the Child. The Working Party wishes to stress the importance of this principle also in the context of SNS.

Some interesting initiatives have been undertaken by Data Protection Authorities world wide which focus mostly on awareness-raising regarding SNS and possible risks. The Working Party encourages further research on how to address the difficulties surrounding adequate age verification and proof of informed consent in order to better address these challenges.

Based on the considerations made so far, the Working Party believes that a multi-pronged strategy would be appropriate to address the protection of children's data in the SNS context. Such a strategy might be based on:

- awareness raising initiatives, which are fundamental to ensure the active involvement of children (via schools, the inclusion of DP-basics in educational curricula, the creation of ad-hoc educational tools, the collaboration of national competent bodies);
- fair and lawful processing with regard to minors such as not asking for sensitive data in the subscription forms, no direct marketing aimed specifically at minors, the prior consent of parents before subscribing, and suitable degrees of logical separation between the communities of children and adults;
- implementation of Privacy Enhancing Technologies (PETs) – eg privacy-friendly settings by default, pop-up warning boxes at appropriate steps, age verification software);
- self-regulation by providers, to encourage the adoption of codes of practice that should be equipped with effective enforcement measures, also disciplinary in nature;
- if necessary, ad-hoc legislative measures to discourage unfair and/or deceptive practices in the SNS context".[60]

Children: Problems with the EU Data Protection Directive 1995

There is no express reference to children in the EU Data Protection Directive 1995. It is as if children were not even in contemplation when the main EU data protection measure was being drafted. Commenting in relation to the prior information and

[59] *Opinion 2/2010 on Online Behavioural Advertising*, Article 29 Data Protection Working Party, WP 171, Adopted on 22 June 2010.

[60] *Opinion 5/2009 on Online Social Networking*, Article 29 Data Protection Working Party, 01189/09EN, WP 163. Adopted on 12 June 2009, at 11–12.

consent requirements specified in the EU Data Protection Directive 1995,[61] it has been queried:

> "[How] are children expected to understand the likely implications for them of providing their data? How can they judge whether the data collection process is in their best interests? To this extent the requirement to inform websites' users before collecting any personal data is not relevant as it stands if applied to children's personal data. It should at least be specified that web users are to inform their users in terms understandable by any class of age".[62]

One of the rights provided in Article 12 of the EU Data Protection Directive 1995 is a right of access to the data subject to the data held by the data controller (eg websites) in relation to them. This should also apply equally to children. However, is this access right given to the child directly or to their parent?[63] Or indeed a guardian? A further complication is the line and balance between a child's privacy rights in relation to his or her parent.[64] Can children have an overriding interest as and above that of the parents in the details of their online activities, including their personal data held by social networks?

Also, with spyware (filtering/monitoring) software being installed by parents on the computer devices being used by their children, the issue of free speech, children's rights, children's' privacy and data protection rights and proportionality will need to be considered. Consider, for example, whether it may be more proportionate for a parent to ensure that a child uses a laptop, for example, only while in the kitchen or living room, as opposed to installing spyware monitoring software if he or she were to be permitted to use the laptop in the bedroom unsupervised. Which is more proportionate? Is installing blocking and filtering software (and availing of device and internet browser settings), a more graduated and proportionate response? Is one to be preferred under the data protection regime? It is also queried how effective the provisions in relation to unsolicited commercial communications are as regards children. "[H]ow can one expect [that] a child [is] mature enough to [understand and] request ... not to have his/her personal data used to receive unsolicited mail?"[65] If children decide to assert or claim rights, there is clearly potential for some difficult court litigation.

EU Commission: No Children in Data Protection

The EU Commission recognises the threats and issues raised by children's social networking and has stated that it will "consider ... introducing specific obligations for data controllers on the type of information to be provided and on the modalities for providing it, including in relation to children."[66] It will also consider introducing

---

61 Directive 95/46/EC of the European Parliament and of the Council of 24 October 1995 on the protection of individuals with regard to the processing of personal data and on the free movement of such data.

62 Bartoli, *op. cit*, 40.

63 *ibid.*

64 *ibid*, 40–41.

65 *ibid*, 41.

66 Communications from the Commission to the European Parliament, the Council, the Economic and Social Committee of the Regions, A Comprehensive Approach on Personal Data Protection in the European Union, 4 November 2010, COM (2010) 609 Final, 6.

standard data protection notification forms for data controllers and also a framework for breach notifications.[67]

One of the proposals in the data protection Regulation is to allow the EU Commission to specify and introduce specific measures or detailed acts pursuant to the Regulation, once passed.

There are, however, other measures to consider. The Lisbon Treaty expressly recognises children's rights in Article 2.3. The EU Charter also refers to the protection of children's data.[68] The 1981 Council of Europe Convention Concerning the Processing of Personal Data refers to children's data privacy concerns. The Council of Europe Convention on Cybercrime 2001 incorporates a criminal offence in relation to the production of child pornography.[69] In addition, the EU Framework Decision on combating the sexual exploitation of children and child pornography 2004 creates offences in relation to child pornography.[70] It has been indicated that this decision also attaches liability to websites "who directly allow sexually explicit material to be made available to young persons".[71] Corporate liability can also arise under the above Convention.[72] We also wait to see how the constitutional referendum dealing with constitutional children's rights in Ireland may also effect these issues.

US Responses to Children

One study, which was commissioned in advance of the Children's Online Privacy Protection Act 1998 (COPPA), suggested that of the 212 websites targeted at children which were examined, 89 percent gathered children's personal data; 12 percent notified parents of their data collection activities; and the majority disclosed personal data obtained to third parties.[73] There does not appear to be equivalent research here.

The first US effort to deal with these concerns was the Communications Decency Act 1996 (CDA).[74] This was held, however, to be an overbroad infringement of free-speech rights in the case *Reno v ACLU*.[75] The balancing of competing constitutional rights, even in Ireland, is always a difficult exercise.

The second US effort in relation to this area was the COPPA. The Child Pornography Prevention Act 1996 (CPPA) was also enacted, although the Supreme Court held that it too was overly broad.[76]

---

67 *ibid*, 6–7

68 Article 24 of the EU Charter of Fundamental Rights of the European Union provides that a child's best interests must be a primary consideration and that children shall have the right to such protection and may express their views freely.

69 Referred to in Reid, *op. cit*, 218.

70 Framework Decision 2004/68 on combating the sexual exploitation of children and child pornography [2004] OJ L13/44. Referred to *ibid*. This may even be updated under proposals made by the Commission, see *ibid*, 220.

71 Reid, *op. cit*, 218

72 Article 26. Referred to *ibid*, 219.

73 *Privacy: A Report to Congress*, Federal Trade Commission, June 1998, available at http://www.ftc.gov/reports/privacy3/priv-23c.pdf. Referred to in Bartoli, *op. cit*, 37.

74 Groppe, *op. cit*, 229.

75 *Reno v ACLU* 521 US 844 (1997), referred to in Groppe, *op. cit*, 229.

76 See *Ashcroft v Free Speech Coalition* 535 US 234, 240 (2002), referred to in Groppe, *op. cit*,

The US Children's Internet Protection Act 2000 requires schools and libraries to install pornography-filtering software.[77] Liberties groups have raised free-speech concerns in relation to many library restrictions.

The US Adam Walsh Child Protection and Safety Act 2006 provides for a public national register of sex offenders.[78] John McCain also proposed legislation enhancing reporting obligations on websites.[79]

The COPPA, and the rules established by the FTC pursuant to it, make clear that they apply to websites targeting children.[80] The factors that will assist in determining this include:

- the website subject matter;
- the audio or visual content on the website;
- the age of models on the website;
- the website language;
- whether there is advertising on the website;
- other empirical evidence relating to the age of actual or intended users, including the use of animated characters or child-orientated features.[81]

The COPPA rules also set the age threshold for children at 13. However, one commentator questions the plausibility of websites being able to know and verify this in practice.[82] A further difficulty raised is the importance of whether the website must be targeted solely at children under 13.[83] What happens if there is a mixed-age audience? There may also be so-called general websites, which do not target children but which have users who are children.[84] Children may also provide false information, including a false age.[85] This is a difficult practical issue.

One commentator states in the context of COPPA that "research indicates that children are willing to trade away personal information for speculative reasons—for instance in order to win a prize or to enter a contest. This suggests that many young people do not care about privacy."[86]

The US federal approaches seek to restrict the download of inappropriate content for children as well as the uploading of impermissible material by children.[87] There have been at least two state efforts to establish "controversial" registers of children's email addresses.[88]

220.

77 Groppe, *op. cit*, 224–225 and 231–233.

78 *ibid*, 235–236.

79 The Stop the Online Exploitation of Our Children Act 2006, referred to in Groppe, *op. cit*, 236.

80 Bartoli, *op. cit*, 37–38.

81 *ibid*, 38.

82 *ibid*, 38.

83 *ibid*, 38.

84 *ibid*, 38–39.

85 *ibid*, 38.

86 *ibid*, 39.

87 Munukutla-Parker, *op. cit*, 641.

88 Referred to *ibid*, 641.

There are also a number of local state laws in the US, apart from federal initiatives. An example is a law in New York, the Electronic Security and Targeting of Online Predators Act (eSTOP Act), which seeks to oblige registered sex offenders to also register all of their email accounts and identifiers, including social networking details, with the New York State Division of Criminal Justice.[89] Then these details will be passed to social networking websites to screen, block and remove them from these websites.[90] It remains to be seen how these measures may deal with constitutional challenges.

Children and Commercial Matter

There is other potentially relevant legislation that can affect what commercial matters and transactions children might engage with. One example is the Unfair Commercial Practices Directive.[91] Commenting on the Directive, Reid states:

> "[i]n the case of vulnerable consumers, the threshold at which a practice becomes unfair is significantly lower than that for the average consumer, thus it is essential that not only is significant information about the products and services offered to the young person but that that information is as clear, accessible and understandable as possible. Information provided to young children must be communicated to them in easy to read, comprehensible language, rather than in small print legalese, to enable these rights to be meaningful and indeed to avoid legal action".[92]

UN Convention on Children

The UN Convention on the Rights of the Child[93] sets out special protection and entitlements in relation to children. Article 1 of the Convention states that a child is someone under the age of 18, as do "most relevant international instruments".[94] The most fundamental interests in relation to children and children's rights include:

- the best interests of the child;
- protection and care necessary for the wellbeing of the child;
- privacy rights and interests;
- representation;
- balancing privacy and best interests of the child;
- adapting to the degree of maturity of the child; and
- the right to participate.[95]

In relation to privacy, it refers to the right of a child as a human being to have privacy, and in particular Article 16 of the UN Convention on the Rights of the Child provides that no child shall be subject to arbitrary or unlawful interference

89 M Morrissey, "Legislative Update: Banning Sex Offenders from Using Social Networking Websites" (2008) (28) *Children's Legal Rights Journal* 89 at 90.

90 *ibid.*

91 See also Reid, *op. cit*, 224.

92 Generally, see comments of Reid, *op. cit*, 225.

93 Convention on the Rights of the Child, United Nations, adopted General Assembly Resolution 44/25 on 20 November 1989. Referred to in Bartoli, *op. cit*, 37.

94 *Opinion 2/2009 on the Protection of Children's Personal Data (General Guidelines and the Special Case of Schools)*, Article 29 Data Protection Working Party, 398/09/EN, WP 160, Adopted on 11 February 2009, at 3, and references therein.

95 *ibid*, 4–7.

with his or her privacy, family, home or correspondence, nor to unlawful attacks on his or her honour and reputation. We await how the constitutional referendum developments regarding children in Ireland may be interpreted in the internet arena.

Hotlines

The solutions to deal with these concerns can be legal but they can also involve forms of self-regulation and co-regulation. Examples include internet hotlines. Inhope, for example, promotes internet hotlines so that people can alert appropriate agencies and complain when they are concerned in relation to particular online material aimed at or relating to children.[96]

Technology solutions also exist, such as forms of filtering and blocking technology. Software keyword filtering systems block or raise alerts for particular content. There is no fail-safe solution, however. Filtering technologies, etc are not without their own issues. They can be subject to errors and false positives. They are sometimes criticised in that they unjustly interfere with normal commercial activities.[97] Legal issues also surround the competing legal rights. Notwithstanding that, the EU Safer Internet programme 2009–2013 calls for the use of more filtering technologies.[98]

Spyware and its compliance with the data protection regime when used in relation to children, as well as any future enumerated children's constitutional rights, have yet to be fully considered.

Self-regulation by industry is reported to have a number of successes, such as the MySpace software reporting application Zephyr[99] and the Sentinel Safe software, which bans sex offenders from the website.[100] The issue of banning convicted sex offenders is gaining popularity in certain quarters in the US. A question arises as to whether social networking and related websites can act to ban convicted or (certain) registered sex offenders only once mandated or required to do so by a specific law or court order. Can industry access and act on registered sex offender lists voluntarily? Can they be mandated to? Under what circumstances can they access registered sex offender lists? As the concepts of internet rights and rights of access to the internet increasingly come to the fore, to what extent will defendant or convicted persons' rights of access to the internet have to be balanced against other competing rights?

Age Verification

One of the proposed solutions refers to chat and discussion board moderation. This involves people actually examining and vetting the content of communications online. Another solution involves developing age-verification software.[101] However, there are issues with proposed suggestions for children's age-verification systems. While adults (and students) can verify their age, it is quite difficult for a child to

---

96 See www.inhope.org.
97 Munukutla-Parker, *op. cit*, 221.
98 Referred to *ibid*.
99 See Groppe, *op. cit*, 237–240.
100 *ibid*, 239.
101 *ibid*, 221.

prove their age.[102] Other alternatives are design related, for example, having children pass a series of knowledge questions online.[103]

There have been unsuccessful attempts to force social networks to implement age-verification systems.[104] However, the Communications Decency Act 1996 in the US affords some protection to these websites by providing defences for third-party materials.

Age and Website Rules/Settings

Both Facebook and MySpace have minimum age restrictions of 13.[105] However, there are significant numbers of underage users of social networks generally.[106]

MySpace is reported as requiring a click agreement from users that they are at least 14 years old.[107] There have also been calls to have stricter default privacy setting for those under 16 years of age.[108] Subsequent protections were introduced whereby an adult must be able to provide details of person under 16 before being able to contact them and must already be that person's friend on MySpace.[109] That is, there must be some prior context or connection.

Age and Technology Solutions

Some might suggest that any solution involving technology should be the least expensive.[110] Various website access options can be triggered once a person keys in his or her date of birth. These can include blocking access or guiding the child through a course on safety awareness.[111] Of course this on its own does not deal with people keying in a false age. However, tests and questions can also be added on to help limit underage applicants for particular services.

Self-Regulation/Soft Law

One avenue to consider is "soft law" or regulation, which can involve a number of potential avenues.[112] An example is the UK Direct Marketing Association (DMA) Code of Practice for Commercial Communications to Children Online. Ireland also has the Irish Direct Marketing Association.[113]

---

102 Stedman, *op. cit*, 394–395.
103 *ibid*, 395.
104 See for example MD Martin and CV Popov, "*Doe v MySpace*: Liability for Third Party Content on Social Networking Sites" (Spring 2007) *Communications Law* at 3, referred to in Nelson *et al.*, *op. cit*, 24. See also, F Gilbert, "Age Verification as a Shield for Minors on the Internet: A Quixotic Search?" (2008) *Shilder Journal of Law Communications & Technology* 6.
105 Nelson, *et al.*, *op. cit*, 24.
106 *ibid*.
107 See Stedman, *op. cit*, 369–371, and references therein.
108 *ibid*, 369–371 and references therein.
109 *ibid*, 371.
110 *ibid*, 397.
111 See *ibid*, 395.
112 Bartoli, *op. cit*, 35.
113 Irish Direct Marketing Association, see http://www.idma.ie/.

Another solution relates to attempts to label and categorise children's content centrally, for example under the umbrella of a central generic descriptive .kid domain name.[114]

In 2009 MySpace removed 90,000 registered sex offenders from its website.[115] This is an example of websites banning or restricting access. This is clearly one possible solution. However, a number of legal as well as practical issues arise. For example, there is the increasing prospect of competing rights being litigated with the arrival of the concept of a human right of access to the internet. Free-speech issues also arise.

The US has a number of (proposed or enacted) laws which seek directly or indirectly to deal with online sexual predators, eg tort law; the Communications Decency Act 1996; the Child Online Protection Act (COPA) 1998; the Deleting Online Predators Act 2007; and state laws.[116] It has been argued that self-regulation is a better option.[117] Possibly, it may be that hard law and soft law are needed in conjunction.

Regulation/Liability

Can and should social networks be liable for third-party content? How do intermediary defences interact with privacy and data protection? There is insufficient research of this issue.

In *Doe v MySpace*[118] the plaintiff mother failed in claiming that MySpace was negligent in not preventing the communications of sexual predators. The court upheld the Communications Decency Act (CDA) immunities[119] and ruled that no duty towards users arose.[120] One court stated that imposing "a duty under these circumstances for MySpace to confirm or determine the age of each applicant, with liability resulting from negligence in performing or not performing that duty, would of course stop MySpace's business in its tracks and close this avenue of communication".[121] The CDA exemptions were also upheld in a case where the plaintiff complained of being introduced to an underage person.[122] Section 30 of the CDA protects the social networks in terms of the defamatory statements of their users. In the case of a prank which went wrong and resulted in death threats, the victim unsuccessfully sued AOL for not taking the prank material down when notified.[123]

There is, however, increasing adverse publicity and pressure on social networks to

---

114 Reid, *op. cit*, 223–224.
115 Montes, *op. cit*, 513.
116 Referred to in van der Heide, "Social Networking and Sexual Predators: The Case for Self-Regulation" (2008–2009) (31) *Hastings Communications & Entertainment Law Journal* 173 at 179–186.
117 *ibid*, 187–191.
118 *Doe v MySpace Inc* 528 F.3d 413, 416 (5th Circuit 2008), referred to in Nelson *et al.*, *op. cit*, 24.
119 *Doe v MySpace Inc* at 420.
120 *Doe v MySpace Inc* 474 F Supp 2d 843, 850–852 (WD Texas 2007), referred to in Nelson *et al.*, *op. cit*, 25.
121 *Doe v MySpace Inc* at 851, as referred to in Nelson *et al.*, *op. cit*, 25.
122 *Doe v Sexsearch.com* 502 F Supp 2d 719, 722 (ND Ohio 2007) 724.
123 Nelson *et al.*, *op. cit*, 25.

be more proactive.[124] We now see that there can also be indirect pressure applied to advertisers. One law in Illinois, for example, bans registered sex offenders from using social networks.[125] It remains to be seen whether such laws will withstand constitutional challenges.

Child Education and Awareness

There is increasing awareness of the importance of informing and educating children in relation to internet and social networking issues. In Ireland, education workshop talks are organised for children in schools in relation to internet safety and internet risks.[126] At an EU level, a report was published on 18 April 2011 in relation to children's social networking issues and dangers, *Social Networking, Age and Privacy*, which compared comparative research issues across 25.[127] It refers to some of the risks of social networking for children, including pornography and sexual images,[128] bullying,[129] "sexting,"[130] meeting contacts offline,[131] sending and or receiving sexual images and content,[132] potentially harmful user-generated content (UGC),[133] and misuse of personal data.[134]

The Parent Gap

One of the problems for many parents is that they are not technology aware and, therefore, are not in a position to assess for themselves the risks that face their children online. This has been referred to as the "generational divide".[135] Frequently, parents are not aware of children's (and teenagers') online activities.[136] Parents need to take responsibility in terms of becoming aware of what their children are doing and the technology they are using. However, part of this educational role must also rest with policy makers in assisting and educating parents. Parents must be assisted in keeping or becoming connected.[137]

---

124 *ibid*, 26.

125 HR 1314, 96th General Assembly, Reg Sessions (Illinois 2009) available at www.ilga.gov/legislation/96/HB/09600HB131enr.ht, referred to in Nelson *et al.*, *op. cit*, 26.

126 See "Safer Internet Day: Talks in Schools," National Centre for Technology in Education, available at http://ncte.ie/, referring to workshops organised for 2011.

127 Livingston *et al.*, *op. cit*. The report is substantial. See reference at Social Networking, Age and Privacy, referred to in EU Kids Online, available at www2.lse.ac.uk/media@lse/research/EUKidsOnline/Home.aspx. See also www.eukidsonline.net.

128 *ibid*, 6, 49 *et seq*.

129 *ibid*, 6, 61 *et seq*.

130 *ibid*, 7.

131 *ibid*, 7, 85 *et seq*.

132 *ibid*, 73 *et seq*.

133 *ibid*, 97–99.

134 *ibid*, at 99.

135 Bartoli, *op. cit*, 36.

136 See, for example, Press Release, "New Study Reveals 14% of Teens Have Had Face-to-Face Meetings With People They've Met on the Internet," National Centre for Missing & Exploited Children (11 May 2006) at http://us.missingkids.com/missingkids/servlet/NewsEventServlet?LanguageCountry=en_US&PageId=2383, referred to in Stedman, *op. cit*, 373.

137 See generally K Bielenberg, "Why Parents Must Stay Connected to their Children" *Irish Independent* 31 August 2013.

Child Development/Child Rights

It has been suggested that the number of underage users of social networking provides not just legal issues for social networks, but also moral issues.[138]

There are also other issues to consider when we contemplate child protection and children's rights. One of these is the issue of how society should protect children's privacy but without adversely affecting or curtailing their development and learning.[139] What free speech and privacy rights do children possess, and against whom may these rights be enforced?[140] Do children's rights of free speech exist, and do children shed these rights when they go online?[141] These developing concerns are difficult and complex issues.

Child Criminals

We often think of those who are infringing privacy and data protection as adults hacking, spamming or seeking to promote their sexual intentions, or as organisations, some of which are legitimate but lean a little too much in favour of direct marketing and advertising. However, we infrequently consider that children can commit crimes[142] and acts of infringement too. Children can be victims and perpetrators.[143] These can include a whole variety of activities that can impinge on social networking, privacy and data protection.[144] This area gets infrequent attention in the literature and deserves further research. Most laws also fail to differentiate between adult and child perpetrators.[145] However, the nature of social networking and its increasing popularity with children and young persons will most likely mean that there will be increasing instances of non-adults engaging in activity, such as making, posting or distributing material that on its face offends a specific law. Currently, most laws "fail to adequately protect juveniles from the harsh penalties".[146]

Children and Defamation

There are already instances where both the parents and the child who made alleged defamatory comments have been sued.[147]

---

138 Nelson *et al.*, *op. cit*, 24.

139 Bartoli, *op. cit*, 35.

140 IG Cram "'Minors' Privacy and Freedom of Expression" in *Yearbook of Media and Entertainment Law* (Oxford University Press, Oxford, 1997), 31–52.

141 V Lei, "Students' Free Speech Rights Shed at the Cyber Gate" (2009–2010) *Richmond Journal of Law & Technology* 1.

142 CA Lee, "When Children Prey on Children: A Look at Hawai'i Version of Megan's Law and Its Application to Juvenile Sex Offenders" (Summer/Fall 1998) (1) *University of Hawai'i Law Review* 477.

143 JL Barry, "The Child as Victim and Perpetrators: Laws Punishing Juvenile 'Sexting'" (2010–2011) *Vandenberg Journal of Entertainment & Technology Law* 129.

144 In relation to state paternal roles, see, for example, EF Emens, "Intimate Discrimination: The State's Role in the Accidents of Sex and Love" (March, 2009)(122) *Harvard Law Review* 1307.

145 Barry, *op. cit*, 129.

146 *ibid*, 129.

147 See references at KM Gurney, "MySpace, Your Reputation: A Call to Change Libel Laws for Juveniles Using Social Networking Sites" (2009) (82) *Temple Law Review* 241 at 257. One example is *Draker v Schreiber* 271 SW3d 318 (Texas App 2998).

There have also been calls for specific amendments to defamation laws to provide a defence for defamatory statements made by children and juveniles. Such liability could follow them for the rest of their lives.[148] In addition, it is argued that younger people speak in a parlance that is not properly understood by adults[149] and is easily misunderstood by adults,[150] which needs to be acknowledged in defamation law. On this topic, Gurney writes:

> "Woefully out-of-date defamation law needs to be fundamentally remodelled for an internet world where social networking [web]sites dominate other online outlets, including blogs. True reform requires careful consideration of the variety of online speakers as well as their subjects, and of defamation defendants in addition to plaintiffs. Thoughtful change, rather than a quick fix like § 230, will require time.
>
> But the problem of juveniles' activities on social networking [web]sites simply cannot wait, as evidenced by the spike in defamation and student speech lawsuits. Teenagers may receive harsh discipline at school for their online speech, and be punished again when the same teachers and school administrators file lawsuits against them. Recent Supreme Court cases authorize, and even encourage, school officials to maximize their oversight of student speech that occurs either on or off campus by minimizing these students' First Amendment rights. Reading this line of Supreme Court precedent in tandem with the Court's much older defamation cases produces a clear call to change the way juveniles are treated in libel lawsuits: Because these students have fewer free speech rights than adults, it is unfair to hold them equally responsible for their speech in a court of law. Out of deference to the Court's direction as well as solicitude for immature teenagers facing dual punishments, judges should implement some simple solutions familiar to the rest of defamation and tort law while awaiting more comprehensive legislative action."[151]

Also:

> "the unique characteristics of social networking [web]sites and individuals' behavior there demand a different legal standard in defamation cases. Interactions on the [web]sites are casual and smack more of a spur-of-the-moment conversation than thoughtful prose.[302] Social networking culture puts a premium on witty, almost boastful, repartee—not accuracy or sensitivity.[303] As Daniel Solove wrote in *The Future of Reputation,* in a passage on blogging that is particularly applicable to social networking [web]sites:
>
> > One of the main differences between blogs and mainstream media publications is style. Blog posts are edgy, not polished and buffed into the typical prefabricated write-by-the-numbers stock that often gets produced by the mainstream media. Discourse on the internet is pungent. In many respects, this is a virtue .... But blog posts are created with no editors and published with no time delays. There's little time to cool down before sounding off. Just click the Publish button and unleash it to the world .... It goes without saying that this is a recipe for some problems.
>
> The law also needs to consider that readers do not expect the level of care from an obviously juvenile profile on a social networking [web]site as they do from the *New York Times.* Although the accuracy of postings on social networking [web]sites may be questionable, and defamatory content therefore more likely, readers are also less apt to believe what they see there, reducing reputational damage. As Glenn Reynolds suggested, '[t]he blogosphere ... is a low-trust culture. ... Newspapers, on the other hand, used to operating in a higher-trust environment, more commonly require readers to take their word regarding factual assertions.' Courts should account for the fact that even though content on a social

---

148 Gurney, *op. cit*, 241.

149 D Boyd, "Why Youth (Heart) Social Network Sites: The Role of Networked Publics in Teenage Social Life" in D Buckingham, *Youth, Identity and Digital Media* (Chambridge, Mass., 2008) 119 at 134. Referred to in Gurney, *op. cit*, 244.

150 Gurney, *op. cit*, 247.

151 Gurney, *op. cit*, 267–268.

> networking [web]site might be defamatory, libel law's framework for awarding damages based on limited evidence of injury is inappropriate."[152]

However, if there is reduced defamatory responsibility for children and or juveniles, might there also be reduced levels of free speech rights for children?[153] Rights and balancing of rights are an issue to be fully considered.

Many argue in favour of net neutrality, especially in relation to free speech online.[154]

However, a school student who posted a false profile and comments about the school principal and was suspended was unsuccessful in arguing that the activity was out of school, that it did not disrupt the school and that his *suspension* was unconstitutional.[155] Nelson comments:

> "The decision to post inappropriate comments is likely tied to the false sense of privacy a user believes to be attached to social networking, whether from perceived anonymity or the fact that the individual is communicating with a machine rather than a person. Thus, the rule of thumb, think through each posting and its possible legal implications before posting".[156]

Spyware

Spyware is a form of software program whose functionality allows an individual to monitor and see what activities individuals are undertaking on their computers. It is required to be installed on an individual's computer. Spyware is often recommended as a solution for parents concerned about the risks that their children or teenagers may encounter online.

However, if the software is limited to monitoring, by definition it means that the child is not actually protected in the sense of perceived bad websites being blocked. Equally, the same arises in terms of online solicitation and inappropriate pop-up ads, websites, online services, etc. None of these are precluded from being seen or accessed by the child. The risks remain. However, if parents in subsequently reviewing what their child has been doing see something they disapprove of, they can caution, reprimand or ban the child as they deem appropriate. They may also seek to use filtering or blocking technology to prevent access to or from certain websites, which could include (certain) social networks. These later solutions are not fool-proof, however, for a tech-savvy teenager. There can frequently be ways to get around such additional technical solutions.[157]

As noted elsewhere, the growing literature in relation to children's rights, free speech

---

[152] *ibid*, 273.

[153] *ibid*, 268–269. Other organisations, such as CBS, NBC, Universal, BMG and Warner Music, embrace YouTube and upload content, even receiving increased ratings; see *Zeran v America Online Inc* 129 F3d 327, 330–335 (4th Circuit 1997).

[154] JL Newman, "Keeping the Internet Neutral: Net Neutrality and Its Role in Protecting Political Expression on the Internet" (2008) (31) *Hastings Communications & Entertainment Law Journal* 153.

[155] See *JS v Blue Mountain School District No 3:07CV585*, 2008 WL 4279517 (MD Pa, 11 September 2008).

[156] Nelson, *et al*., *op. cit*, 31.

[157] One example being using proxys or third-party sites to access indirectly the websites that may be blocked directly.

and potential rights of access to the internet may mean that ultimately there may be countering arguments and rights to be balanced against a parent's intention to install spyware monitoring and surveillance software. One could conceivably have a situation where data protection rules are bolstered by these "new" rights, making it more difficult for parents to seek to restrict or monitor children's access to the internet, websites and or social networking.

REFERENDUM

Recently children have been expressly recognised as having rights under the Irish Constitution. While there was a lot of discussion at the time, there was an absence of any discussion of the effect of such amendment and the issue of children using social networks and related websites. Neither was there discussion of these new children's rights as regards children and content and online abuse on social networks and related websites. This is potentially a rich and fruitful area for research, discussion and literature.

CRIMINAL OFFENCE OF CYBERBULLYING

The Sixth Report of the Special Rapporteur on Child Protection, A Report Submitted to the Oireachtas[158] by the Special Rapporteur Dr. Geoffrey Shannon recommends that cyberbullying be a criminal offence. The report highlights the advent of online abuse, as well as such issues as the possibility of anonymous reporting by victims. It states:

> "The impact and effect of bullying on children has been tragically thrown into the media spotlight ... Whilst bullying has always been an unfortunate aspect of our society, the growth of 'Cyber-bullying' has almost overnight created a readily accessible forum for bullies to target children with little or no regulation or sanction. The Irish legal system has been somewhat taken unawares as to the manner and means through which children have fallen victim to cyber-bullying. Whilst there are some legislative provisions in being that might be interpreted in such a manner as to tackle this growing problem, a focused response is required."[159]

It adds:

> "However, in order for a system of legal recourse to be effective victims of such bullying need to be able to feel that they can come forward and express their concerns without fear of retribution. Thus, provision also needs to be made for the protection of child victims of such behaviour, eg the means of retaining their anonymity when making a complaint as to such bullying."[160]

The report also highlights the issue of potential liability for schools and educational organisations for online abuse, etc. It states that the "extent of a school's liability

---

158 G Shannon, *Sixth Report of the Special Rapporteur on Child Protection, A Report Submitted to the Oireachtas*, (Dublin, 23 January 2013).

159 *ibid*, 9.

160 *ibid*, 9.

arising from an incident of bullying between students is a topic of some considerable debate and one that has been thrown into the fore in recent months."[161]

It notes recent guidelines published in Ireland for schools, but cautions that "in the era of online technology and cyber-bullying a new focus must be brought to bear on this issue. Lessons can be learnt from the developments in New South Wales and Massachusetts in attempting to set a legislative basis to tackle this problem in schools."[162]

The Recommendations refer to "Cyber-bullying as a Criminal Offence." It states:

> "On review of reported cases of harassment involving social networking, email and SMS, there appear to be very few criminal prosecutions taken for this type of harassment under the Non-Fatal Offences Against the Person Act, 1997 despite the suitability of that Act. When cyber-bullying is being described as an epidemic, we need to examine why this is the case. Specifically, is there reticence to investigate complaints of cyber-bullying?
>
> Responding to calls for new criminal legislation to tackle cyber-bullying, the Minister for Justice identified our existing laws against harassment as being suitable. However, the Minister has directed the Law Reform Commission to examine difficulties in prosecuting for cyber-bullying and, in particular, the necessity to show persistence in the harassment.
>
> Existing laws regarding harassment can be used to incorporate cyber-bullying incidents. A review of the Post Office (Amendment) Acts should be undertaken with a view to incorporating emerging means of cyber-bullying."[163]

Anonymity for victims of online abuse or at least cyberbulling online abuse is favoured. The Recommendations continue as follows:

> "The current Irish legal position would appear to suggest that an application for anonymity in the context of cyber-bullying litigation would be unsuccessful. However, it is difficult to be definitive in respect of the legal position because Mr Justice Peart's decision in *McKeogh v John Doe* may well have been different if the applicant had been a child or teenager seeking to rely on the right to privacy of children, and able to invoke the general social interest in protection of children from cyber-bullying. The ideal solution would be an agreement of co-operation to be entered into between ISPs (and potentially other entities such as Facebook) and the Gardaí to provide IP addresses where complaints of cyber-bullying have been received."[164]

Single Body to Oversee Social Networking

The Irish Oireachtas Joint Committee on Transport and Communications which held parliamentary hearings and submissions during 2013 *inter alia* in relation to online abuse and cyberbullying, has recommended that a single body should be given responsibility for co-ordinating the regulation of social media content.[165]

Paul C Dwyer of the National Anti-Bullying Coalition told the Committee that just

---

161 *ibid*, 9.
162 *ibid*, 9.
163 *ibid*, 20.
164 *ibid*, 20.
165 Oireachtas Joint Committee on Transport and Communications, *Houses of the Oireachtas, Joint Committee on Transport and Communications Report Addressing the Growth of Social Media and Tackling Cyberbullying*, (Government Publications: Dublin, 18 July 2013).

one social network provider received some 100,000 reports or requests per day but dedicated just 90 staff to process such requests.[166] The Committee and the Report recommends that the online abuse report data be furnished by the social networks to the Irish Data Protection Commissioner.[167]

In Recommendation 3, the Committee supports the recommendation contained in the Action Plan on Bullying that the definition of bullying in the new national procedures for schools should include a specific reference to cyberbullying. Also, guidelines for cyberbullying should be put in place, so that school principals dealing with instances of cyberbullying have a clear protocol to follow.[168]

Recommendation 4 refers to employers. It states that employers be made aware of the importance of introducing a social media policy, ie outlining what constitutes cyberbullying and what actions will be taken if there is a breach of such a policy.[169] Employers should be aware that cyberbullying falls under "harassment" and Section 10 of the Non-fatal Offences Against the Person Act 1997 may apply in such cases.[170]

Recommendation 6 states as follows:

> "The Committee recommends that a single body be given responsibility for co-ordinating the regulation of social media content. Funding and organisational models for this agency should be agreed with the industry. It is noted that other examples of industry-led partnerships between stakeholders and government have been established in other sectors in recent years."[171]

Conclusion

The issue of children's use of social networks (and other website services) is at the forefront of concerns regarding safety and regard for the personal details of children. This is not just a single neat issue and involves quite a number of problems and concerns, some of which are new and developing. Indeed, social networking is not that old itself. It is also the case that there is no one solution to these concerns. A combination of self-regulation, technical solutions as well as more enhanced recognition in the data protection regime for children, etc. is likely to be required. As with so many areas involving technology, any solution or combination of solutions cannot be a stand-still endeavour. These matters require constant attention as the underlying technology and its uses change.

---

166 *ibid*, 8.
167 *ibid*.
168 *ibid*, 9.
169 *ibid*.
170 *ibid*.
171 *ibid*, 10.

CHAPTER 26

AN IRISH PERSPECTIVE

Aisling McMahon

HEADLINE OF ISSUES

- Children social networking
- An Irish perspective
- Data protection
- Ireland
- Europe
- Child consent
- Age verification
- Recommendations

INTRODUCTION

In 2009, a quarter of a million users signed up to social networkings worldwide every day.[1] Social networks offer a means of interactive communication, allowing users to register and create profiles generally free of charge. On these pages information such as names, telephone numbers, addresses, schools and pictures may be posted.[2] In addition, users may access each other's profiles, add photographs of friends with captions or tags, or on some websites write on an interactive area of an individual's profile called a "wall". Privacy settings may be amended and there is generally an option to make one's profile "public" or "private". Profiles set to "public" allow other users to access them and are searchable on the internet, whereas profiles set to "private" restrict access to one's "friends" or in some cases users in the same group. Variations of "public" or "private" accessibility may also be adopted. Given the extent of real personal information which may be displayed on social networks, data protection concerns arise. These concerns are greater in relation to young users, who may fail to appreciate the risks of excessive disclosure of personal information online. Furthermore, although many social networks specify 13 as the minimum age

---

1 V Redding, "First European Agreement of Social Networks – A Step Forward to Child Safety Online" Speech 09/46, Safer Internet Day, 10 February 2009 at 2. Available at http://europa.eu/rapid/pressReleasesAction.do?reference=SPEECH/09/46.

2 B Sullivan, "Kids, Blogs and Too Much Information," 29 April 2005. Available at www.msnbc.msn.com/id/7668788.

limit for membership[3] this limit does not appear to be actively enforced.[4] A study in 2008, by Ofcom showed that 27 percent of eight- to 11-year-olds in the UK who were aware of social networks said that they had a profile.[5] Similarly, in Ireland the 2011 EU Kids Online Ireland Report found that 32 percent of boys and 41 percent of girls under the age of 12 have a social networking profile.[6]

This chapter will focus on the data protection issues surrounding the use of social networks by children under the age of 18. First, it looks at the research on the use of social networks in Ireland by 9- to 16-year-olds. Secondly, it examines briefly the benefits and risks of social networking for young users. Thirdly, it examines the Data Protection Directive 1995,[7] analysing its application to social network providers and young users of such websites. Fourthly, the chapter looks at the use of age verification techniques to prevent under age users from gaining access to social networks. Fifthly, it examines the recommendations of the European Safer Internet Forum,[8] the EU Article 29 Data Protection Working Group[9] and the EU Kids Online Report[10] in relation to social networking use and children. This chapter concludes by arguing that a multi-pronged approach[11] involving the adoption of safety measures and educational awareness initiatives should be implemented in order to ensure children are using social networks in the safest environment possible.

---

3 Bebo, Facebook and MySpace specify a minimum age of 13. See www.bebo.com/TermsOfUse2.jsp, www.facebook.com/terms.php?ref=pf and http://www.myspace.com/Help/Terms. As to the reason for this age limit, O'Neill and Dinh note that because in the United States the online collection of personal information for persons under the age of 13 must comply with the Children's Online Privacy Protection Act 1998, which has strict rules on age verification and consent, many countries set the age limit at 13. See B O'Neill and T Dinh, "Social Networking Among Irish 9–16 Year Olds" *Reports* (2012) Paper 29, available at http://arrow.dit.ie/cserrep/29 at 4, n2

4 Waters, "Children Flock to Social Networking Sites," *BBC News*, 2 April 2008, available at http://news.bbc.co.uk/2/hi/technology/7325019.stm.

5 Office of Communications, "Social Networking A Quantitative and Qualitative Research Report into Attitudes, Behaviours and Use" (2 April 2008), available at http://stakeholders.ofcom.org.uk/binaries/research/media-literacy/report1.pdf.

6 B O'Neill, S Grehan and K Ólafsson, "Risks and Safety for Children on the Internet: The Ireland Report" in *EU Kids Online* (LSE: London, 2011), 24. Available at http://eprints.lse.ac.uk/46444/.

7 Commission Directive 1995/46/EC of the European Parliament and of the Council of the 24 October 2000 on the protection of individuals with regard to the processing of personal data and on the free movement of such data [1995] OJ L281. Available at http://eur-lex.europa.eu/LexUriServ/LexUriServ.do?uri=CELEX:31995L0046:EN:HTML.

8 European Commission and Social Network Providers, "*Safer Social Networking Principles for the European Union,*" 10 February 2009. Available at http://ec.europa.eu/information_society/activities/social_networking/docs/sn_principles.pdf at 1.

9 Article 29 Data Protection Working Party, *Opinion on Online Social Networking*, 01189/09/EN, June 2009, at 11. Available at http://ec.europa.eu/justice/policies/privacy/docs/wpdocs/2009/wp163_en.pdf.

10 B O'Neill, S Livingstone and S McLaughlin, "Final Recommendations for Policy, Methodology and Research" in *EU Kids Online* (LSE: London, 2011).

11 As recommended by Article 29 Data Protection Working Party, *Opinion on Online Social Networking*, 01189/09/EN, June 2009. Available at http://ec.europa.eu/justice/policies/privacy/docs/wpdocs/2009/wp163_en.pdf, last accessed 25 August 2011.

Social Networks and Children

The safety of children online was recently examined in the EU Kids Online European Project,[12] which offered specific country reports, including one for Ireland.[13] This report included some findings on social networking use for Irish children.[14] Further, the use of social networks by Irish children was explored in a dedicated piece entitled Social Networking among Irish 9–16 year olds by Brian O'Neill and Thuy Dinh.[15] Some of the main findings of this research are outlined in this section. The report found that social networking is a "near universal feature"[16] of Irish children's lives: one in five children at nine years of age have a social networking profile, rising to over half of all 11- to 12–year-olds, three-quarters of 13- to 14-year-olds and almost 90 percent of all 15- to 16-year-olds.[17] However, the research illustrated an increasing awareness on the part of Irish children of privacy on the internet[18]: 63 percent of the respondents claimed to have private profiles, 22 percent had partially private profiles and 12 percent had profiles that were publicly accessible.[19] The authors noted that the number of Irish children who placed their profiles on private is among the highest in Europe (the European average being 43 percent[20]), which they claim suggests that "education and awareness raising efforts have paid off."[21] Nonetheless, it is of note that the younger and arguably most vulnerable age group, the nine- to 10-year-olds, have the highest percentage of recorded public profiles at 18 percent.[22]

In relation to the information disclosed on social networks by the Irish nine- to 16-year-olds surveyed, O'Neill and Dinh found that 76 percent of Facebook users displayed a photograph that showed their face, compared with 68 percent of Bebo users. The user's full last name was displayed by 77 percent of Facebook users compared with 52 percent of Bebo users, and location address details were displayed by 8 percent of Facebook and 6 percent of Bebo users.[23] Overall, O'Neill and Dinh concluded that Facebook users display more personal information than Bebo users and those with profiles set to full public visibility.[24] They claimed this might be

---

12 See http://www2.lse.ac.uk/media@lse/research/EUKidsOnline/Home.aspx.

13 See http://www2.lse.ac.uk/media@lse/research/EUKidsOnline/ParticipatingCountries/ireland.aspx.

14 O'Neill, Grehan and Ólafsson, *op. cit*, 4.3

15 O'Neill and Dinh, *op. cit*. See also O'Neill, Grehan and Ólafsson, *op. cit*.

16 O'Neill and Dinh, *op. cit*, 1.

17 *ibid*, 1.

18 There has been an increasing awareness of privacy on such websites in comparison to earlier statistics. For instance, a study conducted in 2007 by Anchor Ireland found that Irish young people were more likely than their counterparts in Europe and the United States to make their online profiles public, as 71% of the respondents had a publicly accessible profile compared with 56% of other European teenagers and 66% of teenagers in the United States. Anchor attributed this to the technical features of Bebo, which at the time of the survey was the most popular Irish site for young people. See, Anchor Ireland, *The Anchor Watch_Your_Space Survey: Survey of Irish Teenagers' Use of Social Networking Websites* (2007). Available at www.webwise.ie/GenPDF.aspx?id=1744, at 4–5.

19 O'Neill and Dinh, *op. cit*., 6.

20 O'Neill, Grehan and Ólafsson, *op. cit*, 25.

21 O'Neill and Dinh, *op. cit*., 1.

22 *ibid*, 6.

23 *ibid*, 7.

24 *ibid*.

attributed in part to Facebook's policy of real names.[25] It is arguable, given that Bebo and Facebook as surveyed were operating in the same environment but had different levels of information displayed on their websites, that the social network provider's own policies and technological interface influence the type and amount of personal data displayed.

The authors made a number of interesting findings in relation to the social networking safety skills of Irish nine- to 16-year-olds.[26] They noted that 60 percent of children knew how to block messages from people they did not want to receive messages from, while 54 percent were able to change privacy settings on their profiles. However, again the age of users appeared a significant factor in relation to such knowledge, as 79 percent of 15- to 16-year-olds claimed to be able to change privacy settings, whereas only 31 percent of 11- to 12-year-olds said they were able to do so.[27] These findings suggest the need for continued support and educational initiatives to augment safety skills and privacy awareness, particularly of younger children.[28]

Given the extent of social networking use by Irish children and the level of real personal information that can and is being displayed on such websites, it is useful at this juncture to consider the risks and benefits of social networking use.

Benefits and Risks of Social Network Use by Children

There are a number of claimed benefits of social networking use for children. First, such websites provide an outlet for people to communicate with others and to express themselves[29]: users may personalise their profiles and create blogs or other content and then display it to others. Secondly, the anonymous nature of social networking enables teenagers to experiment with different identities; they can have an identity online which they might not expose elsewhere due to fear of stereotype or stigma.[30] Thirdly, social networks may prove useful in terms of social interaction, as there are various communities for users with different interests and chat-room discussions can occur on diverse topics, helping to give teenagers a sense of belonging.[31] Social networkings fulfil the basic human need to socialise[32] and create a private social space for young people.[33]

Nonetheless, young users can also be exposed to a number of risks on social

---

25 *ibid.*

26 *ibid*, 8.

27 *ibid.*

28 *ibid.*

29 S Rapacki,, "Social Networking Sites – Why Teens Need Places like MySpace," *Young Adult Library Services* (2007) at 28.

30 D Boyd, "Address at American Association for the Advancement of Science: Identity Production in a Networked Culture: Why Youth Heart MySpace" (19 February 2006), available at http://danah.org/papers/AAAS2006.html.

31 SH Duncan, "MySpace is Also Their Space: Ideas for Keeping Children Safe from Sexual Predators on Social Networking Sites" (2007) (96) *Kentucky Law Journal* 527 at 536.

32 V Redding, "First European Agreement of Social Networks – a Step Forward to Child Safety Online" Speech 09/46, Safer Internet Day, 10 February 2009 at 3.

33 Duncan, *op. cit*, 537.

networks.[34] These risks were divided into four categories in the Safer Social Networking Principles for the European Union[35] document, which was developed by social networking providers in collaboration with the EU Commission. These principles were adopted in June 2009 by 20 social networking providers in Europe. The risks were categorised as follows:

- the risk of encountering "illegal content";
- the risk of "age inappropriate content", referring to pornography or sexual content or other content with adult themes that would be inappropriate for children;
- "contact" risk, which refers to the potential for inappropriate contact from adults or other young people online;
- "conduct" risk, referring to how young people themselves behave online. This includes behaviours such as posting sexually provocative photographs of themselves and divulging excessive personal information. It may also include engaging in cyber-bullying or soliciting other young people online.[36] In this vein, it is important to consider that while young people may be victims and experience harm online, they may also be participants in harmful or anti-social activities on social networking [web] sites.[37]

Another risk is the potential for identity theft on social networks, as discussed by the International Working Party on Telecommunications.[38] This risk was confirmed by Watchdog, a BBC consumer programme, which conducted a study by creating a Facebook profile with a cartoon picture and then inviting 100 selected at random to join as a friend. The programme showed how the identities of such users could be stolen and used to open a bank account.[39]

Recently, in Ireland, concerns have been raised about the potential exposure of young people to risks on social media, particularly in relation to the risks of cyberbullying.[40] At the time of writing, it has been reported that following a number of tragic cases where deaths were linked to comments posted on social media, an Oireachtas Group

---

34 For a discussion of such risks, see House of Lords Debate, "Children: Social Networking Sites," Moved by Lord Harris of Haringey, 12 February 2009. Column 1287. Available at www.publications.parliament.uk/pa/ld200809/ldhansrd/text/90212-0009.htm#09021268000035.

35 European Commission and Social Network Providers, *Safer Social Networking Principles for the European Union*, 10 February 2009, available at http://ec.europa.eu/information_society/activities/social_networking/docs/sn_principles.pdf.

36 Redding, "First European Agreement of Social Networks – a Step Forward to Child Safety Online," *op. cit*, 2.

37 *ibid*, 2.

38 R Verkaik, "*New Front in the Battle Against Identity Theft*," *Independent*, 23 November 2007, available at www.independent.co.uk/life-style/gadgets-and-tech/news/new-front-in-the-battle-against-identity-theft-760107.html. This was also discussed in Wong, "Social Networking: A Conceptual Analysis of a Data Controller" (2009) 15(5) *Communications Law* 142–149

39 P Boyes, "And This is Me on Facebook Helping with Brain Surgery," *Times*, 18 August 2008.

40 See "Minister Pledges to Investigate Websites After Deaths Linked to Cyber Bullying" *Irish Examiner*, 2 November 2012, available at http://www.irishexaminer.com/breakingnews/ireland/minister-pledges-to-investigate-website-after-deaths-linked-to-cyber-bullying-572731.html. See also, O'Doherty, "Online Bullying Exposes Children to Dangers Beyond the School Yard," *Irish Times*, 30 November 2012, available at http://www.irishtimes.com/newspaper/ireland/2012/1030/1224325896632.html.

would be set up to investigate abuses of social media in Ireland.[41] Furthermore, the Law Reform Commission in Ireland has been asked to look into the difficulties in prosecuting cyberbullying Ireland.[42]

The EU Data Protection Directive and Social Networks

The risks posed to children on social networks may in some cases be attributed to, or at least exacerbated by, excessive disclosure of personal information, so it is apt to examine how data protection law operates in this area. At the outset, it is useful to discuss some of the more general principles which apply. Data protection in Europe is governed by the Data Protection Directive 1995[43] implemented into Irish law by the Data Protection Acts.[44] The Directive applies to "the processing of personal data wholly or partly by automatic means, and to the processing or otherwise than by automatic means of personal data which form part of a filing system."[45] Personal data refer to "any information relating to an identified or identifiable natural person ('data subject')".[46] The data subject (generally) must be a living person and a data controller is defined as:

> "a natural or legal person, public authority, agency or any other body which alone or jointly with others determines the purposes and means of the processing of personal data; where the purposes and means of processing are determined by national or Community laws or regulations, the controller or the specific criteria for his nomination may be designated by national or Community law".[47]

All data controllers must obey relevant data protection principles or face liability.

The EU Article 29 Working Party, an advisory body set up following the adoption of the Directive, produced its Opinion on Online Social Networking[48] in 2009, which confirmed that social network providers are data controllers under the Directive and as such owe duties to social networking users.[49] This position was reiterated in the Report of the Audit of Facebook Ireland Ltd. published by the Office of the Irish Data Protection Commissioner in December 2011.[50] The report considered

---

41 O'Regan, "Oireachtas Committee to Report to Rabitte on Abuse of Social Media," *Irish Times*, 28 December, 2012, available at http://www.irishtimes.com/newspaper/ireland/2012/1228/1224328227058.html.

42 O'Regan, "Law Reform to Tackle Cyber Bullying," *Irish Times*, 8 November 2012, available at http://www.irishtimes.com/newspaper/ireland/2012/1108/1224326308706.html.

43 Commission Directive 1995/46/EC of the European Parliament and of the Council of the 24 October 2000 on the protection of individuals with regard to the processing of personal data and on the free movement of such data. [1995] OJ L281. Available at http://eur-lex.europa.eu/LexUriServ/LexUriServ.do?uri=CELEX:31995L0046:EN:HTML.

44 Data Protection Act 1988 and Data Protection Act 2003.

45 Article 3(1) Directive 95/46/EC.

46 Article 2 (a) Directive 95/46/EC.

47 Article 2 (d) Directive 95/46/EC.

48 Article 29 Data Protection Working Party, 01189/09/EN, Opinion on Online Social Networking, June 2009. Available at http://ec.europa.eu/justice/policies/privacy/docs/wpdocs/2009/wp163_en.pdf.

49 *ibid*, 5. For a discussion of the term "data controller" as it applies to social networking, see Wong, *op. cit*, 142–149.

50 Office of the Data Protection Commissioner, Facebook Ireland Ltd: Report of Audit, 21 December 2011. Available at http://dataprotection.ie/viewdoc.asp?DocID=1182&m=f.

whether Facebook Ireland Ltd. as a data controller was compliant with relevant Irish Data Protection Acts 1988 and 2003, which implemented the Data Protection Directive into Irish law. The report is particularly significant given that the European headquarters of Facebook are in Ireland, so there is an onus on the Irish Data Protection Commissioner to monitor compliance with EU law.

A discussion of this report is beyond the scope of this chapter, but for the sake of completeness some of the main points should be noted. The report set out a number of recommendations to ensure Facebook's compliance with specific data protection laws. In September 2012, the office published a review of compliance with these recommendations. It found that the majority of the recommendations were implemented to its full satisfaction. In particular, it was satisfied with:

> "the provision of better transparency for the user in how their data is handled, the provision of increased user control over settings, the implementation of clear retention periods for the deletion of personal data or an enhanced ability for the user to delete items, the enhancement of the user's right to have ready access to their personal data and the capacity of FB-I to ensure rigorous assessment of compliance with Irish and EU data protection requirements".[51]

Facebook also agreed to turn off the controversial "tag suggest"/"facial recognition" feature for all new EU users and to delete existing templates for existing users by 15 October 2012.[52] However, in some areas full implementation was not yet achieved, particularly with regard to the education of new users, the deletion of social plug-in data for EU users, fully verified account deletion, and minimising the potential for ad targeting based on words that could be considered sensitive personal data.[53] A four-week deadline was set for the implementation of these recommendations. These reports highlight the need for social networking operators to be aware of their responsibilities under data protection law and comply with them.

Nonetheless, it is not only social networking providers that have responsibilities under data protection law. The EU Article 29 Working Party stated that individual users might also in some limited cases be considered to have taken on the responsibilities of data controllers. It noted that the duties of data controller are not applied on individuals who process personal data "'in the course of a purely personal or household activity' – the so-called 'household exemption.'"[54] The Opinion stated, however, that in some cases this exemption would not apply to user activities.[55] A number of examples of when the exemption may not apply are given, including where the social networks is used as a collaboration forum for a company or association, or where the user has a large number of contacts.[56] The EU Article 29 Working Party notes that once "access to profile information extends beyond self-selected contacts,

---

51 Press Release, *Report of Review of Facebook Ireland's Implementation of Audit Recommendations Published – Facebook Turns Off Tag Suggest in the EU*, 21 September 2012, available at http://dataprotection.ie/viewdoc.asp?DocID=1233&m=f.

52 *ibid.*

53 Office of the Data Protection Commissioner, *Facebook Ireland Ltd, Report of Re-audit*, 21 September 2012, 3. Available at http://dataprotection.ie/docs/Facebook_Audit_Review_Report/1232.htm.

54 Article 29 Data Protection Working Party, 01189/09/EN, Opinion on Online Social Networking, June 2009. Available at http://ec.europa.eu/justice/policies/privacy/docs/wpdocs/2009/wp163_en.pdf.

55 *ibid.*

56 *ibid*, 6.

such as when access to a profile is provided to all members within the SNS or the data is indexable by search engines, access goes beyond the personal or household sphere"[57] or "[e]qually, if a user takes an informed decision to extend access beyond self-selected 'friends' data controller responsibilities come into force."[58]

In such cases, the Working Party notes that the same legal regime will "apply as when any person uses other technology [forms] to publish personal data on the web."[59] Hence, individual users could face liability if considered to be data controllers and if they fail to comply with relevant laws.

However, holding users of social networks liable as data controllers, even in limited cases, is not without its difficulties and such an approach has been argued by Garrie *et al*[60] to be highly problematic.[61] They argue that data controllers have many obligations and to try to impose and enforce these on social networking users would be unrealistic, especially given the number of users that exist.[62] They also claim that some of the requirements of data controllers are more suited to imposing on an organisation, such as the social networking provider, rather than an individual user. Furthermore, the authors note that the application of data protection law to social networks is uncertain, as much personal information is already available on such websites, which users may have consented to being made available.[63] They claim that applying the definition of data controller to include users of social networks could lead to the possibility of widespread litigation ensuing.[64] It is submitted that the problems would be compounded in the case of child users, as one would also have to prove that they understood the potential for being a data controller and the responsibilities placed on such controllers if deemed to be in breach of same.

Case Law

In terms of relevant case law, in *Bodil Lindqvist*[65] the European Court of Justice held that data protection laws applied to websites.[66] It held that:

> "referring on an internet page to various people and identifying them by name or by other means, for instance by giving their telephone number...constitutes the processing of personal data wholly or in part by automatic means within the meaning of Art 3(1) of Directive 95/46".[67]

Two English decisions, albeit not relevant to the application of the Directive, are useful in demonstrating the potential for claims against ISP and users for the content of posts on social networks. In *Godfrey v Demon Internet Service Provider* (ISP)[68] a

---

57 *ibid.*
58 *ibid.*
59 *ibid.*
60 D Garrie, M Duffy-Lewis, R Gillespie and R Wong, "Data Protection: the Challenges Facing Social Networking" (2010) *Bingham International Law and Management Review* 127– 152
61 *ibid*, 128.
62 *ibid*, 132.
63 *ibid*, 133.
64 *ibid*, 134.
65 C-101/01, *Bodil Lindqvist v Sweden* [2004] 1 CMLR 20.
66 *ibid*, para 26.
67 *ibid*, para 27.
68 [1999] 4 All ER 342, [2001] QB 201.

post was placed on an online discussion forum that was claimed to be from Godfrey and was defamatory of him. Godfrey sent a letter informing the ISP that he was not the author of the post and requested it be removed. The ISP ignored this and the post was not deleted for an additional 10 days. In a pre-trial motion the judge ruled that the ISP could be sued for libel, as it would be a publisher for any transmission by a website of defamatory content under the s 1 of the Defamation Act 1996.[69] The case was subsequently settled.

In another case, *Applause Store Productions Ltd v Raphael*,[70] a user Mathew Firsht brought a legal action against a former friend, Grant Raphael. A Facebook profile was set up in the name of Matthew Firsht that contained defamatory material, and the evidence showed that the profile was set up using a computer with Mr Raphael's IP address. The court found in favour of the claimant on grounds of "misuse of private information".[71]

One issue that should be noted in terms of liability under the EU Data Protection Directive 1995 is that the application of the Directive is determined by the state in which the data controller is established.[72] Therefore, an application of the Directive to social networks based outside the EU could be challenged on the grounds that the law that should apply is the law of the state in which the social networking provider or user is established. Arguably, however, if the actions of social network providers as data controllers would have an impact on European data subjects, the Directive would still apply. In fact, the EU Article 29 Working Party has stated that the Directive "generally applies to the processing of personal data by SNS even when their headquarters are outside the EEA."[73]

Data Protection Directive and Children's Data on Social Networking

The material above relates to the general application of data protection law to social networks; however, some further considerations are noteworthy in terms of children's data. In 2008, the EU Article 29 Working Party completed a report on the protection of children's data,[74] noting that although there is no specific reference to children in the Data Protection Directive, it still applies to such data by virtue of the child being a natural person.[75] It stated that a child "enjoys all the rights of a person including the right to the protection of their personal data."[76] The EU Article 29 Working Party's Opinion on Online Social Networking, stressed the importance

---

69 "Demon Settles Net Libel Case," *BBC News*, 20 March 2000, available at http://news.bbc.co.uk/2/hi/science/nature/695596.stm.

70 *Applause Store Productions Ltd v Raphael* [2008] EWHC 1781.

71 For a discussion of the different types of actions that may arise in relation to harmful content posted on social networking sites, see L McDermott, "Legal Issues Associated with Minors and Their Use of Social Networking Sites" (2012) 17(1) *Communications Law* 19–24 at 20.

72 D Kelleher, *Privacy and Data Protection Law in Ireland* (Tottell: Dublin, 2006).

73 Article 29 Data Protection Working Party, *Opinion on Online Social Networking*, June 2009, 01189/09/EN, at 12. Available at http://ec.europa.eu/justice/policies/privacy/docs/wpdocs/2009/wp163_en.pdf.

74 *Working Document 1/2008 on the Protection of Children's Personal Data (General Guidelines and the Special Case of Schools)*, Article 29 Data Protection Working Party, 00483/08, (Brussels, 2008) Available at http://ec.europa.eu/justice/policies/privacy/docs/wpdocs/2008/wp147_en.pdf.

75 *ibid.*

76 *ibid*, 2.

of the best interests of the child principle and the UN Convention on the Rights of the Child in the context of children's use of social networks.[77] This suggests that the general principles of the Directive should be applied even more stringently to children's data in this context. The EU Article 29 Working Party states that data controllers must be aware that the child is not yet mature and controllers should "act with the utmost good faith when processing their data."[78] The Working Party states that data controllers should pay "special attention to the situation of the child, as they must respect their best interests at all times."[79] It further notes in relation to data retention, that a "droit á l'oubli" or right to ensure data are not retained, must be borne in mind, which covers every data subject "especially children".[80] According to the Working Party, this right is particularly important in relation to children, as they are still developing and maturing; therefore, data in relation to them can quickly change and "become out-dated and irrelevant to the original purpose of collection",[81] and in such cases data should not be kept.

A specific difficulty in applying data protection law strictly to children's activities on social networks is ascertaining whether the appropriate consent has been given for data processing on such websites. Article 7 of the Directive sets out the criteria needed to legitimise data processing, and Article 7(a) acknowledges that data may be processed if the "data subject has unambiguously given his consent."[82] On registering for a social network, users must consent to the terms and conditions of the website. Consent is defined as any "freely given specific and informed indication of his wishes by which the data subject signifies his agreement to personal data relating to him being processed."[83] It is questionable whether a child can give informed and free consent in this context, as some may not be mature enough to appreciate the risks of processing data in this context. The terms and conditions of registration on social networks may also encompass requests for consent to use this information for other purposes, such as advertising, and it is questionable whether children would appreciate this.

Furthermore, as discussed by the EU Article 29 Working Party, child users of social networks are under the age required of consent for contract law, and consent is valid only if it comes from someone that is legally capable of giving it.[84] Children can enjoy certain legal rights to conclude contracts, but these generally refer to marriage, employment, etc.[85] Such rights may extend to social networks; however,

---

77 *Opinion on Online Social Networking*, June 2009, Article 29 Data Protection Working Party, 01189/09/EN, at 11. Available at http://ec.europa.eu/justice/policies/privacy/docs/wpdocs/2009/wp163_en.pdf.

78 *Working Document 1/2008 on the Protection of Children's Personal Data" (General Guidelines and the Special Case of Schools)*, Article 29 Data Protection Working Party, 00483/08 (Brussels, 2008) at 7. Available at http://ec.europa.eu/justice/policies/privacy/docs/wpdocs/2008/wp147_en.pdf.

79 *ibid*, 7.

80 *ibid*, 8.

81 *ibid.*

82 Article 7 Directive 95/46/EC.

83 Article 2(h) Directive 95/46/EC.

84 Article 29 Data Protection Working Party, *Working Document 1/2008 on the Protection of Children's Personal Data (General Guidelines and the Special Case of Schools)*, 00483/08, (Brussels, 2008). Available at http://ec.europa.eu/justice/policies/privacy/docs/wpdocs/2008/wp147_en.pdf, at 8.

85 *ibid*, 9.

the maturity of the child must be considered[86] and parental authorisation may be needed. In the context of data protection, parents as representatives may "facilitate data processing by giving their consent".[87] Parents should consider ways in which excessive disclosure of data could "pose a threat to their child's privacy and vital interests".[88] However, the Working Party state that their status as the child's representative's will not take priority over the child's rights as, data protection rights "belong to the child and not to their representatives who merely exercise them".[89]

In some instances there may be uncertainty in terms of who should consent in order for a child to register for a social networks. In this respect, the EU Article 29 Working Party recommends that children be treated in accordance with their level of maturity.[90] The Working Party notes that the "solution can progress from mere consultation of the child, to a parallel consent of the child and the representative, and even to the sole consent of the child if he or she is already mature."[91] This suggests that an on-going evaluation of the child's maturity is required in order to assess what form of consent is applicable, although this would be difficult for social network providers to assess and operate in practice, as maturity can differ from child to child at varying ages.

Age-Verification Techniques

One issue often discussed as part of a solution to ensuring the safety of children on social networks is adopting age-verification techniques.[92] These are imposed in order to prevent underage users gaining access to social networks. Age-verification techniques confirm the identity and ages of individuals attempting to use services where age limitations are imposed.[93] There are a number of methods of age verification, but social networks tend to employ self-certification in combination with semantic analysis.[94] Self-certification is where users are asked about their age on entering a website. It relies solely on the information provided by the user, and additional methods are often employed to increase its effectiveness. For instance, "cookies" are used to try to prevent users from re-registering with different ages; however, users can often bypass these by turning cookies off or deleting them. "Walled gardens" are also used where children who try to register as adults to gain access to adult content are then denied access to areas of the website accessible only to minors. However, this can be evaded in some cases by setting up two profiles. Overall, the main shortcoming with self-certification techniques is that users can lie about their age to evade requirements. A 2008 study showed that over one quarter of children between eight and 12 were evading the age restrictions imposed by

---

86 *ibid.*
87 *ibid*, 8.
88 *ibid.*
89 *ibid*, 5.
90 *ibid*, 6.
91 *ibid.*
92 For a discussion such techniques see, European Commission, Information Society and Media Directorate General, "*Background Report on Cross Media Rating and Classification and Age Verification Solutions*" (Luxembourg, 2008). Available at http://ec.europa.eu/information_society/activities/sip/docs/pub_consult_age_rating_sns/reportageverification.pdf.
93 *ibid*, 16.
94 *ibid*, 18.

websites such as Bebo, Facebook and MySpace.[95] Similarly, a 2012 study of Irish nine- to 16-year-olds, discussed above, found that almost one third of Facebook users surveyed and a quarter of Bebo users surveyed lied about their age on their social networking profile.[96]

Another method of age verification is semantic analysis, which has been explained as "automated text analysis for age verification purposes which employs a search algorithm using terms commonly used by underage users to find under aged profiles on social network [web]sites."[97] The difficulty with this method is that people have different levels of maturity, so one cannot identify an exact age, merely an age range. It is also very difficult to operate in multilingual environments.[98] Other techniques include offline verification and parental controls that use face-to-face identification controls to verify age. Such methods are commonly used by mobile phone operators, but it has been argued that they would be very costly and cumbersome to use in the social networking context.[99] Biometric verification may also be used to verify age by means of fingerprints, iris scans and other identifiable characteristics.[100] The use of biometric technology, however, is controversial, as much personal information is disclosed in the process. Physical identification could also be used. This was experimented by the online website Second Life, which requested that all users provide a one-time physical identification.[101]

Age-verification models have been introduced in some countries, generally on a voluntary basis but in some jurisdictions are enforced by law. Germany, the United Kingdom and France have introduced legal requirements for age verification by specific online services and ISPs.[102] The German model is useful to examine, given its extensive provisions. It requires the use of age-verification technologies by providers of specific services and prescribes the pre-approval mechanism by the state of age-verification technologies.[103] Article 4(2) of the Interstate Treaty on the Protection of Minors in the Media (JMStV) provides that content that may impair the development of children and adolescents is legal only if it can be proven that it is inaccessible by such young people.[104] Content is classified under three headings: content that is illegal; content endangering minors; and content harmful to minors.[105] Basic age verification is used for harmful content. This uses credit card numbers,

---

95 See Carvel, "Facebook: Children Evade Social Websites' Age Limits," *Guardian*, 7 August 2008, available at www.guardian.co.uk/technology/2008/aug/07/socialnetworking.facebook.

96 O'Neill and Dinh, *op. cit*, 7.

97 European Commission, Information Society and Media Directorate General, "*Background Report on Cross Media Rating and Classification and Age Verification Solutions*" (Luxembourg, 2008) at 21. Available at http://ec.europa.eu/information_society/activities/sip/docs/pub_consult_age_rating_sns/reportageverification.pdf.

98 *ibid*, 21.

99 *ibid*, 23.

100 *ibid*, 22. This technique has been used by the social networking site Anne's Diary; see www.annesdiary.com.

101 See http://lindenlab.com/press/releases/08_29_07.

102 See European Commission, Information Society and Media Directorate General *Background Report on Cross Media Rating and Classification and Age Verification Solutions* (Luxembourg, 2008) at 17. Available at http://ec.europa.eu/information_society/activities/sip/docs/pub_consult_age_rating_sns/reportageverification.pdf at para 3.2

103 *ibid.*

104 *ibid*, 23.

105 *ibid*, 23.

ID control numbers and web camera checks. Strict age verification is required for content that endangers minors, entailing a one-time physical identification by the user whose identity is checked against an identity card. Every time the user accesses the website thereafter, a subsequent authentication process occurs. In order to prevent multiplication of access data to third parties, the subsequent authentication process includes unique identifiers and may also use bank or identification cards with age criteria.[106]

As to the use of age-verification techniques for access to social networks, it is submitted that they do not appear to be the most appropriate or effective solution to the difficulties faced. The UK Byron Report noted that age-verification solutions should not be focused on too much to the detriment of the role of education and parents.[107] Another issue is that some age-verifying techniques, particularly identity cards and national identifiers, raise their own data protection problems. There is a concern that methods for the collection of data for age verification could undermine accepted privacy norms in the EU.

Recommendations to Ensure Safety of Children on Social Networks

A number of recent reports have offered recommendations regarding ensuring children's safety on social networks. Some of the main reports and recommendations are outlined below.

European Safer Internet Forum Recommendations

As noted previously, on 10 February 2009 20 social network providers in consultation with the European Commission developed and adopted seven good-practice recommendations to enhance children's safety on social networks.[108]

The seven recommendations are as follows. First, social networking providers should raise awareness of safety on social networks to users, parents and carers.[109] Providers should create targeted educational materials to enable young people navigate their services safely.[110] Messages should be presented in child-friendly language in a prominent easily accessible location. Also, clear information should be given on what constitutes inappropriate behaviour. This should be communicated outside the terms of service.

Secondly, providers should ensure that services are age-appropriate for the intended audience.[111] Age restrictions should be clear, and providers should identify and

106 *ibid*, 24.

107 Bryon Review, Children and New Technology, "Safer Children in a Digital World" (2008). Available at http://webarchive.nationalarchives.gov.uk/20100202100434/dcsf.gov.uk/byronreview/.

108 *Safer Social Networking Principles for the European Union*, European Commission and Social Network Providers, 10 February 2009. Available at http://ec.europa.eu/information_society/activities/social_networking/docs/sn_principles.pdf at 1.

109 *ibid*, 6.

110 *ibid*.

111 *ibid*.

remove under-age users. They should ensure users cannot re-register with a false age after being rejected. Parents' involvement should also be promoted, and parents should manage their children's use of the service.[112]

Thirdly, technology should be used to assist young people in using websites.[113] Technical measures should limit the exposure to inappropriate contact with adults. Furthermore, profiles of users under the age of 18 should be placed on private, and users should easily be able to block others from their profiles.

Fourthly, users should be provided with mechanisms for reporting illegal content or conduct.[114] Such reports should be acknowledged and dealt with efficiently.

Fifthly, websites should have procedures in place to respond to notifications of illegal conduct and to share reports of illegal behaviour with relevant law enforcement agencies.[115]

Sixthly, social network providers should encourage users to adopt a safe approach to personal information.[116] This would include providing a range of privacy options along with information to ensure that users understand the consequences of posting material online. Providers should reconsider the practice of automatically displaying or mapping information given in the registration process onto user profiles. Upon registration, all information sought should have an option alongside it to make it public or private. Furthermore, users should be able to access privacy settings at all times.[117]

Seventhly, it was recommended that there should be a means to assess or review illegal or prohibited content.[118]

The implementation of these recommendations was evaluated by the European Commission Safer Internet Programme in January 2010.[119] The evaluation report considered 19 self-declaration statements submitted by signatories of the principles (the social networking companies) along with evaluating 25 services provided by these companies. Overall, it found that principles three (empowering users) and six (encouraging safe approach to privacy) had the highest level of compliance. The first principle (raising awareness) also had a high level of compliance. It found that principle four (easy to use mechanisms for reporting violation) and principle two (age-appropriate services) had the lowest compliance levels between that which was stated in the self-declaration forms and that observed in relation to services, with the majority of such services assessed to be only partially compliant.[120]

---

112 *ibid*, 7.

113 *ibid*, 7.

114 *ibid*, 8.

115 *ibid*.

116 *ibid*, 9.

117 *ibid*.

118 *ibid*.

119 E Staksrud and B Lobe, *Evaluation of the Implementation of the Safer Social Networking Principles for the EU Part I: General Report* (European Commission Safer Internet Programme, Luxembourg, 2010).

120 *ibid*, 5

Some of the specific findings relevant for the purposes of this chapter were as follows. In regard to the first principle (raising awareness), it found that while 17 social networks provide safety information for children who sign up to websites, the information could be found easily on only nine websites.[121] The safety information for younger children was assessed as difficult or not possible to understand in one-third of services. In relation to the second principle (age-appropriate services), the report found that all social networks asked for a birth date on registration. On some websites with a minimum age limit, an experiment was conducted whereby following attempts at registering as an 11-year-old a subsequent attempt was made to register the same profile but with an age of 15. In seven websites this was enough to gain registration.[122] In two other websites, access was granted under the same process once a cookie was removed.[123] In all cases, users were able to sign up later to such websites using a different profile but on the same computer.[124] As to the third principle (empowering users), it was found that users can delete pictures on their profiles in 18 websites, while 22 websites allow users to delete postings.[125] Finally, regarding the sixth principle (encouraging safe approach to privacy), the report revealed that the typical information required on registration is the user's real name, gender and email address.[126]

EU Article 29 Working Party Recommendations

The EU Article 29 Working Party's[127] Opinion on Online Social Networking[128], published in 2009, also offered some recommendations in relation to children's use of such websites. It recommended that a multi-pronged approach should be adopted, and advocated for awareness-raising initiatives, which were deemed crucial to attaining the active involvement of children.[129] It suggested the adoption of privacy-enhancing technologies such as "privacy-friendly settings by default, pop-up warning boxes at appropriate steps, age verification software)"[130] and self-regulation by providers encouraging the adoption of codes of practice. The EU Article 29 Working Party emphasised the need for fair and lawful processing of minors' data; in particular, it stated that social networking providers should refrain from asking for sensitive information in subscription forms and direct marketing aimed at children. It recommended that providers maintain "suitable degrees of logical separation between the communities of children and adults."[131]

Furthermore, the Working Party made a number of recommendations concerning the functionality of websites. It recommended that social network providers when dealing with child users should try to give layered notices containing "simple,

---

121 *ibid*, 6
122 *ibid*, 7
123 *ibid.*
124 *ibid.*
125 *ibid.*
126 *ibid*, 8
127 See http://ec.europa.eu/justice/data-protection/article-29/index_en.htm.
128 *Opinion on Online Social Networking*, Article 29 Data Protection Working Party, 01189/09/EN, June 2009. Available at http://ec.europa.eu/justice/policies/privacy/docs/wpdocs/2009/wp163_en.pdf.
129 *ibid*, 11.
130 *ibid*, 12.
131 *ibid.*

concise and educational language that can be easily understood."[132] Language used should be child-friendly and a shorter notice should be used, with a link to a more detailed notice via hyperlink.[133] Privacy notices should also be given in the right place at the right time. According to the Working Party, the timing of notices is a crucial factor in raising children's awareness of risks, as in an online environment these may be the child's only opportunity to apprise dangers.[134]

Recommendations of the EU Kids Online Report

Finally, the EU Kids Online Project offered 20 recommendations in relation to children's internet usage generally.[135] A discussion of all these is beyond the purview of this chapter; however, some of the most relevant recommendations in terms of social networking use, were as follows. It recommended that safety messages should be tailored and adapted to new modes of access,[136] highlighting the need to monitor new technological developments, which may pose further/different risk factors and call for a need to update policies. It also emphasised that while children need to be protected online, they also need to take responsibility for keeping safe and respecting others online.[137] The report stressed the need to raise parental awareness of risks and safety online, without being alarmist.[138] It found that policy makers need to be aware of new risks which are posed online especially by peer-to-peer conduct, with user-generated content and data misuse posing significant difficulties for policy makers.[139] Furthermore, it recommended that awareness-raising strategies should "highlight effective coping strategies in safety messages, emphasising social supports such as talking to parents, friends and teachers, as well as the use of online tools."[140]

Conclusion

The use of social networks by children raises many data protection concerns, particularly given the level of real personal information that can be disclosed. Children may fail to perceive the risks of excessive data disclosure on the internet, disclosing information online that they would not disclose in an offline environment. Policies in the area should be constantly monitored and updated in order to keep up with advancements in technology. Data protection law on its own is not an appropriate solution to alleviate such risks. Instead, it is submitted that a multi-pronged approach[141] incorporating the recommendations of the EU Article 29 Working Party, the EU Kids Online Report and the European Safer Internet Forum, as discussed above, should be adopted. Given the complexity of issues involved, it is imperative that educational measures play a significant role in any reform of the

---

132 *ibid.*
133 *ibid*, 10.
134 *ibid.*
135 O'Neill, Livingstone and McLaughlin, *op. cit.*
136 *ibid*, 6.
137 *ibid*, 5.
138 *ibid*, 7.
139 *ibid*, 8
140 *ibid.*
141 A multi-pronged approach was recommended by the *Opinion on Online Social Networking*, Article 29 Data Protection Working Party, 01189/09/EN, June 2009. Available at http://ec.europa.eu/justice/policies/privacy/docs/wpdocs/2009/wp163_en.pdf.

area,[142] as a key to minimising and hopefully alleviating the risks posed is to equip children with sufficient tools and knowledge to protect their own data and the data of others in a social networking environment.

[142] For further discussion of the importance of education in this area, see, McLaughlin, "Education the Solution to Cyber Bullying Scourge," *Irish Times*, 2 November 2012, available at http://www.irishtimes.com/newspaper/opinion/2012/1102/1224326036363.html. This was also emphasised by O'Neill, Grehan and Ólafsson, *op. cit*, 10.

PART VIII: SOCIAL NETWORKING AND INTERNET ACCESS

Chapter 27

SOCIAL NETWORKING AND INTERNET ACCESS

Headline of Issues

- Internet bans and access restrictions
- Social networks and contracts
- Blacklists
- Civil law
- Criminal law
- Convicts
- Adults
- Children
- Children's Referendum
- Laws and judicial discretion
- Hacking and peer to peer (P2P)

Introduction

One of the emerging issues in relation to social networking is whether it is permissible to impose a ban or sanction against someone convicted that they cannot access the internet, or cannot access certain websites. For example, can someone be banned from social networks? Can they be banned from using the internet entirely? This issue applies in the context of, for example, hacking, internet fraud and online child sex offences.

Social Networks: Contract

The primary relationship between a user or member and a particular social network is governed by the contract relationship between them. In most instances this is governed by or incorporates the contract terms and conditions of the website. As these are on the website, these will be drafted in favour of the website. It is possible, therefore, that the contract relationship provides that the website can suspend or terminate the member's right to access and use the website. Such a provision could provide for such action in the event of a breach of the website rules by the member. On the basis that there is a valid and existing contract, the social network would have a strong argument is seeking to ban or suspend a given member.

Social Networks: Blacklists and Civil Law

Those who may appear on a register of sex offenders, or some other blacklist, may not be members of a social network. Can the list be used to pre-vet or ban them in advance from becoming members? Effectively, a condition of membership becomes being a non-convict or not being convicted of certain offences. While these raise particular issues in and of themselves, it would certainly appear that these are matters not expressed or contemplated in the current version of the contract terms and conditions of most social networks.

Assuming, for instance, that the website has access to a blacklist, is it entitled as a matter of civil law to use the list to vet or ban its applicant members? Do issues of constitutional free speech or rights to association arise? These issues have yet to be fully considered and ventilated in court.

Social Networks: Blacklists and Criminal Law

In terms of criminal law and quasi-criminal law, it is possible for legislators to *inter alia* draft a law that bans those on a sexual offenders blacklist, for example, from using the internet or from accessing social networks. How practical it would be in actuality can certainly be queried. Consider, for example, a law saying that "blacklist category X cannot access websites which children frequent". Even adding "often frequent" would hardly delimit any aspect of the internet. Further still, if it sought to focus on "social networks," can we identify any social networks that do not have at least some children accessing it?

Social networks might justify their decision to ban members or applicants contained on a blacklist by saying that they are legally obliged to do so. This could arise in two instances. First, there might be a specific law, such as referred to above. The second situation might involve a judge imposing such a ban or sanction as part of his or her sentencing decision at the time of initial conviction. Issues such as mandatory sentencing and sentencing discretion arise.[1]

Internet Access Sanctions

It is increasingly recognised that alternative and creative sanctions can be imposed on convicted persons other than imprisonment. These include community service, curfews and electronic tagging.

More recently, the issue arises as to whether a court sanction can be imposed to restrict or prevent a person using and accessing the internet. Already there are examples of cases where such internet access restrictions have been imposed.

It is increasingly common to try to impose creative sanctions on certain convicted paedophiles and convicted online child sex offenders. For example, a child sex

1 On these important issues see, for example, T O'Malley, *Sentencing: Towards a Coherent System* (Round Hall: Dublin, 2011).

offender could have used social network to make contact with children, solicit them and groom them.

Restricting those convicted in relation to online child predatory activities is arguably not without technological precedent.

Hacking Internet Access Sanctions

There are already examples where those convicted of hacking and other computer crimes have had judicial sanctions imposed not to access the internet. This might seem surprising, but there are a number of examples where this has occurred.

Under the Irish Criminal Justice (Theft and Fraud Offences) Act 2001 unlawful use of a computer can be an offence, namely, where a person dishonestly operates or causes to be operated a computer within the State with the intention of making a gain for himself or another.[2] An offence of creating a false instrument arises if it is done with the intention that it shall be used to induce another person to accept it as genuine and, by reason of so accepting it, to do some act—in this case to track and profile a subscriber online.[3]

The Criminal Damage Act 1991 creates an offence of unauthorised access to a computer and it is also an offence to damage data.[4]

Child Sex Offender Internet Access Sanctions

It is a step further again to impose access restrictions against those convicted in relation to child sex crimes emanating from social networking.

These can of course be "real" crimes and "internet crimes". The former would be where a child is murdered, raped or attacked after meeting with somebody they were introduced to through a social network. An example of the latter is someone convicted of an offence relating to accessing, storing and or creating animation child pornography—and which they may have downloaded, uploaded and or distributed online or electronically.[5]

This is a developing area in Ireland and the UK. Some instances do exist elsewhere.

For example, Lori David was banned by a court in Texas from (1) using the internet; and (2) texting anyone other than a family member.[6] She was convicted of an

---

2 Criminal Justice (Theft and Fraud Offences) Act 2001, s 9.

3 *ibid*, s 25.

4 Criminal Damage Act 1991, s 5.

5 See the Child Trafficking and Pornography Act 1998 (amended by s 6 of the Criminal Law (Sexual Offences)(Amendment) Act 2007). Note also the harassment offence in s 10 of the Non-Fatal Offences Against the Person Act 1997.

6 "Katy Mom Banned from Internet After 'Sexting' Son's Friend," *CBS Houston*, 14 November 2011, available at http://houston.cbslocal.com/2011/11/14/texas-housewife-banned-from-internet-over-sexting-sons-friend/; "Mother Banned from the Internet After Pleading Guilty to

offence which involved sexting, by sending nude photograph of herself (aged 38) to a 16-year-old boy. He was a friend of her son.

A court in the UK banned an alleged hacker, Jake Davis, from using the internet pending his trial.[7] Prosecutors in a US case also demanded that an internet ban be imposed on an alleged hacker, a Mr Cooper, as a bail condition.[8] An original request that he be obliged to install computer and internet monitoring software on his computer was dropped.[9] Jerome Heckenkamp, an alleged US hacker, also had internet bail restrictions imposed pending trial, which he sought to challenge during the long delay between charge and trial.[10]

A 17-year-old French hacker (known as DKD) is also reported to have been sentenced with an internet ban for hacking.[11]

Four other alleged hackers in the UK were banned from using their online user pseudonyms on the internet or internet relay chat (IRC, a messaging system).[12]

UK Prime Minister David Cameron indicated that he would like to see rioters and those planning such activities banned from social networking.[13] There is also a proposed cyber-security strategy initiative in the UK, which, *inter alia*, proposes internet and social networking bans for criminals ("criminals who commit offences online") and cyberbullies.[14]

A man in Michigan was charged with hacking, after he hacked his wife's Gmail email account (and discovered evidence of her having an affair). The Leon Walker case was predicted to have potential repercussions for investigations that occur in a significant number of US family and divorce cases.[15]

Child conviction internet restriction cases are few in number, but they may grow in

---

'Sexting' 16 Year Old Son's Classmate Naked Pictures of Herself," *Daily Mail*, 14 November 2011.

7 E Oswald, "LulzSec's 'Topiary' Released on Bail, Banned from Internet," *Betanews*, 1 August 2011, available at http://betanews.com/2011/08/01/lulzsec-s-topiary-released-on-bail-banned-from-internet/.

8 P Roberts, "Alleged Anonymous Member Faces Ban, Monitoring Software," *ThreatPost*, 25 July 2011, available at http://threatpost.com/en_us/blogs/anonymous-members-face-internet-bans-monitoring-software-072511.

9 *ibid.*

10 K Poulsen, "Kechenkamp Challenges Computer Ban," *SecurityForces.com*, 3 December 2003, available at www.securityfocus.com/news/7576.

11 "Hacker Banned from the Internet," *GovernmentSecurity.org*, 12 July 2003, available at www.governmentsecurity.org/forum/topic/714-hacker-banned-from-the-internet/.

12 G Cluley, "Anonymous Suspects Bailed – Banned from Using Online Nicknames and IRC," *NakedSecurity.Sophos.com*, 7 September 2011, available at http://nakedsecurity.sophos.com/2011/09/07/anonymous-suspects-bailed-banned-from-using-online-nicknames-or-irc/.

13 "UK Prime Minister Wants to Ban Suspected Rioters From Facebook & Twitter," *TechDirt*, 11 August, 2011, available at www.techdirt.com/articles/20110811/11531615478/uk-prime-minister-wants-to-ban-suspected-rioters-facebook-twitter.shtml.

14 *The UK Cyber Security Strategy*, CabinetOffice.gov, available at www.cabinetoffice.gov.uk/resource-library/cyber-security-strategy. C Williams, "Criminals and Cyber Bullies to be Banned from the Web," *Daily Telegraph*, 25 November 2011.

15 C McGreal, "American Charged With Hacking After Snooping on Wife's Emails," *Guardian*, 27 December 2010.

frequency. In the US different courts can take different approaches. Adkins[16] refers to the cases of *United States v Paul*[17] and *United States v Brigham*[18] in the Fifth Circuit, which tend to uphold internet restrictions for convicted child pornography offences, while the Second Circuit is reluctant to impose restrictions on internet usage as a parole or probations restriction, such as in *United States v Peterson.*[19]

Challenges to Internet Sanctions

If these types of sanctions continue to grow in popularity, it may only be a matter of time before objections are made on the jurisdiction of a court to impose such a restriction or on the enforcement by a court or the police of such a restriction. These objections could conceivably come from a number of such constitutional and legal arguments.

Exploring these potential arguments is beyond the space and scope of this current work. However, we should explore one such possible argument: the theory of internet access as a human right.

A Human Right to Internet Access

There is an increasing view that access to the internet is, or should be, a human right. To use the words of Adkins, "[i]ncreasingly, being connected to society means being connected to the Internet."[20] A call has also been made to link data protection rules and the human rights regime.[21] Adkins continues later that "[d]ue to recent advances which have caused a surge in Internet popularity and utility, the Internet is nothing less than essential to our modern way of life."[22] A growing literature relates to the argument that access by persons to the internet is a human right.[23]

Extensive international jurisprudence and academic literature is devoted to fundamental human rights. In some ways this can sometimes be argued to take precedence over certain national laws. On occasion, competing rights have to be carefully balanced. This has often been recognised in terms of Irish constitutional rights. There are now suggestions that existing laws and technologies, such as

---

16 J Adkins, "Unfriended Felons: Reevaluating the Internet's Role for the Purpose of Special Conditions in Sentencing in a Post-Facebook World" (2011) *Journal of Telecommunications & High Technology Law* 263.

17 *United States v Paul* 274 F3d 155, 169–170 (5th Cir 2001).

18 *United States v Brigham*, 569 F3d 220 (5th Cir 2009).

19 *United States v Peterson*, 248 F3d 79, 83 (2d Cir 2001).

20 Adkins, *op. cit*, 264.

21 C Pounder, "Why Privacy is at Risk" (2009)(25) *Computer Law & Security Review* 285.

22 *ibid*, 284.

23 F La Rue, *Report of the Special Rapporteur on the Promotion and Protection of the Right to Freedom of Opinion and Expression*, United Nations, 16 May 2011. D Kravets, "UN Report Declares Internet Access a Human Right," *Wired.com*, 2 June 2011. ML Best, "Can the Internet be a Human Right?" (2004)(4) *Human Rights & Human Welfare* 23–31. "Top French Court Declares Internet Access 'Basic Human Right,'" *FoxNews.com*, 12 June 2009, available at www.foxnews.com/story/0,2933,525993,00.html.

technologies and laws relating to competition law and intellectual property, should be balanced to accommodate human rights.[24]

There has already been a call in Ireland to recognise internet access as a human right in this jurisdiction.[25] While this argument and the support for it is growing, including in Ireland, it has not generally — been linked with the issues and concerns relating social networking, child protection and related statute crimes. It is suggested that it is only a matter of time until these issues become more central.

The increasing use, if not reliance, by individuals on the internet for news, information and communications might enhance the argument for recognition of the internet as an essential technology; and separately of a human right of access to the internet.

The European Convention on Human Rights has also been relevant in terms of interpreting associational type rights. For example, the European Court of Human Rights in the case *Niemitz v Germany* stated as follows:

> "Respect for private life must also comprise to a certain degree the right to establish and develop relationships with other human beings. There appears, furthermore, to be no reason of principle why this understanding of the notion of private life should be taken to exclude activities of a professional or business nature since it is, after all, in the course of their working lives that the majority of people have a significant, if not the greatest, opportunity of developing relationships with the outside world. This view is supported by the fact that, as was rightly pointed out by the Commission, it is not always possible to distinguish clearly which of an individual's activities form part of his professional or business life and which do not".[26]

Broadband Internet

In many places there is on-going consternation in relation to the slow pace of broadband availability and roll-out. If internet access is recognised as a human right, this may then place an obligation on government to ensure that it is properly rolled out. This would have obvious political and cost issues.

Children's Rights to Access Internet

Just as we are considering expressly enshrining children's right in the Irish Constitution, the issue of internet access and human rights raises an altogether new issue.

Let us assume that there is a human right of access to the internet. The question then

24 See, for example, AEL Brown, "Access to Essential Technologies: The Role of the Interface Between Intellectual Property, Competition and Human Rights" (2010)(24) *International Review of Law Computers & Technology* 51. Brown calls for a draft Access to Knowledge Treaty, *ibid.*

25 See "Calls to Make Internet a Human Right Under Irish Law," *Silicon Republic*, 15 April 2011, referring to calls by Ronan Lupton, the chairman of ALTO.

26 *Niemitz v Germany*, ECHR, 23 November 1992, Series A No. 251/B, para. 29.

arises as to who the recipient of this right is. Is it adults only? Is it children, young persons and teenagers? If we assume that children are recipients of internet access rights, can they assert this right against parents or schools to be allowed to access the internet, social networking or other websites? Indeed, can they assert the right in order to access websites without supervision and without internet safety filtering software? These issues have yet to be considered.

Children's Referendum

The discussion regarding the recent Irish Children's Referendum, whereby children's rights were expressly recognised in the Constitution, was entirely devoid of the possible implications as regards the internet, social network and relates issues.

The new Constitutional Article reads as follows:

> "Article 42A
>
> 1 The State recognises and affirms the natural and imprescriptible rights of all children and shall, as far as practicable, by its laws protect and vindicate those rights.
>
> 2 1° In exceptional cases, where the parents, regardless of their marital status, fail in their duty towards their children to such extent that the safety or welfare of any of their children is likely to be prejudicially affected, the State as guardian of the common good shall, by proportionate means as provided by law, endeavour to supply the place of the parents, but always with due regard for the natural and imprescriptible rights of the child.
>
> 2° Provision shall be made by law for the adoption of any child where the parents have failed for such a period of time as may be prescribed by law in their duty towards the child and where the best interests of the child so require.
>
> 3 Provision shall be made by law for the voluntary placement for adoption and the adoption of any child.
>
> 4 1° Provision shall be made by law that in the resolution of all proceedings—
>
> i. brought by the State, as guardian of the common good, for the purpose of preventing the safety and welfare of any child from being prejudicially affected, or
>
> ii. concerning the adoption, guardianship or custody of, or access to, any child, the best interests of the child shall be the paramount consideration.
>
> 2° Provision shall be made by law for securing, as far as practicable, that in all proceedings referred to in subsection 1° of this section in respect of any child who is capable of forming his or her own views, the views of the child shall be ascertained and given due weight having regard to the age and maturity of the child."

This is an area which may well be worthy of considered analysis and research in future, and may have to be as internet rights issues evolve.

Conclusion

While the issue of internet restrictions has yet to be considered here, it is only a matter of time. It is to be recommended, however, that any such measures be fully and properly debated, and if implemented, that they be done so in a principled manner.

Whether a human right of access to the internet is recognised or not, it is quite a draconian step regardless to restrict access, whether judicially or via statute. In terms of content, there are developing issues of contention regarding peer to peer

(P2P), filtering and three strikes. Three strikes is the concept promoted by music (and film) industries that internet access provider should block users when they have been notified for a third time that the user is illegally downloading copyright music or film materials. These are sometimes known as graduated responses. Any such step should be considered at a policy level and not in an instant or reactive manner to a hard-case example.

The subject matter of possible internet access sanctions can also differ considerably. Internet restrictions in relation to P2P are quite different from child sex offender restrictions. While copyright infringement is an important issue, P2P infringement issues have until recently been viewed more as civil wrongs than criminal wrongs.[27] In addition, there are many reasons to say that P2P infringement is less serious than physical sex offences arising through sex offenders using social networks.

Indeed, in the case of P2P filtering, three strikes, etc, the copyright infringement is only alleged and may never come to court. The telecommunications companies and ISPs are acting on foot of allegations of infringement made by the content industries. The extent to which internet access is recognised as a human right might be argued to be more significant in the hierarchy of rights than an allegation of copyright infringement, notwithstanding that copyright is acknowledged now as a property right.[28]

A further issue to be considered in terms of sentencing restrictions is the extent to which judicial discretion[29] presently encompasses the scope to impose internet access restrictions. Is there a need for this to be permitted expressly in a new statute? This is not an easy question to answer, and may require an appeal case to decide the point in the absence of a statutory provision arising.

Child safety online is an important issue. However, as we are recognising and expanding the rights of children, there may be an unintended consequence of recognising the human right of internet access. It is always difficult to get the right proportion and balance in sentencing.

Clearly, these are also issues which are important and which need to receive greater consideration in future.

---

27 In relation to copyright offences, see Chapter 13, Copyright and Related Rights Act 2000.

28 As provided in section 17(1) of the Copyright and Related Rights Act 2000. See also A Murphy and C Kelly, *Copyright and Related Rights Act 2000* (Round Hall Sweet and Maxwell: Dublin, 2002).

29 See generally A Barak, *Judicial Discretion* (Yale University Press: Yale, 1989); O'Malley, *op. cit.*

PART IX: SOCIAL NETWORKING, PEER TO PEER AND PRIVACY

Chapter 28

SOCIAL NETWORKING, PEER TO PEER AND PRIVACY

Headline of Issues

- The P2P content wars and social networks
- Reactions
- Balancing rights and conduits
- Private spaces
- Internet monitoring and surveillance
- Internet lockers
- Notice and takedown (NTD)
- Contact listings
- YouTube and copyright
- YouTube, etc, user-generated content (UGC) and copyright
- Identity theft and personal name squatting
- Privacy and data protection

Introduction

The interface between the internet, social networking and intellectual property rights (IPRs) contains many new problems for privacy and data protection rights. That digital download of music has overtaken music physically sold in shops emphasises the changing environment.[1]

One of these arises as a consequence of peer-to-peer (P2P) litigation, whereby the music and film industries are pursuing intermediaries such as internet service providers (ISPs) to reveal the personal identity of individual internet users. More recently, the content industries have been litigating to force ISPs to filter the internet use of individual end users. There are also attempts to force ISPs to cut individual internet users off the internet where the content industries allege three times that the end user has infringed their rights. This is sometimes known as three strikes. While there are privacy (and other) concerns for individuals with all of these, there are particular concerns if the identities being revealed to content companies from ISPs.

While there are data protection and privacy concerns, the ISPs can take a view that they are permitted to do so if there is a court order in existence.

In the UK and Ireland the (increasingly) recognised procedure is to apply for a

---

1 J Halliday, "Digital Downloads Overtake Physical Music Sales in the US for First Time," *Guardian*, 6 January 2012.

Norwich Pharmacal order (NPO)[2] which directs the ISP to reveal specified personal data in relation to the end user. This is deemed to comply with data protection. In the US there is a line of John Doe type cases where proceedings are issued but the music industry plaintiff does not need a name (as it is not yet aware of the actual name of the defendant), and on foot of issuing such proceedings and interim orders, seeks to access the identity of an end user from an ISP. One would assume that NPOs may be applied for by Lord McAlpine in the UK, if they have not already, to identify those anonymous users whom have defamed Lord McAlpine in online comments. Frequently, however, NPOs are sought in relation to copyright music and film litigation. In one UK case, the porn star Ben Dover obtained an NPO in relation to 9,000 individuals alleged to be infringing.[3] There have been various NPOs granted in Ireland, initially in relation to intellectual property, but more recently in relation to online abuse issues.[4]

The P2P Content Wars and Social Networks

By way of context setting, we need to look at the P2P wars and the intellectual property issues, and then the privacy and data protection concerns. There are significant and increasing copyright-related issues with social networking.[5] The arrival of digital copies and the internet broke the traditional chain of delivering hardcopy copyright materials to users. The significance is that content owners had less control, and arguably have lost control, of the distribution of their works. More importantly, they face significant problems in collecting remuneration for the use of their works.

The US file sharing website Napster[6] was accused of facilitating massive P2P music copyright infringement by end users. This resulted in protracted litigation in the US. Ultimately, the website was shut down. Subsequent websites and software providers sought to tailor their business models to avoid being found liable for infringement or contributory infringement. These include P2P websites and software services such as KaZaA, Morpheus, Grokster, eDonkey, BitTorrent, Gnuttella, FasTrack, LimeWire, Pirate Bay and others.

The line of cases against P2P infringers, including websites and website services, culminating in the *Napster* cases[7] and the US Supreme Court *Grokster* decision[8]

---

2 Named after the UK case of *Norwich Pharmacal Co v Customs and Excise Commissioners* [1974] AC 133.

3 See *Golden Eye v Telefonica*, 26 March 2012, available at http://www.bailii.org/cgi-bin/markup.cgi?doc=/ew/cases/EWHC/Ch/2012/723.html&query=golden+and+eye&method=boolean.

4 For example, *McKeogh v Doe*, IEHC, unreported, 2012 (various dates); *US Oil & Gas plc*, unreported, 2012; and various Ryanair cases.

5 See, for example, J Naughton, "Sopa and Pipa: Don't Let Big Business Break the Internet, Legislation on Internet Piracy Presented to Congress Last Year is the Typical Kneejerk Response of the 'Content' Industry to Change," *Guardian*, 8 January 2012. Also, S Nelson, J Simek and J Foltin, "The Legal Implications of Social Networking" (2009–2010) (22) *Regent Law Review* 1t at 27 *et seq*.

6 *A&M Records Inc v Napster* 239 F3d 1004 (9th Circuit 2001).

7 *A&M Records Inc v Napster*.

8 *Metro Goldwyn Mayer Studios Inc v Grokster* 545 US 913. This decision relied on the point that the website's business model appeared to induce users to engage in or share pirated materials.

and more recent UK website blocking cases on balance appear to favour the content industries in their litigation.[9]

The Reactions

The P2P music file-sharing wars led to three main reactions:

- new laws and copy-rights;
- digital technology protection measures;
- reprographic copying laws and related levies.

The main reaction was to promote new reactive copyright laws. These include the two World Intellectual Property Organisation (WIPO)[10] copyright treaties,[11] the EU Copyright Directive[12] and the US Digital Millennium Copyright Act (DMCA).[13]

On foot of these new laws, there followed a worldwide litigation war against alleged large-scale individual music P2P infringers, ie individuals uploading significant amounts of allegedly infringing music files. Websites and software entities that are argued to facilitate illegal P2P infringement are also targeted, eg Napster and follow-on websites. A further variation is P2P software or software services. These business models seek to avoid liability, *inter alia*, on the basis of not hosting infringing music files, or storing user databases of infringing music files.

Later still, general individual end users (ie non-serial uploaders of infringing music) and intermediaries such as schools, universities and even internet cafes were also sued by the content industries.

More recently, the content industries sought to attack the "gatekeeper role of the ISP".[14] The content industries have argued that ISPs, etc, can be liable for

9 One should be aware, however, of significant debates as to the boundaries of copyright laws and separate debates as to whether all information, digital information and software should be "free," in the sense of freely available and payment free. These are sometimes referred to as the principles (or philosophies) of open source and copyleft. Note, however, that some would strongly distinguish between copyleft and open source, for example, Richard M Stallman. Such discussions are beyond the scope of this work. See, for example, SH Laddie, "Copyright: Over-Strength, Over-Regulated, Over-Rated?" (1997)(1) *Intellectual Property Quarterly* 3–15; E Raymond, "The Cathedral and the Bazaar," available at http://catb.org/~esr/writings/homesteading/; Electronic Frontier Foundation at www.eff.org; and GNU project at www.gnu.org.

10 WIPO or the World Intellectual Property Organisation is an international body under the auspices of the UN.

11 WIPO Copyright Treaty, adopted in Geneva on 20 December 1996 (WCT); and the WIPO Performances and Phonograms Treaty (WPPT).

12 Directive 2001/29/EC of the European Parliament and of the Council of 22 May 2001 on the harmonisation of certain aspects of copyright and related rights in the information society.

13 Digital Millennium Copyright Act 1998. It has been argued that under new laws, arguably each time is opened to view it an infringement occurs, because a copy must be made and also because there is arguably a public performance as referred to in the laws. See, for example, K Hunt, "Copyright and YouTube: Pirate's Playground or Fair Use Forum?" (2007)(14) *Michigan Telecommunications and Technology Law Review* 197 at 204.

14 SK Katyal, "The New Surveillance" (2004)(54) *Case Western Law Review* 297 at 371.

infringement in a vicarious or secondary liability capacity.[15] One of the advantages for the content industries is that the number of ISPs they may have to sue is significantly smaller than hundreds of thousands of users all over the world.

In US law there is a possibility for secondary infringers or contributory infringers to (sometimes) be held liable for the infringing acts of the main or primary infringer. However, there is arguably "vague standards governing contributory liability for intellectual property infringements ... [given] [t]he unstable legal environment both preceding and following the Supreme Court's *Grokster* decision has cast a shadow over all user-generated content businesses."[16] Social networks, including virtual websites, could be held liable for the alleged infringing acts of their users.[17] Already Marvel comics sued City of Heroes because users were creating avatars that resembled Marvel characters such as Spiderman, the Incredible Hulk and Wolverine. Ultimately this case settled.[18]

The content industries are pushing and lobbying for ISPs to implement copyright leaning policies in terms of alleged and repeat P2P infringers.[19] One example is a three-strikes policy.

Ireland is at the coalface of this ISP-related phase of the litigation. Irish telecommunications companies (telcos) and ISPs have been sued in order to try to force them to adopt a three-strikes policy of cutting off internet users whom the music industry allege are infringers, and or to upload the filtering (blocking) software of the music industry.[20] These issues are still being hotly debated and litigated with varying success for the content industries.[21]

Only later did new (lawful) models of digital music distribution arrive, such as iTunes, MusicNet, Pressplay and HMV Online. Arguably, the music industry can be criticised for not providing user-friendly lawful means of digital downloading music until late in the day.

New technology created the problem (as perceived by the content industries). Technology measures could also provide solutions.[22] These include technology restrictive control or access mechanisms (eg password access; encryption; anti-

15 JC Breen, "YouTube or YouLose: Can YouTube Survive a Copyright Infringement Lawsuit?" (2007)(16) *Texas Intellectual Property Law Journal* 151 at 173 *et seq*.

16 G Lastowska, "User-Generated Content and Virtual Worlds" (2007–2008)(10) *Vanderbilt Journal of Entertainment and Technology Law* 893 at 904.

17 But note the intermediary defences.

18 *Mervel Enterprises Inc v NCSoft Corp* 2004 WL 3770845 (CD California 10 November 2004) (No 04-CV-9253); and A Veiga, "Marvel Sues Two Companies Over Role-Playing Game," *USA Today.com*, 11 November 2004, http://usatoday.com/tech/news/2004-11-11-marvel-sues-over-avatars_x.htm?loc=interstitialskip as referred to in Lastowska, *op. cit*, at 913–914.

19 See Breen, *op. cit*, 161–162.

20 See the cases of *EMI v Eircom* [2010] IEHC 108 (16 April 2010) and *EMI Records (Ireland) Ltd v UPC Communications Ireland Ltd*. [2010] IEHC 377 (11 October 2010).

21 Note, in to the Irish cases of *IRMA v Eircom* and *IRMA v UPC*, the ECJ (pro-privacy-leaning) case of *Sabam v Tiscali/Scarlet (Scarlet Extended SA v Société Belge des Auteurs, Compositeurs et Editeurs SCRL (SABAM)* Case C-70/10). The Data Protection Commissioner is also considering the data protection implications of the Eircom three-strikes deal with the music industry.

22 Breen, *op. cit*, 162–163.

copying mechanisms), and separately identification and data information labelling systems. Both of these fall under the umbrella of digital right management (DRM).[23] The legal origin for these measures lies in the TRIPS Agreement and the WIPO Treaties, namely the WIPO Copyright Treaty[24] and WIPO Phonograms Treaty.[25] These ultimately led to the EU Copyright Directive, in particular Article 6, and related national implementing measures.[26] The hacking or decrypting of these DRM protective measures is deemed to be an offence—in addition to any separate copyright infringement.[27] A number of cases have related to such legislative measures.[28]

Balancing Rights and Conduits

WIPO began looking at the protection of IPRs in the online context, in particular in the WIPO Copyright Treaty of 1996. In addition to providing the basis of enhanced and more appropriately internet-focused copyright laws among Member States, it also provides that certain defences or safe harbours be provided to certain communications intermediaries. This is on the basis that these intermediaries do not, and cannot, know and be responsible for third-party communications that they facilitate but do not create. They merely assist the communication from third party A to third party B. They provide a communication conduit, but without creating the content passing on it. This analogy is often made of a post office's service of facilitating the delivery of third-party letter communications from A to B.

The EU eCommerce Directive[29] provides three separate limited defences, namely:

- mere conduit (Article 12);
- caching (Article 13); and
- hosting (Article 14).[30]

Mere conduit refers to where an information society service is provided that consists of the transmission on a communication network of information provided by a recipient of the service (user), or the provision of access to a communication network. Member States shall ensure that the website is not liable for the information transmitted, on condition that the website:

23 Katyal, *op. cit*, at 351–356.
24 Article 12.
25 Article 19.
26 See national implementation in s 375 of the Copyright and Related Rights Act 2000. Note also UK Copyright, Designs and Patents Act 1988.
27 See, for example Article 12 of the WIPO Copyright Treaty; Article 6.2 of the EU Copyright Directive; ss 375(1), 370 and 371 of the Copyright and Related Rights Act 2000.
28 These include the *Elcomsoft* case (*US v ElcomSoft and Dmitry Sklyarov* (2002)) and the *KaZaA* case in the Netherlands (*Buma/Stemra* (2003)); and also a case in Canada (*BMG Canada Inc v John Doe* (2004)).
29 Directive 2000/31/EC of the European Parliament and of the Council of 8 June 2000 on certain legal aspects of information society services, in particular electronic commerce, in the Internal Market.
30 These are transposed in Regulations 16, 17 and 18 respectively of the Irish E-Commerce Regulations 2003.

- does not initiate the transmission;
- does not select the receiver of the transmission; and
- does not select or modify the information contained in the transmission.

Caching refers to where an information society service is provided which consists of the transmission in a communication network of information provided by a recipient of the service (user). Member States shall ensure that the website is not liable for the automatic, intermediate and temporary storage of that information, performed for the sole purpose of making more efficient the information's onward transmission to other recipients of the service on their request, provided that:

- the provider does not modify the information;
- the provider complies with conditions on access to the information;
- the provider complies with rules regarding the updating of the information, specified in a manner widely recognised and used by industry;
- the provider does not interfere with the lawful use of technology, widely recognised and used by industry, to obtain data on the use of the information; and
- the provider acts expeditiously to remove or to disable access to the information it has stored upon obtaining actual knowledge of the fact that the information at the initial source of the transmission has been removed from the network, or access to it has been disabled, or that a court or an administrative authority has ordered such removal or disablement.

Hosting refers to where an information society service is provided that consists of the storage of information provided by a recipient of the service (user). Member States shall ensure that the website is not liable for the information stored at the request of a recipient of the service, on condition that:

- the provider does not have actual knowledge of illegal activity or information and, as regards claims for damages, is not aware of facts or circumstances from which the illegal activity or information is apparent; or
- the provider, upon obtaining such knowledge or awareness, acts expeditiously to remove or to disable access to the information.

If material is infringing, the ISP must remove the material on receipt of a complaint by the copyright owner. This is known as "notice and takedown" (NTD). If the offending material is not removed, or removed in a timely manner, the liability immunity may be lost. These intermediary defences were introduced in US law as amendments the US Copyright Act in 1998. However, the US laws been indicated to provide more content owner protection for online content than envisaged under the WIPO Copyright Treaty.[31]

The US Digital Millennium Copyright Act 1998 (DCMA) provides safe-harbour

---

31 J Cobia, "The Digital Millennium Copyright Act Takedown Notice Procedure: Misuses, Abuses, and Shortcomings of the Process" (2009)(10(1)) *Minnesota Journal of Science and Technology* 387 at 388.

defences to ISPs for what might otherwise be copyright infringement.[32] It was introduced to implement the two WIPO Treaties of 1996. The safe-harbour provisions for intermediaries were included in 17 USC SS 512 (a)–(d) so long as the works were transitory, caching, information residing on systems or networks at user discretion and information location tools.[33] Originally envisaged as applying to ISPs, the DCMA has a wide ambit and can apply to social networking websites.[34] The DCMA was held to apply when eBay was sued in relation to alleged copyright infringement activities of users.[35] However, there is also a developing vein of litigation where content owners seek to fix IPR liability on social networking websites despite the DCMA. One example is where Viacom issued proceedings against YouTube and Google.[36] When Google purchased YouTube for $1.65 billion it apparently set aside a $200 million fund to defend infringement cases.[37] The Football Association Premier League Limited also issued proceedings against YouTube.[38] One plaintiff, Robert Tur, is also suing YouTube over police video footage he filmed but which was being uploaded to YouTube without his consent.[39]

There have been suggestions that the DCMA requires amendment.[40] Some have argued that intermediaries effectively have (great) power but without any of the responsibility.[41] The content industries argue for a rebalancing in favour of content owners. Currently issues of intermediary liability are described as a "patchwork of different rules for different substantive areas."[42]

One of the issues which arises is gain or financial benefit under the respective ISP and social networking defences. In many instances a social networking is free. Therefore, it argues that there is no financial gain as might bring it outside the defences. Some argue that certain advertising may be a trigger for liability.[43] More

---

32 It has been argued that the DCMA does not provide full defences to intermediaries but only limits the reliefs available to plaintiffs. See Breen, *op. cit*, 173. There is debate in some quarters, however, as to whether YouTube is an information society service provider as set out in the eCommerce Directive, or alternatively avail of the US safe-harbour legislation, or alternatively again whether it is a content provider itself. See Flint, *op. cit*. There is also increasing arguments in favour of protecting and expanding (US) social networking business models. See RM Groves, "Facebook 2 Blackberry and Database Trading Systems: Morphing Social Networking to Business Growth in a Global Recession" (2009–2010)(112) *West Virginia Law Review* 153.

33 See, for example, BG Meyers, "Filtering Systems or Fair Use? A Comparative Analysis of Proposed Regulations for User-Generated Content" (2008–2009)(26) *Cardozo Arts & Entertainment Law Journal* 935 at 938.

34 See LB Patten, "Note, From Safe Harbor to Choppy Waters; YouTube, the Digital Millenium Copyright Act, and a Much Needed Change of Course" (2007)(10) *Vanderbilt Journal of Entertainment and Technology Law* 179 at 118–190 as referred to in Nelson *et al., op. cit*, 27.

35 *Hendrickson v eBay Inc* 165 F Supp 2d 1082, 1093 (CD California 2001).

36 See Complaint for Declaratory and Injunctive Relief and Damages at 5, *Viacon International Inc v YouTube Inc* 540 F Supp 2d 461 (SDNY 2008)(No 07 CV 2103).

37 WN Davis, "Downloading a File of Copyright Woes, Google's Buyout of YouTube Shows Federal Laws Still Lag Behind Technology," *ABA Journal*, March 2007 at 10.

38 See Class Action Complaint at 2, Football Association Premier League Limited v YouTube Inc 633 F Supp 2d 159 (SDNY 2009)(No 07 CV 3582).

39 Davis, *op. cit*, 10.

40 See Patten, *op. cit*, at 118–190 as referred to in Nelson *et al., op. cit*, 29.

41 See R Tushnet, "Power Without Responsibility: Intermediaries and the First Amendment" (2007–2008)(76) *George Washington Law Review* 986.

42 See *ibid*, 987.

43 See K Fayle, "Understanding the Legal Issues for Social Networking Sites and Their Users," *FindLaw.com* (2007) available http://technology.findlaw.com/articles/00006/010966.html.

recent is the advent and use of behavioural advertising or targeted advertisements based on a user's activity, preferences or previous search results. These histories are used to build profiles and then to target advertisements to users.

Online website service provider immunity defences are also recognised in the US Communications Decency Act and have been upheld in cases such as *Doe v Myspace*, *Zeran v America Online* and *Carafano v Metrosplash*.[44]

Private Spaces

P2P assists the rapid distribution of (legitimate and illegal) copyright materials.[45] However, P2P and part of the reaction "reconfigure[s] the boundaries of private and public space".[46] What were once private activities are now carried out in public or online. This can have consequences, such as where the private enforcement of copyright law[47] by music companies means that private internet activities can be made public, or internet access can even be cut off.

The content industries now threaten normal non-multiple-uploading users and intermediaries such as schools, universities and ISPs,[48] and more recently telcos.

There is a serious issue to the extent to which an individual's personal details or identity can be revealed online or as a result of P2P litigation processes. In addition, in what circumstances can or should ISPs reveal customer personal details?

Internet Monitoring and Surveillance

A further P2P concern relates to the "evidence" and intelligence which the content industries may seek to rely on in making an application for an NPO, or in making demands (eg a three-strikes strike-off) of an ISP relating to an end user. Frequently, such evidence is a report from a third-party firm that undertakes internet usage monitoring activities. Some of this may be legitimate, but without transparency in relation to all the methods of gathering such evidence, privacy and data protection concerns remain.

As referred to above, part of the music industry's response has involved the surveillance of individuals' internet activities. The music and film content industries routinely search the internet with web crawlers for suspected illegal or pirate

44 *Doe v Myspace*, 474 F Supp 2d 843 (WD Texas 2007); *Zeran V America Online* 129 F 3d 327 (4th Circuit 1997); and *Carafano v Metrosplash* 339 F3d 1119 (9th Circuit 2003). Referred to in Y Hashemi, "Facebook's Privacy Policy and Its Third Party Partnerships: Lucrativity and Liability" (2009)(15) *Bolton University Journal of Science and Technology Law* 140 at 1158–160.

45 SK Katyal, "The New Surveillance" (2004) (54) *Case Western Law Review* 297 at 300. Also 309–320.

46 *ibid*, 314.

47 As referred to in Katyal, *op. cit*, 320–326.

48 *ibid*, 325.

materials and evidence of infringement.[49] Katyal traces the history and origins of internet piracy surveillance and P2P surveillance.[50] Lessig also comments:

> "If you walked into a store, and the guard at the store recorded your name; if cameras tracked your every step, noting what items you looked at and what items you ignored; if an employee followed you around, calculating the time you spent in any given aisle; if before you could purchase an item you selected, the cashier demanded that you reveal who you were – if any and all of these things happened in real space, you would notice. You would notice and could then make a choice about whether you wanted to shop in such a store ... .
>
> In cyberspace, you would not. You would not notice such monitoring because such tracking in cyberspace is not similarly visible".[51]

Piracy surveillance is also critical as it "unilaterally permits private copyright owners to interpret the rules governing copyright and to prevent their violation."[52] (Snowden, NSA and GCHQ raise separate but important issues.)

Katyal, when referring to P2P, states that "[t]he effect of piracy surveillance without probable cause affects a person's right to receive information and runs the risk of chilling legitimate expression and fair use of copy-righted materials in both real space and cyberspace."[53] Questions arises as to the extent of this "right to receive information", when it may be possible to curtail this right, and under what circumstances.

Internet Lockers

A new online private space is the online cloud services known as digital lockers or cloud lockers. These can be used for storing personal music files, some of which it may be alleged to be illegal or unpaid for. Variations of cloud lockers are offered by websites such as Sideload.com, Google and Amazon.

In a case taken by EMI against Sideload.com, the New York District Court held that the ISP safe-harbour defences of the DMCA were available to it against a claim of infringement.[54] While the issue relates to the intermediary liability in the first instance, and may yet be appealed, there remain many privacy issues in relation to the end users, in particular whether their privacy, usage and identities will be revealed.

Notice and Takedown (NTD)

Cobia highlights some of the problems with the DMCA NTD procedure.[55] These

---

49 *ibid*, 298. Also 341–350.

50 *ibid*, 326–339.

51 L Lessing, "The Law of the Horse: What Cyberlaw Might Teach" (1999)(113) *Harvard Law Review* 501 at 504–505, referred to in Katyal, *op. cit*, 350.

52 Katyal, *op. cit*, 382–383.

53 *ibid*, 374.

54 *EMI v Sideload.com*, referred to in 1709 copyright blog, 24 August 2011. Available at http://the1709blog.blogspot.ie/2011/08/cloud-lockers-protected-by-safe-harbor.html.

55 J Cobia, "The Digital Millennium Copyright Act Takedown Notice Procedure: Misuses, Abuses, and Shortcomings of the Process" (2009)(10(1)) *Minnesota Journal of Science and Technology* 387.

include an inadequate balance between content right-holders and intermediaries; that it contributes to infringement; and that it is used to censor or chill otherwise legitimate criticism.[56] It is also a threat to the traditional fair-use defences in the US.[57]

The NTD remedies are meant to be efficient and cost effective. The content owner simply informs the website in question and the website, as part of the trade-off and in order to maintain the safe-harbour defence, takes down the allegedly offending material. It is therefore described as a self-policing solution.[58]

It should be noted that the website defences under EU law do not specify a formal NTD procedure, unlike the position in the US.

Contact Listings

In 2008 a UK recruitment company sued a former employee to restrain the employee from making use of information on a social network to establish a competing business.[59] Hays Recruitment claimed that its former employee, Mark Ions, had copied details from its client lists onto his LinkedIn contact list. He was ordered to disclose his list of contacts on LinkedIn.[60]

This served to highlight the importance of company commercial information and databases. Most business will have lists, databases and commercially sensitive information. Examples include supplier and customer listings. These are most acute for technology, software and online entities. "At its legal core, Facebook is a database. Its core business is not the sale of tangible products like furniture or equipment. Rather, it selects and arranges information in a format that allows interactive use by its online customers."[61] The EU database right protection model is also recommended in the US.[62]

Contact lists of online social networking could be considered trade secrets, as the information is not readily accessible; is valuable (ie has value); is compiled at the employer's expense; and reasonable safeguards and protection were taken.[63] The issue of investment and expenditure can also come up in discussion of trade secrets.[64]

---

56 *ibid*. Also see examples at *ibid*, 391–393.

57 *ibid*, 395.

58 *ibid*, 388.

59 See B Van Wyk, "We're Friends, Right? Client List Misappropriation and Online Social Networking in the Workplace" (2008–2009)(11) *Vanderbilt Journal of Entertainment and Technology Law* 743 at 743 and 746–747; and R Tyler, "Court Orders Ex-employee to Hand Over LinkedIn Contacts," *Daily Telegraph*, 17 June 2008, www.telegraph.co.uk/finance/newsbysector/mediatechnologyandtelecons/2791724/Court-orders-ex-employee-to-hand-over-LinkedIn-contacts.html.

60 See Van Wyk, *op. cit*, 743 and 746–747. Also see R Paul and LH Chung, "Brave New Cyberworld: The Emperor's Guide to the Interactive Internet" (2008)(2) *Labour Law* 109, referred to *ibid*.

61 Groves, *op. cit*, 160.

62 *ibid*, 186. The EU Database Directive, Directive 96/9/EC of the European Parliament and of the Council of 11 March 1996 on the legal protection of databases, is available at http://eur-lex.europa.eu/LexUriServ/LexUriServ.do?uri=CELEX:31996L0009:EN:HTML.

63 Van Wyk, *op. cit*, 768.

64 See *ibid*, 762.

More recently, a US company is pursuing an ex-employee for allegedly diverting Twitter followers to his new Twitter address. The company, PhoneDog, is claiming that the list of Twitter followers constitutes a database.[65] It is claiming $340,000 in relation to the lost 17,000 Twitter followers.[66]

The internet, email, digital copying and now social networking pose a serious threat to the maintenance and safeguarding of these materials by organisations.

However, sometimes overlooked is the importance of privacy and data protection in databases. Corporate and organisational databases can include personal data. This can be inward-facing, such as employee personal data, or outward-facing, such as customer personal data. It also includes prospective customer and employee personal data. The issue of security for hospital records is highly topical. Another example of outward-facing personal data contained in databases is patient data.[67] Indeed, patient data can constitute the more important category of personal information, known as sensitive personal data. This imposes more stringent obligations on data controllers processing personal data.

YouTube and Copyright

YouTube[68] faces "daunting legal challenges"[69] from the giants of the media and content industries in relation to copyright claims, such as from Time Warner,[70] Fox,[71] Viacom[72] and the Recording Industry Association of America.[73] Others include NBC, TVT, Epic Records, Atlantic Records, E! Entertainment, MTV2 and Fox Searchlight.[74] It remains to be seen what the final result will be.

However, while claims may continue, as well as take-down requests, some feel that

---

65 R Booth, "Company Sues Ex-Employee For His Twitter Followers," *Guardian*, 27 December 2011.

66 *ibid.*

67 Under the Data Protection (Amendment) Act 2003 in Ireland, personal data now includes both manual and electronically stored personal data.

68 For some brief comments in relation to the development of YouTube, see JC Breen, "YouTube or YouLose: Can YouTube Survive a Copyright Infringement Lawsuit?" (2007)(16) *Texas Intellectual Property Law Journal* 151 at 155–156, 158–159.

69 K Hunt, "Copyright and YouTube: Pirate's Playground or Fair Use Forum?" (2007)(14) *Michigan Telecommunications and Technology Law Review* 197 at 198.

70 DB Wood, "The YouTube World Opens an Untamed Frontier for Copyright Law," *The Christian Science Monitor*, 18 December 2006, http://csmonitor.com/2006/1218/p01s03-usju.html, referred to in Hunt, *op. cit*, 198.

71 N Carson, "Fox Offloads Suit Against YouTubers," *InternetNews.com*, 5 March 2007, www.intenretnews.com/bus-news/article.php/3663671, referred to in Hunt, *op. cit*, 198.

72 C Lombardi, "YouTube Takes Down Comedy Central Clips," *CNET News.com*, 30 October 2006, http://news.com/YouTube-takes-down-Comedy-Central-clips/2100-1030_3-6130868.html, referred to in Hunt, *op. cit*, 198.

73 E Bangeman, "YouTube, Google Videos Latest Targets of RIAA's Wrath," *Ars Technica*, 15 June 2006, http://arstechnica.com/news.ars/post/20060615-7065.html, referred to in Hunt, *op. cit*, 198; see also 215–216.

74 Breen, *op. cit*, 153.

much of the contentious content is used in a non-commercial manner.[75] YouTube and social networks also blur traditional lines between conversation and publication.[76]

YouTube content often comprises user-generated original content, mixed own and third-party materials, and third-party content.[77]

It has been argued that "fair use"[78] defences (which seek to protect new types of use which do not undermine the commercial value of the original) should protect YouTube against claims of infringement.[79] Fair use permits certain uses of copyright material, such as commentary, criticism, news reporting and parody.[80]

The hosting intermediary defence, as referred to in s 512(c) of the (US) Copyright Act, is argued as being a defence to YouTube for a copyright infringement case arising from user postings.[81]

However, there are also substantial arguments that YouTube does not fit into the website defences, or that if it does, it can lose the defence. Google (which own YouTube) had some of its executives arrested and found guilty of breaching data protection in Italy for not taking down an abusive video in relation to a child with Down's syndrome. Interestingly, the Italian court relied on evidence from a court hearing and documentation in Ireland. This was successfully appealled, and may be further appealed still.

Furthermore, there are cases in Australia, New Zealand, Germany and elsewhere which hold that YouTube, Google, etc can be liable, or indeed are liable, for content and materials on their websites. Max Mosley has also been successful in a French Google case. The ECJ/CJEU Spanish case ruling is awaited.

UGC and Copyright

Copyright laws struggle to keep up and deal with user-generated content (UGC), such as much of the content materials on many websites.[82] Katyal states:

> "A few years ago, it was fanciful to imagine a world where intellectual property owners – such as record companies, software owners, and publishers – were capable of invading the most sacred areas of the home in order to track, deter, and control uses of their products. Yet, today, precisely that is taking place. Emboldened by courts and legislators, copyright owners now undertake a widening degree of control over cultural products through the guise of piracy detection. As is now clear, the internet is no longer a smooth-functioning

75 Hunt, *op. cit*, 199.
76 *ibid*, 200.
77 Hunt, *op. cit*, 201.
78 See *Campbell v Acuff Rose Music Inc* 510 US 569; *Falsom v Marsh* 9 F Cas 342 (CCD Mass 1841); (US) Copyright Act 1976, section 107.
79 Hunt, *op. cit*, 206–210, 220–221.
80 BG Meyers, "Filtering Systems or Fair Use? A Comparative Analysis of Proposed Regulations for User-Generated Content" (2008–2009)(26) *Cardozo Arts & Entertainment Law Journal* 935 at 949.
81 Breen, *op. cit*, 154.
82 S Seidenberg, "Copyright in the Age of You Tube, As User Generated Sites Flourish, Copyright Law Struggles to Keep Up," *ANA Journal*, February 2009, 46.

> patchwork of anonymous possibilities for peer-to-peer communication. Instead, lurking behind the façade of such potential connections lies an increasing and subtle host of opportunities for legal accountability and detection, particularly where the use (or misuse) of intellectual property is concerned".[83]

The Recording Industry Association of America and the Business Software Alliance are very active in terms of litigating their members' rights in terms of music content licensing and software content licensing respectively. There is argued to be increasing conflict and even a "paradox"[84] between consumer privacy and the owners of content IPRs. Katyal adds that:

> "[In a] myriad of ways in which private entities have successfully monitored transmissions to control uses of their copyrighted materials. Piracy surveillance enables copyright owners to utilize a type of monitoring that demonstrably trespasses on a person's expectations of informational privacy and anonymity. These regimes take on three basic types: monitoring, which involves the use of automated systems to search for copyrighted material; management, which involves a host of actions taken in real space and cyberspace to limit certain uses of cultural products; and interference, which involves a degree of preventative actions taken to disable peer-to-peer file sharing from occurring.
>
> [The] private regimes of copyright enforcement carry significant disadvantages, among them the risk of transforming copyright law into a regime of 'panoptic publication,' where potential creators are monitored by third parties for the infringement potential of their activities. Because these systems of copyright enforcement are largely unregulated and fall outside of state control, piracy surveillance measures are capable of an unprecedented scope of invasion and control over the expressive activities of ordinary citizens, particularly with respect to the protection of fair use, free speech, and due process".[85]

It has been argued that ultimately piracy surveillance carries the potential to transform the nature of copyright law from a liability-based regime into a regime that governs the creation and use of all cultural products in cyberspace, whether illegitimate and legitimate.[86]

Unfortunately, "the nature of peer-to-peer cyberspace also ushers a contradictory complication: We act as though we have perfect anonymity in cyberspace, when in fact, much of the information we produce is also subject to a great degree of surveillance."[87] This was written in advance of recent NSA revelations.

Katyal states:

> "since the advent of computer technology, information has become a valuable commodity in and of itself, leading to an immense shift towards its commercialization. As a result, the economic base of society has shifted from industry to information, giving rise to such labels as the 'Information Revolution' or the 'Information Society.' Vast amounts of personal information are now primed for harvest, distribution, and disclosure to third parties on the internet, often without the individual's knowledge. Use of this information al-lows companies to perfect the creation of a 'virtual persona,' or 'electronic persona,' which comprises a profile of an individual user's tastes, purchasing habits, Web sites visited, and other identifying information.
>
> This transition towards third-party ownership, has, in turn, radically altered the preexisting balance between privacy and property contemplated in real space by

83 Katyal, *op. cit*, 297.
84 *ibid*, 299.
85 *ibid*, 301.
86 *ibid*, 301.
87 *ibid*, 314.

> subordinating the protection of informational privacy to the accumulation of database property. Today, techniques of data collection are especially pernicious because they are subtle, ongoing, largely unregulated, and inextricably linked to a person's online activities. Various entities collect an enormous amount of personal information from users with scant attention to the moral and legal privacy implications raised by its collection. Web sites use 'tracking software' that logs information about users, which is then used for a variety of purposes. ISPs are capable of tracking software downloaded by individuals. These records are a form of identification: Web server logs show that an individual using a particular ISP visited a Web site on a certain date and time, and the ISP usually keeps re-cords of the identity of the IP address holders. Others use 'Web bugs,' which are small, invisible graphics placed on Web sites or email messages to monitor the activities of individual users. On email messages, Web bugs allow the creator of the message to know when the message was read, to detect the IP address of an anonymous user, and to determine if and when the message is for-warded to others. Such methods of collection are also important for another reason: They can often provide the blueprint for strategies of piracy surveillance ...".[88]

What differentiates social networking from other websites is that much of the audiovisual content is owned, created and uploaded by the individual users: UGC. It includes videos, pictures, photographs, reviews, as well as UGC in virtual worlds.[89] There are "significant practical and legal problems that accompany user-generated content."[90]

We might distinguish also between old and new forms of UGC. For instance:

> "[u]ser-generated content, per se, has been around for a long time. After all, email is user generated content. What is different is the newfound importance and volume UGC is taking on. Policy issues concerning UGC have been percolating for a few years. For example, Cass Sunstein's book Republic.com, which was published in 2002, discusses the political significance of blogs, which are a form of UGC. It is only in the past few years, however, with the emergence of UGC mega-sites such as YouTube, MySpace, Facebook, Digg, and Revver, that UGC has taken on a new level of social significance, due to the sheer number of participants and the new ways in which they are interacting."[91]

However, there are problems with the websites permitting UGC, according to some authors. For example:

> "Many Web 2.0 companies are designed to allow tool generators to monetize user-created value. Technology and contract facilitate these business models. In order to use most online services, users generally must indicate that they assent to multi-page terms of service. If one reads those terms, they often require that the user provide the … owner with a licence to use all content generated during the use of the content to exclude the user from access at any time, thereby potentially denying the user access to the content that has been generated ... If these licence terms are enforceable, they essentially set up these online services as walled gardens, where users are invited in to create content for the benefit of the owners".[92]

While there are significant issues with mainstream social networking UGC, there is less acknowledged about UGC and new virtual worlds. A virtual world is a "software platform that provides users with access to simulated three-dimensional

---

88 *ibid*, 316–317. References omitted.

89 G Lastowska, "User-Generated Content and Virtual Worlds" (2007–2008)(10) *Vanderbilt Journal of Entertainment and Technology Law* 893 at 895.

90 *ibid*.

91 S Hetcher, "User-Generated Content and the Future of Copyright: Part One-Investiture of Ownership" (2008)(10) *Vanderbilt Journal of Entertainment and Technology Law* 863 at 865.

92 Lastowska, *op. cit*, 901.

space." Within this simulated space, individuals are represented by "avatars". Avatars are software-rendered and somewhat customisable representations of humans or humanoids."[93] These virtual worlds can also have their own economies and currency. Some of these are also very valuable, with real money and sometimes significant real money being exchanged for the virtual currency or virtual property.[94] Some of the best-known examples of virtual worlds are World of Warcraft and Second Life. The former is more proprietary. However, the later fully embraced UGC. Many UGC creators have profited from their creations on Second Life. Apparently, over a hundred users are earning over $60,000 per year from selling their UGC items on Second Life.[95] There is now also a virtual currency, Bitcoins.

However, not all UGC is of a commercial standard, with varying quality as well as some offensive or illegal UGC creations.[96] The possibility of virtual worlds for educational uses is also being explored.[97] For example:

> "[A parallel to] Napster and Grokster is that unauthorized commercial content is uploaded by some users and downloaded by other users. There are differences (eg Napster was music only), whereas now most of these [web]sites contain video. Thus, now it is not just the record labels attacking this activity as criminal infringement; rather, the TV studios, film studios, and other owners of video are also claiming infringement".[98]

Similar websites or services included Aimster.

Hatcher adds:

> "Another feature these [web]sites share is that they were created by young people for next to nothing, rather than by the titans of online commerce, such as Ebay, Amazon.com, Google, Yahoo!, or Microsoft."[99]

Users include small professional, amateurs and "amateurs aspiring to become professionals".[100] The cost of broadband and the tools required are significantly cheaper.[101]

An important difference, however, is that there is significantly less of a proportion of infringing materials than appear on social networking and related websites.[102]

The US Supreme Court in the *Sony Betamax* case[103] relied to a great extent on the extent of the non-infringing uses in order for a defence to arise to an infringement

---

93 *ibid*, 904.
94 See E Castronova, "Synthetic Worlds: The Business and Culture of Online Games" (2005) (University of Chicago Press) 17-160, as referred to in Lastowska, *op. cit*, 905.
95 Lastowska, *op. cit*, 911, and references therein.
96 *ibid*, 911–913.
97 See, for example, USC Centre on Public Diplomacy, Public Democracy and Virtual Worlds Project, http://uscpublic diplomacy.com/index.php/virtualworlds/about_cpd_vw, as referred to in Lastowska, *op. cit*, 913.
98 Hetcher, *op. cit*, 867.
99 *ibid*, 866.
100 *ibid*, 863.
101 *ibid*, 878.
102 *ibid*, 867.
103 *Sony v Universal City Studio* 464 US 417 (1984).

claim. The House of Lords reached a similar decision in the UK case of *CBS Songs v Amstrad*.[104] Both cases found that there was no infringement because the technologies discussed in the respective cases permitted non-infringing uses.

Viacom has sued YouTube and Google in New York in a copyright case regarding UGC, user postings and intermediary liability.[105] It refers to over 150,000 allegedly infringing clips of YouTube.[106]

The "form agreements between users and the UGC mega-sites are highly questionable. If these agreement turn out to be invalid and nullities, ... then the copying of the users' creative content by the mega-sites will be unauthorized and, thus, an infringement". Yet another problem presented by some UGC content is that there can be more than one person contributing to the work. This can include different people working on it, or different people presenting different elements of the overall work, including pictures, video, music, creative, productions and editing. Where more than one person is involved in creating a copyright work, there can be joint copyright ownership.[107] This can, therefore, create a problem in dealing with these works. Further still, even where there may be an original copyright work, if someone adds significantly to it, a whole new copyright work can be created.

It has also been suggested that there may be copyright subsisting in certain content on Twitter, even though tweets are limited to 140 characters, while copyright infringement generally requires substantial copying to have occurred.[108]

There are various solutions proposed for copyright problems presented by UGC.[109] There are also proposed voluntary and industry solutions to the UGC infringing issues, such as the Microsoft Principles for User Generated Content Services; Google YouTube Video Identification; and EFF The Fair Use Principles.[110]

Identity Theft and Personal Name Squatting

Identity theft and using and registering under other people's names are a growing problem. This can include fraud, theft, quasi-personality and IP rights.

---

104 *CBS Songs v Amstrad* (1988) RPC 567. Note general commentary in, for example, S Holmes, "Comment on the Recent *Grokster* Judgment by the US Supreme Court" (2005) (1) *Journal of Intellectual Property Law & Practice* 23–26.

105 *Viacon v YouTube* No 07-CV-2103 (SDNY 13 March 2007) http://viacom.com/news/News_Docs/Viacom%20YouTube%20Federal%20Complaint.pdf, referred to in Hetcher, *op. cit*, 882–883. Also, BG Meyers, "Filtering Systems or Fair Use? A Comparative Analysis of Proposed Regulations for User-Generated Content" (2008–2009) (26) *Cardozo Arts & Entertainment Law Journal* 935 at 941.

106 See Meyers, *op. cit*, at 941.

107 Hetcher, *op. cit*, 888.

108 See ST North, "Twitteright: Finding Protection in 140 Characters or Less" (2010–2011) *Journal of High Technology Law* 333.

109 For example, see E Castanova, "Synthetic Worlds: The Business and Culture of Online Games" (March 2008) (121) *Harvard Law Review* 1387.

110 See Meyers, *op. cit*, 936–937.

In some instances, in particular in the US, identity theft in relation to financial transactions has been made a specified statute offence.

Many readers will have heard of the problem of parties registering the website domain name (ie website address) of a well-known or famous company. Indeed, the names of celebrities, sports stars and politicians (eg Bertie Ahern) have been registered by third parties. Sometimes the registrants will then demand a payment from the brand owner.

This latter practice became known as domain name squatting and domain name infringement. There have been many important cases around the world in relation to this problem, many of which have resulted in the original entity or individual getting an order that the domain name be returned (ie transferred) to them.

Given the growing nature of the problem and the high cost of litigation, a number of specialist arbitration mechanisms were established specifically to deal with these domain disputes in an efficient and cost-effective manner. The best known of these is the WIPO Arbitration and Mediation Centre's Domain Name Resolution Procedure.[111]

However, given the increase in social networking and the increasing incidents of false registrations of profiles in other peoples' and organisations' names, it is important that this additional problem be examined and addressed.

This problem has already been described as "username-squatting".[112] It should be noted that while domain name disputes have included personal names, the issue of social networking username squatting is much more likely to involve personal names that commercial names. While social network increasingly permit organisational users, the vast majority of social networking users are individuals.

Conclusion

These issues are contentious and are being litigated, and lobbied over, around the world. It is quite easy to say that the so-called defences are absolute and are clear. However, analysis of the history and logic of the defences makes clear that current technology and dispute issues may not always match the original interpretations. Each of the defences is distinct and standalone, and each covers very different activities. The issues are increasingly nuanced.

---

[111] See www.wipo.int/amc/en/domains/.

[112] Z Pesochinsky, "Almost Famous: Preventing Username-Squatting on Social Networking Websites" (2010)(28) *Cardoza Arts & Entertainment Law Journal* 223.

PART X: SOCIAL NETWORKING AND SPORT

Chapter 29

SOCIAL NETWORKING AND SPORT

Headline of Issues

- Social networking
- The use of social networking by athletes
- Amateurs
- Students
- Professionals
- The entitlement to regulate athletes use of social networking

Introduction

There is a growing issue and conflict in relation to athletes and social networking. This relates in particular to whether athletes can be stopped from using social networking such as Facebook and Twitter. There are growing instances where organisations seek to stop and even discipline athletes for using and posting on social networks. It is, perhaps, surprising to learn that this includes not only professional sports organisations but college and amateur organisations also.

Social Networking and Sport

Given the popularity of social networking it was inevitable that sports organisations would seek to exploit it for advertising, marketing and other commercial purposes. However, it is also used for other activities, in particular in relation to the athletes themselves. Some of these examples include the recruitment of students to sports through social networking websites and text messages.[1] The use and content of text messaging between athletes and their coaches is receiving increased attention.[2] Obviously there are advantages, such as ease of contact, training time updates, cost, group texts, etc, to the use by athletes of social networks.[3] Some of the evolving concerns, however, are highlighted below.

Some concerns centre on the safety of athletes. Safety dangers can arise from unruly fans[4] threatening athletes on the latter's social network pages, or otherwise

1 M Maher, "You've Got Messages: Modern Technology Recruiting Through Text-Messaging and the Intrusiveness of Facebook" (2007)(8) *Texas Review of Entertainment and Sports Law* 125 at 127.

2 *ibid*, 127.

3 *ibid*, 127.

4 *ibid*, 147.

threatening them as a result of something that the athlete may have said online. Equally, clubs, organisations, schools and colleges can be concerned that their athletes and sports stars may say or do something controversial online, whether in a social networking post, photograph, etc.[5]

Issues and Concerns

There are evolving issues in terms of the ability of organisations to regulate and monitor their athletes' online activities. For example:

- Do colleges have a right to stop their student athletes posting on Facebook?
- Do professional sports clubs have the right to control the use by athletes of social networking and what they may post?[6]
- Is there a right to regulate?
- Is there a right to monitor?
- What rights so athletes have in terms of personal privacy to post to their own private and public social networking pages?
- Do athletes have free-speech rights (such as under the US First Amendment[7] for example) that encompass Facebook and Twitter postings and may outweigh the purported claims of colleges and sporting organisations?
- What privacy and data protection rights do athletes retain in relation to their online private and online public postings, and which rights may be breached by their organisation in terms of monitoring, or indeed in terms of seeking to regulate and prevent them entirely?

These issues will be increasingly contested and are evolving. While there are recent examples in Ireland of athletes' litigation in relation sporting issues, such as a boxing case regarding which boxer should be deemed to qualify for competition,[8] there does not appear to be a case involving these social networking issues.

Social Networking and Professional/Amateur Athletes

Sporting organisations have been increasingly expressing concerns about what their sports stars may be saying via social networking.

One American football player, Chad Ochocino, was fined $25,000 for tweeting during a game.[9] The NFL now bans players from using social networking up to 90

---

5 One instance of a controversial sports star tweet was that of Joey Barton referring to another soccer player made on 9 January 2012. Referred to on the Newstalk sports show, 10 January 2012.

6 Maher, *op. cit*, 127.

7 *ibid*, 127. See also D McLaren, "Freedom of Speech for Sports Stars on Social Media?" *UK Sports Network*, Social Media and Sport, available at www.theuksportsnetwork.com/freedom-of-speech-for-sports-stars-on-social-media.

8 *O'Reilly v Irish Amateur Boxing Association*, High Court, 19 August 2011, Cooke J.

9 McLaren, *op. cit*.

minutes before games and during games.[10] The UK under-19 cricketer Azeem Rafiq criticised a coach in an online post and was dropped as a result.[11]

On occasion players have been reprimanded for photographs that are leaked or taken by third parties, sent on to friends, re-tweeted, etc. American Football player Matt Stafford was reprimanded over a social networking photograph of him lifting a beer keg.[12] Other American Football players have been criticised for the recording of a song with sexual references.[13] Some players are also reported as being dismissed, such as at the Big 12 teams Texas and Oklahoma.[14]

This is an increasing issue in UK sports.[15] Liverpool are reported as investigating Nathan Ecclestone in relation to a tweet in bad taste which referred to 9/11.[16]

The Football Association in the UK is having to concern itself with social media comments by soccer players. Rio Ferdinand, for example, was fined £45,000 for a particular tweet perceived as being racist.[17] Blackpool fined Michael Chopra £10,000.

The issue of social media controversies are not immune to GAA[18] athletes. The GAA president responded to certain comments on Twitter as follows:

> "I wouldn't call it banter, it was one-sided and it was outrageous to suggest that a draw would be rigged ... They called into question the honesty of the entire TV3 crew, the games section in Croke Park ... They called into question my honesty and the honesty of Liam Hayes and the two cameras and that is outrageous, absolutely outrageous ... It's not a random chat. If you want a random chat you pick up your mobile – those players put it on record, it was done for effect and done to suggest that in some way we would collude to be dishonest ... I can't see how they can justify their actions."[19]

The concern from the club (and organisational) perspective is that the comments, innocent or otherwise, can adversely reflect on the player and the club. Revenue, sponsorship and fan goodwill can all be jeopardised. This is also an issue for individual athletes. Australian Olympic swimmer Stephanie Rice lost a sponsorship

---

10 *ibid.*

11 *ibid.*

12 See, for example, C Robinson, "Social Networking a Potential Trap for Prospects," *Yahoo Sports Tuesday*, 7 April 2009, available at http://sports.yahoo.com/nfl/news?slug=cr-socialnetowrking040709.

13 *ibid.*

14 *ibid.*

15 S Rice, R Rai and J Charlton, "Silly Twits: Sports Stars in Social Networking Controversy," *Independent on Sunday*, 14 September 2011.

16 "Liverpool Investigate Nathan Eccleston Over Controversial 9/11 Tweet," *Independent*, 14 September 2011.

17 J Jackson, "Rio Ferdinand Warned by Sir Alex Ferguson After $45,000 Twitter Fine," *Guardian*, 17 August, 2012, available at http://www.guardian.co.uk/football/2012/aug/17/rio-ferdinand-alex-ferguson-warned-twitter.

18 The Gaelic Athletics Association.

19 Referred to in "GAA president Liam O'Neill rejects 'fix' allegations," Joe.ie, 4 July 2012, available at http://www.joe.ie/gaa/gaa-news/gaa-president-liam-oneill-rejects-fix-allegations-0026545-1.

contract with Jaguar after tweeting "Suck on that faggots!" after Australia scored a try against South Africa in a rugby game.[20]

Another aspect of concern relates to athletes looking to be signed by professional teams. Many such individuals will naturally have their own private social networking profiles. However, there are reports that certain sports clubs in the US regularly use false profiles of pretty girls to make friend requests to these unsigned athletes.[21] This is known as "ghosting".[22] Therefore, good prospective athletes may have lost contracts and been de-selected as a result of what clubs feel about their social networking comments, friends, etc. One should be aware that while regular or blanket monitoring of employees appears to be permissible in the US, this is not permitted under EU data protection law. It may be that blanket monitoring and false-profile friend requests in relation to athletes may also be in breach of EU data protection.

Social Networking and College Athletes

The prevalence of text messages, etc from sports coaches to potential and actual athletes has growing issues. Some of these are seen as negative. The disadvantages include imposing unjustified pressures on students, interfering with students' education and threats to student privacy.[23] Effectively, students are seen by some coaches as being available to contact 24/7.

Some academic institutions have banned student athletes from using social networks.[24] Others are actively monitoring these issues as they come to an organisational policy position on these communications. Some also keep an eye on student and athlete postings.[25]

Once an age issue (ie an underage user issue) is triggered for the website , there may arguably be a legal or duty of care issue.[26] One suggestion has been that there should be two versions of a social network, one for children and one for adults.[27]

Obviously athletes must take responsibility for own postings.[28] However, it is quite a different thing to say that an organisation has a *per se* right to regulate or prevent an athlete from accessing and posting via social networks. It can be argued, for example, that in the US the First Amendment[29] rights of the individual present a constitutional

---

20 M Cowley, "Twitter Turns into Anti-Social Networking Trap for Sport Stars," *Sydney Morning Herald*, 9 September 2010.

21 See, for example, C Robinson, "Social Networking a Potential Trap for Prospects," *Yahoo Sports* Tuesday, 7 April 2009, available at http://sports.yahoo.com/nfl/news?slug=cr-socialnetowrking040709.

22 *ibid.*

23 Maher, *op. cit*, 129–131.

24 *ibid*, 139–140, and examples therein.

25 *ibid*, 140.

26 EP Stedman, "MySpace, But Whose Responsibility? Liability of Social-Networking Websites When Offline Sexual Assault of Minors Follows Online Interaction" (2007)(14) *Villanova Sports & Entertainment Law Journal* 363 at 395.

27 *ibid*, 395.

28 Maher, *op. cit*, 144.

29 *ibid*, 142–143.

bar to organisations preventing an individual from making statements online. This opens up a new line for First Amendment litigation. Privacy rights are also an issue if the organisation seeks to routinely monitor the athlete online. Issues that may also be considered are the extent to which such rights can be contracted away, for example, in a contract of engagement or playing contract. Does a professional playing contract have the same status as a student athlete's scholarship or student playing agreement? Are there legitimate reasons for saying that student athletes have more concern in protecting the private aspects of their being, including online postings, than commercial professional players? Should students' privacy and free-speech interests be protected more so than those of older famous professionals who may have professional agents and lawyers? Organisations also have obligations to protect their employees, which also need to be balanced.

Social Networking and Journalists

Journalists also have to consider social networking. Ethical issues arise in terms of what they may use from social networking, Twitter, etc as sources for sports news stories. Not all Twitter accounts are bona fide who they say they are. The Irish presidential election debate turned into controversy when an unverified tweet was read out live on TV but subsequently turned out to be incorrect. Can a journalist use a comment from a source he or she has not verified?

The number of social networks vastly escalates the potential scale of news sources available to the sports journalist. However, authenticity is again an issue. So too is news values and news judgments. Is there real news quality to online posts? Are quality and professionalism affected? Some social networking profile pages may be set to private or have a restricted set of friends. Issues of ethics, hacking, privacy and data protection arise.[30]

In Ireland there is sometimes a reluctance in certain organisations to fully engage with social media. In the case of RTE, the national broadcaster, scandals such as the fake presidential debate tweet and the Fr Reynolds scandal where a priest was defamed have perhaps led to the adoption of a more cautious approach. Media organisations have to develop social media policies.[31] A further issue is that of ownership of user and follower databases.

Competing Rules

One of the problems also to be considered is that there may be competing or complementary rules, codes, etc applicable to the same incident. There may be the club or college rules as well as the rules of the national sports representative

---

[30] See generally, S Reed, "Sports Journalists' Use of Social Media and Its Effects on Professionalism" (2011) *Journal of Sports and Media* 43 at 57 and *passim*.

[31] One newspaper indicated to its journalists that they should not comment via social media on the Leveson Report at the time of the report's release. The BBC told its staff not to refer to any of its difficulties and investigations on social media or in the press. See M Hennessy, "BBC Chief Tells Staff Not to Air Its Difficulties in Press and Social Media," *Irish Times*, 14 November 2012.

organisation.[32] This is in addition to certain activities being potentially criminal while others are potentially civil.

Transparency

Also, from the athletes' point of view, it is reasonable for them to expect that if certain matters are officially deemed to be inappropriate or otherwise not permissible, these matters should be clearly and transparently set out in advance. They need to be able to know what is and is not permitted.

Separately, in deciding whether a particular penalty or sanction is enforceable, it can be a factor that the "offence" was made known in a transparent and explicit manner.

Tracy notes these issues when stating that "[f]or athletes engaging in non-sport misconduct, there is no baseline penalty scheme. Punishments run the gamut, without deference to type of conduct, sport, level, gender, or even existing policy."[33]

Conclusion

These issues are only coming to be contested presently. The final outcome remains to be seen. Particular nuances may mean there are different results between college students and professionally paid sports stars; between public and private internet spaces; and between the particular jurisdictions involved. Indeed, a further point relates to the extent that something that can be viewed or accessed worldwide can be restricted in terms of the law that may apply in one particular jurisdiction.

The Olympics in London showed that national icons and sporting heroes are not immune from online abuse, including death threats. While certain abusers have already been identified and prosecuted, the Crown Prosecution Service in the UK has indicated that it is willing to appeal unduly lenient sentences for such online abuse where deemed appropriate.[34]

It remains to be seen whether similar prosecutions will arise in Ireland. Separately, at least one High Court Judge has called for further criminal offences for online abuse, as well as politicians.

32 A Tracy, "Athletic Discipline for Non-Sport Player Misconduct: the Role of College Athletic Department and Professional League Discipline and the Legal System's Penalties and Remedies" (2009) *Va Sports & Entertainment Law Journal* 254 at 255–256.

33 Tracy, *op. cit*, 270.

34 E Davey, "London 2012: Stiffer Sentences Possible for Olympic Criminals," BBC, 25 July 2012, available at http://www.bbc.co.uk/news/uk-england-london-18957632.

CHAPTER 30

SOCCER PLAYERS ON SOCIAL MEDIA

Gary Madden

HEADLINE OF ISSUES

- Social networking
- Soccer players
- Social medial
- Regulation
- The Football Association and regulation

INTRODUCTION

Social media has exploded in recent years.[1] Social networks and related websites have gripped people and organisations alike. This is highlighted by the fact that Twitter, a social media website, has accumulated over half a billion users to date.[2] It has changed the way in which people obtain news, conduct business, communicate with one another and how they socialise.[3] It's subscribers herald from a variety of backgrounds and a variety of positions within modern society. Professional sports persons are amongst those with huge exposure and fan-bases who have engaged in this social media frenzy.

This chapter endeavours to provide an overview of professional sports persons on social networks in order to determine who should regulate their behaviour on these social media websites.

To start, the regulation of social media websites in a general (non-sporting) context will be outlined. This will be followed by an exploration of examples of how the law has became involved in the regulation of social media. Throughout this chapter the English position will be the primary focus, due to the fact that the Football Association (FA) are a body operating in England. The focus of this chapter will then switch towards the regulation of social media in relation to footballers and the role of the English FA in this regulation. In delineating the approach of the English FA, their guidelines and code of conduct pertaining to social media will be considered.

1 S Kierkegaard, "Twitter Thou Doeth?" (2010)(26(6)) *Computer Law & Security Review* 577

2 C Smith, "Twitter Approaching 500m Users, Growth Far Outpacing Facebook: Catching Facebook at a Rate of Knots" (TechRadar, 30 January 2013) http://www.techradar.com/news/internet/web/twitter-approaching-500m-users-growth-far-outpacing-facebook-1128483.

3 Sanja Kelly and Sarah Cook, "Evolving Tactics of Internet Control and the Push for Greater Freedom" in Sanja Kelly and others (eds), *Freedom on the Net 2012: A Global Assessment of Internet and Digital Media* (New York: Freedom House, 2012)

Specific examples of the FA regulating players associated with their organisation will directly follow this, in order to provide a more detailed analysis.

Next this chapter argues that the English FA are not suitable regulators of footballers on social media. Issues including inconsistent fines for players on social networks, undesirable reasons for the inconsistencies, inconsistencies seen in other areas of the FA, a lack of accountability and the right to freedom of expression all contribute to this view. An analysis of the regulation of other professionals will take place with the aim of ascertaining suitability of the role of the English FA as regulators of footballers on social media. Potential alternatives will be offered to conclude this chapter. It is submitted at this point, and at several points throughout this chapter that the FA, in its current capacity are unsuitable as regulators in this area. The reasons for this will be explained throughout the chapter.

Social Media is Regulated

As one would expect, many social media websites operate user content policies which enable users to report offensive or bullying content in order to have it removed, or to have the infringer's account closed down.[4] However, the regulation of social media is to a large extent achieved by virtue of the fact that online communications are subject to many of the same laws as offline communications. In the UK in 2012, guidelines were drafted for cases which involve communications which have been sent online via social media.[5] The guidelines established some of the areas of law which are most likely to be utilised in dealing with communications sent via social media. Each of the offences serve to highlight the fact that a person may be criminally liable for communications sent online, such as on Twitter or Facebook. Online offences which may result in a criminal prosecution include: credible threats,[6] communications targeting specific individuals (harassment),[7] breach of court order[8] and communications which are grossly offensive, indecent, obscene or false.[9] Notably, the latter have a higher threshold, and based on the public interest, will be unlikely to result in a prosecution.[10] Simply put, an individual may be liable by law, for communications despite the fact that these communications are on social media websites.

---

4 S Birkbeck, "Can the Use of Social Media be Regulated?" (2013)(19(3)), *Computer and Telecommunications Law Review*, 83, 83

5 Director of Public Prosecutions, *Interim Guidelines on Prosecuting Cases Involving Communications Sent via Social Media* (Crown Prosecution Service, 19 December 2012) 1 http://www.cps.gov.uk/consultations/social_media_consultation.pdf.

6 Legislation including the Offences Against the Person Act 1861, Protection from Harassment Act 1997, Crime and Disorder Act 1998, Criminal Justice Act 2003 and the Communications Act 2003 all have relevant sections which may be used.

7 Protection from Harassment Act 1997, s 7.

8 Contempt of Court Act 1981 and Sexual Offences (Amendment) Act 1992, s 5.

9 Legislation including the Malicious Communications Act 1988 and the Communications Act 2003 have relevant sections which may be used.

10 Director of Public Prosecutions, *Interim Guidelines on Prosecuting Cases Involving Communications Sent via Social Media* (Crown Prosecution Service, 19 December 2012) 4 http://www.cps.gov.uk/consultations/social_media_consultation.pdf.

The Role of the Law in Social Media

Despite the absence social network/media specific legislation, the law has still assumed a role online. This lack of social media specific legislation in England is understandable due to the fact that trying to formulate, and then apply, new black-and-white law in this area may be likely to fail.[11] The reasoning for this is rooted in the fact that "[i]f you regulate for specific technologies, different ones will proliferate and your technologically specific policy or legislation will be useless".[12] As a result English law has taken the approach of utilising the legislation which already exists, and applying this to internet.

One of the most well known examples of this is the "Twitter Joke Trial" where Paul Chambers was convicted under s 127(1) of the Communications Act 2003, for sending by means of a public electronic communications network a message of "menacing character".[13] Mr Chambers had commented on Twitter that "Robin Hood Airport is closed. You've got a week and a bit to get your s*** together otherwise I am blowing the airport sky high!!"[14] However, upon appeal the communication was deemed not to be menacing.[15]

It is worth noting at this point that s 127 is hardly a lone legislative bulwark against internet trolls and harassers.[16] The law has equipped itself with an abundance of legislative provisions which enable it to charge social media content.[17] For example, The Protection Against Harassment Act 1997 prescribes that any two "acts" which form a course of harassing conduct can be charged as a crime.[18] This was succesfully used to win a Norwich Pharmacal order against Facebook to require the names and identities of a womans online trolls to be revealed, to enable proceedings to commence.[19] Furthermore, The Sexual Offences (Amendment) Act 1992 was used to charge a number of people who revealed on Twitter the identity of a woman who was raped, as the naming of victims of sexual assault is forbidden in the media or by social media users.[20]

---

11 D Snow and J Manning, "Modern-day Droogs are Free to Roam: Can Social Media Content Really be Effectively Regulated?" *The Sydney Morning Herald* (Sydney, 15 September 2012) http://www.smh.com.au/technology/technology-news/modernday-droogs-are-free-to-roam-20120914-25xhf.html.

12 *ibid.*

13 D Carney, "Case Comment: Football Banning Orders and Twitter - Bomb Joke on Twitter" *Police Journal*, (2012)(85(3)), 255, 257

14 R Griffiths, "Social Media and the Criminal Law" (2013)(24(2)) *Entertainment Law Review* 57, 58

15 Alisdair Gillespie, "Case Comment Twitter, Jokes and the Law" (2012)(76(5)) *Journal of Criminal Law* 364, 365

16 L Edwards, "Section 127 of the Communications Act 2003: Threat or Menace?" (2012)(23(4)) SLJ 3 http://papers.ssrn.com/sol3/papers.cfm?abstract_id=2200166.

17 L Edwards, "Section 127 of the Communications Act 2003: Threat or Menace?" (23(4)) SLJ 3 (2012) http://papers.ssrn.com/sol3/papers.cfm?abstract_id=2200166.

18 The Protection Against Harassment Act 1997.

19 J Swift, "Bains Cohen Takes on Facebook in Internet Bullying Case" (12 June 2012) *The Lawyer*, http://www.thelawyer.com/bains-cohen-takes-on-facebook-in-internet-bullying-case/1012919.article.

20 L Scaife, "The DPP and Social Media: A New Approach Coming Out of the Woods?" (2013) (18(1)) *Communications Law* 5, 7

However, the law's adaptation to the dangers of unfettered social media comment in England is perhaps best epitomised by the Crown Prosecution Service's (CPS) Guidelines on Prosecuting Cases Involving Communications Sent by Social Media (the Guidelines).[21] These guidelines attempt to build upon the Protection from Harassment Act 1997, the Malicious Communications Act 1988 and Communications Act 2003, in the quest to provide greater protection.[22] Their succesful use was highlighted in the Fabrice Muamba decision, where a 21 year old student was sentenced to 56 days imprisonment under s 127 of the Communications Act 2003 for posting racially aggravated abuse on Twitter.[23]

Therefore, it is evident that there exists a number of legal provisions which provide a medium for taking action under English law. A number of other legal provisions apply which may be used in relation to social media offences. This chapter will now focus on the issues centred around professional footballers, social media and the regulation of these players.

The Role of the English FA

The English FA is the governing and regulatory body of English football.[24] As a result, the FA have adopted a number of guidelines and rules regarding footballers on social media networks. The FA published charging guidelines for social networking cases which outline the types of comments which will be subject to a disciplinary process. These guidelines state that cases involving comments made on social networking websites will be tried under FA Rule E3(1).[25] FA Rule E3 provides as follows:

> "(1) A Participant shall at all times act in the best interests of the game and shall not act in any manner which is improper or brings the game into disrepute or use any one, or a combination of, violent conduct, serious foul play, threatening, abusive, indecent or insulting words or behaviour.[26]
>
> (2) In the event of any breach of Rule E3(1) including a reference to any one or more of a person's ethnic origin, colour, race, nationality, faith, gender, sexual orientation or disability (an 'aggravating factor'), a Regulatory Commission shall consider the imposition of an increased sanction.[27] This allows for a Regulatory Commission to consider the imposition of a double or treble sanction.[28] However, specific sanctions are not expressly outlined".[29]

---

21 L Silkin, "Social Media Tamed? Trepidation in the Upper Echelons of Sports Organisations' *Law in Sport* (19 February 2013), http://www.lawinsport.com/blog/lewis-silkin-sports-law-blog/item/social-media-tamed.

22 *ibid.*

23 *ibid.*

24 Public and Regulatory Law Group Alert (11 October 2012) http://www.legalcitation.ie/page5/files/OSCOLA%20Ireland%20QuickRef.pdf.

25 The Football Association, *Media comments and Social Networking cases – Charging guidelines* http://www.thefa.com/~/media/Files/TheFAPortal/governance-docs/analysis/media-comments-and-social-media-guidelines.ashx

26 The FA, Rules and Regulations of the Associaiton Season 2011-2012, 119 available at http://www.thefa.com/thefa/~/media/Files/PDF/TheFA/FA%20Handbook%202010-11/FAHandbook-update-1011.ashx/FAHandbook-update-1011.pdf

27 *ibid.*

28 *ibid.*

29 The Football Association, *Media Comments and Social Networking Cases – Charging Guidelines* http://www.thefa.com/~/media/Files/TheFAPortal/governance-docs/analysis/media-comments-and-social-media-guidelines.ashx.

Additionally, the Premier League — following several months work which included consultation with the Professional Footballers' Association and the FA — now put together guidelines which set out clear direction to players on the use of social media, however it is the FA who remain in charge of the disciplinary process.[30] The areas of focus for these guidelines include: the benefits of using social media to engage with supporters, understanding the potential audience of social media websites like Twitter and Facebook, understanding that it is possible to commit offences online via social media. The guidelines also outline the FA's regulatory role in respect of disciplinary action that can be taken against players who make improper comments on social media websites.[31] Unfortunately, the specific details included in the guidelines have not been released.

The FA's proactive approach towards protection of social media use by its members was further illustrated when they issued the English national team with rules on their use of social media. The FA rules which were administered to the players, give particular mention to the players' use of Twitter and Facebook. This may be construed as an attempt to control the instant and unfiltered use of social media by soccer stars.[32] The new code of conduct states that England players must "not publish (on Twitter or Facebook) anything that may cause or embarrass a member of the FA, the England squad and management." No criticism on Twitter or Facebook is allowed at all, nor is use of Twitter or Facebook permitted a day before or on the day of a match.[33] Again, the full text of this code of conduct has not been made available.

It is, therefore, clear that the English FA have attempted to use the powers bestowed upon them as self-regulators, to reduce the negative ramifications which may stem from unwise use of social networking websites by its members. As has been illustrated, the FA have attempted to nullify the threat of exposure by means of guidelines, rules and disciplinary procedures. However, the question arises as to the whether the FA should have such power to regulate its members use of social networks? An exploration of the disciplinary procedure will, in the view of this writer, highlight the inconsistencies in this process. It is submitted that these inconsistencies provide one of the reasons why the FA may not be well placed to regulate their members activities on Twitter and Facebook.

Why the English FA Should Not Regulate Players on Social Media

Inconsistent English FA Disciplining

Joining social networks such as Twitter and Facebook can be highly beneficial for professional footballers. It provides the footballer with avenues to interact with fans on a level playing field and allows them to stay in touch with reality, from the perspective that it enables the reception of authentic opinions outside their sporting

---

30 Mirror Football, "Twitter Ye Not: Premier League Issue Tweeting Guidelines for Players" *Mirror* (UK, 24 July 2012) http://www.mirror.co.uk/sport/football/news/premier-league-twitter-guidelines-revealed-1163286.

31 *ibid.*

32 L Witherington, "England's FA Gives Players New Rules on Social Media" *The Wall Street Journal* (Europe, 17 October 2012) http://online.wsj.com/article/SB10000872396390444734804578062641765330554.html.

33 *ibid.*

vacuum.[34] Moreover from a commercial perspective, social media can develop player exposure, raise public awareness, build brands, and ultimately enhance the sports industry's profitability.[35] However, there is little doubt that the irresistible march of social media has been met with trepidation in the upper echelons of many sports organisations, of which football is one.[36] The English FA have, as a result been quite lively in their disciplinary procedures for footballers behaviour on Twitter.

The FA has taken a strong stance on Twitter under the far reaching term of bringing the game into disrepute (Rule E3).[37] This (overly) broad claim leaves players with little room to maneuvere in the construction of their comments, when they wish to express their dissatisfaction by means of a tweet. The result has been the imposition of a number of charges by the FA, and it is the inconistencies of these charges which will now be explored.

The FA have been quite fortright in their application of disciplinary measures regarding activities on social networks since their first charge[38] in early 2011. The FA charged Ryan Babel with improper conduct accompanied by a fine of £10,000 for questioning decisions made by a referee.[39] Prior to the Ryan Babel decision, athletes had only been warned for posting inappropriate comments on Twitter, but this was the first time a governing body held a specially convened hearing (and indeed imposed what was a considerable fine, which was believed in many quarters to be disproportionate).[40] Since this decision to charge Mr Babel, there has been a number of disciplinary proceedings involving other players. However, it is argued that there has been a high degree of inconsistency in the charges which have been imposed for similar "offences".

Another £10,000 charge involved Liverpool footballer Suso. Suso posted a satirical tweet based on the sexual orientation of his Liverpool teammate and friend.[41] The FA, in a statement, noted that the charge was "that he acted in a way which was improper and/or brought the game into disrepute".[42] Here, we see two charges for

---

34 L Silkin, "Social Media in Sport" *Law in Sport* (27 November 2012) http://www.lawinsport.com/blog/item/social-media-in-sport.

35 *ibid.*

36 L Silkin, "Social Media Tamed? Trepidation in the Upper Echelons of Sports Organisations" *Law in Sport* (19 February 2013), http://www.lawinsport.com/blog/lewis-silkin-sports-law-blog/item/social-media-tamed.

37 N Talbott, "A Sportsperson's Dilemma: To Tweet or Not to Tweet?" (WrightHassall, 25 January 2013) http://www.wrighthassall.co.uk/articles/2013/01/25/sportspersons-dilemma-tweet-or-not-tweet/.

38 D Geey and H Cohen, "Being Tweeted Fairly? Footballers, Clubs & Social Media" (*The Tomkins Times*, 20 January 2011) http://tomkinstimes.com/2011/01/being-tweeted-fairly-footballers-clubs-social-media/.

39 "Liverpool's Ryan Babel Accepts FA Twitter Charge" (BBC Sport Football, 13 January 2011) http://news.bbc.co.uk/sport2/hi/football/teams/l/liverpool/9352443.stm.

40 A Nixon, "The Sport Lawyer – The Top 5 Cases of 2011" *Law in Sport* (08 January 2012) http://www.lawinsport.com/articles/regulation-a-governance/item/the-sport-lawyer-the-top-5-cases-of-2011.

41 "FA Fines Liverpool's Suso £10,000 for Twitter Jibe at José Enrique" *The Guardian* (UK, 18 December 2012) http://www.guardian.co.uk/football/2012/dec/18/fa-liverpool-suso-jose-enrique.

42 S Peach, "Liverpool Midfielder Suso Fined by FA for Calling Jose Enrique 'Gay' on Twitter" *The Independent* (UK, 18 December 2012) http://www.independent.co.uk/sport/football/premier-

bringing the game into disrepute with identical fines. A consistent precedent appeared to have been created. However the consistency ends here.

Rio Ferdinand was fined £45,000 on the same grounds as Suso, ie improper conduct and bringing the game into disrepute. However, in Mr Ferdinand's tweet, there was a reference to "ethnic origin, colour or race".[43] One might infer that the gross increase in the amount of the fine may perhaps be attributed to the ethnic origin, colour or race element which was not seen in Suso's tweet. However, the potential validity of this reasoning is negated by the fine which was imposed on Arsenal midfielder Emmanuel Frimpong. In stark contrast to the fine imposed on Mr Ferdinand, a fine of £6,000 was levied upon Mr Frimpong, who retweeted a derogatory term which included a reference to faith.[44]

Leaving aside the ethnicity, religion, etc elements for a moment, the fine imposed on Chelsea footballer Ashley Cole, is the fine which has received the greatest amount of commentary. Ashley Cole was fined £90,000 for using an expletive on Twitter to describe the FA.[45] The was comment was deemed to be improper and/or brought the game into disrepute.[46] By contrast, a Grimsby Town footballer[47] was also charged by the FA. The charge against Mr Colbeck was for four breaches of FA Rule E3 relating to Twitter comments.[48] Again, the tweets were deemed to be improper and/or brought the game into disrepute. Notably, his four tweets also fell under FA Rule E3(2) as each of the breaches included a reference to a person's or persons' disability and/or sexual orientation.[49] Mr Colbeck was fined £1,500.[50]

From the aforementioned list of cases involving fines being placed on players for their tweets, it is clear that consistency in severity of punishment is a virtue which appears to be antonymous with the English FA. It is opined that this clear unpredicatability and indeed inconsistency of fines which players are required to pay, reinforce the viewpoint that the FA are not, in their current capacity acting sufficiently in their regulation of footballers on social media.

Undesirability of the FA (A Self-Regulatory Body) Reasoning and Inconsistency

First, if we re-visit the charges placed on Suso, Rio Ferdinand and Emmanuel Frimpong, the lack of consistency is particularly evident. Despite the fact that each

---

league/liverpool-midfielder-suso-fined-by-fa-for-calling-jose-enrique-gay-on-twitter-8424216.html.

43 "FA Fines Rio Ferdinand for Twitter Comment" (Premium Sports Center, 17 August 2012) http://www.premiumsportscenter.com/2012/08/fa-fines-rio-ferdinand-for-twitter.html.

44 S Blaquiere, "FA Fines Arsenal Midfielder Frimpong £6,000 for Twitter Comments" (Goal, 1 August 2012) http://www.goal.com/en-gb/news/2896/premier-league/2012/08/01/3279815/fa-fines-arsenal-midfielder-frimpong-6000-for-twitter

45 L Silkin, "Social Media in Sport" *Law in Sport* (27 November 2012) http://www.lawinsport.com/blog/item/social-media-in-sport.

46 *ibid.*

47 Grimsby play a number of Divisions below Chelsea.

48 Football Association Regulatory Commission, *Reasons for the Regulatory Commission Decision in the Matter of Joe Colbeck of Grimsby Town FC* (2012).

49 *ibid.*

50 "Grimsby Town: Joe Colbeck Twitter Fine was Disproportionate, says Paul Hurst" *Grimsby Telegraph* (Grimsby, 11 January 2013) http://www.thisisgrimsby.co.uk/story-17827037-detail/story.html#axzz2QlHcPP7r.

of the charges involving the above, were imposed by virtue of Rule E3, the main method of distinction which appears to exist between the charges is the means by which the tweets are deemed to bring the game into disrepute. In terms of severity of the fine, it appears that Mr Frimpongs' charge, which was based on religion, falls at the lower end of the spectrum. This is followed by Suso's tweet regarding sexual orientation. This is proceeded by Mr Ferdinand's tweet which involved issues of race at the top of the spectrum. Perhaps the FA may attempt to justify the varying fines on the basis of differing subject matter. However, it is the view of the writer that this should not be tolerated. It is opined that from a policy perspective the classification of severity of tweets regarding delicate issues such as religious beliefs, sexual orientation and race should not be placed in the hands of a private body, without a body to oversee these decisions.

Notably, under FA Rule E3(2) the Regulatory Commission have the power to vary the sanction according to the aggravating or mitigating factors present in each case. Perhaps factors such as wages, number of followers on Twitter, and previously disciplinary record may be used as the reasoning behind the inconsistencies mentioned above. In fact, it is worth noting that in the Joe Colbeck decision, the Regulatory Commission cited players wages, previous conduct and admittance of the charge as factors to be considered when deciding the sanction.[51] It is the view of the writer that in any decision relating to a charge, both admittance of the charge and previous conduct should be used as factors in deciding the appropriate sanction.

However, it is further suggested that factors such as wages, amount of followers, etc, should not be decisive factors. Rather, there should be equal punishment for the same offence. Where a body is granted the power to charge its members, the consistency of charges is of paramount importance. Procedural fairness cannot occur where members are being charged different sums of money based on their earnings. If two individuals commited a minor assault, it would not be fair to order compensation of £1,500 to be paid by one individual, but £90,000 to be paid by the other, based on their earnings. The FA charged Mr Cole £88,500 more than Mr Colbeck due to the fact that he has higher earnings than Mr Colbeck, despite the fact that Mr Colbeck had four tweets as opposed to Mr Cole's solitary tweet. It is submitted that issuing greater fines despite committing the "same" or "less serious" offence(s) is highly undesirable due to the lack of consistency and fairness which stems from this practice. It is strongly argued that this should not be permitted, and that there should be equal charges.

The reasoning for this is four-fold. First, similar charges for similar offences should be a standard which all bodies exercising judicial power meet. Second, this standard would force the FA to provide greater consistency in their charging of players. Third, equal charges for equal offences would force the FA to potentially reaffirm the opinion of the writer ie their fines are currently disproportionate.[52] Finally, it is the

51 Football Association Regulatory Commission, *Reasons for the Regulatory Commission Decision in the Matter of Joe Colbeck of Grimsby Town FC* (2012).

52 If equal charges were necessary, the more likely scenario would be a reduction of the fines which were levied upon Ashley Cole and Rio Ferdinand, rather than an increase in fines for Joe Colbeck. If they cannot justify the imposition of £45,000 or £90,000 fines for all players, this indicates the disproportionate nature of the fines which Mr Ferdinand and Mr Cole were required to pay.

view of this writer that similar charges should be imposed from a policy perspective as it would reduce the opportunity for the FA to potentially issue arbitrary fines for their own benefit. The FA could potentially charge players excessive amounts when ever the organisation is in need of an influx of money. As Grimsby Town manager pointed out, "They've got people monitoring the players, which is a job in itself with how many professionals are out there, and I wonder how much money that person is being paid".[53]

Therefore, it is argued that a private, self-regulatory body should not be the sole body that decides on the classification of sensitive issues including race, sexual orientation, etc. It is submitted that placing this power in the hands of a private body who have displayed a clear inability to show equality in their charging of players on social media is undesirable. It is undesirable as a result of the aforementioned inconsistent disciplinary measures administered for social media offences, as well as the inconsistency which is evident across other areas of the FA's disciplinary process.

Lack of Consistency is Prevalent in Other Areas that the FA Act in a Self-Regulatory Capacity

In every industry, including sport, it is of paramount importance that there is integrity emanating from the rules and regulations which govern that sport.[54] It has long been posited that the FA lacks transparency in many of its operations, such as its decision-making processes and in cases of disciplinary hearings in general.[55] This lack of transparency can be said to contribute to the lack of consistency displayed by the FA across a wide range of their disciplinary procedures, thus the rules and regulations appear to be lacking integrity.

The inconsistency of the English FA in its disciplinary proceedings and sanctions is evident in another case beyond footballers actions on social media. One such decision, which sparked much debate was the John Terry case.[56] This case involved the alleged racial online abuse of Anton Ferdinand during a football match. Mr Terry was subsequently charged by the FA with breaking rule E3(1) and E3(2) and received a four match ban. However, in the case involving Luis Suarez, who was charged on identical grounds to Mr Terry for the racial online abuse of Patrice Evra, an eight match ban was the penalty administered.[57] This level of inconsistency is of such an unsatisfactory nature that it prompted former English FA compliance officer Graham Beam to state that "the FA can't be trusted to run the disciplinary process. It's time to overhaul it because the FA can't be trusted to be consistent with penalties".[58]

---

[53] "Grimsby Town: Joe Colbeck Twitter Fine was Disproportionate, says Paul Hurst" *Grimsby Telegraph* (Grimsby, 11 January 2013) http://www.thisisgrimsby.co.uk/story-17827037-detail/story.html#axzz2QlHcPP7r.

[54] House of Commons Culture Media and Sport Committee, *Football Governance: Seventh Report of Session 2010-2012 Volume 2* (HC 792 II, The Stationary Office 2011) 187.

[55] The Independent Football Commission, *Report on Self Regulation* (2004) 9.

[56] For a full desription see http://www.thefa.com/News/governance/2012/oct/~/media/22A83175745E44468105B57232F085B7.ashx.

[57] See "Extracts from the FA Report on the Luis Suárez Patrice Evra Racism Case" *Guardian* (1 January 2012) http://www.guardian.co.uk/football/2012/jan/01/fa-report-luis-suarez-patrice-evra accessed 12 December 2012.

[58] S Tongue, "FA Disciplinary Process is 'A joke'" *Independent* 7 October 2012 http://

Lack of Accountability — Can the FA Act as it Pleases?

Thomas Paine once noted that "A body of men holding themselves accountable to nobody ought not to be trusted by anybody". The level of accountability within the English FA is minimal, and given the fact that accountability is central to effective self-regulation, question marks must be raised as to whether this lack of accountability is indicative of the inadequacy of the FA as a self regulatory body.

Reverting back to the case involving Mr Terry, there is also an issue of accountability. The issue here is why the FA charged and banned Mr Terry despite the fact that he had been already been acquitted in a court of law. Firstly, it is submitted that the prosecuting standard in FA disciplinary proceedings is too low. At present each case hinges on the balance of probabilities test. The inefficiency of such a test is emphasised by the fact that in 2011, there were 473 FA disciplinary cases with a conviction rate of 99.5 percent.[59] It is submitted that the FA should be held accountable as to the adoption of this test.

Secondly and more importantly, Rule 6.8 of the FA's rules and regulations states that "[w]here the subject matter of a complaint or matter before the Regulatory Commission has been the subject of previous civil or criminal proceedings, the result of such proceedings and the facts and matters upon which such result is based shall be presumed to be correct and the facts presumed to be true unless it is shown, by clear and convincing evidence, that this is not the case".[60] However, Mr Terry was charged by the FA on the balance of probabilities test, yet, to have the FA hearing, they require clear and compelling evidence. This appears to be somewhat contradictory. This is indicative of the FA's determination to self-regulate this area, even in defiance of their own rulebook.[61]

Thus the FA have exercised a lack of accountability in issues outside of the regulation of its members on social media. However, given the already clear precedent of inconsistency displayed by the FA, and the filtering of this inconsistency into the regulation of its members on social media, it is forseeable that this lack of accountability will follow a similar pattern. Furthermore, whilst the John Terry and Luis Suarez cases do not involve social media, it is interesting to note that the charges arose by virtue of the same provisions as those of Ashley Cole, Rio Ferdinand, etc, namely, FA Rule E3(1) and FA Rule E3(2). Thus, there is commonality of charge. In the view of the writer this example of the FA being inconsistent and unaccountable for the disciplinary proceedures and charges which they levy upon their members serves as justification for the view that the FA are not well positioned, in their current capacity, to regulate its members actions on social media.

---

www.independent.co.uk/sport/football/news-and-comment/fa-disciplinary-process-is-a-joke-8200705.html,

59 M Samuel, "Others Had Made Up Their Minds so Terry Had to Quit England" Mail Online 23 September 2012 http://www.dailymail.co.uk/sport/article-2207528/John-Terry-quit-England-captain-FA-guilty--Martin-Samuel.html.

60 The FA, Rules and Regulations of the Associaiton Season 2011-2012, 418 available at http://www.thefa.com/thefa/~/media/Files/PDF/TheFA/FA%20Handbook%202010-11/FAHandbook-update-1011.ashx/FAHandbook-update-1011.pdf.

61 M Samuel, "Others Had Made Up Their Minds So Terry Had to Quit England" Mail Online 23 September 2012 http://www.dailymail.co.uk/sport/article-2207528/John-Terry-quit-England-captain-FA-guilty--Martin-Samuel.html.

Should the FA be Allowed to Regulate Members Speech?

Freedom of expression is provided for in the UK by virtue of Article 10 ECHR.[62] Furthermore, the European Court of Human Rights has long held that the freedom of expression includes opinions which offend, shock or disturb the state or the general population.[63] Moreover, Article 19(2) of the International Covenant on Civil and Political Rights, to which the United Kingdom (UK) is a party further provides for the freedom of expression.[64] However, limitations are placed upon this freedom. Examples of where limitations may be imposed include credible threats of violence to persons or damage to property and communications which are grossly offensive, indecent, obscene or false.[65]

In determining whether freedom of expression is to be protected, a balancing act in which the fundamental right of free speech and the need to prosecute serious wrongdoing has to be undertaken.[66] It is submitted that it is acceptable when bodies such as the legislature and the courts engage in the restriction of the freedom of expression, due to the level of accountability and transparency associated with these bodies. However, it is suggested that the FA, a private self-regulating body, should not be afforded a free-reign to limit this freedom for the same reasons. Consequently, placing the power to limit speech by its members on social networks into the hands of a private body is undesirable. The reasoning behind this is largely attributed to the fact that the FA could abuse this power. When the courts carry out the balancing act of balancing the social good against the potential harms, they will do so with societal standards in mind, evidenced by the differing thresholds for differing limitations.[67] However, it is not unforseeable that the FA could restrict the freedom of expression for the purpose of improving the reputation of their body regardless of societies desire for all types of information as well as the individuals right to express their opinions. Simply put, whilst limitation on the freedom of expression is required, it is submitted that this restriction should not be placed in the hands of a private body.

An International Perspective—The NFL

The National Football League ("NFL"), the premier American football league has also adopted policies in relation to Twitter. The NFL's Twitter policy, which applies to players, coaches and other team personnel, prohibits these parties from using Twitter ninety minutes before the game or until the traditional post game interviews are completed.[68] However, the NFL does not interfere with the Twitter activity of the players in its organisation outside of this.[69] This is a restriction which is enforced strictly by the NFL, as evidenced by the $25,000 fine which Cincinnati Bengals

---

62 European Convention on Human Rights 2001, s 10.

63 *Handyside v United Kingdom* [1976] 1 EHRR 737.

64 D McGoldrick, "The Limits of Freedom of Expression on Facebook and Social Networking Sites: A UK Perspective" (2013)(13) *Human Rights Law Review* 125, 127.

65 *ibid*, 125, 136.

66 *ibid*, 125, 135.

67 *ibid*, 125, 136.

68 J Thomas, "Twitter: The Sports Media Rookie" (2011)(6(1)) *Journal of Sports Media* 115, 116.

69 *ibid*.

wide receiver Chad Ochocinco was ordered to pay for two violations — possessing an electronic device and posting messages on Twitter during a game.[70]

However, the NFL have remained loyal to its Twitter policy by refusing to fine NFL players who tweet outside of the times which are prohibited. This lack of interference by the NFL is perhaps best illustrated by Green Bay Packers guard TJ Lang's tweet which stated "F**k it NFL.. Fine me and use the money to pay the regular refs" - this tweet came as a result of a questionable call by the replacement referees in a match involving Green Bay.[71] A similar tweet by a Premier League footballer would undoubtedly result in a hefty fine under FA Rule E3(1). However, the NFL decided against fining TJ Lang. Their reluctance to interfere with NFL players freedom to tweet as they see fit, was highlighted by their dismissive response, which noted that "we're not looking at that".[72]

Notably, the individual franchise's (equivalent to a Premiership team) may fine its players where they see fit. This was seen when the San Diego Chargers fined Cornerback Antonio Cromartie $2,500 for using Twitter to complain about the food served at the team's training camp. Not only did the tweet complain about the food available at the Chargers' training facilities, but it also insinuated that it contributed to the team's failure to make it to the Super Bowl in recent years.[73] Therefore, unlike the FA, there is a clear desire on behalf of the NFL to regulate its members Twitter activity as little as possible.

The English FA are Insufficient Regulators of its Members on Social Media

From the aforementioned, it is clear that the FA, in its current capacity are unsuitable regulators of their members on Twitter, Facebook and other social networks. As has already been alluded to the English FA lack consistency and accountability, two virtues which should be synonymous with both regulation and disciplinary processes. Regardless of the fact that it is much more preferable if the football industry is able to develop effective systems of self-regulation, it is opined that the inability of the FA to self-regulate social media in an effective and acceptable manner renders alternative approaches desirable, if not essential.

Alternative Approach—Allow the Issue to be Dealt with Internally

As has been seen in the NFL, social networking issues are often dealt with internally. In the Premier League, a number of clubs have already formulated their own social

---

70 K Armstrong, "Chad Ochocinco Fined $25,000 for Being on Twitter During Cincinnati Bengals Preseason Game", *Daily News America* (New York, 24 August 2010) http://www.nydailynews.com/sports/football/chad-ochocinco-fined-25-000-twitter-cincinnati-bengals-preseason-game-article-1.201993.

71 K Linendoll, "Inside Twitter, Sports' Digital Locker Room" (*ESPN The Magazine*, 27 January 2013) http://espn.go.com/blog/playbook/tech/post/_/id/3918/inside-twitter-sports-digital-locker-room#more.

72 R Demovsky, "NFL Won't Fine Packers Players" (*Packers News*, 26 September 2012) <http://blogs.greenbaypressgazette.com/blogs/gpg/insider/2012/09/26/nfl-wont-fine-packers-players/.

73 J Thomas, "Twitter: The Sports Media Rookie" (2011)(6(1)) *Journal of Sports Media* 115, 116.

media policies.[74] Perhaps allowing the clubs to deal with social media issues on an internal basis may be favourable. Internal disciplinary procedures are the norm within the Premier League, with clubs often fining players for getting sent off in matches, as seen when Manchester City fined Mario Balotelli two weeks wages for getting sent off in an important match.[75]

One of the main advantages this approach is that the club can judge the most suitable means of punishment. Arguably, the most empowering facet in a sport is the trust a team places in each of its individual members.[76] Given the bond which can grow between team-mates, there are not many things which may hit a sportsperson harder than the feeling of disappointment in letting their team down.[77] Thus the club may issue match suspension instead of fines. This may result in the penalties imposed having a greater effect, and perhaps may deter future actions which will lead to such sanctions.

Another advantage of this approach is that appeals could be made to higher bodies such as the Premier League and the FA.[78] Furthermore, appeals beyond the club, the Premier Leage and the FA could be taken to an independent body above the FA, which in the view of the writer should be established. Having this process of appeals available to the members would undoubtedly improve accountability.

Alternative Approach — An Independent Body

It is submitted that the most desirable approach would be the establishment of an independent body, set up by the State, to review the FA's decisions on contentious issues involving social media and other areas. Despite the fact that it is preferable for the football industry to develop effective systems of self-regulation[79] it is the view of the writer that in order to ensure it's effective and legitimate regulation, State intervention should be welcomed in certain areas of football, such as the regulation of footballers on social media.

State intervention has proved succesful before in English football, as seen with the improvement of stadia and security.[80] This provides a very clear precedent for

74 A Nixon, "FA Code of Conduct to be Introduced" *Law in Sport*, 20 October 2012 http://www.lawinsport.com/blog/the-sport-lawyer-blog/item/fa-code-of-conduct-to-be-introduced.

75 A Hunter, "Mario Balotelli Goes Head to Head with Manchester City Over Club Fine" *Guardian* (UK, 18 December 2012) http://www.guardian.co.uk/football/2012/dec/18/mario-balotelli-manchester-city.

76 L Silkin, "Social Media in Sport" *Law in Sport*, 27 November 2012 http://www.lawinsport.com/blog/item/social-media-in-sport.

77 *ibid.*

78 This is already permitted as Premier League rules allow for players to appeal disciplinary decisions under Section K.

79 House of Commons Culture Media and Sport Committee, Football Governance (London: Stationery Office 2011) 251.

80 The Football Spectators Act 1989 was implemented in order to help with the problem of security at stadia. This Act established the Football Licensing Authority (FLA) which was a body with the objective of ensuring reasonable safety and management of spectators in stadia through a number of different mechanisms. The result was improved security, coupled with greater attendances at matches. For a detailed analysis see: Steve Greenfield and Guy Osborn, *Regulating Football: Commodification, Consumption and the Law* (London: Pluto Press, 2001) 20-22.

succesful government intervention in the governance of football.[81] It is undisputable that at that time, the English FA were not legitimately and effectively self-regulating, and the intervention of the State was required. The same applies in relation to the FA's regulation of Twitter.

Therefore, the establishment of this independent review body should result in a greater degree of consistency in the the administration of charges and penalties. Furthermore, an independent body should also lead to accountability and confidence in the decisions relating to footballers on social networks.

Recommendations Using Social Media

Various methods of avoiding and dealing with the problems associated with professional sports persons social networking activity arise. The following is a set of ten recommendations which, if followed by professional sports persons, could ensure that the problems associated with social netoworks are avoided.

Recommendations For Organisations, Clubs And Franchises

Recommendations include:

(a) Create a social media policy for your members to follow;
(b) Ensure that the social media policy is drafted in a manner which incorporates all aspects of your members social networking activity which you desire to direct;
(c) Ensure that the social media policy is drafted with legal standards in mind;
(d) Ensure that social media policies are in line with other policies which are also applicable to your members. A conflict between two policies should not occur where the member is required to abide by both policies;
(e) Inform members of the existence of the social media policy, and the educate them on what they are and are not allowed to do on social networks as part of that policy;
(f) Delineate the consequences which will arise from acting outside of the social media policy;
(g) Hold workshops at regular intervals throughout the year to re-emphasise the importance of following the social media policy;
(i) Outline the legal consequences which may stem from inappropriate use of social media;
(j) Encourage members to use social media;
(k) Explain the positive effects which astute use of social networking website platforms can have for both the member and the organisation in both monetary and non-monetary terms.

Recommendations For Sports Persons Using Social Media

Recommendations include:

81 House of Commons Culture Media and Sport Committee, Football Governance (London: Stationery Office, 2011) 251.

(a) Read, understand and follow the guidelines which the club, franchise or organisation that you are a part of provide you with;
(b) Take part in and digest all the information which is made available to you on any social media education days;
(c) Familiarise yourself with the legal consequences which may arise as a result of your social networking activity;
(d) Understand the negative ramifications which may be caused to yourself, other individuals or organisations as a result of your social networking activity;
(e) Afford comments which you make on social networking websites the same level of consideration as you would public comments made to the media in interviews;
(f) Allow a cooling off period. Whatever comment that you feel like making, allocate a period of time that you will wait before posting that comment. This should ensure that any irrational, heat of the moment comments are avoided;
(g) Do not respond to negative or abusive comments on social networking sites;
(h) Avail of the report abuse button on social networking websites such as Twitter and Facebook;
(i) Report any communications of a malicious nature to local authorities;
(j) Embrace social networking sites. Engage with fans in a positive manner and enjoy any of the positive effects or opportunities which this creates.

Conclusion

Human beings, by nature, are social. Throughout history, man has always created means of communication with his fellow man, starting in ancient civilisation when the Phoenicians and the Egyptians created alphabet, later the Morse code was developed, then the telephone and now social networking.[82] Restrictions or limitations placed on this desire for social interaction should not be allowed without sufficient checks and balances in place.

In modern society, the creation of social networking websites such as Twitter have opened up a Pandora's box of new opinions.[83] Whilst we cannot have a "wild west"[84] scenario with completely unregulated speech, any regulation of this expression must be adequate and fair. As has been thematic throughout this essay, it is the view of this writer that the FA, in its current capacity is not regulating in a sufficient manner. The lack of consistency in the fines which the FA has charged footballers for their misdemeanours on social networking sites is sufficient justification to demand an alternative disciplinary process. Moreover, it is often suggested that self-regulation

---

82 Timothy Liam Epstein, "Student Athlete.O: Regulation of Student Athletes' Social Media Use: A Guide to Avoiding NCAA Sanctions and Related Litigation" (2012)(1(1)) *Missisipi Law Journal*, http://papers.ssrn.com/sol3/papers.cfm?abstract_id=1998315.

83 D Geey and H Cohen, "Being Tweeted Fairly? Footballers, Clubs & Social Media" (*The Tomkins Times*, 20 January 2011) http://tomkinstimes.com/2011/01/being-tweeted-fairly-footballers-clubs-social-media/.

84 L Silkin, "Social Media in Sport" (*Law in Sport*, 27 November 2012) http://www.lawinsport.com/blog/item/social-media-in-sport.

leads to groups not being accountable through normal democratic demands,[85] and it is argued that this is the case in relation to the FA and its disciplinary process.

To conclude, self-regulation whilst beneficial in many sporting situations, given the fact that they have the greatest knowledge in this area[86], is most effective when a sporting institution amends a true rule of the game, such as the backpass rule.[87] Sporting bodies who self-regulate are on less steady ground when they are required to regulate on areas outside of their core competencies or on sensitive legal topics.[88] Therefore, the establishment of an independent body to oversee the decisions of the FA involving footballers on social media, should lead to an improved, consistent and accountable disciplinary process.

Despite the problems associated with it, it is obvious that social media is a force to be reckoned with when it comes to marketing, sponsorship, reputational management, image building, creating fan bases and the engagement of those fans in a direct manner.[89] The gains for organisations as well as the individual can be significant, both in economic, personal or social terms. There exists an opportunity at presesnt to avail of these unprecedented opportunities. Harnessed correctly, social media, and indeed professional sportspersons use of social networking websites will be beneficial for all parties involved. Adequate social media policies as well as education of the professional sportsperson are the tools which should be utilised in order to harness this opportunity. Sportspersons use of social networking websites is a double-edged sword. However, if organisations and clubs implement policies and educate their members, it is submitted that one side of this sword will be significantly unsharpened, leaving the holders of the sword with a far more powerful weapon.

---

85 G Graham, "Self-regulation" in G Richardson and H Genn (eds), *Administrative Law and Government Action:The Courts and Alternative Mechanisms of Review* (Oxford: Clarendon, 1994) 190.

86 S Thorp, "Governance: Self-regulation of Sport: Arguments For and Against" (2010)(8(8)) *World Sports Law Report* 7, 9.

87 *ibid.*

88 *ibid.*

89 I Kishner and B Crescenti, "The Rise of Social Media:What Professional Teams and Clubs Should Consider" (2010)(27(4)) *Entertainment and Sports Lawyer* 24, 24.

PART XI: SOCIAL NETWORKING AND COURTS

Chapter 31

SOCIAL NETWORKING AND COURTS

Headline of Issues

- Witnesses
- Jurors
- Lawyers and judges
- Reporting
- UK consultation
- UK Contempt Consultation

Introduction

Social networking is increasingly being used by lawyers.[1] One of the areas which is at the fore of the social networking debate is the use of social networking in court, and in relation to courts. This might seem surprising at first glance, given the historical stereotype of courts being conservative and traditional.

Yet the legal process in courts is at the cutting edge of the regulation of social networking. The first issue arising relates to how courtroom actors or participants may use social networking. Are they permitted to? Can a witness, lawyer or even judge tweet or post comments in relation to a case? Can or should they do so in relation to a case they were involved in? One would think that they should certainly not do so in relation to an active case in which they are participating. Courts are having to deal with all of these issues.

In-Court: Witnesses

In one case a CEO texted his CFO who was in the witness stand while the judge was distracted with a bench conference.[2] A mistrial was declared by the judge when he was alerted to what had occurred. The judge stated that the text was:

> "underhanded and calculated to undermine the integrity of this court and the legal process ... Regretfully, plaintiff through its unacceptable conduct has reached into the court's quiver

---

1 See, for example, S Stine and J Poie, "The Good, the Bad and the Ugly, Blogging, Microblogging and Social Media for Public Lawyers" (2009)(17) *Public Law* 13.

2 DC Espana, "Judge Tosses Fraud Suit After Witness Is Texted by Boss During Trial," *Law.com*, 17 August 2009, http://law.com/jsp/law/LawArticleFriendly.jsp?id=1202433074669, referred to in S Nelson, J Simek and J Foltin, "The Legal Implications of Social Networking" (2009–2010) (22) *Regent Law Review* 1 at 5.

> of sanctions, drawn the bowstring taut and aimed the arrow at the heart of its own case. This court has justifiably released the string".[3]

Costs were also awarded against the plaintiff company.[4]

In-Court: Juror Postings

It is easy to contemplate how a party in legal proceedings could be prejudiced if one of the jurors was to start posting details of the cases, confidential information from the jury room or to solicit opinions or feedback, all of which could prejudice that party.

In the UK a woman sitting on a jury polled her Facebook friends to see which way she should vote in the case.[5]

Pennsylvania Senator Vincent Fumo appealed a conviction, arguing that a juror was posting trial details on Twitter, Facebook and blogs.[6]

Another juror posted eight tweets during a trial, one of which stated "oh and nobody buy Stoam. Its bad mojo and they'll probably cease to [e]xist, now that their wallet is 12m lighter."[7] This last tweet was before the jury announcement.

In-Court: Lawyers and Judges

Lawyers are not immune from the advent of online social networking, albeit perhaps a little later than others.[8]

In at least one instance, it has been found unethical to have a friend or colleague purport to make a friend request on a lawyer's behalf with the intention of obtaining information and details from a witness's social networking profile.[9]

There are even examples now where lawyers and judges themselves have fallen foul of social media. In one instance a lawyer requested an adjournment in a case due to a family death but their Facebook account referred to social parties appearing to indicate that they were socialising and that no one had died.[10] The same report

---

3 *ibid.*

4 *ibid.*

5 "Juror Dismissed After Asking Facebook Friends How She Should Vote on Trial," *MailOnline*, 25 November 2008, http://dailymail.co.uk/sciencetech/article-1089228/Juror-dismissed-asking-Facebook-friends-vote-trial.html, referred to in Nelson *et al.*, *op. cit*, 3.

6 *United States v Fumo*, No. 06-319, slip op. 115, 116–116, 125, (ED Pa, June 17 2009), available at http://paed.uscourts.gov/documents/opinions/09d0710p.pdf, referred to in Nelson *et al.*, *op. cit*, 3–4.

7 J Gambrell, "Appeal Claims Jurors Bias in 'Tweets' Sent During $12 Million Case," *Law.com*, 16 March 2009, www.law.com/jsp/article.jsp/article.?id=1202429071686, referred to in Nelson *et al.*, *op. cit*, 4–5.

8 Lawyers are being advised to use social networking for their business. See, for example, C Barnes, "Social Networking: Not Just for Youngsters Anymore," *Bar Leader*, January-February 2009, at 19.

9 TM Williams, "Facebook: Ethics, Traps, and Reminders" (2007–2008)(36) *Student Law* 24.

10 M McDonough, "Facebook Judge Catches Lawyer in Lie, Sees Ethical Breaches," *ABA*

refers to other lawyers who posted complaints about clients, lawyers and a judge.[11] In another instance a lawyer and a client were found to be exchanging text messages while the client was giving a video deposition.[12] There was found to be a breach of Federal Rule of Civil Procedure Rule 30.[13] This issue was discovered because the defence attorney inadvertently sent a text to the plaintiff lawyer saying, "doing fine".[14]

In Florida the judicial Ethics Advisory Committee issued guidance on 9 November 2009 advising that judges should not become social networking friends with lawyers who appear in their courts.[15]

A lawyer was suspended after being found to be blogging during a case when they were serving on a jury.[16] Furthermore, the defendant's conviction was also reversed because of the blogging and the comments made.[17] This would not happen in those jurisdictions where lawyers are not permitted to act on a jury.

In another example a judge and a lawyer became Facebook friends during a case they were both involved in, and exchanged comments on the case and when it would conclude and speculated on whether one of the parties had had an affair.[18] The judge eventually disqualified himself, and was later found to have breached the judicial code for researching one of the party's websites.[19]

Lawyers also need to be extra vigilant to not disclose case or instruction details online or via social networking[20]:

Nelson, Simek and Foltin recommend the following rules for law firms in relation to social networking.[21]

- Remind lawyers that they should avoid the appearance of establishing a lawyer/client relationship. The rule of thumb should be: do not give legal advice – speak about the issues of law generally and factually instead;
- Confidential information must at all times remain confidential. Firms

---

Journal, 31 July 2009, http://abajournal.com/news/facebooking_judge_catches_lawyers_in_lies_crossing_ethical_lines_abachicago/, referred to in Nelson *et al.*, *op. cit*, 8.

11 *ibid.*

12 *Ngai v Old Navy*, No 07-5653 (KSH)(PS) 2009 WL 2391282, at *1 (DNJ 31 July 2009).

13 *ibid.*

14 *ibid.*

15 C Gray, "The Too Friendly Judge? Social Networks and the Bench" (May-June 2010)(93) *Judicature* 236.

16 M Neil, "California Lawyer Suspended Over Trial Blogging While Serving as Juror," *ABA Journal*, 4 August 2009, http://abajournal.com/news/calif._layer_suspended_over_trial_blog_while_serving_as_juror/, referred to in Nelson *et al.*, *op. cit*, 9.

17 *ibid.*

18 R Jones, "Judge Reprimanded for Discussing Case on Facebook," *The-Dispatch.com*, 1 June 2009, http://the-dispatch.com/article/20090601/articles/905319995/1005?Title=Judge-reprimanded-for-discussing-case-on-Facebook, referred to in Nelson *et al.*, *op. cit*, 10.

19 *ibid.*

20 In relation to one US restriction, see Y Ostolaza and R Pellafone, "Applying Model Rule 4.2 to Web 2.0: The Problem of Social Networking Sites" (2010) *Journal of High Technology Law* 56.

21 Nelson *et al.*, *op. cit*, 33–34.

must have a rule that explicitly forbids any posting of confidential information. Attorneys should be required to request permission to post any information that may even remotely seem private.

- Strict privacy settings should be employed when joining new social networks. Do not rely on the default settings for the social network, which are generally very open and public.
- Require lawyers to use disclaimers when publishing any content that relates to work performed by the firm.
- Request good judgment. Ask lawyers to be polite and avoid sensitive subjects.
- Any use of a firm's insignia and logo should be run past the law firm's marketing department.
- Remind lawyers that copyright and financial disclosure laws apply equally to online conduct and offline conduct.
- Firms should take steps to educate their attorneys on these guidelines. Whether through a video presentation or a quick, informal seminar, attorneys should be given an opportunity to learn of these guidelines and ask questions about the guidelines if needed.

TWITTER

The UK Press Complaints Commission is considering whether to regulate journalists' Twitter use.[22] A complaint to the Press Complaints Commission in the UK by a blogger that her privacy was breached by a newspaper article publishing her blog comments was not upheld.[23] Courts are also debating whether Twitter should be allowed in court for reporting purposes, and, if so, by when.

Reporting: Twitter In Court

A Kansas court permitted a reporter to tweet from court in a criminal gang-related case, apparently on the basis that it opened the legal process to the public.[24] Other courts have expressly prohibited the use of mobile telephones, smartphones, email, Twitter, etc.[25] Twitter has been allowed in UK and Irish courts.

---

22 D Sabbagh, "PCC Seeks to Regulate Press Twitter Feeds, Watchdog to Consult on How Tweets can be Brought Under its Remit, Asking Each Newspaper to Draw up a 'Twitter Policy,'" *Guardian*, 6 May 2011, available at www.guardian.co.uk/media/2011/may/06/pcc-press-twitter-feeds.

23 Adjudication – *Sarah Baskerville v Daily Mail*, available at http://www.pcc.org.uk/cases/adjudicated.html?article=NjkzNA==.

24 LarrysWorld.com, "Twitter in the court: Federal Judge Gets It", http://www.pcanswer.com/2009/03/09/twitter-in-the-court-federal-judge-get-it/ 9 March 2009, referred to in Nelson *et al.*, *op. cit*, 7.

25 Order Regarding Media Conduct and Electronic Equipment Access, *United States v UBS AG*, No 1:09-cv-20423-ASG (SD Florida 9 July 2009), available at 7http://www.flsd.uscourts.gov/viewer.asp?file=/cases/pressDocs/109cv20423_106.pdf, referred to in Nelson *et al.*, *op. cit*, 8–9.

Court Reactions: Rules, Regulations, Consultations

How should we deal with such issues? Some courts ban mobile telephones in court.[26] Other courts appear to ban electronic devices while in the jury box or during case deliberations.[27] Some courts permit certain mobile devices.[28] New Jersey apparently permits jurors to bring mobile telephones to court so long as they are turned off; in one Alaskan court jurors must "check" the mobile telephones with the bailiff at the deliberations stage; an Oregon court and the United States District Court for the Western District of Louisiana ban juror mobile telephones.[29] The courts in Ramsey County, Minnesota, prohibit jurors from bringing any wireless device to court, and have even declared two mistrials when mobile telephones were used during deliberations in breach of the ban.[30]

In Multnomah County, Oregon the jury instruction states: "Do not discuss this case during the trial with anyone, including any of the attorneys, parties, witnesses, your friends, or members of your family. 'No discussion' also means no emailing, text messaging, tweeting, blogging or any other form of communications."[31] The juror instruction also warns against internet searching:

> "In our daily lives we may be used to looking for information on-line and to 'Google' something as a matter of routine. Also, in a trial it can be very tempting for jurors to do their own research to make sure they are making the correct decision. You must resist that temptation for our system of justice to work as it should".[32]

An Arkansas court also issues a juror instruction as follows:

> "[D]uring your deliberations, please remember you must not provide any information to anyone by any means about the case. Thus, for example, do not use any electronic device or media, such as the telephone, a cell or smart phone, Blackberry, PDA, computer, the internet, and internet service, any text or instant messaging service, any internet chat room, blog, or website such as Facebook, My[]Space, YouTube or Twitter, to communicate to anyone any information about this case until I accept your verdict."[33]

Apparently also, similar such instructions have been given by judges in individual cases.[34]

---

26 For example, the United States District Court for the Eastern District of Virginia; see S Nelson and J Simek, "Three Strikes and You're Out: Judges Talk About Technology in the Courtroom" (July–August 2005) *Law Pract* at 24–25.

27 Michigan Supreme Court; see A Ramasastry, "Why Courts Need to Ban Jurors' Electronic Communications Devices," *FindLaw.com*, 11 August 2009, http://writ.news.findlaw.com/ramasastry/20090811.html, referred to in Nelson *et al.*, *op. cit*, 6.

28 Such as the experimental rules in the United States District Court for the Southern District of New York, referred to in AH Helm, "Courtrooms All Atwitter," *National Law Journal* (New York City), 10 August 2009, at 34.

29 Ramasastry, *op. cit.*

30 *ibid.*

31 "Cell Phone Policies/Instructions for Jurors," JUR-E Bull (National Centre for State Courts, Centre for Jury Studies, Williamsburg, Va.) 1 May 2009, www.ncsonline.org/WC/Publications/KIS_JurInnJurE05-01-09.pdf, referred to in Nelson *et al.*, *op. cit*, 6.

32 *ibid.*

33 This was on 21 April 2009, see "Ride the Lightening: Web 2.0 Jury Instructions in Arkansas," http://ridethelightening.senseient.com/2009/05/web-20-jury-instructions-in-arkanss.html, referred to in Nelson *et al.*, *op. cit*, 7.

34 See Nelson *et al.*, *op. cit*, 7, giving an example of *People v Jamison*, No 8042/06, 2009 WL

Overall, there is no universal norm or consistency of approach to these developing issues. In most instances there is no defined formal written policy. Where policies do exist, they vary greatly in their form and what they specify. "We have clearly identified the problem, but we certainly have not standardized a solution."[35] We might equally say that where policies do exist, we are not altogether familiar with how successful individual policies are. Are some better defined than others? Are some more appropriate? Are some more successful? Research is needed in this area. The US National Center for State Courts has at least begun the first stage of this research, in terms of gathering the different written policies as may exist in the US into one resource bank.[36] Analysing and comparing these should be the next phase. Researching and monitoring the effectiveness is a further stage still, which may require more complex empirical research, at least in part.

A further point, and one which is critically important, is how user-friendly the policies are. Those aimed at lay jurors and witnesses should, as far as possible, be user-friendly and drafted in plain English. This issue does not appear to have been considered expressly in the literature to date.

Tweeting and UK Courts

The Contempt of Court Act 1981 prohibits the making of sound recordings in court without judicial permission. It also makes it an offence to take photographs in court. The 2005 Constitutional Reform Act made an amendment whereby cameras are permitted in the new Supreme Court. More recently, Court of Appeal cameras are permitted.

One commentator states that the "difference between scribbling notes (published later) and filing copy instantly from the courtroom using an electronic device is self-evidently slight."[37]

Another commentator states that "[o]f course, despite this development, the same small laptops that may be permitted to be used to live-blog court cases in England and Wales cannot be used to type up notes from the proceedings using a word processor, Notebook and paper is needed for that."[38] He concludes that while "Julian Assange's court appearances have brought about one partial thawing of court reporting restrictions, but there are many more ice blocks remaining."[39]

In announcing the tentative official advent in courts, the UK Lord Chief Justice is reported as saying that live text-based communications may be permitted so long as the judge feels that it will not interfere.[40] However, Laurence Eastham states that:

2568740, at *6 (NY Supreme Court, 18 August 2009).

35 Nelson *et al.*, *op. cit*, 7.

36 *ibid*, 7.

37 S Butterworth, "Can Live Blogs and Twitter Take Court Reporting into the 21st Century?" *Guardian*, 28 July 2010, available at www.guardian.co.uk/law/afua-hirsch-law-blog/2010/jul/28/live-blogging-tweeting-court-reporting.

38 "Tweeting in Court (With Permission) in England and Wales Only for Now," Slugger O'Toole, available at http://sluggerotoole.com/2010/12/21/tweeting-in-court/.

39 *ibid*.

40 L Eastham, "Contempt," Editor's Blog, *Society of Computers & Law*, 20 December 2010, available at www.scl.org/site.aspx?i=bp18241.

> "Of course Lord Judge is right in principle, but I am not sure he has taken prison overcrowding into account. The history of Twitter is littered with the ill-considered tweet's that had unexpected and unfortunate effects – look at poor old Paul Chambers. My immediate reaction to the report is to wonder which profession will end up in prison first – will it be the careless journalist looking for a cheap laugh, the bored barrister awaiting his turn and revealing to his followers what he really thinks about the judge or the trainee solicitor who is supposed to be taking notes but who really doesn't want to be there?"[41]

This was in December 2010. It is very prescient in relation to what was to occur in May 2011 with the Ryan Giggs affair, where details were released, accessed and commented on by approximately 70,000 Twitter users despite the existence of a super injunction.

The Paul Chambers case involved a conviction and fine under s 127 of the Communications Act 2003 for tweeting that he was going to blow up a named airport.[42]

One issue is that Twitter limits tweets to 140 characters. Therefore, there is a concern that this brevity cannot possibly give a full, fair and accurate report of what has occurred in court.[43]

A concern for journalists is that they would have the full defences available for journalistic reporting under normal contempt-of-court rules if and when they tweet from court.[44] This is despite the possibility and difficulty of tweets being instantaneous, very short and considerably less than a normal considered court report.

Equally, journalists want to have the defamation defences for fair and accurate court reports available to them when tweeting.[45] It is recognised that the size restriction of 140 characters can pose a problem in terms of court tweets being full, fair and accurate.[46] This can be an issue generally for all court tweet reports as well as for particular tweets. "Can they fairly sum up what might be complex legal points in 140 characters?"[47] Is a tweet report of a case fair and reasonable? Equally, is a tweet on the court process generally also fair and accurate? What educational effects are actually being researched and recorded?

There are certainly real issues as to whether tweets can be fair and accurate, or indeed whether they can be in every instance. However, in certain (but not all) contexts these issues can perhaps be ameliorated by the technology and setting. For example, the use of links in tweets, known as Tweetlonger, can enable the reader to click through to more extensive content which, taken as a whole, can provide a much fuller and more detailed explanation of a case. However, this also poses

---

41 *ibid.*

42 L Eastham, "The Twitter Bomb Joke and the Big Issues," Editor's Blog, *Society of Computers & Law*, 23 November 2010, available at www.scl.org/site.aspx?i=bp18241.

43 D Banks, "Tweeting in Court: Why Reporters Must be Given Guidelines, A District Judge's Decision to Allow Journalists to Use Twitter in the Julian Assange Hearing Raises Interesting Legal Questions," *Guardian*, 15 December 2010, available at www.guardian.co.uk/law/2010/dec/15/tweeting-court-reporters-julian-assange.

44 *ibid.*

45 *ibid.*

46 *ibid.*

47 *ibid.*

a problem, as there is no guarantee that readers will actually click through to the more extensive content reports. Indeed, depending on the configuration adopted, the likelihood may be reduced that many or any click-throughs will occur. One of the reasons why official music-downloading websites were initially so unsuccessful was that there were too many click-through steps for a user to access and download music. This was in contrast to the more user-friendly unofficial and pirate music websites and peer-to-peer (P2P) services.[48] One commentator also suggests that "[i]t might also be solved by the use of liveblogs ... which publish tweets and other material, thus giving adequate context".[49] The implication appears to be that the full stream or thread of all the tweets is instantly available for a reader. Thus the reader is not looking at one single post about a case, possibly out of context, but can see a whole stream of tweets about it. However, the nature of live tweets means that there is no longer article (yet) available to link to.

Another danger is that members of the public, citizen reporters or bloggers may wish to tweet from court. The risk is that "the tweeting citizen journalist, unaware of court reporting laws, may include material which should be excluded."[50] It is also unclear if journalistic defences will be extended to other parties.

Other issues arise from the particular hardware being used, for example, camera telephones. For example:

> "[T]weets will often be sent from a smartphone which has a very good camera. Will the temptation to tweet a picture of someone be too much? While the courts appear to be considering opening up to reporting via use of such technology, there has been no indication that that includes sending pictures or video".[51]

Soon after Twitter was permitted in the Julian Assange case, the UK Lord Chief Justice announced interim guidance in relation to the permitting of live, text-based communications in court pending a more detailed formal consultation in relation to the issues presented, and permitting such communications including Twitter.[52]

One could argue that the issuance of the guidelines was appropriate, and even overdue. Alternatively, one can argue that the interim guidelines were premature and unnecessary, and a knee-jerk reaction to one case, as opposed to maintaining a status quo while research and policies are considered.

The President of the UK Supreme Court, Lord Phillips, stated:

> "The rapid development of communications technology brings with it both opportunities and challenges for the justice system. An undoubted benefit is that regular updates can be shared with many people outside the court, in real time, which can enhance public interest in the progress of a case and keep those who are interested better informed.
>
> We are fortunate that, by the time a case reaches the Supreme Court there is very

48 Note separate efforts recently to expand anti-piracy legislative protections in new extra territorial law. See "US Firms Back Crackdown on Piracy," *Irish Times*, 26 May 2011.

49 Banks, *op. cit.*

50 *ibid.*

51 *ibid.*

52 C Dougan-Bacchus, "Interim Practice Guidance on Use of Live Text-Based Forms of Communication (Including Twitter) from Court," *All England Reporter* (December 2010) (D) 228.

> seldom any reason for any degree of confidentiality, so that questions about what should and should not be shared with those outside the courtroom do not usually arise. This means that we can offer a green light to tweeting and other forms of communication, as long as this does not disrupt the smooth running of the court".[53]

The Supreme Court guidance is meant to be "limited to the Supreme Court" in part because it is an appeal court and does not interact with witnesses or jurors, and therefore "[d]ifferent considerations" and risks apply as from other courts.[54]

It is noted already that the interim guidelines refer explicitly to only one form of technology service, namely Twitter.[55]

It has been suggested now that the "default position" is that "tweeting is allowed".[56] However, such comments can appear as being overbroad. The guidelines are interim.

A consultation process in terms of considering the issues in greater detail and also in relation to what rules may be applied was also launched (see below). Regardless of what the finding or recommendations will be, this is undoubtedly an area that will have to be further developed in practice, research and regulation for some time to come.

UK Supreme Court Guidance

The UK Supreme Court also addressed the issue of tweeting and reporting from its chamber in its own policy, issued in February 2011.

The Supreme Court notes that the legislation applicable to it is "materially different" from other courts, as well as the fact that it is an appeal chamber and does not interact with witnesses or jurors.[57]

It is noted that the legislative prohibitions of broadcasting and photography in court were "specifically exempted" in an amendment to the Act for the new UK Supreme Court.[58]

The new rules in relation to the Supreme Court provide that, subject to exceptions, lawyers as well as the public can used text-based communication from the Supreme Court provided that "these are silent" and "there is no disruption".[59] However, no mobile calls are permitted.[60]

---

[53] Press Notice, Guidance Issued for Tweeting the Twists and Turns of Supreme Court Cases, The Supreme Court of the United Kingdom, Reference Number 02/2011, 3 February 2011, available at www.supremecourt.gov.uk/docs/pr_1102.pdf.

[54] *ibid.* Also "Supreme Court to Allow Tweeting," www.loughboroughecho.net.

[55] J Griffin, "Tweeting Allowed in Supreme Court," *Suite 1010*, available at www.suite101.com.

[56] "Tweeting Allowed in Supreme Court," http://ukscblog.com/tweeting-allowed-in-supreme-court.

[57] *The Supreme Court of the United Kingdom Policy on the Use of Live Text Based Communications from Court* (February 2011). Available at www.supremecourt.gov.uk/docs/live-text-based-comms.pdf.

[58] *ibid.*

[59] *ibid.*

[60] *ibid.*

The exceptions referred to above are that the person must observe any reporting restrictions that may apply; and that such communications in cases involving children must maintain anonymity.[61] A "breach of anonymity will be treated as a contempt of court."[62]

There is also a catch-all-type provision whereby the Supreme Court notes that on occasion an order may restrict publication of a judgment in order to not influence current proceedings in lower courts.[63]

In terms of such restrictions, these "will be notified to court visitors by a notice at the door of the courtroom, and, where appropriate, by verbal instructions from a Justice."[64]

The UK Twitter Consultation

A consultation paper, *Consultation on the Use of Live, Text-Based Communications from Court for the Purposes of Fair and Accurate Reporting*, was issued by the Judicial Office for England and Wales on Behalf of Lord Chief Justice on 7 February 2011. Respondents were called to direct their views to the Courts Reporting Consultation at the Royal Courts of Justice. It relates to the possible use of live text-based communications in court. Therefore, it excludes dealing with non-live tweeting or text-based communications.

The Consultation

The consultation set out some of the issues and considerations, and then invited comments and responses in relation a list of predetermined questions, namely:

- Is there a legitimate demand for live, text-based communications to be used from the courtroom?
- Under what circumstances should live, text-based communications be permitted from the courtroom?
- Are there any other risks which derive from the use of live, text-based communications from the court?
- How should the courts approach the different risks to proceedings posed by different platforms for live, text-based communications from court?
- Who should be permitted the use of live, text-based communications from court? Is this reconciled with the blanket prohibition against the use of mobile telephones in court?
- Should the use of live, text-based communications from court be principally for the use of the media? How should the media be defined? Should persons other than the accredited media be permitted to engage in live, text-based communications from court?

---

61 *ibid.*

62 *ibid.* Generally, in relation to contempt law, see Borrie and Lowe, *The Law of Contempt* (LexisNexis, London, 2010); *Arlidge, Eady & Smith on Contempt* (Sweet and Maxwell: London, 2010).

63 *ibid.*

64 *ibid.*

In December 2011 the UK courts, following the consultation, decided to permit or relax the possibility of tweeting in court, at the discretion of individual judges.[65]

Contempt Consultation

In England and Wales, the Law Commission has issued an extensive consultation in relation to contempt issues,[66] including:

- contempt by publication;
- the impact of new media;
- contempts committed by jurors;
- contempt in the face of the court.

The consultation document states that various:

> "high profile cases ... underscore the need for this project. These include,
> (1) A juror who was found to have researched the defendant on the internet;
> (2) The first internet contempt by publication, which concerned the posting of an incriminating photograph of a defendant on a website;
> (3) Contempt proceedings for the vilification of Chris Jeffries during the investigation into the murder of Joanna Yeates; and
> (4) Proceedings for contempt by publication following the collapse of the prosecution of Levi Bellfield".[67]

It adds:

> "[s]uch cases illustrate the challenge that is posed by the new media to the existing laws on contempt of court which pre-date the internet age. They also illustrate the continuing need for limits on media coverage in order to protect the administration of justice and the right to a fair trial".[68]

CONCLUSION

These issues are only coming to be considered in various courts internationally. The UK consultation and what might result from it in terms of policy have yet to be seen. It may also be the case that the News of the World phone hacking scandal and the police and parliamentary investigations have some influence on the ultimate results. The final UK policy on these issues may have some influence on the ultimate consideration and discussion of these issues elsewhere, albeit not in any binding way. While there are similarities between Ireland and the UK, there are numerous legal and constitutional differences. It is understood that there may be a forthcoming official consideration of some of these issues at Irish judicial level; no details are currently available.

---

65 See *Practice Guidance: The Use of Live Text-based Forms of Communications (Including Twitter) from Court for the Purposes of Fair and Accurate Reporting*, Lord Chief Justice of England and Wales, 14 December 2011.

66 Law Commission, Consultation Pater No 209, *Contempt of Court, A Consultation Paper*.

67 *ibid*, 1. Footnotes omitted.

68 *ibid*.

PART XII: DATA PROTECTION: THE FUTURE

CHAPTER 32

PRIVACY BY DESIGN

HEADLINE OF ISSUES

- The Privacy by Design (PbD) solution
- The Origins of PbD – Dr. Ann Cavoukian, Information and Privacy Commissioner of Ontario, Canada
- Pre-problem solving
- EU Article 29 Working Party
- EU PbD

INTRODUCTION

Privacy concerns are real and are growing as technology grows. Yet, technology also offers solutions in many instances, such as incorporating data protection pre-problem solving into product and service design from the very beginning.

Traditionally, data protection is frequently glossed over from a compliance perspective and looked at in detail only if and when it is necessary to react to a particular issue or complaint arising later on. In effect, it is often the case that organisations do not have to think about data protection in advance in a proactive manner. It is only after an event that detailed compliance is considered. Privacy by design (PbD) seeks to reconfigure the treatment of data protection concerns.

ORIGINS OF PRIVACY BY DESIGN

The concept of Privacy by Design or PbD is complementary to data protection law and regulation. The idea is acknowledged to have originated with Ann Cavoukian Ph.D, the Information & Privacy Commissioner for Ontario, Canada. She states that,

> "the increasing complexity and interconnectedness of information technologies [requires] building privacy right into system design ... the concept of Privacy by Design (PbD), ... describe[s] the philosophy of embedding privacy proactively into technology itself – making it the default."[1]

In *Privacy by Design, The 7 Foundational Principles, Implementation and Mapping of Fair Information Practices*, Commissioner Cavoukian maps the PbD principles (ie the 7 Foundational Principles of PbD) against the Fair Information Practices, or FIPs and answers the question of why we need PbD in the first place.

---

1 Available at http://privacybydesign.ca/about/, accessed on 21 August, 2012.

PbD affirms but also enhances the FIPs.[2] Elements such as PbD's proactive approach, the fact that privacy must be embedded in design and that the approach is inherently positive-sum (ie the notion that all interests must be satisfied – privacy AND security, for example) are the obvious extensions to the FIPs.

Part of the justification for PbD is the ongoing changes to how products and services are provided as well as the rapid increase in modern innovation, its complexity and the inherent challenges which this brings for informational privacy protection.[3] While we can enjoy the benefits of innovation and technology, freedom of choice and control of our personal data must be preserved.[4] "[P]rivacy has nonetheless evolved over the years, beyond being viewed solely as a legal compliance requirement, to also being recognized as a market imperative and critical enabler of trust and freedoms in our present-day information society."[5]

Commenting on the need for the PbD design approach, the Commissioner states that "[t]here is a growing understanding that innovation, creativity and competitiveness must be approached from a 'design-thinking' perspective – namely, a way of viewing the world and overcoming constraints that is at once holistic, interdisciplinary, integrative, innovative, and inspiring."[6] Data protection and privacy also "must be approached from the same design-thinking perspective."[7] The Commissioner advises that "[p]rivacy must be incorporated into networked data systems, technologies and business processes, by default. Privacy must become integral to organizational priorities, project objectives, design processes, and planning operations. Privacy must be embedded into every standard, protocol and process that touches our lives."[8]

The Commissioner sets out 7 Foundational Principles for PbD. These are,

1 Proactive not Reactive; Preventative not Remedial;
2 Privacy as the Default Setting;
3 Privacy Embedded into Design;
4 Full Functionality – Positive-Sum, Not Zero-Sum;
5 End to End Security – Full Lifecycle Protection;
6 Visibility and Transparency – Keep it Open;
7 Respect for User Privacy – Keep it User-Centric.[9]

These 7 Foundational Principles for PbD are further detailed by the Commissioner as follows:

---

2 Ann Cavoukian, PhD, *Privacy by Design, The 7 Foundational Principles, Implementation and Mapping of Fair Information Practices* (Information & Privacy Commissioner Ontario, Canada) (May 2010, and revised January 2011), at 1. The Commissioner separately describes the PbD Principles as being "considerably broader in scope and extend well beyond the Fair Information Practices," see Ann Cavoukian, Ph.D, *Operationalizing Privacy by Design: A Guide to Implementing Strong Privacy Practices*, Information and Privacy Commissioner, Ontario, Canada (December 2012) at 2.

3 *ibid*, 2.

4 *ibid.*

5 *ibid.*

6 *ibid.*

7 *ibid.*

8 *ibid*, original emphasis.

9 *Ibid*, 2-5.

"Proactive not Reactive; Preventative not Remedial

The Privacy by Design approach is characterized by proactive rather than reactive measures. It anticipates and prevents privacy invasive events before they happen. PbD does not wait for privacy risks to materialize, nor does it offer remedies for resolving privacy infractions once they have occurred – it aims to prevent them from occurring. In short, Privacy by Design comes before-the-fact, not after.

Whether applied to information technologies, organizational practices, physical design, or networked information ecosystems, *PbD* begins with an explicit recognition of the value and benefits of proactively adopting strong privacy practices, early and consistently (for example, preventing (internal) data breaches from happening in the first place). This implies:

- A clear commitment, at the highest levels, to set and enforce high standards of privacy – generally higher than the standards set out by global laws and regulation.
- A privacy commitment that is demonstrably shared throughout by user communities and stakeholders, in a culture of continuous improvement.
- Established methods to recognize poor privacy designs, anticipate poor privacy practices and outcomes, and correct any negative impacts, well before they occur in proactive, systematic, and innovative ways.

Privacy as the Default Setting

We can all be certain of one thing – the default rules! Privacy by Design seeks to deliver the maximum degree of privacy by ensuring that personal data are automatically protected in any given IT system or business practice. If an individual does nothing, their privacy still remains intact. No action is required on the part of the individual to protect their privacy – it is built into the system, by default.

This *PbD* principle, which could be viewed as **Privacy by Default,** is particularly informed by the following FIPs:

- **Purpose Specification** – the purposes for which personal information is collected, used, retained and disclosed shall be communicated to the individual (data subject) at or before the time the information is collected. Specified purposes should be clear, limited and relevant to the circumstances.
- **Collection Limitation** – the collection of personal information must be fair, lawful and limited to that which is necessary for the specified purposes.
- **Data Minimization** – the collection of personally identifiable information should be kept to a strict minimum. The design of programs, information and communications technologies, and systems should begin with non-identifiable interactions and transactions, as the default. Wherever possible, identifiability, observability, and linkability of personal information should be minimized.
- **Use, Retention, and Disclosure Limitation** – the use, retention, and disclosure of personal information shall be limited to the relevant purposes identified to the individual, for which he or she has consented, except where otherwise required by law. Personal information shall be retained only as long as necessary to fulfill the stated purposes, and then securely destroyed.
- Where the need or use of personal information is not clear, there shall be a presumption of privacy and the precautionary principle shall apply: the default settings shall be the most privacy protective.

Privacy Embedded into Design

Privacy by Design is embedded into the design and architecture of IT systems and business practices. It is not bolted on as an add-on, after the fact. The result is that privacy becomes an essential component of the core functionality being delivered. Privacy is integral to the system, without diminishing functionality.

Privacy must be embedded into technologies, operations, and information architectures in a holistic, integrative and creative way. Holistic, because additional, broader contexts must always be considered. Integrative, because all stakeholders and interests should be consulted. Creative, because embedding privacy sometimes means re-inventing existing choices because the alternatives are unacceptable.

- A systemic, principled approach to embedding privacy should be adopted – one that relies upon accepted standards and frameworks, which are amenable to external reviews and audits. All fair information practices should be applied with equal rigour, at every step in the design and operation.
- Wherever possible, detailed privacy impact and risk assessments should be carried out and published, clearly documenting the privacy risks and all measures taken to mitigate those risks, including consideration of alternatives and the selection of metrics.
- The privacy impacts of the resulting technology, operation or information architecture, and their uses, should be demonstrably minimized, and not easily degraded through use, misconfiguration or error.

Full Functionality – Positive-Sum, Not Zero-Sum

Privacy by Design seeks to accommodate all legitimate interests and objectives in a positive-sum 'win-win' manner, not through a dated, zero-sum approach, where unnecessary trade-offs are made. Privacy by Design avoids the pretence of false dichotomies, such as privacy vs security, demonstrating that it is possible, and far more desirable, to have both.

Privacy by Design does not simply involve the making of declarations and commitments – it relates to satisfying all of an organization's legitimate objectives – not only its privacy goals. *Privacy by Design* is doubly-enabling in nature, permitting full functionality – real, practical results and beneficial outcomes to be achieved for multiple parties.

- When embedding privacy into a given technology, process, or system, it should be done in such a way that full functionality is not impaired, and to the greatest extent possible, that all requirements are optimized.
- Privacy is often positioned in a zero-sum manner as having to compete with other legitimate interests, design objectives, and technical capabilities, in a given domain. *Privacy by Design* rejects taking such an approach – it embraces legitimate non-privacy objectives and accommodates them, in an innovative positive-sum manner.
- All interests and objectives must be clearly documented, desired functions articulated, metrics agreed upon and applied, and trade-offs rejected as often being unnecessary, in favour of finding a solution that enables multi-functionality.

Additional recognition is garnered for creativity and innovation in achieving all objectives and functionalities in an integrative, positive-sum manner. Entities that succeed in overcoming outmoded zero-sum choices are demonstrating first-class global privacy leadership, having achieved the Gold Standard.

End to End Security – Full Lifecycle Protection

Privacy by Design, having been embedded into the system prior to the first element of information being collected, extends securely throughout the entire lifecycle of the data involved — strong security measures are essential to privacy, from start to finish. This ensures that all data are securely retained, and then securely destroyed at the end of the process, in a timely fashion. Thus, Privacy by Design ensures cradle to grave, secure lifecycle management of information, end-to-end.

Privacy must be continuously protected across the entire domain and throughout the life-cycle of the data in question. There should be no gaps in either protection or accountability. The 'Security' principle has special relevance here because, at its essence, without strong security, there can be no privacy.

- **Security** – Entities must assume responsibility for the security of personal information (generally commensurate with the degree of sensitivity) throughout its entire lifecycle, consistent with standards that have been developed by recognized standards development bodies.
- **Applied security** standards must assure the confidentiality, integrity and availability of personal data throughout its lifecycle including, *inter alia*, methods

of secure destruction, appropriate encryption, and strong access control and logging methods.

Visibility and Transparency – Keep it Open
Privacy by Design seeks to assure all stakeholders that whatever the business practice or technology involved, it is in fact, operating according to the stated promises and objectives, subject to independent verification. Its component parts and operations remain visible and transparent, to both users and providers alike. Remember, trust but verify!

Visibility and transparency are essential to establishing accountability and trust. This PbD principle tracks well to Fair Information Practices in their entirety, but for auditing purposes, special emphasis may be placed upon the following FIPs:

- **Accountabilty** – The collection of personal information entails a duty of care for its protection. Responsibility for all privacy-related policies and procedures shall be documented and communicated as appropriate, and assigned to a specified individual. When transferring personal information to third parties, equivalent privacy protection through contractual or other means shall be secured.
- **Openness** – Openness and transparency are key to accountability. Information about the policies and practices relating to the management of personal information shall be made readily available to individuals.
- **Compliance** – Complaint and redress mechanisms should be established, and information communicated about them to individuals, including how to access the next level of appeal. Necessary steps to monitor, evaluate, and verify compliance with privacy policies and procedures should be taken.

Respect for User Privacy – Keep it User-Centric.
Above all, Privacy by Design requires architects and operators to keep the interests of the individual uppermost by offering such measures as strong privacy defaults, appropriate notice, and empowering user-friendly options. Keep it user-centric!

The best *Privacy by Design* results are usually those that are consciously designed around the interests and needs of individual users, who have the greatest vested interest in the management of their own personal data.

Empowering data subjects to play an active role in the management of their own data may be the single most effective check against abuses and misuses of privacy and personal data. Respect for User Privacy is supported by the following FIPs:

- **Consent** – The individual's free and specific consent is required for the collection, use or disclosure of personal information, except where otherwise permitted by law. The greater the sensitivity of the data, the clearer and more specific the quality of the consent required. Consent may be withdrawn at a later date.
- **Accuracy** – personal information shall be as accurate, complete, and up-to-date as is necessary to fulfil the specified purposes.
- **Access** – Individuals shall be provided access to their personal information and informed of its uses and disclosures. Individuals shall be able to challenge the accuracy and completeness of the information and have it amended as appropriate.
- **Compliance** – Organizations must establish complaint and redress mechanisms, and communicate information about them to the public, including how to access the next level of appeal.
- *Respect for User Privacy* goes beyond these FIPs, and extends to the need for human-machine interfaces to be human-centered, user-centric and user-friendly so that informed privacy decisions may be reliably exercised. Similarly, business operations and physical architectures should also demonstrate the same degree of consideration for the individual, who should feature prominently at the centre of operations involving collections of personal data."[10]

---

[10] *ibid.*

The Commissioner also documents a recent survey of the application areas of PbD. This is entitled *Operationalizing Privacy by Design: A Guide to Implementing Strong Privacy Practices*.[11] The Foundational Principles are reproduced at the beginning.

The document reiterates the justification and need for PbD. For example, "the individual should be the one to determine the fate of his or her personal information."[12] It is even more important today, "in an age characterized by far-reaching online social media and ubiquitous computing."[13] This applies across all types of organisations and sectors, not just multinationals. Technology and the internet mean that "relatively small organizations may control disproportionately large volumes of PII"[14] and personal data. The Commissioner indicates that "what matters is that someone is charged with the responsibility of being accountable for the organization's privacy protection."[15]

PbD is important in its approach as it tries to ensure that problems, e.g. breaches, do not occur at all. It is pre-problem solving. The Commissioner also indicates that "[d]oing it right, the first time, has long been recognized as a cost-saving strategy in multiple domains. Most importantly, however, the approach fosters an environment where privacy harms are minimized or entirely prevented from happening, in the first place. Imagine the cost savings in avoiding data breaches."[16] PbD is a "'build it early' approach to privacy"[17] and data protection.

The Commissioner states that "[c]omprehensive privacy programs are an essential component of building trusting, longterm relationships with existing customers and attracting opportunity in the form of new ones. Privacy breaches can have profound and long-term adverse consequences, including significant financial impacts and damage to the brand and reputation of organizations."[18]

The rest of the paper is fleshed out with examples of the Commissioner's collaboration with numerous organisations and how each of the principles informed that particular exercise. The examples and case studies of applications are:

- CCTV/Surveillance Cameras in Mass Transit Systems;
- Biometrics Used in Casinos and Gaming Facilities;
- Smart Meters and the Smart Grid;
- Mobile Devices & Communications;
- Near Field Communications (NFC) ;
- RFIDs and Sensor Technologies;
- Redesigning IP Geolocation Data;
- Remote Home Health Care;
- Big Data and Data Analytics.

---

11 Ann Cavoukian, Ph.D, *Operationalizing Privacy by Design: A Guide to Implementing Strong Privacy Practices*, Information and Privacy Commissioner, Ontario, Canada (December 2012).
12 *ibid*, 2.
13 *ibid*.
14 *ibid*.
15 *ibid*.
16 *ibid*.
17 *ibid*, 5.
18 *ibid*, 5.

The case studies present best practices in relation to the application of a particular Principle.[19] In addition to analysing the issues and making best practice recommendations, they also incorporate positive actions that should be taken as well as allocating task responsibility to particular personnel within the organisation. Indeed, in the EU it is increasingly emphasised that data protection compliance is a board room issue.

The document also encompasses a very useful resource of reference papers organised according to application area and separately organised by Principle.

This serves to highlight the ever increasing popularity as well as endorsement of the PbD Principles, including the International Association of Data Protection Authorities and Privacy Commissioners, the US Federal Trade Commission (FTC), the EU and various privacy and industry professionals,[20] market leaders, technology leaders and regulators.[21]

EU & Privacy by Design

Obviously there are many data protection concerns posed by social networking. Various solutions have been suggested for some of these problems, from legislation to technical solutions to education. One of the new suggested solutions is known as privacy by design (PbD). While this concept could be applied to all data-processing activities, it can also be applied to social networking. To date, however, it does not appear to have been.

PbD is relevant to the privacy concerns with social networking. This is also a solution applicable in terms of many second-generation internet (Web 2.0) and cloud internet issues. Indeed, others have also been raising the possibility of emphasising privacy as a "product safety" issue.[22]

The review of the European data protection legal regime being undertaken presently the EU Commission is understood to encompass the promotion of the concept of PbD solutions. It should be recalled that the present EU review is aimed at addressing the problems created by social networking and cloud computing as well as just updating the Data Protection Directive1995.

In Europe the EU Article 29 Working Party expressly recognises the existence and problems posed by social networking. As part of dealing with these issues, it proposed greater adoption for the PbD concept.

By making PbD a more explicit legal obligation "this would ... bind technology designers and producers and data controllers when using ICT technologies, such that 'privacy by default' would become the norm and not the exception".[23]

---

19 *ibid*, 2.
20 *ibid*, 1.
21 *ibid*, 5.
22 J Grimmelmann, "Privacy as Product Safety" (2010) *Widener Law Journal* 793.
23 R Wong, "Data Protection: The Future of Privacy" (2011) (27) *Computer Law & Security Review* 53 at 55.

Separately, the EU Article 29 Working Party suggests that "privacy should be embedded into information processing technologies and systems".[24]

Some have argued that the social networks are in the best position to assist users in dealing with and protecting privacy.[25] There is a criticism that the eCommerce legal defences "intermediaries an incentive to be as little involved as possible in what goes on their web servers".[26]

Pre-Problem Solving

At its essence PbD is about pre-problem solving. It seeks to incorporate the consideration of privacy and data protection issues and concerns to the concept stage of the design of new products and services.

The *Future of Privacy* opinion document addresses PbD, referring to it as a "new principle" and stating:

> "41 The basic concepts of Directive 95/46/EC were developed in the nineteen seventies, when information processing was characterized by card index boxes, punch cards and mainframe computers. Today computing is ubiquitous, global and networked.
>
> Information technology devices are increasingly miniaturized and equipped with network cards, WiFi or other radio interfaces. In almost all offices and family homes users can globally communicate via the internet. Web 2.0 services and cloud computing are blurring the distinction between data controllers, processors and data subjects.
>
> 42 Directive 95/46/EC has stood well the influx of these technological developments because it holds principles and uses concepts that are not only sound but also technologically neutral. Such principles and concepts remain equally relevant, valid and applicable in today's networked world.
>
> 43 While it is clear that technological developments described above are generally good for society, nevertheless they have strengthened the risks for individuals' privacy and data protection. To counterbalance these risks, the data protection legal framework should be complemented. First, the principle of 'privacy by design' should be introduced in the new framework; second, as the need arises, regulations for specific technological contexts should be adopted which require embedding data protection and privacy principles into such contexts".[27]

While the principle of PbD itself is new, similar ideas have been anticipated before. The EU Article 29 Working Party states:

---

24 Wong, *op. cit*, 56, referring to Article 29 Working Party, *Opinion 1/2010 on the Concept of "Controller" and "Processor,"* adopted on 16 February 2010 at www.cbpweb.nl/dpwnloads_med/med20100219_C.03%20DC-DP_Opinion_Adopted.pdf. Also, M Schmidl and D Krone, "The EU Art. 29 Working Party's Guidance on Data 'Controllers' and 'Data Processors'," available at www.bnai.com/EUArticle29/default.aspx.

25 BL Mann, "Social Networking Websites – A Concentration of Impersonation, Denigration, Sexual Aggressive Solicitation, Cyber-Bullying or Happy Slapping Videos" (2009)(17) *International Journal of Law & Information Technology* 252 at 256.

26 Mann, *op. cit*, 252–257, and referring to C George and J Scerri, "Web 2.0 and User-Generated Content: Legal Challenges in the New Frontier" (2008) *Journal of Information, Law and Technology* at http://go.warick.ac.uk/iilt/2007_2/george_scerri.

27 *The Future of Privacy*, Joint Contribution to the Consultation of the European Commission on the Legal Framework for the Fundamental Right to Protection of Personal Data, Article 29 Data Protection Working Party, Working Party on Police and Justice, WP 168. Adopted 1 December 2009.

> "44 The idea of incorporating technological data protection safeguards in information and communication technologies ('ICT') is not completely new. Directive 95/46/EC already contains several provisions which expressly call for data controllers to implement technology safeguards in the design and operation of ICT. This is the case of Article 17 which lays down the data controllers' obligation to implement appropriate technical and organizational measures. Recital 46 calls for such measures to be taken, both at the time of the design of the processing system and at the time of the processing itself. Article 16 establishes the confidentiality of processing, a rule which is mirrored and complemented in regulations regarding IT security. Apart from these articles, the principles relating to data quality as contained in Article 6 (lawfulness and fairness, purpose limitation, relevance, accuracy, time limit of storage, responsibility) also apply.
>
> 45 Whereas the above provisions of the Directive are helpful towards the promotion of privacy by design, in practice they have not been sufficient in ensuring that privacy is embedded in ICT. Users of ICT services – business, public sector and certainly individuals – are not in a position to take relevant security measures by themselves in order to protect their own or other persons' personal data. Therefore, these services and technologies should be designed with privacy by default settings".[28]

However, the Opinion continues:

> "46 It is for these reasons that the new legal framework has to include a provision translating the currently punctual requirements into a broader and consistent principle of privacy by design. This principle should be binding for technology designers and producers as well as for data controllers who have to decide on the acquisition and use of ICT. They should be obliged to take technological data protection into account already at the planning stage of information-technological procedures and systems. Providers of such systems or services as well as controllers should demonstrate that they have taken all measures required to comply with these requirements.
>
> 47 Such principle should call for the implementation of data protection in ICT (privacy by design or 'PbD') designated or used for the processing of personal data. It should convey the requirement that ICT should not only maintain security but also should be designed and constructed in a way to avoid or minimize the amount of personal data processed. This is in line with recent case law in Germany.
>
> 48 The application of such principle would emphasize the need to implement privacy enhancing technologies (PETs), 'privacy by default' settings and the necessary tools to enable users to better protect their personal data (eg, access controls, encryption).
>
> It should be a crucial requirement for products and services provided to third parties and individual customers (eg WiFi-Routers, social networks and search engines). In turn, it would give DPAs more powers to enforce the effective implementation of such measures.
>
> 49 Such principle should be defined in a technologically neutral way in order to last for a long period of time in a fast changing technological and social environment. It should also be flexible enough so that data controllers and DPAs will, on a case by case basis, be able to translate it in concrete measures for guaranteeing data protection.
>
> 50 The principle should emphasize, as current Recital 46 does, the need for such principle to be applied as early as possible: 'At the time of the design of the processing system and at the time of the processing itself'. Safeguards implemented at a late stage are inconsistent and insufficient as regards the requirements of an effective protection of the rights and freedoms of the data subjects.
>
> 51 Technological standards should be developed and taken into consideration in the phase of system analysis by hardware and software engineers, so that difficulties in defining and specifying requirements deriving from the principle of 'privacy by design' are minimized. Such standards may be general or specific with regard to various processing purposes and technologies".[29]

PbD is recognised as being important in future data protection compliance and

---

[28] *ibid.*

[29] *ibid.*

solutions. Various examples are referred to the EU Article 29 Working Party as demonstrating how PbD should enable successful data protection. It states:

> "• Biometric identifiers should be stored in devices under control of the data subjects (ie smart cards) rather than in external data bases;
> • Video surveillance in public transportation systems should be designed in a way that the faces of traced individuals are not recognizable or other measures are taken to minimize the risk for the data subject. Of course, an exception must be made for exceptional circumstances such as if the person is suspected of having committed a criminal offence;
> • Patient names and other personal identifiers maintained in hospitals' information systems should be separated from data on the health status and medical treatments. They should be combined only in so far as it is necessary for medical or other reasonable purposes in a secure environment;
> • Where appropriate, functionality should be included facilitating the data subjects' right to revoke consent, with subsequent data deletion in all servers involved (including proxies and mirroring)".[30]

The EU Article 29 Working Party refers to how implementation of PbD may occur in practice. It states:

> "53 In practice, the implementation of the privacy by design principle will require the evaluation of several, concrete aspects or objectives. In particular, when making decisions about the design of a processing system, its acquisition and the running of such a system the following general aspects/objectives should be respected:
>
> - Data Minimization: data processing systems are to be designed and selected in accordance with the aim of collecting, processing or using no personal data at all or as few personal data as possible;
> - Controllability: an IT system should provide the data subjects with effective means of control concerning their personal data. The possibilities regarding consent and objection should be supported by technological means;
> - Transparency: both developers and operators of IT systems have to ensure that the data subjects are sufficiently informed about the means of operation of the systems. Electronic access / information should be enabled;
> - User Friendly Systems: privacy related functions and facilities should be user friendly, ie they should provide sufficient help and simple interfaces to be used also by less experienced users;
> - Data Confidentiality: it is necessary to design and secure IT systems in a way that only authorised entities have access to personal data;
> - Data Quality: data controllers have to support data quality by technical means.
>
> Relevant data should be accessible if needed for lawful purposes.
>
> - Use Limitation: IT systems which can be used for different purposes or are run in a multi-user environment (ie virtually connected systems, such as data warehouses, cloud computing, digital identifiers) have to guarantee that data and processes serving different tasks or purposes can be segregated from each other in a secure way".[31]

Regulations for Specific Technological Contexts

However, the "privacy by design principle may not be sufficient to ensure, in all cases, that the appropriate technological data protection principles are properly

---

[30] *ibid.*
[31] *ibid.*

included in ICT".[32] In some cases there may be a need for a "more concrete 'hands on approach'".[33] The EU Article 29 Working Party states:

> "To facilitate the adoption of such measures, a new legal framework should include a provision enabling the adoption of specific regulations for a specific technological context which require embedding the privacy principles in such context.
>
> 55 This is not a new concept; Article 14 (3) of the ePrivacy Directive, contains a similar provision: 'Where required, measures may be adopted to ensure that terminal equipment is constructed in a way that is compatible with the right of users to protect and control the use of their personal data, in accordance with Directive 1999/5/EC and Council Decision 87/95/EEC of 22 December 1986 on standardization in the field of information technology and communications).'
>
> 56 The above would facilitate the adoption, in specific cases, of specific legislative measures embedding the concept of 'privacy by design' and ensuring that adequate specifications are provided. For example, this may be the case with RFID technology, social networks, behavioural advertisement, etcetera".[34]

The EU Article 29 Working Party adds in conclusion that the "increasing significance of data protection when creating and operating IT systems is posing additional requirements to IT-specialists. This causes the need to firmly incorporate data protection into the curricula of IT-professions".[35] In addition, the "technological data protection principles and the ensuing concrete criteria should be used as a basis for awarding labels of quality (certification schemes) in a framework of a data protection audit".[36]

Expectations for the Future

There are undoubtedly "potent, landscape-changing threats[s] to privacy".[37] Findlay asks the following questions:

- Is it unreasonable to expect privacy in places where such an expectation would have been completely warranted just 10 years ago?
- Is it fair to ask people to change their behaviour in the face of such rapid technological change?
- Does the emergence of small, sophisticated and mobile image-capturing devices paired with the explosion of social networking expose new privacy risks deserving of protection?
- To what extent must law enforcement standards change and adapt in light of these changes?[38]

Findlay feels that the choice for solutions to the problem is between individuals' own behaviour or new or reformulated legal protection.[39]

---

32 *ibid.*
33 *ibid.*
34 *ibid.*
35 *ibid.*
36 *ibid.*
37 D Findlay, "Tag! Now You're 'It.' What Photographs on Social Networking Sites Mean for the Fourth Amendment" (2008) (10) *North Carolina Journal of Law & Technology* 171 at 200.
38 *ibid.*
39 *ibid*, 200.

Publication in a social networking context can have "severe and dramatic consequences".[40]

The view is expressed that "[c]urrent constructs of privacy law do not prove adept at adequately protecting sensible notions of privacy expectations".[41]

Garrie, Duffy-Lewis, Wong and Gillespie feel that education, more proactive data protection commissioners and a more enhanced data protection legal regime are required to address the problems with social networking.[42]

Some authors also suggest that there is not a legally recognised concept of a "digital identity" in which individuals have and can seek to protect rights.[43] This is argued to be evident as a consequence from the UK Identity Cards Act 2006 and what is referred to as "an individual's transactional identity".[44]

> "Arguably, a concept of transactional identity which consists of a defined set of information has been evident in commercial practice for several years. However, its presence in legislation which establishes a national identity scheme is a significant development which confirms its emergence as a new legal concept".[45]

Conclusion

Ann Cavoukian Ph.D, the Information & Privacy Commissioner for Ontario, Canada states that "[r]egardless of their size and structure, however, any organization that encounters personal information must effectively manage and protect it."[46] Those within the organisation should all understand whom is responsible for what tasks in relation to ensuring this. The Commissioner adds that a "properly defined set of privacy policies forms a backdrop against which application owners and product developers develop specific sets of privacy requirements to be embedded into their offerings."[47] A wide variety of organisations already "undertake significant PbD-based implementations."[48] This will no doubt only increase in popularity and across even more applications and sectors.

PbD offers a fundamental mind shift in the practical and legal mechanics of privacy and data protection. In the context of social networking (and Cloud, etc) we should embrace it because these are technologies which affect more individuals, and more rapidly, than any technology before. The scale and pace of growth mean that

---

40 *ibid*, 201.

41 *ibid*, 201.

42 DB Garrie, M Duffy-Lewis, R Wong and RL Gillespie, "Data Protection: The Challenges Facing Social Networking" (2009–2010) (131) *International Law & Management Review* 127 at 151–152.

43 C Sullivan, "Digital Identity – The Legal Person?" (2009)(25) *Computer Law & Security Review* 227.

44 *ibid*.

45 *ibid*, n11 at 228.

46 Ann Cavoukian, PhD, *Privacy by Design, The 7 Foundational Principles, Implementation and Mapping of Fair Information Practices* (Information & Privacy Commissioner Ontario, Canada) (May 2010, and revised January 2011), at 9.

47 *ibid*, 10.

48 *ibid*, 11.

it is very difficult indeed to stop and think about all the privacy implications. It is commendable, therefore, to engage in pre-problem solving at the early design stage before the new website, product or service goes live.

CHAPTER 33

DATA PROTECTION AUDITS

HEADLINE OF ISSUES

- Facebook
- Complaints to Data Protection Commissioner
- Multiple complaint issues
- Dublin audit review and report
- Agreed changes
- Rolling changes to privacy practices
- Global significance

INTRODUCTION

The instances of official data protection audits will increase in future. In Ireland this will be at the instance of the Data Protection Commissioner. In the UK it will be the Information Commissioner's Office. Other EU countries have their own respective data protection authorities.

In the case of Ireland, the issue of official audits has increased prominence because of the many international technology company (EU) headquarters located in Ireland. Currently LinkedIn is being audited for data protection issues by the Irish Data Protection Commissioner. Inevitably other tech organisations and non-tech organisations will come to be audited also.

The most notable such audit thus far has been the Facebook audit and subsequent re-audit. In this instance, the audit occurred at least in part due to a number of complaints received by the Irish Data Protection Commissioner. However, it must be noted that the Irish Data Protection Commissioner as well as other data protection authorities, are entitled to undertake investigations and audits even without any instant complaint arising.

Notwithstanding the somewhat specific circumstances leading to the Facebook audit, it is still instructive to consider further in relation to the process and issues that may arise. Obviously, once the LinkedIn audit and report issue, we will have further audit process issues available to consider. LinkedIn is also arguably a more regular example of the issues that may arise.

The Facebook audit arises, at least in part, on foot of a number of complaints received by the Irish Data Protection Commissioner's Office. It undertook a review audit of certain Facebook practices and procedures.

This is significant in that it is the most detailed review thus far. More importantly, however, it is significant because it will affect and have relevance to the policies, practices and procedures of Facebook everywhere outside the US and Canada. Dublin is the headquarters of Facebook outside of the US and Canada.

The Austria Complaint

The Austrian complaint was issued by an organisation established by an Austrian law student entitled Europe Against Facebook. The complaint involves a number of discrete and specific areas. These are summarised by the Irish Data Protection Commissioner's Office in its report issued on 21 December 2011.[1]

The complaints are summarised as follows:

> "Complaint 1 – Pokes
> A poke is a type of short message sent from one Facebook user to another. Complainant stated that while Facebook allows for the removal of old pokes, they are not, in fact, being deleted. As part of an access request the complainant was provided with a copy of all pokes ever sent or received going back over a 2 year period.
>
> Complaint 2 – Shadow Profiles
> Complainant contended that Facebook is gathering information in relation to non-Facebook users. This information primarily consists of email addresses, but may also include names, telephone numbers and addresses. Facebook typically collects this information when a user synchronises their phone or imports their email contact list to their Facebook account. Complainant contended that Facebook is using this data to create profiles of non-users. The complainant also stated that, on foot of an access request, Facebook did not provide any details in relation to Facebook users who may have uploaded his email or telephone details to their Facebook account.
>
> Complaint 3 – Tagging
> Friends on Facebook have the facility to 'tag' photos of another user (friend) and display them on their Facebook page and within the 'news feed' section. While the other user may subsequently remove the tag, the issue is that the user is unable to prevent friends tagging photos to their Facebook page in the first place.
>
> Complaint 4 – Synchronising
> This is related to Complaint 2. When a Facebook user synchronises their mobile phone or other device with Facebook, the complainant states that all personal data on the device are transferred to Facebook. This may result in invitations being issued by Facebook to those individuals whose data have been transferred. The individuals are not aware that their personal data has been disclosed in this way.
>
> Complaint 5 – Deleted Posts
> Facebook provides a facility whereby a user can delete old posts. The complainant stated that, while the act of deleting a post does remove the post from view, it is not, in fact, deleted. As part of an access request, the complainant was provided with posts which he had deleted. The deleted posts in question go back over a period of 3 years.
>
> Complaint 6 – Posting on other Peoples Pages
> When posting a comment on another person's Facebook page, the information posted is subject to the other person's privacy settings. The issue for the complainant is that the person posting the comment is unaware of the other user's privacy settings and, accordingly, will

---

1 *Facebook Ireland Limited, Report of Audit*, 21 December 2011, Data Protection Commissioner, available at http://dataprotection.ie/viewdoc.asp?DocID=1182&m=f.

not know who can see the comment being posted – it could be restricted to friends only, but equally, could be viewed by everyone on the internet, including search engines.

Complaint 7 – Messages
It is possible for Facebook users to send instant messages to other users who are online. It is also possible to delete these messages if the user so chooses. However, the complainant contended that the act of hitting the delete button provided merely removes the message from view and does not, in fact, delete it.

Complaint 8 – Consent and Privacy Policy
There are a number of aspects to this complaint set out under the following headings:

Access: the complainant stated that Facebook's Privacy Policy is not easily accessible – the link 'privacy' provided at the bottom of the user's Facebook page is merely a link to a privacy guide, containing limited information. There is a link within this document to the actual Privacy Policy.

Role of FB-I and the User: the complainant stated that the user is not provided with any clear information on who is data controller (Facebook Irl or Facebook Inc).

Extent of Privacy Information: the complainant was dissatisfied that, in order to get a grasp of Facebook's privacy policies, a user must deal with multiple documents and links, with many specific provisions difficult to locate.

Contradictions: the complainant highlighted contradictions he has identified within the Privacy Policy. He stated that the contradictions identified run to 6 pages and has provided some sample issues in the complaint in relation to the deletion of data.

Vague Provisions: the complainant has highlighted a number of provisions in the Privacy Policy which he considered to be vague and general in nature.

Unambiguous Consent: the complainant has highlighted a number of issues with the process of consenting to the Privacy Policy including the use of small text and lack of a check box to be ticked.

Freely Given Consent: this complaint is in relation to the monopoly Facebook has on business and personal users and that there should be a high bar in terms of privacy terms and conditions given the limited competition.

Specific Consent: the complainant contended that there is no specific consent being provided by users for the use of their personal data.

Informed Consent: the complainant considered that the purpose for which personal data is processed is not properly explained.

Consent obtained by deception or misinterpretation: this again relates to how Facebook uses personal data and the complainant has highlighted a number of examples where he considered Facebook to be providing false or misleading information.

Complaint 9 – Face Recognition201
In relation to Facebook's use of tagged photos, the complainant contended that there has never been a specific consent provided to users availing of this feature, and particularly in relation to users who would have provided consents to Facebook prior to the introduction of the feature.

Complaint 10 – Access Requests
This complaint relates to an incomplete access request. The complainant stated that his

access request resulted in only limited data being provided. He outlined the areas – 19 of them – under which he contended Facebook did not provide information.

Complaint 11 – Removal of Tags
A user is provided with the option 'remove tag' from a tagged photo on their Facebook page. However, the complainant contended that removing the tag is not deleting the tag data and that Facebook is not transparent in terms of informing users on the retention of this information following the use of the 'remove tag' option.

Complaint 12 – Data Security
The complainant set out a number of security concerns in relation to the security of personal data – no encryption on private data (other than passwords and credit cards), not taking enough responsibility for data security in its privacy statements and a lack of control over data being provided to third party applications.

Complaint 13 – Applications
This relates to third party applications which sit on the Facebook Platform. The complainant outlined a number of issues including a lack of informed user consent when accessing a third party application, a lack of oversight by Facebook in terms of privacy compliance among third parties and the non-notification to users by Facebook in a case where a third party has no privacy policy.

Complaint 14 – Removed Friends
Facebook provides a facility to add friends and to 'unfriend' friends. The issue here is that when a user clicks on the 'unfriend' option, the friend information is not deleted, but is retained in the background – the complainant saw no justification for the retention and considered that Facebook is not transparent in terms of informing users on the retention of the information.

Complaint 15 – Excessive Processing
This covers a number of earlier complaints in terms of the non-deletion of information (pokes, tags, etc) which a user may have removed from their page. The complainant considered the amount of data Facebook holds and processes to be excessive and a security risk.

Complaint 16 – Opt Out
The complainant argued that there is no specific consent when signing up to Facebook (see ... Complaint 8) and that personal data is being collected prior to a new user being able to set their privacy settings. The complainant also contended that the security settings themselves are too liberal in nature and that the settings pages and links provided discourage the new user from applying certain security settings.

Complaint 17 – Like Button 202
The complainant stated that when a user visits a website which contains a 'social plug in' – the Like button – the following information is being recorded: date, time, URL, IP address, browser and operating system information. The complainant considered that the information is being collected unfairly and is excessive.

Complaint 18 – Obligations as Processor
The complainant considered that FB-I is a data processor while the Facebook user is the data controller. He contended that Facebook's operation as a processor is at variance with both Irish Data Protection legislation and Directive 95/46/EC.

Complaint 19 – Pictures Privacy Settings
Facebook allows a user to upload photographs to their Facebook page and apply security settings. The complainant stated that Facebook has outsourced the delivery of the picture content to a company (Akamai Technologies) and, by using the source code from the

> pictures page of Facebook.com and identifying certain URLs, that it is possible to view some photographs that should be hidden from view.
>
> Complaint 20 – Deleted Pictures
> This complaint relates to the previous complaint (19). Facebook users are given the option to delete pictures they have uploaded to Facebook. Again, by using the source code from the pictures page of Facebook.com and identifying certain URLs, the complainant stated that it was possible to view a photograph for up to 48 hours after he had deleted it from Facebook.
>
> Complaint 21 – Groups
> Facebook allows users to add friends to groups which are found on the user's Facebook page and within 'news feeds.' The issue raised in the complaint is that a user can be added to other users groups without their consent.
>
> Complaint 22 – New Policy
> This relates to recent changes made to Facebook's Privacy Policy. The complainant contended that it is difficult to understand the changes in conjunction with the previous policy and that users have not had any opportunity to consent to the changes made".[2]

Norwegian Complaint

A separate complaint was also received by the Irish Data Protection Commissioner in relation to Facebook from the Norwegian Consumer Council. Originally, a complaint was made in Norway but was transmitted to Ireland, given that Facebook was located in Dublin.

The complaint is summarised by the report as follows:

> "The complaint is generally described as being in relation to the collecting, processing and storing of personal data on Facebook. In particular, the complaint examines Facebook's privacy settings and information passed to third party applications accessible from the Facebook platform.
>
> Privacy Settings
> The complainant highlights a number of changes made by Facebook to privacy settings functionality. In one instance in December 2009, the Council considers that the new privacy settings recommended by Facebook would allow certain information, for example 'posts by me' and 'religious views' to be available to a wider user audience and that 'members were urged to accept the new privacy settings'.
>
> The Council also takes issue with another change, stating that, formerly, it was possible for a user to block all third party applications with a simple click, but now they had to be removed individually.
>
> Third Party Applications
> The Council highlights the fact that when a Facebook user signs up to a third party application that the user's data is provided to the application. The Council contends, from information collected from a survey it carried out, that 'many people believe the applications to be part of Facebook and they are therefore not even aware that they are interacting with a third party.' The Council also considers that many of the terms and conditions of third party applications are complex or unclear.
>
> The Council states that a user signing up to a third party application must accept the application's terms and conditions in order to use the service. The Council contends that

---

2 Appendix 2.

Zynga, a third party application providing 37 different games, collects and holds the following information when you sign up,

- Name
- Address
- Gender

The Council has concerns in relation to additional data subsequently collected,

- Information about you from other Zynga users
- Information on those you invite to use a Zynga game

The Consumer Council states that there is no information provided on,

- How long this data is stored
- What it is used for
- Whether it is shared with others

The Council also contends that Zynga retains personal data even after a user account has been closed. The Council highlighted the use of this retention of data with an example from the Zynga game Café World, providing a screenshot of the game which shows a profile photograph of a Facebook user continuing to appear in the game after the user had previously blocked the application.

Conclusion

The Norwegian Consumer Council sets out a number of areas under which it considers Facebook and Zynga to be in breach of Norwegian Data Protection Law and raises issues which may be summarised by the following questions:

- Are Facebook and Zynga legally entitled to collect, store and process sensitive personal data such as race and political affiliation?
- What responsibility does Facebook take for third party applications offered via its platform?
- Given the complexity of third part terms and conditions, can a user be deemed to have provided free and informed consent to the processing of their data?
- Are Facebook and Zynga complying with data protection law in terms of limitations to the processing of personal data?
- Is the processing of personal data by Facebook and Zynga compatible with and relevant to the purpose for which it was collected?
- Is the data being retained for longer than is necessary, given the purpose for which it was originally collected?
- Is the disclosure of data by both Facebook and Zynga in breach of data protection law?
- The Council states that while Facebook is on the 'Safe Harbour' list, Zynga is not.

Accordingly, does Facebook's processing of personal data in the context of its relationship with Zynga conflict 'Safe Harbor' rules?"

More recently, some doubts have been raised in relation to whether the EU-US Safe Harbor data transfer arrangement should continue, in light of the Snowden revelations.

The Report and Decisions

The Irish Data Protection Commissioner report and accompanying press release refer to the following issues to be addressed by Facebook:

"• a mechanism for users to convey an informed choice for how their information is used and shared on the [web]site including in relation to Third Party Apps;

- a broad update to the Data Use Policy/Privacy Policy to take account of recommendations as to where the information provided to users could be further improved;

- transparency and control for users via the provision of all personal data held to them on request and as part of their everyday interaction with the [web]site;
- the deletion of information held on users and non-users via what are known as social plugins and more generally the deletion of data held from user interactions with the [web]site much sooner than presently;
- increased transparency and controls for the use of personal data for advertising purposes;
- an additional form of notification for users in relation to facial recognition/'tag suggest' that is considered will ensure Facebook ... is meeting best practice in this area ...;
- an enhanced ability for users to control tagging and posting on other user profiles;
- an enhanced ability for users to control whether their addition to Groups by friends;
- the Compliance management/Governance function ... which will be further improved and enhanced to ensure that the introduction of new products or new uses of user data take full account of ... data protection law".

These are to be addressed on a rolling-review basis, culminating in a further detailed re-audit review carried out in July 2012.

While the audit process is wide in scope, the audit arose because of a formal complaint, comprising numerous individual complaints, made by an Austrian law student, a privacy group called Europe Against Facebook and also a complaint from Norway.

The full report is detailed and consisted of 149 pages plus appendices. It will have implications not just for Facebook but other internet and social networks which collect and process personal data. As with the growing trend of EU data privacy law potentially becoming the *de facto* international standard, the report will also have implications for the operators and users of websites outside the EU.

Re-Audit Report

The Irish Data Protection Commissioner also issued an updated Re-Audit Report.[3] Again, this is detailed. However, it was confined to the same issues as the initial report. While a full analysis is not possible here, it is worth mentioning that the Data Protection Commissioner required various amendments by Facebook, including:

- the decommissioning of the Facebook facial recognition feature in the EU;
- that Facebook be much more transparent with users in relation to its data protection related activities;
- that Facebook allow users to fully and completely delete their accounts with it.

The Irish Data Protection Commissioner also highlighted that the review was a moment-in-time analysis and that it was inevitable that further issues would arise. Indeed, this was somewhat prophetic, given that the Data Protection Commissioner

---

3 See *Facebook Ireland Limited, Report of Re-Audit*, Data Protection Commissioner, 21 September 2012, available at www.dataprotection.ie.

has since been required to call on Facebook to delay and make changes in relation to a subsequent proposal by Facebook to amend its privacy-related policies.[4]

Conclusion

While data privacy rules may differ widely between the EU and the US, there are increasing examples of EU law becoming the *de facto* standard for privacy and data protection internationally. The announcement of the EU investigation report of Facebook's data protection practices in the EU, via the Office of the Irish Data Protection Commissioner, in December 2011 compliments the global importance of the EU data protection regime. The compliance steps outlined in the report, which must be undertaken by Facebook, have implications for Facebook in relation to its users in the EU but also in other countries. Facebook will be required to make its data-protection processing activities more transparent. It will also have to ensure stronger consent from its users to those processes. This could apply to all countries outside the US and Canada.

The progress of the implementation of the recommendations, as well as the subsequent reports from the Irish Data Protection Commissioner can be viewed as important guides. As the reports make clear, they are time and issue specific and compliance can change over time. Compliance and vigilance are on-going issues.

What happens to social networks generally is also important, as this could indicate what will happen in relation to other service providers also.[5]

The Irish Data Protection Commissioner is now currently progressing with a similar audit review in relation to LinkedIn.

While the Facebook and LinkedIn examples are instances of official audits, the nature of the security, processing, collection, and other issues that may arise can be investigated by or for the organisation even without an official audit arising. Indeed, these may even be recommended and beneficial for the organisation depending on the circumstances.

---

4 P Flanagan, "Data Protection Group Seeking Change to Facebook Privacy Policy," *Irish Independent*, 29 November 2012, available at http://www.independent.ie/business/technology/data-protection-group-seeking-change-to-facebook-privacy-policy-3309757.html.

5 Y Hashemi, "Facebook's Privacy Policy and Its Third Party Partnerships: Lucrativity and Liability" (2009)(15) *Bolton University Journal of Science and Technology Law* 140 at 149.

Chapter 34

THE FUTURE

Headline of Issues

- Online liability
- Defences
- CJEU – Spanish case
- Future-proofing solutions
- Spam solutions
- Official data protection review
- Regulation and social networking

Introduction

Social networking brings may benefits. Yet a portion of social networking activities bring difficult and contentious issues around certain problem content. Issues such as online abuse, teen suicides and cyber-bullying clearly draw significant media attention. It is correct that social and policy attention should be concerned to dealing with these issues. No one solution will be successful on its own. A further point is that there is a lack of research which addresses all of the potential solutions. Further research is required. As the popularity of social networking increases yet further, we will see further issues and concerns arising.

Photograph Software

New software may be developed which will increase user control over photographs. Individuals may be able to control or implement use settings of their photographs. This could include setting restrictions on where the photographs can appear. It could also include preventing third parties from copying photographs or altering photographs. Additionally, content including photographs may be set to delete after a specified time or after being received.

Future-Proofing Solutions

The new wired and wireless world presents many new difficulties for preserving privacy and maintaining respect for individuals' data protection rights.

Various solutions are being discussed and proposed. Optimists feel that some of the solutions will be useful, while more pessimistic commentators might feel that laws and solutions can never fully catch up with the new data protection and second-generation internet (Web 2.0) concerns.

However, as many of these problems have their origin in new technologies, it is sometimes felt that technology itself can provide a solution. One solution is security software to prevent hacking or the harvesting of personal information on computer. Filtering software is another example. There is a new trend to attempt to address privacy and data protection problems at the very earliest stages of designing new technology. New and amended laws are also frequently argued to be a necessary solution to the new 2.0 issues. There is increasing discussion of "Do Not Track" solutions to deal with online monitoring by organisations.

Spam Solutions

Unsolicited commercial communications are a widespread issue for everyone. The volume of spam grows exponentially.[1] Indeed, this is now also an increasing concern for mobile telephones and mobile devices.

This spam problem is an inconvenience to individuals and a financial cost to industry (in terms of lost productivity, security and bandwidth costs). There is a large literature in relation to the general spam problem discussed elsewhere.[2] Spam affects privacy and data protection when individuals' personal details are used to target spam at them. Also, personal details are often hacked and stolen to provide targets for spam communications. There is a large illicit industry in selling on databases of stolen personal details, for spam, identity theft and other fraudulent activities.

While spam is included in existing EU law,[3] there is still no dedicated spam laws in the EU. There are, however, spam laws in the US at federal[4] and local level.[5] This could be said to be one of the few areas where US data protection law is more refined and explicit than EU law.

There is already some recognition in copyright law for self-help remedies, such as

1 VJ Reid, "Recent Developments in Private Enforcement of the CAN-SPAM Act" (2010) (4) *Akron Intellectual Property Journal* 281 at 298.

2 See, for example, J Kennedy, "'Unprecedented' Complaints Over Automated Abortion Calls," *Irish Times*, 23 November 2012; T Greene, "Study: Microsoft Repeatedly Ranks as Top US Spammer; University of Texas Project Calls Attention to Problem in Effort to Reduce Spam, Improve Security," *Network World*, 26 July 2012; SJ Delany, M Buckley and D Greene, "SMS Spam Filtering: Methods and Data" (2012) (39) *Expert Systems With Applications* 9899; D Lorentz, "The Effectiveness of Litigation Under the CAN-SPAM Act" (2011) (30) *Rev Litigation* 559; DJ Rutenberg, "Silence of the Spam: Improving the CAN-SPAM Act by Including an Expanded Private Cause of Action" (2011) (14) *Vanderbilt Journal Entertainment & Technology Law* 225; MS Kirsh, "Do-Not-Track: Revising the EU's Data Protection Framework to Require Meaningful Consent for Behavioural Advertising" (2011) (18) *Rich Journal Law & Tech* 2.

3 Article 7, E-Commerce Directive, Directive 2000/31/EC of the European Parliament and of the Council of 8 June 2000 on certain legal aspects of information society services, in particular electronic commerce, in the Internal Market.

4 Controlling the Assault of Non-Solicited Pornography and Marketing (CAN-SPAM) Act 2003, Pub L No 108-187, 117 Stat 2699-2719 (codified as amended at 15 USC S 7701-7713).

5 See SpamLaws.com, available at www.spamlaws.com/state/index.shtml. However, the local spam laws in the US have been described as a "patchwork regulatory approach." See Reid, *op. cit*, 288–289.

private piracy seizure and private prosecutions.[6] Some of the new tailored spam laws follow suit. In a number of these laws there is an explicit right for the individual recipients of unsolicited commercial communications to sue the sender.[7]

The US federal law, the CAN-SPAM Act 2003,[8] outlaws spamming, and provides that unsolicited commercial emails must provide an opt-out mechanism, and prohibits deceptive headers and subject lines.[9] The CAN-SPAM Act provides the primary enforcement ability to the Federal Telecommunications Commission (FTC). State Attorneys General are also permitted to take enforcement actions.

ISPs may also take action under the CAN-SPAM Act. Indeed, the right to sue may even be wider than what might be described as traditional ISPs. Growing case law indicates that other parties, such as Earthlink, Microsoft and AOL, are also able to sue.[10] Such cases include *MySpace v Globe.com*[11] (providing that a social network could sue for spam); *Facebook v ConnectU*[12]; *Haselton v Quicken Loans*[13]; *MySpace v Wallace*[14]; and *Facebook v Guerbuez*.[15] In *MySpace v The Globe.com* and *Facebook v Guerbuez* the courts awarded damages of $230 million and $873 million respectively.[16]

Certain case law in relation to US federal law is argued to recognise that individual spam recipients can also sue the spammers. For example in *Gordon v Virtumundo*[17] the recipient plaintiff was found not to have standing to sue in circumstances where the plaintiff set and organised his online presence with the intention of receiving spam and suing on foot of it.[18] Indeed, one can compare this to the recent practice of patent trolls who seek to register, buy or act in relation to patents with the intention of taking infringement actions rather than seeking to exploit the patents commercially. The plaintiff in this case was arguably similarly opportunistic.[19]

Generally also, spam laws raise penalties for spammers. A new Chinese law, for example, provides that spammers sending over 5,000 spam messages, or spamming

6 N Kounoupias, "Private Prosecution for Copyright Infringement," *Society of Computers and Law* available at www.scl.org/site.aspx?=ed1106.

7 For example, the Californian law, § 17529.5. California Business and Professions Code Division 7, Part 3, Chapter 1, Article 1.8. Restrictions On Unsolicited Commercial Email Advertisers (added by Stats. 2003 ch. 487 (S.B. 186), approved September 23, 2003; amended by Stats. 2004 ch. 183 (A.B. 3082), approved July 19, 2004; and Stats. 2004 ch. 571 (S.B. 1457), approved 17 September 2004. Available at www.spamlaws.com/state/ca.shtml.

8 Controlling the Assault of Non-Solicited Pornography and Marketing (CAN-SPAM) Act 2003, Pub L No 108-187, 117 Stat 2699-2719 (codified as amended at 15 USC S 7701-7713).

9 Reid, *op. cit*, 289.

10 *ibid*, 291.

11 *MySpace v The Globe.com, Inc* 2007 WL 1686966 a5 *5 (CD California 27 February 2007).

12 *Facebook Inc v ConnectU LLC* 489 F Supp 2d 1087, 1094 (ND California 2007).

13 *Haselton v Quicken Loans Inc* 2008 WL 3046980 at S2.1.1 (WD Washington 2008).

14 *MySpace Inc v Wallace* 498 F Supp 2d 1293, 1301 (CD California 2008).

15 *Facebook Inc v Guerbuez* 2008 US Dist Lexis 108921 (ND California 2008). All referred to in Reid, *op. cit*, 291–298.

16 Albeit, in default judgements where the defendants did not mount full defences.

17 *Gordon v Virtumundo Inc* 575 F 3d 1040, 1040-1046 (9th Circuit 2009).

18 Reid, *op. cit*, 298–299.

19 *ibid*, 305.

over 500 people, can receive a 10-year prison sentence.[20] The Washington State Law provides a fine of $500 per spam communication.[21]

EU Official Data Protection Review

The EU is also in the process of updating the EU Data Protection Directive 1995,[22] in particular to update the data protection regime as regards technological development since 1995, including the internet and social networking. Viviane Reding, the EU Commissioner for Information Society and Media, said at the time of launching the proposals that the world has changed greatly since the Directive was introduced in 1995 and robust protection was needed in response.[23] The amount of data being processed continues to grow exponentially.[24] International data transfers also increase.

The EU Article 29 Working Party has also issued an Opinion in relation to developing data protection law in light of these developing issues, entitled *The Future of Privacy*.[25] One of the issues it recommends is greater prominence for the concept of privacy by design (PbD) or data protection by design (DPbD).

However, while the EU Data Protection Directive 1995 is well over 10 years old, "revising the Directive is the beginning. Recognising how the Data Protection Directive 1995 can be applied effectively to Web 2.0, cloud computing and identity management systems are also necessary."[26] Also, "the demand for personal data continues to grow massively, and so should our determination to reinforce the rights of individuals over the use of their personal data.[27] Privacy by design and privacy-enhancing technologies (known as PETs) are indicated to be important parts

---

20 See "Ten Year Prison Sentence for Sending 5000 Fraud SMS in China," *eChinacities*, 25 April 2011, available at www.echinacities.com/aroundtown/china-in-pulse/ten-year-prison-sentence-for-sending-5-000-fraud-sms-in.html.

21 § 19.190.040 (1) of the Revised Code of Washington, Title 19. Business Regulations – Miscellaneous, Chapter 19.190. Commercial Electronic Mail (as amended by 2003 Acts ch. 137 (H.B. 2007)). Available at www.spamlaws.com/state/wa.shtml.

22 See, for example, "EU Commission Outlines Plans to Strengthen Privacy Law," *Out-Law.com*, 29 January 2010, available at www.out-law-com/page-10712; Article 29 Data Protection Working Party press release regarding the review of the data protection regulatory framework, available at http://ec.europa.eu/justice/policies/privacy/news/docs/pr_15_07_10_en.pdf, 15 July 2010.

23 Reported in "EU Commission Outlines Plans to Strengthen Privacy Law," *Out-Law.com*, 29 January 2010, available at www.out-law-com/page-10712.

24 *ibid*; and also C Kuner, "An International Legal Framework for Data Protection: Issues and Prospects" (2009) (25) *Computer Law & Security Review* 307.

25 Article 29 Working Party, The Future of Privacy: Joint contribution to the Consultation of European Commission on the legal framework for the fundamental right to protection of personal data, 1 December, 2009, WP 168, available at http://ec.europa.eu/justice/policies/privacy/docs/wpdocs/2009/wp168_en.pdf. See also R Wong, "Data Protection: The Future of Privacy" (2011) (27) *Computer Law & Security Review* 53. In relation to laws and technology generally, see for example R Jones and R Moore, "Introduction: An Uncomfortable Marriage: The Challenges 'New' Technology Is Posing or 'Old' or Established Legal Concepts?" (March-July 2009) (23) *International Review of Law Computers & Technology* 1.

26 Wong, *op. cit*, 57.

27 *ibid.*

of the proposed update.[28] The EU Article 29 Working Party also issued a headline document in relation to detection technologies.[29] There is also some discussion of global legal standards for data protection.[30]

New EU Regulation

The EU has outlined it proposed Regulation for updating the EU data protection regime.[31] The explanatory memorandum summarises the Regulation as follows:

- Article 5 sets out the principles relating to personal data processing, which correspond to those in Article 6 of Directive 95/46/EC. Additional new elements are in particular the transparency principle, the clarification of the data minimisation principle and the establishment of a comprehensive responsibility and liability of the controller;
- Article 6 sets out, based on Article 7 of Directive 95/46/EC, the criteria for lawful processing, which are further specified as regards the balance of interest criterion, and the compliance with legal obligations and public interest;
- Article 7 clarifies the conditions for consent to be valid as a legal ground for lawful processing;
- Article 8 sets out further conditions for the lawfulness of the processing of personal data of children in relation to information society services offered directly to them;
- Article 9 sets out the general prohibition for processing special categories of personal data and the exceptions from this general rule, building on Article 8 of the Directive 95/46/EC;
- Article 10 clarifies that the controller is not obliged to acquire additional information in order to identify the data subject for the sole purpose of complying with any provision of this Regulation;
- Article 11 introduces the obligation on controllers to provide transparent and easily accessible and understandable information, inspired in particular by the Madrid Resolution on international standards on the protection of personal data and privacy;
- Article 12 obliges the controller to provide procedures and mechanism for exercising the data subject's rights, including means for electronic requests, requiring response to the data subject's request within a defined deadline, and the motivation of refusals;

---

28 *ibid.*

29 *Opinion 1/2007 on the Green Paper on Detection Technologies in the Work of Law Enforcement, Customs and Other Security Authorities*, 9 January 2007, available at http://ec.europa.eu/justice/policies/privacy/docs/wpdocs/2007/wp129_en.pdf.

30 For example, the Madrid Resolution adopted by the International Conference of Data Protection and Privacy Commissioners on 6 November 2009, as referred to in Wong, *op. cit*, 55. Also, C Kuner, "An International Legal Framework for Data Protection: Issues and Prospects" (2009) (25) *Computer Law & Security Review* 307.

31 Proposal for a Regulation of the European Parliament and of the Council on the Protection of Individuals with regard to the Processing of Personal Data and on the Free Movement of Such Data (General Data Protection Regulation), COM(2012) 11 final, available at http://ec.europa.eu/justice/data-protection/document/review2012/com_2012_11_en.pdf.

- Article 13 provides rights in relation to recipients, based on Article 12(c) of Directive;
- Article 14 further specifies the controller's information obligations towards the data subject, building on Articles 10 and 11 of Directive 95/46/EC, providing additional information to the data subject, including on the storage period, the right to lodge a complaint, in relation to international transfers and to the source from which the data are originating. It also maintains the possible derogations in Directive 95/46/EC, eg there will be no such obligation if the recording or disclosure are expressly provided by law. This could apply for example in proceedings by competition authorities, tax or customs administrations, or services competent for social security matters;
- Article 15 provides the data subject's right of access to their personal data, building on Article 12(a) of Directive 95/46/EC and adding new elements, such as to inform the data subjects of the storage period, and of the rights to rectification and to erasure and to lodge a complaint. Article 16 sets out the data subject's right to rectification, based on Article 12(b) of Directive 95/46/EC;
- Article 17 provides the data subject's right to be forgotten and to erasure. It further elaborates and specifies the right of erasure provided for in Article 12(b) of Directive 95/46/EC and provides the conditions of the right to be forgotten, including the obligation of the controller which has made the personal data public to inform third parties on the data subject's request to erase any links to, or copy or replication of that personal data. It also integrates the right to have the processing restricted in certain cases, avoiding the ambiguous terminology "blocking";
- Article 18 introduces the data subject's right to data portability, ie to transfer data from one electronic processing system to and into another, without being prevented from doing so by the controller. As a precondition and in order to further improve access of individuals to their personal data, it provides the right to obtain from the controller those data in a structured and commonly used electronic format;
- Article 19 provides for the data subject's rights to object. It is based on Article 14 of Directive 95/46/EC, with some modifications, including as regards the burden of proof and its application to direct marketing;
- Article 20 concerns the data subject's right not to be subject to a measure based on profiling. It builds on, with modifications and additional safeguards, Article 15(1) of Directive 95/46 on automated individual decisions, and takes account of the Council of Europe's recommendation on profiling;
- Article 30 obliges the controller and the processor to implement appropriate measures for the security of processing, based on Article 17(1) of Directive 95/46/EC, extending that obligation to processors, irrespective of the contract with the controller;
- Articles 31 and 32 introduce an obligation to notify personal data breaches, building on the personal data breach notification in Article 4(3) of the e-privacy Directive 2002/58/EC;
- Article 33 introduces the obligation of controllers and processors to carry out a data protection impact assessment prior to risky processing operations;

- Article 34 concerns the cases where authorisation by, and consultation of, the supervisory authority is mandatory prior to the processing, building on the concept of prior checking in Article 20 of Directive 95/46/EC;
- Article 35 introduces a mandatory data protection officer for the public sector, and, in the private sector, for large enterprises or where the core activities of the controller or processor consist of processing operations which require regular and systematic monitoring. This builds on Article 18(2) of Directive 95/46/EC, which provided the possibility for Member States to introduce such requirement as a surrogate of a general notification requirement;
- Article 36 sets out the position of the data protection officer;
- Article 37 provides the core tasks of the data protection officer.[32]

Raising Awareness of Dangers

It is important to continue to raise awareness of data protection, risks, etc. The Canadian Privacy Commissioner, for example, issued a video raising awareness of social media dangers, entitled *What Does a Friend of a Friend Need to Know About You.*[33] This will be an ongoing task.

Regulation and Social Networking

The EU Commission refers specifically to the potential effects of the Regulation in the area of social networks (and related websites). It states that "72% of internet users are worried that they give away too much personal data online. They feel they do not have complete control of their data".[34]

It adds:

> "The Commission is proposing a strengthened right to be forgotten so that if you no longer want your personal data to be processed, and there is no legitimate reason for an organisation to keep it, it must be removed from their system. Data controllers must prove that they need to keep the data rather than you having to prove that collecting your data is not necessary. Providers must take account of the principle of 'privacy by default,' which means that the default settings should be those that provide the most privacy. Companies will be obliged to inform you as clearly, understandably and transparently as possible about how your personal data will be used, so that you are in the best position to decide what data you share.
>
> The proposals will make it easier for you to access your data and give you a right to data portability, which means it will be easier to transfer personal data from one service provider to another. They will also make sure that when users give their consent for companies to use their personal data, that agreement is given explicitly and with their full awareness. This will give users control over their data, and help foster trust in the online environment".[35]

---

32 *ibid.*

33 Referred to in DB Garrie, M Duffy-Lewis, R Wong and RL Gillespie, "Data Protection: The Challenges Facing Social Networking" (2009–2010) (131) *International Law & Management Review* 127 at 136.

34 "How will the Data Protection Reform Affect Social Networks?" available at http://ec.europa.eu/justice/data-protection/document/review2012/factsheets/3_en.pdf.

35 *ibid.*

The key proposed changes in relation to social networking are referred to by the EU Commission as follows:

> "• Strengthening the 'right to be forgotten' to help people better manage data protection risks online. When individuals no longer want their data to be processed and there are no legitimate grounds for retaining it, the data will be deleted. The rules are about empowering people, not about erasing past events or restricting the freedom of the press;
> • Guarantee easy access to your own data;
> • Establishing a right for individuals to freely transfer personal data from one service provider to another (data portability);
> • Ensuring that consent must be given explicitly by individuals when it is required for certain types of data processing;
> • Increasing the responsibility and accountability of those processing data by introducing data protection officers for companies over 250 employees, and the principles of 'privacy by default' and 'privacy by design' to ensure that individuals are informed in an easily understandable way about how their data will be processed".[36]

Special Rapporteur on Child Protection

The Sixth Report of the Special Rapporteur on Child Protection[37] by the Irish Special Rapporteur Mr Geoffrey Shannon recommends that cyberbullying be a criminal offence. The report highlights the advent of online abuse, as well as such issues as the possibility of anonymous reporting by victims. It states:

> "The impact and effect of bullying on children has been tragically thrown into the media spotlight ... Whilst bullying has always been an unfortunate aspect of our society, the growth of 'Cyber-bullying' has almost overnight created a readily accessible forum for bullies to target children with little or no regulation or sanction. The Irish legal system has been somewhat taken unawares as to the manner and means through which children have fallen victim to cyber-bullying. Whilst there are some legislative provisions in being that might be interpreted in such a manner as to tackle this growing problem, a focused response is required."[38]

It adds:

> "However, in order for a system of legal recourse to be effective victims of such bullying need to be able to feel that they can come forward and express their concerns without fear of retribution. Thus, provision also needs to be made for the protection of child victims of such behaviour, eg the means of retaining their anonymity when making a complaint as to such bullying."[39]

The report also highlights the issue of potential liability for schools and educational organisations for online abuse, etc. It states that the "extent of a school's liability arising from an incident of bullying between students is a topic of some considerable debate and one that has been thrown into the fore in recent months."[40]

---

36 *ibid.*

37 G Shannon, *Sixth Report of the Special Rapporteur on Child Protection, A Report Submitted to the Oireachtas*, (Dublin, 23 January 2013).

38 *ibid*, 9.

39 *ibid*, 9.

40 *ibid*, 9.

It notes recent guidelines published in Ireland for schools, but cautions that "in the era of online technology and cyber-bullying a new focus must be brought to bear on this issue. Lessons can be learnt from the developments in New South Wales and Massachusetts in attempting to set a legislative basis to tackle this problem in schools."[41]

The Recommendations refer to "Cyber-bullying as a Criminal Offence." It states:

> "On review of reported cases of harassment involving social networking, email and SMS, there appear to be very few criminal prosecutions taken for this type of harassment under the Non-Fatal Offences Against the Person Act, 1997 despite the suitability of that Act. When cyber-bullying is being described as an epidemic, we need to examine why this is the case. Specifically, is there reticence to investigate complaints of cyber-bullying?
>
> Responding to calls for new criminal legislation to tackle cyber-bullying, the Minister for Justice identified our existing laws against harassment as being suitable. However, the Minister has directed the Law Reform Commission to examine difficulties in prosecuting for cyber-bullying and, in particular, the necessity to show persistence in the harassment.
>
> Existing laws regarding harassment can be used to incorporate cyber-bullying incidents. A review of the Post Office (Amendment) Acts should be undertaken with a view to incorporating emerging means of cyber-bullying."[42]

Anonymity for victims of online abuse or at least cyberbulling online abuse is favoured. The Recommendations continue as follows:

> "The current Irish legal position would appear to suggest that an application for anonymity in the context of cyber-bullying litigation would be unsuccessful. However, it is difficult to be definitive in respect of the legal position because Mr Justice Peart's decision in *McKeogh v John Doe* may well have been different if the applicant had been a child or teenager seeking to rely on the right to privacy of children, and able to invoke the general social interest in protection of children from cyber-bullying. The ideal solution would be an agreement of co-operation to be entered into between ISPs (and potentially other entities such as Facebook) and the Gardaí to provide IP addresses where complaints of cyber-bullying have been received."[43]

The Irish Oireachtas Joint Committee on Transport and Communications which held parliamentary hearings and submissions during 2013 *inter alia* in relation to online abuse and cyberbullying, has recommended that a single body should be given responsibility for co-ordinating the regulation of social media content.[44]

Paul C Dwyer of the National Anti-Bullying Coalition told the Committee that just one social network providers received some 100,000 reports or requests per day but dedicated just 90 staff to process such requests.[45] The Committee and the Report recommends that the online abuse report data be furnished by the social networks to the Irish Data Protection Commissioner.[46]

In Recommendation 3 the Committee supports the recommendation contained

---

41 *ibid*, 9.

42 *ibid*, 20.

43 *ibid*, 20.

44 Oireachtas Joint Committee on Transport and Communications, *Houses of the Oireachtas, Joint Committee on Transport and Communications Report Addressing the Growth of Social Media and Tackling Cyberbullying*, (Government Publications: Dublin, 18 July 2013).

45 *ibid*, 8.

46 *ibid*.

in the Action Plan on Bullying that the definition of bullying in the new national procedures for schools should include a specific reference to cyberbullying. Also, guidelines for cyberbullying should be put in place, so that school principals dealing with instances of cyberbullying have a clear protocol to follow.[47]

Recommendation 4 refers to employers. It states that employers be made aware of the importance of introducing a social media policy, ie outlining what constitutes cyberbullying and what actions will be taken if there is a breach of such a policy.[48] Employers should be aware that cyberbullying falls under "harassment" and Section 10 of the Non-fatal Offences Against the Person Act 1997 may apply in such cases.[49]

Recommendation 6 states as follows:

> "The Committee recommends that a single body be given responsibility for co-ordinating the regulation of social media content. Funding and organisational models for this agency should be agreed with the industry. It is noted that other examples of industry-led partnerships between stakeholders and government have been established in other sectors in recent years."[50]

Data Loss

Unfortunately the issue of data loss and data breach appears to be continuing in frequency and volume of personal data involved. At the time of writing new data loss stories are occurring: a data breach by an Irish company involving personal credit card data of approx 70,000 Irish citizens and reportedly 500,000 across the EU; Adobe is also reported to be the subject of a data loss incident involving 150 million individuals; Target 40m; Snapchat 4.6m; etc.

The dangers are increasing and therefore the imperative increases to tackle the issues.

Employer/University Access

Increasingly individuals, be they employees or students are under pressure to reveal their passwords to prospective employers, employers and universities in order that the organisation can vet or monitor the individual and their activities. This raises real privacy and data protection concerns. Certainly in Ireland and the EU, this is not something that would appear to be permitted under privacy and data protection laws. Neither does there appear to be any clear legal or business case for such intrusiveness.

This also applies to the practice where an organisation may request (or demand) that an individual join or befriend the social networking profile of the organisation. In practical terms, this allows the organisation to view and access the profile, comments, photographs, etc of the employee or student.

---

[47] *ibid*, 9.
[48] *ibid*.
[49] *ibid*.
[50] *ibid*, 10.

Of course, the situation may differ as between the US and elsewhere, in particular the EU.

Cloud

There is significant promotion of cloud services by commercial organisations. Equally, there as many queries being raises, such as security, electronic evidence, access, discovery, business continuity, etc. More recently, the Snowden developments have enhanced arguments for the local storage of internet related personal data, including if not in particular personal data on cloud related services and social networks. Germany, Brasil and even the EU are actively promoting these considerations.

Politicisation of Data Protection

Even before the Snowden developments, there has been an increasing politicisation of data protection and data protection reform. The proposed EU Data Protection Regulation is understood to be the most heavily lobbied legal measure in the EU ever.

The Snowden developments emphasise potentially divergent positions between the US (and UK) and other nations as regards policy, privacy and data protection.

Separately, the fact that data breach and data loss incidents are not limited to the commercial world, but include many official and government organisations means that data protection is increasingly moving up the political agenda.

That data protection and social networking are front page stories and no longer back page stories, means that policy makers must take cognisance of media and public attention on data protection.

Conclusion

We must evolve beyond "first generation information privacy law"[51] to address the new second-generation internet and the new privacy and data protection concerns developing with social networking and other activities.

Social networking offers many opportunities. It is clearly changing how people interact socially, online and offline. In increasing connectivity it changes privacy also. How should society respond to the "changing face of privacy on the internet"?[52]

New issues are emerging. It is reported that financial (and possibly other) organisations are now using social networking content, "likes", your "friends, etc,

---

[51] M Burdon, "Privacy Invasive Geo-Mashups: Privacy 2.0 and the Limits of First Generation Information Privacy Laws" (2010) *University of Illinois Journal of Law, Technology and Policy* 1.

[52] Miller, "The Facebook Frontier: Responding to the Changing Face of Privacy on the Internet" (2008–2009) *Kentucky Law Journal* 541.

to make financial decisions and rate users", eg, credit scores.[53] In Canada there are reported to be charges against two teenagers for distributing images of child pornography relating to an incident of cyber-bullying.[54] The 17 year old victim, Rehtaeh Parsons, committed suicide. It is salutary when we consider the Slane concert sex matter in Ireland, where certain images were posted and distributed on social networks.[55] Soccer fans in the UK can now face prosecution for their online trolling, abuse, etc, as new UK Crown Prosecution Service Guidelines are issued.[56] Issues are emerging a between EU and the US as regards data protection laws, which may have far reaching consequences.[57] However, perhaps the development which has most significance, perhaps even greater than the updated EU Data Protection regime (via the Regulation), will be the impact of all of the NSA Snowden revelations. This is a story which has yet to run its full course. Already it has led to many political tensions, cross Atlantic diplomacy and Brazilian and German proposals to the UN in relation to a resolution for greater recognition of privacy and data protection.

In conclusion, this is an area which never stands still.

[53] K Lobosca, "Facebook Friends Could Change Your Credit Score," *CNN Money*, 27 August 2013.

[54] "Rehtaeh Parsons Suicide: Two Charged Over Photos in Cyberbullying Case, Child Pornography Charges Laid in Case Where Girl Killed Herself After Images of Her Alleged Rape Were Posted Online", *Guardian,* 9 August 2013.

[55] C O'Brien, "Slane Sex Act Photos: A Salutary Lesson of How Social Media Can Exploit and Abuse", *Irish Times,* 21 August 2013.

[56] "Football Fans Face Prosecution for 'Online Hooliganism'", *Guardian,* 23 August 2013.

[57] K Lillington, "Internet Privacy Breaches Sound Alarm Bells for Worried Businesses", *Irish Times,* 22 August 2013.

AUTHOR AND CONTRIBUTORS

Gary Kovacs

Gary Kovacs is the CEO of Mozilla Corporation with the responsibility for leading the overall direction of the organization and the Firefox Web browser. Prior to joining Mozilla, Gary held senior leadership roles as Senior VP of Markets, Solutions & Products at Sybase (through its acquisition by SAP earlier this year), as General Manager and VP of Mobile & Devices at Adobe and as VP of Product Marketing at Macromedia (through its acquisition by Adobe). Previously, he led the successful creation and growth of Zi Corporation, a company specializing in embedded software and services for mobile and consumer devices. Prior to Zi Corporation, Gary spent 10 years at IBM in leadership positions in product management, sales, marketing and operations within the global software division.

Andrew Harbison

Andrew Harbison is one the most experienced computer forensics investigators in private practice in Ireland. He has completed in excess of 400 separate computer investigations for clients ranging from multinational companies and major financial services companies to small and medium sized enterprises and private individuals. He has carried out forensic IT evidence acquisitions in many countries. He has innovated a number of important IT investigative techniques and seen them put into Irish precedent. He is also Ireland's most experienced electronic discovery practitioner and has completed dozens of e-discovery assignments under Irish, UK and US rules of evidence. He recently led the litigation technology team in the largest electronic discovery in Irish legal history.

Andrew is also Adjunct Lecturer in Digital Investigation at UCD. He worked with the UCD Cybercrime Institute to develop their highly successful MSc in Digital Investigation. He also lectures on the Law Society of Ireland Higher Diploma course in Intellectual Property and Information Technology Law and also lectures on the Advanced Diploma in Corporate, White Collar & Regulatory Crime at the Honorable Society of Kings Inns. He is currently co-writing the chapters on IT Fraud and Cloud Computing for the latest edition of the Law Society of Ireland's Professional Practice Guides.

Andrew holds a BE in Electronics Engineering and Masters Degrees in Business Administration and Information Technology.

Aisling McMahon

Aisling McMahon graduated with a BCL (first class honours degree) and an LLM (first class honours) in Law, Technology and Governance from the National University of Ireland Galway. She held the Michael MacNamara Scholarship during her LLM year. She tutored law in NUI Galway for two academic years and subsequently worked as a Judicial Researcher in the Judges' Library, Four Courts. She is currently a PhD candidate in the University of Edinburgh and recipient of the Principal's Career Development Award. Doctoral Candidate. Managing Editor of SCRIPT-ed.

Peggy Valcke

Peggy Valcke is research professor at the Interdisciplinary Centre for Law & ICT at the University of Leuven (ICRI - iMinds - KU Leuven). She is visiting professor at the University of Tilburg and teaches media law at the University of Brussels and in the Florence School of Regulation. In 2006, she was visiting professor at Central European University in Budapest and in 2011, she was appointed member of the scientific committee of the newly created Centre for Media Freedom and Pluralism at the Robert Schumann Centre of the European University Institute. Her research focuses on media, communications, IT and competition law, with a particular emphasis on media pluralism. In 2008-2009, she served as project leader for the Independent Study on Indicators for Media Pluralism in the Member States – Towards a Risk-Based Approach, financed by the European Commission. Peggy is the editor the International Encyclopaedia for Media Law (Kluwer Law International) and is a member of the editorial board of a.o. The Journal of Media Law (Hart Publishing), Computer, Law and Security Review (Elsevier), and Journal of Information Policy (Fordham University). Peggy is one of the five members of the General Chamber of the Flemish Media Regulator and is part-time member of the Belgian Competition Council.

Aleksandra Kuczerawy

Aleksandra Kuczerawy (LLM) is a PhD candidate at the Katholieke Universiteit Leuven, Belgium. She works as a legal researcher at the Interdisciplinary Centre for Law and ICT (KU Leuven – ICRI – iMinds) since 2007. She works in a number of independent studies and FP7 projects, mainly in the areas of: Spatial Data Infrastructures (One Geology Europe), Privacy and Identity Management (PrimeLife), Media law (Independent study on European Media Pluralism Indicators), User Generated Content and Internet of Services (SocIoS, Experimedia). She also wrote several publications focusing on Social Networking Sites and data protection. Currently she has expended her research field to Liability of Internet Intermediaries and the topic of her PhD is: 'Private enforcement of public policies: Freedom of expression in the era of online gatekeeping'. Moreover, Aleksandra is an assistant editor of the International Encyclopedia of Law (IEL) - Cyber Law.

Claire Wallace

Claire Wallace (LLB (Dub), LLM (NUI)) is currently a trainee solicitor with Maples and Calder Solicitors, Dublin. She graduated with a First Class Honours degree in Law from Trinity College Dublin in 2009, having spent the academic year 2007/08 at Washington and Lee School of Law, Virginia, USA. During her time spent at Trinity College, Claire was the recipient of the Sweet and Maxwell Prize in her Senior Freshman year, as well as the Julian Prize for her final year examination results. She holds an LLM in Law, Technology and Governance from the National University of Ireland, Galway, where she completed her thesis on "Protecting the Data of the Dead." Claire also tutored in Constitutional Law whilst studying at the National University of Ireland, Galway. Claire has worked in the area of risk management for solicitors, as well as for number of commercial law firms.

Damien McCallig

PhD candidate at the School of Law, National University of Ireland, Galway (NUIG). His research, which is funded by the Irish Research Council, is entitled *The Law of Digital Remains: Reconciling the dignity and interests of the deceased with those of the living*. He is currently the module coordinator for Internet Regulation and Governance on the LLM in Law, Technology and Governance at NUIG and regularly contributes to IRIS – Legal Observations of the European Audiovisual Observatory, which addresses many of the cutting-edge issues in the media and communications fields.

Cáit Brennan

BSc, Dip IT, MTOPRA. Originally from Co. Tipperary, Cáit Brennan graduated from The University of Limerick with a degree in Industrial Chemistry and has worked in the regulatory affairs and research and development areas of the generic pharmaceuticals industry since 1994. She also deals with intellectual property, patenting and trademark issues. Currently employed by a multinational organisation, she is studying part-time in commercial compliance and regulation in NUI Galway. Cáit has played music in various bands as a hobby over the years and has written and recorded many of her own songs. She was President of her local Lions Club in 2012. She lived in Australia for a year where she made bio-diesel, music and friends. She currently lives in Galway.

Europe versus Facebook

Europe versus Facebook is a privacy and data protection advocacy group, in particular concerned with the personal data issues relating to the Facebook social networking website. Europe versus Facebook is organised by a small group of about 10 Facebook users. The starting point was an article Max Schrems (Law Student, University of Vienna) wrote during his semester abroad at Santa Clara University, California, where a Facebook representative held a talk about European privacy laws. After finding that Facebook was breaching these laws and after returning to Vienna, Max and his friends decided that someone had to take action against these obvious breaches of European laws. This loose group of students is not aiming for any financial gain or other personal interest. In spring 2012 we funded an Austrian NGO that manages financial support to keep their fight against Facebook running.

Max Schrem

Max Schrems, an Austrian law student and founder of the *Europe versus Facebook* group, has had an ongoing battle for privacy with the social networking giant Facebook. It all started with him asking Facebook for all the personal data it stored relating to his Facebook account, exercising his right to access as laid down in European data protection law.

After going through the more than 1200 pages long PDF document he got on a CD, Schrems started wondering why Facebook had data about him that by European law it should not have and what could be done about this.

The US based Electronic Privacy Information Centre (EPIC) has given the 2013 International Privacy Champion Award to Max Schrems, the organizer of Europe v Facebook. EPIC called Max "an innovative and effective spokesperson for the right to privacy." EPIC cited his work to obtain his personal information collected by Facebook, which has inspired more than 40,000 users around the world to make similar access requests, helping to ensure greater transparency of internet websites. Previous award recipients include Canadian Privacy Commissioner Jennifer Stoddart, European Parliamentarian Sophie In't Veld, Australian Jurist Michael Kirby, and Constitutional Law Scholar Stefano Rodotà. The award is given by EPIC annually in recognition of January 28, International Privacy Day.

José Maria Baño Fos

José Maria Baño Fos is an Adjunct Professor of Administrative Law at the Instituto de Empresa Law School in Madrid. José Maria is a member of the Madrid bar since 2008 and the New York since 2009 and combines his academic position with his private practice at José María Baño León Abogados. Prior to that, José María worked as an associate at Cleary Gottlieb (Brussels) and Perez-Llorca (Madrid) where he specialised in competition and EU law including the Spanish Google ECJ/CJEO case. José María obtained his Bachelor of Laws with the highest honours from the University of Valencia and received an LL.M. from Fordham University, where he was Caja Madrid scholar. José María has published several articles on the fields of directors' liability, damages actions for antitrust infringements, minority shareholdings and legitimate expectations. José María has also been a visiting researcher at Columbia University School of Law and guest lecturer at NUI Galway.

Donnacha O'Sullivan

Donnacha O Sullivan received his Bachelor of Civil Law from NUI Galway in 2012. He is a past winner of the "Best Submission" prize for the UCC Student Online Law Review. He most recently completed a Masters in Law, Technology and Governance in NUI Galway, composing a thesis focusing on Graduated Response Mechanisms aimed at combating digital piracy and preserving copyright holders rights in an online age.

Gary Madden

Gary Madden graduated with an LLB in Law and Economics from University of Limerick and an LLM. in Law, Technology and Governance from National University of Ireland Galway. Originally from Galway, having grown up in a sporting environment, his primary research interest is the interconnection between the law and sporting issues. He recently completed his Masters dissertation, "The Developing Problems Facing Individuals and Organisations Resulting from Sports Persons' Activity on Social Networks and Related Websites." He intends to pursue a career in this area.

Sara Fernández Castedo (Lugo)

Sara graduated from the Santiago de Compostela University in Spain with an honours law degree, specializing in business law. She also attended the University of Padova in Italy. After working as an attorney at the council of Santiago de Compostela, she moved to Australia. Sara currently works for CitiBank, at the E-banking Department in Dublin, Ireland.

Paul Lambert

BA, LLB, LLM, CTMA, Solicitor, Merrion Legal Solicitors. Adjunct Lecturer in Law, National University of Ireland Galway. Paul is the author of *Courting Publicity, Twitter and Television Cameras in Court* (Bloomsbury UK); *Television Courtroom Broadcasting, Distraction Effects and Eye-Tracking* (Intellect UK); *Television Courtroom Broadcasting Effects: The Empirical Research and the Supreme Court Challenge* (University Press of America); and books on data protection in the UK (Bloomsbury) and Ireland (Clarus). Paul frequently publishes academic articles and speaks at seminars in Europe and elsewhere as well as being interviewed in trade and media publications. Paul is a solicitor and specialises in data protection, media, communications, internet, information technology and intellectual property law, both contentious and non-contentious. Board, Copyright Association of Ireland; Legal Working Group, IIA; Member, Society of Computers and Law; and Irish Computer Society (e: paul.lambert@merrionlegal.com)

INDEX